CANADIAN EDITION

VISUALIZING

PSYCHOLOGY

VISUALIZING
PSYCHOLOGY

Karen Huffman
Palomar College

Alastair Younger
University of Ottawa

Claire Vanston
Capilano University

WILEY

In collaboration with
THE NATIONAL GEOGRAPHIC SOCIETY

CREDITS

VICE PRESIDENT AND PUBLISHER Veronica Visentin
VICE PRESIDENT, PUBLISHING SERVICES Karen Bryan
MANAGING DIRECTOR Helen McInnis
ACQUISITIONS EDITOR Rodney Burke
DIRECTOR OF DEVELOPMENT Barbara Heaney
MARKETING MANAGER Patty Maher
CREATIVE DIRECTOR, PUBLISHING SERVICES Ian Koo
EDITORIAL MANAGER Karen Staudinger
DEVELOPMENTAL EDITOR Gail Brown
EDITORIAL ASSISTANT/PERMISSIONS COORDINATOR Sara Tinteri
EDITORIAL ASSISTANT Laura Hwee
CREATIVE DIRECTOR Harry Nolan
COVER DESIGNER Harry Nolan
INTERIOR DESIGN Vertigo Design
PHOTO RESEARCHER Stacy Gold,
National Geographic Society
COVER
Main image: © iStockphoto.com/Vasiliy Yakobchuk
Smaller images (left to right): Huy Lam Photography/First Light;
© Copyright Media Bakery; Cary Wolinsky/National Geographic
Stock; Jimmy Chin/National Geographic Stock; LWA-JDC/Corbis

This book was set in Times New Roman by GGS Higher Education Resources, a Divison of PreMedia Global, Inc., printed and bound by World Color Press Inc. The cover was printed by Lehigh Phoenix.

Library and Archives Canada Cataloguing in Publication

Huffman, Karen
    Visualizing psychology / Karen Huffman, Alastair Younger, Claire Vanston. —Canadian ed.

ISBN 978-0-470-15576-9

1. Psychology–Textbooks. I. Younger, Alastair II. Vanston, Claire III. Title.

BF121.H784 2010   150   C2009-907031-6

To order books or for customer service, please call 1.800.567.4797.

ISBN 978-0-470-15576-9
BRV ISBN 978-0-470-67917-3

Printed and bound in the United States of America

1 2 3 4 5 WC 14 13 12 11 10

Visualizing Psychology, Canadian Edition, is designed to help your students learn effectively. Created in collaboration with the National Geographic Society and our Wiley Visualizing Consulting Editor, Professor Jan Plass of New York University, *Visualizing Psychology* integrates rich visuals and media with text to direct students' attention to important information. This approach represents complex processes, organizes related pieces of information, and integrates information into clear representations. Beautifully illustrated, *Visualizing Psychology* shows your students what the discipline is all about, its main concepts and applications, while also instilling an appreciation and excitement about the richness of the subject.

Visuals, as used throughout this text, are instructional components that display facts, concepts, processes, or principles. They create the foundation for the text and do more than simply support the written or spoken word. The visuals include diagrams, graphs, maps, photographs, illustrations, schematics, animations, and videos.

Why should a textbook based on visuals be effective? Research shows that we learn better from integrated text and visuals than from either medium separately. Beginners in a subject benefit most from reading about the topic, attending class, and studying well-designed and integrated visuals. A visual, with good accompanying discussion, really can be worth a thousand words!

Well-designed visuals can also improve the efficiency with which information is processed by a learner. The more effectively we process information, the more likely it is that we will learn. This processing of information takes place in our working memory. As we learn, we integrate new information in our working memory with existing knowledge in our long-term memory.

Have you ever read a paragraph or a page in a book, stopped, and said to yourself: "I don't remember one thing I just read."? This may happen when your working memory has been overloaded, and the text you read was not successfully integrated into long-term memory. Visuals don't automatically solve the problem of overload, but well-designed visuals can reduce the number of elements that working memory must process, thus aiding learning.

You as the instructor, facilitate your students' learning. Well-designed visuals, used in class, can help you in that effort. Here are six methods for using the visuals in *Visualizing Psychology* in classroom instruction.

1. **Assign students to study visuals in addition to reading the text.**
   It is important to make sure your students know that the visuals are just as essential as the text.

2. **Use visuals during class discussions or presentations.**
   By pointing out important information as the students look at the visuals during class discussions, you can help focus students' attention on key elements of the visuals and help them begin to organize the information and develop an integrated model of understanding.

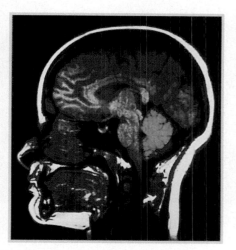

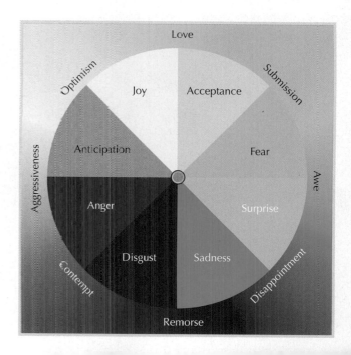

3. **Use visuals to review content knowledge.**
Students can review key concepts, principles, processes, vocabulary, and relationships displayed visually. Better understanding results when new information in working memory is linked to prior knowledge.

4. **Use visuals for assignments or when assessing learning.**
Visuals can be used for comprehension activities or assessments. For example, students could be asked to identify examples of concepts portrayed in visuals. Visuals can be very useful for drawing inferences, for predicting, and for problem solving.

5. **Use visuals to situate learning in authentic contexts.**
Learning is made more meaningful when a learner can apply facts, concepts, and principles to realistic situations or examples. Visuals can provide that realistic context.

6. **Use visuals to encourage collaboration.**
Collaborative groups often are required to practise interactive processes. These interactive, face-to-face processes provide the information needed to build a verbal mental model. Learners also benefit from collaboration in many instances, such as decision making or problem solving.

Visualizing Psychology not only aids student learning with extraordinary use of visuals, but it also offers remarkable photos, media, and film from the National Geographic Society collections.

Given all of its strengths and resources, *Visualizing Psychology* will immerse your students in the discipline, its main concepts, and applications, while also instilling an appreciation and excitement about the subject area.

Additional information on learning and instructional design is provided electronically, including an *Instructor's Resource Guide* that provides guidelines and suggestions on using the text and visuals most effectively. Other supplementary materials include the Test Bank; PowerPoint slides; Image Gallery to provide you with the visuals used in the text; web-based learning materials for homework and assessment including images, video, and media resources from National Geographic.

PREFACE

People are complicated and diverse. We think differently, act differently, and feel differently from one another. Our behaviour differs from one day to the next. We do things for reasons we can explain and often for reasons we cannot. As we age, our views and perspectives change, and we feel differently about the world around us. Across evolutionary time, we have changed as a species—with our expanding frontal lobes came new skills, more complex thought, and more diverse behaviours. These, and a wide variety of related topics, constitute the domain of psychology. We study humans (and nonhumans), their similarities, differences, and peculiarities; why they do things and how they think and feel. The study of psychology truly is the study of the human experience. *Visualizing Psychology*, Canadian Edition, invites you to explore this remarkable area and learn about a field that has interested people since they first began to wonder about themselves and the world they live in.

As you might expect, the compelling nature of psychology has attracted the attention of millions of readers, along with a multitude of psychology books. So, what makes *Visualizing Psychology* unique? Why did we write this book? The answer is simple—we believe this book does psychology differently. First, we think that *active learning* and *critical thinking* (two closely related concepts), in conjunction with meaningful and relevant examples, are key ingredients to true understanding and lifelong learning. Therefore, we have developed and incorporated a large set of active learning and critical thinking pedagogical tools designed to help you with the material. We have also taken a keen interest in providing examples that are relevant to students. Moreover, in developing the book, we subjected it to the critical eye of student focus groups in a variety of campuses across Canada. Many of their insights have been incorporated into the book, and we are most grateful for their participation. Their input has made our book better.

As the name implies, *Visualizing Psychology* is unique in its focus on visuals. Students today are different from those of 20 or 30 years ago. Many have been raised with bright and vivid screens projecting images and information—screens that let you quickly and readily look at our colourful world and its people. This textbook acknowledges you as a new breed of learner, by covering the basic content of a standard psychology text, but enhancing it with an educationally sound and carefully designed visual art program. For example, each chapter contains a unique *Visualizing* feature and *Process Diagram* that present a key concept and then explore it in detail using a combination of illustrative photos or figures. As you read through the text, we encourage you to take full advantage of these and other special study tools, including *Learning Objectives*, *What a Psychologist Sees*, *Applying Psychology*, *Psychological Science*, *Study Organizers*, *Concept Checks* and *Summaries*. Take a look at the Illustrated Book Tour for samples of these special features. In addition, we have chosen images that you will find engaging,

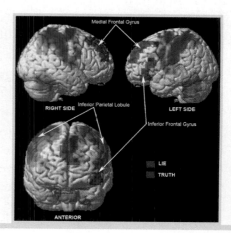

relevant, and sometimes even a bit provocative. Our partnership with National Geographic Society has given us access to thousands of award-winning photographs, many of which have never before been seen in a psychology textbook.

This textbook is intended to serve as a broad overview of the entire field of psychology. Despite its shortened and condensed nature, *Visualizing Psychology*, like most other survey textbooks, contains a large number of unfamiliar terms and complex concepts. We understand that the language of psychology is new to all but the most seasoned scholars, and we have used care with our terms and definitions to make them uncomplicated and clear. Unlike some other textbooks in psychology, this one is written for every student, and not just those intending to major in psychology.

As you can see, we feel passionately about psychology and about our textbook. We believe that psychology is indeed the finest discipline. The study of psychology offers us all an incomparable window into not only the human experience, but also the world that sustains us. As you will see, psychology offers many keys to understanding people and what they think and do. We're eager to share our passion for psychology with you, so let's get started.

ORGANIZATION

While psychology is renowned for its diversity, if you're like most new introductory psychology students, you probably think of psychology as primarily the study of abnormal behaviour and therapy. You'll be quite surprised to discover that our field is much larger, richer, and variable than just these two areas. To organize such a diverse and complex field, our book is divided into 15 chapters that are arranged in a "micro" to "macro" fashion. Generally, we tend to move from the smallest element of behaviour (the neuron and neuroscience) out to the largest (the group, culture, and social psychology). Here is a brief summary of the major topics we explore in each chapter:

- **CHAPTER 1** describes psychology's history, its different theoretical perspectives and fundamental questions, and how psychologists go about answering those questions.

- **CHAPTER 2** explains the evolutionary, neural, and other biological bases of behaviour, and lays the groundwork for further discussions of biological foundations that appear in later chapters.

- **CHAPTER 3** examines interactions among stress, health, thinking, and behaviour.

- **CHAPTERS 4** through **8** present aspects of cognition (thinking), including sensation, perception, consciousness, learning, memory, language, and intelligence. These chapters examine both typical cognitive processes and cases where thinking goes awry.

- **CHAPTERS 9** and **10** of *Visualizing Psychology* explore human development across the lifespan, from prenatal development to the post-retirement years, including physical, cognitive, social, moral, and personality development.

- **CHAPTERS 11** and **12** discuss processes and qualities that are integral to our most basic experiences and interactions with one another: motivation, emotion, and personality.

- **CHAPTER 13** begins by discussing what constitutes "abnormal behaviour" and how psychological disorders are identified and classified. We discuss the major disorders, their symptoms, how they develop, and, finally, how psychological disorders vary across cultures.

- **CHAPTER 14** describes and evaluates major forms of therapy, organizing them into three groups: insight therapies, behaviour therapies, and biomedical therapies. We also discuss the different "types" of therapists and counsellors in Canada who provide psychological help.

- **CHAPTER 15** discusses how we think about, feel about, and act around other people. In this chapter, we explore a range of social psychological phenomena, ranging from perceptions of others' intentions, to romantic attractions, to prejudice and discrimination.

- **STATISTICS MODULE** is a stand-alone section that introduces you to the powerful tools psychologists and other researchers use to analyze their research findings.

FEATURES OF THE CANADIAN EDITION

Visualizing Psychology Canadian Edition is dedicated to enhancing the student learning experience through several unique features, including:

- **Visuals.** Throughout the text, photos, figures, diagrams, and other illustrations have been carefully selected or created to provide effective illustrative aids to learning.

- **Coverage of important topics.** *Visualizing Psychology* contains, explores, and discusses topics such as critical thinking in everyday life, neural plasticity, gay families, circadian rhythms and aging, IQ testing, bilingualism and French immersion, attachment in infancy and adulthood, bullying and victimization, the not criminally responsible defence (the insanity plea), and herbal treatments for psychological problems.

- **Applying Psychology features.** These application sections help students relate psychological concepts to their own lives and understand how these concepts are applied in various sectors of society, such as school or the workplace.

- *Psychological Research* **features**. *Visualizing Psychology* emphasizes the empirical, scientific nature of psychology, and provides descriptions of current research findings, explanations of their significance, and applications.

- **Opportunities for critical thinking**. Each *Applying Psychology* and *Psychological Science* feature is accompanied by questions designed to encourage students to critically evaluate the topic discussed within the context of what they have learned in the text. Many figure captions also include critical thinking questions to further enhance student comprehension and critical thinking skills.

- **Study aids.** Carefully developed *Study Organizers* make it easy to compare different aspects of a topic, thus providing students with a useful tool for enhancing their understanding of the topic and preparing for exams. Among the topics treated in this way are the major psychological perspectives, properties of vision and hearing, schedules of reinforcement, stages of language development, main categories of psychological disorders, and defence mechanisms.

As well, we have included a very student-friendly, stand-alone statistics module.

ILLUSTRATED

FEATURES THAT HELP STUDENTS VISUALIZE PSYCHOLOGY

A number of pedagogical features using visuals have been developed specifically for *Visualizing Psychology*. Presenting the highly varied and often technical concepts woven throughout psychological science raises challenges for reader and instructor alike. This Illustrated Book Tour provides a guide to the diverse features contributing to the book's pedagogical plan.

CHAPTER INTRODUCTIONS illustrate certain concepts in the chapter with concise stories that underscore some of psychology's most compelling questions. These narratives are featured alongside striking accompanying photographs. The chapter openers also include **CHAPTER OUTLINES** listing the main sections and features of the chapter.

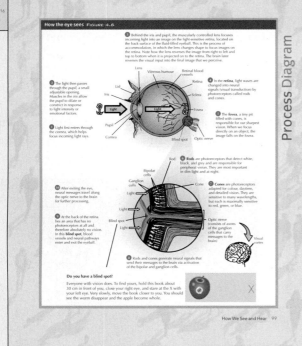

PROCESS DIAGRAMS present a series of figures or a combination of figures and photos that describe and depict a complex process, helping students to observe, follow, and understand the process.

VISUALIZING features are specially designed multipart visual spreads that focus on a key concept or topic in the chapter, exploring it in detail or in broader context using a combination of photos and figures.

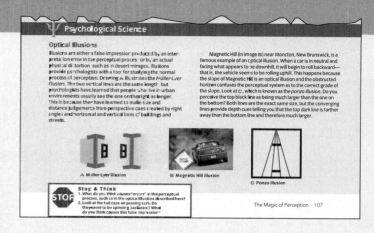

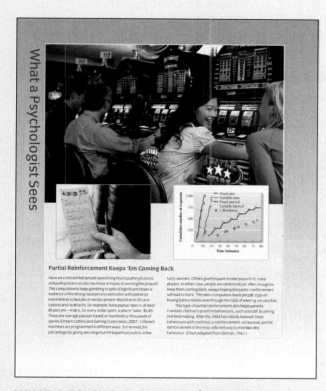

WHAT A PSYCHOLOGIST SEES features highlight a concept or phenomenon, using photos and figures that would stand out to a professional in the field, and helping students to develop observational skills.

PSYCHOLOGICAL SCIENCE features emphasize the empirical, scientific nature of psychology by presenting expanded descriptions of current research findings, along with explanations of their significance and possible applications.

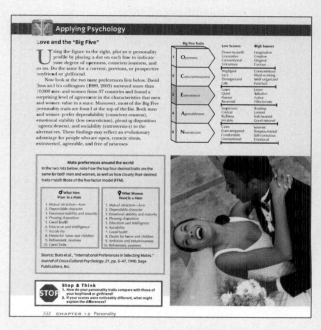

APPLYING PSYCHOLOGY sections help students relate psychological concepts to their own lives and understand how these concepts are applied in various sectors of society, such as school or the workplace.

WHAT IS HAPPENING IN THIS PICTURE? is an end-of-chapter feature that presents students with a photograph relevant to chapter topics but that illustrates a situation students are not likely to have encountered previously. The photograph is paired with questions designed to stimulate creative thinking.

PROVIDE STUDENTS WITH PROVEN LEARNING TOOLS

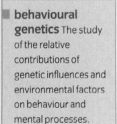

Language

LEARNING OBJECTIVES

Identify the building blocks of language.

Describe the prominent theories of how language and thought interact.

Describe the major stages of language development.

Review the evidence that non-human animals are able to learn and use language.

Language enables us to mentally manipulate symbols, thereby expanding our thinking, and to communicate our thoughts, ideas, and feelings. To produce language, we first build words using **phonemes** and **morphemes**. Then we string words into sentences using rules of

■ **language** A form of communication that uses sounds and symbols combined according to specific rules.

■ **phoneme** [FO-neem] The smallest basic unit of

STUDY ORGANIZERS present material in a format that makes it easy to compare different aspects of a topic, thus providing students with a useful tool for enhancing their understanding of the topic and preparing for exams.

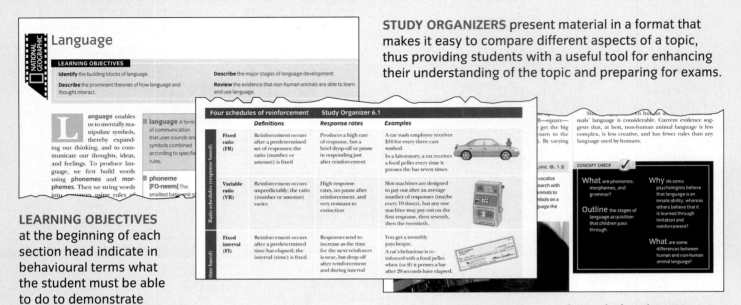

Study Organizer 6.1

Four schedules of reinforcement		Definitions	Response rates	Examples
Ratio schedules (response based)	**Fixed ratio (FR)**	Reinforcement occurs after a predetermined set of responses; the ratio (number or amount) is fixed	Produces a high rate of response, but a brief drop-off or pause in responding just after reinforcement	A car wash employee receives $10 for every three cars washed. In a laboratory, a rat receives a food pellet every time it presses the bar seven times.
	Variable ratio (VR)	Reinforcement occurs unpredictably; the ratio (number or amount) varies	High response rates, no pause after reinforcement, and very resistant to extinction	Slot machines are designed to pay out after an average number of responses (maybe every 10 times), but any one machine may pay out on the first response, then seventh, then the twentieth.
(time based)	**Fixed interval (FI)**	Reinforcement occurs after a predetermined time has elapsed; the interval (time) is fixed	Responses tend to increase as the time for the next reinforcer is near, but drop off after reinforcement and during interval	You get a monthly paycheque. A rat's behaviour is reinforced with a food pellet when (or if) it presses a bar after 20 seconds have elapsed.

Still ... en human animals' language is considerable. Current evidence suggests that, at best, non-human animal language is less complex, is less creative, and has fewer rules than any language used by humans.

CONCEPT CHECK

What are phonemes, morphemes, and grammar?

Why do some psychologists believe that language is an innate ability, whereas others believe that it is learned through imitation and reinforcement?

Outline the stages of language acquisition that children pass through.

What are some differences between human and non-human animal language?

LEARNING OBJECTIVES at the beginning of each section head indicate in behavioural terms what the student must be able to do to demonstrate mastery of chapter material.

CONCEPT CHECK questions at the end of each section encourage students to test their comprehension of the learning objectives.

■ **behavioural genetics** The study of the relative contributions of genetic influences and environmental factors on behaviour and mental processes.

■ **evolutionary psychology** A branch of psychology that studies the ways in which natural selection and evolution can help to explain behaviour and mental processes.

■ **neuroscience** An interdisciplinary field that studies how biological processes interact with behaviour and mental processes.

The human brain FIGURE 2.16

This drawing summarizes key functions of some of the brain's major structures. The brainstem, which includes parts of the hindbrain, midbrain, and forebrain, provides a handy geographical landmark.

VIEW THIS IN ACTION
in your WileyPLUS course

Forebrain
Higher-level structures and functions

Cerebral cortex
Thin outer layer responsible for most complex behaviours and higher mental processes

Corpus callosum

Limbic system
Collection of structures involved in emotions, drives, and memory

Hypothalamus
Controls the endocrine system and the ANS, and regulates behaviours (feeding, fighting, fleeing, and mating)

Reticular formation
Helps screen incoming sensory information and controls arousal

Midbrain

Brainstem
Helps regulate reflex activities critical for survival (e.g., heartbeat and respiration)

Spinal cord
Responsible for transmitting information between brain and rest of body; handles simple reflexes

Thalamus
Relays sensory messages to cortex

Hippocampus
Limbic system structure involved in memory

Pons
Involved with respiration, movement, waking, sleep, and dreaming

Cerebellum
Coordinates fine muscle movement, balance, and some perception and cognition

Medulla
Responsible for breathing, heartbeat, emesis, and other vital life functions

Hindbrain

Daum, 2004; Sacchetti, Sacco, & Strata, 2007).

(car, concert) or abstract *(intelligence, pornography)*. They are

ILLUSTRATIONS AND PHOTOS support concepts covered in the text, elaborate on relevant issues, and add visual detail. Many of the photos originate from National Geographic's rich sources.

MARGINAL GLOSSARY TERMS (IN GREEN BOLDFACE) introduce each chapter's most important terms. Other terms appear in black boldface and are defined in the text.

Mental imagery FIGURE 8.1

Some of our most creative and inspired moments come when we're forming and manipulating mental images. This mountain climber is probably visualizing her next move, and her ability to do so is critical to her success.

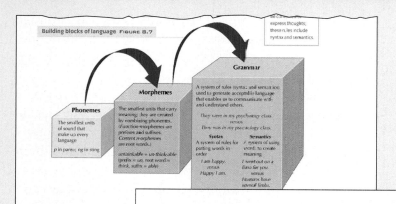

Building blocks of language **FIGURE 8.7**

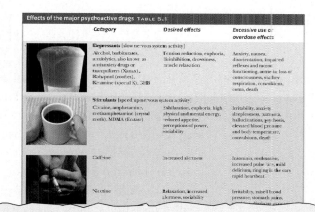

Effects of the major psychoactive drugs **TABLE 5.1**

SUMMARY

TABLES AND GRAPHS, with data sources cited at the end of the text, summarize and organize important information.

The end-of-chapter **SUMMARY** revisits each learning objective and each marginal glossary term, featured in boldface here, and included in a list of **KEY TERMS**. Students are thus able to study vocabulary words in the context of related concepts. Each portion of the Summary is illustrated with a relevant photo from its respective chapter section.

CRITICAL AND CREATIVE THINKING QUESTIONS encourage critical thinking and highlight each chapter's important concepts and applications.

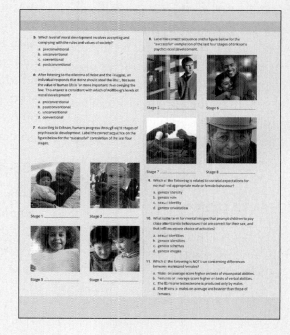

SELF-TESTS at the end of each chapter provide a series of multiple-choice questions, many of them incorporating visuals from the chapter, that review the major concepts.

MEDIA AND SUPPLEMENTS

Visualizing Psychology is accompanied by an array of media and supplements that incorporate the visuals from the textbook extensively to form a pedagogically cohesive package. For example, a Process Diagram from the book appears in the *Instructor's Resource Guide* with suggestions on using it as a PowerPoint in the classroom; it may be the subject of a short video or an on-line animation; and it may also appear with questions in the Test Bank, as part of the chapter review, homework assignment, assessment questions, and other on-line features.

WileyPLUS

This on-line teaching and learning environment integrates the entire digital textbook with the most effective instructor and student resources to fit every learning style. With **WileyPLUS**:

- Students achieve concept mastery in a rich, structured environment that's available 24/7.

- Instructors personalize and manage their course more effectively with assessment, assignments, grade tracking, and more.

WileyPLUS can be used with or in place of the textbook.

INSTRUCTOR RESOURCES

VIDEOS

A collection of videos, many from the award-winning National Geographic Film Collection, have been selected to accompany and enrich the text. Each chapter includes at least one video clip, available on-line as digitized streaming video that illustrates and expands on a concept or topic to aid student understanding. A full list of the National Geographic videos is on page xv. Accompanying each of the videos are contextualized commentary and questions that can further develop student understanding. The videos are available in **WileyPLUS**.

POWERPOINT PRESENTATIONS AND IMAGE GALLERY

A complete set of highly visual PowerPoint presentations is available on-line to enhance classroom presentations. Tailored to the text's topical coverage and learning objectives, these presentations are designed to convey key text concepts, illustrated by embedded text art.

Image Gallery Photographs, figures, maps, and other visuals from the text are on-line and can be used as you wish in the classroom. These on-line electronic files allow you to easily incorporate them into your PowerPoint presentations as you choose, or to create your own overhead transparencies and handouts.

TEST BANK (AVAILABLE IN WileyPLUS AND ELECTRONIC FORMAT)

Some visuals from the textbook are also included in the Test Bank. The Test Bank contains approximately 1,200 test items, including multiple-choice and essay questions that test a variety of comprehension levels. The Test Bank is available in two formats: on-line in MS Word files and as a Computerized Test Bank. The easy-to-use test-generation program fully supports graphics, printed tests, student answer sheets, and answer keys. The software's advanced features allow you to create an exam to your exact specifications.

INSTRUCTOR'S MANUAL (AVAILABLE IN ELECTRONIC FORMAT)

The Instructor's Manual begins with the special introduction *Using Visuals in the Classroom*, prepared by Matthew Leavitt of the Arizona State University, in which he provides guidelines and suggestions on how to use the visuals in teaching the course. Each chapter includes suggestions and directions for using web-based learning modules in the classroom and for homework assignments, as well as creative ideas for in-class activities.

WEB-BASED LEARNING MODULES

A robust suite of multimedia learning resources have been designed for *Visualizing Psychology* focusing on and using the visuals from the book. Delivered via the web, the content is organized into Tutorial animations. These animations visually support the learning of a

difficult concept, process, or theory, many of them built around a specific feature such as a Process Diagram, Visualizing feature, or key visual in the chapter. The animations go beyond the content and visuals presented in the book, providing additional visual examples and descriptive narration.

NATIONAL GEOGRAPHIC SOCIETY VIDEOS

National Geographic videos accompany *Visualizing Psychology*. Below is a brief description of the videos available for each chapter.

Chapter 1 Introduction and Research Methods

1. Among Wild Chimpanzees (3:48) A young Jane Goodall speaks about her work in the wilds of Africa with primates.
2. What Is Psychology? (0:54) What makes us act the way we do? Psychology explores individual differences.

Chapter 2 Neuroscience and Biological Foundations

3. Brain Surgery (4:33) Brain surgery is performed on a young man's tumour while he is awake.
4. Cool Quest (3:59) MRIs map the activity of the brain, exposing "cool" and "uncool" images.
5. Brain Bank (3:08) The Harvard Brain Tissue Resource Center, known as the "Brain Bank," is the largest brain repository in the world.

6. Brain Tumor Surgery (3:14) A patient suffering from seizures discovers he has a massive brain tumour near the part of the brain that controls motor activity.
7. MRI (0:38) An actual patient undergoing an MRI, showing the various images that the MRI produces.

Chapter 3 Stress and Health Psychology

8. Science of Stress (3:31) How stress affects the body.

Chapter 4 Sensation and Perception

9. Eye Trick Town (2:35) In Italy, Trompe L'oeil paintings that "trick" the eye into a perception of depth.
10. Camels (1:25) Photography of camels walking in the desert presents an interesting exploration into the relative nature of sensation and perception.

Chapter 5 States of Consciousness

11. Sleep Walking (1:57) The video suggests that during slow wave, non-REM sleep some people's lower part of the brain wakes up while the upper part of the brain responsible for awareness stays asleep.
12. Bali: Trance (3:24) Highlights of a festival in Bali where villagers come close to stabbing themselves while in a trance state.
13. Peyote and the Huichol People (4:17) The Huichol people ingest peyote, a mind-altering drug to enter the spirit world.

Chapter 6 Learning

14. Animal Minds (1:15) Rats are able to learn their way through a maze, implying they may have a cognitive map.
15. Thai Monkey (2:11) Monkeys are taught how to retrieve coconuts through an official monkey training school, using both operative conditioning and modelling.

Chapter 7 Memory

16. Taxi Drivers (4:06) Video on the role that the hippocampus plays in consolidating memories, suggesting that there is a structural change to the brains of London taxi drivers.

Chapter 8 Thinking, Language, Intelligence

17. Orangutan Language (3:23) The orangutan language project at the National Zoo provides a stimulating environment where they learn a vocabulary of symbols and construct simple sentences.

ABOUT THE AUTHORS

Karen Huffman

Karen Huffman is a professor of psychology at Palomar College in San Marcos, California, where she teaches full-time and serves as the Psychology Student Advisor and Co-Coordinator for Psychology Faculty. Karen received the National Teaching Award for Excellence given by Division Two of the American Psychological Association (APA). She also was recognized with the first Distinguished Faculty Award for Excellence in Teaching from Palomar College, and an Outstanding Teaching award from the University of Texas at Austin. Karen's special research and presentation focus is in active learning and critical thinking, and she has presented numerous on-line web seminars and workshops throughout the United States, Canada, and Puerto Rico. Karen is the author of Wiley introductory psychology texts including, *Psychology in Action* and *Living Psychology*.

Alastair J. Younger

Alastair Younger is Professor of Psychology at the University of Ottawa, Canada's largest bilingual university. He received his B.A. in Psychology from Carleton University in Ottawa in 1976, after which he studied clinical and developmental psychology at Concordia University in Montreal, completing his M.A. in 1979 and his Ph.D. in 1984. He is registered as a clinical psychologist with the College of Psychologists of Ontario and is a member of the Canadian Psychological Association and the Society for Research in Child Development. He is co-author of the first and second Canadian editions of *Child Psychology* (Wiley). In addition, he has authored more than 15 student study guides for courses in introductory psychology, child psychology, and abnormal psychology. He has been a professor at the University of Ottawa for more than 25 years, where he coordinates the introductory psychology courses in both English and French and has taught courses for many years in child psychology, theories of development, social development, and research methods and ethics. His research focuses on children's peer relations, especially shyness/withdrawal and aggression in children.

Claire Vanston

Claire Vanston is a Psychology Instructor at Capilano University in North Vancouver, British Columbia. She earned her B.A. (Hons.) in Psychology in 1997, and completed a Master of Science in biological psychology in 2000, and a Ph.D. in 2005. She has been the recipient of four national-level research scholarships and is a published research psychologist. Her doctoral studies investigated the effects of steroid hormones on cognition and behavior, and she continues working part-time in this area. She also holds a position as a Sexual Health Educator with Options for Sexual Health B.C. (previously Planned Parenthood) teaching elementary and high school sex education. She has authored a half a dozen student study guides and instructor manuals, and has taught a number of courses in community and seniors' education programs. Dr. Vanston has taught courses for many years at Capilano University and elsewhere in the areas of introductory psychology, biological psychology, human neuropsychology, lifespan development, research methods, and human sexuality. She is a mother of daughters, rides a Ducati Monster and is described by her students as "not your average Psych Prof."

ACKNOWLEDGEMENTS

PROFESSIONAL FEEDBACK

Throughout the process of writing and developing this text and the visual pedagogy, we benefited from the comments and constructive criticism provided by the instructors listed below. We offer our sincere appreciation to these individuals for their helpful review:

Cheryl Berezuik, *Grand Prairie Regional College*

Judy Berger, *John Abbott College*

Rena Borovilos, *Humber College*

Kimberley Clow, *University of Ontario Institute of Technology*

Jill Esmonde Moore, *Georgian College*

Renee Ferguson, *Georgian College*

Robin Gagnon, *Dawson College*

Tom Hanrahan, *Canadore College*

Sue Honsberger, *Algonquin College*

Naomi Kestenbaum, *Seneca College*

Linda Lysynchuk, *Laurentian University*

Dawn Moore, *Algonquin College*

Luigi Pasto, *John Abbott College*

Susana Phillips, *Kwantlen Polytechnic University*

Jonah Santa-Barbara, *Mohawk College*

Donald Sharpe, *University of Regina*

Karen Taylor, *NorQuest College*

Karen Tee, *Vanier College*

Mary Trant, *Seneca College*

Paul Valliant, *Laurentian University*

Stephen White, *Champlain College*

Frank Winstan, *Vanier College*

FOCUS GROUPS PARTICIPANTS

A number of students participated in focus groups, providing feedback on the text, visuals, and pedagogy. Our thanks to the following for their helpful comments and suggestions.

Capilano University

Erin Des Mazes, Khorshied Fazel-Bastami, Taraneh Hamzeh, Caroline Leung, Elnaz Shoghi, Carly Thornton

John Abbott College

Amanda Blackburn, Gabriel Charbonneau-Berube, Tanvir Dhanuta, Amelia Giroux, Andrew Halarides, Marie Lachapelle, Lina Malki, Teodora Niculae, Charlotta Prigent, Caroline Ravacley, Zackary Rocha, Nathan Wong

NorQuest College

Sabah Adad, Aida Garibovic, Amanda Gnutle, Janet Hak, Sarah-Lynn Nowell, Janine Tremblay

University of Ontario Institute of Technology

David Ampofo, Candice Anderson, Patience Asante, Mohamed Awad, Leo Benyamin, Neha Bhatia, Mathisan Chandrakumar, Deirdra Cheeseman, Amanda D'Aurelio, Dylan Dever, Jessica England, Jonelle Felix, Larissa Ferguson, Victoria Freitag, Michael Fronte, Stephanie Gloin, Glenn Hanley, Ben Hedley, Keitha Holt, Adeera Khilji, Devon Lasher, Cathlin Martin, Kirsten Moore, Robert Nayer, Jennifer Oliver, Sharif Opoku, Zeleco Persaud, Clive Pires, John Primeau, Jenova Reginold, Sandeep Sahdra, Jenella Satarah James, Abida Sayed, Bhumika Shah, Asra Siddiqui, Talha Tariq, Ashley Yaworski

Vanier College

Joseph Allen Adjei, David Campbell, Nora Chau, Chi Yan Chee, Natasha Garizzi, Andreas Katravas, Gabrielle Lupien, Khushbu Patel, Damiano Raveenthiran, Robert Toto, Karen Vuong

SPECIAL THANKS

Thank you to the team at Wiley for your commitment to excellence and your professionalism. Very special thanks to Gail Brown, our developmental editor, who worked tirelessly to transform our ideas into this beautiful book—without your patience, conscientiousness, commitment, and expertise, this book would not be what it is. We also owe heartfelt thanks to our Acquisitions Editor, Rodney Burke—it was your vision and effort that started this project and expertly directed it to completion; to Helen McInnis, Managing Director, Wiley Visualizing, who oversaw the concept of the book and Barbara Heaney, Director of Product and Market Development.

We wish also to acknowledge the contributions of Vertigo Design for the interior design concept, and Harry Nolan, Creative Director who gave art direction, refined the design and other elements and the cover.

Stacy Gold, Research Editor and Account Executive at the National Geographic Image Collection, also deserves our thanks for her valuable expertise in selecting NGS photos, as does Julie Pratt, photo researcher, who searched for and found additional wonderful photos to help illustrate concepts in this text. As well, the editorial and proofreading contributions of Dawn Hunter and Laurel Hyatt are also very much appreciated.

Our sincerest thanks are also offered to those who worked on and contributed to the wide assortment of supplements and ancillaries, including Jill Esmonde Moore (Georgian College), Renee Ferguson (Georgian College), Kristine Peace (Grant MacEwan University), Jonah Santa-Barbara (Mohawk College), and Amy Walther-Ford (Georgian College).

All the writing, producing, and marketing of this book would be wasted without an energetic and dedicated sales staff. We wish to sincerely thank all the publishing representatives for their tireless efforts and good humour. It's a true pleasure to work with such a remarkable group of people.

From Alastair Younger: To my wife, Manal—thank you for all your wonderful ideas and advice as we discussed the content of each chapter, and for your encouragement and steadfast support throughout the production of this book. To my son Daniel—thank you for your special insight into the world of college students and for taking the time to discuss ideas with me. To my daughter Melanie—thank you for inspiring many of the creative examples that I used in this book and for always being so supportive.

From Claire Vanston: Thanks first to all my students— you are my source of inspiration. To Jill Fikowski— your research skills were among the finest I have ever encountered. And to my family: Dwayne, I could not have done this without you and your unwavering support. Bianca and Alex thanks for understanding that I need to be more than a Mum, and Sophie, this book is for you.

CONTENTS *in Brief*

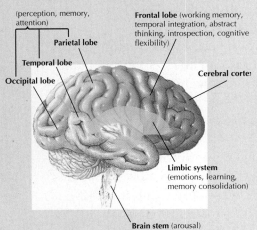

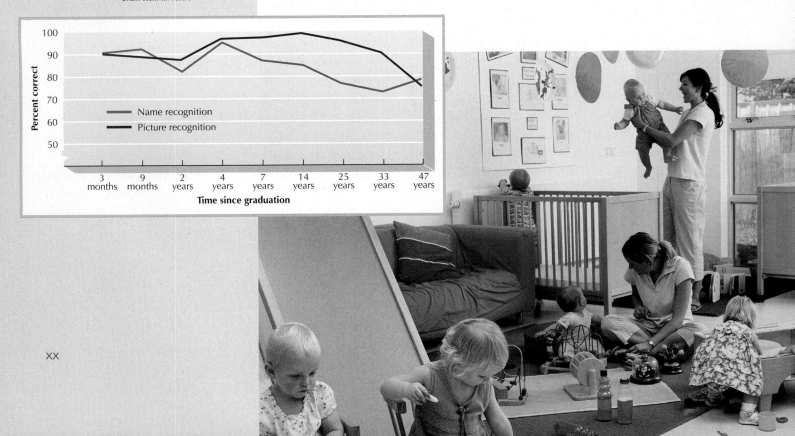

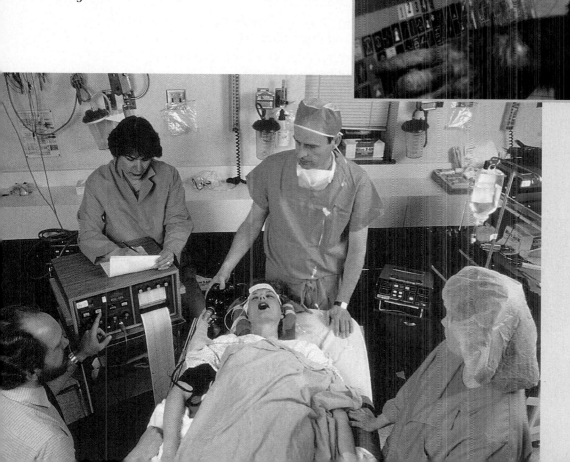

CONTENTS

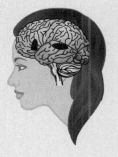

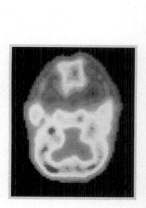

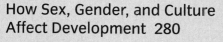
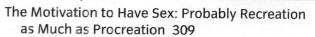
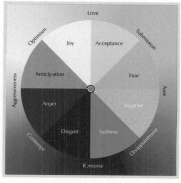

VISUALIZING FEATURES

Visualizing Features: Multi-part visual presentations that focus on a key concept or topic in the chapter

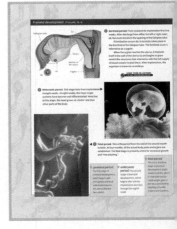

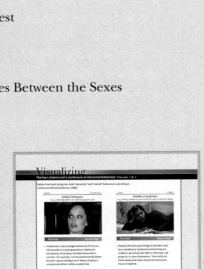

PROCESS DIAGRAMS

Process Diagrams: A series or combination of figures and photos that describe and depict a complex process

CANADIAN EDIT

VISUALIZING

PSYCHOLOGY

What might *compel* a person to willingly dangle hundreds of feet above the ground? What binds mothers—human and non-human alike—to their young? How can chronic stress contribute to serious health problems such as cancer and heart disease? Why are men and women so sexually different? What happens when ancient cultural practices and evolved preferences collide with the demands of modern living? All these questions, and countless more, are the province of psychology.

Psychology is a dynamic field that affects every part of our lives. It encompasses our most private thoughts, our relationships, our physiology, our politics, our gut feelings, and our deliberate decisions. It examines complex interactions that affect us at every level, from the cellular to the cultural, across evolutionary time and into the future. It is truly the study of the human experience. Psychology encompasses not only humankind but also our non-human compatriots—from sea snails and pigeons to cats and chimps.

Psychologists work in an incredible range of areas, perhaps more than you realize. In addition to studying and treating abnormal behaviour, psychologists study sleep, dreaming, stress, health, drugs, personality, sexuality, motivation, emotion, learning, memory, childhood, aging, death, love, conformity, intelligence, creativity, and much, much more.

NATIONAL GEOGRAPHIC

3

Introducing Psychology

LEARNING OBJECTIVES

Describe seven key guidelines for critical thinking.

Describe how scientific psychology differs from pseudopsychologies.

Outline psychology's four main goals.

Identify some of the diverse professional roles that psychologists fill.

WHAT IS PSYCHOLOGY?

psychology The scientific study of behaviour and mental processes.

The term **psychology** derives from the roots *psyche*, meaning "mind," and *logos*, meaning "word." Modern psychology is the scientific study of **behaviour** and **mental processes**. Behaviour is anything we do—from sleeping to rock climbing. Mental processes are our private, internal experiences: thoughts, perceptions, feelings, memories, and dreams.

For many psychologists, the most important part of the definition of psychology is the word *scientific*. Psychology places very high value on empirical evidence and critical thinking, and we have included a detailed discussion of both these terms later in this chapter. First, we want to differentiate psychology from its cheap imitator: pseudopsychology (**TABLE 1.1**).

Be careful not to confuse scientific psychology with pseudopsychologies, which may claim to be scientific but on investigation do not have scientific support, have not been empirically validated, and have not been scrutinized by trained researchers. (*Pseudo* means "false.") Pseudopsychologies include claims made by psychics (who purport to be able to read thoughts and foretell the future), palmistry (reading people's character from the markings on their palms), psychometry (determining facts about an object by handling it), psychokinesis (moving objects by purely mental means), astrology (the study of how the positions of the stars and planets influence people's personalities and affairs), and other similar fields (**FIGURE 1.1**).

PSYCHOLOGY IS ABOUT CRITICAL THINKING; LIFE IS ABOUT CRITICAL THINKING

In his book *Challenging your Preconceptions: Thinking Critically about Psychology*, Randolf A. Smith (2002) begins the preface with the heading you have just read (Smith, 2002). In this book he outlines seven essential guidelines

Test your knowledge of psychology TABLE 1.1

Answer true or false to the following statements:

1. The best way to learn and remember information is to cram, or study it intensively during one concentrated period.

2. Most brain activity stops during sleep.

3. Advertisers and politicians often use subliminal persuasion to influence our behaviour.

4. Punishment is the most effective way to permanently change behaviour.

5. Eyewitness testimony is often unreliable.

6. Polygraph (lie detector) tests can accurately and reliably reveal whether a person is lying.

7. Behaviours that are unusual or that violate social norms indicate a psychological disorder.

8. People with schizophrenia have two or more distinct personalities.

9. Similarity is one of the best predictors of long-term relationships.

10. In an emergency, as the number of bystanders increases, your chance of getting help decreases.

Answers: 1. False (Chapter 1). **2.** False (Chapter 1). **3.** False (Chapter 5). **4.** False (Chapter 4). **5.** True (Chapter 6). **6.** False (Chapter 7). **7.** False (Chapter 11). **8.** False (Chapter 13). **9.** True (Chapter 13). **10.** True (Chapter 15).

critical thinking The ability to accurately analyze information and be able to draw rational, fact-based conclusions based on the empirical evidence provided.

for critical thinking. The term **critical thinking** is defined as the ability to accurately analyze information and be able to draw rational, fact-based conclusions based on the empirical evidence provided. This type of thinking is not only required for psychology but is also essential for everyday life. Every day we are bombarded with advertising claims, news reports, anecdotes, and apparent facts provided by "experts," all purported to be truths. Critical thinking allows us to evaluate these claims.

1. *Critical thinkers are flexible and can tolerate ambiguity and uncertainty.* The process of scientific discovery is neither linear nor perfect nor quick. Understanding the world and the people in it takes time and patience. Critical thinkers appreciate that it takes many studies to understand a psychological phenomenon, and seldom does one single study solve the problem or answer the question. Critical thinkers also acknowledge there is diversity and variation in most areas. They resist the urge to neatly compartmentalize the world and always appreciate that knowledge has grey areas more often than black and white ones.

bias When a belief prevents fair judgement.

2. *Critical thinkers can identify inherent biases and assumptions.*

A **bias** occurs when a belief prevents fair judgement on an issue. An **assumption** is something taken for granted to be true. It takes skill to identify biases and assumptions in claims and even greater skill to identify them in ourselves. We are much less likely to question statements or evidence that fit with an existing belief than those that do not. For example, the statement "yoga improves concentration" is much more likely to be accepted without question than the statement "raspberry ice-cream improves concentration." The former fits with our general beliefs. Although we are much more likely to question the latter statement, we should question *both* claims.

assumption Something taken for granted to be true.

3. *Critical thinkers are sceptical.* Critical thinkers must maintain an air of cautious suspicion when evaluating the claims of others. If it sounds too convenient, too good, or too simplistic to be true, then it probably is. Never accept anything on authority; insist that claims must be supported with empirical evidence; and be careful of statements that appear to be derived from received wisdom. It is perfectly okay to ask, "How do you know that?" Base your decision on the response to that question. Be wary of such responses as "everybody knows" or "my friend/mom/aunt/teacher told me." Neither are empirical sources.

empirical evidence
Information acquired by formal observation, experimentation, and measurement by using systematic scientific methods.

4. *Critical thinkers separate facts from opinion.* A major difference between scientists and non-scientists is that scientists are trained to ignore opinions and look for quality evidence. The standard of evidence in psychological science is **empirical evidence**. This is evidence obtained from experimentation, formal observation, or measurement. Opinions, urban myths, old wives tales, good stories, and fables are not empirical sources and are therefore not valid forms of scientific evidence. Likewise, critical thinkers do not fall into the trap of *argument by anecdote*, which is evidence provided as a personal story or word-of-mouth description. Simply because someone told you it worked for them is not evidence that it has worked. Often in first-year college and university courses students are challenged when general psychological principles and findings contradict their personal experiences and beliefs. If this happens to you, look for the empirical evidence.

5. *Critical thinkers do not oversimplify.* Although simple explanations are often appealing, and many of us want to find solutions to problems quickly, the world generally does not work that way. People, their thinking, and their behaviours are complex, diverse, and ambiguous. Scientific questions are often complicated. Psychological problems are not solved in one hour of therapy, or before the next commercial break (as some afternoon TV shows would have you believe). Critical thinkers understand that although simple explanations can be appealing, they are often too simple to be correct.

6. *Critical thinkers make logical inferences.* If your friend told you he was going to school at 8 a.m. today when he normally leaves at noon, you might infer he wanted to study, go to the library, or work on a project. Your logical inference follows on from the information given. It would not be logical for you to infer your friend was going to school early because he was going to be teleported to Jupiter. Similarly, critical thinkers use logical inference processes in their own thinking and in evaluating the claims of others. If it sounds weird, inconsistent, or illogical, then ask more questions.

7. *Critical thinkers examine the available evidence.* This is probably the most important of all seven guidelines and good critical thinkers generally use this one the most. Because empirical evidence is the general standard used to evaluate claims, ideas, and information, if someone cannot support a claim with some proof, the statement should be discounted. If you are in doubt, ask questions and always look at the quality of the evidence (**FIGURE 1.2**).

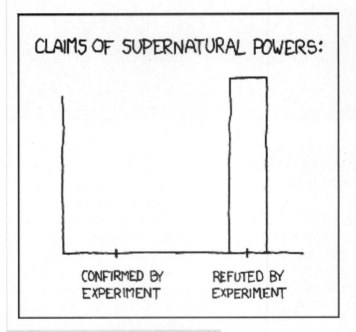

The data so far FIGURE 1.2

As this cartoon humorously illustrates, empirical evidence is often the best test of the facts.

Sources of empirical psychology evidence
Scholarly journal articles
Psychology textbooks

Sources that should be verified
Websites
News programs
Newspapers
Documentary TV shows

Sources that should not be used to make empirical claims
Anecdotes
Urban myths
Old wives tales
Fables and legends
Horoscopes
Television shows, including sitcoms

Psychological Science

The Goals of Psychology

Scientific psychology has four basic goals: to describe, explain, predict, and change behaviour or mental processes through the use of scientific methods. Let's consider each within the context of aggressive behaviour.

Psychologists usually attempt to *describe*, or name and classify, particular behaviours by making careful scientific observations. For example, if someone says, "Men are more aggressive than women," we would ask what is meant by the term *aggressive*. Does *aggressive* mean angry? Prone to yelling? Likely to throw the first punch? Scientific description requires specificity in terms.

To *explain* a behaviour or mental process, we need to discover and understand its causes. One of the most enduring debates in science has been the nature-nurture controversy (Gardiner & Kosmitski, 2005; McCrae, 2004). To what extent are we controlled by biological and genetic factors (the nature side), or by environment and learning (the nurture side)? Today, almost all scientists agree that most psychological, and even physical, qualities reflect an interaction between nature and nurture. For example, research indicates that there are numerous interacting causes or explanations for aggression, including culture, learning, genes, nervous systems, and high levels of testosterone (e.g., Dodge, Coie, & Lynam, 2008; Juntii, Coats, & Shah, 2008; Kelly et al., 2008; Temceff et al., 2008).

> **nature-nurture controversy**
> Dispute over the relative contributions of nature (heredity) and nurture (environment) in the development of behaviour and mental processes.

After describing and explaining a behaviour, an event, or a mental process, psychologists try to *predict* the conditions under which it is likely to occur. For instance, knowing that excessive alcohol consumption leads to increased aggression (Tremblay, Graham, & Wells, 2008), we might predict that more fights will erupt in places where alcohol is consumed than in those where alcohol isn't consumed.

The final goal of psychology is to *change* behaviour. To psychologists, change means applying psychological knowledge to prevent unwanted outcomes or to bring about desired goals. In almost all cases, change as a goal of psychology is positive. For example, psychologists help people stop addictive behaviours, improve their work environments, learn better, become less depressed, improve their family relationships, and so on.

Stop & Think
1. How would you explain the behaviour illustrated in the photo?
2. Can you predict the conditions under which such behaviour is likely to occur?

Many people think of psychologists only as therapists and counsellors, but many psychologists have no connection with therapy at all. Instead, they work as researchers, teachers, and consultants in academic, business, industry, and government settings, or in a combination of settings (**TABLE 1.2**). For more information about what psychologists do—or how to pursue a career in psychology—visit the websites of the Canadian Psychological Association (CPA; www.cpa.ca), the American Psychological Association (APA; www.apa.org), and the Association for Psychological Science (APS; www. psychologicalscience.org).

Areas of specialization in psychology TABLE 1.2

Area of Specialization	What a Psychologist Does
Biopsychology or neuroscience	Investigates the relationship among biology, behaviour, and mental processes, including how physical and chemical processes affect the structure and function of the brain and nervous system
Clinical psychology	Specializes in the evaluation, diagnosis, and treatment of mental and behavioural disorders
Cognitive psychology	Examines higher mental processes, including thought, memory, intelligence, creativity, and language
Counselling psychology	Overlaps with clinical psychology, but practitioners tend to work with less seriously disturbed individuals and conduct more career and vocational assessment
Developmental psychology	Studies human growth and development from conception until death
Educational and school psychology	Studies the process of education and works to promote the intellectual, social, and emotional development of children in the school environment
Experimental psychology	Examines processes, such as learning, conditioning, motivation, emotion, sensation, and perception, in humans and other animals. (The term *experimental psychologist* is somewhat misleading because psychologists working in almost all areas of specialization also conduct research.)
Forensic psychology	Applies principles of psychology to the legal system, including jury selection, psychological profiling, and so on
Gender and/or cultural psychology	Investigates how men and women and different cultures differ from one another and how they are similar
Health psychology	Studies how biological, psychological, and social factors affect health and illness
Industrial/organizational psychology	Applies the principles of psychology to the workplace, including personnel selection and evaluation, leadership, job satisfaction, employee motivation, and group processes within the organization
Social psychology	Investigates the role of social forces and interpersonal behaviour, including aggression, prejudice, love, helping, conformity, and attitudes

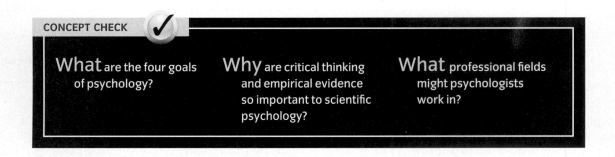

CONCEPT CHECK ✓

What are the four goals of psychology?

Why are critical thinking and empirical evidence so important to scientific psychology?

What professional fields might psychologists work in?

Origins of Psychology

Although people have always been interested in human nature (think about why you took this course), it was not until the first psychological laboratory was founded in 1879 that psychology as a science officially began. As interest in the new field grew, psychologists adopted various perspectives on the "appropriate" topics for psychological research at the time and the "proper" research methods. These diverse viewpoints and subsequent debates have shaped modern psychological science.

A BRIEF HISTORY: PSYCHOLOGY'S INTELLECTUAL ROOTS

Wilhelm Wundt [VILL-helm Voont; (1832–1920)], generally acknowledged as the "father of psychology," established the first psychological laboratory in Germany in 1879. Wundt helped train the first scientific psychologists and wrote one of psychology's most important books, *Principles of Physiological Psychology*, which was published in 1874.

Wundt and his followers were primarily interested in how we form sensations (from our senses), images, and feelings. Their chief methodology was termed "*introspection*," which involved monitoring and reporting on our inner world or conscious experiences (Goodwin, 2009). Edward Titchener, a student of Wundt, brought his ideas to the United States. Titchener's approach, now known as **structuralism**, sought to identify the basic building blocks, or structures, of thoughts through introspection and then to determine how these elements combine to form the whole experience. Because introspection could not be used to study animals, children, or more complex mental disorders, structuralism failed as a working psychological approach. Although short-lived, structuralism established a model for studying mental processes scientifically. In fact, James Mark Baldwin, who in 1889 established the first

psychological laboratory in Canada at the University of Toronto, was influenced by this approach, having done some of his graduate training in Germany with Wundt (Cairns & Cairns, 2006; Wright & Myers, 1982).

Structuralism's intellectual successor, **functionalism**, studied how the mind functions to help humans and other animals adapt to their environment. Functionalism, led by American William James (**FIGURE 1.3**), was strongly influenced by Charles Darwin's theory of evolution by natural selection (Chapter 2) (Segerstrale, 2000). Although functionalism also eventually declined, it expanded the scope of psychology to include research on emotions and observable behaviours, initiated the psychological testing movement, and influenced modern education and industry.

William James (1842–1910) FIGURE 1.3

William James broadened psychology to include the study of animal behaviour, the influence of biological processes, and observable behaviours. His book *Principles of Psychology* (1890) was the first textbook in psychology and took him 12 years to write.

During the late nineteenth and early twentieth centuries, while functionalism was prominent in the United States, the **psychoanalytic school** was forming in Europe (Gay, 2000). Its founder, Austrian physician Sigmund Freud, believed that many psychological problems are caused by conflicts between "acceptable" behaviour and "unacceptable" unconscious sexual or aggressive motives (Chapter 12). The theory provided a basis for a system of therapy known as *psychoanalysis* (Chapter 14).

Freud's non-scientific approach and emphasis on sexual and aggressive impulses have long been controversial, and today few strictly Freudian psychoanalysts are left. But the broad features of his theory profoundly influenced psychotherapy and psychiatry and modern psychodynamic psychologists, who focus on the importance of unconscious processes and unresolved past conflicts.

In the early twentieth century, another major perspective appeared that dramatically shaped the future course of psychology. Unlike earlier approaches, the **behaviourist perspective** emphasizes objective, observable environmental influences on overt behaviour. Behaviourism's founder, John B. Watson (1913), vociferously rejected the practice of introspection as a method of research and also the notion that unconscious forces influence behaviour. Instead, Watson adopted Russian physiologist Ivan Pavlov's concept of *conditioning* (Chapter 6) to explain behaviour in terms of observable stimuli (in the environment) and observable responses (behavioural actions).

Most early behaviourist research was focused on learning, and non-human animals were ideal subjects for this research. One of the best-known behaviourists, B. F. Skinner, was convinced that behaviourist approaches could be used to "shape" human and other animal behaviour. Therapeutic techniques rooted in the behaviourist perspective have been most successful in treating observable behavioural problems, such as phobias and alcoholism (Chapter 13) (**FIGURE 1.4**).

Although the psychoanalytic and behaviourist perspectives dominated North American psychology for some time, in the 1950s a new approach emerged, the **humanistic perspective**, which stressed *free will* (voluntarily chosen behaviour) and *self-actualization* (a state of self-fulfillment). According to Carl Rogers and Abraham Maslow, two central humanist figures, all individuals naturally strive to develop and move toward self-actualization. Like psychoanalysis, humanist psychology developed an influential theory of personality and a form of psychotherapy (chapters 12 and 14).

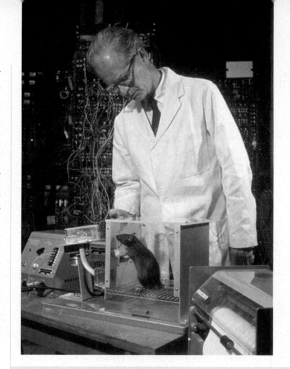

B. F. Skinner (1904–1990) and the conditioning box he developed FIGURE 1.4

B. F. Skinner was one of the most influential psychologists of the twentieth century. He believed that by using basic learning principles to shape human behaviour, we could change what he perceived as the negative course of humankind.

One of the most powerful influential modern approaches, the **cognitive perspective**, recalls psychology's earliest years by emphasizing thoughts, perceptions, and information processing. Modern cognitive psychologists, however, study how we gather, encode, and store information using our vast array of mental processes. These include perception, memory, imagery, concept formation, problem solving, reasoning, decision-making, and language. Many cognitive psychologists employ what is called an *information-processing approach*, likening the mind to a computer that sequentially takes in information, processes it, and then produces a response.

During the last few decades, scientists have explored the role of biological factors in almost every area of psychology. Using sophisticated tools and technologies, scientists who adopt this **neuroscientific** or **biopsychological perspective** examine behaviour through the lens of genetics and biological processes in the brain and nervous system.

The **evolutionary perspective** stresses natural selection (Chapter 2), adaptation, and the evolution of behaviour and mental processes. Its proponents argue that natural selection has favoured human and other animal behaviours that enhance an organism's reproductive success, thereby ensuring that their genes are passed on to subsequent generations.

Finally, the **sociocultural perspective** emphasizes social interactions and cultural determinants of behaviour and mental processes. Although we are often unaware of their influence, such factors as ethnicity, religion, occupation, and socio-economic class have an enormous psychological impact on our mental processes and behaviour.

Early schools of psychological thought, such as structuralism and functionalism, have almost entirely disappeared or have been blended into newer, broader perspectives. Contemporary psychology reflects seven major perspectives: psychoanalytic/psychodynamic, behaviourist, humanistic, cognitive, neuroscientific/biopsychological, evolutionary, and sociocultural (STUDY ORGANIZER 1.1). Yet the complex behaviours and mental processes humans and other animals exhibit require complex explanations. That is why most contemporary psychologists do not adhere to one single intellectual perspective. Instead, a more integrative, unifying theme—the **biopsychosocial model**—has gained wide acceptance. This model views biological processes (e.g., genetics, the nervous system, and evolution), psychological factors (e.g., learning, thinking, emotion, personality, and motivation), and social forces (e.g., family, school, culture, ethnicity, social class, and politics) as interrelated, inseparable influences (see *What a Psychologist Sees*).

> **biopsychosocial model** A unifying theme of modern psychology that considers biological, psychological, and social processes.

The Biopsychosocial Model

Look at the young person in this photo. What might be the cause of her emotional arousal? Now look at the photo below, which shows her within a broader context. With this "bigger picture" (the immediate surroundings, her parents' guiding influence, and her culture's enthusiasm for exciting sporting events) in mind, can you better understand why she might be feeling and behaving as she is? The biopsychosocial model recognizes that there is usually no single cause for our behaviour or our mental states. For example, our moods and feelings are often influenced by genetics and neurotransmitters (biology), our learned responses and patterns of thinking (psychology), and our socio-economic status and cultural views of emotion (social).

Perspectives   *Major Emphases*

Psychoanalytic/Psychodynamic   Unconscious processes and unresolved past conflicts

Behaviourist   Objective, observable environmental influences on overt behaviour

Humanistic   Free-will, self-actualization, and human nature as naturally positive and growth-seeking

Cognitive   Thinking, perceiving, problem solving, memory, language, and information processing

Neuroscientific/Biopsychological   Genetics and biological processes in the brain and other parts of the nervous system

Evolutionary   Natural selection, adaptation, and evolution of behaviour and mental processes

Sociocultural   Social interaction and the cultural determinants of behaviour and mental processes

VIEW THIS IN ACTION
in your WileyPLUS course

THE BIOPSYCHOSOCIAL MODEL

The biopsychosocial model combines and interacts with the seven major perspectives.

CONCEPT CHECK ✓

Which early schools of psychological thought are reflected in modern perspectives?

Why did structuralism decline in popularity?

What modern perspective views biological, psychological, and social forces as interrelated influences on behaviour?

The Science of Psychology

In science, research strategies are generally categorized as either basic or applied. **Basic research** is typically conducted in universities or research laboratories by researchers who are interested in advancing general scientific understanding. Basic research meets the first three goals of psychology (description, explanation, and prediction). Complementing basic research is **applied research**. Applied research can be conducted either outside or inside the laboratory, and it meets the fourth goal of psychology—to change existing real-world problems.

Basic and applied research often interact, with one building on the other. For example, after basic research identified how chronic sleep deprivation impairs performance, more applied research showed how sleep extensions (that is, getting more sleep) improve both reaction time and mood in people (Kamdar, Kaplan, Kezirian, & Dement, 2004). Findings like this have important implications for sports medicine and academic settings.

> **basic research**
> Research conducted to advance scientific knowledge rather than for practical application.

> **applied research**
> Research designed to solve practical real-world problems.

THE SCIENTIFIC METHOD: AN ORGANIZED WAY OF DISCOVERING

Like scientists in any field, psychologists follow strict, standardized scientific procedures so that others can understand, interpret, and repeat or retest their findings.

Most scientific studies involve six basic steps (**FIGURE 1.5**). The **scientific method** is cyclical and additive, and scientific progress comes from repeatedly challenging and revising existing theories and creating new ones. When different scientists, using different participants in different settings, can partially repeat, completely repeat, or *replicate*, a study's findings, there is much greater confidence in the accuracy of the results. If the findings cannot be replicated, researchers look for explanations and conduct further studies. Similar to a jigsaw puzzle, scientific discovery involves putting together many little pieces of information to reveal the whole picture.

> **scientific method**
> A systematic and orderly procedure for understanding and learning about the world.

ETHICAL GUIDELINES: PROTECTING THE RIGHTS OF OTHERS

The largest professional organization of psychologists in Canada is the Canadian Psychological Association (CPA). Its first objective is to improve the health and welfare of all Canadians. This objective is achieved by a mandate to promote excellence in psychological research, psychological education, and psychological practice. The CPA outlines four ethical principles, listed in order of weight, intended to guide Canadian psychologists and others in the field of psychology:

Principle I: Respect the dignity of all people.
Principle II: Provide responsible caring.
Principle III: Demonstrate integrity in relationships.
Principle IV: Be responsible to society.

Process Diagram

Cycle continues ➤

Step 1
Literature review
The scientist conducts a *literature review,* reading what has been published in major professional, scientific journals on her subject of interest.

Cycle begins ➤

Step 6
Theory
After one or more studies on a topic, researchers generally advance a *theory* to explain their results. This new theory then leads to new (possibly different) hypotheses and new methods of inquiry.

Step 2
Operationally defined hypothesis
The scientist makes a testable prediction or *hypothesis* about how one factor or variable interacts with another. To be scientifically testable, the variables must be *operationally defined*—that is, stated very precisely and in measurable terms.

SCIENTIFIC METHOD

Step 5
Peer-reviewed scientific journal
The scientist writes up the study and its results and submits it to a *peer-reviewed scientific journal.* (Peer-reviewed journals ask other scientists to critically evaluate submitted material before publication.) On the basis of these peer reviews, the study may then be accepted for publication.

Step 3
Research design
The scientist chooses the best *research design* to test the hypothesis and collect the data. She might choose naturalistic observations, case studies, correlations, surveys, experiments, or other methods.

Step 4
Statistical analysis
The scientist performs *statistical analyses* on the raw data to describe, organize, and numerically summarize them. Additional statistical analyses are performed to make inferences about the study to the more general population. This allows the researcher to determine whether the findings support or refute the hypothesis.

Respecting the Rights of Human Participants

One of the primary principles governing research with human participants requires a researcher to obtain a research participant's **informed consent** (FIGURE 1.6) *before* initiating an experiment. The researcher must fully inform the participant as to the nature of the study, including any physical risks, discomfort, or unpleasant emotional experiences. The researcher must also explain to the participant that he or she can refuse to participate in the study and can withdraw from the research even after the study has started.

One of the outcomes of informed consent is that participants are aware of the purpose of the study. This can often change the actions of the participants and they may not respond naturally in the research setting. Therefore, the CPA acknowledges the need sometimes for some minor deception in certain research areas. When deception is used, important guidelines and restrictions apply, including **debriefing** participants at the end of the experiment.

CPA guidelines also stipulate that all information acquired about people during a study must be held confidential and not published in such a way that individuals' privacy is compromised.

Finally, an institutional research ethics board must first approve all research that uses human participants conducted at a college, a university, or any other reputable institution. Most scholarly journals in North America will not publish a study without a statement from the researcher confirming the research was compliant with its in-house institutional research board. If a Canadian researcher receives federal money to help fund the costs of his or her research, the researcher must comply with the ethical rules of the federal funding agency. Should a researcher violate the ethical rules, his or her funding can be cancelled.

Respecting the Rights of Non-human Animals

Although they are involved in only 7 to 8 percent of psychological research (American Psychological Association, 1984) non-human animals—mostly rats and mice—have made significant contributions to almost every area of psychology, including the brain and nervous system, health and stress, sensation and perception, sleep, learning, memory, and emotion. Non-human animal research (FIGURE 1.7) has also produced significant gains for animals themselves—for example, by suggesting more natural environments for zoo and lab animals and more successful breeding techniques for endangered species.

Informed consent FIGURE 1.6

Research participants must be fully informed of the nature of a study, including the potential risks involved, before agreeing to participate.

Non-human animal research FIGURE 1.7

Although guidelines provide instructions for the care, housing, and socialization of animals in non-human animal research, the issue remains hotly debated.

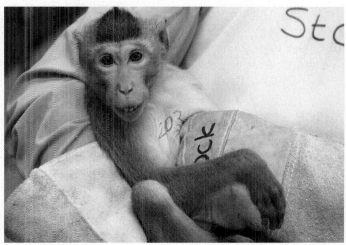

The Canadian Council on Animal Care (CCAC) (www.ccac.ca) supervises research involving non-human animals. The mandate of the CCAC emphasizes both high ethical standards and research excellence (Canadian Council on Animal Care [CCAC], 2005). The CCAC provides clear guidelines for the use of animals in research, testing, and teaching (it has no jurisdiction over animals used for human consumption). Its guidelines contain instructions on how to care for research animals, including such factors as housing, diet, socialization, transportation, veterinary care, anaesthesia, and surgical procedures (CCAC, 2005). Should researchers violate these guidelines, they risk losing the federal funding. Each year the CCAC publishes summary documents on its website that include statistics regarding the numbers of animals used in biomedical research in Canada, the types of species used, and the types of procedures conducted. As with human research, all animal research must be approved before the study's inception by an Institutional Animal Care Committee. This committee compares the proposed research to the CCAC guidelines to ensure compliance. Any non-compliant proposals must be changed or the research cannot be conducted.

While the ethical debate surrounding the use of non-human animals in research is ongoing and has been a topic of considerable media attention (Saucier & Cain, 2006), it is often overlooked that psychologists do, in fact, take great care with their research animals. Researchers also actively search for new and better ways to protect animals (Appiah, 2008; CCAC, 2005; Guidelines for Ethical Conduct, 2008). For example, the CCAC requires researchers to test their proposed research against the three Rs when using research animals (Russell & Burch as cited in CCAC, 2005): *reduce* the numbers of animals used in research; *replace* animals with other types of research models wherever possible, and *refine* experiments such that animal suffering and discomfort is minimized.

Respecting the Rights of Psychotherapy Clients

Like psychological scientists, therapists must also maintain the highest of ethical standards and uphold their clients' trust. All personal information and therapy records must be kept confidential, with records being available only to authorized persons and with the client's permission. However, the public's right to safety ethically outweighs the client's right to privacy. If a therapist believes a client might harm herself or himself or others, the therapist is legally required to report the information. In general, however, a psychologist's primary obligation is to protect client disclosures (Sue & Sue, 2008). Clinicians who violate the ethical guidelines risk severe sanctions and can permanently lose their licences to practise.

Plagiarism: The Dark Side of Research

In most artistic and academic arenas, individuals who create and publish documents own these works as part of their intellectual property. It is the same in research. When researchers publish a study, idea, or theory they have created, they must be acknowledged or credited when another discusses or uses their research. In psychology, we acknowledge the work of another by using citations. These typically include the name of the authors and the year of publication of the work in parentheses following the discussion of the work. Citations are then listed in full in the references section at the end of the document. A person who does not acknowledge the work of another with proper citations and references is guilty of **plagiarism**. Plagiarism is a form of academic dishonesty and a serious ethical violation. It is generally uncommon in most research areas, but with the electronic age, it has become more common among post-secondary students (Badge, Cann, & Scott, 2007). While most students do not plagiarize, some do. A variety of factors have been shown to foster this form of cheating, such as poor academic skill, time management issues, ineffective deterrence, or simply student ignorance (Park, 2007). Despite the explanations, however, there is no acceptable excuse for plagiarism. It is a serious and risky infraction and should never be considered let alone practised.

> ■ **plagiarism**
> A form of academic dishonesty in which a person takes credit for the work or ideas of another person.

Psychology as a Discipline that Has Helped but also Harmed

Although psychology has done a great deal to help improve the quality of life for many; in the past psychology has also inadvertently harmed people. For example, it was psychologists who developed and administered the first intelligence tests. Although these tests have served many valid and useful purposes, IQ scores have also been misused to legitimize racial and cultural bigotry, force sterilizations, and justify mass murder (Murdoch, 2007). Another example of inadvertent harm can be seen in the work of psychoanalyst Frieda Fromm-Reichmann, who gave us the early, and incorrect, theory that mothers could cause their children to become schizophrenic. The *schizophrenogenic* mother was described as a dominant, overprotective, and rejecting mother who, by her behaviour, could induce psychosis in her child. This explanation persisted for a number of years, and caused untold guilt and stress for many families (Parker, 1982). Psychologists have also supported surgical procedures that while creating more compliant mental health patients, in many cases also resulted in their permanent brain damage (Baker & Pickren, 2007).

While psychology does not have a perfect track record as a helping profession, it is a discipline that is self-critical (Danziger, 1994) and does attempt to ultimately undo some of the harm it has caused. Sadly, it is only in hindsight that these mistakes are generally identified. Consider this as you read the chapters in this text. Is there a current therapy, theory, or procedure about which future generations of psychologists might say, "That hurt a lot of people—what were they thinking back then?"

CONCEPT CHECK ✓

What is the primary purpose of basic research? Of applied research?

How do scientists generate and refine hypotheses?

What is informed consent? Debriefing? Confidentiality?

What procedures are in place to protect human and non-human research participants?

Research Methods

LEARNING OBJECTIVES

Explain why only experiments can identify the cause and effect underlying particular patterns of behaviour and mental processes.

Differentiate the independent variable from the dependent variable.

Describe the three key types of descriptive research.

Explain how correlational research identifies relationships between variables.

Explain what is meant by the statement "correlation is not causation."

Identify some important research methods used in biological studies.

Psychologists draw on four major types of psychological research: experimental, descriptive, correlational, and biological (**STUDY ORGANIZER 1.2**). All have advantages and disadvantages, so most psychologists use several methods to study a single problem. In fact, when multiple methods lead to similar conclusions, the accuracy of research findings is strengthened.

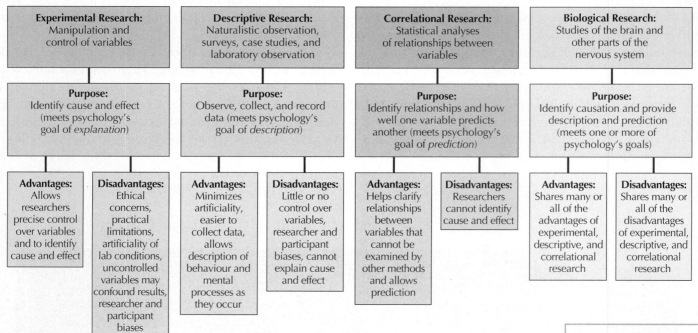

Note that the four methods are not mutually exclusive. Researchers may use two or more methods to explore the same topic.

EXPERIMENTAL RESEARCH: A SEARCH FOR CAUSE AND EFFECT

experiment
A carefully controlled scientific procedure that determines whether variables manipulated by the experimenter have a causal effect on the experiment result.

The most powerful research method is the **experiment**, in which a researcher manipulates and controls the experimental variables to determine cause and effect. Only through an experiment can researchers isolate and examine a single factor's effect on a particular behaviour (Goodwin, 2009). That's because the only way to discover which of many possible factors has an effect is to experimentally isolate each one. As illustrated in **FIGURE 1.8**, an experiment has a number of critical components, including an **independent variable (IV)**, a **dependent variable (DV)**, an experimental group, and a control group. See **TABLE 1.3** for help with understanding the difference between the independent and dependent variable.

independent variable (IV)
A variable that is manipulated by the researcher to determine its effect on the dependent variable. The IV is the *cause* variable.

dependent variable (DV)
A variable that is measured; it is affected by (or dependent on) the independent variable and is the outcome or *effect* variable.

Differentiating the independent variable from the dependent variable   TABLE 1.3

IV	Independent variable	Cause variable	Manipulated by experimenter
DV	Dependent variable	Effect variable	Measured by the experimenter

As a memory aid, remember that *dependent* starts with the letter *d* and *data* (that are measured and collected by the experimenter) also starts with the letter *d*.

Process Diagram

To test the hypothesis that watching violent television increases aggression, experimenters might randomly assign children to one of two groups: **experimental group** participants, who watch a prearranged number of violent television programs, and **control group** participants, who watch the same amount of television, except the programs that they watch are nonviolent. (*Having at least two groups— a control group and an experimental group— allows the performance of one group to be compared with that of another.*)

Experimenters then observe the children and count how many times—say, within one hour—each child hits, kicks, or punches a punching bag (an operational definition of aggression).

■ **experimental group** The group that receives the experimental manipulation.

■ **control group** The group that does not receive the experimental manipulations but is treated the same way as the experimental group in all other areas.

Hypothesis
"Watching violence on TV increases aggression."*

Participants are **randomly selected** from the population and **randomly assigned** to the experimental group or control group.

Experimental Group

Control Group

Independent Variable (IV)
(Violent or nonviolent program)

Dependent Variable (DV)
(Number of times child hits the punching bag)

Groups Compared

* If this were a real experiment, we would operationally define the type and amount of violent TV and what is meant by "aggression." In this example, aggression is the number of times the child hits the bag.

VIEW THIS IN ACTION
in your WileyPLUS course

The goal of any experiment is to learn how the dependent variable is affected by (or depends on) the independent variable. Experiments can also have different *levels* of an independent variable. For example, consider the experiment testing the effect of TV violence on aggression described in Figure 1.8. Two experimental groups could be created, with one group watching two hours of mixed martial arts fighting and the other watching six hours; the control group would watch only non-violent programming. Then a researcher could relate differences in aggressive behaviour (DV) to the *amount* of violent programming viewed (IV).

In experiments, all extraneous variables (such as time of day, lighting conditions, and participants' age and sex) must be held constant across experimental and control groups so that they are exactly the same between the two groups. This ensures these **confound variables** do not affect the groups' results.

> **confound variables** Nuisance variables that can affect the outcome of the study and lead to erroneous conclusions about the effects of the independent variable on the dependent variable.

In addition to the scientific controls mentioned (e.g., operational definitions, a control group, and controlled confound variables), a good scientific experiment protects against potential sources of error from both the researcher and the participants. Experimenters can unintentionally let their beliefs and expectations affect participants' responses, producing flawed results. For example, imagine what might happen if an experimenter breathed a sigh of relief when a participant gave a response that supported the researcher's hypothesis. One way to prevent such **experimenter bias** from destroying the validity of participants' responses is to establish objective methods for collecting and recording data. For example, an experimenter might use computers to present stimuli and record responses.

Another option is to design a **double-blind study** in which neither the researcher nor the participant knows which group received the experimental treatment. In a **single-blind study**, the researcher knows who is in the experimental and the control groups, but the participants do not (**FIGURE 1.9**).

Single-blind study
The experimenter knows who is in the experimental versus the control groups and the participants do not.

Double-blind study
Neither the experimenter nor the participants know who is in which group.

Single-blind versus double-blind study
FIGURE 1.9

Participants can also add error or bias into an experiment. First, **sample bias** can occur if the sample of participants does not accurately reflect the composition of the larger population that they have been drawn from. For example, in psychology, critics have argued that the subject pool used for most of our research has been biased because it has historically used either young, white male post-secondary students or young, white male rats—not to suggest these mammals are interchangeable as research subjects, of course. One way to minimize sample bias is to randomly select participants who constitute a representative sample of the entire population of interest. Logically, this process is called **random selection**. Once the sample has been obtained, assigning participants to experimental groups by using a chance, or random, system, such as a coin toss, also helps prevent sample bias. **Random assignment** ensures that each participant is equally likely to be assigned to either the experimental group or the control group.

> **random selection** Everyone in the population of interest has an equal chance of being in the sample.

> **random assignment** Everyone selected to be in the study has an equal chance of being put in either the control group or the experimental group.

Bias can also occur when participants are influenced by the experimental conditions. For example, participants may try to present themselves in a good light (the **social desirability response**) or deliberately attempt to mislead the researcher. This type of bias is especially common with controversial research topics, such as infidelity, drinking and driving behaviours, illegal drug use, and cheating. Researchers attempt to control for this type of participant bias by allowing respondents to answer anonymously.

DESCRIPTIVE RESEARCH: FORMAL OBSERVATION AND RECORDING

descriptive research Research methods used to observe, record, and describe behaviour (without producing cause–effect explanations).

We all watch others, think about their behaviour, and try to explain and understand what we see; but in conducting **descriptive research**, psychologists do it systematically and scientifically. The key types of descriptive research are naturalistic observation, laboratory observation, surveys, and case studies. Most of the problems and safeguards discussed for the experimental method also apply to these non-experimental techniques.

When conducting **naturalistic observation**, researchers systematically measure and record a subject's behaviour, without trying to manipulate anything. Many settings lend themselves to naturalistic observation, from supermarkets to airports to outdoor settings (**FIGURE 1.10**).

The main advantage of naturalistic observation is that researchers can obtain data about natural behaviour, rather than about behaviour that is a reaction to an artificial experimental situation. But naturalistic observation can be difficult and time-consuming, and the lack of control by the researcher makes it difficult to conduct observations for behaviour that occurs infrequently. If a researcher wants to observe behaviour in a controlled setting, **laboratory observation** has many of the advantages of naturalistic observation but with greater control over the variables. In this type of observation the psychologist brings participants into a specially prepared room in the laboratory and, while hidden from view, observes the behaviour of the participants (**FIGURE 1.11**).

Naturalistic observation FIGURE 1.10

Canadian primatologist Dr. Birute Galdikas, shown here with orangutans, studied them in the jungles of Borneo. Studying behaviour in its natural environment allows behaviour to unfold naturally (without interference).

Laboratory observation: observing behaviour in a controlled setting FIGURE 1.11

Why is this researcher observing the children's behaviour through a window from outside the room?

research is plagued by this **volunteer effect**, where those who participate tend to be more liberal and sexually active than those who do not (Wiederman, 1999). Surveys also suffer the problem of large non-response rates. Sometimes those who choose not to participate can outweigh those who do. If it takes 20 different requests to get one participant, the results of the survey clearly will not reflect the larger population and the results will likely be biased. Although they can help predict behaviour, survey techniques cannot explain causes of behaviour.

What if a researcher wants to investigate porphyrophobia (fear of the colour purple)? In such a case, it would be difficult to find enough participants to conduct an experiment or to use surveys or naturalistic observation. For rare disorders or phenomena, researchers try to find someone who has the problem and then study him or her intensively. Such in-depth studies of a single research participant are called **case studies** (FIGURE 1.13).

CORRELATIONAL RESEARCH: IDENTIFYING RELATIONSHIPS

We all know that certain things go together—for example, hot weather and fewer clothes; higher annual income and more toys; height and weight; and so on. Researchers can formally observe and measure these types of relationships by using a non-experimental technique called **correlational research**. Correlational research determines what the degree of relationship (or correlation) is between two variables. As the name implies, when any two variables are correlated, a change in one is accompanied by a change in the other.

correlational research A research method in which variables are observed or measured (without directly manipulating) to identify possible relationships between them.

By using the correlational method, researchers measure participants' responses or behaviours on variables of interest. Next, the researchers analyze their results by using a statistical formula that gives a **correlation coefficient**, a numerical value that provides two pieces of information: the *strength* and the *direction* of the relationship between the two variables. Correlation coefficients are

Surveys FIGURE 1.12

In conducting surveys, researchers often use questionnaires to gather data from a wide selection of people. Under what conditions would you be willing to participate in such research?

Psychologists use **surveys** (FIGURE 1.12) to measure a variety of psychological behaviours, thoughts, interests, and attitudes. The survey technique includes tests, questionnaires, polls, and interviews. This research method is probably the one you are most familiar with—especially in the evening when unsolicited calls from survey companies interrupt your dinner. One key advantage of surveys is that researchers can gather data from many more people than is possible with other research methods. Unfortunately, surveys have a number of disadvantages: most surveys rely on self-reported data, and not all participants are completely honest. In addition, if the survey topic is a bit edgy or personal, those who volunteer to participate and form the survey sample may not be representative of the larger population. Human sexuality

In 1848, a railroad worker named Phineas Gage had a metal rod (6 kg, 3 cm in diameter, and 1 m long) blown through the front of his face and brain and out the top of his head. Amazingly, Gage was not knocked unconscious and was soon up and moving around. Moreover, he didn't receive any medical treatment until 1½ hours later. However, Gage suffered a serious personality transformation. Before the accident, he had been capable, energetic, and well liked. Afterward, he was described as "fitful, capricious, impatient of advice, obstinate, and lacking in deference to his fellows" (Macmillan, 2000, p. 13). Women were instructed to not remain long in his presence in case his frequent fits of profanity might offend their sensibilities (Damasio, 2006). Gage's injury and recovery were carefully documented and recorded by his physician, Dr. J. M. Harlow. As his story illustrates, the case study method offers unique advantages—a researcher could not do such an experiment nor find any volunteers willing to participate in a study that required a penetrating brain injury. However, the case study has serious research limits, including a lack of generalizability to the larger population and inadvertent bias in recording the case study details.

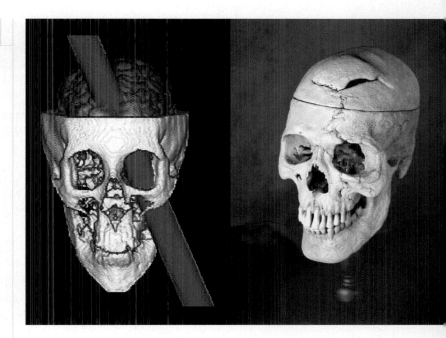

expressed as a number ranging from +1.00 to –1.00. The sign (+ or –) indicates the direction of the correlation, positive or negative (**FIGURE 1.14A** on the next page). The closer the number is to –1.00 or +1.00, the stronger the relationship. Both +1.00 and –1.00 are the strongest possible relationships. Thus, if you had a correlation of +.92 or –.92, you would have a *strong correlation*. By the same token, a correlation of +.15 or –.15 would represent a *weak correlation*. Correlation coefficients close to zero are often interpreted as representing no relationship between the variables—as is the relationship between broken mirrors and years of bad luck. Correlations can be represented numerically with the correlation coefficient but they can also be represented graphically in a **scatter plot** (**FIGURE 1.14A**).

Correlational research is an important research method for psychologists, and understanding correlations can also help people live safer and more productive lives. For example, correlational studies have repeatedly found high correlations between birth defects and amount of alcohol drank by the pregnant mother (Bearer et al., 2004–2005; Gunzerath et al., 2004). This kind of information enables us to make predictions about relative risks and fosters more informed decisions (**FIGURE 1.14B**).

However, people do not always understand that a correlation between two variables does not mean that one variable causes another (**FIGURE 1.14C**). For example, some critics of global warming research have argued that the evidence in its support is based on correlational rather than experimental research and therefore does not establish cause and effect (Solomon, 2008). Although correlational studies do sometimes point to possible causes, only the experimental method manipulates the independent variable under controlled conditions and, therefore, can support conclusions about cause and effect.

BIOLOGICAL RESEARCH: WAYS TO DESCRIBE AND EXPLORE THE NERVOUS SYSTEM

Biological research studies the brain and other parts of the nervous system to examine the biological processes that are involved in our mental processes and behaviour.

biological research Scientific studies of the brain and other parts of the nervous system.

The earliest explorers of the nervous system dissected the brains of cadavers (deceased humans) and conducted experiments on other animals by using *lesioning* techniques (systematically destroying brain tissue to study the effects

Three types of correlation

A Each dot on these graphs (called *scatter plots*) represents one participant's score on two factors, or variables. (Note: For simplicity we have not included values on the graph axes.) ▼

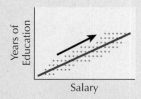

Years of Education / Salary

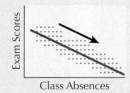

Exam Scores / Class Absences

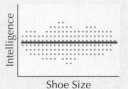

Intelligence / Shoe Size

In a positive correlation, the two factors move (or vary) in the same direction.

In a negative correlation, the two factors vary in opposite directions— that is, as one factor increases, the other factor decreases.

Sometimes no relationship exists between two variables— a zero correlation.

Pregnancy and smoking ◀

B Research shows that cigarette smoking is strongly correlated with fetal harm. The more the mother smokes the greater the damage to the fetus (Chapter 9). Is this a positive or negative correlation?

Correlation is not causation ◀

C Does a high correlation (+.84) between ice cream production and sexual assaults mean eating ice cream causes men to sexually assault women? Or does sexual assault cause an urge to eat more ice cream? Obviously not! Instead both are being caused by a third variable—summertime or warm weather, when days are longer and people are outside more.

NATIONAL GEOGRAPHIC

on behaviour and mental processes). By the mid-nineteenth century, this research had produced a rudimentary map of the nervous system, including some areas of the brain. Early researchers also relied on clinical observations and case studies of living people who had experienced injuries, diseases, and disorders that affected brain functioning. The case study of Phineas Gage was one such example.

Modern researchers still use such methods, but they also employ other techniques to examine biological processes that underlie our behaviour (**TABLE 1.4**). Recent advances in neuroscience have led to various ways to image the living brain, which can be used in both clinical and laboratory settings (Haller et al., 2005). Most of these methods are relatively *non-invasive*—that is, their use does not involve breaking the skin or entering the body.

Tools for studying the brain and other parts of the nervous system TABLE 1.4

Each biological method has strengths and weaknesses, but all provide invaluable insights. Findings from these tools are discussed in a number of chapters in this text.

Method	Description	Sample Results
Brain dissection 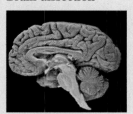 *Structures of the brain can be examined by dissecting the brains of deceased people who donated their bodies for scientific study.*	Careful cutting and study of a cadaver's brain to reveal structural details.	Brain dissections of deceased Alzheimer's disease patients often show identifiable changes in a variety of brain regions (Chapter 7).
Ablation or lesions  *This stereotaxic instrument is commonly used in small animal lesion studies; it provides accurate placement of lesions in anaesthetized animals.*	Surgically removing parts of the living brain (ablation), or destroying specific areas of the brain (lesioning), followed by observation for changes in behaviour or mental processes.	Lesioning specific parts of a rat's hypothalamus has a remarkable effect on its eating behaviour (Chapter 11).
Observation and case studies 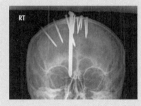 *A CT scan (described later in this table) confirmed that the nails in this self-inflicted injury had penetrated deep into the patient's brain. He presented with left-sided weakness and an unsteady gait. The nails were removed and he made an uneventful recovery (James et al., 2006).*	Observing and recording changes in personality, behaviour, or sensory capacity associated with brain disease or injuries.	Damage to one side of the brain often causes numbness or paralysis on the opposite side of the body.
Electrical recordings  *Electrical activity throughout the brain sweeps in regular waves across its surface. The electroencephalogram (EEG) is a readout of this activity. Unfortunately, because the electrodes record only from the surface of the scalp, they provide little precision about the location of deep brain activity.*	By using electrodes attached to a person's or animal's scalp or skin, brain activity is recorded to produce an electroencephalogram (EEG).	The EEG reveals areas of the brain most active during a particular task or changes in mental states, like sleeping and meditation (Chapter 5). It can also trace abnormal brain activity caused by neural anomalies, like epilepsy or tumours.
Electrical stimulation of the brain 	By using an electrode, a weak electric current stimulates specific areas or structures in the brain.	In the 1950s Canadian neurosurgeon Wilder Penfield mapped the surface of the brain and found that different areas have different functions.

(continued on next page)

Tools for studying the brain and other parts of the nervous system (continued) TABLE 1.4

Method	Description	Sample Results
CT (computed tomography) scan 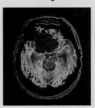 *This CT scan used X-rays to locate a brain tumour, which is the deep purple mass at the top left.*	Computer-created cross-sectional X-rays of the living brain. It is the least expensive type of imaging and is widely used in research.	CT reveals the effects of strokes, injuries, tumours, and other brain disorders.
PET (positron emission tomography) scan 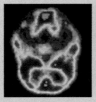 *PET scans and brain functions. The left scan shows brain activity when the eyes are open, whereas the right scan is with the eyes closed. Note the increased activity (red and yellow regions) in the top of the photo when the eyes are open.*	A radioactive form of glucose is injected into the bloodstream and the scanner records the amount of glucose used in particularly active areas of the living brain. It then produces a computer-constructed picture of the brain.	PET scans were originally designed to detect neural abnormalities, but they are also used to identify brain areas active during ordinary activities (reading, singing, etc.).
MRI (magnetic resonance imaging) scan 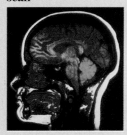 *Note the fissures (valleys) and internal structures of the brain. The throat, nasal airways, and fluid surrounding the brain are dark.*	Powerful electromagnets produce a high-frequency magnetic field that is passed through the brain.	The MRI produces high-resolution three-dimensional pictures of the living brain and is useful for identifying abnormalities and for mapping brain structures and function.
fMRI (functional magnetic resonance imaging) scan	A newer, faster version of the MRI that detects blood flow by detecting magnetic signals from blood that has given up its oxygen to active neural cells.	The fMRI measures blood flow, which indicates areas of the brain that are active or inactive during ordinary activities or responses (like reading or talking). It also shows changes associated with various disorders.
TMS (transcranial magnetic stimulation) 	A method of brain stimulation that exposes the brain to powerful magnet fields via a wire coil held near the skull. The magnetic field changes neural activity in the brain.	TMS can be used to elicit a motor response or to temporarily inactivate brain regions and then observe their effects. It is also used to treat depression (Chapter 14).

CONCEPT CHECK

How do psychologists guard against bias?

Which type of psychological research involves observing participants' behaviour in the real world?

What is the difference between a positive and a negative correlation?

What does it mean to call a procedure *non-invasive*?

Getting the Most from Your Study of Psychology

LEARNING OBJECTIVES

Describe the steps you can take to read more accurately.

Explain how visual features can enhance learning.

Examine your current time-management habits, and identify how you might improve them.

Explain the benefits of distributed study and overlearning.

Summarize the grade-improvement and test-taking strategies that you can use to ensure success in your courses.

We've looked so far at psychology as a science, its history, its major fields, and its methods of research. Psychology also has valuable practical information to offer in terms of how to be a successful student. In this section, we will offer several well-documented techniques that will help you work smarter—not just longer or harder (Dickinson, O'Connell, & Dunn, 1996), so that you can get the most from your study of psychology (and any other subject). Mastering these skills will initially take some time, but you'll save hundreds of hours later on.

FAMILIARIZATION

Have you ever noticed that you can read a paragraph many times and still remember nothing from it? Often you must make a conscious effort to learn. There are a number of ways to actively read (and remember) information in a text. The first step is to familiarize yourself with the general text so that you can take full advantage of its contents. In *Visualizing Psychology*, the Preface, Table of Contents, Glossary (Key Terms in each chapter), and Subject Index will give you a bird's-eye view of the rest of the text. In addition, as you scan the book to familiarize yourself with its contents, you should also take note of the many tables, figures, photographs, and special feature boxes, all of which will enhance your understanding of the subject.

ACTIVE READING

The most important tool for higher education academic success is the ability to read and master the assigned class text. One of the best ways to read actively is to use the **SQ4R method** originally developed by Francis Robinson (1970). The initials stand for the six steps in effective reading: **s**urvey, **q**uestion, **r**ead, **r**ecite, **r**eview, and **w**rite. As you might have guessed, *Visualizing Psychology* was designed to incorporate each of these steps (**FIGURE 1.15**).

VISUAL LEARNING

Our brains are highly tuned to visual, as well as verbal cues. Photographs, drawings, and other graphical information help us solidify our understanding, organize and internalize new material, recognize patterns and interrelationships, and think creatively.

In some books, photographs and illustrations merely repeat, visually, the concepts that are also stated in words. *Visualizing Psychology* is different. We have explicitly designed the book to take advantage of your capacity to process information through both visual and verbal channels. The text is tightly integrated with a rich array of visual features that will help you solidify your understanding of the concepts contained in the text. (The Illustrated Book Tour in the preface describes these features in detail.) The photographs, drawings, diagrams, and graphs in this book carry their own weight—that is, they serve a specific instructional purpose, above and beyond what is stated in words. They are as essential as the text itself; be sure to pay attention to them (they will probably also appear on tests).

Process Diagram

Survey
Each chapter of the text opens with an illustrated Chapter Outline, and each section includes Learning Objectives. Together they provide an overview, or survey, of the chapter. Knowing what to expect from a chapter can help you focus on the main points.

wRite
In addition to the writing you do in the previous steps, take brief notes in the text margins or on a separate sheet of paper. This will help keep you focused during your reading.

Question
To maintain your attention and increase comprehension, each chapter includes a number of Learning Objectives. Use them to form questions, then keep the questions in mind while reading each of the chapter's sections.

Review
Carefully review and answer the Concept Checks that conclude each major section and the Critical and Creative Thinking Questions at the end of each chapter. Upon finishing the chapter, review your questions and answers from the earlier steps and the end-of-chapter summary. Repeating this review process before each quiz or exam will dramatically improve your exam scores!

Read
Try to answer the questions you formed in the previous step as you read the chapter. Read carefully—in short, concentrated time periods.

Recite
After you have read one small section, stop and silently recite what you've just read or make a written summary. To better retain the material, think of personal examples of major concepts and how you might apply a certain concept to real-life situations.

VIEW THIS IN ACTION
in your WileyPLUS course

Improving Your Grade

If you are a student, the general learning tools outlined here will make you more efficient and successful in your courses. In addition, the following list includes several specific strategies for grade improvement and test taking that will further improve your performance:

- *Take good notes.* Effective note taking depends on active listening. Ask yourself what the main idea is. Write down key ideas and supporting details and examples.

- *Understand your professor.* The amount of lecture time spent on various topics is usually a good idea of what the instructor considers important.

- *General test taking.* On multiple-choice exams, carefully read each question and all the alternative answers before responding. Be careful to respond to all questions and make sure that you have recorded your answers *correctly.* Finally, practise your test taking by responding to the Concept Check questions, the Stop & Think Questions, and the Self-Test in each chapter.

- *Skills courses.* Improve your reading speed and comprehension and your word-processing or keyboarding skills by taking additional study skills, computer, and academic writing courses designed to develop these specific abilities.

- *Additional resources.* Don't overlook important human resources. Your instructors can provide useful tips. Enlist roommates, classmates, friends, and family members to help you with your studying.

Stop & Think
1. What factors might prevent you from reading test questions carefully and responding accurately?
2. How could a friend or roommate help you improve your grades on tests?

TIME MANAGEMENT

If you have trouble balancing work, study, and social activities or budgeting your time, these four time-management strategies may help:

- *Establish a baseline.* Before attempting any changes, record your day-to-day activities for one to two weeks. You may be surprised by how you spend your time.

- *Set up a realistic schedule.* Make a daily and weekly "to do" list, including all required activities, basic maintenance tasks (like laundry, cooking, child care, and eating), and a reasonable amount of "down time." Then create a daily schedule of activities that includes time for each of these. To make permanent time-management changes, shape your behaviour, starting with small changes and building on them.

- *Reward yourself.* Give yourself immediate, tangible rewards (such as watching a favourite TV show or movie) for sticking with your daily schedule.

- *Maximize your time.* Time-management experts, like Alan Lakein (1998), suggest that you should try to minimize the amount of time you spend worrying and complaining and fiddling around getting ready to study ("fretting and prepping"); it's the actual studying that really matters. Also be on the lookout for hidden "time opportunities"— spare moments that normally go to waste, which you could use more productively, such as time spent riding on the bus to school or sitting in the waiting room of the dentist or doctor.

DISTRIBUTED STUDY

Spaced practice is a much more efficient way to study and learn than massed practice (Chapter 7). That is, you will learn material more thoroughly if you distribute your study over time, rather than trying to cram all the information in at once (such as the night before the exam).

OVERLEARNING

Many people tend to study new material just to the point at which they can recite the information and do not attempt to understand it more deeply. For best results, you should know how key terms and concepts are related to one another. You should also be able to generate examples other than the ones in the text. You should repeatedly review the material by visualizing the phenomena that are described and explained in the text and by rehearsing what you have learned until the information is firmly locked in place. You will find this confidence-building exercise particularly important if you suffer from test anxiety.

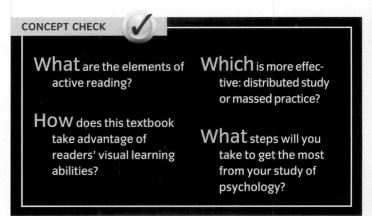

CONCEPT CHECK ✓

What are the elements of active reading?

How does this textbook take advantage of readers' visual learning abilities?

Which is more effective: distributed study or massed practice?

What steps will you take to get the most from your study of psychology?

SUMMARY

1 Introducing Psychology

1. **Psychology** is the scientific study of **behaviour** and **mental processes**. The discipline places high value on **empirical evidence** and **critical thinking**. One of the most enduring controversies in science has been the **nature-nurture controversy**.

2. Psychology's four basic goals are to describe, explain, predict, and change behaviour and mental processes through the use of **scientific methods**.

3. Psychologists work as therapists, researchers, teachers, and consultants in a wide range of settings.

2 Origins of Psychology

1. Wilhelm Wundt, the father of psychology, and his followers, including Edward Titchener, were interested in studying conscious experience. Their approach, **structuralism**, sought to identify the basic structures of mental life through introspection.

2. **Functionalism**, led by William James, was the school that studied how the mind functions to adapt humans and other animals to their environment.

3. Contemporary psychology reflects seven major perspectives: **psychoanalytic or psychodynamic, behaviourist, humanistic, cognitive, neuroscientific or biopsychological, evolutionary,** and **sociocultural**. Most contemporary psychologists embrace a unifying perspective known as the **biopsychosocial model**. This model views biological processes, psychological factors, and social forces as interrelated influences on behaviour.

3 The Science of Psychology

1. **Basic research** is aimed at advancing general scientific understanding, whereas **applied research** works to address real-world problems.

2. Most scientific investigations involve six basic steps, collectively known as the **scientific method**. Scientific progress comes from repeatedly challenging and revising existing theories and building new ones.

3. **Critical thinking** emphasizes objectively evaluating information and drawing conclusions based on **empirical evidence**. It is essential not only in psychological science but also in real life.

4. Psychologists must maintain high ethical standards. This includes respecting the rights of both human and non-human research participants and of psychotherapy clients. **Informed consent** and **debriefing** are critical elements of any research that involves human participants. Researchers and clinicians are held ethically and professionally responsible for their actions by the CPA, by their institutions (Research Ethics Boards and Institutional Animal Care Committees), and by government agencies.

4 Research Methods

1. Experimental research manipulates and controls variables to determine cause and effect. An **experiment** has two critical components: **independent** and **dependent variables**, and **experimental** and **control groups**. A good scientific experiment protects against potential sources of error from both the researcher and the participants.

2. **Descriptive research** involves systematically observing and describing behaviour without manipulating variables. The four major types of descriptive research are **naturalistic observation, laboratory observation, surveys**, and **case studies**.

3. **Correlational research** allows researchers to observe the relationship between two variables. Researchers analyze their results using a **correlation coefficient**. Correlations can be positive or negative. A correlation between two variables does not necessarily mean that one causes the other.

4. **Biological research** focuses on internal, biological processes that are involved in our feelings, thoughts, and behaviour. Recent advances in brain imaging have improved scientists' ability to examine these processes and to do so non-invasively.

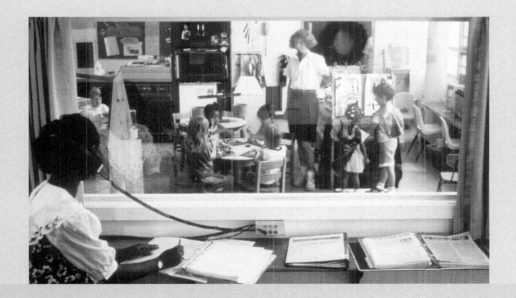

5 Getting the Most from Your Study of Psychology

1. Several well-documented techniques will help you understand and absorb the material in this book most completely. These include familiarization, active reading, visual learning, time management, distributed study, and overlearning.

2. For students, several additional strategies for grade improvement and test taking can further improve course performance. These include more effective note taking, understanding the professor, general test-taking strategies, study skills courses, and using other helpful resources.

KEY TERMS

- applied research p. 13
- assumption p. 5
- basic research p. 13
- behaviour p. 4
- behaviourist perspective p. 10
- bias p. 5
- biological research p. 23
- biopsychosocial model p. 11
- case studies p. 22
- cognitive perspective p. 10
- confound variables p. 20
- control group p. 19
- correlation coefficient p. 22
- correlational research p. 22
- critical thinking p. 5
- debriefing p. 15
- dependent variable (DV) p. 18
- descriptive research p. 21

- double-blind study p. 20
- empirical evidence p. 6
- evolutionary perspective p. 10
- experiment p. 18
- experimental group p. 19
- experimenter bias p. 20
- functionalism p. 9
- humanistic perspective p. 10
- independent variable (IV) p. 18
- informed consent p. 15
- laboratory observation p. 21
- mental processes p. 4
- naturalistic observation p. 21
- nature-nurture controversy p. 7
- neuroscientific (biopsychological) perspective p. 10

- plagiarism p. 16
- psychoanalytic school p. 10
- psychology p. 4
- random assignment p. 20
- random selection p. 20
- sample bias p. 20
- scatter plot p. 23
- scientific method p. 13
- single-blind study p. 20
- social desirability response p. 21
- sociocultural perspective p. 11
- SQ4R method p. 27
- structuralism p. 9
- surveys p. 22
- volunteer effect p. 22

CRITICAL AND CREATIVE THINKING QUESTIONS

1. Scientific psychologists are among the least likely to believe in psychics, palmistry, astrology, and other paranormal phenomena. Why might that be?

2. This chapter noted how one goal of psychology is to attempt to change undesirable behaviours or mental processes. What human behaviours do you think could be modified by applying the first three psychological goals?

3. Which psychological perspective would most likely be used to study and explain why some animals, such as newly hatched ducks or geese, follow and become attached to (imprinted on) the first large moving object they see or hear?

4. Why is the scientific method described as a cycle, rather than as a simple six-step process?

5. Imagine that a researcher recruited research participants from among her friends, and then assigned them to experimental or control groups based on their sex. Why might this be a problem?

6. It is not uncommon for the media to incorrectly report research correlations as though they are cause and effect relationships. Why are these types of errors particularly troubling to scientific discovery?

7. Which modern methods of examining how the brain influences behaviour are non-invasive?

8. What do you think keeps most people from fully employing the active learning strategies and study skills presented in this chapter?

9. Why is critical thinking important in everyday life?

What is happening in this picture ?

Non-human animals are sometimes used in psychological research when it is impractical or unethical to use human participants. What types of research questions might meet this criterion?

Opinions are sharply divided on the ethical question of whether non-human animals should be used in research at all. What safeguards are in place in Canada to help ensure the proper treatment of these animals?

SELF-TEST

(Check your answers in Appendix A.)

1. In this textbook, psychology is defined as the
   _____.

   a. science of conscious and unconscious forces on behaviour
   b. empirical study of the mind
   c. scientific study of the mind
   d. scientific study of behaviour and mental processes

2. According to this textbook, the goals of psychology are to
   _____.

   a. explore the conscious and unconscious functions of the human mind
   b. understand, compare, and analyze human behaviour
   c. improve psychological well-being in all individuals, from conception to death
   d. describe, explain, predict, and change behaviour and mental processes

3. Whereas Edward Tichener was associated with the structuralist school of psychology, William James was a _____.

   a. humanist
   b. psychoanalyst
   c. functionalist
   d. behaviourist

4. The father of modern psychology is _____.

   a. Sigmund Freud   c. Wilhelm Wundt
   b. B. F. Skinner   d. William James

5. Which of the following research questions would interest a psychologist from the behaviourist perspective?

   a. Is there a correlation between self-esteem and anxiety?
   b. Does crowding influence acts of aggression?
   c. Is depression related to intelligence?
   d. Can motivation be increased by positive self-talk?

6. The biopsychosocial model is known as _____.

   a. an integrative, unifying model
   b. a concept formation
   c. a consolidation model
   d. an eclectic conceptualization

7. The term *basic research* is *best* defined as research that
   _____.

   a. is basic to one field only
   b. is intended to advance scientific knowledge rather than being done for practical applications

   c. is done to get a grade or a tenured teaching position
   d. solves basic problems encountered by humans and animals in a complex world

8. When researchers can specify the conditions under which a behaviour or event is likely to occur, they have accomplished which psychological goal?

   a. explanation
   b. influence
   c. description
   d. prediction

9. Identify and label the six steps in the scientific method: choose the best research design to test the hypothesis; after more studies, advance a theory to explain the results; perform statistical analysis; conduct a review of the literature; make a testable prediction; write up the study and its results and submit the study to a scientific journal

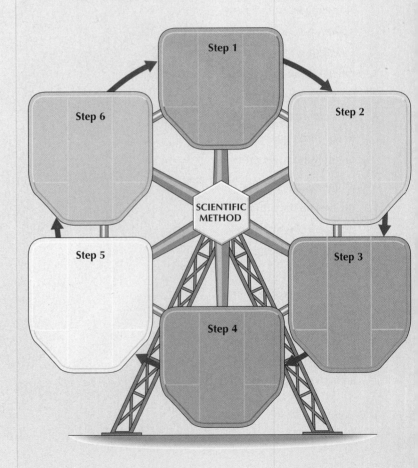

10. According to this textbook, debriefing is _____.

   a. interviewing subjects after a study to find out what they were thinking during their participation
   b. explaining the purpose of the study, anticipated results, and deception used when the study is over
   c. disclosing potential physical and emotional risks, and the nature of the study before it begins
   d. interviewing subjects after a study to determine whether any deception was effective in preventing them from learning the true purpose of the study

11. _____ are manipulated; _____ are measured.

   a. Dependent variables; independent variables
   b. Surveys; experiments
   c. Statistics; correlations
   d. Independent variables; dependent variables

12. A researcher has developed a new treatment for smoking which combines hypnosis and acupuncture. He randomly assigns participants to two groups and administers his new treatment to one group, while the other group receives no treatment. He measures the number of cigarettes participants smoke in the two weeks following treatment. This study is best described as:

   a. experimental.
   b. correlational.
   c. laboratory observation.
   d. naturalistic observation.

13. What is the *dependent* variable in the previous study?

   a. The two groups of participants
   b. The 2 weeks following treatment
   c. Hypnosis and acupuncture
   d. The number of cigarettes smoked

14. A researcher conducts a study assessing the frequency of aggressive acts displayed by Grade 2 students during their lunch break. What type of research would the researcher likely employ?

   a. a case study
   b. naturalistic observation
   c. an experiment
   d. laboratory observation

15. The *best* definition of a double-blind study is research in which _____.

   a. nobody knows what they are doing
   b. neither the participants in the treatment group nor the control group knows which treatment is being given to which group
   c. both the researcher and the participants are unaware of who is in the experimental and control groups
   d. two control groups (or placebo conditions) must be used

16. Which of the following is generally considered to be empirical evidence?

   a. websites
   b. scholarly journal articles
   c. news programs
   d. personal anecdotes

17. Who supervises the use of research animals in Canada?

   a. The research institution where the animals are housed
   b. The Canadian Council on Animal Care
   c. The Canadian Psychological Association
   d. The Canadian Wildlife Association

18. The number that indicates the direction and strength of the relation between two variables is referred to as a:

   a. correlation score.
   b. positive correlation.
   c. scatter plot.
   d. correlation coefficient.

19. List the six steps of the SQ4R study method.

20. Rebecca studies for her psychology course by carefully considering how different concepts of human behaviour are related, by thinking about examples and applications of such behaviour, and then continually reviewing this material afterward. What study skill is Rebecca using?

   a. massed practice
   b. overlearning
   c. time-management
   d. distributed practice

Neuroscience and Biological Foundations

Nicknamed "The Next One," Sidney Crosby is a Canadian hockey legend. Born in Cole Harbour, Nova Scotia, he started skating at the age of three. One of his first coaches said he'd never seen a five-year-old skate like Crosby. But even these early skills could not have predicted Crosby's remarkable later achievements. In his first season in the National Hockey League (NHL), he finished sixth overall, scoring 102 points. In his second season he scored 120 points and earned three of the most prestigious awards in professional hockey: the Art Ross Trophy, the Lester B. Pearson Award, and the Hart Memorial Trophy. He was 19 years old and is the youngest player ever to have won a scoring title in a North American professional sports league and currently the youngest player to be named a full team captain. In 2009 he captained the Pittsburgh Penguins to a remarkable Stanley Cup victory.

What makes the extraordinary achievements of Crosby (and Wayne Gretzky, Mario Lemieux, and Bobby Orr) possible? Are these players genetically gifted? What parts of their brain allow them to so superbly control the puck and consistently score? Are there special chemicals in their brains that make it possible for them to cope with the continual physical and mental exertion that characterizes training and high-level competition? In this chapter, we will look at the biological processes that make it possible for great achievers like Sidney Crosby—as well as the rest of us—to absorb, organize, and respond to the massive influx of sights, sounds, thoughts, emotions, and memories that compete, every minute, for the brain's attention.

NATIONAL GEOGRAPHIC

Our Genetic Inheritance

behavioural genetics The study of the relative contributions of genetic influences and environmental factors on behaviour and mental processes.

evolutionary psychology A branch of psychology that studies the ways in which natural selection and evolution can help to explain behaviour and mental processes.

neuroscience An interdisciplinary field that studies how biological processes interact with behaviour and mental processes.

Hundreds of thousands of years of evolution have contributed to who we are today. Our ancestors foraged and scavenged for food, fought for survival, and passed on some traits that were selected and transmitted down through vast numbers of generations. How do these transmitted traits affect us today? For answers, psychologists often turn to **behavioural genetics** (the relative involvement of genes and environment on our behaviour and mental processes) and **evolutionary psychology** (how our current behaviours and mental processes can be understood in terms of the evolution of our species).

BEHAVIOURAL GENETICS: BOTH NATURE AND NURTURE CONTRIBUTE DIFFERENTIALLY

Ancient cultures, such as the Egyptians, Indians, and Chinese, believed the heart was the centre of all thoughts and emotions. We now know that the brain and the rest of the nervous system are the driving force behind our psychological life and our physical being. This chapter introduces you to the field of **neuroscience** and

biopsychology, the scientific study of the biology of behaviour and mental processes. In this chapter we will discuss genetics and heredity, the nervous system, and the functions of each part of the brain.

No one really wants to think about his or her parents having sex, but it obviously did happen and at the moment of your conception, your mother and father each contributed 23 *chromosomes* to begin the process of making you. Some chromosomes have thousands of genes on them and others have fewer than a hundred, but all are necessary to make a human being (**FIGURE 2.1**). For some traits, such as blood type, a single pair of genes (one from each parent) determines what characteristics you will possess. But most traits are determined by a combination of many genes.

When the two genes for a given trait differ, the outcome depends on whether the gene is a *dominant* or *recessive* gene. A dominant gene expresses its trait whenever the gene is present. In contrast, the gene for a

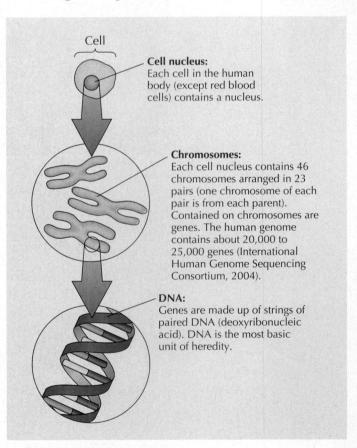

Cell

Cell nucleus: Each cell in the human body (except red blood cells) contains a nucleus.

Chromosomes: Each cell nucleus contains 46 chromosomes arranged in 23 pairs (one chromosome of each pair is from each parent). Contained on chromosomes are genes. The human genome contains about 20,000 to 25,000 genes (International Human Genome Sequencing Consortium, 2004).

DNA: Genes are made up of strings of paired DNA (deoxyribonucleic acid). DNA is the most basic unit of heredity.

Hereditary code FIGURE 2.1

recessive trait will normally be expressed only if the other gene in the pair is also recessive.

It was once assumed that such characteristics as eye colour, hair colour, and height were the result of either one dominant gene or two paired recessive genes. But today most geneticists believe that each of these characteristics is *polygenic,* meaning they are controlled by multiple genes. Many polygenic traits, like height and intelligence, are also affected by environmental and social factors (**FIGURE 2.2**). How do scientists research human genetic inheritance? To determine the influences of heredity or environment on complex traits, like aggressiveness, intelligence, and sociability, scientists rely on indirect methods, such as twin, family, and adoption studies, and studies of genetic abnormalities.

Psychologists are especially interested in the study of twins because twins have a uniquely high proportion of shared genes. Identical (*monozygotic*—one ovum) twins share 100 percent of the same genes, whereas fraternal (*dizygotic*—two ova) twins share, on average, 50 percent of the same genes, just like any other pair of siblings (**FIGURE 2.3**).

Because both identical and fraternal twins have the same parents and develop in a similar environment, they

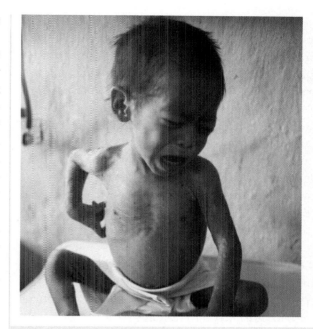

Gene-environment interaction FIGURE 2.2

Children who are malnourished may not reach their full potential genetic height or maximum intelligence. Can you see how environmental factors interact with genetic factors to influence many traits?

Identical and fraternal twins FIGURE 2.3

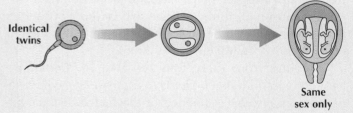

A Monozygotic, or identical, twins develop from a single ovum fertilized by a single sperm. They share the same sex and the same genetic makeup.

B Dizygotic, or fraternal, twins are formed when two separate sperm fertilize two separate ova. They can be the same or opposite sex and share some of the same genetic makeup.

provide a valuable "natural experiment." If genes influence a trait or behaviour to some degree, identical twins should be more alike than fraternal twins on that trait or behaviour. Twin studies have provided a wealth of information on the relative effects of heredity on behaviour. For example, studies of intelligence show that identical twins have almost identical IQ scores, whereas fraternal twins are only slightly more similar in their IQ scores than are non-twin siblings (Bouchard, 2004; Plomin, 1999). This difference suggests a genetic influence on intelligence.

Psychologists interested in behavioural genetics also study entire families. If a specific trait is inherited, blood relatives should show greater trait similarity, compared with unrelated people. Also, closer relatives, like siblings, should be more similar than distant relatives. Family studies have shown that many traits, such as intelligence and sociability, and psychological disorders, such as depression, do indeed run in families.

Studying families with children who have been adopted provides valuable information for researchers. If adopted children are more like their biological family than their adoptive family on some trait, then genetic factors probably had the greater influence. Conversely, if adopted children resemble their adopted family even though they do not share similar genes, then environmental factors may be more influential.

Finally, research in behavioural genetics explores disorders and diseases that result when genes malfunction. For example, researchers believe that genetic or chromosomal abnormalities are important factors in Alzheimer's disease and schizophrenia (Borenstein et al., 2006; O'Tuathaigh et al., 2006).

Findings from these four research methods have allowed behavioural geneticists to estimate the *heritability* of various traits; that is, the degree to which individual differences are a result of genetic, inherited factors rather than differences in the environment. If genes contributed nothing to the trait differences, it would have a heritability estimate of 0 percent. If trait differences were completely due to genes, it would have a heritability estimate of 100 percent. Keep in mind, however, that heritability estimates apply to the *differences* seen in traits and not the actual traits per se. For example, a height heritability estimate would calculate the relative genetic contribution of differences between the shortest and tallest person in a population (**FIGURE 2.4**). Heritability estimates also apply to groups, and not to individuals—so we do not speak of a heritability estimate for a single person.

As we've seen, behavioural genetics studies help explain the role of heredity (nature) and the environment (nurture) in our individual behaviour. To increase our understanding of genetic dispositions, we also need to look at universal behaviours transmitted to us from our evolutionary past.

EVOLUTIONARY PSYCHOLOGY: APPLYING NATURAL SELECTION TO BEHAVIOUR AND MENTAL PROCESSES

Evolutionary psychology is based on the premise that many behavioural commonalities, from mating to fighting, emerged and remain in human populations today because they helped our ancestors (and their descendents) survive and reproduce. This perspective stems from the writings and research of Charles Darwin (1859) who theorized that environmental forces select traits that are adaptive to the organism's survival. This process of **natural selection** occurs when a particular genetic trait

natural selection Across a wide range of inherited trait variation, the mechanism by which those traits that confer a survival or reproductive advantage will increase in the population.

Height and heritability FIGURE 2.4

Height has one of the highest heritability estimates—around 80 to 90 percent (Plomin, 1990; Silventoinen et al., 2008). However, it's impossible to predict with certainty a single individual's height from a heritability estimate. The same is true regardless of whether the trait in question is athletic ability, intelligence, depression, or risk of developing cancer. What other factors might have contributed to the difference in height between this mother and daughter?

Charles Darwin and natural selection FIGURE 2.5

Despite popular belief, Charles Darwin (A) (1809–1882) did not originate the theory of evolution. The theory of evolution—the process of genetic change in a population—predated Darwin by many years (his grandfather Erasmus Darwin had written about it in the eighteenth century). What Darwin did was to propose the *mechanism* by which evolution occurs; that is, through *natural selection*. Darwin noted that across a wide range of inherited (genetic) trait variation, those traits that confer a survival or reproductive advantage will increase in the population (Darwin, 1859). Look at the images of these two finches. These finches evolved from a common ancestor. The beak of the large ground finch (B) is big for cracking large seeds, and the beak of the i'iwi finch (C) is long and curved to extract nectar from flowers. The genes of those birds with beaks that were slightly better adapted to getting food in their local environments slowly increased in the population and ultimately gave rise to new finch species.

gives an individual a survival and reproductive advantage over others of the same species (**FIGURE 2.5**). Some people mistakenly believe that natural selection means "survival of the fittest." It is not necessarily the fittest (or strongest) who survive, rather, it is those who can adapt best to their environment and make the greatest genetic contribution to succeeding generations. What really matters then is *reproduction*—the survival of the genome. Because of natural selection, the individual with the most adaptive traits will be most likely to live long enough to pass on his or her genes to the next generation.

When we think of natural selection we often think of its effects in terms of anatomy. For example, a beneficial gene might cause an organism to run a little faster, have better vision, or use food or oxygen more efficiently. But natural selection also acts on behaviour—genes influence what we do and how we

act, and if those genes confer a behaviour that is adaptive, that behaviour will also increase in a population.

Genetic mutations help explain the evolution of behaviour. It's likely that everyone carries at least one gene that has mutated, or changed from the original. This is probably also true of ancestral humans and other organisms. Very rarely, a mutated gene will be significant enough to change an individual's behaviour, but if it happens, it might cause someone to be more sociable, more of a risk-taker, shyer, or more careful. If the gene then gives the person a reproductive advantage, he or she will be more likely to pass on the gene to future generations. However, this mutation doesn't guarantee long-term survival. A well-adapted population can perish if its environment suddenly changes. This is because environments select for adaptive traits; if environments change, the trait may no longer be adaptive.

CONCEPT CHECK

What is the difference between a dominant and a recessive trait?

What does knowing the heritability of a trait tell us about that trait?

What is evolution by natural selection?

How are heredity and evolution linked to human behaviour?

Neural Bases of Behaviour

Your brain and the rest of your nervous system consist of billions of **neurons.** Each one is a tiny information-processing system with thousands of connections for receiving and sending electrochemical signals to other neurons. Each human body may have as many as one *trillion* neurons. (Be careful not to confuse the term *neuron* with the term *nerve.* Nerves are large bundles of axons—defined below—outside the brain and spinal cord.)

Neurons are held in place, supported, and nurtured by **glial cells**. Glial cells surround neurons and perform a variety of tasks, including cleaning up and insulating one neuron from another so their neural messages aren't scrambled. Glial cells also have a wide array of other duties, such as playing a direct role in nervous system communication and neural signalling (Arriagada et al., 2007; Wieseler-Frank, Maier, & Watkins, 2005; Zillmer, Spiers, & Culbertson, 2008).

No two neurons are identical, but most share three basic features: **dendrites**, the **cell body**, and an **axon** (**FIGURE 2.6**). To remember how information travels through the neuron, think of these three in reverse alphabetical order: *dendrite →* *cell body → a*xon.

neuron A nervous system cell that receives and conducts electrochemical impulses.

glial cell A nervous system cell that supports, nourishes, insulates, and protects neurons.

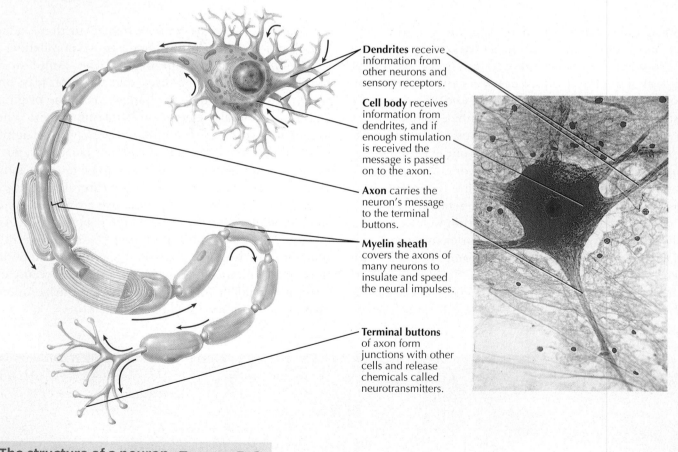

Dendrites receive information from other neurons and sensory receptors.

Cell body receives information from dendrites, and if enough stimulation is received the message is passed on to the axon.

Axon carries the neuron's message to the terminal buttons.

Myelin sheath covers the axons of many neurons to insulate and speed the neural impulses.

Terminal buttons of axon form junctions with other cells and release chemicals called neurotransmitters.

The structure of a neuron FIGURE 2.6

Arrows indicate direction of information flow: dendrites → cell body → axon → terminal buttons of axon.

How Toxins and Drugs Affect Our Brain

Poisons, toxins, and mind-altering (psychoactive) drugs have their effect in the nervous system by interacting with neurotransmitter systems.

Normal neurotransmitter activation

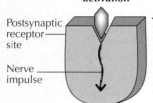

Postsynaptic receptor site

Nerve impulse

◄ **A** Like a key fitting into a lock, receptor sites on receiving neurons' dendrites and cell bodies recognize particular neurotransmitters by their distinctive shapes.

Blocked neurotransmitter activation

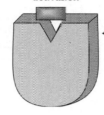

◄ **B** Neurotransmitter and other molecules without the correct shape won't fit a particular receptor, so they cannot stimulate the receiving neuron.

Agonist drug "mimics" neurotransmitter

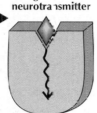

C Some *agonist drugs*, like the poison in the black widow spider or the nicotine in cigarettes, are similar enough in structure to a certain neurotransmitter (in this case, *acetylcholine*) that they can mimic its effects on the receiving neuron. ►

Antagonist drug fills receptor space and blocks neurotransmitter

D Some *antagonist drugs* block neurotransmitters like acetylcholine. Because acetylcholine is vital in muscle action, blocking it paralyzes muscles, including those involved in breathing, which can be fatal. ►

Examples of antagonists to acetylcholine include most snake venom and some poisons, like *botulinum toxin*. This is one of the most poisonous naturally occurring substances, but when used in tiny doses in the form of Botox®, it is effective in treating painful muscle contractions and excessive sweating. It is also used for cosmetic purposes to improve the appearance of frown lines and crow's feet wrinkles. Another example of an acetylcholine antagonist is curare, a plant toxin that has been widely used by South American hunter-gatherer peoples as an arrow poison. When the curare-tipped arrowhead breaks the skin it paralyzes the respiratory muscles and the animal quickly dies by asphyxiation.

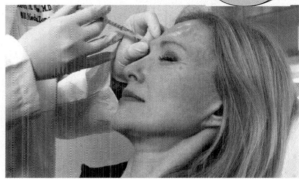

HOW DO NEURONS COMMUNICATE?

A neuron's basic function is to transmit information throughout the nervous system. Neurons communicate in a type of electrical and chemical language. The process of neural communication begins within the neuron itself, when the dendrites and cell body receive electrical messages. These messages move along the axon in the form of a neural impulse, or **action potential** (FIGURE 2.7 on pages 44–45).

A neural impulse travels along a bare axon at only about 10 metres per second. This is much slower than the speed at which electricity moves through a wire. Many mammalian axons, however, are enveloped in fatty insulation called a **myelin sheath**. This sheath blankets the axon, except in places called *nodes* where the myelin is very thin or absent. In a myelinated axon, the neural impulse moves about 10 times as fast as on a bare axon. This is because the action potential jumps from node to node rather than travelling along the entire length of the axon membrane.

Communication *within* the neuron (FIGURE 2.7A) is not the same as communication *between* neurons (FIGURE 2.7B). Within the neuron, messages travel electrically. But messages are transmitted chemically from

action potential
The voltage change across an axon membrane when an impulse is transmitted.

myelin sheath
The fatty insulation that segmentally wraps an axon and serves to speed neural transmission.

NATIONAL GEOGRAPHIC

How neurons communicate: Communication *within* the neuron FIGURE 2.7A

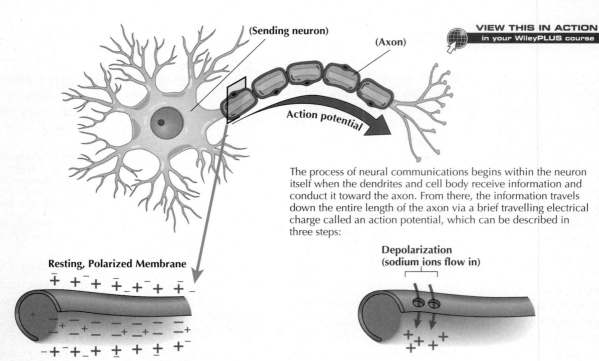

(Sending neuron)

(Axon)

Action potential

VIEW THIS IN ACTION
in your WileyPLUS course

The process of neural communications begins within the neuron itself when the dendrites and cell body receive information and conduct it toward the axon. From there, the information travels down the entire length of the axon via a brief travelling electrical charge called an action potential, which can be described in three steps:

Resting, Polarized Membrane

❶ Resting potential
When an axon is not stimulated, it is in a polarized state, called the *resting potential.* "At rest," the fluid inside the axon has more negatively charged ions than the fluid outside. This results from the selective permeability of the axon membrane and a series of mechanisms, called *sodium-potassium pumps*, that pull potassium ions in and pump sodium ions out of the axon.
The inside of the axon has a charge of about −70 millivolts relative to the outside.

**Depolarization
(sodium ions flow in)**

❷ Action potential initiation
When an "at rest" axon membrane is stimulated by a sufficiently strong signal, it produces an *action potential* (or depolarization). This action potential begins when the first part of the axon opens its "gates" and positively charged sodium ions rush through. The additional sodium ions change the previously negative charge inside the axon to a positive charge—thus depolarizing the axon.

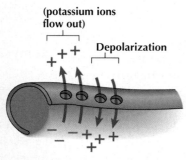

(potassium ions
flow out)

Depolarization

❸ Spreading of action potential and repolarization
The initial depolarization (or action potential) of Step 2 produces a subsequent imbalance of ions in the adjacent axon membrane. This imbalance thus causes the action potential to spread to the next section. Meanwhile, "gates" in the axon membrane of the initially depolarized section open and potassium ions flow out, thus allowing the first section to repolarize and return to its resting potential.

Flow of depolarization

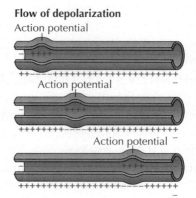

Action potential

Action potential

Action potential

❹ Overall summary
As you can see in the figure above, this sequential process of depolarization, followed by repolarization, transmits the action potential along the entire length of the axon from the cell body to the terminal buttons. This is similar to an audience at an athletic event doing "the wave." One section of fans initially stands up for a brief time (action potential). This section then sits down (resting potential), and the "wave" then spreads to adjacent sections.

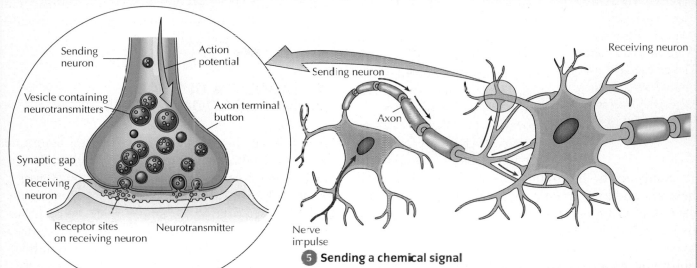

6 Receiving a chemical signal

After neurotransmitters diffuse across the synaptic gap, they bind to the membrane of a specific receiving neuron. Each receiving neuron gets large numbers of neurotransmitter messages. As you can see in the photo, the axon terminals from thousands of other nearby neurons almost completely cover the cell body of the receiving neuron. Neurotransmitters deliver either excitatory or inhibitory messages, and the receiving neuron will produce an action potential and pass along the message only if the number of excitatory messages outweigh the number of inhibitory messages (in a process called *summation*). Why do we need competing messages? Like an accelerator and brake on a car, your body needs similar on (excitatory) and off (inhibitory) mechanisms. By using these two switches, your body manages an amazing balance between overexcitation, leading to seizures, and underexcitation, leading to unconsciousness and death.

5 Sending a chemical signal

When action potentials reach the branching axon terminals, they trigger the terminal buttons at the axon's end to release thousands of neurotransmitter molecules into the *synaptic gap*, the tiny space between the sending and receiving neuron. These chemicals then move across the synaptic gap and attach to receptors on the membranes of the receiving neuron. In this way, they carry the message from the sending neuron to the receiving neuron.

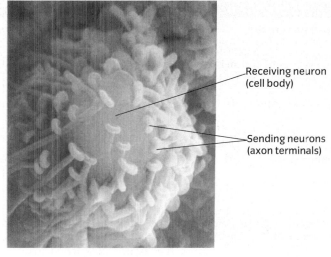

7 Dealing with leftovers

Neurotransmitters do not remain attached to their receptors forever—they bind and release. When unbound they are either taken back up into the terminal button of the sending neuron for breakdown and recycling in a process called "reuptake," or are destroyed right in the synapse by a variety of degradation enzymes.

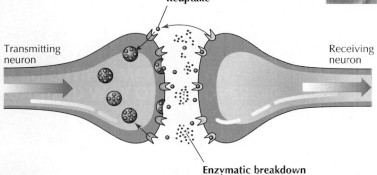

Process Diagram

one neuron to the next. The chemicals that transmit these messages are called **neurotransmitters**.

Researchers have discovered hundreds of substances that function as neurotransmitters. These substances regulate a wide variety of physiological processes. See *What a Psychologist Sees* on page 43 for a description of some of these effects.

Studying the brain and its neurotransmitters will help you understand some common medical problems. (STUDY ORGANIZER 2.1 discusses some of the better understood neurotransmitters.) For example, we know that decreased levels of the neurotransmitter dopamine are associated with Parkinson's disease (PD), whereas excessively high levels of dopamine appear to contribute to some forms of schizophrenia.

One of the better-known brain chemicals are the endogenous opium-like peptides, commonly known as **endorphins** (a contraction of *endogenous*, meaning

"self-produced," and *morphine*). These nervous system chemicals mimic the effects of opium-like drugs, such as morphine: They elevate mood and reduce pain. They also affect memory, learning, blood pressure, appetite, and sexual activity.

HORMONES: A GLOBAL COMMUNICATION SYSTEM

We've just seen how the nervous system uses neurotransmitters to rapidly transmit messages across synapses to have widespread effects throughout the body. A second type of communication system exists. This second system is made up of a network of glands, called the **endocrine system** (FIGURE 2.8). Rather than neurotransmitters in synapses, this system uses **hormones** in blood to carry its messages (see FIGURE 2.9).

Study Organizer 2.1	How neurotransmitters affect us	
Neurotransmitter	**Behaviours and/or Mental Processes Affected**	
Serotonin	Sleep, mood, appetite, sensory perception, temperature regulation, sex drive, pain suppression, and impulsivity. Low levels associated with depression.	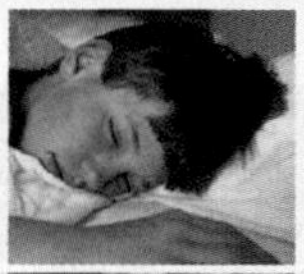
Acetylcholine (ACh)	Muscle action, cognitive functioning, memory, rapid-eye-movement (REM) sleep, emotion. Suspected role in Alzheimer's disease.	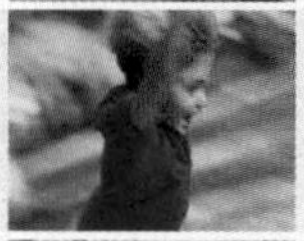
Dopamine (DA)	Movement, attention, memory, learning, and emotion. Excess DA associated with schizophrenia, too little with Parkinson's disease. Also plays a role in addiction and pleasure systems in the brain.	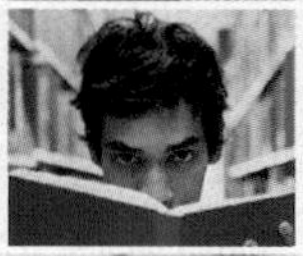
Norepinephrine (NE) (or noradrenaline)	Learning, memory, dreaming, emotion, waking from sleep, eating, alertness, wakefulness, reactions to stress. Low levels of NE associated with depression, high levels with agitated, manic states.	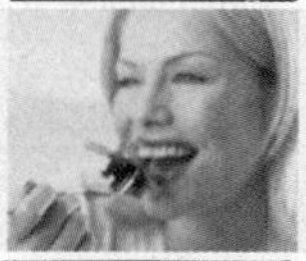
Epinephrine (or adrenaline)	Emotional arousal, memory storage, and metabolism of glucose necessary for energy release.	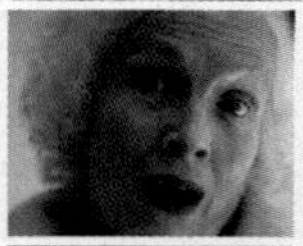
Gamma aminobutyric acid (GABA)	Neural inhibition in the central nervous system. Tranquilizing drugs, like Ativan or Xanax, increase GABA's inhibitory effects and thereby decrease anxiety.	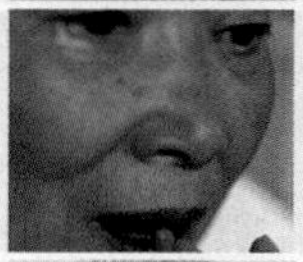
Endorphins	Mood, pain, memory, and learning.	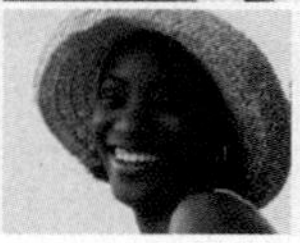

The endocrine system
FIGURE 2.8

This figure shows the major endocrine glands, along with some internal organs to help you locate the glands.

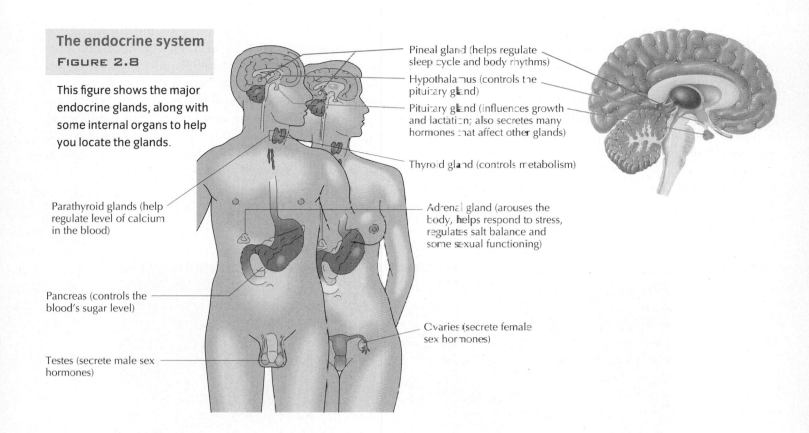

Pineal gland (helps regulate sleep cycle and body rhythms)

Hypothalamus (controls the pituitary gland)

Pituitary gland (influences growth and lactation; also secretes many hormones that affect other glands)

Thyroid gland (controls metabolism)

Adrenal gland (arouses the body, helps respond to stress, regulates salt balance and some sexual functioning)

Parathyroid glands (help regulate level of calcium in the blood)

Pancreas (controls the blood's sugar level)

Ovaries (secrete female sex hormones)

Testes (secrete male sex hormones)

Neurotransmitters send individual messages

To...	Jean Bean
CC...	
Subject:	Lunch Tomorrow?
Attach...	

Hi Jean,
Are you free for lunch tomorrow? If so, want to meet at noon at the Hong Kong Cafe? Hoping to see you then.

Hormones send global messages

To...	Friends; family; co-workers
CC...	
Subject:	Party!
Attach...	

Hi Everybody,
Jean Bean and I are hosting a party on Saturday night at 9 p.m. Please come, and tell your friends!

Why do we need two communication systems? FIGURE 2.9

You can think of neurotransmitters as individual e-mails, like those you send to particular people. Neurotransmitters deliver messages to specific receptors across specific synapses, which other neurons nearby probably don't "overhear." Hormones, in contrast, are like a global e-mail message that you send to everyone in your address book. Endocrine glands release hormones directly into the bloodstream. The hormones travel throughout the body, carrying messages to any cell that will accept them (that is, it has the appropriate hormone receptors). Hormones also function like your global e-mail recipients forwarding your message to yet more people. For example, a small part of the brain called the hypothalamus releases hormones that signal the pituitary gland, which then stimulates or inhibits the release of other downstream hormones.

Your endocrine system has several important functions. It helps regulate long-term bodily processes, such as growth and sexual characteristics. For example, if testosterone were to be removed from a healthy young man, his genitals would get smaller and his sex drive would decrease (Brett et al., 2007). Hormones also maintain ongoing bodily processes (such as digestion and elimination), and they control the body's response to emergencies. In times of crisis and arousal, the hypothalamus sends messages through two pathways: the neural system and the endocrine system (primarily via the pituitary gland). The pituitary gland sends hormonal messages to the adrenal glands (which sit on top of each kidney, shaped similar to a Hershey's chocolate kiss). The adrenal glands then release three hormones: *cortisol*, a stress hormone that boosts energy and blood sugar levels; *epinephrine* (adrenaline); and *norepinephrine*. These last two hormones also serve as neurotransmitters, but, as you will see, they have different functions in the endocrine system.

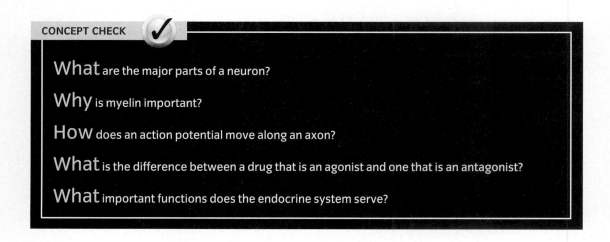

CONCEPT CHECK ✓

What are the major parts of a neuron?

Why is myelin important?

How does an action potential move along an axon?

What is the difference between a drug that is an agonist and one that is an antagonist?

What important functions does the endocrine system serve?

Nervous System Organization

LEARNING OBJECTIVES

Identify the major components of the nervous system.

Explain how the spinal cord initiates reflexes.

Explain why research investigating neuroplasticity and neurogenesis are important.

Describe the opposing roles of the sympathetic and parasympathetic nervous systems.

Have you heard the expression "Information is power"? Nowhere is this truer than in the human body. Without information, we could not survive. Neurons within our nervous system must take in sensory information from the outside world and then process and respond to it. Just as the circulatory system handles blood, which conveys chemicals and gases around the body, our nervous system uses electrical signals and chemicals to convey information.

The nervous system is divided and subdivided into several branches (**FIGURE 2.10**). One main part of our nervous system includes the brain and a large bundle of nerves that form the *spinal cord*. Because this system is located in the centre of your body (within your skull and spine), it is called the **central nervous system (CNS)**.

central nervous system (CNS) The brain and spinal cord.

The second major part of your nervous system includes all the nerves outside the brain and spinal

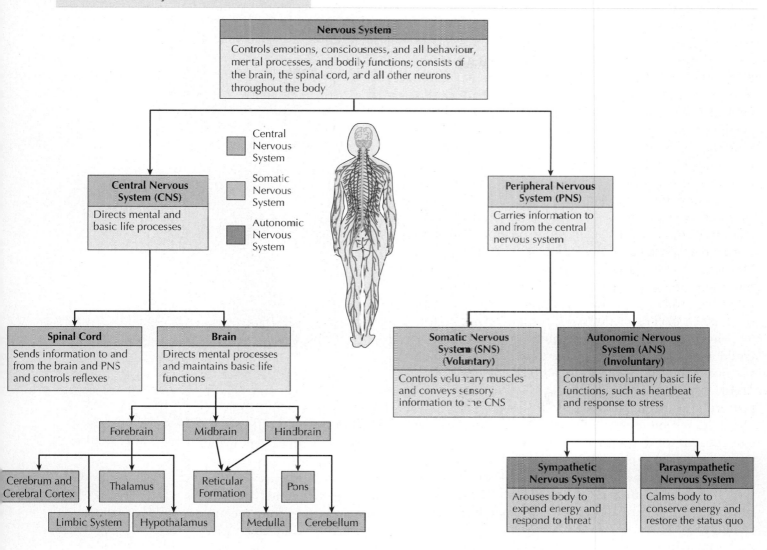

Nervous System

Controls emotions, consciousness, and all behaviour, mental processes, and bodily functions; consists of the brain, the spinal cord, and all other neurons throughout the body

Central Nervous System
Somatic Nervous System
Autonomic Nervous System

Central Nervous System (CNS)
Directs mental and basic life processes

Peripheral Nervous System (PNS)
Carries information to and from the central nervous system

Spinal Cord
Sends information to and from the brain and PNS and controls reflexes

Brain
Directs mental processes and maintains basic life functions

Somatic Nervous System (SNS) (Voluntary)
Controls voluntary muscles and conveys sensory information to the CNS

Autonomic Nervous System (ANS) (Involuntary)
Controls involuntary basic life functions, such as heartbeat and response to stress

Forebrain
Midbrain
Hindbrain

Cerebrum and Cerebral Cortex
Thalamus
Reticular Formation
Pons

Limbic System
Hypothalamus
Medulla
Cerebellum

Sympathetic Nervous System
Arouses body to expend energy and respond to threat

Parasympathetic Nervous System
Calms body to conserve energy and restore the status quo

CENTRAL NERVOUS SYSTEM (CNS): THE BRAIN AND SPINAL CORD

Although the central nervous system (CNS) is incredibly versatile and remarkably powerful, it is also incredibly fragile. Unlike neurons in the PNS that can regenerate and require less protection, serious cord. This **peripheral nervous system (PNS)** carries messages (action potentials) to and from the central nervous system to the periphery of the body.

damage to neurons in the CNS is usually permanent. However, new research is revealing the brain is not as "hard wired" as we once thought. Scientists had long believed that after the first few years of life, humans and most animals are unable to repair or replace damaged neurons in the brain or spinal cord. We now know that the brain is capable of lifelong **neuroplasticity** and **neurogenesis**.

Neuroplasticity: Changes in the Brain's Architecture

Rather than being a fixed, rigid organ, the brain is capable of changing its structure (anatomy) and function (physiology) through usage and experience (Deller et al., 2006; Kinsley & Lambert, 2008; Mateer & Kerns, 2000; Romero et al., 2008; Rossignol et al., 2008). It was once thought that this malleability occurred only during childhood and that by puberty the brain had its permanent adult form and function. Now, decades of research have shown the brain has the lifelong capacity to reorganize its neural pathways in response to new experiences and to compensate for lost function after damage. It is this dynamic rewiring that makes brains so wonderfully adaptive. For example, it makes it possible for us to learn a new sport, computer game, or foreign language. Moreover, neuroplasticity is the mechanism by which our brain can structurally and functionally modify itself following strokes and trauma (Taub, 2004; Whishaw et al., 2008; Wolf et al., 2008).

The idea that changes in neuronal architecture could account for changes in thinking and behaviour was first demonstrated in the 1940s by Dr. Donald Hebb (1904–1985) (**FIGURE 2.11**), a Canadian psychologist and the principal pioneer of neuropsychology. Hebb's description of how the brain and neural signals can account for the higher functions of the mind and consciousness was extremely influential. He believed the human conscious experience could be described in terms of patterns of neural signals (Hebb, 1949). Hebb suggested that neurons that are simultaneously active would tend to become associated with each other, such that activity in one would facilitate activity in the other (Hebb, 1949). Repeated stimulation ultimately strengthens the synapses, and associated neurons fire more readily, translating into some mental task. At the time, the idea was revolutionary; scientists had long wondered how the 1.5-kilogram gelatinous organ in our heads could initiate behaviour, interact with the environment, and form cohesive thoughts. Hebb's early work gave psychology the basic mechanism of synaptic plasticity. Many of Hebb's ideas have been subsequently supported by research findings.

Neurogenesis: The Making of New Neurons

The brain continually replaces lost cells with new cells. These cells originate deep within the brain and migrate to become parts of specific

Donald Hebb FIGURE 2.11

circuitries. The source of these newly created cells is neural **stem cells**—rare, immature cells that can grow and develop into any type of cell in the nervous system. Their fate depends on the chemical signals they receive (Abbott, 2004; Kim, 2004; Vaillend et al., 2008). Stem cell research has come a long way since the 1960s, when it was first described in transplanted mouse bone marrow cells by Canadian scientists Ernest McCulloch and James Edgar Till (Becker, McCulloch, & Till, 1963). These special cells are now used for a variety of purposes, such as bone marrow transplants. Clinical trials that have used transplanted stem cells to replace cells destroyed by strokes, Alzheimer's, Parkinson's, epilepsy, stress, and depression show their tremendous potential in treating neural injury and disease (Chang et al., 2005; Fleischmann & Welz, 2008; Hampton, 2006, 2007; Leri, Anversa, & Frishmann, 2007; Waldau & Shetty, 2008).

> **stem cells** Precursor (immature) cells that can develop into any type of new specialized cells; a stem cell holds all the information it needs to make bone, blood, brain—any part of a human body—and can also copy itself to maintain a stock of stem cells.

Does this mean that people paralyzed from spinal cord injuries might be able to walk again? At this time, neurogenesis in the brain and spinal cord appears to be minimal. However, one possible option might be to transplant embryonic stem cells into the damaged area of the spinal cord. Researchers have transplanted mouse embryonic stem cells into a damaged rat spinal cord (Jones, Anderson, & Galvin, 2003; McDonald et al., 1999). When the damaged spinal cord was viewed several weeks later, the implanted cells had survived and spread throughout the injured cord area. More important, the rats also showed some movement in the previously paralyzed parts of their bodies. Similar findings have been reported by other research teams (Feng et al., 2008). Preliminary human clinical trials have shown that some spinal nerve regeneration can occur after a spinal cord injury has been treated with cell-growth-promoting substances (Wu et al., 2008).

The Spinal Cord
Beginning at the base of the brain and continuing down the back, the spinal cord carries vital information from the rest of the body to and from the brain. But the spinal cord doesn't just relay messages. It can also initiate some automatic behaviours on its own. We call these involuntary, automatic behaviours **reflexes** or **reflex arcs** because the response to the incoming stimuli is automatically "reflected" back (FIGURE 2.12).

We're all born with numerous reflexes, many of which fade over time. But even as adults, we still blink in response to a puff of air in our eyes, gag when something touches the back of the throat, and urinate and defecate in response to pressure in the bladder and rectum. Reflexes even influence our sexual responses. Certain stimuli, such as touching the genitals, can lead to clitoral and penile erection (see *Psychological Science*). However, to have the passion, sexual thoughts, and emotion, or to get aroused by sexy sights or sounds, the sensory information must ultimately include the brain.

> **reflexes or reflex arcs** Involuntary, automatic behaviour initiated by the spinal cord in response to some stimulus.

The workings of the spinal cord FIGURE 2.12

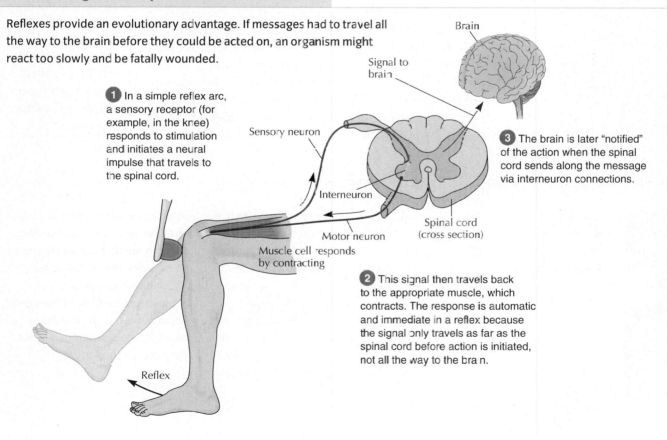

Reflexes provide an evolutionary advantage. If messages had to travel all the way to the brain before they could be acted on, an organism might react too slowly and be fatally wounded.

1 In a simple reflex arc, a sensory receptor (for example, in the knee) responds to stimulation and initiates a neural impulse that travels to the spinal cord.

Brain

Signal to brain

Sensory neuron

Interneuron

Motor neuron

Muscle cell responds by contracting

Spinal cord (cross section)

3 The brain is later "notified" of the action when the spinal cord sends along the message via interneuron connections.

2 This signal then travels back to the appropriate muscle, which contracts. The response is automatic and immediate in a reflex because the signal only travels as far as the spinal cord before action is initiated, not all the way to the brain.

Reflex

Psychological Science

The Brain Isn't Necessary for an Erection

Direct tactile (touch) stimulation of the penis or clitoris can trigger an erection. This occurs because of a spinal reflex that forms a loop from the genitals to the spinal cord and back. Sensory nerve endings in the genital area detect the tactile stimulation, and this information is then conveyed to the spinal cord. Nerves then transmit the output signal back to the penis or clitoris, and this signal causes the changes in blood flow in the genitals that account for an erection. Although the spinal cord does send sensory information onward to the brain, this role is not essential. People with spinal injuries that sever communication between the lower regions of the spinal cord and the brain can usually achieve erection with tactile stimulation alone.

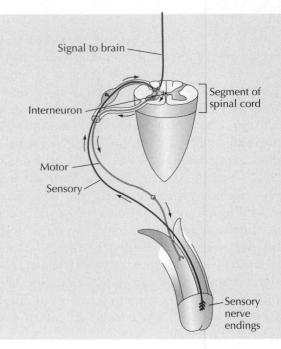

Signal to brain

Segment of spinal cord

Interneuron

Motor

Sensory

Sensory nerve endings

PERIPHERAL NERVOUS SYSTEM (PNS): CONNECTING THE CNS TO THE REST OF THE BODY

■ **somatic nervous system (SNS)** Subdivision of the peripheral nervous system (PNS). The SNS receives incoming sensory information and controls the skeletal muscles.

The main function of the peripheral nervous system (PNS) is to carry information to and from the central nervous system. It links the brain and spinal cord to the body's senses, muscles, and glands.

The PNS is subdivided into the somatic nervous system and the autonomic nervous system.

In a kind of "two-way street," the **somatic nervous system (SNS)** first carries sensory information to the CNS and then carries messages from the CNS to skeletal muscles (FIGURE 2.13).

The other subdivision of the PNS is the **autonomic nervous system (ANS)**. The ANS is responsible for involuntary tasks, such as heart rate, digestion, pupil dilation, and breathing. Like an automatic

■ **autonomic nervous system (ANS)** Subdivision of the peripheral nervous system (PNS) that controls involuntary functions of tissues, organs, and glands. It is subdivided into the *sympathetic* nervous system and the *parasympathetic* nervous system.

The relationship between sensory and motor neurons FIGURE 2.13

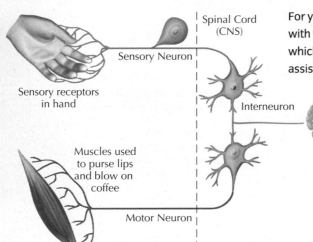

Spinal Cord (CNS)

Sensory Neuron

Sensory receptors in hand

Interneuron

Muscles used to purse lips and blow on coffee

Motor Neuron

For you to be able to function, your brain must communicate with your body. This is the job of the *somatic nervous system*, which receives sensory information, sends it to the brain, and assists in the brain's response. *Sensory neurons* carry messages to the CNS. *Motor neurons* carry messages *away* from the CNS. *Interneurons* communicate within the CNS and link up the sensory inputs and the motor outputs. Most of the neurons in the brain are interneurons.

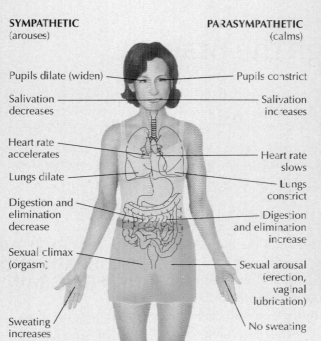

SYMPATHETIC (arouses)		PARASYMPATHETIC (calms)
Pupils dilate (widen)		Pupils constrict
Salivation decreases		Salivation increases
Heart rate accelerates		Heart rate slows
Lungs dilate		Lungs constrict
Digestion and elimination decrease		Digestion and elimination increase
Sexual climax (orgasm)		Sexual arousal (erection, vaginal lubrication)
Sweating increases		No sweating

Stress, high activity, fight or flight

Relaxation, low stress, rest and digest

Actions of the autonomic nervous system (ANS) FIGURE 2.14

pilot, the ANS can sometimes be consciously overridden. But as its name implies, the autonomic system normally operates on its own without conscious effort (autonomously).

The autonomic nervous system is further divided into two branches: the sympathetic and parasympathetic, which tend to work in opposition to regulate the functioning of organs, like the heart, the intestines, and the lungs (**FIGURE 2.14**). Like two children playing on a teeter-totter, one branch will be up while the other is down, but they essentially balance each other.

During stressful times, either mental or physical, the **sympathetic nervous system** mobilizes bodily resources to respond to the stressor. This emergency response is often called the fight-or-flight response. If you saw a deadly snake coiled and ready to strike, your sympathetic nervous system would, among other things, increase your heart rate, respiration, and blood pressure; stop your digestive and eliminative processes; and release hormones, such as cortisol, into the bloodstream. The net result of sympathetic activation is to get more oxygenated blood and energy to the skeletal muscles and to prepare you to deal with the stressor—whether you defend yourself (fight) or escape (flight).

The sympathetic nervous system provides an adaptive, evolutionary advantage. Early in evolution, when an organism faced a dangerous predator or an aggressive intruder, there were only two reasonable responses: fight or flight.

This evolved automatic mobilization of bodily resources is still essential today. However, non-life-threatening events, such as traffic jams and pressing deadlines, also activate our sympathetic nervous system. Our bodies respond to these sources of stress with sympathetic arousal. As the next chapter discusses, ongoing sympathetic activation to such chronic stress can damage our health.

In contrast to the sympathetic nervous system and its fight or flight response, the **parasympathetic nervous system** functions to rest and digest. It is responsible for returning the body to its normal functioning by slowing heart rate, lowering blood pressure, and increasing digestive and eliminative processes. In non-arousing activities (such as reading or talking on the phone), this branch of the nervous system is involved in energy storage and conservation.

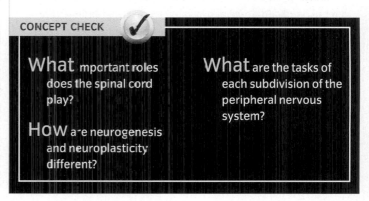

CONCEPT CHECK

What important roles does the spinal cord play?

How are neurogenesis and neuroplasticity different?

What are the tasks of each subdivision of the peripheral nervous system?

A Tour Through the Brain

LEARNING OBJECTIVES

Identify the major structures of the hindbrain, midbrain, and forebrain, and of the cerebral cortex.

Summarize the major roles of the lobes of the cerebral cortex.

Describe what scientists have learned from split-brain research.

Explain why it's a mistake to believe that the right brain is usually "neglected."

Describe some examples of localization of function in the brain.

We begin our exploration of the brain at the lower end, where the spinal cord joins the base of the brain, and move upward toward the skull. As we move from bottom to top, vital reflexes, like breathing, generally give way to more complex mental processes, like making social judgements and planning (**FIGURE 2.15** and **FIGURE 2.16**).

Damage to the brain FIGURE 2.15

The 2005 debate over Terri Schiavo was largely about whether her husband should be allowed to remove her feeding tube. Although Terri was still able to move and breathe on her own, she had no higher-level brain functions. Terry's parents believed that the lower-level brain functions she exhibited were sufficient proof of life. Advocates on the other side felt that once the cerebral cortex ceases functioning, the "person" is gone and there is no reason to keep the body alive. What do you think? A lengthy court battle granted permission to remove her feeding tube. Terri Schiavo died on March 31, 2005, after nearly 14 days without food or water. She was 41 years old.

LOWER-LEVEL BRAIN STRUCTURES: THE HINDBRAIN, MIDBRAIN, AND PARTS OF THE FOREBRAIN

The billions of neurons that make up the human brain control most of what we think, feel, and do. Certain brain structures are specialized to perform certain tasks, a process known as **localization of function**. However, most parts of the brain perform integrative, interdependent functions.

localization of function Specialization of various parts of the brain for particular functions.

The Hindbrain
The **hindbrain** includes the medulla, pons, and cerebellum and functions collectively to generate most of your vital bodily processes.

The **medulla** is effectively an extension of the top of the spinal cord, carrying information to and from the brain. It also controls many essential automatic bodily functions, such as respiration and heart rate, so damage to this brain region is often fatal. But for your medulla you would also not be able to swallow, vomit, or defecate—all clearly essential functions.

The **pons** is involved in respiration, movement, sleeping, waking, and dreaming (among other things). The pons also has a role in relaying sensory information from the periphery to higher brain structures. For example, auditory information first enters the brain at the level of the pons.

The cauliflower-shaped **cerebellum** at the back of the brain ("little brain" in Latin) is, evolutionarily, a very old structure. It coordinates fine muscle movement and balance. The cerebellum also has the rather interesting task of taking a sequence of movements that always runs in the same order and packages them as a single automatic output. While executing complex martial arts moves or acrobatic movements nicely illustrate

The human brain FIGURE 2.16

This drawing summarizes key functions of some of the brain's major structures. The brainstem, which includes parts of the hindbrain, midbrain, and forebrain, provides a handy geographical landmark.

VIEW THIS IN ACTION
in your WileyPLUS course

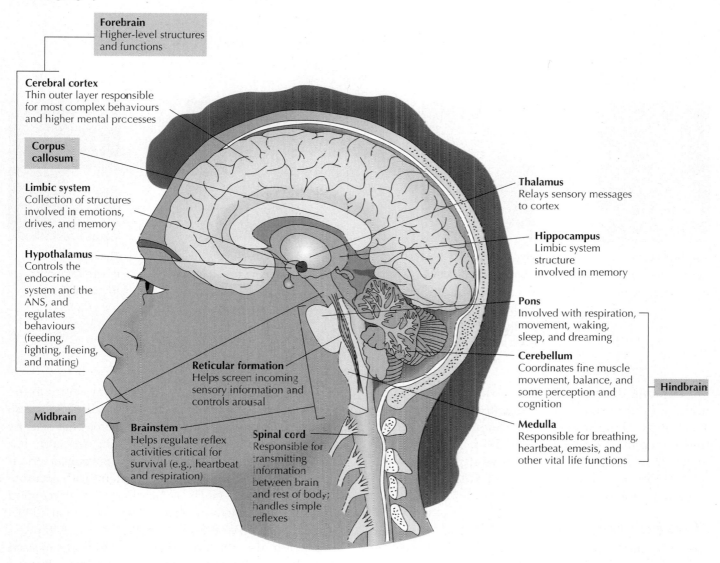

Forebrain
Higher-level structures and functions

Cerebral cortex
Thin outer layer responsible for most complex behaviours and higher mental processes

Corpus callosum

Limbic system
Collection of structures involved in emotions, drives, and memory

Hypothalamus
Controls the endocrine system and the ANS, and regulates behaviours (feeding, fighting, fleeing, and mating)

Midbrain

Reticular formation
Helps screen incoming sensory information and controls arousal

Brainstem
Helps regulate reflex activities critical for survival (e.g., heartbeat and respiration)

Spinal cord
Responsible for transmitting information between brain and rest of body; handles simple reflexes

Thalamus
Relays sensory messages to cortex

Hippocampus
Limbic system structure involved in memory

Pons
Involved with respiration, movement, waking, sleep, and dreaming

Cerebellum
Coordinates fine muscle movement, balance, and some perception and cognition

Medulla
Responsible for breathing, heartbeat, emesis, and other vital life functions

Hindbrain

the cerebellum at work, it is best demonstrated when a person is learning to drive a standard transmission car. For most, this process is initially very difficult, requiring tremendous concentration to get the clutch, gas, and gear change in the correct order. After a bit of practice, however, the driver is able to change gears effortlessly, without being distracted by music, conversation, or other variables: the cerebellum has tuned into the repetitive behaviours involved in the gear changing process and runs them as a single smooth behaviour.

This ability then frees up higher brain regions to do more complex tasks, like concentrating on road conditions and other drivers (and not changing radio stations, searching for music, or texting friends!).

The Midbrain
The **midbrain** helps us orient our eye and body movements to visual and auditory stimuli, and works with the pons to help control sleep and level of arousal. When you are visually tracking a moving object, it is the midbrain—among other regions—that is active.

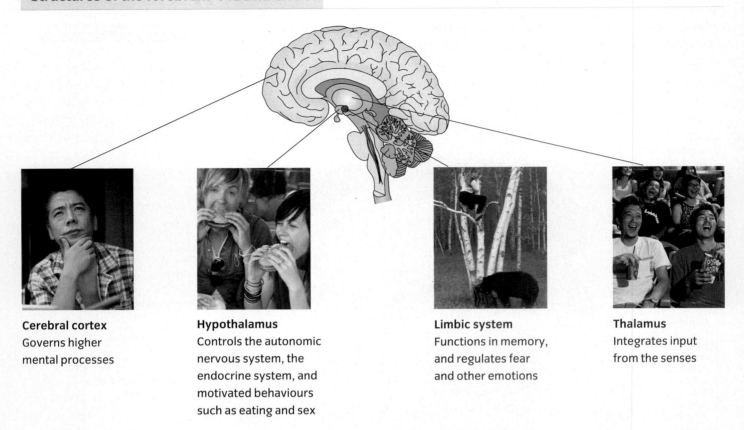

Cerebral cortex
Governs higher
mental processes

Hypothalamus
Controls the autonomic
nervous system, the
endocrine system, and
motivated behaviours
such as eating and sex

Limbic system
Functions in memory,
and regulates fear
and other emotions

Thalamus
Integrates input
from the senses

Running through the core of the hindbrain, midbrain, and brainstem is the **reticular formation** (RF). This diffuse, long, finger-shaped network of neurons filters incoming sensory information and alerts the higher brain centres to important events. Without your reticular formation, you would not be alert or attentive or perhaps even conscious.

The Forebrain
The **forebrain** is the largest and most prominent part of the human brain. It includes the thalamus, hypothalamus, limbic system, cerebrum, and cerebral cortex (**FIGURE 2.17**). The first three structures are located near the top of the brainstem. The cerebrum is wrapped above and completely around the other three structures, and the cerebral cortex (discussed separately in the next section) is the outermost layer of the cerebrum. (*Cerebrum* is Latin for "brain" and *cortex* is Latin for "covering" or "bark.")

The **thalamus** receives input from nearly all sensory systems and directs the information to the appropriate cortical areas. It may also have a role in learning and memory (Bailey & Mair, 2005; Ridley et al., 2005). Because the thalamus is the brain's major sensory relay centre to the cerebral cortex, damage or abnormalities can cause the cortex to misinterpret or not receive vital sensory information. Interestingly, brain-imaging research has linked thalamus abnormalities to schizophrenia, a serious psychological disorder involving problems with accurate sensory processing (such as hearing) and perception (Chapter 13) (Andreasen et al., 2008; Byne et al., 2008; Clinton & Meador-Woodruff, 2004; Preuss et al., 2005).

Beneath the thalamus lies the kidney-bean-sized **hypothalamus** (*hypo* means "under" or "below"). It is the control centre for many essential survival behaviours, such as hunger, thirst, sex, and aggression (Hinton et al., 2004; Williams et al., 2004; Zillmer, Spiers, & Culberton, 2008). It controls the autonomic nervous system and the body's internal environment, including temperature control, which it achieves by controlling the endocrine system. Looking as if it is dripping from the bottom of the hypothalamus is the *pituitary gland*. The pituitary is often wrongly referred to as the master endocrine gland, but this gland is actually a slave to the hypothalamus. After instruction from the hypothalamus, it releases hormones that activate the other endocrine glands in the body. The hypothalamus influences the pituitary in two ways: (1) through direct neural connections and (2) by releasing its own hormones into the blood supply of the pituitary.

An interconnected group of forebrain structures, known as the **limbic system**, is located roughly along the border between the cerebral cortex and the lower-level brain structures.

In general, the limbic system is responsible for emotions, learning, and memory and includes the *hippocampus* and the *amygdala* (some neuroanatomists also include parts of the thalamus, the hypothalamus, and the pituitary in the limbic system). The amygdala has been a major focus of research interest in the limbic system, particularly its involvement in aggression and fear (Asghar et al., 2008; Carlson, 2008; LeDoux, 1998, 2002, 2007). Another well-known function of the limbic system is its role in pleasure and reward (Dackis & O'Brien, 2001; Olds & Milner, 1954; Torta & Castelli, 2008). Even though limbic system structures and neurotransmitters are instrumental in emotional behaviour, the cerebral cortex also tempers and modulates emotion in humans.

The hippocampus is important in long-term memory and spatial navigation. It is one of the first brain regions to be affected in Alzheimer's patients, and this is probably why early symptoms of the disease involve memory loss and disorientation, which progressively worsen.

THE CEREBRAL CORTEX: THE CENTRE OF OUR HIGHER PROCESSING

cerebral cortex
Thin surface layer on the cerebral hemispheres that regulates most complex behaviour, including processing sensations, motor control, and higher mental processes.

The grey, wrinkled **cerebral cortex** is responsible for most of our complex behaviours and higher mental processes. It plays such a vital role in our sense of self that many consider it the essence of our subjective experience of life and the embodiment of exactly who we are. In fact, physicians can declare a person legally dead when the cortex dies, even when the lower-level brain structures and the rest of the body are fully functioning.

Although the cerebral cortex is only about 3 millimetres thick, it's made up of approximately 30 billion neurons and nine times as many glial cells. It contains numerous wrinkles called *convolutions* (think

of a crumpled-up newspaper), which allow it to maximize its surface area while still fitting into the restricted space of the skull.

The full cerebral cortex and the two cerebral hemispheres beneath it closely resemble an oversized walnut. The deep valley, or *fissure,* down the centre marks the left and right *hemispheres* of the brain. The hemispheres make up about 80 percent of the brain's weight. They are mostly filled with axon connections between the cortex and the other brain structures. Each hemisphere gets signals from and controls the opposite side of the body.

The cerebral hemispheres are divided into eight distinct areas or lobes, with four in each hemisphere (**FIGURE 2.18**). Like the lower-level brain structures, each lobe specializes in somewhat different tasks—another example of localization of function. However, some functions are shared between the lobes.

The Frontal Lobes The large **frontal lobes** coordinate messages received from the other three lobes. An area at the very back of the frontal lobes, known as the *motor cortex,* initiates all voluntary movement (which is different from the largely automatic motor tasks performed by the cerebellum). In the lower left frontal lobe lies *Broca's area.* In 1865, French physician Paul Broca discovered that damage to this area causes difficulty in speech production but not language comprehension. This type of impaired language ability is known as *Broca's aphasia.* Finally, the frontal lobes control most of the higher functions that distinguish humans from other animals, such as thinking, personality, emotional judgements, and memory. Abnormalities in the frontal lobes are often observed in patients with schizophrenia (Chapter 13). As seen in the case of Phineas Gage (Chapter 1) and in other research, damage to the frontal lobe affects motivation, creativity, self-awareness, initiative, reasoning, and suitable emotional behaviour. Our ability to function normally and respond appropriately in social situations is also a function of the frontal lobes (**FIGURE 2.19**).

The Parietal Lobes, the Temporal Lobes, and the Occipital Lobes The **parietal lobes** interpret bodily sensations including pressure, pain, touch, temperature, and location of body parts. A band of tissue on the front of the parietal lobe, called the *somatosensory cortex,* receives information about touch and other skin and visceral senses (**FIGURE 2.20**).

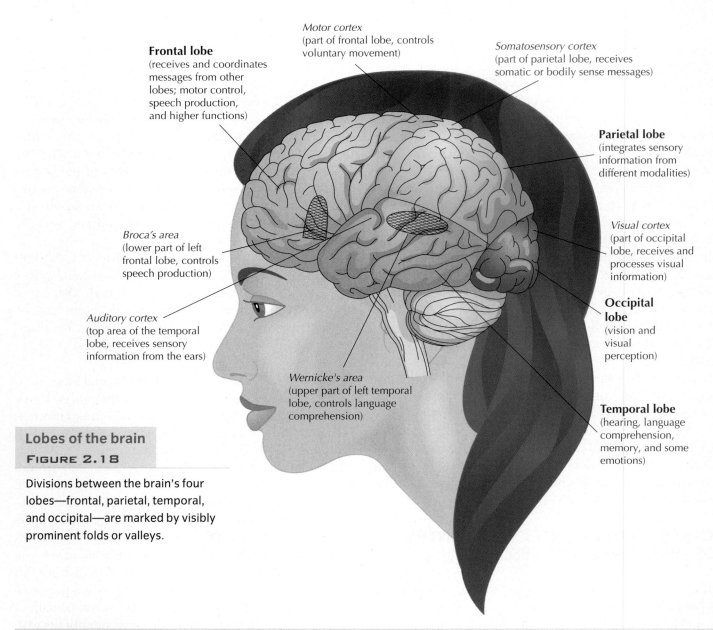

Motor cortex
(part of frontal lobe, controls voluntary movement)

Somatosensory cortex
(part of parietal lobe, receives somatic or bodily sense messages)

Frontal lobe
(receives and coordinates messages from other lobes; motor control, speech production, and higher functions)

Parietal lobe
(integrates sensory information from different modalities)

Broca's area
(lower part of left frontal lobe, controls speech production)

Visual cortex
(part of occipital lobe, receives and processes visual information)

Occipital lobe
(vision and visual perception)

Auditory cortex
(top area of the temporal lobe, receives sensory information from the ears)

Wernicke's area
(upper part of left temporal lobe, controls language comprehension)

Temporal lobe
(hearing, language comprehension, memory, and some emotions)

Lobes of the brain

FIGURE 2.18

Divisions between the brain's four lobes—frontal, parietal, temporal, and occipital—are marked by visibly prominent folds or valleys.

Accidental evidence of specialized brain functions? FIGURE 2.19

In 1998, construction worker Travis Bogumill was accidentally shot with a nail gun near the rear of his right frontal lobe. Remarkably, Bogumill experienced only an impaired ability to perform complex mathematical problems. This case study is consistent with experimental research showing that the frontal lobes and short-term memory are responsible for mathematical calculations, reasoning, problem solving, and thinking about future rewards or actions (Evans, 2003; Hill, 2004; Neubauer et al., 2004).

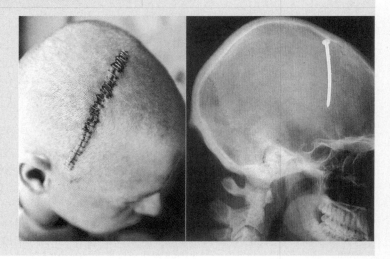

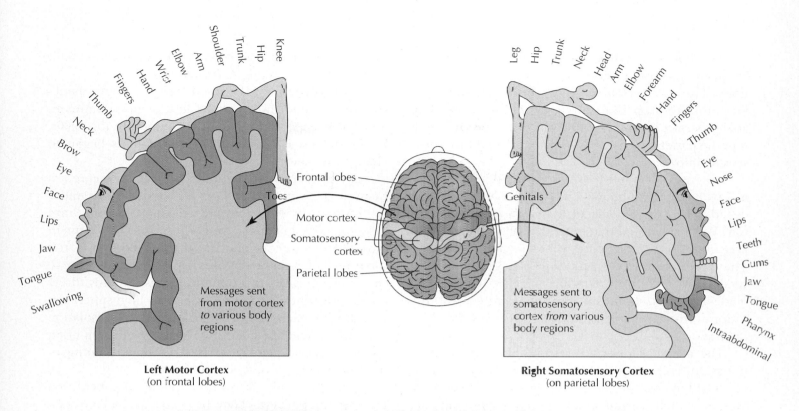

Left Motor Cortex
(on frontal lobes)

Right Somatosensory Cortex
(on parietal lobes)

Frontal lobes

Motor cortex

Somatosensory cortex

Parietal lobes

Messages sent from motor cortex *to* various body regions

Messages sent to somatosensory cortex *from* various body regions

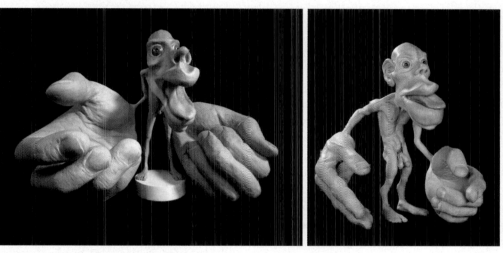

Body representation of the motor cortex and somatosensory cortex FIGURE 2.20

This drawing represents a vertical cross-section taken from the left hemisphere's motor cortex and right hemisphere's somatosensory cortex. If body areas were truly proportional to the amount of tissue on the motor and somatosensory cortices, our bodies would look like the oddly shaped human figures draped around the outside edge of the cortex. Notice that the most sensitive regions of the body and the regions of the body that have the greatest fine motor precision (such as the fingers and the lips) have the largest representations on the motor and somatosensory strip. This is superbly illustrated by clay homunculi ("little men") made to demonstrate the relative space body parts occupy on the motor and sensory strips. Newer research suggests the discrete mapping of the fingers onto the motor cortex may in fact be a bit of an oversimplification. It seems the representation of the fingers actually mingle and overlap suggesting a more accurate motor homunculus would look like a naked little man wearing mittens. Moreover, the body part position on the cortex appears to be organized according to the behaviours to be performed rather than simply a static map of the individual body parts (Graziano, 2006).

The **temporal lobes** are responsible for hearing, language comprehension, memory, and some emotions. The *auditory cortex* (which processes sound) is located at the top front of each temporal lobe. This area processes incoming sensory information and sends it to the parietal lobes, where it is combined with other sensory information.

An area of the left temporal lobe, *Wernicke's area,* is involved in language comprehension. About a decade after Broca's discovery, German neurologist Carl Wernicke noted that patients with damage in this area could not understand what they read or heard. They could, however, speak quickly and easily. Their speech was often unintelligible because it contained made-up words, sound substitutions, and word substitutions. This syndrome is now referred to as *Wernicke's aphasia.*

The **occipital lobes** are responsible, among other things, for vision and visual perception. Damage to the occipital lobe can produce blindness, even though the eyes and their neural connection to the brain are perfectly functional.

The Association Areas
One of the most popular and enduring myths in psychology is that we use only 10 percent of our brain. This myth might have begun with early research showing that approximately three quarters of the cortex is *uncommitted* (that is, it had no precise, specific function responsive to electrical brain stimulation). Abundant research has shown these areas are not dormant, however. They are clearly involved in interpreting, integrating, and acting on information processed by other parts of the brain. They are called **association areas** because they associate, or connect, various areas and functions of the brain. The association areas in the frontal lobe, for example, help in decision-making and task planning. Similarly, the association area right in front of the motor cortex is involved in the planning of voluntary movement.

TWO BRAINS IN ONE? THE SPLIT SCREEN

We mentioned earlier that the brain's left and right cerebral hemispheres control opposite sides of the body. Each hemisphere also has separate areas of specialization.

(This is another example of *localization* of function, yet it is technically referred to as *lateralization*.)

Early researchers believed that the right hemisphere was subordinate to the left, or non-dominant, and had few special functions or abilities. In the 1960s, landmark research with *split-brain* patients began to change this view.

The primary connection between the two cerebral hemispheres is a thick, ribbon-like band of axons under the cortex called the **corpus callosum.** In some rare cases of severe epilepsy, when other forms of treatment have failed, surgeons cut the corpus callosum to stop the spread of epileptic seizures from one hemisphere to the other. Because this operation cuts the only direct communication link between the two hemispheres, it reveals what each half of the brain can do in isolation from the other. The resulting research with split-brain patients has profoundly improved our understanding of how the two halves of the brain function.

If you met and talked with a split-brain patient, you probably wouldn't even know he or she had had the operation. The subtle changes in split-brain patients normally appear only with specialized testing (**FIGURE 2.21**).

Dozens of studies on split-brain patients, and newer research on people whose brains are intact, have documented several differences between the two brain hemispheres (**FIGURE 2.22** on page 62). Interestingly, left and right brain specialization is not usually reversed in left-handed people. About 68 percent of left-handers and 97 percent of right-handers have their major language areas on the left hemisphere. This suggests that even though the right side of the brain is dominant for movement in left-handers, other skills are often localized in the same brain areas as for right-handers.

What about the popular conception of the neglected right brain? Courses and books directed at "right-brain thinking" often promise to increase your intuition, creativity, and artistic abilities by waking up your "neglected" and "underused" right brain (e.g., Brady, 2004; Edwards, 1999). This myth of the neglected right brain arose from popularized accounts of split-brain patients and exaggerated claims and unwarranted conclusions about differences between the left and right hemispheres. Research has clearly shown that the two hemispheres work together in a coordinated, integrated way, with each making important contributions. Simply said, you cannot get by without your right or your left hemisphere.

Experiments on split-brain patients often present visual information to only the patient's left or right hemisphere, which leads to some intriguing results. For example,

"What did you see?"

"I saw nothing."

Verbal left hemisphere   Non-verbal right hemisphere

A When a split-brain patient is asked to stare straight ahead while a photo of a screwdriver is flashed only to the right hemisphere, he will report that he "saw nothing."

"With your left hand, pick up what you saw"

B However, when asked to pick up with his left hand what he saw, he can reach through and touch the items hidden behind the screen and easily pick up the screwdriver.

"What did you see?"

"I saw a baseball."

C When the left hemisphere receives an image of a baseball, the split-brain patient can easily name it.

Assuming you have an intact, unsevered corpus callosum, if the same photos were presented to you in the same way, you could easily name both the screwdriver and the baseball. Can you explain why? The answers lie in our somewhat confusing visual wiring system:

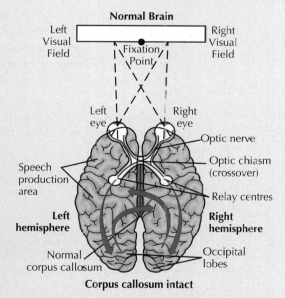

Normal Brain

Left Visual Field — Right Visual Field

Fixation Point

Left eye — Right eye

Optic nerve
Optic chiasm (crossover)
Relay centres

Speech production area

Left hemisphere   **Right hemisphere**

Normal corpus callosum   Occipital lobes

Corpus callosum intact

D As you can see, our eyes connect to our brains in such a way that, when we look straight ahead, information from the left visual field (the blue line) travels to our right hemisphere, and information from the right visual field (the red line) travels to our left hemisphere. The messages received by either hemisphere are then quickly sent to the other across the corpus callosum.

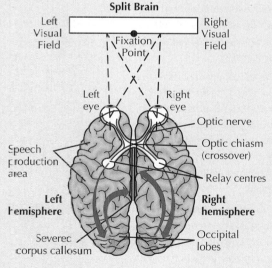

Split Brain

Left Visual Field — Right Visual Field

Fixation Point

Left eye — Right eye

Optic nerve
Optic chiasm (crossover)
Relay centres

Speech production area

Left hemisphere   **Right hemisphere**

Severed corpus callosum   Occipital lobes

Corpus callosum severed

E When the corpus callosum is severed, and information is presented only to the right hemisphere, a split-brain patient cannot verbalize what he sees because the information cannot travel to the opposite (verbal) hemisphere.

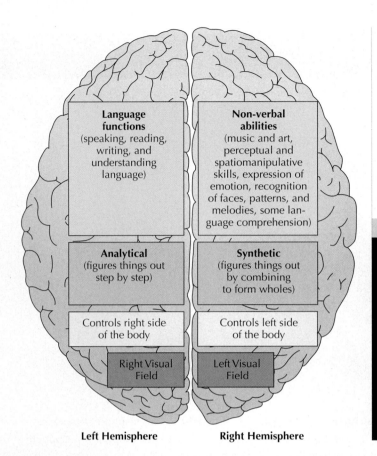

Language functions (speaking, reading, writing, and understanding language)	Non-verbal abilities (music and art, perceptual and spatiomanipulative skills, expression of emotion, recognition of faces, patterns, and melodies, some language comprehension)
Analytical (figures things out step by step)	**Synthetic** (figures things out by combining to form wholes)
Controls right side of the body	Controls left side of the body
Right Visual Field	Left Visual Field

Left Hemisphere   **Right Hemisphere**

Functions of the left and right hemispheres
FIGURE 2.22

In general, the left hemisphere specializes in verbal and analytical functions; the right hemisphere focuses on non-verbal abilities, such as spatiomanipulative skills (the ability to locate and manipulate objects in three-dimensional space), art and musical abilities, and visual recognition tasks. Keep in mind, however, that both hemispheres are activated when we perform almost any task or respond to any stimuli.

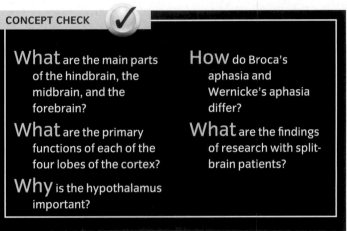

CONCEPT CHECK ✓

What are the main parts of the hindbrain, the midbrain, and the forebrain?

What are the primary functions of each of the four lobes of the cortex?

Why is the hypothalamus important?

How do Broca's aphasia and Wernicke's aphasia differ?

What are the findings of research with split-brain patients?

SUMMARY

1 Our Genetic Inheritance

1. **Neuroscience** studies how biological processes relate to behavioural and mental processes.

2. Genes (dominant or recessive) hold the code for inherited traits. Scientists use **behavioural genetics** methods to determine the relative influences of heredity and environment (heritability) on complex traits.

3. **Evolutionary psychology** suggests that many behavioural commonalities emerged and remain in human populations through natural selection because they were adaptive and improved survival and reproductive success.

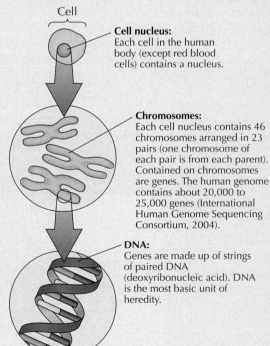

Cell

Cell nucleus: Each cell in the human body (except red blood cells) contains a nucleus.

Chromosomes: Each cell nucleus contains 46 chromosomes arranged in 23 pairs (one chromosome of each pair is from each parent). Contained on chromosomes are genes. The human genome contains about 20,000 to 25,000 genes (International Human Genome Sequencing Consortium, 2004).

DNA: Genes are made up of strings of paired DNA (deoxyribonucleic acid). DNA is the most basic unit of heredity.

2 Neural Bases of Behaviour

1. **Neurons**, supported by **glial cells**, receive and send electrochemical signals to other neurons and to the rest of the body. Their major components are **dendrites**, a **cell body**, and an **axon**.

2. Within a neuron, a neural impulse, or **action potential**, moves along the axon.

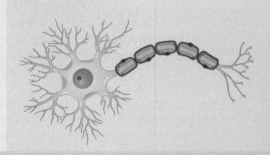

3. Neurons communicate with each other by using **neurotransmitters**, which are released at the synapse and bind to receptors on the receiving neuron. Neurons receive input from many synapses, some excitatory and some inhibitory. Hundreds of different neurotransmitters regulate a wide variety of physiological processes. Many poisons, toxins, and drugs act by mimicking or interfering with neurotransmitters.

4. The **endocrine system** uses **hormones** to broadcast messages throughout the body. The system regulates long-term bodily processes, maintains ongoing bodily processes, and controls the body's response to emergencies.

3 Nervous System Organization

1. The **central nervous system (CNS)** includes the brain and spinal cord. The CNS allows us to process information and adapt to our environment in unique and versatile ways. The spinal cord transmits information between the brain and the rest of the body, and initiates involuntary **reflexes**. Although the CNS is very fragile, recent research shows that the brain is capable of lifelong **neuroplasticity** and **neurogenesis**. Neurogenesis is made possible by **stem cells**.

2. The **peripheral nervous system (PNS)** includes all the nerves outside the brain and spinal cord. It links the brain and spinal cord to the body's senses, muscles, and glands. The PNS is subdivided into the **somatic nervous system (SNS)** and the **autonomic nervous system (ANS)**.

3. The ANS includes the **sympathetic nervous system** and the **parasympathetic nervous system**. The sympathetic nervous system mobilizes the body's fight-or-flight response. The parasympathetic nervous system returns the body to its normal functioning.

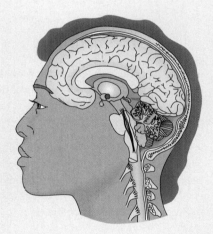

- Central Nervous System
- Somatic Nervous System
- Autonomic Nervous System

4 A Tour Through the Brain

1. The brain is divided into the **hindbrain**, the **midbrain**, and the **forebrain**. The brainstem includes parts of each of these. Certain brain structures are specialized to perform certain tasks (**localization of function**).

2. The hindbrain (including the **medulla**, **pons**, and **cerebellum**) controls automatic behaviours and vital reflexes.

3. The midbrain helps us orient our eye and body movements, and helps control sleep and arousal. The **reticular formation** runs through the core of the hindbrain, midbrain, and brainstem.

4. Forebrain structures (including the **thalamus**, **hypothalamus**, and **limbic**

system) integrate input from the senses, control survival behaviours, and regulate the body's internal environment, emotions, learning, and memory.

5. The **cerebrum** and **cerebral cortex** are part of the forebrain and govern most higher processing and complex behaviours. It is divided into two hemispheres, each controlling the opposite side of the body. The **corpus callosum** links the hemispheres. Each hemisphere is divided into **frontal**, **parietal**, **temporal**, and **occipital** lobes. Each lobe specializes in somewhat different tasks, but a large part of the cortex is devoted to integrating actions performed by different brain regions.

6. Split-brain research shows that each hemisphere performs somewhat different functions, although they work closely together, communicating through the corpus callosum.

KEY TERMS

- action potential p. 43
- association areas p. 60
- autonomic nervous system (ANS) p. 52
- axon p. 42
- behavioural genetics p. 38
- cell body p. 42
- central nervous system (CNS) p. 48
- cerebellum p. 54
- cerebral cortex p. 57
- corpus callosum p. 60
- dendrites p. 42
- endocrine system p. 46
- endorphins p. 46
- evolutionary psychology p. 38
- forebrain p. 56

- frontal lobes p. 57
- glial cell p. 42
- hindbrain p. 54
- hormones p. 46
- hypothalamus p. 56
- limbic system p. 57
- localization of function p. 54
- medulla p. 54
- midbrain p. 55
- myelin sheath p. 43
- natural selection p. 40
- neurogenesis p. 49
- neuron p. 42
- neuroplasticity p. 49
- neuroscience p. 38

- neurotransmitters p. 46
- occipital lobes p. 60
- parasympathetic nervous system p. 53
- parietal lobes p. 57
- peripheral nervous system (PNS) p. 49
- pons p. 54
- reflexes or reflex arcs p. 51
- reticular formation p. 56
- somatic nervous system (SNS) p. 52
- stem cells p. 50
- sympathetic nervous system p. 53
- temporal lobes p. 60
- thalamus p. 56

CRITICAL AND CREATIVE THINKING QUESTIONS

1. Imagine that scientists were able to identify specific genes linked to criminal behaviour, and it was possible to remove or redesign these genes. Would you be in favour of this type of gene manipulation? Why or why not?

2. In considering the gene-environment interaction, what are some ways in which you are very similar to your parents or your siblings? What ways are you very different? Can you think of environmental factors such as events and experiences, which might contribute to this variation?

3. Why is it valuable for scientists to understand how neurotransmitters work at a molecular level?

4. What are some everyday examples of neuroplasticity—that is, of how the brain is changed and shaped by experience?

5. Which part of the nervous system allows you to type on your keyboard and which part allows you to recognize that it is indeed a keyboard beneath your fingers?

6. As neuroscience continues to understand the marvels of the human nervous system many answers about the causes of disease and disorders are revealed. We know the many benefits of these findings in helping to treat and cure. Can you think of any disadvantages?

7. When you experience different emotions, from anger to pleasure, what system of the brain is active? Imagine if neuroscience could surgically change this system so that we only felt positive emotions. What would be the advantages and disadvantages of this type of manipulation?

8. If you were in a car accident that damaged your left temporal lobe, what type of behavioural and cognitive deficits would you experience?

What is happening in this picture ?

The complexities of sexual interaction—and in particular, the difficulties that men and women sometimes have in achieving sexual arousal or orgasm—illustrate the balancing act between the sympathetic and parasympathetic nervous systems.

Sexual arousal and excitement require that the body be relaxed enough to allow increased blood flow to the genitals. During parasympathetic dominance, nerves carry messages from the central nervous system directly to the sexual organs, allowing for increased blood flow and genital arousal.

During sympathetic dominance, blood flow to the genitals and organs decreases as the body readies for a fight or flight response. As a result, the person is less likely to become sexually aroused or maintain an erection. What types of circumstances surrounding dating and sexuality might trigger sympathetic dominance? In what ways might a person overcome it? Do you think such intimate topics should be the domain of psychological research?

(Check your answers in Appendix A.)

1. Behavioural genetics is the study of _____.
   a. the relative effects of behaviour and genetics on survival
   b. the relative effects of heredity and environment on behaviour and mental processes
   c. the relative effects of genetics on natural selection
   d. how genetics affects correct behaviour

2. Evolutionary psychology studies _____.
   a. the ways in which humans adapted their behaviour to survive and evolve
   b. the ways in which humankind's behaviour has changed over the millennia
   c. the ways in which humans can evolve to change behaviour
   d. the ways in which natural selection and adaptation can explain behaviour and mental processes

3. This is a measure of the degree to which a characteristic is related to genetic, inherited factors.
   a. Heritability   c. The biological ratio
   b. Inheritance   d. The genome statistic

4. The term _____ refers to the evolutionary concept that those with adaptive genetic traits will survive and reproduce and their genes will spread in the population.
   a. natural selection   c. survival of the fittest
   b. evolution   d. all of these options

5. Label the following parts of a neuron, the cell of the nervous system responsible for receiving and transmitting electrochemical information:
   a. dendrites   d. myelin sheath
   b. cell body   e. terminal buttons of axon
   c. axon

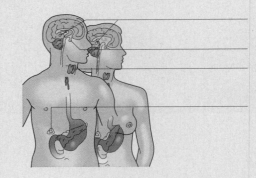

6. Your textbook defines the *action potential* as _____.
   a. the likelihood that a neuron will take action when stimulated
   b. the tendency for a neuron to be potentiated by neurotransmitters

   c. a neural impulse that carries information along the axon of a neuron
   d. the firing of a nerve, either toward or away from the brain

7. Why is the myelin sheath so important for proper neural functioning?
   a. Myelin allows neurotransmitters to travel smoothly from the dendrites to the cell body.
   b. Myelin allows significantly faster neural communication.
   c. Myelin allows neurotransmitters to travel smoothly from the cell body to the axon.
   d. Myelin supports the fundamental metabolic, life-sustaining functions of the neuron.

8. Which of the following neurotransmitters would be released if we experienced a severe and painful injury such as a broken bone?
   a. Serotonin, as it helps with pain relief
   b. Dopamine, as it helps us feel less stressed during traumatic situations
   c. Norepinephrine, as it helps with recovery
   d. Endorphins, as they help with pain relief

9. Too much of this neurotransmitter appears to be related to schizophrenia, whereas too little may be related to Parkinson's disease.
   a. Acetylcholine   c. Norepinephrine
   b. Dopamine   d. Serotonin

10. Chemicals that are manufactured by endocrine glands and circulated in the bloodstream to change or maintain bodily functions are called _____.
   a. vasopressors   c. hormones
   b. gonadotropins   d. steroids

11. Label the main glands of the endocrine system:
   a. pineal   c. adrenal
   b. pituitary   d. thyroid

12. The central nervous system _____.
  a. consists of the brain and spinal cord
  b. is the most important nervous system
  c. includes the automatic and other nervous systems
  d. all of these options

13. The peripheral nervous system _____.
  a. is composed of the spinal cord and most of the peripheral nerves
  b. is less important than the central nervous system
  c. is contained within the skull and spinal column
  d. includes all the nerves and neurons outside the brain and spinal cord

14. The _____ nervous system is responsible for fight or flight, whereas the _____ nervous system is responsible for maintaining calm.
  a. central; peripheral
  b. parasympathetic; sympathetic
  c. sympathetic; parasympathetic
  d. autonomic; somatic

15. Driving on the highway late one night, Jason's car nearly collided with another vehicle. The sudden shock of this near-fatal experience made Jason's heart rate increase dramatically, his breathing quicken, and his entire body break into a sweat. Which division of the nervous system was activated by this experience?
  a. the sympathetic nervous system
  b. the peripheral nervous system
  c. the parasympathetic nervous system
  d. the central nervous system

16. Label the following structures or areas of the brain:
  a. forebrain   d. thalamus
  b. midbrain   e. hypothalamus
  c. hindbrain   f. cerebral cortex

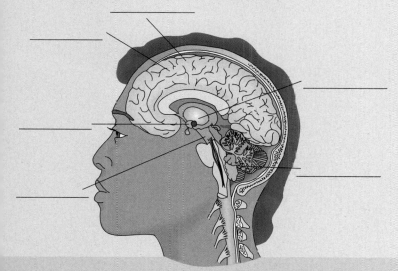

17. Label the four lobes of the brain:
  a. frontal lobe   c. temporal lobe
  b. parietal lobe   d. occipital lobe

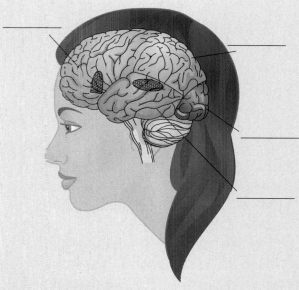

18. A serious car accident has left Janice with an inability to speak normally (she can still understand everything said to her however). She also has difficulty with many simple, everyday cognitive tasks. Which part of her brain has likely sustained the most damage?
  a. the frontal lobes
  b. the left hemisphere
  c. the hindbrain
  d. the limbic system

19. Identify the following functions of the brain with either the left or right hemisphere.
  a. language function, _____ hemisphere
  b. nonverbal abilities, _____ hemisphere
  c. control of left side of the body and the right visual field, _____ hemisphere
  d. control of right side of the body and the left visual field, _____ hemisphere

20. What has newer research shown regarding the bodily representation on the motor and somatosensory cortex?
  a. Only men have these structures
  b. The representation of the fingers mingle and overlap
  c. The most sensitive regions have the largest representation
  d. All of the above

Stress and Health Psychology

uesday, September 11, 2001, likely started in the usual way for you, but while at school or on your way to school, you heard the news of the attacks. Even now, years later, you can probably recall in detail the events of that morning: the suddenness of the terrorist attacks, the buildings burning and tumbling to the ground, even the clear, beautiful skies above the destruction. Of the more than 90 countries that lost citizens, 24 Canadians were killed that day. Those families who were directly affected—and even many who were not—remember the day and its aftermath as the most stressful time in their lives. How does such extreme stress affect people's health and well-being, both immediately and later on? How do people cope with stress of such magnitude? What about life's more mundane aggravations: slow drivers, bad wireless connections, unreliable friends? Do these also take a toll on our well-being? If so, to what extent and what can we do about it?

Throughout most of history, people have understood that emotions and thoughts affect physical health. However, it wasn't until the late nineteenth century, after discovering the causes of the infectious diseases typhoid and cholera, that scientists began to focus on the physiological causes of disease in general. Today, the major causes of death have shifted from contagious diseases (such as pneumonia, influenza, tuberculosis, syphilis, and measles) to non-contagious diseases (such as cancer, cardiovascular disease, and diabetes), diseases that are caused in part by psychological factors and lifestyle choices (Leventhal et al., 2008; Straub, 2007). In this chapter, we explore how biological, psychological, and social factors (the *biopsychosocial model*) affect illness, health, and well-being.

NATIONAL GEOGRAPHIC

Understanding Stress

A nything that places a demand on the body can cause **stress**. The trigger that prompts the stressful reaction is called a **stressor**. Stress reactions can occur in response to internal cognitive stimuli, such as chronic worrying, for example, or external (environmental) stimuli, such as ongoing loud noise (Sarafino, 2008; Straub, 2007).

Pleasant or beneficial stress, such as moderate exercise, is called **eustress**. Stress that is unpleasant or objectionable, as might occur when a person is stuck in a traffic jam, is called **distress** (Selye, 1974).

SOURCES OF STRESS

Early stress researchers Thomas Holmes and Richard Rahe (1967) believed that any life change that required some adjustment or compensation in behaviour or lifestyle could cause some degree of stress (**FIGURE 3.1**). They also believed that exposure to several stressful events within a short period could have a direct detrimental effect on health.

To measure the relationship between change and stress, Holmes and Rahe created a Social Readjustment Rating Scale (SRRS) and then asked people to check off all the life events on the SRRS they had experienced in the previous year (**TABLE 3.1**).

stress The body's non-specific response to any demand made on it; the physical and mental arousal to circumstances that we perceive as threatening or challenging.

stressor An event that places demands on an organism that tax its resources.

eustress Pleasant, beneficial, or curative stress.

Seven major sources of stress FIGURE 3.1

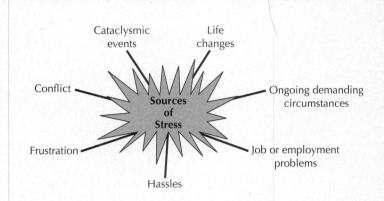

The SRRS scale is an easy and popular way to measure stress caused by life change. Cross-cultural studies have shown that most people rank the magnitude of stressful events in similar ways (De Coteau, Hope, & Anderson, 2003; Scully, Tosi, & Banning, 2000). But the SRRS is not perfect. For example, it shows only the correlation between stress and illness; it does not show that stress actually causes illnesses. Moreover, not all people respond to life's challenges in the same way, and not all stressful situations arise from a single devastating event, such as the death of a family member. **Chronic stressors**, such as a bad relationship or an intolerable political climate, can be significant too. Even the stress of low-frequency noise is associated with measurable sleep disturbances, and hormonal and cardiac changes (Waye, 2004; Waye et al., 2002). Our social lives can also be chronically stressful, because making and maintaining friendships involves considerable thought and energy (Sias et al., 2004). The original SRRS from 1967 is now quite old and has been improved and updated by other researchers. The scale we present here is the newer version (Hobson et al., 1998).

Perhaps the largest source of chronic stress is work. People often experience stress associated with keeping or changing jobs or with job performance (Moore, Grunberg, & Greenberg, 2004). The most stressful jobs are those that make great demands on performance and concentration but allow little control, creativity, or opportunity for advancement (Smith et al., 2008; Straub, 2007).

Stress at work can also cause serious stress at home, not only for the worker but for other family members as well. In our private lives, divorce, child and spousal

Social Readjustment Rating Scale (SRRS)

Holmes and Rahe (1967) and others (Hobson et al., 1998) believe that higher scores on the SRRS are correlated with greater risks of illness and disease. Below is the list of life events derived from their scale that require some readjustment and are therefore believed to cause stress. Life events are listed from most to least stressful. Each life event has an associated numerical value (not reprinted here) with the death of a spouse/partner having the highest score of 100. Values then decrease down the list.

Life Event

1. Death of a spouse/partner
2. Death of a close family member
3. Major injury/illness to self
4. Detention in jail or other institution
5. Major injury/illness to close family member
6. Foreclosure on loan/mortgage
7. Divorce
8. Being the victim of crime
9. Being the victim of police brutality
10. Infidelity
11. Experiencing domestic violence/sexual abuse
12. Separation or reconciliation with spouse/partner
13. Being fired/laid off/unemployed
14. Experiencing financial problems/difficulties
15. Death of close friend
16. Surviving disaster
17. Becoming a single parent
18. Assuming responsibility for sick or elderly loved one

19. Loss of, or a major reduction in, health insurance/benefits
20. Self/close family member being arrested for violating the law
21. Major disagreement over child support/custody/visitation
22. Experiencing/involved in auto accident
23. Being disciplined at work/demoted
24. Dealing with unwanted pregnancy
25. Adult child moving in with parent/parent moving in with adult child
26. Child developing behaviour or learning problem
27. Experiencing employment discrimination/sexual harassment
28. Attempting to modify addictive behaviour of self
29. Discovering/attempting to modify addictive behaviour of close family member
30. Employer reorganization/downsizing
31. Dealing with infertility/miscarriage
32. Getting married/remarried
33. Changing employers/careers

34. Failing to obtain/qualify for a mortgage
35. Pregnancy of self/spouse/mate
36. Experiencing discrimination/harassment outside the workplace
37. Release from jail
38. Spouse/partner begins/ceases work outside the home
39. Major disagreement with boss/co-worker
40. Change in residence
41. Finding appropriate child care/daycare
42. Experiencing a large unexpected monetary gain
43. Changing positions (transfer, promotion)
44. Gaining a new family member
45. Changing work responsibilities
46. Child leaving home
47. Obtaining a home mortgage
48. Obtaining a major loan other than home mortgage
49. Retirement
50. Beginning/ceasing formal education
51. Receiving a ticket for violating the law

abuse, alcoholism, and money problems can place severe stress on all members of a family (Aboa-Éboulé, 2008; Aboa-Éboulé et al., 2008; DiLauro, 2004; Luecken & Lemery, 2004; Orth-Gomer, 2007).

In addition to chronic stressors, the minor **hassles** of daily living can pile up and become a major source of stress.

We all experience many hassles in a day, such as project deadlines, annoyances (gas prices), organizational irritations (conflicting exam schedules), and inconveniences (people walking too slowly in front of us). But our reactions to these hassles vary (Linzer et al., 2002; Sarafino, 2005) (FIGURE 3.2).

Which occupation is associated with more psychological distress and poorer mental health? FIGURE 3.2

Canadian research addressing mental health in the workplace has shown machine operators in the manufacturing sector experience far greater stress and psychological strain than do police officers (Marchand, 2007). Can you explain why this might be?

Type	Description	Example
Approach-approach	The person must choose between two or more favourable alternatives. Either choice will have positive results; the requirement to choose is the source of stress.	You must choose between two jobs: one that will be inherently interesting and one that pays very well.
Avoidance-avoidance	The person must choose between two or more unpleasant alternatives that will lead to negative results no matter which choice is made.	You must choose between missing a vital project deadline and missing an important job interview.
Approach-avoidance	The person must choose between alternatives that will have both desirable and undesirable results. Such situations lead to a great deal of ambivalence.	You want to spend more time in a new intimate relationship, but that means you won't be able to see your old friends as much.

In the book (and film) *Sophie's Choice*, Sophie and her two children are sent to a German concentration camp. A soldier demands that Sophie give up either her daughter or her son, or else both children will be killed. Obviously, both alternatives will have tragic results. What kind of conflict does this example illustrate?

Some researchers have shown that daily hassles can be as significant as major life events in creating stress (Kraaij, Arensman, & Spinhoven, 2002; Kubiak et al., 2008). The death of a loved one might indeed be a very stressful event, but the accumulation of daily hassles can also trigger significant stress reactions. In fact, scales, such as the Hassles and Uplifts Scales (Kanner et al., 1981), have been developed to assess the health impact of the stresses of everyday living.

As with hassles, **frustration** can cause stress. And the more motivated we are, the more frustrated we are when our goals are blocked.

Finally, stress can arise when we experience **conflict**— that is, when we are forced to make a choice between at least two incompatible alternatives. The three basic types of conflict are shown in **Study Organizer 3.1**.

The longer any conflict exists or the more important the decision, the more stress a person experiences. Generally, approach-approach conflicts are the easiest to resolve and produce the least stress. Avoidance-avoidance conflicts are usually the most difficult because all choices lead to unpleasant results.

HOW STRESS AFFECTS THE BODY

When stressed, your body undergoes several physiological changes. The **sympathetic nervous system**, or **SAM system**, and the **HPA axis** control the most significant of these changes (**Figure 3.3** and **Figure 3.4**).

Under stress, the sympathetic nervous system prepares us for immediate action—to fight or flee. Parts of the brain and endocrine system then kick in to maintain our arousal. How does this happen?

1 The **SAM system** (short for *sympatho-adreno-medullary*) provides an initial, rapid-acting stress response thanks to co-operation between the sympathetic nervous system and the adrenal medulla.

2 The **HPA axis** (short for the *hypothalamic-pituitary-adrenocortical* system) responds more slowly but lasts longer. It also helps restore the body to its baseline state, *homeostasis*.

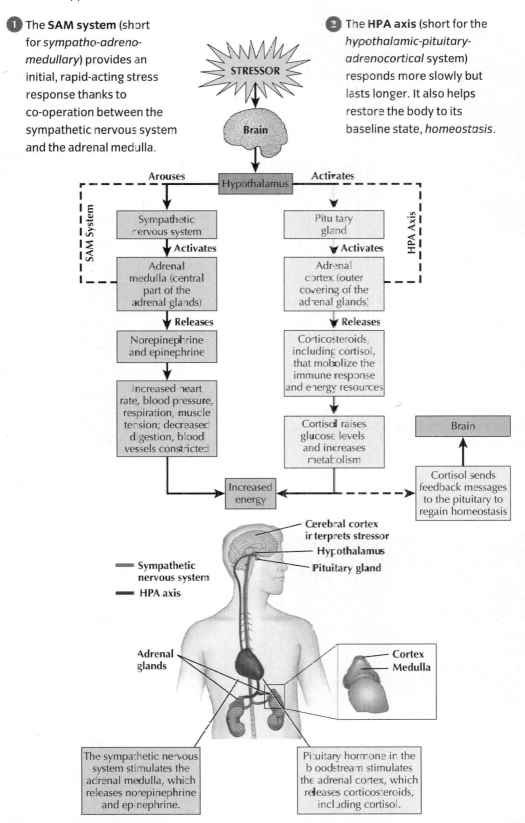

STRESSOR

Brain

Arouses — Hypothalamus — Activates

SAM System

Sympathetic nervous system
↓ **Activates**
Adrenal medulla (central part of the adrenal glands)
↓ **Releases**
Norepinephrine and epinephrine
↓
Increased heart rate, blood pressure, respiration, muscle tension; decreased digestion, blood vessels constricted

HPA Axis

Pituitary gland
↓ **Activates**
Adrenal cortex (outer covering of the adrenal glands)
↓ **Releases**
Corticosteroids, including cortisol, that mobilize the immune response and energy resources
↓
Cortisol raises glucose levels and increases metabolism

Brain

Increased energy ← Cortisol sends feedback messages to the pituitary to regain homeostasis

Cerebral cortex interprets stressor
Hypothalamus
Pituitary gland

— Sympathetic nervous system
— HPA axis

Adrenal glands

Cortex
Medulla

The sympathetic nervous system stimulates the adrenal medulla, which releases norepinephrine and epinephrine.

Pituitary hormone in the bloodstream stimulates the adrenal cortex, which releases corticosteroids, including cortisol.

The general adaptation syndrome (GAS) FIGURE 3.4

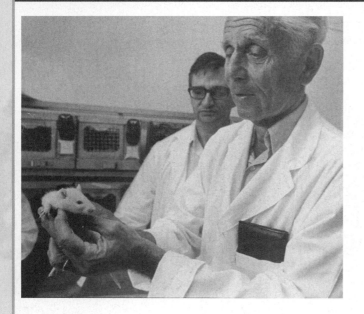

Stress causes a number of detrimental physiological changes. Canadian physician Hans Selye [SELL-yay], renowned for his work on stress, described a generalized, three-part physiological reaction to stressors. He termed it the **general adaptation syndrome (GAS)** (Selye, 1936). Selye was a tireless and committed researcher and dedicated his life to understanding the physiological basis of stress, publishing more than 1,700 articles and 39 books on the subject. He was made a Fellow of the Royal Society of Canada and a Companion of the Order of Canada, and received honorary fellowships in more than 60 scientific societies. He was nominated for a Nobel Prize 10 times (Loriaux, 2008).

■ **general adaptation syndrome (GAS)** Selye's three-part model of how organisms characteristically react to stressors.

Note how the three stages of this syndrome (*alarm*, *resistance*, and *exhaustion*) focus on the biological response to stress—particularly the "wear and tear" on the body with prolonged stress. As a critical thinker, can you see how the alarm stage corresponds to the SAM system, whereas the resistance and exhaustion stages are part of the HPA axis?

1 Alarm Reaction (SAM system) In the initial *alarm reaction*, your body experiences a temporary state of shock, and your resistance to illness and stress falls below normal limits.

2 Stage of Resistance (HPA axis) If the stressor remains, your body attempts to endure the stressor, and enters the *resistance phase*. Physiological arousal remains higher than normal, and there is a sudden outpouring of hormones. Selye maintained that one outcome of this stage for some people is the development of *diseases of adaption*, including asthma, ulcers, and high blood pressure.

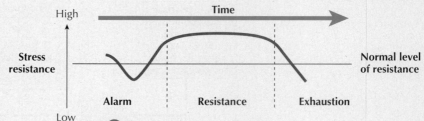

3 Stage of Exhaustion (HPA axis) Long-term exposure to the stressor eventually leads to the exhaustion phase if the resistance is not successful. In this phase, you become more susceptible to illness. In severe cases, long-term exposure to stressors can be life threatening because you become vulnerable to serious illness, such as heart attack, stroke, and cancer.

◄ **Stress in ancient times** As shown in these ancient cave drawings, the automatic fight-or-flight response was adaptive and necessary for early human survival. However, in modern society it occurs as a response to ongoing situations in which we often cannot fight or flee. This repeated arousal could be detrimental to our health.

Cortisol, a key element of the HPA axis, plays a critical role in the long-term effects of stress. Prolonged elevation of cortisol has been linked to increased levels of depression, post-traumatic stress disorder (PTSD), memory problems, unemployment, and drug and alcohol abuse (Ayers et al., 2007; Bremner et al., 2004; Johnson, Delahanty, & Pinna, 2008; Sarafino, 2008). Perhaps most important, increased cortisol is directly related to impairment of immune system functioning. When the immune system is impaired, we become more susceptible to opportunistic infections, such as the viruses that cause colds, and are at an increased risk of developing a number of diseases, including bursitis, colitis, Alzheimer's disease, rheumatoid arthritis, and periodontal disease (Cohen et al., 2002; Cohen & Lemay, 2007; Dantzer et al., 2008; Gasser & Raulet, 2006; Segerstrom & Miller, 2004).

psychoneuro-immunology The interdisciplinary field that studies the interaction among the mind, the nervous system, and the immune system.

Knowledge that psychological factors can influence both the nervous system and the immune system upset the long-held assumption in biology and medicine that infectious diseases are "strictly physical." The clinical and theoretical implications of this relationship are so important that a new field of biopsychology has emerged in the last 20 years called **psychoneuroimmunology**. This area studies the interaction between the mind, the nervous system, and the immune system.

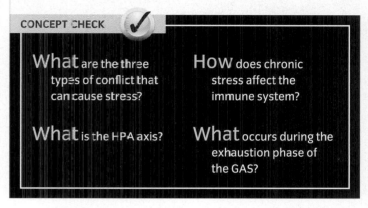

CONCEPT CHECK

What are the three types of conflict that can cause stress?

What is the HPA axis?

How does chronic stress affect the immune system?

What occurs during the exhaustion phase of the GAS?

Stress and Illness

LEARNING OBJECTIVES

Explain why an immune system compromised by stress might be more vulnerable to cancer growth.

Describe the personality trait that can influence how we respond to stress.

Describe the key symptoms of post-traumatic stress disorder (PTSD).

Explain how biological and psychological factors can jointly influence the development of gastric ulcers.

As we've just seen, stress can have a dramatic effect on the body. This section explores how stress is related to four serious illnesses: cancer, coronary heart disease, post-traumatic stress disorder, and gastric ulcers.

CANCER: A VARIETY OF CAUSES, INCLUDING STRESS

Cancer is the second leading cause of death for adults in Canada (Statistics Canada, 2004). It occurs when a particular type of immature body cell begins rapidly dividing unchecked and then forms a mass or tumour that invades surrounding healthy tissue. Unless destroyed or removed, the tumour eventually damages organs and ultimately causes death. More than 100 types of cancer have been identified and they appear to be caused by an interaction between environmental factors and genetic predispositions.

In a healthy person, whenever cancer cells start to multiply, the immune system checks the uncontrolled growth by attacking and killing the abnormal cells (**FIGURE 3.5**). As mentioned earlier, stress causes the adrenal glands to release hormones that suppress the immune system. In times of ongoing stress, the

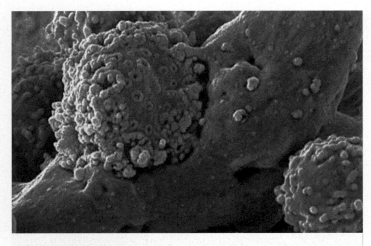

The healthy immune system in action

FIGURE 3.5

Stress can compromise the immune system, but a healthy immune system can readily deal with invaders, as shown here. The round structure near the left centre of this photomicrograph is a T-lymphocyte, a type of white blood cell produced by the immune system. It has just killed a cancer cell, the larger, elongated structure.

compromised immune system is less able to contain the development of cancers (Ben-Eliyahu et al., 2007; Kemeny, 2007).

We might be able to reduce our risk of developing cancer by making changes that reduce our stress levels and enhance our immune systems. For example, researchers have found that interrupting people's sleep significantly decreased the number of their *natural killer cells,* a type of

immune system cell (Irwin et al., 1994). These researchers also found that a normal night's sleep after the deprivation returned the killer cells to their normal levels. These laboratory findings are intriguing, but they have not yet been replicated in natural settings (Shakhar et al., 2007), so the results should be interpreted cautiously.

CARDIOVASCULAR DISORDERS: THE LEADING CAUSE OF DEATH IN CANADA

Cardiovascular disorders, including heart attacks and stroke, are the leading cause of death in Canada (Statistics Canada, 2004). Understandably, health professionals are concerned because stress is a major contributor to cardiovascular disease. *Heart disease* is a general term for all disorders that eventually affect the heart muscle and lead to heart failure. *Coronary heart disease* occurs when the walls of the coronary arteries thicken, reducing or blocking the blood supply to the heart. Symptoms of such disease include *angina* (chest pain caused by insufficient blood supply to the heart) and *heart attack* (death of portions of heart muscle tissue). Controllable factors that contribute to heart disease include stress, smoking, certain personality characteristics, obesity, a high-fat diet, and lack of exercise (Aboa-Éboulé, 2008; Ayers et al., 2007; Sarafino, 2008). However, for young adults heart disease is not a leading cause of premature death. In this age group suicide and accidents top the list (**FIGURE 3.6**).

Controllable risk factors for premature death FIGURE 3.6

Heart disease and cancer are the leading causes of death for Canadians, but among young adults, suicide and accidents are the biggest killers. Why do you think there are these types of age-related differences? In what ways might suicide and accidents, such as those caused by texting while driving, be considered somewhat controllable?

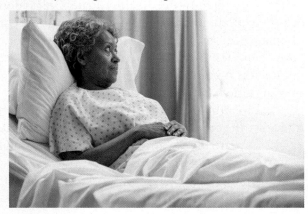

When the body is under stress, the autonomic nervous system releases epinephrine and cortisol into the bloodstream. These hormones increase heart rate and release fat and glucose from the body's stores to give muscles a readily available source of energy. If no physical "fight-or-flight" action occurs (and this is likely in our modern lives), the fat that was released into the bloodstream is not burned as fuel. Instead, it can adhere to the walls of blood vessels. These fatty deposits are a major cause of blood supply blockage, which causes heart attacks.

hardiness Resilient personality with a strong commitment to personal goals, control over life, and viewing change as a challenge rather than a threat.

Have you ever wondered why some people survive in the face of great stress (personal tragedies, demanding jobs, and even a poor home life) while others do not? Suzanne Kobasa was among the first to study this question (Kobasa, 1979; Maddi et al., 2006; Vogt et al., 2008). By examining male executives who were experiencing high levels of stress, she found that some people are more resistant to stress than others because of a personality factor called **hardiness**, a resilient type of optimism that comes from three distinctive attitudes.

First, hardy people feel a strong sense of commitment to both their work and their personal life. They also make intentional commitments to purposeful activity and problem solving. Second, these people see themselves as being in control of their lives, rather than as victims of their circumstances. Finally, hardy people look at change as a challenge to overcome and not as a threat to their well-being. As outlined in *What a Psychologist Sees*, there are other personality variables that have been implicated in stress effects and well-being.

Smoking, obesity, and lack of exercise are important contributory and controllable factors associated with heart disease. Smoking restricts blood circulation, and obesity stresses the heart by causing it to pump more blood to the excess body tissue. A high-fat diet, especially one that is high in cholesterol, contributes to the fatty deposits that clog blood vessels. Lack of exercise contributes to weight gain and prevents the body from obtaining important exercise benefits, including strengthened heart muscles, increased heart efficiency, and the release of endorphins and neurotransmitters, such as serotonin, that alleviate stress and promote well-being.

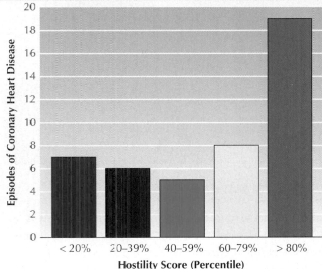

Source: Niaura et al. (2002).

The Personality Trait of Hostility

Among personality traits, the strongest predictor of developing heart disease is *hostility* (Krantz & McCeney, 2002; Mittag & Maurischat, 2004). In particular, the constant stress associated with cynical hostility—the hypervigilant, constantly being "on watch" for problems—is linked to poor physiological outcomes such as higher blood pressure, heart attacks, and production of excess stress-related hormones. People who are hostile, suspicious, argumentative, and cynical tend to have more interpersonal conflicts. This can heighten autonomic activation, leading to increased risk of cardiovascular disease (Boyle et al., 2004; Bundle & Suls, 2006; Eaker et al., 2007). While most of us do not suffer from this form of cynical hostility, getting angry does seem to affect us physiologically, so when you find yourself irritated with another driver, a friend, or family member, remember your anger might be more detrimental to your health than just getting you red in the face.

POST-TRAUMATIC STRESS DISORDER (PTSD): NOT JUST A DISORDER OF MODERN TIMES

One of the most powerful examples of the effects of severe stress is **post-traumatic stress disorder (PTSD)**. Children and adults can experience the symptoms of PTSD, which include feelings of terror and helplessness during the trauma, and recurrent flashbacks, nightmares, impaired concentration, and emotional numbing afterward. These symptoms may continue for months or years after the event. Some victims of PTSD self-medicate with alcohol and other drugs as a way to relieve their emotional pain. This often compounds their problems and harms valuable interpersonal relationships (Kaysen et al., 2008: Sullivan & Holt, 2008).

During the Industrial Revolution, workers who survived horrific railroad accidents sometimes developed a condition very similar to PTSD. It was called *"railway spine"* because experts thought the problem resulted from a twisting or concussion of the spine. Later, doctors working with combat veterans referred to the disorder as *"shell shock"* because they believed it was a response to the physical concussion caused by exploding artillery. Today, we know that PTSD is caused by any exposure to extraordinary stress (**FIGURE 3.7**).

PTSD's essential feature is *severe anxiety* (a state of constant or recurring alarm and fearfulness) that develops after experiencing a very traumatic event, such as learning about the violent or unexpected death of a family member, experiencing war first-hand as either a soldier or a civilian, or being a victim of or witness to violence (American Psychiatric Association, 2002). **TABLE 3.2** summarizes the primary symptoms of PTSD and offers five important tips for coping with traumatic events.

Coping with extreme trauma FIGURE 3.7

Roméo Dallaire, a retired Canadian lieutenant general, was head of the United Nations (U.N.) Peacekeeping Force during the 1994 conflict in Rwanda. While there, he witnessed the gruesome slaughter of over 800,000 Tutsis and Hutus by Hutu extremists in the space of about 100 days. The genocide and the unspeakable horrors Dallaire encountered in Rwanda left him battling depression, substance abuse, and post-traumatic stress disorder (PTSD) for a number of years afterwards, culminating in a suicide attempt in 2000. He has since received treatment and now speaks openly about PTSD and his recovery process.

GASTRIC ULCERS: ARE THEY CAUSED BY STRESS?

Beginning in the 1950s, psychologists reported evidence that stress can lead to ulcers—painful lesions to the lining of the stomach and upper part of the small intestine. Correlational studies found that people who live in stressful situations develop ulcers more often than people who don't live with stress. And numerous experiments with laboratory animals have shown that stressors, such as shock or confinement to a very small space, can produce ulcers (Andrade & Graeff, 2001; Bhattacharya & Muruganandam, 2003; Gabry et al., 2002; Landeira-Fernandez, 2000).

The relationship between stress and ulcers was generally accepted until researchers reported a particular bacterium (*Helicobacter pylori* or *H. pylori*) was also associated with ulcer formation. Most ulcer patients have the *H. pylori* bacterium in their stomachs, and it has been

Identifying PTSD and coping with crisis TABLE 3.2

Primary symptoms of post-traumatic stress disorder (PTSD)

- Re-experiencing the event through vivid memories or flashbacks
- Feeling "emotionally numb"
- Feeling overwhelmed by what would normally be considered everyday situations
- Having diminished interest in performing normal tasks or pursuing usual interests
- Crying uncontrollably
- Isolating oneself from family and friends and avoiding social situations
- Relying increasingly on alcohol or drugs to get through the day
- Feeling extremely moody, irritable, angry, suspicious, or frightened
- Having difficulty falling or staying asleep, sleeping too much, and experiencing nightmares
- Feeling guilty about surviving the event or being unable to solve the problem, change the event, or prevent the disaster
- Feeling fear and sense of doom about the future

Five important tips for coping with crisis

1. Recognize your feelings about the situation and talk to others about your fears. Know that these feelings are a normal response to an abnormal situation.
2. Be willing to listen to family and friends who have been affected and encourage them to seek counselling if necessary.
3. Be patient with people. Tempers are short in times of crisis, and others may be feeling as much stress as you are.
4. Recognize normal crisis reactions, such as sleep disturbances and nightmares, withdrawal, reverting to childhood behaviours, and trouble focusing on work or school.
5. Take time with your children, spouse, life partner, friends, and co-workers to do something you enjoy.

Source: American Counseling Association, 2006, and adapted from Pomponio, 2002.

---

shown to damage the stomach wall. However, approximately 75 percent of normal control subjects' stomachs also have the bacterium. This suggests that ulcers are not purely the result of an infection by *H. pylori* and that other factors—psychological factors—must also contribute. It seems that the bacterium can cause ulcers, but they develop more readily in people whose systems are compromised by stress. Behaviour modification and other psychological treatments, along with antibiotics, have been shown to be effective in treating patients with ulcers.

Studies of the amygdala (a part of the brain involved in emotional responses) show that it appears to play an important role in gastric ulcer formation as well (Aou, 2006; Tanaka et al., 1998). It seems stressful situations, which activate the amygdala, cause an increase in stress hormones synthesis and hydrochloric acid secretion, and a decrease in blood flow in the stomach walls. This combination leaves the stomach more vulnerable to attack by the *H. pylori* bacteria.

In sum, it appears that the presence of *H. pylori* and stressful situations that cause increased hydrochloric acid, increased stress hormones, and decreased blood flow lead to the formation of gastric ulcers. Once again, we see how biological, psychological, and social forces influence one another (the biopsychosocial model) (Overmier & Murison, 2000).

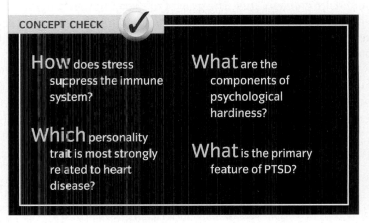

CONCEPT CHECK

How does stress suppress the immune system?

Which personality trait is most strongly related to heart disease?

What are the components of psychological hardiness?

What is the primary feature of PTSD?

Health Psychology in Action

Health psychology is the study of how biological, psychological, and social factors affect health and illness. One of the roles of the health psychologist is to reduce psychological distress and unhealthy behaviours. In this section, we consider three unhealthy

> ■ **health psychology**
> The study of how biological, psychological, and social factors interact in health and illness.

behaviours that contribute to death and disease states: tobacco use, excessive alcohol consumption, and an inactive lifestyle.

TOBACCO: A WELL-KNOWN NOXIOUS SUBSTANCE

Most people today know that smoking is bad for their health and that the more they smoke, the more at risk they are. This has not always been the case. When considering the substances to outlaw in the Canadian Opium and Drug Act of 1911, tobacco was excluded because it was not considered to be a habit-forming drug (Alexander, 1990). Today, we know that tobacco use endangers both smokers and those who breathe in second-hand smoke, and it is no surprise that most health psychologists and medical professionals are interested in preventing smoking and getting those who already smoke to stop.

Ψ Psychological Science

What Does a Health Psychologist Do?

Health psychologists are interested in how people's lifestyles and activities, emotional reactions, ways of interpreting events, and personality characteristics influence their physical health and well-being.

As researchers, they are particularly interested in the relationship between stress and the immune system.

As practitioners, health psychologists can work as independent clinicians or as consultants with physicians, physical and occupational therapists, and other health care workers. The goal of the health psychologist is to reduce psychological distress and unhealthy behaviours. They also help patients and families make critical decisions and prepare psychologically for surgery or other treatment.

Health psychologists educate the public about health maintenance. They provide information about the effects of stress, smoking, alcohol, and lack of exercise, and about other health issues. In addition, health psychologists help people cope with chronic problems, such as pain, diabetes, and high blood pressure, as well as unhealthful behaviours, such as anger expression and lack of assertiveness.

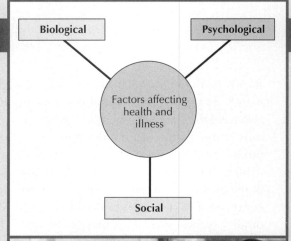

Stop & Think
1. How might the health psychologist in this photo help a patient coping with a serious illness?
2. What biological, psychological, and social factors would need to be addressed in this case?

Applying Psychology

Preventing Teenage Smoking

For adolescents, the long-term health disadvantages of smoking seem irrelevant compared with its short-term social rewards and the addictive, reinforcing properties of the nicotine. Therefore, as shown in this photo, many smoking prevention programs focus on more immediate problems with smoking. Films and discussion groups try to educate teens about peer pressure and the media's influence on smoking, as well as to help them hone their decision-making and coping skills. Unfortunately, the effect of such psychosocial programs is small (Hatsukami, 2008; Pierce, 2007; Vijgen et al., 2008). To have even a modest effect, these programs must begin early and continue for many years. To reduce the health risk and help fight peer pressure, many schools ban smoking in college and university buildings. The rising cost of cigarettes—now averaging $10 per pack in most

WARNING
TOBACCO USE CAN MAKE YOU IMPOTENT

Cigarettes may cause sexual impotence due to decreased blood flow to the penis. This can prevent you from having an erection.

Health Canada

provinces and territories when taxes are included—may also deter many young people from smoking. For a person who smokes a half a pack or 10 cigarettes a day, the annual cost is more than $1,800.

> **STOP** **Stop & Think**
> 1. Why do you think teenagers tend to disregard the health risks associated with smoking, even when they are aware of the risks?
> 2. Do you think the cost of cigarettes is a sufficient deterrent to teenage smoking? Can you think of a more effective deterrent?

The first puff on a cigarette is rarely pleasant, so why do people ever start smoking? The answer is complex. First, smoking usually starts when people are young. According to the 2006–07 Youth Smoking Survey sponsored by Health Canada, 21 percent of young people in grades 5 through 9 report experimenting with some form of tobacco product (Health Canada, 2008). Peer behaviour and imitation of celebrity role models (such as actors and musicians) are particularly strong factors in young people's decision to begin smoking.

Second, nicotine is addictive; once a person begins to smoke, there is a biological need to continue. Nicotine addiction appears to be very similar to cocaine and alcohol addiction (Brody et al., 2004). When a person inhales tobacco smoke, the nicotine quickly increases the release of acetylcholine and norepinephrine in his or her brain. These neurotransmitters (see Chapter 2) increase alertness, concentration, memory, and feelings of pleasure. Nicotine also stimulates the release of dopamine, the neurotransmitter that is most closely associated with the reward centres of the brain (Fehr et al., 2008; Yang et al., 2008). Finally, smokers learn to associate smoking with pleasant things, such as good food, relaxation, friends, enjoyable social activities, and sex. This makes quitting even harder as the smoker now has to break the connection between these pleasurable activities and smoking.

In addition to these social and psychological associations, smokers also learn to associate the act of smoking

with the "high" that nicotine gives them. When smokers are deprived of cigarettes, they go through an unpleasant *withdrawal*. Nicotine relieves the withdrawal symptoms, so smoking is reinforced.

The best way to reduce the number of smokers is to stop people from ever taking that first puff. As a way to discourage both smoking and young people from starting smoking, the Canadian Tobacco Act prohibits the sale of cigarettes to minors and the display of cigarettes in stores, and bans cigarette advertisements on television, radio, and in Canadian magazines (American editions of many magazines available in Canada do not have to comply with Canadian law, however). In addition, all cigarette packets sold in Canada are required by law to carry an anti-smoking statement. As of 2008, 18 percent of Canadians continued to smoke—a percentage that has been steadily decreasing.

In 2005, British Columbia had the lowest smoking prevalence (12.6 percent) and Nunavut had the highest (46.1 percent). The remaining provinces had percentages between 15 and 19 percent, and the territories had percentages much higher. All provinces have experienced a large drop in smoking prevalence since 1985 (**Figure 3.8**).

Some people find that the easiest way for them to stop smoking is to suddenly and completely stop. However, the success rate for this "cold turkey" approach is extremely low. Even with medical aids, such as nicotine patches, gum, or pills, it is still very difficult to quit. Any

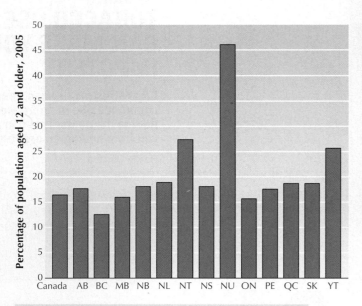

Smoking rates by province and territory

FIGURE 3.8

Smoking rates have been decreasing in Canada. What do you think accounts for this decrease? Do you think it is the result of effective anti-smoking campaigns?

Source: Statistics Canada. Data retrieved from http://www40.statcan. ca/l01/cst01/health07a-eng.htm and http://www40.statcan.ca/l01/cst01/health07b-eng.htm.

Smokers unite? FIGURE 3.9

It is ironic that anti-smoking laws may have made quitting smoking even more difficult for some. Being forced to gather together outside to smoke may forge stronger social bonds among smokers and strengthen their resolve to "suffer the tyranny" of anti-smoking laws. In addition, having to wait longer for their next nicotine dose increases the severity of withdrawal symptoms (Palfai et al., 2000). In effect, the smoker gets repeated previews of just how unpleasant quitting would be. What might be an alternative to our current anti-smoking laws, which make it difficult for people to smoke but at the same time indirectly support continued smoking behaviour?

program designed to help smokers break their habit must combat the social rewards of smoking, the social bonds among smokers (**FIGURE 3.9**), the paired associations, and the physical addiction to nicotine (Koop, Richmond, & Steinfeld, 2004).

Some smoking cessation programs combine nicotine replacement therapy with cognitive and behavioural techniques. This helps smokers identify stimuli or situations that make them feel like smoking and then change or avoid them (Brandon et al., 2000). Smokers can also be trained to refocus their attention on something other than smoking or remind themselves of the benefits of not smoking (Taylor et al., 2000). Behaviourally, they might cope with the urge to smoke by chewing gum, exercising, or chewing a mint after a meal instead of lighting a cigarette.

ALCOHOL: BOTH A PERSONAL HEALTH AND A SOCIAL ISSUE

Alcohol-related death and disability account for 9 percent of the overall toll on life and longevity in Canada and alcohol is among the top three risk factors contributing to disease, disability, and death. This compares with tobacco at 12 percent and high blood pressure at 11 percent (Canadian Centre on Substance Abuse, 2007). The American Medical Association (2008) considers *alcohol* to be the most dangerous and physically damaging of all drugs. After tobacco, it is the leading cause of premature death in America and most European countries (Abadinsky, 2008; Cohen et al., 2004; Maisto, Galizio, & Conners, 2008). Excessive alcohol consumption may cause serious brain damage (Crews et al., 2004). In addition, alcohol consumption seems to increase aggression, which helps explain why it's a major factor in many murders, suicides, spousal assaults, incidents of child abuse, and accidental deaths in North America (Levinthal, 2008; Sebre et al., 2004; Sher, Grekin, & Williams, 2005).

Most people are now aware of the major risks associated with drinking alcohol and driving: heavy fines, loss of driver's licence, jail time, serious injuries, and death. The effects of heavy alcohol consumption in itself can also be fatal. Because alcohol depresses neural activity throughout the brain, if blood levels of alcohol rise to a critical level, the brain's respiratory

Applying Psychology

Do You Have an Alcohol Problem?

In our society, drinking alcohol (within limits) is generally considered acceptable. However, many people abuse alcohol. To assess your own drinking behaviour, place an X next to each of the symptoms below that best describes your current drinking behaviour.

Seven Signs of Alcohol Dependence

_____ • Significant drinking occurs regularly, sometimes to the point of almost continuous daily consumption.

_____ • Drinking is given a higher priority than other activities, in spite of its negative consequences.

_____ • More and more alcohol is required to produce behavioural, subjective, and metabolic changes; large amounts of alcohol can be tolerated well.

_____ • Even short periods of abstinence bring on withdrawal symptoms, such as sweatiness, trembling, and nausea.

_____ • Withdrawal symptoms are relieved or avoided by further drinking, especially in the morning.

_____ • The individual is subjectively aware of a craving for alcohol and has little control over the quantity and frequency of intake.

_____ • If the person begins drinking again after a period of abstinence, he or she rapidly returns to the previous high level of consumption and other behavioural patterns.

Source: World Health Organization (2008).

> **Stop & Think**
> 1. Why is it important to determine whether you have an alcohol problem?
> 2. In what ways might alcoholism be a greater social problem than addiction to heroin or methamphetamines?

Binge drinking FIGURE 3.10

Unfortunately, many college and university students believe that heavy drinking is harmless fun and a natural part of post-secondary life. But excessive alcohol consumption, including binge drinking, carries serious health consequences and can even be fatal. While you have probably not engaged in the form of "drinking" shown in the picture, have there been occasions when your alcohol consumption met the criteria for binge drinking? Do you think these amounts are too high, too low, or about right? Why?

binge drinking When a man consumes five or more drinks in a row or a woman consumes four or more drinks in a row on at least three occasions during the previous two weeks.

centre stops functioning and the person dies. This is why **binge drinking** is so dangerous (**FIGURE 3.10**).

Binge drinking is of particular concern on college and university campuses. A survey of Canadian campuses by the Centre for Addiction and Mental Health found in 2004 that 32 percent of undergraduates drink at a dangerous level. Ten percent of those surveyed reported having experienced an alcohol-related assault, 9.8 percent reported alcohol-related sexual harassment, and 14.1 percent reported having unplanned sex because of their alcohol consumption (Binks, 2008).

College and university administrators are increasingly aware of the problems of binge drinking and other types of alcohol abuse. For example, Queen's University in Ontario suspended its homecoming celebrations for two years because excessive drinking and its consequences had become too serious a problem to ignore

Health Psychology in Action 83

(Binks, 2008). Many institutions are developing policies and programs that go beyond traditional educational programs to include the physical, social, legal, and economic environment on post-secondary campuses and the surrounding communities (Kapner, 2004).

INACTIVITY: THE RISKS OF A SEDENTARY LIFESTYLE

The Canadian Community Health Survey has estimated that approximately 50 percent of Canadians are inactive (**FIGURE 3.11**), meaning they participate in no formal exercise program. Another study put this number as high as 62 percent (Craig et al., 1999). For many Canadians the only exercise they get is walking to and from the vehicles that take them to work or school and home again. Research has shown a strong relationship between time spent watching television and computer use, and obesity in both men and women (Statistics Canada, 2008).

A sedentary lifestyle increases the risk of developing a number of diseases and disorders, including obesity, type II diabetes, some cancers, heart disease, and premature death. Research has estimated the direct health care costs attributable to physical inactivity in Canada at about $2.1 billion per year (Katzmarzyk et al., 2000). Health

Canada recommends three types of activities to keep healthy: endurance activities, such as walking or running (four to seven times per week); flexibility activities, such as stretching (four to seven times per week); and strength activities, such as weight training (two to four times per week) (Public Health Agency of Canada, 2003). A person should get about 60 minutes of activity each day. This does not have to be done in one session; research has shown breaking activity into 10-minute intervals has a similar beneficial effect on health (Public Health Agency of Canada, 2003). Everyday activities, such as clearing the mail and running errands, can also be beneficial.

Here are some simple ways to increase your activity levels around campus:

- Park away from a building entrance in a parking lot. Spots farther away from a building entrance are usually more readily available, and you gain the exercise benefits of walking a few minutes more.

- Use the stairs rather than an elevator or escalator. If this is difficult for you, start by taking the stairs when you are going down.

- Avoid using automatic door buttons. You use more muscles by pulling or pushing a door than by simply tapping a door opener.

- Get up and walk around during the break in your class, and if time allows, go outside. A 10-minute class break can allow for a small bout of exercise.

- Walk whenever possible: between classes, to the cafeteria, to the library or to the lecture hall.

- Use a pedometer to track the number of steps you walk. Aim for 10,000 steps each day.

- Visit the school gym and see what fitness classes are offered. These are a healthful and smart way to fill time between classes.

Inactivity FIGURE 3.11

The same Health Canada (2008) study that identified a link between time spent watching television and computer use and obesity in men and women found no such association between reading and obesity. All three activities are sedentary, so what might explain the different findings?

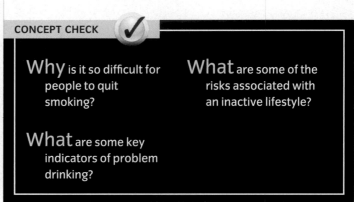

CONCEPT CHECK

Why is it so difficult for people to quit smoking?

What are some of the risks associated with an inactive lifestyle?

What are some key indicators of problem drinking?

Health and Stress Management

LEARNING OBJECTIVES

Compare emotion-focused and problem-focused forms of coping.

Explain the role that interpretation plays in shaping our responses to stressors.

Review some major resources for combating stress.

COPING WITH STRESS

coping Adaptive or compensatory strategies designed to reduce the effects of a stressor.

Because we can't escape stress, we need to learn how to effectively cope with it. Simply defined, **coping** is an attempt to manage stress in some effective way that minimizes its negative effect on the body and mind. It is not one single act but a process that allows us to deal with the various stressors when they present themselves (see **FIGURE 3.12** on the next page).

Our level of stress generally depends on both our interpretation of and our reaction to the stressors. **Emotion-focused forms of coping** are emotional or cognitive strategies that change how we view or feel about a stressful situation.

emotion-focused forms of coping Coping strategies based on changing one's perceptions of stressful situations.

For example, suppose you were refused a highly desirable, well-paying job. You might reappraise the situation and decide that the job wasn't the right match for you, that you weren't ready for it, or that the time commitment was too large.

Emotion-focused forms of coping that are accurate reappraisals of stressful situations and that do not distort reality may alleviate stress in some situations (Giacobbi, Foore, & Weinberg, 2004; Patterson, Holm, & Gurney, 2004). Many times, however, it is necessary and more effective to use **problem-focused forms of coping**, which deal directly with the situation or the stressor by coming up with practical solutions to eventually decrease or eliminate it (Bond & Bunce, 2000). These direct coping strategies include the following:

problem-focused forms of coping Coping strategies that use problem-solving strategies to decrease or eliminate the source of stress.

- identifying the stressful problem
- generating possible solutions
- selecting the appropriate solution
- applying the solution to the problem, thus eliminating the stress

RESOURCES FOR HEALTHY LIVING: FROM GOOD HEALTH TO HAVING MONEY

A person's ability to cope effectively depends on the stressor itself—its complexity, intensity, and duration—and on the type of coping strategy used. It also depends on available resources. Eight important resources for healthy living and stress management are health and exercise, control, positive beliefs, social skills, social support, material resources, relaxation, and a sense of humour. These are described in **TABLE 3.3** on page 87.

The strong federal support for healthy living is evident by the wealth of resources and information provided by Health Canada. Among other things, the agency encourages individuals to do the following:

1. Eat nutritiously, choosing a variety of foods from all the food groups, as suggested by *Canada's Food Guide.*

2. Build a circle of social contacts to create a supportive environment of people who care for you and respect you.

3. Stay physically active to keep your body strong, reduce stress, and improve your energy.

4. Choose not to smoke.

5. Put an end to other negative lifestyle practices (Health Canada, 2009).

By making healthy living choices, a person has a better chance of maintaining and improving not just physical health but mental health as well.

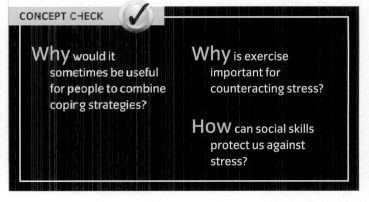

CONCEPT CHECK

Why would it sometimes be useful for people to combine coping strategies?

Why is exercise important for counteracting stress?

How can social skills protect us against stress?

Cognitive appraisal and coping FIGURE 3.12

Research suggests that our emotional response to an event depends largely on how we interpret the event.

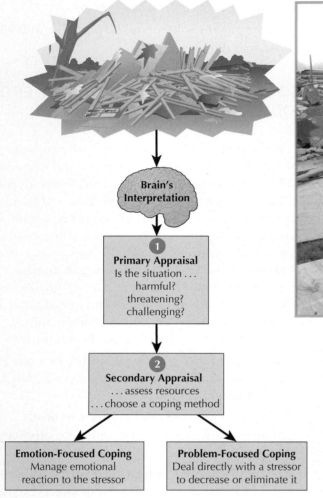

Brain's Interpretation

① Primary Appraisal
Is the situation ...
harmful?
threatening?
challenging?

② Secondary Appraisal
... assess resources
... choose a coping method

Emotion-Focused Coping
Manage emotional
reaction to the stressor

Problem-Focused Coping
Deal directly with a stressor
to decrease or eliminate it

People often combine *emotion-focused* and *problem-focused* coping strategies to resolve complex stressors or to respond to a stressful situation that is in flux. In some situations, an emotion-focused strategy can allow people to step back from an especially overwhelming problem. Then they can reappraise the situation and use the problem-solving approach to look for solutions. Can you see how each form of coping is represented in these two photos?

Health and exercise	Exercising and keeping fit help minimize anxiety, depression, and tension, which are associated with stress. Exercise also helps relieve muscle tension; improves cardiovascular efficiency; and increases strength, flexibility, and stamina.	
Positive beliefs	A positive self-image and attitude can be especially significant coping resources. Even temporarily raising self-esteem reduces the amount of anxiety caused by stressful events. Also, hope can sustain a person in the face of severe odds, as is often documented in news reports of people who have triumphed over seemingly unbeatable circumstances.	
Social skills	People who acquire social skills (such as knowing appropriate behaviours for certain situations, knowing conversation starters, and expressing themselves well) suffer less anxiety than people who do not. In fact, people who lack social skills are more at risk for developing illness than those who have them. Social skills not only help us interact with others but also communicate our needs and desires, enlist help when we need it, and decrease hostility in tense situations.	
Social support	Having the support of others helps offset the stressful effects of divorce, the loss of a loved one, chronic illness, pregnancy, physical abuse, job loss, and work overload. When we are faced with stressful circumstances, our friends and family often help us take care of our health, listen, hold our hands, make us feel important, and provide stability to offset the changes in our lives.	
Control	Believing that you are in charge of your own destiny is an important resource for effective coping. People with an **external locus of control** feel powerless to change their circumstances and are less likely to make healthy changes, follow treatment programs, or positively cope with a situation. Conversely, people with an **internal locus of control** believe that they are in charge of their own destinies and are therefore able to adopt more positive coping strategies.	
Material resources	Money increases the number of options available for eliminating sources of stress or reducing the effects of stress. When faced with the minor hassles of everyday living, or when faced with chronic stressors or major catastrophes, people with money and the skills to effectively use it generally fare better and experience less stress than people without money.	
Relaxation	There are a variety of relaxation techniques. Biofeedback is often used in the treatment of chronic pain, but it is also useful in teaching people to relax and manage their stress. **Progressive relaxation** helps reduce or relieve the muscular tension commonly associated with stress. To use this technique, patients first tense and then relax specific muscles, such as those in the neck, shoulders, and arms. This technique teaches people to recognize the difference between tense and relaxed muscles.	
Sense of humour	Research shows that humour is one of the best ways to reduce stress. The ability to laugh at oneself, and at life's inevitable ups and downs, allows us to relax and gain a broader perspective. In short: "Don't sweat the small stuff."	

SUMMARY

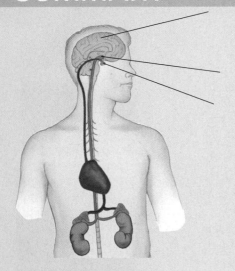

1 Understanding Stress

1. **Stress** is the body's non-specific response to any demand placed on it. Pleasant or beneficial stress is called **eustress**. Stress that is unpleasant or objectionable is called **distress.** Stress can be caused by a variety of factors, such as catastrophes, life changes, intolerable situations, the accumulation of minor **hassles**, **frustrations**, and **conflict**. There are three basic types of conflict: **approach-approach conflict**, **avoidance-avoidance conflict**, and **approach-avoidance conflict.**

2. The **sympathetic nervous system** and the **HPA axis** control significant physiological responses to stress. The sympathetic nervous system prepares us for immediate action; the HPA axis responds more slowly but lasts longer. The understanding that psychological factors influence many disease states have created a new field of biopsychology called **psychoneuroimmunology.**

3. The **general adaptation syndrome (GAS)** describes the body's three-stage reaction to stress. The phases are the initial alarm reaction, the resistance phase, and the exhaustion phase (if the resistance to the stressor was not successful).

2 Stress and Illness

1. Stress makes the immune system less able to resist infection and increases the possibility of cancer development.

2. Increased stress hormones can cause fat to adhere to blood vessel walls, increasing the risk of heart attack. Having the personality trait of hostility amplifies the risk of stress-related heart disease.

3. Exposure to extraordinary stress can cause **post-traumatic stress disorder (PTSD)**, a type of severe anxiety that is characterized by flashbacks, nightmares, and impaired functioning.

4. Stress increases the risk of developing gastric ulcers among people who have the *H. pylori* bacterium in their stomachs.

3 Health Psychology in Action

1. **Health psychology**, the study of how biological, psychological, and social factors affect health and illness, is a growing field in psychology.

2. Most approaches to helping people quit smoking include cognitive and behavioural techniques to aid smokers in their withdrawal from nicotine, along with some form of nicotine-replacement therapy.

3. Excessive alcohol consumption is a leading cause of premature death and may cause brain damage. Alcohol also seems to increase aggression. Although many college and university students believe that heavy drinking is a harmless part of post-secondary life, administrators are becoming increasingly aware of the problems associated with alcohol abuse.

4. A sedentary lifestyle is harmful to general health and is a contributing factor in a variety of disorders and diseases. Health Canada has recommended a number of strategies to improve daily activity levels.

4 Health and Stress Management

1. Our level of stress generally depends on both our interpretation of and our reaction to stressors. **Emotion-focused forms of coping** are emotional or cognitive strategies that change how we view a stressful situation. It is often more effective to use **problem-focused forms of coping** strategies—actual practical solutions to reduce or remove the stressor. People often combine problem-focused and emotion-focused coping strategies to resolve complex stressors or to respond to a stressful situation that is ongoing.

2. Eight important resources for healthy living and stress management are health and exercise, positive beliefs, social skills, social support, material resources, control, relaxation, and a sense of humour. An in-depth look at control tells us that having an **internal locus of control** is a healthier way to manage stress than having an **external locus of control**.

KEY TERMS

- approach-approach conflict p. 88
- approach-avoidance conflict p. 88
- avoidance-avoidance conflict p. 88
- binge drinking p. 83
- chronic stressors p. 70
- conflict p. 78
- coping p. 85
- distress p. 70
- emotion-focused forms of coping p. 87

- eustress p. 70
- external locus of control p. 87
- frustration p. 72
- general adaptation syndrome (GAS) p. 74
- hardiness p. 71
- hassles p. 71
- health psychology p. 80
- HPA axis p. 72
- internal locus of control p. 87

- post-traumatic stress disorder (PTSD) p. 78
- problem-focused forms of coping p. 85
- progressive relaxation p. 87
- psychoneuroimmunology p. 75
- stress p. 70
- stressor p. 70
- sympathetic nervous system (SAM) p. 72

CRITICAL AND CREATIVE THINKING QUESTIONS

1. What are the major sources of stress in your life? Are any of these stressors of the more pleasant type (eustress), or are they all unpleasant (distress)?

2. What types of changes could you make in your life to minimize stress and maximize your health?

3. If you are experiencing a period of high stress, what could you do to avoid becoming ill from the various stressors?

4. Controllable risk factors for premature death include risky behaviour, such as texting while driving. What effect, if any, do you think legislation and legal penalties might have on this and other types of risky behaviour?

5. Why are smoking-prevention efforts often aimed at adolescents?

6. What are some things you could do to have a less sedentary lifestyle? Are there any physical activities that you could easily implement into your life?

7. Which forms of coping do you most often use? Do you use primarily emotion-focused methods or problem-focused forms when dealing with stress?

8. Which of the resources for stress management seem most useful for you?

What is happening in this picture ?

An increasingly health conscious public has generated a demand for healthy alternatives to foods and other items that have traditionally contained significant quantities of chemicals and additives. One such item is cigarettes. In Canada and the U.S. there are now new tobacco products that are being marketed as natural and organic. Although these cigarettes contain more tar and nicotine than conventional smokes, they have none of the additives ordinarily found in tobacco products (Kezwer, 1998). What is the psychological effect on the consumer for this type of product? Do people think they are making a more healthful choice if they switch to an organic, all natural cigarette?

SURGEON GENERAL'S WARNING: Cigarette Smoke Contains Carbon Monoxide.

Sales to Minors Prohibited

SELF-TEST

(Check your answers in Appendix A.)

1. The physical and mental arousal to situations that we perceive as threatening or challenging is called _____.

   a. distress
   b. eustress
   c. stress
   d. stressor

2. Vikram has recently become a father and moved to a different city to start a very high-paying job, both positive things, in his view. What type of stress is Vikram likely to experience with these changes?

   a. Distress
   b. Chronic stress
   c. Eustress
   d. None of the above

3. Holmes and Rahe (1967) and others believe that higher scores on the SRRS are correlated with greater risks of having which of the following?

   a. Ulcers
   b. Heart disease
   c. Disease and illness
   d. Cancer

4. Which of the following is one of the largest sources of CHRONIC stress for adults?

   a. Birth
   b. Work
   c. Bad relationship
   d. Moving

5. Which occupation is associated with more psychological distress and poorer mental health?

   a. Police officers
   b. Fire fighters
   c. Truck drivers
   d. Machine operators

6. In an *approach-approach conflict,* a person must choose between two or more goals that will lead to _____, whereas in an *avoidance-avoidance conflict,* a person must choose between two or more goals that will lead to _____.

   a. less conflict; no conflict
   b. frustration; hostility
   c. a desirable result; an undesirable result
   d. effective coping; ineffective coping

7. Lisa must decide whether to spend the night with old friends in town for a short visit, or stay home and work on her major term paper due the next day. What type of conflict is Lisa likely experiencing?

   a. An approach-approach conflict
   b. An approach-avoidance conflict
   c. A eustress-distress conflict
   d. An avoidance-avoidance conflict

8. Label the structures on the diagram.

   a. hypothalamus
   b. pituitary
   c. cerebral cortex
   d. adrenal glands

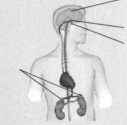

9. Which of the following is the field that studies the interaction among the mind, the immune system, and the nervous system?

   a. Psychosomatology   c. Biopsychology
   b. Neurobiology   d. Psychoneuroimmunology

10. Research suggests that one particular personality trait, illustrated in this photo, is **most** associated with heart disease. What characteristic is this?

    a. Cynical hostility
    b. Road rage
    c. Intense ambition
    d. Time urgency

11. People who experience flashbacks, nightmares, and impaired functioning following a life-threatening or other horrifying event are suffering from which of the following?

    a. A psychosomatic illness
    b. Post-traumatic stress disorder
    c. A nervous breakdown
    d. Depression

12. Which of the following is **not true** of health psychology?

    a. It studies the relationship between psychological behaviour and physical health.
    b. It studies the relationship between psychological behaviour and illness.
    c. It emphasizes wellness and the prevention of illness.
    d. It typically does not include working with people who have chronic or long-term problems.

13. The effects of nicotine on the brain are related to the release of which of the following?

    a. Glutamate   c. Dopamine
    b. Serotonin   d. All of these options

14. At several parties in the past couple of weeks, Arash consumed five drinks in a row and his girlfriend consumed four drinks in a row. This means that _____ met the definition for binge drinking.

    a. Arash   c. both Arash and his girlfriend
    b. his girlfriend   d. neither Arash nor his girlfriend

15. Approximately what percentage of the Canadian public is inactive?

    a. 15–25%   c. 65–80%
    b. 50–55%   d. 75–80%

16. How much activity does Health Canada recommend per day?

    a. 30 minutes   c. 60 minutes
    b. 45 minutes   d. 90 minutes

17. Which of the following activities is NOT correlated with obesity in men and women?

    a. Reading   c. Watching television
    b. Working on a computer   d. Reading and watching television

18. *Emotion-focused forms of coping* are based on changing your _____ when faced with stressful situations.

    a. feelings   c. strategies
    b. perceptions   d. all of these options

19. Hue-Linh generally deals with stressors in her life by considering possible solutions to the problem, choosing the most appropriate solution, and then actually using the solution to deal with the issue. What does Hue-Linh appear to have?

    a. A high level of intrinsic motivation
    b. An external locus of control
    c. An emotion-focused coping style
    d. A problem-focused coping style

20. Research suggests that people with a higher _____ adopt better coping strategies than those with a higher

    _____.

    a. external locus of control; internal locus of control
    b. internal locus of control; external locus of control
    c. emotion-focused coping style; problem-focused coping style
    d. problem-focused coping style; emotion-focused coping style

Sensation and Perception

Imagine that your visual field were suddenly inverted and reversed so that things you expected to be on your right were on your left, and things you expected to be above your head were below it. No doubt you would have trouble getting around. Imagine pouring a cup of coffee or taking notes in class. Do you think you could ever adapt to this distorted world?

To answer that question, about a hundred years ago, psychologist George Stratton (1896) wore special lenses for eight days. For the first few days, Stratton had great difficulty navigating in this environment and coping with everyday tasks. But by the third day, his experience had begun to change—things were easier to do. By the fifth day, Stratton had almost completely adjusted to his strange perceptual environment and his expectations of how the world should be arranged had changed significantly. As Stratton's experiment shows, we are able to adapt even our most basic perceptions by retraining our brains to adapt to unfamiliar physical sensations, creating a newly coherent world.

This chapter focuses on two separate, but inseparable, aspects of how we experience the world: sensation and perception. The boundary between these two processes is not precise but they are generally defined as follows: Sensation is the process of receiving, translating, and transmitting raw sensory data from the external and internal environments to the brain. More simply, it is the gathering up of the information provided from our senses. Perception is the higher-level process of selecting, organizing, and interpreting sensory data into useful mental representations of the world. It is what we do with the sensory information we get in order to understand the world and our experiences. While these definitions might seem a bit dry and confusing, the magic of the concepts comes alive in the examples.

NATIONAL GEOGRAPHIC

CHAPTER OUTLINE

Understanding Sensation

LEARNING OBJECTIVES

Describe how raw sensory stimuli are converted to signals in the brain.

Explain how the study of thresholds helps to explain sensation.

Describe why adapting to sensory stimuli provides an evolutionary advantage.

Identify the factors that govern pain perception.

When presented with a high-pitched tone (such as the sound of a flute), a musician reported, "It looks like fireworks tinged with a pink-red hue. The color feels rough and unpleasant, and it has an ugly taste—rather like that of a briny pickle" (Luria, 1968). This musician was describing a rare condition known as *synesthesia,* which means "mixing of the senses." People with synesthesia routinely blend their sensory experiences. They may "see" temperatures, "hear" colours, or "taste" shapes. To appreciate how extraordinary synesthesia is, we must first understand the basic processes of normal, unblended **sensations**. For example, how do we turn light and sound waves from the environment into something our brain can comprehend? To do this, we must have both a means of detecting stimuli and a means of converting them into a language the brain can understand.

sensation
The process of receiving, translating, and transmitting raw sensory data from the external and internal environments to the brain.

PROCESSING: DETECTION AND CONVERSION

Our eyes, ears, skin, and other sense organs all contain special cells called receptors, which receive and process sensory information from the environment. For each sense, these specialized cells respond to a distinct stimulus, such as sound waves or odour molecules. During the process of **sensory transduction**, the receptors convert the stimulus into neural signals, which are then sent to the brain. For example, with hearing, tiny receptor cells in the inner ear convert the vibrations from sound waves into electrochemical signals. These signals are carried by neurons to the brain, where specific sensory neurons detect and interpret the information. How does our brain differentiate between sensations, such as sounds and smells? Through a process known as **labelled lines** in which different physical stimuli are interpreted as distinct sensations because their neural impulses travel by different routes and arrive at different parts of the brain (**FIGURE 4.1**).

Many animals possess extraordinary sensory abilities. For example, dogs' sense of smell is far more sensitive than humans'. For this reason, specially trained dogs provide invaluable help in sniffing out dangerous plants, drugs, money, and explosives; tracking offenders,

sensory transduction
The process by which a physical stimulus is converted into neural impulses.

labelled lines
The way the brain interprets the type of sensory information based on its neural origin in the body and its destination location in the brain.

Sensory processing within the brain
FIGURE 4.1

Neural impulses travel from the sensory receptors to various parts of the brain.

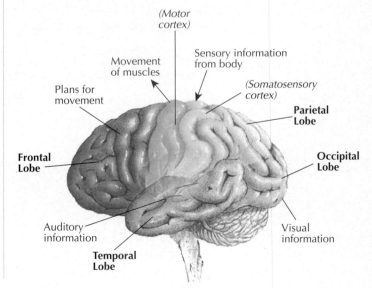

(Motor cortex)

Movement of muscles

Plans for movement

Sensory information from body

(Somatosensory cortex)

Parietal Lobe

Frontal Lobe

Occipital Lobe

Auditory information

Visual information

Temporal Lobe

The trained dogs of Canada Border Services Agency FIGURE 4.2

A dog's superior sense of smell makes it extremely valuable for detecting olfactory stimuli undetectable to humans.

and assisting in search-and-rescue operations. Some researchers have shown dogs can even detect the chemical signs of certain illnesses, such as diabetes or cancer, simply by smelling a person's breath (Pickel et al., 2004).

All species have evolved selective sensory receptors that suppress or amplify information important for their survival (**FIGURE 4.2**). Sensory systems that were advantageous for survival and reproduction have been preferentially selected by the organism's environment. Through evolutionary time, these systems were enhanced, which explains the incredible range of sensory diversity seen across species. Although humans have remarkable sensory systems, uniquely adapted to our world, we cannot sense ultraviolet light, microwaves, the ultrasonic sound of a dog whistle, or infrared heat patterns from warm-blooded animals, as some other animals can.

ADAPTATION: WEAKENING THE RESPONSE

Imagine that friends have invited you to come meet their new cat. As they greet you at the door, you are overwhelmed by the potent odour of cat urine. "How can they live with that smell?" You think. "Can't they smell that?" The answer lies in a well-known sensory phenomenon called **sensory adaptation**. When a stimulus is presented constantly for a length of time, the sensation in the sense receptors often fades or disappears.

Sensory adaptation makes sense from an evolutionary perspective. We can't afford to waste attention, time, and neural energy on unchanging, normally unimportant stimuli. Imagine how big your head would have to be to hold a brain that registered and recorded every sensory event around you. Tuning out repetitive information helps the brain cope with an overwhelming amount of sensory stimuli and allows it the time and space to pay attention to change. Researchers have long been interested in studying the subtleties and nuances of our sensory systems (**FIGURE 4.3**).

> **sensory adaptation**
> Repeated or constant stimulation decreases the number of sensory messages sent to the brain from the sense receptors.

Measuring the senses
FIGURE 4.3

How do we know exactly what humans can see, hear, feel, or smell? The answer comes from research in *psychophysics*, the study of the relationship between events in the physical world and our psychological experiences of them. Researchers study how the strength or intensity of a stimulus affects us. Consider this example:

- To test for hearing loss, a hearing specialist uses a tone generator to produce sounds of differing pitches and intensities.

- You listen over earphones and indicate the earliest point at which you hear a tone. This is your *absolute threshold*, or the smallest amount of a stimulus needed to detect the stimulus half the time.

- To test your *difference threshold*, or *just noticeable difference (JND)*, the examiner gradually changes the volume and asks you to respond when you notice a difference.

- Comparing your thresholds with those of people without hearing loss shows whether you have a hearing loss and, if so, the extent of the loss.

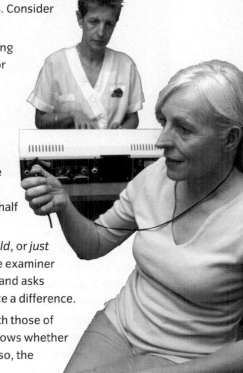

Although some senses, like smell and touch, adapt quickly, we never completely adapt to visual stimuli or to extremely intense stimuli, such as the odour of ammonia or the pain of a bad burn. From an evolutionary perspective, these limitations on sensory adaptation aid survival; for example, they remind us to avoid strong odours and hot objects, or to protect a burn or nurse an injury.

If we don't adapt to pain, how do athletes keep playing despite painful injuries? In certain situations, the body releases natural painkillers called *endorphins* (see Chapter 2), which inhibit pain perception (**FIGURE 4.4**).

In addition to endorphin release, another mechanism of pain perception is described in the **gate-control theory**, first proposed by Canadian psychologist Ronald Melzack and Patrick Wall (1965). According to this theory, the experience of pain depends partly on whether the neural message can get past a "gatekeeper" in the spinal cord. Normally, the gate is kept open either by impulses coming down from the brain or by messages coming from large-diameter nerve fibres that conduct most sensory signals, such as touch and pressure. When tissue is damaged, the pain signal travels along smaller pain fibres, passes through the open gate, and informs the brain. The result is the subjective experience of pain.

> **gate-control theory** The theory that pain sensations are processed and altered by mechanisms within the spinal cord.

According to the gate-control theory, massaging an injury or scratching an itch can temporarily relieve discomfort because pressure on large-diameter neurons interferes with pain signals by closing the gates. Messages from the brain can also close the pain gate, explaining how athletes and soldiers can carry on despite what would normally be excruciating pain. When we are soothed by endorphins or distracted by competition or fear, our experience of pain can be greatly diminished. Conversely, when we get anxious or dwell on our pain, we can intensify it (Roth et al., 2007; Sullivan, 2008; Sullivan, Tripp, & Santor, 1998). Ironically, well-meaning friends who ask chronic pain sufferers about their pain may unintentionally reinforce and increase it (Jolliffe & Nicholas, 2004).

Research also suggests that the pain gate may be chemically controlled, that a neurotransmitter called *substance P* opens the pain gate—pain is felt—and that endorphins close it—pain is reduced (Cesaro & Ollat, 1997; Liu, Mantyh, & Basbaum, 1997). Other research (Melzack, 1999; Vertosick, 2000) has shown that when normal sensory input is disrupted, the brain can generate pain and other sensations on its own. Amputees sometimes continue to feel pain (and itching or tickling) long after a limb has been amputated. This *phantom limb pain* occurs because neurons send conflicting messages to the brain. The brain interprets these messages as pain because it arises in the area of the spinal cord responsible for pain signalling. When amputees are fitted with prosthetic limbs and begin using them, phantom pain generally disappears (Crawford, 2008; Gracely et al., 2002).

The power of the nervous system in inhibiting pain FIGURE 4.4

The body's ability to inhibit pain perception sometimes makes it possible for athletes to play through painful injuries. MMA Champ Randy Couture broke his left arm while deflecting a high kick from opponent Gabriel Gonzaga in 2007. Despite the injury, Couture continued to fight and won the Ultimate Fighting Heavyweight Championship (UFC) by technical knockout later in the third round. Do you think this ability is only seen in elite athletes, or is it in all of us?

CONCEPT CHECK

HOW do we convert sensory information into signals the brain can understand?

Why would we want to limit the amount of sensory information that we receive?

Why is there such a vast range of sensory systems seen across species?

What factors govern pain perception?

How We See and Hear

LEARNING OBJECTIVES

Identify the three major characteristics of light and sound waves.

Explain how the eye captures and focuses light energy, and how it converts it into neural signals.

Describe the path that sound waves take in the ear.

Summarize the two theories that explain how we distinguish among different pitches.

WAVES OF LIGHT AND SOUND

Even the most complex visual and auditory experiences depend on our basic ability to detect light and sound. Both light and sound move in waves, similar to the movement of waves on the ocean (**FIGURE 4.5A**).

Light waves are a form of electromagnetic energy, and different types of waves on the *electromagnetic spectrum* have different wavelengths (**FIGURE 4.5B**).

In contrast to light waves, which are particles (tiny packets) of electromagnetic energy, sound waves are caused by air molecules moving in a particular wave pattern. The waves originate when a vibrating object, such as vocal cords or guitar strings, compress the air molecules (push them together) and then decompress the air molecules (spread them out), resulting in a particular wave pattern. This wave pattern moves away from the vibrating object propagating the sound wave. Sound

Illustrating differences between light and sound waves
FIGURE 4.5

A Watching a fireworks show is one way you've probably learned that light travels much faster than sound. But light also travels differently from sound, which must pass through physical material to be heard. The speed of light is always 300 million metres per second no matter what it passes through. Sound travels through air at 344 metres per second at 21°C. But if you were observing fireworks under fresh water, you'd notice a shorter gap between the burst of light and the arrival of the sound—in water sound will travel at a speed of about 1,500 metres per second, which is about five times its speed in air.

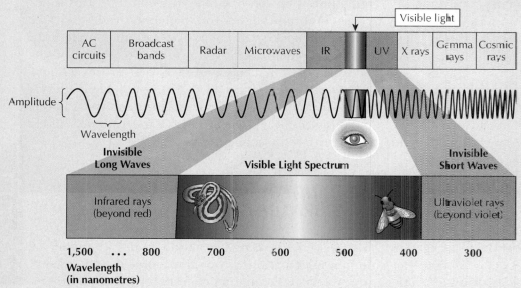

B The human eye can see only visible light, a small part of the full electromagnetic spectrum. Honeybees, however, can "see" in ultraviolet and some rattlesnakes can "see" in infrared. What do you think might be the adaptive significance of this diversity? Visible light with a short wavelength is perceived as blue, visible light with a medium wavelength is green or yellow, and visible light with a long wavelength is red.

Physical Properties	**Wavelength:** The distance between successive peaks	**Wave amplitude:** The height from midline to peak (or midline to trough)	**Range of wavelengths:** the mixture of waves
	Time→ *Long wavelength/low frequency (the number of waves per unit of time)* Time→ *Short wavelength/high frequency*	Time→ *Low amplitude/low intensity* Time→ *High amplitude/high intensity*	Time→ *Low range/low complexity* Time→ *High range/high complexity*
VISION (Light waves)	**Hue:** Short wavelengths that are higher frequency are perceived as bluish; long wavelengths that are lower frequency are perceived as reddish.	**Brightness:** Great amplitude produces more intensity and bright colours; small amplitude produces less intensity and dim colours.	**Saturation:** Wider range produces more complex colour; narrow range produces less complex colour.
AUDITION (Sound waves)	**Pitch:** Shorter wavelengths that are higher frequency are perceived as high-pitched sounds; long wavelengths that are lower frequency are perceived as low-pitched sounds.	**Loudness:** Great amplitude produces louder (more intense) sounds; small amplitude produces soft sounds.	**Timbre:** Wider range produces more complex sound with a mix of multiple frequencies. Narrower range produces less complex sound with one or a few frequencies.

waves can be created in any substance in which particles can be compressed and decompressed—even slightly—such as water or steel.

Both light waves and sound waves vary in wavelength, amplitude (height), frequency, and range—each with a distinct effect on vision and hearing, or audition, as shown in **STUDY ORGANIZER 4.1**.

VISION: OUR DOMINANT SENSE

Most structures in the eye are involved in capturing and focusing light and converting it into neural signals to be interpreted by the brain, as shown in **FIGURE 4.6**.

Thoroughly understanding the processes detailed in Figure 4.6 helps us understand some visual peculiarities. For example, small abnormalities in the eye sometimes cause images to be focused in front of the retina (nearsightedness, also called myopia) or behind it (farsightedness, or hyperopia). Corrective lenses or laser surgery can correct most such visual acuity problems. During middle age, most people's lenses lose elasticity and the ability to adjust or accommodate for near vision, a condition known as presbyopia. This is usually treated with corrective lenses.

If you walk into a dark movie theatre on a sunny afternoon, you won't be able to see at first. This is because in bright light, the pigment inside the rod photoreceptors is bleached, making them temporarily non-functional. It takes a second or two for the rods to become functional enough to see. This process of *dark adaptation* continues for 20 to 30 minutes. Light adaptation, the adjustment that takes place when you go from darkness to a bright setting, takes 7 to 10 minutes and is a property of the cone photoreceptors.

HEARING: TRANSLATING WAVES OF VIBRATING AIR

The sense of hearing, or audition, has a number of important functions, from alerting us to the dangers around us, to facilitating communication with others.

3 Behind the iris and pupil, the muscularly controlled lens focuses incoming light into an image on the light-sensitive *retina*, located on the back surface of the fluid-filled eyeball. This is the process of accommodation, in which the lens changes shape to focus images on the retina. Note how the lens reverses the image from right to left and top to bottom when it is projected on to the retina. The brain later reverses the visual input into the final image that we perceive.

2 The light then passes through the *pupil*, a small adjustable opening. Muscles in the *iris* allow the *pupil* to dilate or constrict in response to light intensity or emotional factors.

1 Light first enters through the *cornea*, which helps focus incoming light rays.

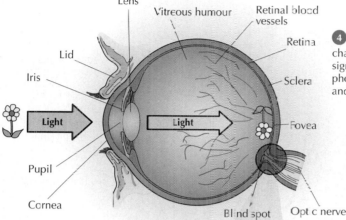

Lens
Vitreous humour
Retinal blood vessels
Lid
Iris
Retina
Sclera
Light
Light
Fovea
Pupil
Cornea
Blind spot
Optic nerve

4 In the **retina**, light waves are changed into neural signals (visual transduction) by photoreceptors called rods and cones.

5 The **fovea**, a tiny pit filled with cones, is responsible for our sharpest vision. When we focus directly on an object, the image falls on the fovea.

10 After exiting the eye, neural messages travel along the optic nerve to the brain for further processing.

9 At the back of the retina lies an area that has no photoreceptors at all and therefore absolutely no vision. In this **blind spot**, blood vessels and neural pathways enter and exit the eyeball.

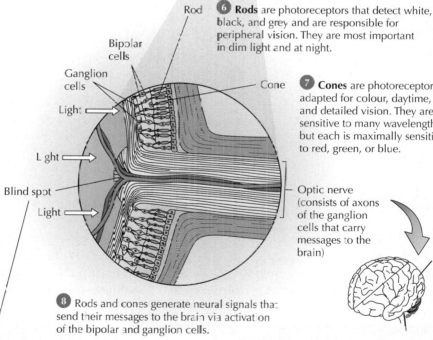

Rod
Bipolar cells
Ganglion cells
Light
Cone
Light
Blind spot
Light
Optic nerve (consists of axons of the ganglion cells that carry messages to the brain)

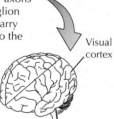

Visual cortex

6 **Rods** are photoreceptors that detect white, black, and grey and are responsible for peripheral vision. They are most important in dim light and at night.

7 **Cones** are photoreceptors adapted for colour, daytime, and detailed vision. They are sensitive to many wavelengths, but each is maximally sensitive to red, green, or blue.

8 Rods and cones generate neural signals that send their messages to the brain via activation of the bipolar and ganglion cells.

Do you have a blind spot?

Everyone with vision does. To find yours, hold this book about 30 cm in front of you, close your right eye, and stare at the X with your left eye. Very slowly, move the book closer to you. You should see the worm disappear and the apple become whole.

How the ear hears FIGURE 4.7

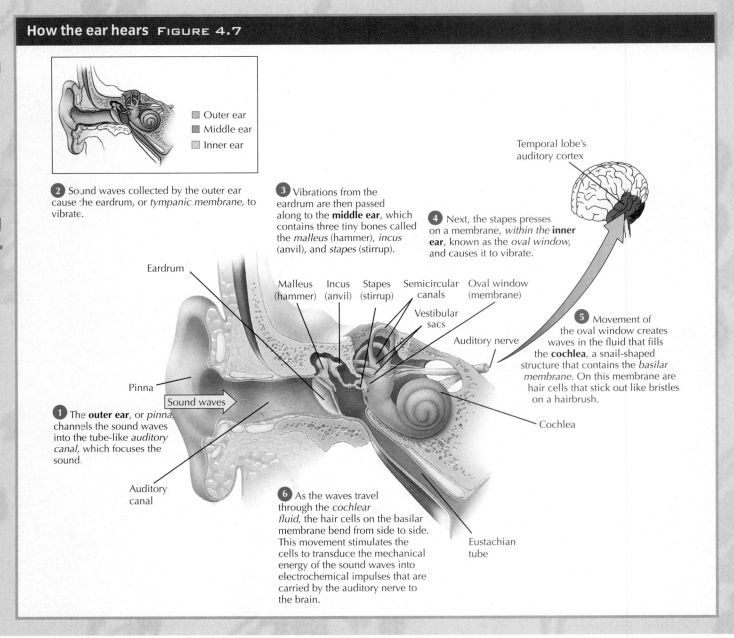

☐ Outer ear
☐ Middle ear
☐ Inner ear

2 Sound waves collected by the outer ear cause the eardrum, or *tympanic membrane,* to vibrate.

3 Vibrations from the eardrum are then passed along to the **middle ear**, which contains three tiny bones called the *malleus* (hammer), *incus* (anvil), and *stapes* (stirrup).

4 Next, the stapes presses on a membrane, *within the* **inner ear**, known as the *oval window,* and causes it to vibrate.

Temporal lobe's auditory cortex

Eardrum

Malleus (hammer) Incus (anvil) Stapes (stirrup) Semicircular canals Oval window (membrane)

Vestibular sacs

Auditory nerve

5 Movement of the oval window creates waves in the fluid that fills the **cochlea**, a snail-shaped structure that contains the *basilar membrane.* On this membrane are hair cells that stick out like bristles on a hairbrush.

Pinna

Sound waves

1 The **outer ear**, or *pinna,* channels the sound waves into the tube-like *auditory canal,* which focuses the sound.

Auditory canal

Cochlea

6 As the waves travel through the *cochlear fluid,* the hair cells on the basilar membrane bend from side to side. This movement stimulates the cells to transduce the mechanical energy of the sound waves into electrochemical impulses that are carried by the auditory nerve to the brain.

Eustachian tube

The ear has three major sections that function as shown in FIGURE 4.7.

The mechanisms determining how we distinguish among sounds of different pitches (low to high) differ depending on the frequency of the sound (TABLE 4.1). According to **place theory**, different high-frequency sound waves (which produce high-pitched sounds) maximally stimulate the hair cells

How the ear distinguishes among sounds of different pitches TABLE 4.1

Theory		Frequency	Pitch	Example
Place theory	Hair cells are stimulated at different locations on basilar membrane.	High frequency	High-pitched sounds	A squeal or a child's voice
Frequency theory	Hair cells fire at the same rate as the frequency for the sound.	Low frequency	Low-pitched sounds	A growl or a man's voice

at different locations along the basilar membrane. Hearing low-pitched sounds works differently. According to **frequency theory**, low-pitched sounds cause hair cells along the basilar membrane to bend and fire neural messages (action potentials) at the same rate as the frequency of that sound. For example, a sound with a frequency of 90 hertz would produce 90 action potentials per second in the auditory nerve. (See FIGURE 4.8.)

Whether we detect a sound as soft or loud depends on its intensity. Waves with high peaks and deep valleys produce loud sounds; those that have relatively low peaks and shallow valleys produce soft sounds. The relative loudness or softness of sounds is measured on a scale of *decibels* (dB) (FIGURE 4.9A).

Can you hear me now? FIGURE 4.8

Stealthy teenagers now have a biological advantage over their teachers: a cellphone ringtone that sounds at 17 kilohertz—too high for adult ears to detect. The ringtone is an ironic by-product of another device that uses the same sound frequency. That invention, dubbed the Mosquito, was designed to help shopkeepers annoy and deter loitering teenagers.

How loud is too loud? FIGURE 4.9

A The loudness of a sound is measured in decibels and the higher a sound's decibel reading, the more damaging it is to the ear. Chronic exposure to loud noise, such as loud music or heavy traffic—or brief exposure to really loud sounds, such as a stereo at full blast, a jackhammer, or a jet engine—can cause permanent nerve deafness. Disease and biological changes associated with aging can also cause nerve deafness.

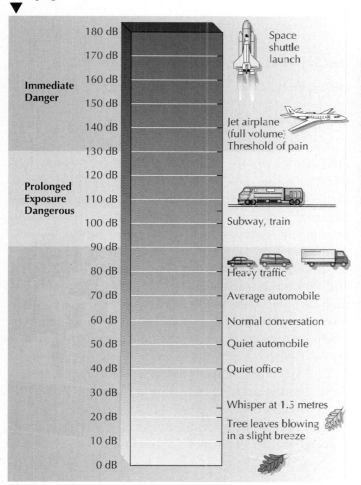

B The Who held the Guinness World Record in 1976 for the loudest rock concert ever with a documented loudness of 126 dB measured at 32 metres from the speakers. Pete Townshend and Roger Daltry both report significant nerve damage hearing loss caused by their prolonged exposure to this type of loud music. Incidentally, Guinness World Records no longer includes this category as it does not want to promote activities that cause hearing loss.

conduction deafness (middle-ear deafness)
Deafness resulting from problems with the mechanical system that conducts sound waves to the inner ear.

nerve deafness (inner-ear deafness)
Damage to the cochlea, hair cells, or auditory nerve.

Hearing loss can stem from two major causes: (1) **conduction deafness**, or **middle-ear deafness**, which results from problems with the mechanical system that conducts sound waves to the inner ear (such as a perforated eardrum), and (2) **nerve deafness**, or **inner-ear deafness**, which involves damage to the cochlea, hair cells, or auditory nerve (such as hearing loss caused by ongoing loud noise) (**FIGURE 4.9B**).

Although most conduction deafness is temporary, damage to the auditory nerve or hair cells is almost always irreversible. The only treatment for severe nerve deafness is a small electronic device called a *cochlear implant*. If the auditory nerve is intact, the implant bypasses hair cells to stimulate the nerve directly. Currently, cochlear implants produce only a rudimentary approximation of hearing, but the technology is improving. Rather than repairing the damage, however, it is best to protect your hearing by avoiding exceptionally loud noises and wearing earplugs when such situations cannot be avoided. Paying attention to bodily warnings of possible hearing loss, including a change in your normal hearing threshold, and *tinnitus,* a whistling or ringing sensation in your ears, are also important in avoiding hearing loss.

CONCEPT CHECK ✓

What are the rods and cones responsible for?

What are the three major parts of the ear?

Why do middle-aged people often need reading glasses?

What are the types of deafness?

Our Other Senses

LEARNING OBJECTIVES

Explain the importance of smell and taste to survival.

Describe how the information contained in odour molecules reaches the brain.

Identify the locations of receptors for the body senses.

Explain the role of our vestibular and kinesthetic senses.

Vision and audition may be the most prominent of our senses, but the others—taste, smell, and the body senses—are also essential for gathering information about our environment.

SMELL AND TASTE: SENSING CHEMICALS

Smell and taste are sometimes referred to as the *chemical senses* because they both involve chemoreceptors that are sensitive to certain chemical molecules. Smell and taste receptors are located near each other and often interact so closely that we have difficulty separating the sensations.

Our sense of smell, olfaction, is remarkably useful and sensitive. We possess more than 1,000 types of olfactory receptors, allowing us to detect more than 10,000 distinct smells (**FIGURE 4.10**). The nose is exquisitely sensitive, more sensitive to smoke than any electronic detector, and malleable—with practice, blind people can learn to quickly recognize others by their unique odours.

Pheromones are compounds found in bodily scents and fluids that can affect the behaviour of organisms such as their courtship and sexual behaviour. Some research evidence suggests that these chemical odours might be able to change sexual behaviours in humans (Savic, Berglund, & Lundström, 2007; Thornhill et al., 2003). However, other research findings challenge these results, arguing that humans do not have this capacity (Hays, 2003). Although research does not as yet have a clear answer on the effects of pheromones in our species, investigators do agree that human sexuality

How the nose smells FIGURE 4.10

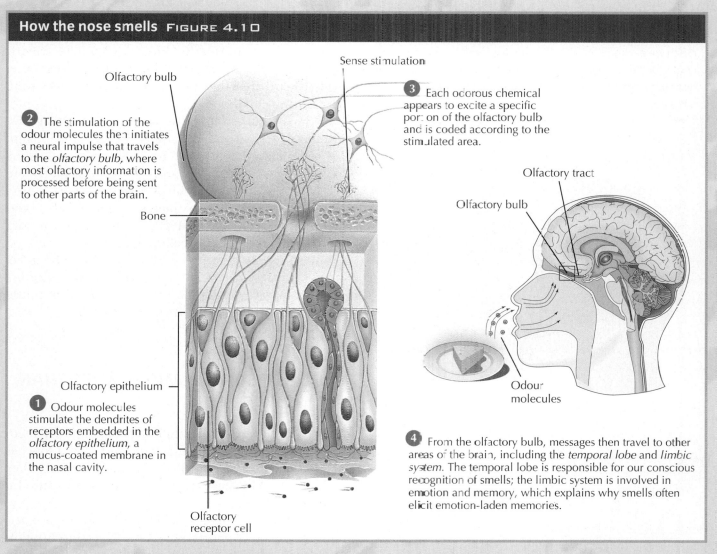

Olfactory bulb

Sense stimulation

2 The stimulation of the odour molecules then initiates a neural impulse that travels to the *olfactory bulb*, where most olfactory information is processed before being sent to other parts of the brain.

3 Each odorous chemical appears to excite a specific portion of the olfactory bulb and is coded according to the stimulated area.

Bone

Olfactory tract

Olfactory bulb

Olfactory epithelium

1 Odour molecules stimulate the dendrites of receptors embedded in the *olfactory epithelium*, a mucus-coated membrane in the nasal cavity.

Odour molecules

4 From the olfactory bulb, messages then travel to other areas of the brain, including the *temporal lobe* and *limbic system*. The temporal lobe is responsible for our conscious recognition of smells; the limbic system is involved in emotion and memory, which explains why smells often elicit emotion-laden memories.

Olfactory receptor cell

---

is far more complex than that of other animals—and much more so than perfume advertisements would have you believe.

Today, the sense of taste, gustation, might be the least critical of our senses. In the past, however, it probably contributed significantly to our survival. Evolutionarily, the major function of taste, aided by smell, was probably to help us avoid eating or drinking harmful substances. Because many plants that contain toxic chemicals taste bitter, an organism would be more likely to survive if it finds bitter-tasting plants distasteful

(Cooper et al., 2002; Kardong, 2008; Skelhorn et al., 2008). Conversely, humans and other animals have a preference for sweet foods, which are generally not poisonous and are good sources of energy.

Children's taste buds are replaced more quickly than adults' taste buds—about every seven days. As we age, taste bud replacement occurs more slowly. Because children have abundant new taste buds compared with adults, they often dislike foods with strong or unusual tastes. Many food and taste preferences are also learned from childhood experiences

When we eat and drink, liquids and dissolved foods flow over bumps on our tongue called *papillae* and into pores where the taste buds are located. The taste buds contain the receptors for taste.

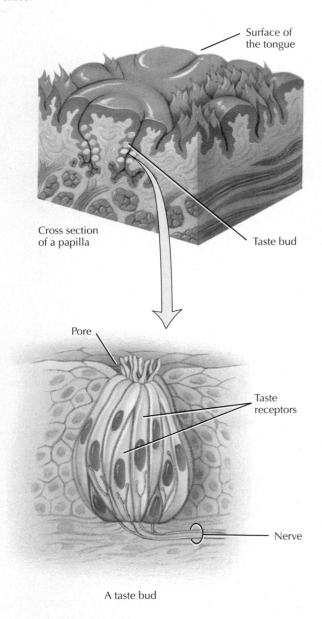

Surface of the tongue

Cross section of a papilla

Taste bud

Pore

Taste receptors

Nerve

A taste bud

the viscosity of axle grease. It is typically spread thinly on toast or crackers but is also used in cooking as a flavour enhancer. Most Canadians who have tried it dislike both the flavour and the texture of Vegemite, primarily because they were not exposed to its strong taste during childhood.

When we take away the sense of smell, there are five distinct tastes: sweet, sour, salty, bitter, and umami. *Umami* means "delicious" or "savoury" and refers to sensitivity to an amino acid called glutamate (Chandrashekar et al., 2006; McCabe & Rools, 2007). Glutamate is found in meats, meat broths, and monosodium glutamate (MSG). It is this flavour in soya sauce that makes it so appealing.

Taste receptors respond differentially to food molecules of different shapes. The major taste receptors (taste buds) are clustered on our tongues within little bumps called *papillae* (FIGURE 4.11).

THE BODY SENSES: MUCH MORE THAN JUST TOUCH

The senses that tell the brain how the body is oriented, where and how the body is moving, and what it touches or is touched by are called the body senses. They include the **skin senses**, the **vestibular sense**, and the kinesthetic sense.

Our skin is sensitive to touch (or pressure), temperature, and pain (FIGURE 4.12A). The concentration and depth of the receptors for each of these stimuli vary. For example, touch receptors are most concentrated on the face, genitals, and fingers and least so on the back and legs. Some receptors respond to more than one type of stimulation—for example, itching, tickling, and vibrating sensations seem to be produced by light stimulation of both pressure and pain receptors. We have more skin receptors for cold than for warmth, and we don't seem to have any receptors for hot at all. The sensation of hot occurs when the cold and warm receptors are simultaneously activated (Craig & Bushnell, 1994).

The *vestibular sense* is responsible for balance—it informs the brain of how the body, and particularly the head, is oriented with respect to gravity and three-dimensional space. When the head moves, liquid in the *semicircular canals*, located in the inner ear, moves and bends hair cell receptors. At the end of the

and cultural influences, so that one person's delicacy can be a source of revulsion to others. For example, most New Zealand and Australian children enjoy the flavour of Vegemite: a thick, black, savoury spread with

A The skin senses are vital. Skin not only protects our internal organs but also provides our brains with survival and attachment information. Both humans and non-human animals are highly responsive to physical contact and touch.

B Part of the thrill of amusement park rides comes from overloading the vestibular sense. This sense is used by the eye muscles to maintain visual fixation and sometimes by the body to change body orientation. We can become dizzy or nauseated if the vestibular sense is overloaded by boat, airplane, or automobile motion. Random versus anticipated movements increase chances of motion sickness, explaining why the driver of the car is generally the least likely to get sick. Children between ages 2 and 12 years have the greatest susceptibility to motion sickness, but this tends to decline with age.

C Without her finely tuned kinesthetic sense to provide information about her bodily posture, orientation, and movement, Canadian gymnast Nansy Damianova would be on her way to the hospital rather than the winner's podium.

semicircular canals are the *vestibular sacs*, which contain hair cells sensitive to the specific angle of the head—straight up and down or tilted. Information from the semicircular canals and the *vestibular sacs* is converted to neural impulses that are then carried to the appropriate section of the brain (**FIGURE 4.12B**).

Kinesthesia is the sense that provides the brain with information about bodily posture, orientation, and movement. Kinesthetic receptors are found throughout the muscles, joints, and tendons of the body. They tell the brain which muscles are being contracted or relaxed, how our body weight is distributed, where our arms and legs are in relation to the rest of our body, and so on (**FIGURE 4.12C**).

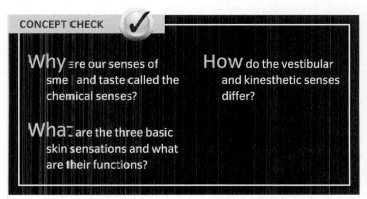

CONCEPT CHECK

Why are our senses of smell and taste called the chemical senses?

What are the three basic skin sensations and what are their functions?

How do the vestibular and kinesthetic senses differ?

The Magic of Perception

LEARNING OBJECTIVES

Describe the relationship among selective attention, feature detectors, and habituation.

Summarize the factors involved in perceptual interpretation.

Describe the limitations of subliminal perception.

While sensation is the process of receiving and translating raw sensory data from the environment, **perception** is the process of selecting, organizing, and interpreting the sensations into useful mental representations of the world. More simply, perception is the meaningful interpretation of our sensations. Certainly, sensation is remarkable, but the real power and creativity of the nervous system is showcased in perception. It is our perceptual system that makes the world feel real, cohesive, and meaningful.

SELECTION: EXTRACTING IMPORTANT INFORMATION

In almost every situation, we encounter more sensory information than we can reasonably pay attention to. Three major factors help us select and focus on some stimuli and ignore others: **selective attention**, **feature detectors**, and **habituation** (FIGURE 4.13).

Visualizing

Selection FIGURE 4.13

A Selective attention

When you are in a group of people, surrounded by various conversations, you can still select and attend to the voices of people you find interesting. Another example of selective attention occurs with the well-known cocktail party phenomenon. Have you noticed how you can suddenly pick up on another group's conversation if someone in that group mentions your name?

B Feature detectors

Cats possess cells, known as feature detectors, that respond to specific lines and angles (Hubel & Wiesel, 1965, 1979). Researchers found that kittens reared in a completely vertical world fail to develop the ability to detect horizontal lines or objects. Conversely, kittens restricted to only horizontal lines cannot detect vertical lines. A certain amount of interaction with the environment is necessary for feature detector cells to develop normally (Blakemore & Cooper, 1970).

C Habituation

After some time, these girls' brains will begin to ignore the sensations of their braces. (Sensory adaptation will also occur at the level of the sensory receptor).

Certain basic mechanisms for perceptual selection are built into the brain. For example, through the process of selective attention (see **FIGURE 4.13A**), the brain picks out the information that is important and relevant to us and ignores the rest (Folk & Remington, 1998; Kramer et al., 2000). Normally, our perceptions agree with our sensations. When they do not, the result is an *illusion*. See *Psychological Science*.

In humans and other animals, the brain contains specialized cells, called feature detectors, that respond only to certain sensory information (see **FIGURE 4.13B**). For example, humans have feature detectors in the temporal and occipital lobes that respond maximally to faces.

Deficits in these brain regions can produce a condition called prosopagnosia (*prospon* means "face" and *agnosia* means "failure to know") (Barton, 2008). People with this condition can recognize that they are looking at a face, but they cannot say whose face it is even if it is the face of a friend or relative. Similarly, they might see their own face in the mirror but do not recognize themselves.

Other examples of the brain's ability to filter experience are evidenced by habituation. The brain is "prewired" to pay more attention to changes in the environment than to stimuli that remain constant. For example, when braces are first applied or when they are tightened, they can be quite uncomfortable. After a while, however, awareness of the pain diminishes (refer back to **FIGURE 4.13C**). Note

Psychological Science

Optical Illusions

Illusions are either a false impression produced by an interpretation error in the perceptual process or by an actual physical distortion, such as in desert mirages. Illusions provide psychologists with a tool for studying the normal process of perception. Drawing A illustrates the *Müller-Lyer illusion*. The two vertical lines are the same length, but psychologists have learned that people who live in urban environments usually see the one on the right as longer. This is because they have learned to make size and distance judgements from perspective cues created by right angles and horizontal and vertical lines of buildings and streets.

Magnetic Hill (in image B) near Moncton, New Brunswick, is a famous example of an optical illusion. When a car is in neutral and facing what appears to be downhill, it will begin to roll backward—that is, the vehicle seems to be rolling uphill. This happens because the slope of Magnetic Hill is an optical illusion and the obstructed horizon confuses the perceptual system as to the correct grade of the slope. Look at C, which is known as the *ponzo illusion*. Do you perceive the top black line as being much larger than the one on the bottom? Both lines are the exact same size, but the converging lines provide depth cues telling you that the top dark line is farther away than the bottom line and therefore much larger.

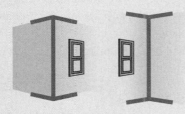

A Müller-Lyer illusion

B Magnetic Hill illusion

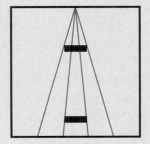

C Ponzo illusion

Stop & Think
1. What do you think causes "errors" in the perceptual process, such as in the optical illusions described here?
2. Look at the hubcaps on passing cars. Do they seem to be spinning backward? What do you think causes this false impression?

the difference between sensory adaptation, in which the diminished response occurs in the sense receptors, and habituation, in which the diminished response occurs in the brain.

As advertisers and political operatives well know, people tend to readily select stimuli that are intense, novel, moving, contrasting, and repetitious. For sheer volume of sales (or votes), the question of whether you like the ad is irrelevant; what matters is whether it gets your attention.

ORGANIZATION: FORM, CONSTANCY, DEPTH, AND COLOUR

Raw sensory data are like the parts of a clock—they must be assembled in a meaningful way before they are functional and useful. Our perceptual system organizes sensory data in terms of form, constancy, depth, and colour.

Form Perception: What Is It? Gestalt psychologists were among the first to study how the brain organizes sensory impressions into a *gestalt*—a German word meaning "form" or "whole." They emphasized the importance of organization and patterning in enabling us to perceive the whole stimulus rather than perceiving its discrete parts as separate entities. The Gestaltists proposed several laws of organization that specify how people perceive form (**FIGURE 4.14**).

Figure–Ground:
The ground is always seen as farther away than the figure. (You see the red shapes as the object and not the spaces between them.)

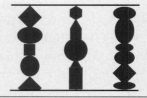

Proximity:
Objects that are physically close together are grouped together. (In this figure, we see 3 groups of 6 hearts, not 18 separate hearts.)

Continuity:
Objects that continue a pattern are grouped together.

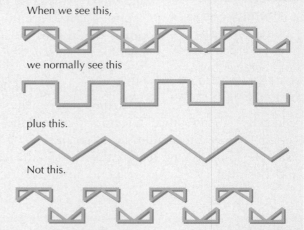

When we see this,

we normally see this

plus this.

Not this.

Closure:
There is the tendency to see a finished unit (triangle, square, or circle) from an incomplete stimulus.

Similarity:
Similar objects are grouped together (the green colored dots are grouped together and perceived as the number 5).

Gestalt principles of organization FIGURE 4.14

Figure-ground, proximity, continuity, closure, and similarity are shown here, but the Gestalt principle of contiguity cannot be shown because it involves nearness in time, not visual nearness. Although the examples of the Gestalt principles in this figure are visual, each principle applies to other modes of perception as well. You probably have experienced aural figure and ground effects; for example, in a lecture, when there was a conversation going on close by you. You might have found it difficult to sort out background sounds from those you wanted to focus on. This is especially difficult if the conversation is interesting or the lecture is boring or difficult.

VIEW THIS IN ACTION in your WileyPLUS course

Reversible and impossible figures FIGURE 4.15

A This Silver Jubilee vase of Queen Elizabeth (right side) and Prince Philip (left side) demonstrates alternating figure-ground relations. In one view the faces are perceived as the figure and in the other view the vase is the figure.

B When you first glance at this famous print by Dutch artist M. C. Escher, you detect specific features of the stimuli and judge them as sensible figures. But as you try to sort the different elements into a stable, well-organized whole, you realize they don't add up—they're impossible. There is no one-to-one correspondence between your actual sensory input and your final perception.

The most fundamental Gestalt principle of organization is our tendency to distinguish between figure (our main focus of attention) and ground (the background or surroundings).

Sometimes, however, it is very hard to distinguish the figure from the ground, as can be seen in FIGURE 4.15A. This is known as a reversible figure. Your perceptual system alternates what it sees as the figure.

Like *reversible figures, impossible figures* help us understand perceptual principles—in this case, the principle of form organization (FIGURE 4.15B).

Constancy: Keeping Sensations Understandable

See *What a Psychologist Sees* on the next page for a discussion of four perceptual constancies.

Depth Perception: How Far Away Is It?

In our three-dimensional world, the ability to perceive the depth and distance of objects—as well as their height and width—is essential. Imagine trying to parallel park or cross the road without the ability to perceive distance and depth. We usually rely most heavily on vision for this perception, but we also use other senses, such as hearing.

Depth perception is primarily learned through experience. However, research using an apparatus called the *visual cliff* (FIGURE 4.16) has shown that

Visual cliff FIGURE 4.16

Crawling infants hesitate or refuse to move to the "deep end" of the visual cliff (Gibson & Walk, 1960), indicating that they perceive the difference in depth. (The same is true for baby animals that walk almost immediately after birth.) Even 2-month-old infants show a change in heart rate when placed on the deep versus shallow side of the visual cliff (Banks & Salapatek, 1983).

Four Perceptual Constancies

As noted earlier with sensory adaptation and habituation, we are particularly alert to change in our environment. However, for some perceptions we also depend on some consistencies. Without this **perceptual constancy**, our world would be totally chaotic.

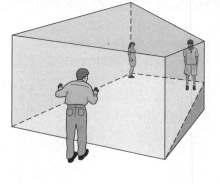

There are four basic perceptual constancies:

1. **Size constancy**. Although the more distant zebras in the photograph appear much smaller than those nearby, we perceive them as similar in size because of size constancy. According to this principle, the perceived size of an object remains the same even though the size of its image on the retina changes. Interestingly, size constancy, like all constancies, appears to develop from learning and experience. Studies of people who have been blind since birth and then have their sight restored find they have little or no size constancy (Sacks, 1995).

> ■ **perceptual constancy**
> Tendency for the environment to be perceived as remaining the same, even with changes in sensory input.

The Ames room illusion is based on the unusual construction of the room, and our perceptual constancies have falsely filled in the wrong details. To the viewer, peering through the peephole, the room appears normal. But in this specially constructed room, the trapezoidal shape and sloping ceilings and floors provide misleading depth cues. Because our brains mistakenly assume the two people are the same distance away, we compensate for the apparent size difference by making the person on the left appear much smaller.

Several Ames room sets were used in *The Lord of the Rings* film series to make the heights of the hobbits appear correct when standing next to Gandalf.

2. **Shape constancy.** As a coin is spun, it appears to change shape, but we still perceive it as the same coin because of shape constancy.

In this photo, the young boy on the right appears to be much larger than the woman on the left. The illusion is so strong that when a person walks from the left corner to the right corner, the observer perceives the person to be growing, even though that is not possible. How can this be?

3. **Colour constancy** and 4. **brightness constancy.** We perceive the dog's fur in this photo as having a relatively constant hue (or colour) and brightness, despite the fact that the wavelength of light reaching our retinas tends to vary as the light changes.

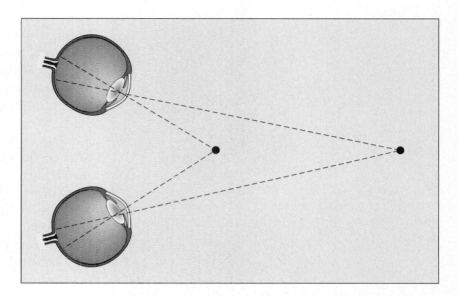

A Stare at your two index fingers a few centimetres in front of your eyes, holding the tips about half a centimetre apart. Do you see the "floating finger"? Move your fingers farther away and the finger will shrink. Move them closer and it will enlarge.

B Because of retinal disparity objects at different distances (such as the floating finger) project their images on different parts of the retina. Far objects project on the retinal area near the nose, whereas near objects project farther out, closer to the ears.

some of depth perception is present from very early in postnatal development.

One mechanism by which we perceive depth relies on having two forward facing eyes to produce **binocular cues**; the other involves **monocular cues**, which work regardless of eye placement.

One of the most important binocular cues for depth perception comes from **retinal disparity** (FIGURE 4.17). Because our eyes are about 6.5 centimetres (or two and a half inches) apart, each retina receives a slightly different view of the world. (Watch what happens when you point at a distant object, closing one eye and then the other.) When both eyes are open, the brain fuses the different images into one, an effect known as *stereoscopic vision*.

As we move closer to an object, a second binocular cue, **convergence**, helps us judge depth. The closer the object, the more our eyes are turned inward. The resulting amount of eye-muscle tension assists in interpreting distance.

The binocular (two eyes) cues of retinal disparity and convergence are inadequate in judging distances longer than about a football field. Luckily, we have a number of monocular cues available separately to each eye. The photo of the Taj Mahal in India (see FIGURE 4.18) contains several monocular cues. Can you identify which ones?

Two additional monocular cues are accommodation of the lens (discussed earlier) and motion parallax. In accommodation, muscles that adjust the shape of the lens as it focuses on an object send neural impulses to the brain, which interprets the signal to assist in distance perception. Motion parallax is the phenomenon that occurs when we are moving; close objects appear to whiz by whereas farther objects seem to move more slowly or remain stationary. This effect can easily be seen when you look out a window while travelling by car or train, and lampposts seem to zoom past while distant buildings move by much more slowly.

Colour Perception: The Vividness of Vision

Our colour vision is as remarkable as our ability to perceive depth and distance. Humans may be able to discriminate among seven million different hues, and research conducted in many cultures suggests that we all seem to see essentially the same coloured world (Davies, 1998). Furthermore, studies of infants old enough to focus and move their eyes show that they are able to see colour nearly as well as adults can (Knoblauch, Vital-Durand, & Barbur, 2000; Werner & Wooten, 1979).

Although we know colour is produced by different wavelengths of light, the actual way in which we perceive colour has been the subject of more than 150 years of scientific debate. There are two theories of colour vision: the trichromatic (three-colour theory) and the opponent-process theory. The **trichromatic theory** (from the Greek word *tri*, meaning "three," and *chroma*, meaning "colour") was first proposed by Thomas Young in the early nineteenth century and was later refined by Herman von Helmholtz and others. Apparently, we have three "colour systems," as they called them: one system that is maximally sensitive to red, another maximally sensitive to green, and another maximally sensitive to blue (Young, 1802). The proponents of this theory demonstrated that mixing lights of these three colours could yield the full spectrum of colours we perceive. Unfortunately this theory has its flaws. One is that it doesn't explain *colour after effects*, a phenomenon you can experience in the following *Applying Psychology* feature.

The **opponent-process theory**, proposed by Ewald Hering later in the nineteenth century, also has the three colour systems, but he suggested that each system is sensitive to two opposing colours—blue and yellow, red and green, black and white—in an "on-off" fashion. In other words, each colour receptor responds either to blue or yellow or to red or green, with the black-or-white systems responding to differences in brightness levels. This theory makes sense because when different-coloured lights are combined, people are unable to

> **trichromatic theory** The theory that colour perception results from mixing three distinct colour systems: red, green, and blue.

> **opponent-process theory** Theory that colour perception is based on three systems of colour receptors, each of which responds in an on-off fashion to opposite-colour stimuli: blue-yellow, red-green, and black-white.

Monocular cues FIGURE 4.18

Linear perspective Parallel lines converge, or angle toward one another, as they recede into the distance.

Interposition Objects that obscure or overlap other objects are perceived as closer.

Relative size Close objects cast a larger retinal image than distant objects.

Texture gradient Nearby objects have a coarser and more distinct texture than distant ones.

Aerial perspective Distant objects appear hazy and blurred compared with close objects because of intervening atmospheric dust or haze.

Light and shadow Brighter objects are perceived as closer than darker objects.

Relative height Objects positioned higher in our field of vision are perceived as farther away.

Applying Psychology

Colour After Effects

Try staring at the dot in the middle of this colour-distorted flag for 60 seconds. Then stare at a plain sheet of white paper. You should get interesting colour after effects—red in place of the green and white in place of black—giving you a "genuine" Canadian flag.

What happened? This is a good example of the opponent-process theory. As you stared at the figure, the green area stimulated only the green channel of the red-green opponent colour cells. Continuous stimulation fatigued the green channel, whereas the unstimulated red channel was not fatigued. When you looked at the piece of white paper, the white stimulated both the red and the green channels equally. Because the green channel was fatigued, the red channel fired at a higher rate and you therefore saw a red after effect. Without first staring at the white dot, the red and green receptors would have cancelled each other out and you would have seen white when you looked at the white paper.

Stop & Think
In what kinds of situations do you think colour after effects are likely to occur?

---

see reddish greens and bluish yellows. In fact, when red and green lights or blue and yellow lights are mixed in equal amounts, we see white.

In 1964, research by Paul Brown and George Wald showed we do have three types of cones in the retina, each responding optimally to red, green, or blue. This confirmed the central component of the trichromatic theory. At nearly the same time, R. L. DeValois (1965) was studying electrophysiological recording of cells in the optic nerve and optic pathways to the brain. He discovered that cells respond to colour in an opponent fashion in the thalamus. The findings reconciled the once-competing trichromatic and opponent-process theories. Now, we know that colour is processed in a trichromatic fashion at the level of the cones in the retina, and in an opponent fashion at the level of the optic nerve and the thalamus in the brain.

Colour-Deficient Vision

Most people perceive three different colours—red, green, and blue—and are called *trichromats*. However, a small percentage of the population has a genetic deficiency in the genes that code for either the red-green system, the blue-yellow system, or both. Those who perceive only two colours are called *dichromats*. People who are sensitive to only the black-white system are called *monochromats*, and they are totally colour blind. If you'd like to test yourself for red-green colour blindness, see FIGURE 4.19.

INTERPRETATION: EXPLAINING OUR PERCEPTIONS

After selectively sorting through incoming sensory information and organizing it, the brain uses this information to interpret, explain, and make judgements

Colour-deficient vision FIGURE 4.19

Are you red-green colour blind? People who suffer red-green deficiency have trouble perceiving the number within this design. Although we commonly use the term *colour blindness* most problems are colour confusion rather than colour blindness. Furthermore, most people who have some colour blindness are not even aware of it.

about the external world. This final stage of perception—interpretation—is influenced by several factors, including perceptual adaptation, perceptual set, frame of reference, and bottom-up or top-down processing.

George Stratton's (1897) experiment, which we discussed in the chapter opener, illustrates the critical role that *perceptual adaptation* plays in how we interpret the information that our brains gather. Without his ability to adapt and change his perceptions to a skewed environment, Stratton would not have been able to function. His brain's ability to "retrain" itself to his new surroundings allowed him to create coherence out of what would otherwise have been chaos. The ability to do this is an example of perceptual adaptation.

Our previous experiences, assumptions, and expectations also affect how we interpret and perceive the world by creating a *perceptual set*, or a readiness to perceive things in a particular manner, based on expectations—in other words, we largely perceive what we expect to perceive. It is perceptual set that influences how we interpret incoming sensory information (FIGURE 4.20).

How we perceive people, objects, or situations is also affected by the *frame of reference*, or context surrounding the object or situation. For example, an elephant is perceived as much larger when it is seen next to a mouse than when it stands next to a giraffe.

Finally, recall that we began this chapter by discussing how we receive sensory information (sensation) and work

Ψ Psychological Science

Subliminal Perception

Is the public under siege by sneaky advertisers and politicians lobbing subliminal (literally, "below the threshold") messages that can undermine our intentions and influence our behaviour? Can you lose weight, stop smoking, or relieve stress by listening to subliminal tapes that promise to solve your problems without your having to pay attention or exert any effort?

It is, in fact, possible to perceive something without conscious awareness (Aarts, 2007; Boccato et al., 2008; Cleeremans & Sarrazin, 2007). For example, in one study the experimenter very briefly flashed one of two pictures subliminally (either a happy or an angry face) followed by a neutral face. They found this subliminal presentation evoked

matching unconscious facial expressions in the participants' own facial muscles (Dimberg, Thunberg, & Elmehed, 2000).

Despite this result and considerable evidence that *subliminal perception* occurs, does it mean that such processes lead to *subliminal persuasion*? That is, is subliminal perception the same as subliminal persuasion—can we be manipulated to do things we are not aware of? Based on considerable research over many decades, the answer to this question is a very clear no. While subliminal stimuli can be detected in a variety of circumstances, at best, it has a minimal (if any) effect on consumer thinking and behaviour and no effect on citizens' voting behaviour (Begg, Needham, & Bookbinder, 1993; Dijksterhuis et al., 2005; Karremans et al., 2006). As for subliminal self-help tapes, you're better off with old-fashioned, tried and tested, conscious methods of self-improvement.

A now-classic Canadian media test of subliminal persuasion was conducted in the 1950s. During a popular Sunday night TV show called *Close-up*, viewers were flashed a subliminal message more than 300 times. When asked to guess what the message was, around 500 people wrote in and about half reported feeling hungry or thirsty during the show. Not one writer got the message correct, however. The subliminal message was simply "telephone now" ("Phone Now," 1958).

> **STOP**
> ### Stop & Think
> 1. Why do you think humans developed the capacity for subliminal perception?
> 2. What role might subliminal perception play in everyday life today?

Perceptual set: Is it a log on the water or the Loch Ness Monster? FIGURE 4.20

Imagine yourself driving along the road beside Loch Ness in the Scottish Highlands at dusk. This large, very deep freshwater lake near Inverness is most famous for the alleged sightings of the Loch Ness Monster or "Nessie." How might your perceptual system interpret this image if you saw it out your car window as you drove by? Is it a log floating on the water or is it the legendary monster? How you perceive it depends in part on your previous assumptions and expectations about the existence of the monster. If you believe in Nessie, then that is what you probably will think you have seen.

Bottom-up, top-down FIGURE 4.21

When first learning to read, you used bottom-up processing. You initially learned that certain arrangements of lines and squiggles represented specific letters. You later realized that these letters combine in memorable chunks to make up words.

Now, yuor aiblity to raed uisng top-dwon prcessoing mkaes it psosible to unedrstnad thsi snterece desipte its mnay mssipllengis.

our way upward to the top levels of perceptual processing (perception). Psychologists refer to this type of information processing as **bottom-up processing**. In contrast, **top-down processing** begins with higher, top-level processing involving thoughts, previous experiences, expectations, language, and cultural background and works down to the sensory level (FIGURE 4.21).

Science and ESP

So far in this chapter, we have talked about sensory input provided to our eyes, ears, nose, mouth, and skin. But is it possible for some people to perceive things that cannot be perceived using the usual sensory channels? Is there such a thing as **extrasensory perception (ESP)**? People who claim to have ESP profess to be able to read other people's minds (telepathy), perceive objects or events that are inaccessible to their normal senses (clairvoyance), predict the future (precognition), or move or affect objects without touching them (psychokinesis).

Scientific investigations of ESP began in the early twentieth century in a number of countries around the world, and some work on the subject continues today. After nearly a hundred years of research on the topic, the results have overwhelmingly found no conclusive evidence for ESP. For example, a meta-analysis of 30 studies using strong scientific controls reported absolutely no evidence of ESP (Milton & Wiseman, 1999, 2001; Valeo & Beyerstein, 2008).

Probably the most important criticism of both experimental and casual claims of ESP is their lack of stability and replication—a core requirement for general scientific acceptance (Hyman, 1996). Even offering a $1-million prize is not a strong enough inducement. As mentioned in Chapter 1, the James Randi Educational Corporation has long offered this prize to anyone who can demonstrate any paranormal event under proper scientific observation conditions. To date, despite many hundreds of applications, no one has ever passed even the preliminary test (Wagg, 2008). In fact, the corporation stopped offering the prize in March 2010 because many other international organizations are now offering similar and larger prizes. If you are interested in applying to one of these organizations, a list can be found at the Skeptic's Dictionary online (http://skepdic.com/ randi.html).

Why do so many people believe in ESP? As mentioned, our motivations and interests often influence our perceptions, driving us to selectively attend to things we want to see or hear. In addition, the subject of extrasensory perception often generates strong emotional responses. When individuals feel strongly about an issue, they sometimes fail to recognize the faulty reasoning underlying their beliefs.

Belief in ESP is particularly associated with failures in critical thinking (Chapter 1). For example, people often fall victim to the *fallacy of positive instances* (also known as the *confirmation bias* (Chapter 8), noting and remembering events that confirm personal expectations and beliefs and ignoring non-supportive evidence. This fallacy of positive instances may explain why some people play the lottery despite the overwhelming odds against winning (**FIGURE 4.22**). For these people, seeing other winners on television or in the newspaper confirms that they too could also win, if they buy a ticket. Finally, human information processing often biases us to notice and remember the most vivid information—such as a detailed (and spooky) anecdote or a heartfelt personal testimonial. A powerful or vivid personal story is far more memorable and convincing for many than a collection of "dry" scholarly negative findings on the subject.

Good luck or bad math skills? FIGURE 4.22

The odds of winning the big 6/49 prize is approximately 1 in millions. Some people believe that a set of six random numbers are more likely to win than a set of six consecutive numbers. However, the odds of a random set of six numbers or a consecutive set of six numbers being drawn from the 49 total numbers are exactly the same. Yet, why do many people think random number sets are more likely to win than consecutive number sets? It's because we often think random number sets are somehow more "random" than consecutive number sets and are therefore more likely to occur.

CONCEPT CHECK

Why do we experience perceptual illusions?

What are the processes that allow us to pay attention to some stimuli in our environments and ignore others?

What kinds of cues do we use to perceive depth and distance?

What factors entice some people to believe in ESP?

SUMMARY

1 Understanding Sensation

1. **Sensation** is the process by which we detect stimuli and convert them into neural signals (**sensory transduction**). **Labelled lines** are the mechanism by which different physical stimuli are interpreted by the brain as distinct **sensations**.

2. In **sensory adaptation**, sensory receptors in the periphery fire less frequently with repeated stimulation so that, over time, sensation decreases.

3. The absolute threshold is the smallest amount of a stimulus needed to detect a stimulus half the time, and the difference threshold, or just noticeable difference, is the smallest change in stimulus intensity that a person can detect.

4. According to the **gate-control theory**, our experience of pain depends partly on whether the neural message gets past a "gatekeeper" in the spinal cord.

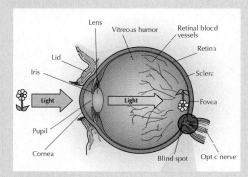

2 How We See and Hear

1. Light and sound move in waves. Light waves are a form of electromagnetic energy, and sound waves are produced when air molecules move in a particular wave pattern. Both light waves and sound waves vary in length, height, and range.

2. Light enters the eye at the front of the eyeball. The cornea protects the eye and helps focus light rays. The iris provides the eye's colour, and muscles in the iris dilate or constrict the pupil. The lens further focuses light, adjusting to allow focusing on objects at different distances. At the back of the eye, incoming light waves reach the **retina**, which contains photoreceptors called **rods** and **cones**. A network of neurons in the retina transmits neural information about light to the brain.

3. The **outer ear** gathers sound waves; the **middle ear** amplifies and concentrates the sounds; and the **inner ear** changes the mechanical energy of sound into neural impulses. The frequency and intensity of the sound wave determine how we distinguish among sounds of different pitches and loudness, respectively.

3 Our Other Senses

1. Smell and taste involve chemoreceptors that are sensitive to certain chemical molecules. In olfaction, odour molecules stimulate receptors in the olfactory epithelium in the nose. The resulting neural impulse travels to the olfactory bulb, where the information is processed before being sent elsewhere in the brain. Our sense of taste (gustation) involves five tastes: sweet, sour, salty, bitter, and umami. The taste buds are clustered on our tongues within the papillae.

2. The body senses tell the brain how the body is oriented, where and how it is moving, and what it touches. They include the **skin senses** the **vestibular sense**, and **kinesthesia**.

4 The Magic of Perception

1. **Perception** is the process of selecting, organizing, and interpreting incoming sensations into useful mental representations of the world. **Selective attention** allows us to filter out unimportant sensory messages. **Feature detectors** are specialized cells that respond only to specific sensory information. **Habituation** is the tendency of the brain to ignore stimuli that remain constant. People tend to automatically select stimuli that are intense, novel, moving, contrasting, and repetitious.

2. To be useful, sensory data must be assembled in a meaningful way. We organize sensory data in terms of form, constancy, depth, and colour. The **trichromatic theory** accounts for colour vision processing in the retina and the **opponent-process theory** accounts for processing in the brain.

3. Perceptual adaptation, perceptual set, frame of reference, and **bottom-up** versus **top-down processing** affect our interpretation of what we experience. Subliminal stimuli, although perceivable, have a minimal effect on thinking and behaviour.

4. Despite considerable scientific evidence against its existence, many people continue to believe in ESP.

KEY TERMS

- binocular cues p. 111
- blind spot p. 99
- bottom-up processing p. 115
- cochlea p. 100
- conduction deafness (middle-ear deafness) p. 102
- cones p. 99
- convergence p. 111
- depth perception p. 109
- extrasensory perception (ESP) p. 115
- feature detectors p. 107
- fovea p. 99
- frequency theory p. 101

- gate-control theory p. 96
- habituation p. 107
- inner ear p. 100
- kinesthesia p. 105
- labelled lines p. 94
- middle ear p. 100
- monocular cues p. 111
- nerve deafness (inner-ear deafness) p. 102
- opponent-process theory p. 112
- outer ear p. 100
- perception p. 107
- perceptual constancy p. 110
- place theory p. 100

- retina p. 99
- retinal disparity p. 111
- rods p. 99
- selective attention p. 107
- sensation p. 94
- sensory adaptation p. 95
- sensory transduction p. 94
- skin senses p. 104
- top-down processing p. 115
- trichromatic theory p. 112
- vestibular sense p. 104

CRITICAL AND CREATIVE THINKING QUESTIONS

1. Sensation and perception are closely linked. What is the primary distinction between the two?

2. If we detected and attended equally to all incoming stimuli, the amount of information would be overwhelming. What sensory and perceptual processes help us reduce and manage incoming sensory information?

3. Knowing that humans adapt to some types of pain, why is it that people can sometimes tune out painful injuries?

4. How might optical illusions contribute to a belief in ESP?

5. What senses would likely be impaired if a person were somehow missing all the apparatus of the ear (including the outer, middle, and inner ear)?

6. Why do you think when we have a bad cold our ability to taste food is severely diminished? What is it that prevents proper taste perception when our sense of smell is compromised?

7. As we age, the ability to hear high frequency sounds deteriorates. Other than the examples used in the text, what advantages and disadvantages could this confer to teenagers?

8. Can you explain how perceptual sets might contribute to the development of prejudice or discrimination?

This man willingly endures what would normally be excruciating pain. What psychological and biological factors might make this possible for him?

Do you think this man would feel more pain, or less, if his friends and family members were frequently and solicitously asking how he was feeling?

SELF-TEST

(Check your answers in Appendix A.)

1. Sensory transduction is the process of converting

_____.

   a. neural impulses into mental representations of the world

   b. receptors into transmitters

   c. a physical stimulus into neural impulses

   d. receptors into neural impulses

2. Labelled lines refer to how _____.

   a. people can reduce their dependence on a single sensory system by developing their ESP

   b. the eye processes visual information before it gets to the thalamus

   c. the brain interprets the type of sensory information by attending to its neural origin and destination in the brain

   d. the sensory receptors can reduce environmental sensations by physically preventing your sensory organs from seeing, hearing, and so on

3. You walk into a nightclub and the music is playing at a comfortable volume. Although the DJ has been slightly increasing the volume for the past hour, you actually only notice this perceptual change when he drastically increases the volume for a particular song. Which perceptual process is illustrated here?

   a. psychophysics   c. sensory deterioration

   b. absolute threshold   d. difference threshold

4. A martial-arts fighter breaks his wrist during a title fight, triggering a surprisingly brief sensation of pain. However, he is able to continue, eventually overcoming this setback to win the fight. Research suggests _____ facilitated the initial feelings of pain, while _____ blocked the feelings of pain so he could continue on and ultimately win the fight.

   a. serotonin; endorphins

   b. substance P; endorphins

   c. phantom limb pain; dopamine

   d. endorphins; substance P

5. HOW THE EYE SEES: Identify the parts of the eye, placing the labels on the figure below:

cornea   blind spot
iris   sclera
pupil   lid
lens   vitreous humour
retina   optic nerve
fovea

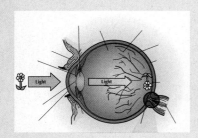

6. What is the visual acuity problem that occurs when the lens focuses an image in front of the retina?

a. farsightedness   c. myopia
b. hyperopia   d. presbyopia

7. When you eat a steak what taste sensation gives it its savoury quality?

a. salty   c. MSG
b. bitter   d. umami

8. HOW THE EAR HEARS: Identify the parts of the ear, placing the labels on the figure below:

pinna   auditory nerve
ear drum   stapes
malleus   oval window
incus   cochlea
auditory canal

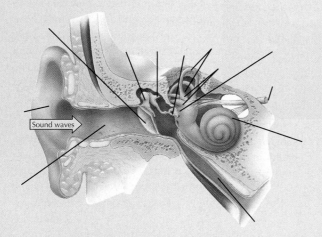

9. Chronic exposure to loud noise can cause permanent
_____ .

a. auditory illusions   c. nerve deafness
b. auditory hallucinations   d. conduction deafness

10. Which brain region contributes little to the processing of olfactory information?

a. the cerebral cortex   c. the olfactory bulb
b. the temporal lobe   d. the limbic system

11. Why is it that children generally dislike foods with strong or unusual tastes?

a. Because their brains are undeveloped
b. Because their taste buds are replaced more quickly than the taste buds of adults
c. Because their parents also dislike the same foods
d. Because their taste buds are replaced less quickly than the taste buds of adults

12. Touch receptors are most densely concentrated on the
_____ .

a. genitals   c. legs
b. back   d. All of the above

13. Identify which of these photos, 1 or 2, illustrates:

a. vestibular sense: photo _____
b. kinesthetic sense: photo _____

14. The *cocktail party phenomenon* is an example of

_____ .

a. sensory adaptation   c. selective attention

b. sensory habituation   d. feature detecting

15. In a(n) _____ , the discrepancy between figure and ground is too vague and you may have difficulty perceiving which is figure and which is ground.

a. illusion

b. reversible figure

c. optical illusion

d. hallucination

16. The tendency for the environment to be perceived as remaining the same even with changes in sensory input is called

_____ .

a. perceptual constancy

b. the constancy of expectation

c. an illusory correlation

d. Gestalt's primary principle

17. The theory of colour vision proposed by Thomas Young that says colour perception results from mixing three distinct colour systems is called the _____ .

a. tricolour theory

b. trichromatic theory

c. colour constancy

d. opponent-process theory

18. The following illustration is an example of _____ .

a. top-down processing

b. frame of reference

c. subliminal persuasion

d. perceptual adaptation

19. A readiness to perceive in a particular manner is known as

_____ .

a. sensory adaptation

b. perceptual set

c. habituation

d. frame of reference

20. Which explanation is one of the reasons given in the textbook to account for why so many people believe in ESP?

a. Failures of good information

b. Failures of education, particularly high school math

c. Failures of media sources to provide accurate and reliable information

d. Failures of critical thinking

States of Consciousness

On November 5, 1999, 16-year-old Erik Ramsey was a passenger in his friend's Camaro when it collided with a minivan. Erik sustained significant injuries but worst among them was the brain trauma that caused the formation of a blood clot near the *pons*. The accident caused an extremely rare and permanent condition known as locked-in syndrome.

While Erik's consciousness, memory, emotions, and reason were all intact, and he could see, hear and feel, he could no longer move or speak. The only muscles that remained under Erik's voluntary command were the ones that controlled the up and down movement of his eyes. Soon after the accident a speech therapist noted that if he could look up and down he could still say yes or no—up for *yes* and down for *no*.

"Erik, are you deaf?" was the first question the therapist asked. Erik looked down. "So you must be tired of people yelling at you?" Erik looked up opening his eyes emphatically (Foer, 2008). What if Erik had not been able to move his eyes? If he couldn't communicate at all, would he still be "conscious"? Contrast Erik's condition with that of Terri Schiavo (Chapter 2) who sustained devastating damage to her cortex but whose brain stem was largely intact. Was Terri conscious?

In this chapter, we begin with a general look at the definition and description of consciousness. Then we examine how consciousness changes because of our circadian rhythms, sleep, and dreams. We also look at psychoactive drugs and their effects on consciousness. Finally, we explore two alternative routes to altered consciousness: meditation and hypnosis.

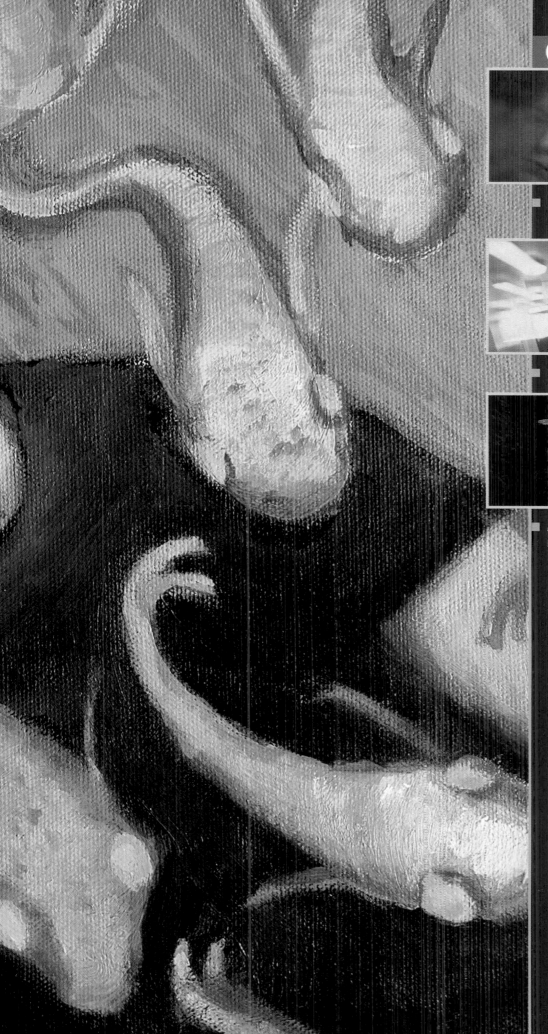

123

Consciousness, Sleep, and Dreaming

LEARNING OBJECTIVES

Explain the difference between controlled and automatic processes.

Describe the effects of sleep deprivation and disruption of circadian rhythms.

Review the stages of sleep.

Compare and contrast the theories of why we sleep and dream.

Summarize the types of sleep disorders.

illiam James, the first American psychologist, likened **consciousness** to a stream that's constantly present, constantly changing, and yet always the same. Like liquid, it meanders and flows, sometimes where the person wills it and sometimes not. Through the process of selective attention (Chapter 4), we can influence our consciousness by deliberately providing focused attention on something or someone. For example, right now, you are awake and concentrating on the words on this page. At times, however, your control may weaken, and your stream of consciousness may drift back to thoughts of Erik Ramsey or forward to a computer or cellphone you want to buy, your work, or a hot classmate.

In addition to meandering and flowing, your "stream of consciousness" also varies in depth. Consciousness is not an either/or phenomenon—conscious or not conscious. Instead, it exists along a continuum. As you can see in **FIGURE 5.1**, this continuum extends from high awareness and sharp, focused alertness at one extreme, to middle levels of awareness, such as during daydreaming, to no awareness and coma at the other extreme.

Other than awake, two of the more common states of consciousness are sleep and dreaming. You may think of yourself as being unconscious while you sleep, but that's not the case. Rather, you are in an **altered state of consciousness (ASC)**.

To understand sleep and dreaming, we need to first explore **circadian rhythms**. Most organisms have adapted to our planet's daily cycle of light and dark by developing a pattern of bodily functions that wax and wane over each 24-hour period. Our activity, alertness, core body temperature, moods, learning efficiency, blood pressure, metabolism, and pulse rate all follow these circadian rhythms (Leglise, 2008; Oishi et al., 2007; Sack et al., 2007). Usually, these processes reach their peak at some point during the day and their low point at night (**FIGURE 5.2**).

Disruptions to circadian rhythms—such as shift work, sleep deprivation, and long international flights—cause increased fatigue, decreased concentration, sleep disorders, and other health problems (James, Cermakian, & Bolvin, 2007; Lader, 2007; Salvatore et al., 2008). Those employees who work on a rotating work schedule or do shift work experience many of these problems. Although security guards, emergency room personnel, police, and others who have these types of schedules can and do function, studies have shown that shift work and sleep deprivation can lead to decreased concentration and impaired productivity—as well as increased numbers of accidents (Dembe et al., 2006; Papadelis et al., 2007; Yegneswaran & Shapiro, 2007). One way to reduce the negative effects of a rotating work schedule is by rolling into the next work schedule clockwise—that is, moving from days to evenings to night shifts. This requires less of an adjustment than doing it the other way around—probably because it's easier to go to bed later when a schedule changes than to do the reverse. Productivity and safety also increase when shifts are rotated once every three weeks versus once per week.

Research has shown that after 17 to 19 hours without sleep, people's test performance, reaction time, and

---

consciousness
An organism's awareness of its own self and surroundings (Damasio, 1999).

altered state of consciousness (ASC) Mental states found generally during sleep, dreaming, psychoactive drug use, and hypnosis.

circadian
[ser-KAY-dee-an]
rhythms Biological, biochemical, and behavioural changes that occur in living organisms on a 24-hour cycle (in Latin, *circa* means "about," and *dies* means "day").

Where Does Consciousness Reside?

One of the oldest philosophical debates is the *mind–body issue*. Is the "mind" (consciousness and other mental functions) fundamentally different from "matter" (the body)? How can a mind influence a physical body and vice versa? Most neuropsychologists today believe the mind *is* the brain and *consciousness* involves an activation and integration of several parts of the brain. But two aspects of consciousness, *awareness* and *arousal*, seem to rely on specific areas. Awareness generally involves the *cerebral cortex*, particularly the frontal lobes. Arousal generally results from *brain-stem* activation (Revonsuo. 2006; Thomson, 2007; Zillmer, Spiers, & Culbertson, 2008).

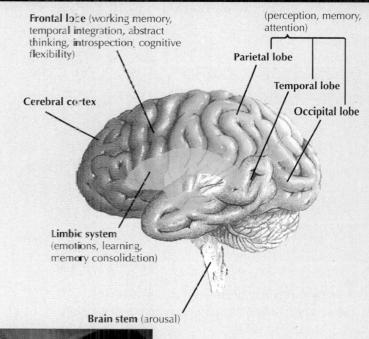

Frontal lobe (working memory, temporal integration, abstract thinking, introspection, cognitive flexibility)

(perception, memory, attention)

Parietal lobe

Temporal lobe

Occipital lobe

Cerebral cortex

Limbic system (emotions, learning, memory consolidation)

Brain stem (arousal)

LEVELS OF AWARENESS

Altered states of consciousness (ASCs) can exist on many levels of awareness, from high awareness to low awareness.

High Awareness

CONTROLLED PROCESSES
Require focused, maximum attention (e.g., studying for an exam, learning to drive a car)

Middle Awareness

AUTOMATIC PROCESSES
Require minimal attention (e.g., walking to class while talking on a cellphone, listening to your instructor while daydreaming)

SUBCONSCIOUS
Below conscious awareness (e.g., sleeping, dreaming)

Low Awareness

NO AWARENESS
Biologically based lowest level of awareness (e.g., head injuries, anaesthesia, coma)

NATIONAL GEOGRAPHIC

What controls circadian rhythms? FIGURE 5.2

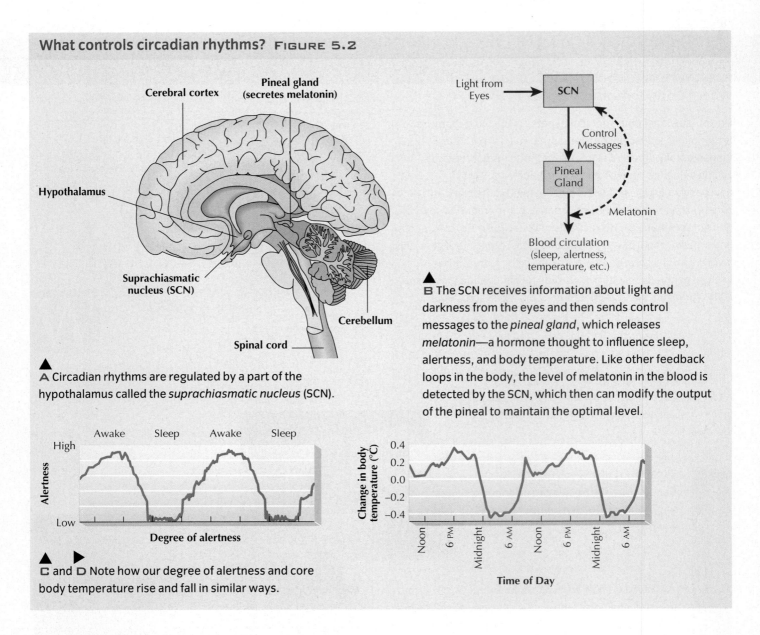

A Circadian rhythms are regulated by a part of the hypothalamus called the *suprachiasmatic nucleus* (SCN).

B The SCN receives information about light and darkness from the eyes and then sends control messages to the *pineal gland*, which releases *melatonin*—a hormone thought to influence sleep, alertness, and body temperature. Like other feedback loops in the body, the level of melatonin in the blood is detected by the SCN, which then can modify the output of the pineal to maintain the optimal level.

C and D Note how our degree of alertness and core body temperature rise and fall in similar ways.

---

accuracy on attention, memory, and other cognitive tasks is actually *worse* than for those with a blood alcohol concentration (BAC) of 0.05! After longer periods without sleep, performance reached levels equivalent to having a BAC of 1.0 (Williamson & Feyer, 2000). As a comparison, in Canada it is a criminal offence to drive with a BAC limit over 0.08. For new drivers this limit is 0.00.

Like shift work, flying across several time zones can also disrupt circadian rhythms. Symptoms of jet lag include fatigue, gastrointestinal problems, and irritability. Jet lag is also correlated with decreased alertness, decreased mental agility, reduced efficiency, and symptom exacerbation of psychiatric disorders (Dawson, 2004; Leglise, 2008; Morgenthaler et al., 2007; Sack et al., 2007). Jet lag generally tends to be worse when we

fly eastward because our bodies find it more difficult to go to bed earlier—as in Eastern time zones, than going to bed later—as in Western time zones.

What about long-term sleep deprivation? Exploring the scientific effects of severe sleep loss is limited by both ethical and practical concerns. For example, historically, many cultures have used chronic sleep deprivation as a form of torture, making it difficult to get ethical approval in a modern research setting to expose participants to it. Moreover, chronically sleep-deprived research participants involuntarily fall into repeated *microsleeps*. These tiny sleep bouts last only seconds at a time but can influence research findings. Sleep-deprived participants are also subject to stress effects, which have their own negative consequences,

Applying Psychology

A Wake-Up Call: Are You Sleep Deprived?

Take the following test to determine whether you are sleep deprived.

Part 1 Set up a small mirror next to the text. Using your non-dominant hand, try to trace the black star pictured here while watching your hand in the mirror. The task is difficult, and sleep-deprived people typically make many errors. If you are not sleep deprived, it may be difficult to trace the star, but you'll probably do it more accurately.

Part 2 Give yourself one point each time you answer yes to the following questions:

Do you often fall asleep . . .
watching TV?
during boring shows or lectures or in warm rooms?
after heavy meals or after a small amount of alcohol?
while relaxing after dinner? within five minutes of getting into bed?

In the morning, do you generally . . .
need an alarm clock to wake up at the right time?
struggle to get out of bed?
hit the snooze bar several times before getting up?

During the day, do you . . .
feel tired, irritable, and stressed out?
have trouble concentrating and remembering?
feel mentally sluggish when it comes to critical thinking, problem solving, and creativity?

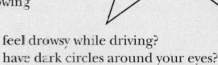

feel drowsy while driving?
have dark circles around your eyes?

If you answered yes to three or more items, you probably are not getting enough sleep.

Renowned sleep researcher and founder of the Stanford University Center for Human Sleep Research Dr. William C. Dement has stated that traditional-age college and university students need more than eight hours of sleep per night—plus or minus one hour depending on individual variation (Dement, 1997). When was the last time you had that amount of sleep at night?

Source: Quiz adapted and reprinted from Maas (1999), with permission.

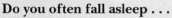

Stop & Think
1. If you are sleep deprived, what steps could you take to get more sleep?
2. Could driving while sleepy be as dangerous as driving after drinking two beers?

and must be separated from the effects of the sleep deprivation variables.

Nonetheless, researchers have learned that, like disrupted circadian cycles, sleep deprivation poses several hazards. These include reduced cognitive and motor performance, irritability and other mood alterations, decreased self-esteem, and elevated levels of the stress hormone *cortisol* (Dembe et al., 2006; Mirescu et al., 2006; Papadelis et al., 2007; Sack et al., 2007; Yegneswaran & Shapiro, 2007). While sleep deprivation has a number of negative effects it does not cause hallucinations and psychosis as was once thought (Coren, 1996).

To underline how essential sleep is, consider this finding: Research has shown when rats are totally sleep deprived, they die on average after 19 days. Letting the animals sleep prevents their death (Rechtschaffen & Bergmann, 2002).

An accumulating total of lost sleep is called a **sleep debt** and the consequences for students are wide ranging and include decreased school performance; reduced vigilance, attention, and concentration; and impairments to physical health. According to Dement (1997) if you are feeling drowsy it is the *last step* before falling asleep and not the first indication of your tiredness. Perhaps the most frightening danger, however, is that lapses in attention among sleep-deprived workers such as pilots, physicians, truck drivers, and other workers cause serious accidents and cost thousands of lives each year (Dembe et al., 2006; de Pinho et al., 2006; Paice et al., 2002; Yegneswaran & Shapiro, 2007).

STAGES OF SLEEP: HOW SCIENTISTS STUDY SLEEP

Surveys and interviews provide only limited information about the nature of sleep, and so researchers in sleep laboratories use a number of sophisticated instruments to study the physiological changes that occur during sleep.

Imagine that you are a participant in a sleep experiment. When you arrive at the sleep lab, you are assigned one of several—usually sparse—bedrooms. The researcher then hooks you up to various physiological recording devices (FIGURE 5.3A). You will need a night or two to "adjust" to the equipment (read: get lousy sleep) before the researchers can begin to monitor your typical night's sleep. As you fall asleep, you first enter a relaxed *presleep* state. As you continue relaxing, your brain's electrical activity slows. Over the next hour or so, you move through four distinct stages of sleep (stages 1 through 4), each progressively deeper (FIGURE 5.3B). Then the sequence reverses itself. Although you don't necessarily go through all sleep stages in this sequence all the time, during the night, people usually complete four to five cycles of light to deep sleep and back, with each complete cycle lasting about 90 minutes.

REM and NREM Sleep   Figure 5.3B also shows an interesting phenomenon that occurs at the end of the first sleep cycle (and subsequent cycles). You reverse back through stages 3 and 2. Scalp recordings then abruptly display a pattern of small-amplitude, fast-wave activity, similar to the cortical activity of an awake, relaxed person. Your breathing and pulse rates become faster and more irregular than during stages 3 and 4, and your genitals likely show signs of arousal. Yet your musculature is deeply relaxed and unresponsive. Because of these contradictory qualities, this stage is sometimes referred to as *paradoxical sleep.*

During this stage of paradoxical sleep, rapid eye movements occur under closed eyelids. Researchers therefore also refer to this same sleep stage as **rapid-eye-movement (REM) sleep**. When awakened from REM sleep, people generally wake refreshed and almost always report dreaming. Because REM sleep is so different from the other periods of sleep, stages 1 through 4 are often collectively referred to as

non-rapid-eye-movement (NREM) sleep. Dreaming can occur during NREM sleep but it's less frequent, and the dreams usually contain a simple idea or emotion, such as "I dreamed of a house" (Hobson, 2002; Squier & Domhoff, 1998). It is usually more difficult to awaken people from stages 3 or 4 than from other sleep stages, and they often wake feeling groggy.

Scientists believe that REM sleep is important for learning and consolidating new memories (Marshall & Born, 2007; Massicotte-Marquez et al., 2008; Silvestri & Root, 2008). Evidence of the importance of REM sleep for complex brain functions comes from the research findings that show the net amount of REM sleep increases after periods of stress or intense learning and that fetuses, infants, and young children—the age ranges involved in the greatest amounts of learning and adaptation—spend a large percentage of their sleep time in this stage. In addition, REM sleep occurs only in higher-order mammals and is absent in non-mammals, such as reptiles (Rechtschaffen & Siegel, 2000). Finally, when deprived of REM sleep, most people "catch up" later by spending more time than usual in this stage, underlining its inherent importance (Dement & Vaughan, 1999). As you will see, however, the exact function of sleep and its various stages is still a bit of a mystery.

NREM sleep may be even more important to our biological functioning than REM sleep. When people are temporarily deprived of *total* sleep, they spend more time in NREM sleep during their first uninterrupted night of sleep, as if they are making up for the time they missed (Borbely, 1982). Only after our need for NREM sleep has been satisfied each night do we begin to devote time to REM sleep. Further, studies show that adults who sleep five or fewer hours each night (*short sleepers*) spend less time in REM sleep than do those who sleep nine or more hours (*long sleepers*). Similarly, infants get much more sleep and have a higher percentage of REM sleep (about 40 percent of total daily sleep during the first six months of life) than do adults (about 20 percent of total daily sleep at

> ■ **rapid-eye-movement (REM) sleep**
> Stage of sleep marked by rapid eye movements, high-frequency brain waves, paralysis of large muscles, and dreaming.
>
> ■ **non-rapid-eye-movement (NREM) sleep**
> Stages 1 to 4 of sleep.

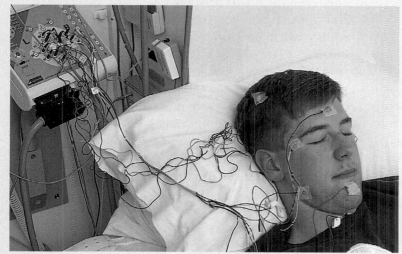

A Sleep research participants wear electrodes on their heads and bodies to measure the brain's and body's behavioural and physiological responses during the sleep cycle.

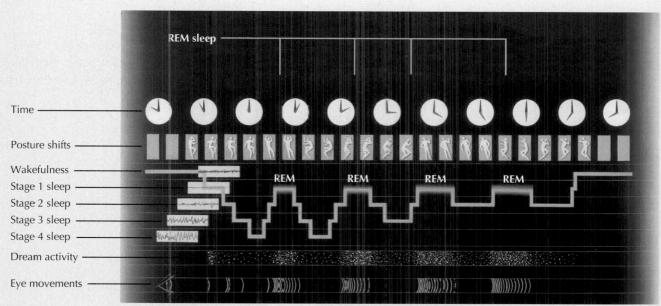

B *An electroencephalogram (EEG)* records neural activity in the outer layers of the cortex by means of small electrodes placed on the scalp. Other electrodes measure muscle activity and eye movements. The stages of sleep are defined by telltale changes in cortical activity and are indicated by the green stepped lines on the figure. The short, compact EEG waves of wakefulness gradually lengthen as people drift into stages 1–4 (red lines). During stage 2 sleep, if awakened the sleeper will often deny sleeping. You have probably encountered this yourself when you try to turn off the TV and your companion, who has had his or her eyes closed sleeping on the couch next to you, then protests loudly. By the end of stage 4, a change in body position generally occurs and heart rate, blood pressure, and respiratory rates all decrease. The sleeper then reverses back through stages 3 and 2 before entering the first REM period of the night. Although the brain and body are giving many signs of active arousal during REM sleep, the major muscle groups are deeply relaxed and temporarily paralyzed. Sleepers awakened from REM sleep often report vivid, bizarre storylike dreams, indicated in the figure by the abundant red and yellow dots beside the dream activity label. Those awakened from stages 1–4 sleep usually report less active thoughts. Note how the length of the REM period increases as the night progresses and the length of stage 3 and 4 sleep diminishes considerably.

age 19, declining to about 14 percent in old age) (**FIGURE 5.4**).

Another developmental change that occurs as we age involves our biological clock. After puberty, and as we get older, our biological clock speeds up, which is why, in general, young adults do not feel like sleeping until much later at night and do not want to wake early in the morning. As we age, the time we start to feel tired gets earlier in the evening, as does our wake-up time. This explains why your grandparents are often up and about when you have only been in bed a few hours and provides some insights why you feel so tired in that 8:30 A.M. class. Incidentally, you are not alone; 60 to 70 percent of Canadian adolescents report that their sleepiest time of the day is between 8 and 10 A.M. (Canadian Institute of Health Research & Institute of Population and Public Health, 2002).

Why Do We Sleep?
There are two prominent theories about why we sleep. The **evolutionary/ circadian theories** emphasize the relationship between sleep and basic circadian rhythms. Sleep keeps animals still and safe when predators are active and allows them to conserve energy when not foraging or finding mates (Siegel, 2008) (**FIGURE 5.5**).

In contrast, the **repair/ restoration theories** stress that sleep helps us recuperate physically, emotionally, and intellectually from daily activities that deplete our reserves (Maas, 1999).

Which theory is correct? Researchers do not currently know. Neither may be correct,

> ■ **evolutionary/ circadian theories** As a part of circadian rhythms, sleep evolved to conserve energy and to serve as protection from predators.
>
> ■ **repair/restoration theories** Sleep serves a recuperative function, allowing organisms to repair or replenish key cognitive and physiological factors.

The relationship between aging and the sleep cycle FIGURE 5.4

Have you ever noticed how much babies sleep and how little sleep older people seem to need? Our biological need for sleep changes throughout our lifetimes. The pie charts in this figure show the relative amounts of REM sleep (dark blue), NREM sleep (medium blue), and awake time (light blue) that the average person experiences as an infant, as an adult, and as an older person.

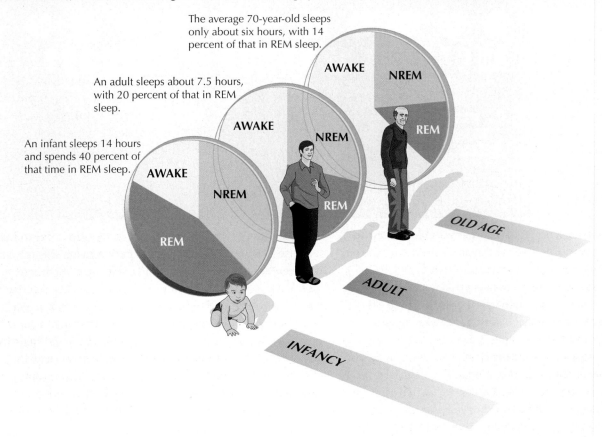

The average 70-year-old sleeps only about six hours, with 14 percent of that in REM sleep.

An adult sleeps about 7.5 hours, with 20 percent of that in REM sleep.

An infant sleeps 14 hours and spends 40 percent of that time in REM sleep.

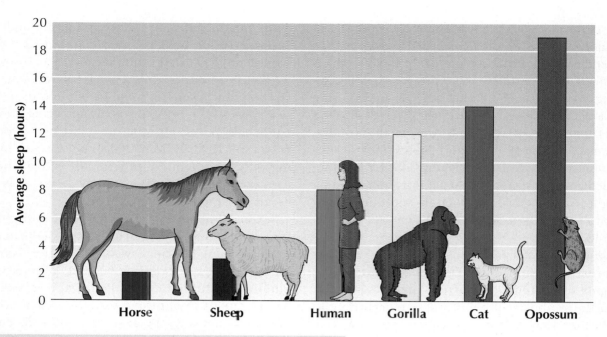

Average daily hours of sleep for different mammals

FIGURE 5.5

According to the evolutionary/circadian theory, differences in diet and number of predators affect different species' sleep habits. Animals that sleep the longest are the least threatened by predators and can easily find food, while animals that must constantly forage or have many predators sleep the least.

or it may be that both are correct—that sleep initially served to conserve energy and keep us out of trouble, but over time it has evolved to allow for repair and restoration.

Why Do We Dream?

The question of why we dream—and whether dreams carry special meaning or information—has fascinated and perplexed psychologists at least as much as the question of why we sleep. Currently there are three theories of why we dream.

The *activation–synthesis* hypothesis suggests that dreams are a by-product of random stimulation of neurons during REM sleep (Hobson, 1999, 2005). Alan Hobson and Robert McCarley (1977) proposed that specific neurons in the brainstem fire spontaneously during REM sleep and these signals are transmitted via the thalamus to the cortex. The cortex then struggles to "synthesize" or make sense out of this random stimulation by manufacturing coherent patterns or dreams. Dreams then, according to this theory, represent random neural brain stem activity that the cortex attempts to apply meaning to. This is not to say that dreams are

meaningless. Hobson (1988, 2005) suggests that even if dreams begin with essentially random brain activity, your individual personality, motivations, memories, and life experiences, stored in your cortex, guide how your brain constructs the dream. This makes sense when we consider how personal our dreams are; we generally dream of friends, family, and personal events—products of our own experiences, stored in our own brains.

A second theory as to why we dream is the *cognitive view*. In this perspective dreams are simply another type of information processing. That is, our dreams help us to periodically sift and sort our daily experiences and thoughts. During sleep the brain shuts out sensory input so that it can process, consolidate, and assimilate information. The body of evidence in support of this theory is the relationship between learning and increased REM sleep mentioned earlier and the strong similarities between dream content and waking thoughts, fears, and concerns (Domhoff, 2005, 2007; Erlacher & Schredl, 2004).

One of the oldest and most scientifically controversial explanations for why we dream is Freud's *psychoanalytic view*. Freud proposed that unacceptable desires, which are normally repressed, rise into consciousness during dreaming. We avoid anxiety, Freud believed, by disguising our forbidden, unconscious needs (what Freud called the dream's latent content) as symbols (the manifest content or the actual storyline of the dream). For example, a journey is supposed to symbolize death; horseback riding and dancing would symbolize sexual intercourse; and a gun might represent a penis. What do you think might represent a vagina? (We discuss Freud's theory further in Chapter 12.)

Most current sleep research does not support Freud's view (Domhoff, 2004; Dufresne, 2007). Critics also argue that Freud's theory is highly subjective and that the symbols can be interpreted according to the particular view or training of the psychoanalyst providing the dream analysis.

SLEEP DISORDERS

Mental health professionals divide sleep disorders into two major diagnostic categories: dyssomnias, which describe problems sleeping, and parasomnias, which describe abnormal sleep disturbances.

The most common of the three **dyssomnias** is *insomnia*. Although it's normal to have trouble sleeping from time to time, such as before an exciting event, as many as 1 in 10 people has persistent difficulty falling asleep or staying asleep, or wakes too early. Most people report some form of clinical insomnia at some point in their life (Pearson, Johnson & Nahin, 2006; Riemann & Voderholzer, 2003; Wilson & Nutt, 2008). A telltale sign of insomnia is feeling poorly rested and tired the next day. Most people with serious insomnia have other medical or psychological disorders, such as depression, anxiety disorders, or addiction, that co-occur with the insomnia (Riemann & Voderholzer, 2003; Taylor, Lichstein, & Durrence, 2003).

Despite advertising claims, non-prescription over-the-counter insomnia pills generally don't do a good job of treating insomnia. Prescription tranquilizers and barbiturates do help people sleep, but they decrease stage 4 and REM sleep and thereby affect sleep quality. In the short term, drugs, such as Ambien, Xanax, Halcion, and Lunesta, seem to be helpful in treating sleep problems related to anxiety and acute, stressful situations; however, chronic use can cause dependency (Leonard, 2003; McKim, 2002). Because of this, sleeping pills are intended only for occasional short-term use, and users should be acutely aware of becoming dependent on them to fall asleep.

Narcolepsy is another serious dyssomnia, characterized by sudden and irresistible sleep bouts that occur during normal waking hours. Narcolepsy afflicts about 1 person in 2,000 and generally runs in families (Billiard, 2007; Pedrazzoli et al., 2007; Siegel, 2000). Symptoms usually appear when the person is between 10 and 20 years old, and once the sleep attacks develop, they continue throughout life. During an attack, REM-like sleep suddenly intrudes into the waking state of consciousness. Victims may experience sudden, incapacitating attacks of muscle weakness or paralysis (known as cataplexy). They may fall asleep while walking, talking, during sex (after sex is normal), or while driving a car. Although long naps each day and stimulant or antidepressant drugs may help reduce the frequency of narcoleptic attacks, researchers are only just beginning to understand the causes and develop possible cures (**FIGURE 5.6**).

Perhaps the most serious dyssomnia is *sleep apnea*. People with sleep apnea repeatedly stop breathing for between 10 seconds and 1 minute or longer during sleep. They then wake up gasping for breath—often quite loudly. When they do breathe during their sleep, they often snore. Although people with sleep apnea are often unaware of it, the repeated awakenings result in insomnia and leave the person feeling tired and sleepy during the day. Sleep apnea seems to result from blocked upper airway passages or from the brain ceasing to send signals to the diaphragm, thus causing breathing to stop. This disorder can lead to high blood pressure, stroke, and heart attack (Billiard, 2007; Hartenbaum et al., 2006; McNicholas & Javaheri, 2007; National Sleep Foundation, 2007).

Treatment for sleep apnea depends partly on its severity. If the problem occurs only when a person sleeps on his or her back, sewing tennis balls to the

dyssomnias
Problems in the amount, timing, and quality of sleep, including insomnia, sleep apnea, and narcolepsy.

Narcolepsy FIGURE 5.6

William Dement and his colleagues at the Stanford Center for Narcolepsy have bred a group of narcoleptic dogs, which increased our understanding of the genetics of this disorder. Research on these specially bred dogs have found degenerated neurons in certain areas of the brain (Siegel, 2000). Whether human narcolepsy results from similar degeneration is a question for future research, but human narcolepsy seems to be caused by a deficiency in hypocretin-1, a type of peptide (protein-based) hormone (Nishino et al., 2000).

back of a pyjama top may encourage the person to sleep on his or her side. This of course would not work if you don't wear pyjamas. Because obstruction of the breathing passages can be related to obesity and heavy alcohol use (Christensen, 2000), losing weight and restricting alcohol are often recommended For others, surgery, dental appliances that reposition the tongue, or machines that provide a stream of air to keep the airway open may be the answer (FIGURE 5.7).

Sleep apnea FIGURE 5.7

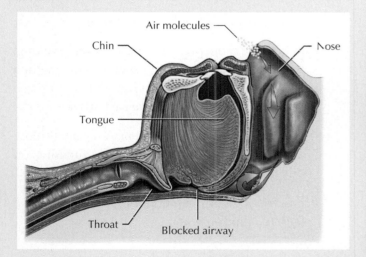

A During sleep apnea, airways are blocked, causing breathing to be severely restricted. To treat this disorder, researchers and doctors have created equipment to promote respiration.

B For some patients, there is help from dental devices that reposition the tongue and open the airway.

C Another treatment for sleep apnea is a machine that provides a steady supply of air to keep the airway open.

Recent findings suggest that snoring alone (without the breathing stoppage characteristic of sleep apnea) can lead to heart disease (Stone & Redline, 2006). Although occasional mild snoring remains somewhat normal, chronic snoring is a potential "warning sign that should prompt people to seek help" (Christensen, 2000, p. 172).

The second major category of sleep disorders, **parasomnias**, includes abnormal sleep disturbances, such as nightmares and *night terrors* (**FIGURE 5.8**).

■ **parasomnias**
Abnormal disturbances occurring during sleep, including nightmares, night terrors, sleepwalking, and sleep talking.

Sleepwalking, which can accompany night terrors, usually occurs during NREM sleep. (Recall that large muscles are paralyzed during REM sleep). Sleep talking can occur during any stage of sleep but is most common during NREM sleep. It can consist of single indistinct words or long, articulate sentences. It is even possible to engage some sleep talkers in a limited conversation.

Nightmares or night terrors? FIGURE 5.8

Nightmares, or bad dreams, occur toward the end of the sleep cycle, usually during REM sleep. More frightening are night terrors, which occur early in the cycle, usually during NREM sleep stages 3 or 4. Night terrors are very common in childhood and typically present with the sleeper suddenly sitting bolt upright, screaming and sweating, walking around, or talking incoherently. The sleeper may also be difficult to awaken. The parent, who is woken by the screaming or crying, usually calms the child and helps him or her settle back to sleep. In the morning the child usually has no memory of the event.

Nightmares, night terrors, sleepwalking, and sleep talking are all more common among young children, but they can also occur to a lesser extent in adults, usually during times of stress or major life events (Billiard, 2007; Hobson & Silvestri, 2009). Patience and soothing reassurance at the time of the sleep disruption are usually the most effective treatments for both children and adults.

A large-scale study reported that behaviour therapy had good success in treating some sleep problems (Constantino et al., 2007; Smith et al., 2005). You can use similar techniques in your own life if you experience transient disordered sleep:

- When you're having a hard time falling sleep, don't keep checking the clock and worrying about your loss of sleep.

- Remove all TVs, stereos, and books from the bedroom and limit use of the room to just sleep.

- Work off tension and stress through exercise (but not too close to bedtime).

- Avoid stimulants, such as caffeine and nicotine.

- Avoid late meals and heavy drinking.

- Follow the same presleep routine every evening. It might include listening to music, writing in a diary, relaxing, or meditating, and try to go to bed at around the same time each night.

- Use *progressive muscle relaxation*. Alternately tense and relax various muscle groups, focusing on one muscle group at a time.

- Practise yoga or deep breathing, or take a warm bath to help you relax.

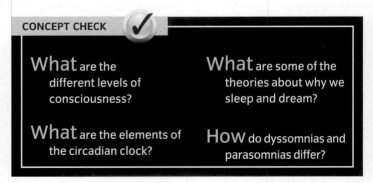

CONCEPT CHECK ✓

What are the different levels of consciousness?

What are the elements of the circadian clock?

What are some of the theories about why we sleep and dream?

How do dyssomnias and parasomnias differ?

Psychoactive Drugs

LEARNING OBJECTIVES

Explain the difference between dependence and addiction.

Summarize the differences among the four major types of psychoactive drugs.

Compare how the different psychoactive drugs affect the nervous system.

Psychoactive drugs influence the nervous system in a variety of ways. Alcohol, for example, has a diffuse effect on neural membranes throughout the nervous system. Most psychoactive drugs, however, act in a more specific way: by either enhancing or mimicking a particular neurotransmitter's effect (an **agonistic drug** action) or blocking or inhibiting it (an **antagonistic drug** action) (see **FIGURE 5.9** on the next page).

In North America the most popular psychoactive drugs are caffeine, tobacco, and ethyl alcohol. Caffeine is the most widely used and is found in hot beverages, soft drinks, and energy drinks (see *Applying Psychology*). Because these drugs are legal drugs, do you think they are somehow better or safer than illegal drugs, such as Ecstasy, marijuana, and heroin? What about prescription drugs, such as antidepressants, or over-the-counter drugs, such as Aspirin and antacids? Because a pharmacist dispenses these drugs, are they "good" as opposed to "bad" drugs?

psychoactive drugs Chemicals that alter perception, conscious awareness, or mood.

agonistic drug A drug that mimics or enhances the activity of neurotransmitters.

antagonistic drug A drug that blocks or inhibits the activity of neurotransmitters.

Applying Psychology

Deja Brew: Energy Drinks Do Caffeine Differently

Since the introduction of Red Bull in North America in 1997, the energy drink market has grown exponentially. These soft drinks contain many different ingredients, such as vitamins and herbs, but their central ingredient is often caffeine. Of the hundreds of different brands marketed, the caffeine content ranges from 50 mg to 500 mg per container (Reissig et al., 2009). In Canada most of these drinks are classified as supplements; the current exception is Red Bull, which is regulated as a natural health product (Health Canada, 2006a). You can check to see whether the energy drink you are consuming is regulated as a natural health product or a supplement by looking on the side of the container for an eight-digit natural product number (NPN). Having an NPN does not necessarily mean a beverage is safe for all people to drink, however.

Although side effects from drinking energy drinks are possible (electrolyte disturbances, nausea, vomiting, and an irregular heartbeat), moderate use by adults is generally considered to be safe. Side effects can occur when energy drinks are abused, such as when they are mixed with alcohol or consumed in large quantities (Health Canada, 2006a). Energy drinks have been aggressively marketed, especially to young men, for their perfor-

mance-enhancing and stimulant effects. Do you drink energy drinks? Consider their effects on your body. Do you feel "recharged" after drinking them?

Adapted from EatRight Ontario. (2009). *Energy drink FAQs*. Retrieved from http://www.eatrightontario.ca/en/ViewDocument.aspx?id=196

How agonistic and antagonistic drugs produce their psychoactive effect FIGURE 5.9

Most psychoactive drugs produce their mood-, energy-, and perception-altering effects by interacting with neurotransmitter systems. They can alter synthesis, storage, and release of neurotransmitters (Step 1). They can also alter the effect of neurotransmitters on the receiving site of the receptor neuron (Step 2). After neurotransmitters diffuse across the synapse, the sending neuron normally deactivates the unbound or excess neurotransmitter (Step 3).

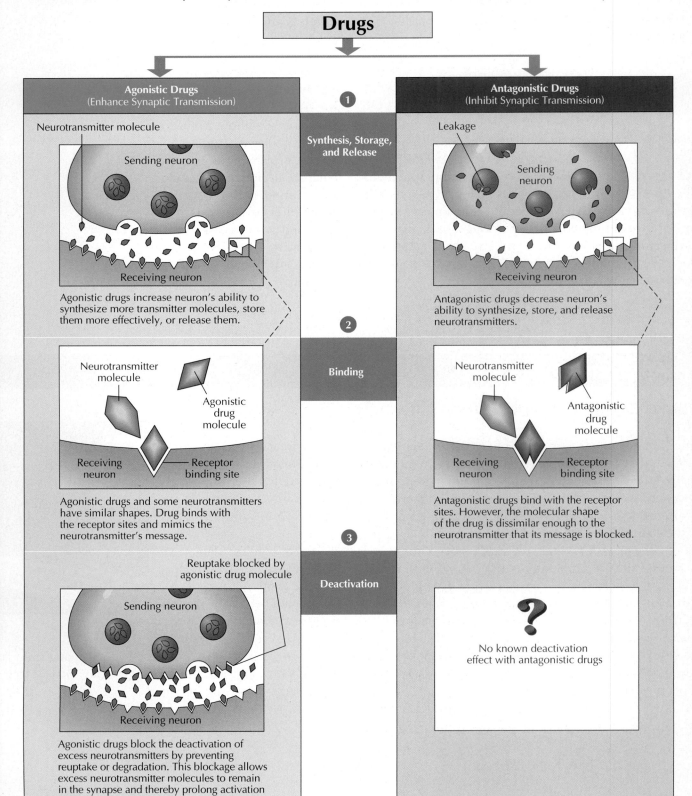

Drugs

Agonistic Drugs
(Enhance Synaptic Transmission)

Antagonistic Drugs
(Inhibit Synaptic Transmission)

1 Synthesis, Storage, and Release

Neurotransmitter molecule

Sending neuron

Receiving neuron

Agonistic drugs increase neuron's ability to synthesize more transmitter molecules, store them more effectively, or release them.

Leakage

Sending neuron

Receiving neuron

Antagonistic drugs decrease neuron's ability to synthesize, store, and release neurotransmitters.

2 Binding

Neurotransmitter molecule

Agonistic drug molecule

Receiving neuron

Receptor binding site

Agonistic drugs and some neurotransmitters have similar shapes. Drug binds with the receptor sites and mimics the neurotransmitter's message.

Neurotransmitter molecule

Antagonistic drug molecule

Receiving neuron

Receptor binding site

Antagonistic drugs bind with the receptor sites. However, the molecular shape of the drug is dissimilar enough to the neurotransmitter that its message is blocked.

3 Deactivation

Reuptake blocked by agonistic drug molecule

Sending neuron

Receiving neuron

Agonistic drugs block the deactivation of excess neurotransmitters by preventing reuptake or degradation. This blockage allows excess neurotransmitter molecules to remain in the synapse and thereby prolong activation of the receptor site.

?

No known deactivation effect with antagonistic drugs

Most neuroscientists and biopsychologists believe that all drugs, regardless of their legal status, have good and bad uses. For example, the illegal drug Ecstasy (or MDMA, which stands for 3-4-methylenedioxymethamphetamine) has potential uses in helping treat post-traumatic stress disorder (Winkelman & Roberts, 2007), and marijuana has many therapeutic applications in a variety of medical settings (see Köfalvi, 2008, for a review). Conversely, legal drugs, such as tobacco, can be very harmful to our health, and other legal drugs can be harmful to the safety of others (such as when alcohol is consumed before a person drives). So in general, it is not a useful dichotomy to lump illegal drugs into a "bad" drugs category and legal drugs into a "good" drugs category. A better way to think about psychoactive drugs is to appreciate that psychoactive substances can be both harmful and beneficial and that a drug's legal status can be unrelated to its usefulness. This distinction, along with how drug *use* differs from drug *abuse* and how chemical alterations in consciousness affect us, are important topics in psychology.

> **drug abuse** Drug use that is necessary for feelings of continued well-being; use continues despite adverse consequences.

> **addiction** A broad term referring to a condition in which a person has an overwhelming commitment to the drug of choice that supplants all other activities.

Is drug abuse the same as drug addiction? The term **drug abuse** generally refers to drug taking that is greater than simple recreational use, continues despite adverse consequences, and is necessary for feelings of continued well-being. **Addiction** is a broad term referring to a condition in which a person has an overwhelming commitment to their drug of choice that supplants all other activities. Addicted individuals feel compelled to use a specific drug to the detriment of all other aspects of their life, such as work, family, and school (Alexander, 1997).

Some researchers use the term **physical dependence** to refer to changes in physical or bodily processes that make a drug necessary for daily functioning. Physical dependence may be evident when the drug is withheld and the user undergoes **withdrawal** reactions, which are the unpleasant symptoms associated with drug cessation, such as discomfort and cravings. After repeated use of a drug, many of the body's physiological processes adjust, requiring more and more of the drug, producing a decreased sensitivity called **tolerance**.

Tolerance leads some users to escalate their drug use and to experiment with other drugs in an attempt to recreate the original pleasurable altered state. Sometimes, using one drug increases tolerance for another. This is known as **cross-tolerance**. For example, cross-tolerance is seen among LSD, mescaline, and psilocybin.

You may have heard of the term *psychological dependence* to refer to the "mental desire" for or craving to obtain a drug's effects. This is a vague and distracting phrase. Researchers have argued this description is not a diagnostic term and is somewhat arbitrary and misleading. Moreover, because "a mental desire"—or any mental desire—is produced by a physical brain, it is therefore not empirically separable from the concept of physical dependence (Alexander, 1997). We discuss substance abuse and substance dependence further in Chapter 13.

> **physical dependence** Changes in physical or bodily processes that make the drug necessary for daily functioning.

> **withdrawal** Characteristic signs that appear in a person when a drug is discontinued after prolonged use.

> **tolerance** A state reached when the physiological reaction to the drug decreases, such that increasing doses are necessary for the same effect.

PSYCHOACTIVE DRUGS: FOUR CATEGORIES

Psychologists typically divide psychoactive drugs into four broad categories: depressants, stimulants, opiates, and hallucinogens. **TABLE 5.1** provides examples of each and describes their effects.

Depressants (sometimes called "downers") act on the central nervous system to suppress or slow bodily processes and to reduce overall responsiveness.

> **depressants** Drugs that slow or depress nervous system activity.

Effects of the major psychoactive drugs TABLE 5.1

	Category	Desired effects	Excessive use or overdose effects
	**Depressants** [slow nervous system activity]		
	Alcohol, barbiturates, anxiolytics, also known as antianxiety drugs or tranquilizers (Xanax), Rohypnol (roofies), Ketamine (special K), GHB	Tension reduction, euphoria, disinhibition, drowsiness, muscle relaxation	Anxiety, nausea, disorientation, impaired reflexes and motor functioning, amnesia, loss of consciousness, shallow respiration, convulsions, coma, death
	**Stimulants** [speed up nervous system activity]		
	Cocaine, amphetamine, methamphetamine (crystal meth), MDMA (Ecstasy)	Exhilaration, euphoria, high physical and mental energy, reduced appetite, perceptions of power, sociability	Irritability, anxiety, sleeplessness, paranoia, hallucinations, psychosis, elevated blood pressure and body temperature, convulsions, death
	Caffeine	Increased alertness	Insomnia, restlessness, increased pulse rate, mild delirium, ringing in the ears, rapid heartbeat
	Nicotine	Relaxation, increased alertness, sociability	Irritability, raised blood pressure, stomach pains, vomiting, dizziness, cancer, heart disease, emphysema
	**Opiates (narcotics)** [have sleep-inducing and pain-relieving properties]		
	Morphine, heroin, opium, codeine, OxyContin	Euphoria, pain relief, sleep, prevention of withdrawal discomfort	Nausea, vomiting, constipation, shallow respiration, convulsions, coma, death
	**Hallucinogens (psychedelics)** [alter consciousness and distort mood and perception]		
	LSD (lysergic acid diethylamide), mescaline (extract from the peyote cactus), psilocybin (magic mushrooms), *Salvia divinorum**	Heightened aesthetic responses, euphoria, mild delusions, hallucinations, distorted perceptions and sensations	Panic, nausea, headaches, longer and more extreme delusions, hallucinations, perceptual distortions ("bad trips"), psychosis * long-term effects of excessive *Salvia* use is currently unknown
	Marijuana	Relaxation, mild euphoria, increased appetite	Perceptual and sensory distortions, hallucinations, fatigue, lack of motivation, paranoia

Alcohol's effect on the body and behaviour FIGURE 5.10

Number of drinks[a] in two hours	Blood alcohol (content (%)[b]	General effect[c]
(2) 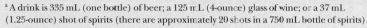	0.05	Relaxed state; increased sociability
(3)	0.08	Everyday stress lessened
(4)	0.10	Movements and speech become clumsy
(7)	0.20	Very drunk; loud and difficult to understand; emotions unstable
(12)	0.40	Difficult to wake up; incapable of voluntary action
(15)	0.50	Coma and/or death

[a] A drink is 335 mL (one bottle) of beer; a 125 mL (4-ounce) glass of wine; or a 37 mL (1.25-ounce) shot of spirits (there are approximately 20 shots in a 750 mL bottle of spirits).

[b] In Canada, the legal blood alcohol level for drinking and driving is below 0.08.

[c] There is considerable variation among people.

Alcohol's effects are determined primarily by the amount that reaches the brain (**FIGURE 5.10**). Because the liver breaks down alcohol at the rate of about 30 mL per hour, the number of drinks and the speed of consumption are both very important. In addition, men's bodies are more efficient at breaking down alcohol. Even after accounting for differences in size and muscle-to-fat ratio, women have a higher blood alcohol level than men following equal doses of alcohol.

While depressants suppress central nervous system activity, **stimulants** (uppers) increase its overall activity and responsiveness. One of the more commonly used legal stimulants is nicotine, which despite its legal status causes serious health problems. Cigarette smoking is the most preventable cause of lung cancer, accounting for 85 percent of all new Canadian cases of this cancer. It has also been implicated in a variety of other cancers and in cardiovascular disease. The use of tobacco kills about 45,000 Canadians a year. That's more than the total number of deaths from AIDS, car accidents, suicide, murder, fires, and accidental poisonings combined (Canadian Lung Association, 2008). Nicotine's effects (relaxation, increased alertness, diminished pain and appetite) are so reinforcing that some people continue to smoke even after having a cancerous tumour removed. For example, psychology's own Sigmund Freud was one such person, continuing to smoke his trademark cigars even after

stimulants Drugs that speed up nervous system activity.

diagnosis and more than 30 surgeries for oral cancer and bone cancer of the jaw.

Opiates (or narcotics) are either derived from the opium poppy (opium, morphine, and heroin) or synthetically produced (Demerol, OxyContin). They are used to relieve severe pain (Kuhn, Swartzwelder, & Wilson, 2003), and are structurally similar to the brain's natural endorphins (Chapter 2), which decrease pain and elevate mood.

opiates Drugs derived from opium or synthetically derived and molecularly similar to opium that relieve pain and induce sleep.

Heroin first got its name from the German word for "heroic," because when heroin was first commercially introduced by Bayer and Co. in 1898, it was hailed as a drug with incredible potential. Not only was it highly effective in treating the coughing, chest pain, and discomfort associated with pneumonia and tuberculosis—two leading causes of death at that time—it also provided relief for severe pain (Alexander, 1997). Because of these tremendous benefits, and a lack of effective alternatives, it was widely prescribed. With its widespread use came the realization of its addictive properties.

Morphine, heroin, and many of the synthetic opiates are addictive because, after repeated flooding with these opiates, the brain eventually reduces the production of its own endorphins. If the user later attempts to stop, the brain lacks both the synthetic and the naturally occurring opiate chemicals, and withdrawal occurs

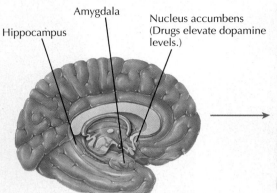

Hippocampus
Amygdala
Nucleus accumbens
(Drugs elevate dopamine levels.)

These key brain areas are associated with reward, pleasure, and addiction.

Opiates (e.g., heroin) mimic endorphins, which elicit euphoria and pain relief. Absence of the drugs triggers withdrawal symptoms (e.g., drug cravings).

(**FIGURE 5.11**). When opiates are used medically to relieve pain, they are generally not habit-forming, although this can happen. However, when repeatedly taken in other circumstances, such as for self-medication to dull the anguish of a marginalized life or dampen emotional pain, they can be extremely addictive (Alexander, 1997; Fields, 2007; Levinthal, 2008).

In the 2007 Ontario Student Drug Use and Health Survey (**FIGURE 5.12**), 21 percent of Ontario students in grades 7 to 12 report using opiate pain relievers, such as Tylenol 3, OxyContin, and Percocet, for non-medical purposes (Adlaf & Paglia-Boak, 2007). Of this group, 72 percent report obtaining the drugs from home.

One of the most intriguing alterations of consciousness comes from **hallucinogens**, drugs that produce sensory or perceptual distortions, including visual, auditory, and kinesthetic hallucinations. Some cultures use hallucinogens for spiritual purposes or as a way to experience "other realities." In Western societies, most people use hallucinogens for their reported "mind-expanding" potential.

Hallucinogens are commonly referred to as psychedelics (from the Greek for "mind manifesting"). They include mescaline (derived from the peyote cactus), psilocybin (derived from mushrooms), phencyclidine (synthetically derived), LSD (lysergic acid diethylamide, derived from ergot, a rye mould) and *Salvia* (*Salvia divinorum*, a herbaceous perennial of the mint family).

LSD, or acid, is a synthetic substance that produces dramatic alterations in sensation and perception. These alterations tend to primarily be visual, such as kaleidoscope-like images, vivid colours, and fantastic pictures. Generally

when on a "trip," users are aware that their altered perceptions are not real. LSD was first synthesized in 1943 by the Swiss chemist Albert Hofmann, who also took the first LSD trip after accidentally licking some of the drug off his finger.

LSD is a serotonin agonist and is usually not considered to be addictive, but it can still be a dangerous drug. Bad LSD trips, while uncommon, can be terrifying and may lead to accidents, deaths, or suicide. Flashbacks may unpredictably recur long after the initial ingestion (Abadinsky, 2008).

LSD use by high school and college students has been increasing (Connolly, 2000; Hedges & Burchfield, 2006; Yacoubian, Green, & Peters, 2003). Psychoactive drugs like Rohypnol (the date-rape drug) and MDMA (Ecstasy) are also increasing in popularity, especially at all-night rave parties. Other "club drugs," like GHB (gamma-hydroxybutyrate), ketamine (Special K), and methamphetamine (crystal meth), are also now more common (Abadinsky, 2008; Weaver & Scholl, 2008).

Although these drugs can produce desirable effects (e.g., Ecstasy's feeling of great empathy and connectedness with others), club drugs can be harmful. For example, they affect the motor coordination, perceptual skills, and reaction time necessary for safe driving. Their use may also lead to risky sexual behaviours. As with all illegal drugs, no quality of product laws protect buyers from unscrupulous practices. Sellers can substitute or cut the drugs with unknown, cheaper, and possibly even more dangerous substances. Some drugs, such as Rohypnol, are odourless, colourless, and tasteless, and they can easily be added to beverages without a person's knowledge (Fernández et al., 2005; National Institute on Drug Abuse, 2005).

Marijuana is also classified as a hallucinogen, even though it has some properties of a depressant (it induces drowsiness and lethargy) and some of an opiate (it acts as a weak painkiller). In low doses, marijuana produces mild euphoria; moderate doses lead to an intensification of sensory experiences and the illusion

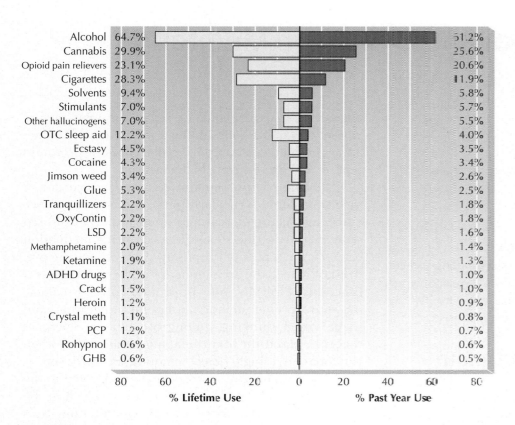

% Lifetime Use		% Past Year Use
Alcohol	64.7%	51.2%
Cannabis	29.9%	25.6%
Opioid pain relievers	23.1%	20.6%
Cigarettes	28.3%	11.9%
Solvents	9.4%	5.8%
Stimulants	7.0%	5.7%
Other hallucinogens	7.0%	5.5%
OTC sleep aid	12.2%	4.0%
Ecstasy	4.5%	3.5%
Cocaine	4.3%	3.4%
Jimson weed	3.4%	2.6%
Glue	5.3%	2.5%
Tranquillizers	2.2%	1.8%
OxyContin	2.2%	1.8%
LSD	2.2%	1.6%
Methamphetamine	2.0%	1.4%
Ketamine	1.9%	1.3%
ADHD drugs	1.7%	1.0%
Crack	1.5%	1.0%
Heroin	1.2%	0.9%
Crystal meth	1.1%	0.8%
PCP	1.2%	0.7%
Rohypnol	0.6%	0.6%
GHB	0.6%	0.5%

Psychoactive drug use among Ontario middle- and high-school students
FIGURE 5.12

The Ontario Student Drug Use and Health Survey, conducted by the Centre for Addiction and Mental Health (CAMH), began in 1977 and is a self-administered, anonymous survey of drug use, mental health, physical activity, and risk behaviour of approximately 6,200 students in grades 7 to 12. The 2007 drug-use results are shown here. By far the most commonly used drug is alcohol, followed by cannabis, and then non-medical use of opioid pain relievers.
Source: Adlaf & Paglia-Boak (2007).

that time is passing slowly. High doses may produce hallucinations, delusions, and distortions of body image (Kölfalvi, 2008; Ksir, Hart & Ray, 2008). The active ingredient in marijuana (cannabis) is THC, or tetrahydrocannabinol, which binds to receptors abundant throughout the brain.

Many researchers and clinicians have found marijuana to be extremely effective in the treatment of glaucoma (an eye disease), in alleviating the nausea and vomiting associated with chemotherapy, and with other health problems, such as chronic pain and the general wasting seen in advanced AIDS (Darmani & Crim, 2005; Fogarty et al., 2007; Health Canada, 2006b; Kölfalvi, 2008).

Medical use of marijuana is legal in Canada. Health Canada grants access to marijuana for patients suffering from the conditions listed above and for other diseases and disorders. It maintains its own supply of both dried marijuana and marijuana seeds via a contract with Prairie Plant Systems. A packet of 30 seeds costs $20 (plus tax) and the dried product costs patients $5.00/gram (Health Canada, 2006b).

As mentioned, a psychoactive drug can be helpful, but it can also be harmful. This is often unrelated to its legal status or its recreational use. While it is somewhat normal to experiment as a young adult, excessive use at the expense of other areas of life, such as friends, family, work, play, and school, signals a problem that needs to be addressed. The excessive drug use may be a visible sign but not necessarily the cause of the problem (Alexander, 1997). If a person is overwhelmingly involved with drugs, their life history and current situation might provide powerful insights into their addiction. Indeed, this might explain why many of Canada's at-risk youth are far more likely than stable teenagers to be involved with illegal psychoactive drugs (Pearce et al., 2008).

CONCEPT CHECK ✓

What are the four types of psychoactive drugs?

What are the differences between drug dependence and drug addiction?

How do psychoactive drugs affect nervous system functioning?

Altering Consciousness through Meditation and Hypnosis

LEARNING OBJECTIVES

Summarize some major forms of meditation.

Explain some of the uses of hypnosis and some of the myths about hypnosis.

As we have seen, such factors as sleep, dreaming, and psychoactive drug use can create altered states of consciousness. Changes in consciousness can also be achieved by means of meditation and hypnosis.

MEDITATION: A RELAXING "HIGH"

Suddenly, with a roar like that of a waterfall, I felt a stream of liquid light entering my brain through the spinal cord. I experienced a rocking sensation and then felt myself slipping out of my body, entirely enveloped in a halo of light. I felt the point of consciousness that was myself growing wider, surrounded by waves of light. (Krishna, 1999, pp. 4–5)

This is how spiritual leader Gopi Krishna described his experience with **meditation**. Although most people in the

meditation
A group of techniques designed to refocus attention, block out all distractions, and produce an altered state of consciousness.

beginning stages of meditation report a simpler, mellow type of relaxation followed by a mild euphoria, some advanced meditators report experiences of profound rapture and joy or strong hallucinations.

The highest functions of consciousness occur in the frontal lobe, particularly in the cerebral cortex. Scientists are seeing increasing evidence that the altered state of consciousness experienced during meditation occurs when a person purposely changes how the prefrontal cortex (the area immediately behind the eyes) functions. Typically, your prefrontal cortex is balancing your working memory, temporal integration, and higher-order thinking, among other tasks. Scientists theorize, based on brain imaging studies, that when you focus on a single object, emotion, or word, you diminish the number of neurons that are devoted to the other tasks, and they instead become involved in the singular focus of your meditation. This narrowing affects other areas of the brain, and since the neurons devoted to time have been temporarily reassigned, you experience a sense of timelessness and mild euphoria (Aftana & Golosheikin, 2003; Castillo, 2003; Harrison, 2005) (**FIGURE 5.13**). Evidence suggests that meditation, and yoga, can help individuals cope better with stress (see *What a Psychologist Sees* and Chapter 3).

How meditation alters consciousness FIGURE 5.13

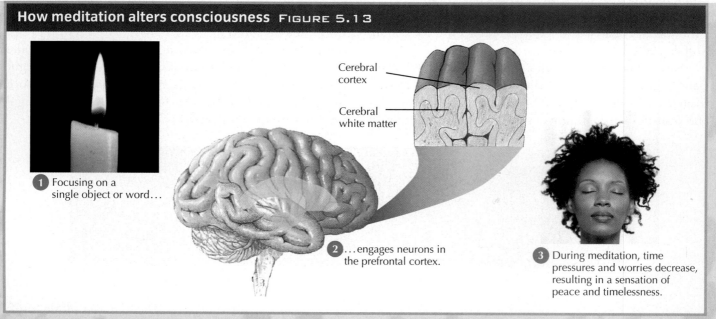

Cerebral cortex

Cerebral white matter

1 Focusing on a single object or word…

2 …engages neurons in the prefrontal cortex.

3 During meditation, time pressures and worries decrease, resulting in a sensation of peace and timelessness.

Process Diagram

Meditation and the Brain

Some meditation techniques, such as Tai Chi and hatha yoga, involve body movements and postures, while in other techniques the meditator remains motionless, chanting or focusing on a single point.

Researchers have recently found that a wider area of the brain responds to sensory stimuli during meditation, suggesting that meditation enhances the coordination between the brain hemispheres (see graphic, right; and Lyubimov, 1992). Researchers have also found that those who meditate use a larger portion of their brain, and that faster and more powerful gamma waves exist in individuals who meditate regularly than in those who do not (Lutz et al., 2004). The increased coordination associated with more powerful gamma waves correlates with improvements in focus, memory, learning, and consciousness.

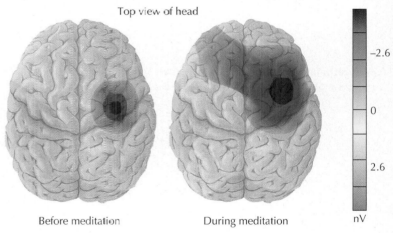

Top view of head

Before meditation

During meditation

−2.6

0

2.6

nV

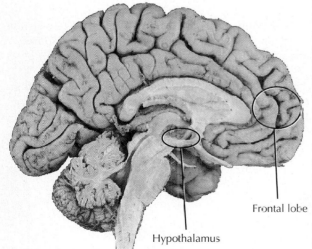

Hypothalamus

Frontal lobe

Research has verified that meditation can produce dramatic changes in basic physiological processes, including heart rate, oxygen consumption, sweat gland activity, and brain activity. Meditation has also been somewhat successful in reducing anxiety and stress and lowering blood pressure (Carlson et al., 2007; Evans et al., 2008; Harrison, 2005). Studies have even implied that meditation can change the body's parasympathetic response (Sathyaprabha et al., 2008; Young & Taylor, 1998) and increase structural support for the sensory, decision-making, and attention-processing centres of the brain (Lazar et al., 2005; Slagter et al., 2007). It seems that during meditation, the part of the brain that is responsible for both sympathetic and parasympathetic responses, the *hypothalamus*, diminishes the sympathetic response and increases the parasympathetic response. Shutting down the so-called fight-or-flight response allows for deep rest, slower respiration, and increased and more coordinated use of the brain's two hemispheres.

HYPNOSIS: MYTHS AND PRACTICAL USES

Relax. . . . Your eyelids are so very heavy. . . . Your muscles are becoming more and more relaxed. . . . Your breathing is becoming deeper and deeper. . . . Relax. . . . Your eyes are closing. . . . Let go.... Relax.

Hypnotists use suggestions like these to begin a **hypnosis** session. Once hypnotized, some people can be convinced that they are standing at the edge of the ocean listening to the sound of the waves and feeling the ocean mist on their faces. Invited to eat a delicious apple that is actually an onion, the hypnotized person may relish the flavour. Told they are watching a very funny or sad movie, hypnotized people may begin to laugh or cry at their self-created visions.

Since the eighteenth century, entertainers, charlatans, and quacks have used (and abused) hypnosis (**TABLE 5.2**); but physicians, dentists, and therapists have also long employed it as a respected clinical tool.

> **hypnosis** A trance-like state of heightened suggestibility, deep relaxation, and intense focus.

Hypnosis myths and empirical facts TABLE 5.2

Myth	Fact
Forced hypnosis: *People can be involuntarily hypnotized or hypnotically "brainwashed."*	Hypnosis requires a willing, conscious choice to relinquish control of one's consciousness to someone else. The best potential subjects are those who are able to focus attention, are open to new experiences, and are capable of imaginative involvement or fantasy (Carvalho et al., 2008; Hutchinson-Phillips, Gow & Jamieson, 2007; Wickramasekera, 2008).
Unethical behaviour: *Hypnosis can make people behave immorally or take dangerous risks against their will.*	Hypnotized people retain awareness and control of their behaviour, and they can refuse to comply with the hypnotist's suggestions (Kirsch & Braffman, 2001; Kirsh, Mazzoni, & Montgomery, 2006).
Faking: *Hypnosis participants are faking it, playing along with the hypnotist.*	There are conflicting research positions about hypnosis. Although many participants are not consciously faking hypnosis, some researchers believe the effects result from a blend of conformity, relaxation, obedience, suggestion, and role playing (Fassler et al., 2008; Lynn, 2007; Orne, 2006). Other theorists believe that hypnotic effects result from a special altered state of consciousness (Bob, 2008; Naisch, 2007; Bowers & Woody, 1996; Hilgard, 1978, 1992). A group of "unified" theorists suggests that hypnosis is a combination of both relaxation/role playing and a unique altered state of consciousness.
Superhuman strength: *Hypnotized people can perform acts of superhuman strength.*	When unhypnotized people are simply asked to try their hardest on tests of physical strength, they generally can do anything that a hypnotized person can (Orne, 2006).
Exceptional memory: *Hypnotized people can recall things they otherwise could not.*	Although the heightened relaxation and focus that hypnosis engenders improves recall for some information, people also are more willing to guess and hypnosis increases the potential for error (Stafford & Lynn, 2002; Wagstaff et al., 2007; Wickramasekera, 2008).

A number of features characterize the hypnotic state (Jamieson & Hasegawa, 2007; Jensen et al., 2008; Nash & Barnier, 2008):

- narrowed, highly focused attention (ability to tune out competing sensory stimuli)

- increased use of imagination and hallucinations

- a passive and receptive attitude

- decreased responsiveness to pain

- heightened suggestibility, or a willingness to respond to proposed changes in perception ("This onion is an apple.")

In psychotherapy, hypnosis can help patients relax, remember some events (which must be cautiously interpreted), and reduce anxiety. It has also been used with modest success in the treatment of phobias and in helping people to lose weight, stop smoking, and improve study habits (Amundson & Nuttgens, 2008; Golden, 2006; Manning, 2007). Hypnosis is also occasionally used in surgery and for the treatment of chronic pain and severe burns (Jensen et al., 2008; Nash & Barnier, 2008). It has found its best use, however, in such areas as dentistry and childbirth, in which patients often have a high degree of anxiety, fear, and misinformation. Because tension and anxiety strongly affect pain, hypnosis, along with any technique that helps the patient relax, is generally medically useful.

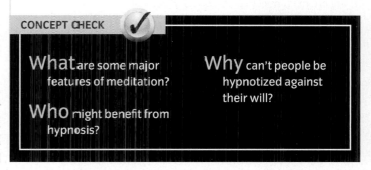

CONCEPT CHECK ✓

What are some major features of meditation?

Who might benefit from hypnosis?

Why can't people be hypnotized against their will?

SUMMARY

1 Consciousness, Sleep, and Dreaming

1. **Consciousness**, an organism's awareness of its own self and surroundings, exists along a continuum, from high awareness to no awareness and coma. Sleep is a particular **altered state of consciousness.**

2. Controlled processes demand focused attention and generally interfere with other ongoing activities. Automatic processes require minimal attention and generally do not interfere with other ongoing activities.

3. Many physiological functions follow 24-hour **circadian rhythms**. Disruptions in circadian rhythms, such as shift work, international travel, and sleep deprivation, cause increased fatigue, cognitive and mood disruptions, and other health problems but not hallucinations and psychosis.

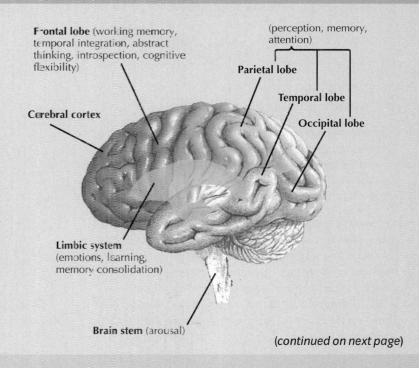

Frontal lobe (working memory, temporal integration, abstract thinking, introspection, cognitive flexibility)

Cerebral cortex

(perception, memory, attention)

Parietal lobe

Temporal lobe

Occipital lobe

Limbic system (emotions, learning, memory consolidation)

Brain stem (arousal)

(continued on next page)

4. The electroencephalogram (EEG) detects and records electrical changes in the neurons of the cerebral cortex. People progress through four distinct stages of **non-rapid-eye-movement (NREM) sleep**, with periods of **rapid-eye-movement (REM) sleep** occurring at the end of each sleep cycle. Both REM and NREM sleep are important for our biological functioning.

5. The **evolutionary/circadian theory** proposes that sleep evolved to conserve energy and as protection from predators. The **repair/restoration theory** suggests that sleep helps us recuperate from the day's events. Three major theories for why we dream are the activation–synthesis hypothesis, the information-processing view, and Freud's psychoanalytic view.

6. **Dyssomnias** are problems in the amount, timing, and quality of sleep; they include insomnia, sleep apnea, and narcolepsy. **Parasomnias** are abnormal disturbances occurring during sleep; they include nightmares, night terrors, sleepwalking, and sleep talking. Although drugs are the most common method of treating sleep disorders, a recent large-scale study reported that behaviour therapy had good success in treating some sleep problems.

2 Psychoactive Drugs

1. **Psychoactive drugs** influence the nervous system in a variety of ways. Alcohol affects neural membranes throughout the entire nervous system. Most psychoactive drugs act in a more specific way, by either enhancing or mimicking a particular neurotransmitter's effect (an **agonistic drug** action) or inhibiting it (an **antagonistic drug** action). Drugs can interfere with neurotransmission at any of four stages: production or synthesis, storage and release, binding, or removal.

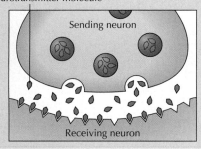

Neurotransmitter molecule
Sending neuron
Receiving neuron

2. The term **drug abuse** refers to drug-taking behaviour that is greater than simple recreational use, continues despite adverse consequences, and is necessary for continued well-being. **Addiction** is a condition in which a person feels an overwhelming commitment to a drug that supplants all other activities. A related term is **physical dependence**, which refers to biological changes in the person that make a drug necessary for minimum daily functioning. Repeated use of a drug can produce decreased sensitivity, or **tolerance**. Sometimes, the use of one drug increases tolerance for another (**cross-tolerance**).

3. Psychologists divide psychoactive drugs into four categories: **depressants** (such as alcohol, barbiturates, Rohypnol, and ketamine), **stimulants** (such as caffeine, nicotine, cocaine, amphetamine, methamphetamine, and Ecstasy), **opiates** (such as morphine, heroin, and OxyContin), and **hallucinogens** (such as marijuana and LSD). Almost all psychoactive drugs—legal or illegal—have beneficial effects but can also cause health problems and, in some cases, even death when abused or misused.

3 Altering Consciousness through Meditation and Hypnosis

1. The term **meditation** refers to techniques designed to refocus attention, block out distractions, and produce an altered state of consciousness. Some followers believe that meditation offers a more enlightened form of consciousness, and researchers have verified that it can produce changes in basic physiological processes.

2. **Hypnosis** is a mild trancelike state of heightened suggestibility, deep relaxation, and intense focus. Although a number of myths surround its use and effectiveness, it is still used in some medical settings. In psychotherapy, hypnosis can help patients relax, remember certain events, and reduce anxiety. It can also be used to help with other circumstances, such as efforts to quit smoking, lose weight, overcome phobias, cope with dentistry, and endure labour.

Top view of head

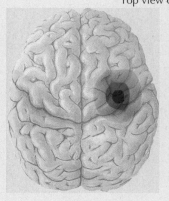
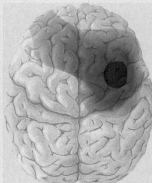

Before meditation   During meditation

KEY TERMS

- addiction p. 137
- agonistic drug p. 135
- altered state of consciousness (ASC) p. 124
- antagonistic drug p. 135
- circadian rhythms p. 124
- consciousness p. 124
- cross-tolerance p. 137

- depressants p. 137
- drug abuse p. 137
- dyssomnias p. 132
- evolutionary/circadian theory p. 130
- hallucinogens p. 140
- hypnosis p. 144
- meditation p. 142

- non-rapid-eye-movement (NREM) sleep p. 128
- opiates p. 139
- parasomnias p. 134
- physical dependence p. 137
- psychoactive drugs p. 135
- rapid-eye-movement (REM) sleep p. 128

- repair/restoration theory p. 130
- sleep debt p. 127
- stimulants p. 139
- tolerance p. 137
- withdrawal p. 137

CRITICAL AND CREATIVE THINKING QUESTIONS

1. Do you believe that people have an unconscious mind? If so, how might it affect thoughts, feelings, and behaviour?

2. Which of the three main theories of dreaming do you most agree with, and why?

3. The medical use of marijuana is legal in Canada, while recreational use is illegal. What factors do you think contribute to a drugs' legal or illegal status? What drugs do you think should be illegal and what drugs do you think should be legal? What factors would contribute to your decision?

4. How much of your week do you spend sleep deprived? After what you have read in this chapter, identify five things you can do to increase the amount of sleep you get.

5. Driving when sleep deprived can be as dangerous as driving after drinking alcohol. In light of this, should driving while sleep deprived be outlawed? What might a device designed to detect sleep deprivation in people look like, and what physiological systems would it need to detect and measure?

6. Why might hypnosis help treat people who suffer from chronic pain?

7. You have read two theories that attempt to explain why sleep evolved. Another way to think about sleep and consciousness is to ask, why did being awake evolve? What could be the answer to this question?

8. Date-rape drugs such as Rohypnol have received considerable media attention; however another drug is used far more often by both the perpetrators and the victims of sexual assault. What is the name of this drug and why has it been implicated in these types of crimes? (See Appendix A for the name of this drug.)

What is happening in this picture ?

During NREM sleep, a cat will often sleep in an upright position like a sphinx. With the onset of REM sleep, the cat rolls over on its side.

- Can you explain why?

- Why might the muscle paralysis of REM sleep serve an important adaptive function?

SELF-TEST

(Check your answers in Appendix A.)

1. *Consciousness* is defined in this text as _____.
   a. ordinary and extraordinary wakefulness
   b. an organism's awareness of its own self and surroundings
   c. mental representations of the world in the here and now
   d. any mental state that requires thinking and processing of sensory stimuli

2. For the past four days, Lisa has been either sleeping and dreaming, or using various psychoactive substances. Which of the following statements applies to Lisa?
   a. She needs to be enrolled in a substance abuse program.
   b. She has been in serious danger of permanently altering her circadian rhythms.
   c. She has recently been in a state of altered consciousness.
   d. She has been lacking any conscious awareness.

3. Mental activities that require focused attention are called _____.
   a. thinking processes
   b. controlled processes
   c. alert states of consciousness
   d. conscious awareness

4. *Automatic processes* require _____ attention.
   a. focused
   b. unconscious
   c. minimal
   d. delta wave

5. *Circadian rhythm*s are _____.
   a. patterns that repeat themselves on a twice-daily schedule
   b. physical and mental changes associated with the cycle of the moon
   c. rhythmical processes in your brain
   d. biological and other changes that occur on a 24-hour cycle

6. Driving home late one night, you find yourself struggling to stay awake, and think you may have fallen asleep for a couple of seconds. What name is given to this shift in your brain activity?
   a. a microsleep
   b. unconscious sleep
   c. a sleep spindle
   d. delta wave shift

7. On the following diagram, identify the main areas of the brain that control circadian rhythms.
   a. hypothalamus
   b. pineal gland
   c. suprachiasmatic nucleus

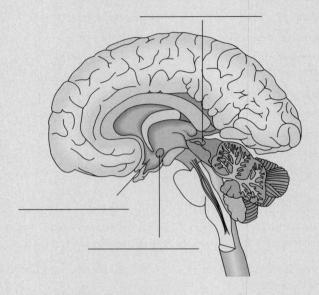

8. The past week has seen Jessica sleep only 3 to 4 hours a night due to studying for exams and her work schedule. What name is given to this type of accumulation of lost sleep?
   a. short sleep bouts
   b. sleep spindles
   c. sleep deprivation
   d. sleep debt

9. This figure displays neural changes tracked by means of small electrodes on the scalp. This research tool is called _____.
   a. an EKG
   b. a PET scan
   c. an EEG recording
   d. an EMG

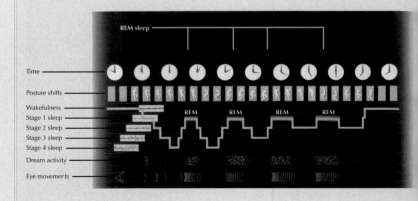

10. The sleep stage marked by irregular breathing, eye movements, high-frequency brain waves, and dreaming is called _____ sleep.
    a. beta
    b. hypnologic
    c. REM
    d. transitional

11. Which of the following people is clearly experiencing insomnia?
    a. Ian frequently cannot fall asleep the night before a final exam.
    b. Enzo regularly sleeps less than eight hours per night.
    c. Adam persistently has difficulty falling or staying asleep.
    d. All of these people are clearly experiencing insomnia.

12. Dieting, restricting alcohol, surgery, dental appliances, and tennis balls are all recommended treatments for _____, a dyssomnia.
    a. insomnia
    b. parasomnia
    c. nightmares
    d. sleep apnea

13. *Psychoactive drugs* _____.
    a. change conscious awareness, mood, or perception
    b. are addictive, mind altering, and dangerous to your health
    c. are illegal unless prescribed by a medical doctor
    d. all of these options

14. Jonathan has used LSD quite regularly for many years, and has more recently started using mescaline. He finds that he can consume significant quantities of mescaline without getting much of an effect. Which of the following terms most accurately describes what Jonathan has developed?
    a. drug abuse
    b. tolerance
    c. cross-tolerance
    d. physical dependence

15. Match the four major categories of psychoactive drugs with the correct photo:
    a. depressants, photo _____
    b. stimulants, photo _____
    c. opiates, photo _____
    d. hallucinogens, photo _____

16. Depressants include all of the following EXCEPT:
    a. anxiolytics
    b. alcohol
    c. nicotine
    d. GHB

17. Psilocybin and Salvia are both:
    a. opiates
    b. hallucinogens
    c. depressants
    d. stimulants

18. Altered states of consciousness can be achieved in which of the following ways?
    a. During sleep and dreaming
    b. Via psychoactive chemicals
    c. Through hypnosis and meditation
    d. All of these options

19. _____ is a group of techniques designed to refocus attention and produce an altered state of consciousness.
    a. Hypnosis
    b. Scientology
    c. Parapsychology
    d. Meditation

20. _____ is an altered state of heightened suggestibility characterized by deep relaxation and intense focus.
    a. Meditation
    b. Amphetamine psychosis
    c. Hypnosis
    d. Daydreaming

Learning

On November 14, 1997, 14-year-old Reena Virk was lured to a secluded area under a bridge in a waterfront park in a suburb of Victoria, British Columbia. There, she was viciously attacked and murdered by a group of eight of her peers, seven of whom were teenage girls. She was hit, kicked, and stomped on so severely that she experienced extensive internal injuries, finally drowning in the water under the bridge (Godfrey, 2005).

What caused this grisly murder? Despite media reports to the contrary, some have speculated that the attack was racially motivated. Reena Virk reportedly had difficulty fitting in. She was of South Asian descent, was slightly overweight, and was the child of immigrants who were not well-to-do (Batacharya, 2004). Whether or not these differences motivated the violence, hate crimes are a serious and growing problem around the world. People are ridiculed, attacked, and even murdered simply because of their ethnicity, sexual orientation, gender, or religious preference. Where does such hatred come from? Is prejudice learned?

We usually think of learning as classroom activities, such as math and reading, or as motor skills, like riding a bike or playing the piano. Psychologists define learning more broadly, as *a relatively permanent change in behaviour or mental processes because of practice or experience*. This relative permanence applies not only to useful behaviours (using a spoon or writing great novels) but also to bad habits, racism, and hatred. The good news is that what is learned can be unlearned, through retraining, counselling, and self-reflection. In this chapter, we discuss several types of conditioning, the most basic form of learning. Then we look at social-cognitive learning and the biological factors involved in learning. Finally, we explore how learning theories and concepts touch everyday life.

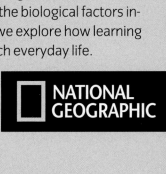
NATIONAL GEOGRAPHIC

Suman Virk, mother of Reena Virk, speaks to reporters.

CHAPTER OUTLINE

Classical Conditioning

One of the earliest forms of learning to be studied scientifically was conditioning. We discuss classical conditioning, made famous by Pavlov's dogs, in this section and a different form of conditioning, known as operant conditioning, in the next section.

THE BEGINNINGS OF CLASSICAL CONDITIONING

Why does your mouth water when you see a large slice of chocolate cake or a hot pizza? The answer to this question was accidentally discovered in the laboratory of Russian physiologist Ivan Pavlov (1849–1936). Pavlov's early work focused on the role of saliva in digestion, and one of his experiments involved measuring salivary responses in dogs by using a tube attached to the dogs' salivary glands.

One of Pavlov's students noticed that many dogs began salivating at the sight of the food or the food dish, the smell of the food, or even the sight of the person who delivered the food long before receiving the actual food. This "unscheduled" salivation was intriguing. Pavlov recognized that an involuntary reflex (salivation) that occurred before the appropriate stimulus (food) was presented could not be inborn and biological. It had to have been acquired through experience—through **learning**.

Excited by their accidental discovery, Pavlov and his students conducted several experiments. Their most basic method involved sounding a tone on a tuning fork just before food was placed in the dogs' mouths. After several pairings of tone and food, the dogs would salivate on hearing the tone, even without receiving food. Pavlov and others went on to show that many things can become conditioned stimuli for salivation if they are paired with food: the ticking of a metronome, a buzzer, a light, and even the sight of a circle or triangle drawn on a card.

The type of learning that Pavlov described came to be known as **classical conditioning** (**FIGURE 6.1**). To understand classical conditioning, you first need to realize that **conditioning** is just another word for learning. You also need to know that some responses are inborn and don't require conditioning. For example, the inborn salivary reflex consists of an **unconditioned stimulus (UCS)** and an **unconditioned response (UCR)**. That is, the UCS (food) elicits the UCR (salivation) without previous conditioning (learning).

Before conditioning occurs, a **neutral stimulus (NS)** does not naturally elicit a relevant or consistent response. For example, as shown in Figure 6.1, Pavlov's dogs did not naturally salivate when a tone sounded. Similarly, as the figure shows, the sight of a cardboard box (neutral stimulus) doesn't naturally make a person hungry for a slice of pizza.

learning A relatively permanent change in behaviour or mental processes because of practice or experience.

classical conditioning Learning that occurs when a neutral stimulus (NS) becomes paired (associated) with an unconditioned stimulus (UCS) to elicit a conditioned response (CR).

conditioning The process of learning associations between environmental stimuli and behavioural responses.

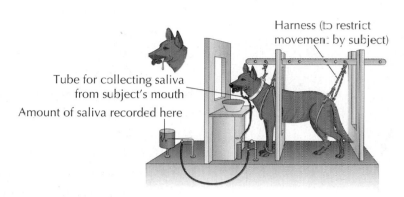

Harness (to restrict movement by subject)

Tube for collecting saliva from subject's mouth

Amount of saliva recorded here

Process Diagram

	Pavlov's example	Modern-day example
Step 1 **Before conditioning** The neutral stimulus (NS) produces no relevant response. The unconditioned (unlearned) *stimulus* (UCS) elicits the unconditioned *response* (UCR).	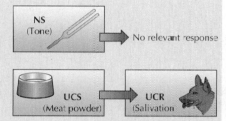	
Step 2 **During conditioning** The neutral stimulus (NS) is repeatedly paired with the unconditioned (unlearned) *stimulus* (UCS) to produce the unconditioned *response* (UCR).	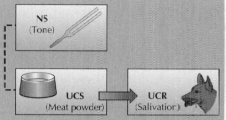	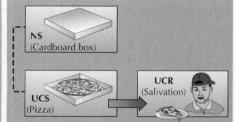
Step 3 **After conditioning** The neutral stimulus (NS) has become a conditioned (learned) stimulus (CS). This CS now produces a conditioned (learned) *response* (CR), which is usually similar to the previously unconditioned (unlearned) response (UCR).	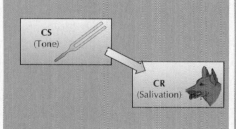	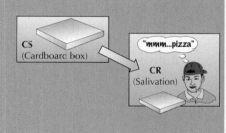
Summary An originally neutral stimulus (NS) becomes a conditioned stimulus (CS), which elicits a conditioned response (CR).	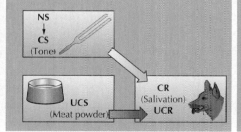	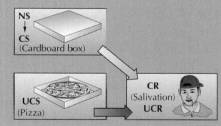

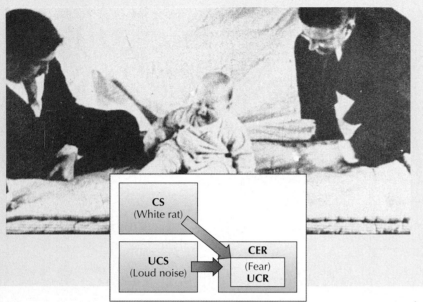

In the famous "Little Albert" study, a healthy 11-month-old child was first allowed to play with a white laboratory rat. Like most infants, Albert was curious and reached for the rat, showing no fear. Watson used the fact that infants are naturally frightened (UCR) by loud noises (UCS). Watson stood behind Albert and again put the rat (NS) near him. When the infant reached for the rat, Watson banged a steel bar with a hammer. The loud noise frightened Albert and made him cry. The white rat (NS) was paired with the loud noise (UCS) only seven times before the white rat alone produced a *conditioned emotional response* (CER) in Albert: fear of the rat.

Pavlov's discovery was that learning occurs when a neutral stimulus, such as a tone (or the cardboard box), is regularly paired with an unconditioned stimulus (food, or the smell of pizza in the cardboard box). The neutral stimulus (tone or the cardboard box) then becomes a **conditioned stimulus (CS)**, which elicits a **conditioned response (CR)**—salivation.

What does a salivating dog have to do with your life? Classical conditioning is the most fundamental way that all animals, including humans, learn many new responses, emotions, and attitudes. Your love for your parents (or boyfriend or girlfriend), your drooling at the sight of chocolate cake or pizza, and even negative reactions, like the hatred and racism that some people display, are largely the result of classical conditioning.

In a famous experiment, John Watson and Rosalie Rayner (1920) demonstrated that fear could also be classically conditioned (**FIGURE 6.2**).

Watson and Rayner's experiment could not be performed today because it violates several ethical guidelines for scientific research (Chapter 1). Moreover, Watson and Rayner ended their experiment without extinguishing (removing) Albert's fear, although they knew that it could endure for a long period. Watson and Rayner also have been criticized because they did not measure Albert's fear objectively. Their subjective evaluation raises doubt about the degree of fear they conditioned (Paul & Blumenthal, 1989).

Despite such criticisms, John Watson made important and lasting contributions to psychology. Unlike other psychologists of his time, Watson emphasized the study of strictly observable behaviours, and he founded the school of *behaviourism*, which explains behaviour as a result of observable stimuli and observable responses.

Watson's study of Little Albert has had legendary significance for many psychologists. Watson showed us that many of our likes, dislikes, prejudices, and fears are **conditioned emotional responses**—classically conditioned emotional responses to previously neutral stimuli. Watson's research in producing Little Albert's fears also led to powerful clinical tools for eliminating extreme, irrational fears known as *phobias* (Chapter 13).

FINE-TUNING CLASSICAL CONDITIONING

Now that you have an understanding of the key concepts of classical conditioning, we can discuss six important principles of classical conditioning: stimulus generalization, stimulus discrimination, extinction, spontaneous recovery, reconditioning, and higher-order conditioning (**FIGURE 6.3**).

Stimulus generalization occurs when an event similar to the original conditioned stimulus triggers the same conditioned response. The more the stimulus resembles the conditioned stimulus, the stronger the conditioned

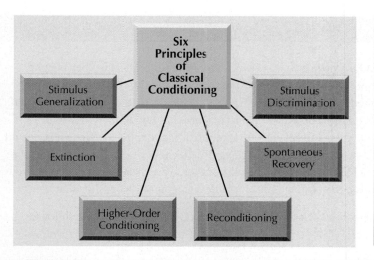

Six principles of classical conditioning FIGURE 6.3

"I don't care if she is a tape dispenser. I love her."

Which of the six basic principles of classical conditioning explain(s) this cartoon?

Answer: Stimulus generalization

response (Hovland, 1937). For example, after first conditioning dogs to salivate at the sound of low-pitched tones, Pavlov later demonstrated that the dogs would also salivate in response to higher-pitched tones. Similarly, after conditioning, the infant in Watson and Rayner's experiment ("Little Albert") feared not only rats but also a rabbit, a dog, and a bearded Santa Claus mask.

Eventually, through the process of **stimulus discrimination** (a term that refers to a learned response to a specific stimulus but not to other similar stimuli), Albert presumably learned to recognize differences between rats and other stimuli. As a result, he probably overcame his fear of Santa Claus, even if he remained afraid of white rats. Similarly, Pavlov's dogs learned to distinguish between the tone that signalled food and those that did not.

Most behaviours that are learned through classical conditioning can be weakened or suppressed through **extinction**. Extinction occurs when the unconditioned stimulus (UCS) is repeatedly withheld whenever the conditioned stimulus (CS) is presented. This gradually weakens the previous association. When Pavlov repeatedly sounded the tone without presenting food, the dogs' salivation gradually declined. Similarly, if you have a classically conditioned fear of cats and later start to work as a veterinary assistant, your fear will gradually diminish.

However, extinction is not unlearning—it does not "erase" the learned connection between the stimulus and the response (Bouton, 1994). In fact, on occasion an extinguished response may spontaneously reappear (**FIGURE 6.4**). This **spontaneous recovery** helps

Extinction and spontaneous recovery FIGURE 6.4

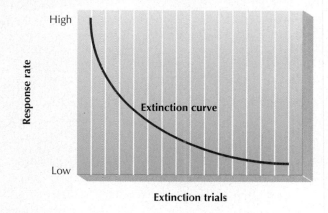

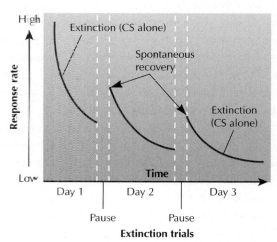

The more often the UCS is withheld whenever the CS is presented, the lower an individual's response rate to the UCS, until extinction occurs.

But an extinguished response may spontaneously reappear, which can trigger a rush of feelings and emotions as though the UCS were present.

Children are not born salivating upon seeing the McDonald's Golden Arches. So why do they beg their parents to stop at McDonald's after simply seeing a billboard for the restaurant? It is because of **higher-order conditioning**, which occurs when a neutral stimulus (NS) becomes a conditioned stimulus (CS) through repeated pairings with a previously conditioned stimulus (CS).

If you wanted to demonstrate higher-order conditioning in Pavlov's dogs, you would first condition the dogs to salivate in response to the sound of the tone (A). Then you would pair a flash of light with the tone (B). Eventually, the dogs would salivate in response to the flash of light alone (C). Similarly, children first learn to pair McDonald's restaurants with food and later learn that two Golden Arches are a symbol for McDonald's. Their salivation and begging to eat at the restaurant on seeing the arches are a classic case of higher-order conditioning (and successful advertising).

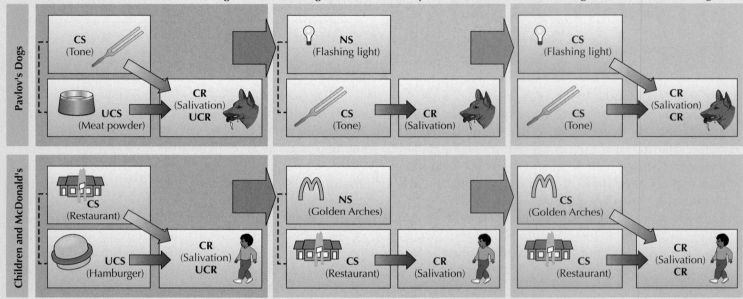

A First-Order Conditioning **B Pairing NS with Previously Conditioned CS** **C Higher-Order Conditioning**

explain why you might suddenly feel excited at seeing a former girlfriend or boyfriend, even though years have passed (and extinction has occurred). It also explains why couples who've recently broken up sometimes misinterpret a sudden flare-up of feelings and return to unhappy relationships. Furthermore, if a conditioned stimulus is reintroduced after extinction, the conditioning occurs much faster the second time around—a phenomenon known as **reconditioning**. Both spontaneous recovery and reconditioning help underscore why it can be so difficult for us to break bad habits (such as eating too many nachos) or internalize new beliefs (such as egalitarian racial beliefs). The phenomenon of **higher-order conditioning** (FIGURE 6.5) further expands and complicates our learned habits and associations.

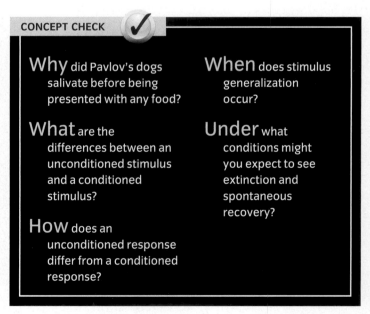

CONCEPT CHECK

Why did Pavlov's dogs salivate before being presented with any food?

What are the differences between an unconditioned stimulus and a conditioned stimulus?

How does an unconditioned response differ from a conditioned response?

When does stimulus generalization occur?

Under what conditions might you expect to see extinction and spontaneous recovery?

Operant Conditioning

LEARNING OBJECTIVES

Explain how reinforcement and punishment influence behaviour.

Describe Thorndike's and Skinner's contributions to research on operant conditioning.

Identify examples of primary and secondary reinforcers.

Explain how different schedules of reinforcement affect behaviour.

Describe the negative side effects of punishment.

C onsequences are the heart of **operant conditioning**. In classical conditioning, consequences are irrelevant—Pavlov's dogs were still allowed to eat whether they salivated or not. But in operant conditioning, the organism performs a behaviour (an *operant*, as in "operation") that produces either reinforcement or punishment. **Reinforcement** strengthens the response, making it more likely to recur. **Punishment** weakens the response, making it less likely to recur.

Classical and operant conditioning also differ in another important way. In classical conditioning, the organism's response is generally passive and involuntary. In operant conditioning, the organism's response is generally active and voluntary. The learner "operates" on the environment and produces consequences that influence whether the behaviour will be repeated. For example, if your friends smile and laugh when you tell a joke, you are likely to joke more with them. If they frown, groan, or ridicule you, you are likely to joke less.

> **operant conditioning**
> Learning in which voluntary responses are controlled by their consequences (also known as instrumental or Skinnerian conditioning).

> **reinforcement**
> A consequence that strengthens a response and makes it more likely to recur.

> **punishment**
> A consequence that weakens a response and makes it less likely to recur.

THE BEGINNINGS OF OPERANT CONDITIONING

Edward Thorndike (1874–1949), a pioneer of operant conditioning, determined that the frequency of a behaviour is modified by its consequences. He developed the **law of effect** (Thorndike, 1911), a first step in understanding how consequences can modify active, voluntary behaviours (**FIGURE 6.6**).

B. F. Skinner (1904–1990) extended Thorndike's law of effect to more complex behaviours. He emphasized that reinforcement and punishment always occur after the behaviour of interest has occurred. In addition, Skinner cautioned that the only way to know how we have influenced someone's behaviour is to check whether the behaviour increases or decreases.

Sometimes, he noted, we think we're reinforcing or we think we're punishing when we're actually doing the opposite. For example, a teacher may think she is encouraging shy students to talk by praising them each time they speak up in class. But what if shy students are embarrassed by this attention? If so, as Canadian researcher Mary Ann Evans (2001) points out, teachers may actually decrease the number of times the students talk in class.

> **law of effect**
> Thorndike's rule that the probability of an action being repeated is strengthened when followed by a pleasant or satisfying consequence.

Thorndike box FIGURE 6.6

In one famous experiment, Thorndike put a cat inside a specially built puzzle box. When the cat stepped on a pedal inside the box (at first, through trial and error), the door opened and the cat could get out to eat. With each additional success, the cat's actions became more purposeful, and it soon learned to open the door immediately (from Thorndike, 1898).

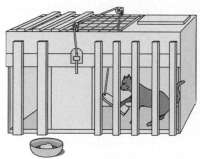

REINFORCEMENT: STRENGTHENING A RESPONSE

Reinforcers, which strengthen a response, can be grouped into two types: primary and secondary. Primary reinforcers satisfy an intrinsic, unlearned biological need (food, water, sex). Secondary reinforcers are not intrinsic; the value of this reinforcer is learned (money, praise, attention). Thus, when we were babies, we most likely found milk (a primary reinforcer) much more reinforcing than a $100 bill. By the time we reached adolescence, however, we most likely had learned to prefer the money (a secondary reinforcer).

Reinforcers can produce **positive reinforcement** or **negative reinforcement**, depending on whether certain stimuli are added or taken away (see TABLE 6.1). It's easy to confuse negative reinforcement with punishment, but the two concepts are actually completely opposite. Reinforcement (whether positive or negative) strengthens a behaviour, whereas punishment weakens a behaviour. If the terminology seems confusing, it may help to think of positive and negative reinforcement in the mathematical sense, that is, in terms of something being added (+) or taken away (−) rather than in terms of good and bad (Table 6.1).

Sometimes we use high-frequency behaviour to reinforce low-frequency responses: making yourself study before going to the movies is a good example. In this case, you are using what is called the **Premack principle,** named after psychologist David Premack. Recognizing that you love to go to movies, you intuitively tie your less-desirable low-frequency activities (making yourself study) to your high-frequency behaviour (going to the movies), thereby positively reinforcing the completion of the less desirable low-frequency behaviour.

Just as you saw in our discussion of classical conditioning, *extinction* can also occur in operant conditioning. In both classical and operant conditioning, removing the original source of learning causes extinction to occur. In classical conditioning, presenting the CS without the UCS eventually leads to extinction of the CR. In operant conditioning, if we remove the reinforcer that follows the response, the animal will eventually stop producing the response. How easy it is to extinguish a response depends on the rate with which we have been reinforcing that response.

What are the best circumstances for using reinforcement? It depends on the desired outcome. To make this decision, you need to understand various **schedules of reinforcement** (Terry, 2009): the rate or interval at which responses are reinforced. Although numerous schedules of reinforcement are possible, the most important distinction is whether they are continuous or partial. When Skinner was training his animals, he

How reinforcement strengthens and increases behaviours TABLE 6.1

	Positive reinforcement *Adds to (+) and strengthens behaviour*	Negative reinforcement *Takes away (−) and strengthens behaviour*
Primary reinforcers Satisfy an unlearned biological need	You hug your baby and he smiles at you. The "addition" of his smile strengthens the likelihood that you will hug him again.	Your baby is crying, so you hug him and he stops crying. The "removal" of crying strengthens the likelihood that you will hug him again, which takes away the crying.
	You do a favour for a friend and she buys you lunch in return.	You take an aspirin for your headache, which takes away the pain.
Secondary reinforcers Value is learned, intrinsic	You increase profits and receive $200 as a bonus.	After high sales, your boss says you won't have to work on weekends.
	You study hard and receive a good grade on your psychology exam.	Your professor says you won't have to take the final exam because you did so well on your in-class tests.

found that learning was most rapid if the response was reinforced every time it occurred—a procedure called **continuous reinforcement**.

As you have probably noticed, real life seldom provides continuous reinforcement. Yet your behaviour persists because your efforts are occasionally rewarded. Most everyday behaviour is rewarded on a **partial (or intermittent) schedule of reinforcement**, which involves reinforcing only some responses, not all (Sangha, McComb, Scheibenstock, Johannes, & Lukowiak, 2002).

Once a task is well learned, it is important to move to a partial schedule of reinforcement. Why? Because under partial schedules, behaviour is more resistant to extinction. Four partial schedules of reinforcement are used: **fixed ratio** (FR), **variable ratio** (VR), **fixed interval** (FI), and **variable interval** (VI). The type of partial schedule selected depends on the type of behaviour being studied and on the speed of learning desired (Kazdin, 2008; Neuringer, Deiss, & Olson, 2000; Rothstein, Jensen, & Neuringer, 2008). A fixed ratio leads to the highest overall response rate, but each of the four types of partial schedules has different advantages and disadvantages (see STUDY ORGANIZER 6.1).

Partial reinforcement is described further in *What a Psychologist Sees*. Each of the four schedules of partial reinforcement is important for *maintaining* behaviour. But how would you teach someone to play the piano or to speak a foreign language? For new and complex behaviours, such as these, which aren't likely to occur naturally, **shaping** is an especially valuable tool. Skinner believed that shaping explains

shaping Reinforcing successively closer and closer approximations to the desired response.

Four schedules of reinforcement — Study Organizer 6.1

		Definitions	Response rates	Examples
Ratio schedules (response based)	**Fixed ratio (FR)**	Reinforcement occurs after a predetermined set of responses; the ratio (number or amount) is fixed	Produces a high rate of response, but a brief drop-off or pause in responding just after reinforcement	A car wash employee receives $10 for every three cars washed. In a laboratory, a rat receives a food pellet every time it presses the bar seven times.
	Variable ratio (VR)	Reinforcement occurs unpredictably; the ratio (number or amount) varies	High response rates, no pause after reinforcement, and very resistant to extinction	Slot machines are designed to pay out after an average number of responses (maybe every 10 times), but any one machine may pay out on the first response, then seventh, then the twentieth.
Interval schedules (time based)	**Fixed interval (FI)**	Reinforcement occurs after a predetermined time has elapsed; the interval (time) is fixed	Responses tend to increase as the time for the next reinforcer is near, but drop off after reinforcement and during interval	You get a monthly paycheque. A rat's behaviour is reinforced with a food pellet when (or if) it presses a bar after 20 seconds have elapsed.
	Variable interval (VI)	Reinforcement occurs unpredictably; the interval (time) varies	Relatively low response rates, but they are steady because the receiver cannot predict when reward will come	In a class with pop quizzes, you study at a slow but steady rate because you can't anticipate the next quiz. A rat's behaviour is reinforced with a food pellet after a response and a variable, unpredictable interval of time.

Partial Reinforcement Keeps 'Em Coming Back

Have you noticed that people spend long hours pushing buttons and pulling levers on slot machines in hopes of winning the jackpot? This compulsion to keep gambling in spite of significant losses is evidence of the strong resistance to extinction with partial (or intermittent) schedules of reinforcement. Machines in Ontario casinos and racetracks, for example, have payout rates of at least 85 percent—that is, for every dollar spent, a player "wins" $0.85. These are average payouts based on hundreds of thousands of games (Ontario Lottery and Gaming Corporation, 2007). Different machines are programmed in different ways. Some meet the percentage by giving very large but infrequent payouts to a few lucky winners. Others give frequent smaller payouts to many players. In either case, people are reinforced just often enough to keep them coming back, always hoping the partial reinforcement will lead to more. The same compulsion leads people to go on buying lottery tickets even though the odds of winning are very low.

This type of partial reinforcement also helps parents maintain children's positive behaviours, such as tooth brushing and bed making. After the child has initially learned these behaviours with continuous reinforcement, occasional, partial reinforcement is the most efficient way to maintain the behaviour. (Chart adapted from Skinner, 1961.)

Momoko, a female monkey, is famous in Japan for her water-skiing, deep-sea diving and other amazing abilities. Can you describe how her animal trainers used the successive steps of shaping to teach her these skills? First, they reinforced Momoko (with a small food treat) for standing or sitting on the water ski. Then they reinforced her each time she put her hands on the pole. Next, they slowly dragged the water ski on dry land and reinforced her for staying upright and holding the pole. Then they took Momoko to a shallow and calm part of the ocean and reinforced her for staying upright and holding the pole as the ski moved in the water. Finally, they took her into the deep part of the ocean.

a variety of abilities that we each possess, from eating with a fork, to playing a musical instrument, to driving a car with a stick shift. Parents, athletic coaches, teachers, and animal trainers all use shaping techniques, which involve successively reinforcing closer and closer approximations to the desired response (FIGURE 6.7).

PUNISHMENT: WEAKENING A RESPONSE

Unlike reinforcement, punishment *decreases* the strength of a response. As with reinforcement, punishment also has two forms: positive and negative (Miltenberger, 2008; Skinner, 1953).

Positive punishment is the addition (+) of a stimulus that decreases (or weakens) the likelihood of the response occurring again. **Negative punishment** is the tak-

ing away (−) of a reinforcing stimulus, which decreases (or weakens) the likelihood of the response occurring again (TABLE 6.2). (To check your understanding of the principles of reinforcement and punishment, see FIGURE 6.3.)

Punishment is a tricky business, and it isn't always intentional. Any process that adds or takes away something and causes a behaviour to decrease is punishment. Thus, if parents ignore all the A's on their child's report card ("taking away" encouraging comments) and ask repeated questions about the B's and C's, they may unintentionally be punishing the child's excellent grade achievement and weakening the likelihood of future A's. Similarly, dog owners who yell at or spank their dogs for finally coming to them ("adding" negative verbal or physical consequences) after being called several times are actually punishing the desired behaviour: coming when called.

How punishment weakens and decreases behaviours TABLE 6.2	
Positive punishment *adds stimulus (+) and weakens the behaviour*	**Negative punishment** *takes stimulus away (−) and weakens the behaviour*
You must run four extra laps in your gym class because you were late.	You're excluded from participating in gym class because you were late.
A parent adds chores following a child's poor report card.	A parent takes away a teen's cellphone following a poor report card.
Your boss chews you out about your performance.	Your boss reduces your pay after a poor performance.

The Skinner box application FIGURE 6.8

To test his behavioural theories, Skinner used an animal, usually a pigeon or a rat, and an apparatus that has come to be called a *Skinner box*. In Skinner's basic experimental design, an animal, such as a rat, received a food pellet each time it pushed a lever, and the number of responses was recorded. Note in this drawing that an electric grid on the cage floor could be used to deliver small electric shocks.

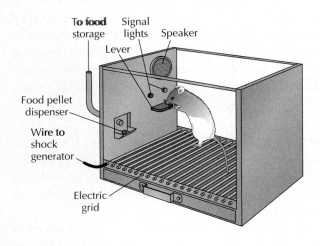

Test yourself

Is this positive reinforcement, negative reinforcement, positive punishment, or negative punishment? Fill in the name of the appropriate learning principle in the spaces provided in each box.

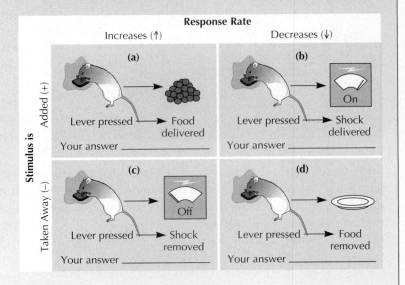

Answers: (a) positive reinforcement, (b) positive punishment, (c) negative reinforcement, (d) negative punishment

Punishment plays an unavoidable role in our social world. Dangerous criminals must be stopped and possibly removed from society. Parents must stop their teenagers from drinking and driving. Teachers must stop disruptive students in the classroom and bullies on the playground. Yet punishment can be problematic (Borrego et al., 2007; Leary et al., 2008; Loxton et al., 2008).

To be effective, punishment should be immediate and consistent. However, in the real world, this is extremely hard to do. Police officers cannot stop all drivers every time they speed. To make matters worse, when punishment is not immediate, the delay can cause the behaviour to be reinforced on a partial schedule, which makes it highly resistant to extinction. Think about gambling. It should be a punishing situation—gamblers usually lose far more than they win. However, the fact that they occasionally win keeps gamblers hanging in there.

Even if punishment immediately follows the misbehaviour, the recipient may learn what not to do but may not necessarily learn what he or she should do. It's much more effective to teach someone by giving a clear examples of correct behaviour than by simply punishing the incorrect behaviour. Finally, punishment can have serious side effects.

The Side Effects of Punishment

1. **Increased aggression.** Because punishment often produces a decrease in undesired behaviour, at least for the moment, the person administering the punishment is actually rewarded for applying punishment. Thus, a vicious circle may be established in which both the punisher and the recipient are reinforced for inappropriate behaviour: the punisher for punishing and the recipient for being fearful and submissive. This side effect partially explains the escalation of violence in family abuse and bullying (Anderson, Buckley, & Carnagey, 2008; Dodge et al., 2008; Fang & Corso, 2007). In addition to fear and submissiveness, the recipient may become depressed or respond with his or her own form of aggression.

2. **Passive aggressiveness.** For the recipient, punishment often leads to frustration, anger, and, eventually, aggression. But most of us have learned from experience that retaliatory aggression toward a punisher (especially one who is bigger and more powerful) is usually followed by more punishment. We therefore tend to control our impulse toward open aggression and instead resort to more subtle techniques, such as showing up late or forgetting to run an errand for someone. This is known as passive aggressiveness (Girardi et al., 2007; Johnson, 2008).

3. **Avoidance behaviour.** No one likes to be punished, and so we naturally try to avoid the punisher. Suppose every time you came home, a parent or spouse started to yell at you. You would delay going home or would find another place to go.

4. **Modelling.** Have you ever seen a parent spank or hit a child for hitting another child? The punishing parent may unintentionally serve as a model for the same behaviour the parent is attempting to stop—hitting.

5. **Temporary suppression.** Do you notice that car drivers quickly slow down when they see a police car but quickly resume their previous speed once the police officer is out of sight? Punishment does not extinguish the behaviour but suppresses it only temporarily during the presence of the punishing person or circumstances.

6. **Learned helplessness.** Why do some people stay in abusive homes or intimate situations? Research shows that people who repeatedly fail in their attempts to control their environment acquire a general sense of powerlessness or *learned helplessness* (Seligman, 1975) and may make no further attempts to escape even if it becomes possible (Bargai, Ben-Shakhar, & Salev, 2007; Diaz-Berciano, de Vicente, & Fontecha, 2008; Kim, 2008; Shea, 2008). (Learned helplessness is discussed in Chapter 13 as one explanation for depression.)

Stop & Think
1. Why do you think drivers quickly slow down when they see a police car, and then quickly resume their previous speed once the police officer is out of sight?
2. Given all the problems associated with punishment, why is it so often used?

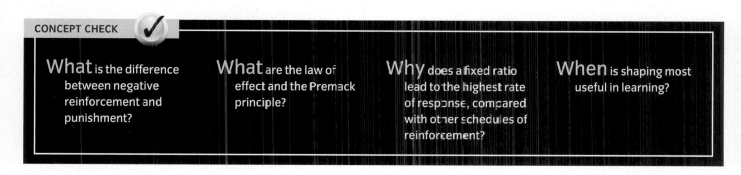

CONCEPT CHECK ✓

What is the difference between negative reinforcement and punishment?

What are the law of effect and the Premack principle?

Why does a fixed ratio lead to the highest rate of response, compared with other schedules of reinforcement?

When is shaping most useful in learning?

Cognitive-Social Learning

LEARNING OBJECTIVES

Explain how insight and latent learning differ from the principles of classical and operant conditioning.

Summarize the evidence that animals (including humans) form internal cognitive maps.

Identify Bandura's necessary conditions for observational learning.

Both operant learning and classical conditioning involve learning associations between a stimulus and an observable behaviour. Although some behaviourists believe that almost all learning can be explained in such stimulus–response terms, other psychologists feel that there is more to learning than can be explained solely by operant and classical conditioning. **Cognitive-social theory** (also called cognitive-social learning or cognitive-behavioural theory) incorporates the general concepts of conditioning, but rather than relying on a simple S–R (stimulus and response) model, this theory emphasizes the interpretation or thinking that occurs within the organism: S–O–R (stimulus–organism–response). According to this view, people have attitudes, beliefs, expectations, motivations, and emotions that affect their learning. Furthermore, both human and non-human animals are social creatures that are capable of learning new behaviours through observation and imitation of others. We begin with a look at the *cognitive* part of cognitive-social theory, followed by an examination of the *social* aspects of learning.

> **Cognitive-social theory** A perspective that emphasizes the roles of thinking and social learning in behaviour.

INSIGHT AND LATENT LEARNING: WHERE ARE THE REINFORCERS?

Early behaviourists likened the mind to a "black box" whose workings could not be observed directly, but German psychologist Wolfgang Köhler wanted to look inside the box. He believed that there was more to learning—especially learning to solve a complex problem—than responding to stimuli in a trial-and-error fashion. In one of a series of experiments, he placed a banana just outside the reach of a caged chimpanzee (**FIGURE 6.9**). To reach the banana, the chimp had to use a stick to extend its reach. Köhler noticed that the chimp did not

Is this insight? FIGURE 6.9

Grande, one of Köhler's chimps, has just solved the problem of how to get the banana. (Also, the thoughtful chimp in the foreground is engaged in observational learning, our next topic.)

solve this problem in a random trial-and-error fashion but, instead, seemed to sit and think about the situation for a while. Then, in a flash of **insight**, the chimp picked up the stick and manoeuvred the banana to within its grasp (Köhler, 1925).

Another of Köhler's chimps, an intelligent fellow named Sultan, was put in a similar situation. This time two sticks were available to him, and the banana was placed even farther away, too far to reach with a single stick. Sultan seemingly lost interest in the banana, but he continued to play with the sticks. When he later discovered that the two sticks could be interlocked, he instantly used the now longer stick to pull the banana within reach. Köhler designated this type of learning **insight learning** because some internal mental event that he could describe only as "insight" went on between the presentation of the banana and the use of the stick to retrieve it.

Like Köhler, Edward C. Tolman (1898–1956) believed that previous researchers underestimated animals' cognitive processes and cognitive learning. He noted that, when allowed to roam aimlessly in an experimental maze with no food reward at the end, rats seemed to develop a **cognitive map** or mental representation of the maze.

To test the idea of cognitive learning, Tolman allowed one group of rats to aimlessly explore a maze with no reinforcement. A second group was reinforced with food whenever they reached the end of the maze. The third group was not rewarded during the first 10 days of the trial, but starting on day 11 they found food at the end of the maze. As expected from simple operant conditioning, the first and third groups were slow to learn the maze, whereas the second group, which had reinforcement, showed fast, steady improvement. However, when the third group started receiving reinforcement (on the 11th day), their learning quickly caught up to the group that had been reinforced every time (Tolman & Honzik, 1930). This showed that the non-reinforced rats had been thinking and building cognitive maps of the area during their aimless wandering and that their **latent learning** only showed up when there was a reason to display it (the food reward).

Cognitive learning is not limited to rats. For example, a chipmunk will pay little attention to a new log in its territory (after initially checking it for food). When a predator comes along, however, the chipmunk heads directly for and hides beneath the log. Recent experiments provide additional clear evidence of latent learning and the existence of internal, cognitive maps in both human and nonhuman animals (Lahav & Mioduser, 2008; McNaughton et al. 2006) (**FIGURE 6.10**).

Is this learning? FIGURE 6.10

This child often rides through her neighbourhood for fun, without a specific destination. Could she tell her mom where the nearest mailbox is located? What type of learning is this?

OBSERVATIONAL LEARNING: WHAT WE SEE IS WHAT WE DO

observational learning Learning new behaviour or information by watching others (also known as social learning or modelling).

In addition to classical and operant conditioning and cognitive processes (such as insight and latent learning), we also learn many things through **observational learning**. From birth to death, observational learning is very important to our biological, psychological, and social survival (the *biopsychosocial model*). Watching others helps us avoid dangerous stimuli in our environment, teaches us how to think and feel, and shows us how to act and interact socially.

Some of the most compelling examples of observational learning come from the work of Canadian-born psychologist Albert Bandura and his colleagues (Bandura, 2003; Bandura, Ross, & Ross, 1961; Bandura & Walters, 1963; Huesman & Kirwil, 2007). Albert Bandura was born and raised in the small town of Mundare, Alberta, not far from Edmonton, and completed his B.A. in psychology at the University of British Columbia. After obtaining his Ph.D. at the University of Iowa, he began a career at Stanford University in California, where he remains today. His award-winning research and theorizing have greatly influenced our understanding of human behaviour.

In several experiments conducted by Bandura and his colleagues, children watched an adult kick, punch, and shout at an inflated Bobo doll. Later, children who had seen the aggressive adult were much more aggressive with the Bobo doll than were those who had not seen the aggression. In other words, "monkey see, monkey do" (**Figure 6.11**). Bandura found that various characteristics of the adult model influenced whether children imitated the behaviour, including whether the model had been rewarded or punished for the aggressive behaviour (Figure 6.11). If the model had been rewarded for the behaviour, the children were more likely to imitate the behaviour. In the same way, if the model had been reprimanded or received other negative consequences for the aggressive behaviour, children were less likely to imitate it.

According to Bandura, observational learning requires at least four separate processes: attention, retention, motor reproduction, and reinforcement (**Figure 6.12**).

Bandura's classic Bobo doll studies
Figure 6.11

Bandura's "Bobo doll" study is considered a classic in psychology. It showed that children will imitate models they observe. Why is this new or important? Are there circumstances in which observational learning (for example, picked up from television) could have positive effects?

1. ATTENTION

Observational learning requires attention. This is why teachers insist on having students watch their demonstrations.

2. RETENTION

To learn new behaviours, we need to carefully note and remember the model's directions and demonstrations.

3. REPRODUCTION

Observational learning cannot occur if we lack the motivation or motor skills necessary to imitate the model.

4. REINFORCEMENT

We are more likely to repeat a modelled behaviour if the model is reinforced for the behaviour.

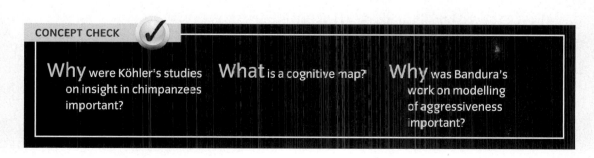

CONCEPT CHECK

Why were Köhler's studies on insight in chimpanzees important?

What is a cognitive map?

Why was Bandura's work on modelling of aggressiveness important?

The Biology of Learning

LEARNING OBJECTIVES

Explain how an animal's environment can affect learning and behaviour.

Identify an example of biological preparedness.

Describe how instinctive drift constrains learning.

So far in this chapter, we have considered how external forces—from reinforcing events to our observations of others—affect learning. But we also know that for changes in behaviour to persist over time, lasting biological changes must occur within the organism. In this section, we will examine neurological and evolutionary influences on learning.

NEUROSCIENCE AND LEARNING: THE ADAPTIVE BRAIN

As Canadian psychologists Joe-Guillaume Pelletier and Denis Paré (2004) have suggested, each time we learn something, either consciously or unconsciously, that experience creates new synaptic connections and alterations in a wide network of brain structures, including the cortex, cerebellum, hypothalamus, thalamus, and amygdala

(see also May et al., 2007; Möhler et al., 2008; Romero, et al., 2008).

Evidence that experience changes brain structure first emerged in the 1960s from studies of animals raised in enriched versus deprived environments. Compared with rats raised in a stimulus-poor environment, those raised in a colourful, stimulating "rat Disneyland" had a thicker cortex, increased nerve growth factor (NGF), more fully developed synapses, more dendritic branching, and improved performance on many tests of learning (Gresack, Kerr, & Frick, 2007; Lores-Arnaiz et al., 2007; Pham et al., 2002; Rosenzweig & Bennett, 1996).

Admittedly, it is a big leap from rats to humans, but research suggests that the human brain also responds to environmental conditions (**FIGURE 6.13**). For example, older adults who are exposed to stimulating environments generally perform better on intellectual and perceptual tasks than those who are in restricted environments (Schaie, 1994, 2008).

Daily enrichment FIGURE 6.13

For humans and non-human animals alike, environmental conditions play an important role in enabling learning. How might a classroom rich with stimulating toys, games, and books foster intellectual development in young children?

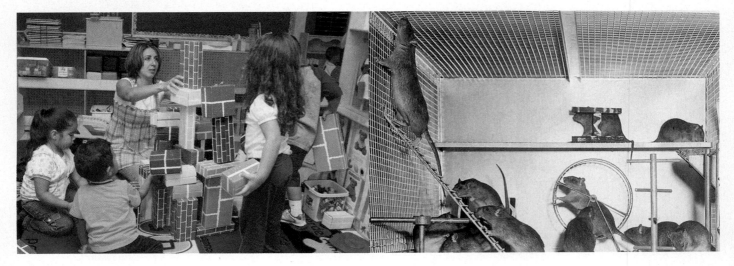

MIRROR NEURONS AND IMITATION

Recent research has identified another neurological influence on learning processes, particularly imitation. By using fMRIs and other brain-imaging techniques (Chapter 1), researchers have identified specific mirror neurons believed to be responsible for human empathy and imitation (Ahlsén, 2008; Fogassi et al., 2005; Hurley, 2008; Jacob, 2008). These neurons are found in several key areas of the brain, and they help us identify with what others are feeling and to imitate their actions. When we see another person in pain, one reason we empathize and "share their pain" is that our mirror neurons are firing. Similarly, if we watch others smile, our mirror neurons make it harder for us to frown.

Mirror neurons were first discovered by neuroscientists who implanted wires in the brains of monkeys to monitor areas involved in planning and carrying out movement (Ferrari, Rozzi, & Fogassi, 2005; Rizzolatti et al., 2002; Rizzolatti, Fogassi, & Gallese, 2006). When these monkeys moved and grasped an object, specific neurons fired, but they also fired when the monkeys simply observed another monkey performing the same or similar tasks.

Mirror neurons in humans also fire when we perform a movement or watch someone else perform it. Have you noticed how spectators at an athletic event sometimes slightly move their arms or legs in synchrony with the athletes, or how newborns tend to imitate adult facial expressions? Mirror neurons may be the underlying biological mechanism for this imitation and for an infant's copying of the lip and tongue movements necessary for speech. They also might help explain the emotional deficits of children and adults with autism or schizophrenia, who often misunderstand the verbal and non-verbal cues of others (Arbib & Mundhenk, 2005; Dapretto et al., 2006; Martineau et al., 2008).

EVOLUTION AND LEARNING: BIOLOGICAL PREPAREDNESS AND INSTINCTIVE DRIFT

Humans and other animals are born with various innate reflexes and instincts. Although these biological tendencies help ensure evolutionary survival, they are inherently inflexible. Only through learning are we able to react to important environmental cues—such as spoken words and written symbols—that our innate reflexes and instincts do not address. Thus, from an evolutionary perspective, learning is an adaptation that enables organisms to survive and prosper in a constantly changing world, or more simply to profit from experience.

Because animals can be operantly conditioned to perform a variety of novel behaviours (like water-skiing), learning theorists initially believed that the fundamental laws of conditioning would apply to almost all species and all behaviours. However, researchers have identified several biological constraints that limit the generality of conditioning principles. These include biological preparedness and instinctive drift.

Years ago, a young woman named Rebecca unsuspectingly bit into a Butterfinger candy bar filled with small, wiggling maggots. Horrified, she ran gagging and screaming to the bathroom. Many years later, Rebecca still feels nauseated when she sees a Butterfinger candy bar (but, fortunately, she doesn't feel similarly nauseated by the sight of her boyfriend, who bought her the candy).

Rebecca's graphic (and true!) story illustrates an important evolutionary process. When a food or drink is associated with nausea or vomiting, that particular food or drink can become a conditioned stimulus (CS) that triggers a conditioned **taste aversion**. Like other classically conditioned responses, taste aversions develop involuntarily (**FIGURE 6.14** on the next page).

Can you see why this automatic response would be adaptive? If one of our ancestral relatives became ill after eating a new plant, it would increase his or her chances for survival if he or she immediately developed an aversion to that plant, but not to other family members who might have been present at the time. Similarly, people tend to develop phobias of snakes, darkness, spiders, and heights more easily than of guns, knives, and electrical outlets presumably because the former were present in the ancestral environment, while the latter were not. We apparently inherit a built-in (innate) readiness to form associations between certain stimuli and responses known as **biological preparedness**.

Laboratory experiments have provided general support for both taste aversion and biological preparedness.

> **biological preparedness**
> Built-in (innate) readiness to form associations between certain stimuli and responses.

Taste aversion in the wild FIGURE 6.14

In applied research, Garcia and his colleagues used classical conditioning to teach coyotes not to eat sheep (Gustavson & Garcia, 1974). The researchers began by lacing freshly killed sheep with a chemical that caused extreme nausea and vomiting in the coyotes that ate the tainted meat. The conditioning worked so well that the coyotes would run away from the mere sight and smell of sheep. This taste aversion developed involuntarily. This research has since been applied many times in the wild and in the laboratory with coyotes and other animals (Aubert & Dantzer, 2005; Domjan, 2005; Workman & Reader, 2008).

For example, John Garcia and Robert Koelling (1966) produced taste aversion in lab rats by pairing flavoured water (NS) and a drug (UCS) that produced gastrointestinal distress (UCR). After being conditioned and then recovering from the illness, the rats refused to drink the flavoured water (CS) because of the conditioned taste aversion. Remarkably, however, Garcia discovered that only certain neutral stimuli could produce the nausea. Pairings of a noise (NS) or a shock (NS) with the nausea-producing drug (UCS) produced no taste aversion. Garcia suggested that when we are sick to our stomachs, we have a natural, evolutionary tendency to attribute it to food or drink. Being biologically prepared to quickly associate nausea with food or drink is adaptive because it helps us avoid that or similar food or drink in the future (Domjan, 2005; Garcia, 2003; Kardong, 2008).

Just as Garcia couldn't produce noise–nausea associations, other researchers have found that an animal's natural behaviour pattern can interfere with operant conditioning. For example, Keller Breland and Marian Breland (1961) tried to teach a chicken to play baseball. Through shaping and reinforcement, the chicken first learned to pull a loop that activated a swinging bat and then learned to actually hit the ball. But instead of running to first base, it would chase the ball as if it were food. Regardless of the lack of reinforcement for chasing the ball, the chicken's natural behaviour took precedence. This biological constraint is known as **instinctive drift**.

instinctive drift The tendency of some conditioned responses to shift (or drift) back toward innate response pattern.

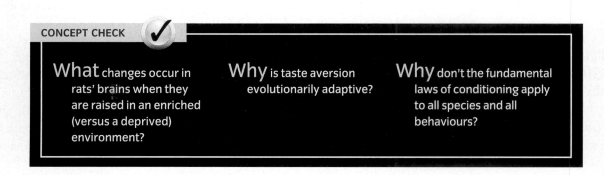

CONCEPT CHECK ✓

What changes occur in rats' brains when they are raised in an enriched (versus a deprived) environment?

Why is taste aversion evolutionarily adaptive?

Why don't the fundamental laws of conditioning apply to all species and all behaviours?

Conditioning and Learning in Everyday Life

In this section, we discuss several everyday applications for classical conditioning, operant conditioning, and cognitive-social learning.

CLASSICAL CONDITIONING: FROM PREJUDICE TO PHOBIAS

One common—and very negative—instance of classical conditioning is prejudice. In a classic study in the 1930s, Kenneth Clark and Mamie P. Clark (1939) found that given a choice, both black and white children preferred white dolls to black dolls. In fact, both groups of children responded that the white doll was good and that the black doll was bad. The Clarks reasoned that the children had learned to associate negative qualities with darker skin and positive qualities with lighter skin. Such learned associations may in part explain racism and prejudice today.

Classical conditioning is also a primary tool for marketing and advertising professionals, filmmakers and musicians, medical practitioners, psychotherapists, and politicians who want to influence our purchases, motivations, emotions, health behaviour, and votes.

Instances of classical conditioning are also found in the medical field. For example, for alcoholic patients, some hospitals pair the smell and taste of alcohol with a nausea-producing drug. Afterward, just the smell or taste of alcohol makes the person sick. Some patients, but not all, have found this treatment successful (Chapter 14).

Finally, researchers have found that classically conditioned emotional responses explain most everyday fears and even most *phobias*, which are exaggerated and irrational fears of a specific object or situation (**FIGURE 6.15**) (Cai et al., 2006; Field, 2006; Ressler & Davis, 2003; Stein & Matsunga, 2006). The good news is that extreme fears—for example, of heights, spiders, or public places—can be effectively treated with *behaviour therapy* (Chapter 14).

Conditioned emotional responses FIGURE 6.15

Classically conditioned emotional responses can explain the development of extreme fears, such as the fear of riding in elevators.

Classical Conditioning as a Marketing Tool

Marketers have mastered numerous classical conditioning principles. For example, TV commercials, magazine ads, and business promotions often pair a company's products or logo (the neutral stimulus/NS) with pleasant images, such as attractive models and celebrities (the conditioned stimulus/CS), which, through higher-order conditioning, automatically trigger favourable responses (the conditioned response/CR). Advertisers hope that after repeated viewings, the previously neutral stimulus (the company's products or logo) will become a conditioned stimulus that elicits a favourable response (CR)—we buy the advertised products. Researchers caution that these ads also help produce visual stimuli that trigger conditioned responses, such as urges to smoke, overeat, and drink alcohol (Kazdin, 2008; Martin et al., 2002; Tirodkar & Jain, 2003; Wakefield et al., 2003).

To appreciate the influences of classical conditioning on your own life, try this:

• Look through a popular magazine and find several advertisements. What images are used as the unconditioned stimulus (UCS) or conditioned stimulus (CS)? Note how you react to these images.

• While watching a movie or a favourite TV show, note what sounds and images are used as conditioned stimuli (CS). (Hint: certain types of music are used to set the stage for happy stories, sad events, and fearful situations.) What are your conditioned emotional responses (CERs)?

 Stop & Think
1. In what way is the ad pictured here an application of psychology?
2. Can you think of other situations in which sounds and images are used as conditioned sitimuli?

OPERANT CONDITIONING: PREJUDICE, BIOFEEDBACK, AND SUPERSTITION

Just as people can learn prejudice through classical conditioning, we also can learn prejudice through operant conditioning. Demeaning and bullying others gains attention and sometimes approval from others. Indeed, as Canadian researchers Debra Pepler and Wendy Craig (Hawkins, Pepler, & Craig, 2001) have noted, the reactions of others can encourage (or discourage) bullying and victimization (we discuss bullying further in Chapter 15). Positive reactions by others can positively reinforce prejudice and discrimination and may increase the instigator's self-esteem, at the expense of the victim (Fein & Spencer, 1997; Rigby, 2008; Kassin, Fein, & Markus, 2008) (**FIGURE 6.16A**). People also may have a single negative (punishing) experience with a specific member of a group, which they then generalize and apply to all members of the group (Vidmar, 1997)—an example of stimulus generalization.

But what explains behaviour that is as extreme as that of the teens who murdered Reena Virk? Why would people do anything that they know could bring a prison sentence? Punishment does weaken and suppress behaviour, but as mentioned before, to be effective it must be consistent and immediate. Unfortunately, it seldom is. Instead, when a person gets away with one or more crimes, that criminal behaviour is put on a partial (intermittent) schedule of reinforcement, making it more likely to be repeated and to become more resistant to extinction.

Biofeedback is another example of operant conditioning in action (**FIGURE 6.16B**). Something is added (feedback) that increases the likelihood that the behaviour will be repeated—positive reinforcement. The biofeedback itself is a secondary reinforcer because of the learned value of the relief from pain or other aversive stimuli (primary reinforcer). Finally, biofeedback involves shaping. A person using biofeedback watches a monitor screen (or other instrument) that provides graphs or numbers indicating some bodily state. Like a

Visualizing

A Prejudice and Discrimination ▶

What reinforcement might these boys receive for teasing this girl? Can you see how operant conditioning, beginning at an early age, can promote unkind or prejudiced behaviour?

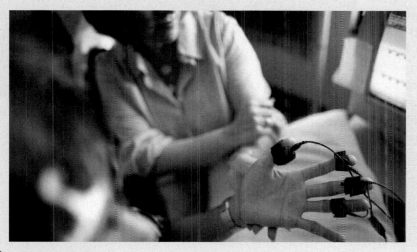

▲ **B Biofeedback**

In biofeedback, internal bodily processes (like blood pressure, muscle tension, or neural activity) are electrically recorded and reported back to the patient. This information helps the person gain control over processes that are normally involuntary. Researchers have successfully used biofeedback (usually in conjunction with other techniques, such as behaviour modification) to treat hypertension, anxiety, epilepsy, urinary incontinence, cognitive functioning, chronic pain, and headache (Andrasik, 2006; Bohm-Starke et al., 2007; Hammond, 2007; Kazdin, 2008; Moss, 2004; Stetter & Kupper, 2002; Tatrow, Blanchard, & Silverman, 2003).

C Superstition ▶

Like Skinner's pigeons, we humans also believe in many superstitions that may have developed from accidental reinforcement: from wearing "something old" during one's wedding, to knocking on wood for good fortune, to performing some bizarre ritual before every athletic competition.

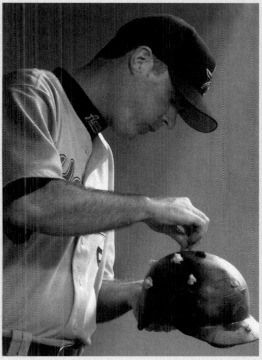

mirror, the biofeedback reflects back the results of the various strategies that the participant uses to gain control. Through trial and error, the participant gets progressively better at making the desired changes.

Even accidental reinforcement can exert a powerful effect, sometimes causing superstitious behaviour (**FIGURE 6.16C**). In a fascinating experiment, B. F. Skinner (1948, 1992) set the feeding mechanism in the cages of eight pigeons to release food once every 15 seconds. No matter what the birds did, they were reinforced at 15-second intervals. Six of the pigeons acquired behaviours that they repeated over and over, even though the behaviours were not necessary to receive the food. For example, one pigeon kept turning in counter-clockwise circles, and another kept making jerking movements with its head. Why did this happen?

Although Skinner was not using the food to reinforce any particular behaviour, the pigeons associated the food with whatever behaviour they were engaged in when the food was originally dropped into the cage.

COGNITIVE-SOCIAL LEARNING: WE SEE, WE DO?

We use cognitive-social learning in many ways in our everyday lives, yet two of the most powerful areas of learning are frequently overlooked: prejudice and media influences. Prejudice and other negative attitudes can be learned through observing others, particularly those whom we admire. For example, a 7-year-old in Winnipeg went to school with a swastika drawn on her arm. Her teacher scrubbed it off, but her mother helped her redraw it the next day. Child and Family Services investigated and found that her parents were involved in white supremacist activities, that she had watched skinhead videos with them, and that her home, where she lived with her 2-year-old brother, contained neo-Nazi symbols and flags (CBC News, 2009a). What kinds of attitudes might be learned through such modelling?

The media also propagate some forms of prejudice. When children watch television, go to the movies, and read books and magazines that portray minorities and women in demeaning and stereotypical roles, they learn to expect these behaviours and to accept them as "natural." Exposure of this kind initiates and reinforces the learning of prejudice (Dill & Thill, 2007; Kassin, Fein, Markus, 2008; Neto & Furnham, 2005; Berenbaum, Martin, & Ruble, 2008).

Both children and adults may be learning other destructive behaviours through observational learning and the media. Correlational evidence from more than 50 studies indicates that observing violent behaviour is related to later desensitization and the performance of violent behaviour (Anderson, Buckley, & Carnagey, 2008; Coyne, Archer, & Eslea, 2004; Kronenberger et al., 2005). In addition, more than 100 experimental studies have also shown a causal link between observing violence and later performing it (Primavera & Herron, 1996). Moreover, the findings of a classic study that investigated the impact of the introduction of television into a Canadian community in the 1970s are telling: the introduction of a single television station into a previously unserved community was associated with increases in both sex-typed attitudes and aggressive behaviour in the child residents of the community (Joy, Kimball, & Zabrack, 1986; Kimball, 1986).

Researchers are just beginning to study how video games (and virtual reality games) affect behaviour (FIGURE 6.17). For example, studies have found that students who play more violent video games in junior high and high school also engage in more aggressive behaviours (Anderson, Gentile, & Buckley, 2007;

Video games and aggression FIGURE 6.17

Researchers hypothesize that video games are more likely to model aggressive behaviour because, unlike TV and other media, they are interactive, engrossing, and require the player to identify with the aggressor. What forms of learning might be involved in this phenomenon?

Carnagey, Anderson, & Bartholow, 2007; Gentile et al., 2004; Wei, 2007). Playing violent video games is associated with increases in aggressive behaviour, aggressive thoughts, aggressive emotions, and physiological arousal (Anderson et al., 2004) Furthermore, playing violent video games has been found to desensitize players to real-life violence, which may then make them less likely to help others in distress (Carnagey, Anderson, & Bushman, 2007). How long these consequences last is unclear. Although it is likely that they dissipate as the effects of the game wear off, the implications for children who consume a steady diet of such violence remain to be examined (Carnagey, Anderson, & Bushman, 2007).

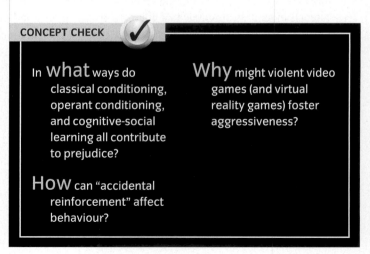

CONCEPT CHECK

In **what** ways do classical conditioning, operant conditioning, and cognitive-social learning all contribute to prejudice?

Why might violent video games (and virtual reality games) foster aggressiveness?

How can "accidental reinforcement" affect behaviour?

1 Classical Conditioning

1. Learning is a relatively permanent change in behaviour or mental processes as a result of practice or experience. Pavlov discovered a fundamental form of **conditioning** (learning) called **classical conditioning**, in which a neutral stimulus becomes associated with an unconditioned stimulus to elicit a conditioned response. In the "Little Albert" experiment, Watson and Rayner demonstrated how many of our likes, dislikes, prejudices, and fears are conditioned emotional responses.

2. Stimulus generalization occurs when an event similar to the originally conditioned stimulus triggers the same conditioned response. With experience, animals learn to distinguish between an original conditioned stimulus and similar stimuli—stimulus discrimination. Most learned behaviours can be weakened through extinction. Extinction is a gradual weakening or suppression of a previously conditioned response. However, if a conditioned stimulus is reintroduced after extinction, an extinguished response may spontaneously recover.

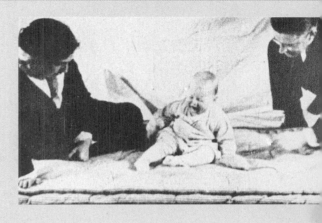

2 Operant Conditioning

1. In **operant conditioning**, an organism performs a behaviour that produces either reinforcement or punishment. **Reinforcement** strengthens the response, while **punishment** weakens the response.

2. Thorndike developed the **law of effect**, a first step in understanding how consequences can modify voluntary behaviours. Skinner extended Thorndike's law of effect to more complex behaviours.

3. Reinforcers can be either primary or secondary, and reinforcement can be either positive or negative.

4. Schedules of reinforcement are the rate or interval at which responses are reinforced. Most behaviour is rewarded on one of four partial schedules of reinforcement: fixed ratio, variable ratio, fixed interval, or variable interval.

5. Organisms learn complex behaviours through **shaping**, in which reinforcement is delivered for successive approximations of the desired response.

6. Punishment weakens the response. To be effective, punishment must be immediate and consistent. Even then, the recipient may learn only what not to do. Punishment can have serious side effects: increased aggression, avoidance behaviour, passive aggressiveness, and learned helplessness.

3 Cognitive-Social Learning

1. **Cognitive-social theory** emphasizes cognitive and social aspects of learning. Köhler discovered that animals sometimes learn through sudden **insight**, rather than through trial and error. Tolman provided evidence of **latent learning** and internal cognitive maps.

2. Bandura's research found that children who watched an adult behave aggressively toward an inflated Bobo doll were later more aggressive than those who had not seen the aggression. According to Bandura, **observational learning** requires attention, retention, motor reproduction, and reinforcement.

4 The Biology of Learning

1. Learning creates structural changes in the brain. Early evidence for such changes came from research on animals raised in enriched versus deprived environments.

2. Learning is an evolutionary adaptation that enables organisms to survive and prosper in a constantly changing world. Researchers have identified biological constraints that limit the generality of conditioning principles: **biological preparedness** and **instinctive drift**.

5 Conditioning and Learning in Everyday Life

1. Classical conditioning is a primary tool for advertisers and others who want to manipulate beliefs, emotions, or behaviour, by pairing a company's product with pleasant images. Classical conditioning is also used in medicine and in the development and treatment of phobias.

2. Operant conditioning plays a role in the development of prejudice, as the reactions of others can encourage (or discourage) demeaning behaviour. Operant conditioning also underlies biofeedback. Even accidental reinforcement can cause superstitious behaviour.

3. Cognitive-social learning plays a role in many areas of everyday life through modelling and observational learning, including the development of prejudice and media influences on our behaviour.

KEY TERMS

CRITICAL AND CREATIVE THINKING QUESTIONS

1. How might Watson and Rayner, who conducted the famous "Little Albert" study, have designed a more ethical study of conditioned emotional responses?

2. What are some examples of ways in which observational learning has benefited you in your life? Are there instances in which observational learning has worked to your disadvantage?

3. Do you have any taste aversions? How would you use information in this chapter to remove them?

4. Most classical conditioning is involuntary. Considering this, is it ethical for politicians and advertisers to use classical conditioning to influence our thoughts and behaviour? Why or why not?

5. Consider the effects of classical conditioning in your own life. Can you think of conditioned stimuli (CS) that elicit conditioned responses (CR) in you?

6. What are some things you use as positive reinforcers? How do you reward yourself after studying hard, completing a paper, exercising and so on?

What is happening in this picture ?

For political candidates, kissing babies seems to be as critical as pulling together a winning platform and airing persuasive campaign ads.

- What principle of learning explains why politicians kiss babies?

- What other stimuli or symbols might elicit similar effects?

SELF-TEST

1. What form of conditioning occurs when a neutral stimulus becomes associated with an unconditioned stimulus (UCS) to elicit a conditioned response (CR)?

   a. reflexive conditioning
   b. instinctive conditioning
   c. classical conditioning
   d. operant conditioning

2. What do we call the process of learning associations between environmental stimuli and behavioural responses?

   a. maturation
   b. contiguity learning
   c. conditioning
   d. latent learning

3. In John Watson's demonstration of classical conditioning with Little Albert, what was the unconditioned stimulus?

   a. symptoms of fear
   b. a rat
   c. a bath towel
   d. a loud noise

4. Which of the following is an example of classical conditioning in everyday life?

   a. treating alcoholism with a drug that causes nausea when alcohol is consumed
   b. the use of seductive women to sell cars to men
   c. politicians associating themselves with families, babies, and the Canadian flag
   d. all of these options

5. *Extinction* _____ .

   a. is a gradual weakening or suppression of a previously conditioned behaviour

   b. occurs when a CS is repeatedly presented without the UCS

   c. is a weakening of the association between the CS and the UCS

   d. all of these options

6. A neutral stimulus is paired with a previously conditioned stimulus (CS) and thereby becomes a conditioned stimulus (CS) itself. What do we call this kind of learning ?

   a. operant conditioning

   b. classical conditioning

   c. higher-order conditioning

   d. secondary conditioning

7. What is the term for learning in which voluntary responses are controlled by their consequences?

   a. self-efficacy

   b. classical conditioning

   c. operant conditioning

   d. higher-order conditioning

8. Match the illustration with the correct label:

   a. Thorndike box: law of effect, photo _____

   b. Skinner box: reinforcement, photo _____

1.

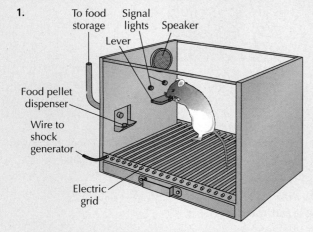

2.

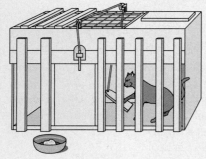

9. The addition of a(n) _____ stimulus results in *positive reinforcement*; whereas the subtraction of a(n) _____ stimulus results in *negative reinforcement*.

   a. desirable; painful or annoying

   b. primary; secondary

   c. operant; classical

   d. higher order; lower order

10. How did the chimpanzee in Köhler's *insight* experiment behave?

   a. It used trial-and-error to reach a banana placed just out of reach.

   b. It turned its back on the banana out of frustration.

   c. It sat for a while, then used a stick to bring the banana within reach.

   d. It didn't like bananas.

11. Learning new behaviour or information by watching others is known as _____ .

   a. social learning

   b. observational learning

   c. modelling

   d. all of the above

12. Garcia and colleagues taught coyotes to avoid sheep by pairing a nausea-inducing drug with freshly killed sheep eaten by the coyotes. This is an example of which of the following?

   a. classical conditioning

   b. operant conditioning

   c. positive punishment

   d. negative punishment

13. Mamie has an EMG attached to her forehead. When tension rises, a computer says, "That's too high." When it drops to normal or lower levels, it says, "That's very good." What is Mamie using to decrease her tension headaches?

   a. primary reinforcement
   b. computerized reinforcement
   c. biofeedback
   d. electromyography monitoring

14. According to the chapter, what is the consequence of exposure to media portrayals of demeaning and stereotypical roles for minorities and women?

   a. It increases critical thinking about minorities and women.
   b. It initiates and reinforces the learning of prejudice.
   c. It increases empathy for minorities and women.
   d. It decreases a child's stereotypical gender-role behaviour.

15. Which of the following increases modelling effects of violent video games?

   a. Videos are interactive.
   b. Videos are engrossing to the player.
   c. Video players identify with the aggressor in the game.
   d. all of these options

16. Which of the following is an example of stimulus generalization?

   a. responding to the conditioned stimulus, but not to other stimuli that closely resemble it
   b. working hard at school to get a financial reward from your dad
   c. responding to other stimuli that closely resemble the conditioned stimulus
   d. getting out of bed at 3 am to turn on the air conditioner because you cannot sleep

17. The Premack principle is best demonstrated by which of the following?

   a. Johnny does his best in school to get the new bike his parents promised him.
   b. Bianca stays away from people who remind her of her ex-boyfriend, to avoid thinking about him.
   c. Jimmy schedules studying time with a girl he likes in the hope that she will become attracted to him.
   d. Lisa does 2 hours of intense studying before allowing herself to watch her favourite TV show.

18. Which of the following best describes an *unconditioned stimulus*?

   a. forgetting a previously strong association between two stimuli
   b. a previously conditioned stimulus that no longer elicits a response
   c. a stimulus you respond to without having to learn its association with another stimulus
   d. trying to show a favourable reaction to a stimulus, regardless of what you think of it

19. After seeing his older brother throw rocks at a nasty dog, Vinny throws some of his toys at it too. Vinny's behaviour is best explained by which of the following?

   a. classical conditioning
   b. operant conditioning
   c. observational learning
   d. insight learning

20. Which researcher discovered that behaviours rewarded with something desirable are likely to be repeated? This is what type of conditioning?

   a. Skinner; operant conditioning
   b. Pavlov; classical conditioning
   c. Pavlov; operant conditioning
   d. Thorndike; operant conditioning

Memory 7

When Henry Molaison was 27 years old, portions of his temporal lobes and limbic system were removed as treatment for severe epilepsy. The surgery was successful—that is, his seizures could now be controlled, but something was clearly wrong with his memory. Two years after the surgery, he still believed he was 27. He had to be repeatedly reminded of events that had occurred after his surgery. As of 2008, more than 50 years later, Henry could not recognize the people who cared for his daily needs or the features of his own room. He would read the same magazines over and over again and laugh at the same old jokes he had been told dozens of times before. Right into his 80s, he still saw himself as a young man and had not recognized a photograph of his own face for decades (Corkin, 2002).

For more than three decades, Dr. Brenda Milner of the Montreal Neurological Institute worked with and studied Henry. Dr. Milner showed that while Henry could not remember one day from the next and could never remember her name, on some of the tasks she administered there were significant improvements in his performance. This occurred even though Henry had no memory of any prior exposure to the task.

Henry Molaison died at the age of 82 in December 2008. For more than 50 years he was recognized as the most important patient in the history of neuroscience. As a case study, he helped researchers and the medical community understand the biological basis of human learning and memory. Two generations of psychology students before you learned about this man, who was known to us only as H.M.

In December 2009, Henry Molaison's brain was sectioned into 2,401 paper-thin slices (see photo) to reveal the nature of the lesion.

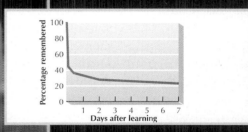

The Nature of Memory

Memory allows us to profit from our experiences and to adjust to ever-changing environments. Without memory we would not learn from past events or adapt to future situations. Consider Henry Molaison for a second as you read this paragraph; it is memory that makes the present meaningful and the future understandable. Yet our memories are also highly fallible. Although some people think of **memory** as a gigantic library or an automatic video recorder, our memories are never perfect records of events. Instead, memory is a *constructive and re-creative process* through which we actively organize and shape information. Memory is malleable. As you might expect, the belief that memory is accurate and precise often leads to serious errors and biases, which we'll discuss throughout this chapter.

memory
An internal record or representation of some prior event or experience.

HOW DOES MEMORY WORK?

Over the years, psychologists have developed numerous models (or representations) of how memory operates. As emerging research has provided insights into memory,

---

Process Diagram

Information-processing model FIGURE 7.1

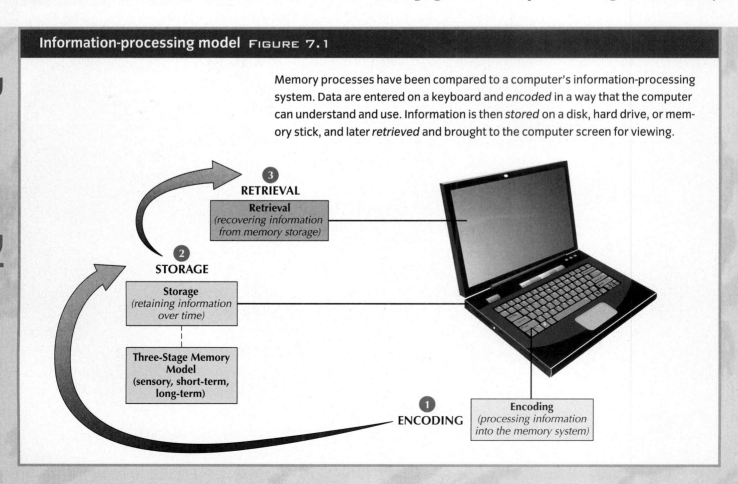

Memory processes have been compared to a computer's information-processing system. Data are entered on a keyboard and *encoded* in a way that the computer can understand and use. Information is then *stored* on a disk, hard drive, or memory stick, and later *retrieved* and brought to the computer screen for viewing.

3 RETRIEVAL
Retrieval
(recovering information from memory storage)

2 STORAGE
Storage
(retaining information over time)

Three-Stage Memory Model
(sensory, short-term, long-term)

1 ENCODING
Encoding
(processing information into the memory system)

many of the older models have largely been abandoned. In this first section, we briefly discuss the two approaches that have the most empirical evidence and have withstood research scrutiny: the information-processing model and the three-stage model.

Information-Processing Model

According to the **information-processing model**, the barrage of information that we encounter every day goes through three basic levels of processing: **encoding**, **storage**, and **retrieval** (FIGURE 7.1).

With this information-processing model of memory, the brain encodes sensory information, such as sounds or visual images, into a neural code that it can understand; stores the information for later use; and retrieves information by searching for the appropriate stored "files" and bringing them back into short-term memory, where they can be worked with. These operations are analogous to incoming information being typed on a keyboard and translated into computer language, stored on a disk, and retrieved when brought to the computer screen to be viewed.

■ **encoding** Processing information into the memory system.

■ **storage** Retaining information over time.

■ **retrieval** Recovering information from memory storage.

The Three-Stage Model

Since the late 1960s, one of the most widely used models in memory research is called the **three-stage memory model** (Atkinson & Shiffrin, 1968). According to this model, memory comprises three different storage "boxes," or stages (sensory, short-term, and long-term), that each hold and process information in a specific way. Each stage has a different purpose, duration, and capacity (FIGURE 7.2). The three-stage memory model remains the leading paradigm in memory research because it offers a convenient way to organize the major research findings. Let's discuss this model in more detail.

The three-stage memory model FIGURE 7.2

Each "box" represents a separate memory system that differs in purpose, duration, and capacity. When information is not transferred from sensory memory or short-term memory, it is assumed to be lost. Information stored in long-term memory can be retrieved and sent back to short-term memory for use.

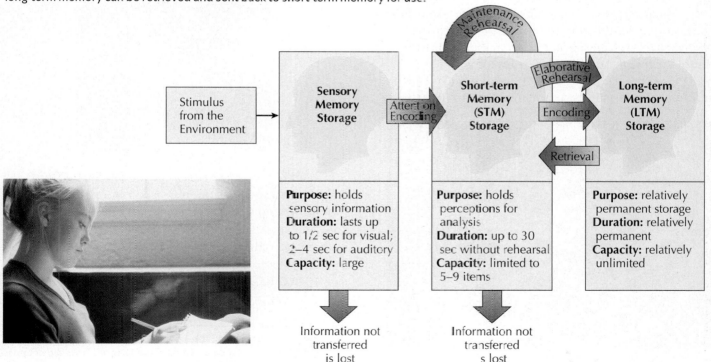

SENSORY MEMORY: FIRST IMPRESSIONS

Everything we see, hear, touch, taste, and smell first enters our **sensory memory**. Information remains in sensory memory momentarily; if we attend to this new information, it is then transferred to the next stage of memory. For visual information, known as *iconic memory*, the visual image (icon) lasts about half a second (**FIGURE 7.3**). Auditory information (what we hear) is held in sensory memory for about the same time, but a weaker "echo," or *echoic memory*, of this auditory information can last up to four seconds (Lu, Williamson, & Kaufman, 1992; Neisser, 1967). Both iconic and sensory memory are demonstrated in *Applying Psychology*.

> **sensory memory**
>
> The first memory stage that holds sensory information and has a relatively large capacity but the duration of only a few seconds.

How do researchers test sensory memory?
FIGURE 7.3

In an early study of sensory memory, George Sperling (1960) flashed an arrangement of letters, like these, for 1/20th of a second. When told to recall the total arrangement in free recall, most people, he found, could recall only four or five letters. But when instructed to report just the top, middle, or bottom row, depending on whether they heard a randomly presented high, medium, or low tone after seeing the matrix, they reported almost all the letters correctly. It seems that all 12 letters are held in sensory memory right after they are viewed, but only those that are immediately attended to are noted and processed.

Applying Psychology

Demonstrating Iconic and Echoic Memory

As mentioned, visual and auditory information remains in sensory memory for a short time. For a simple demonstration of the duration of visual, or *iconic memory*, wave a lit sparkler when it is dark outside. Because the image, or icon, lingers for a fraction of a second after the sparkler is moved, you see the light as a continuous stream, similar to the image in this photo.

Auditory, or *echoic memory*, works similarly. Think back to a time when someone asked you a question while you were deeply absorbed in a task. Did you say "What?" and then immediately find you could answer them before they repeated the statement? Now you know why. A weaker "echo" (echoic memory) of auditory information can last up to four seconds.

 Stop & Think
1. What do you think would happen if we did not possess iconic or echoic memory?
2. What might happen if visual or auditory sensations lingered not for seconds but for minutes?

Early researchers believed that sensory memory had an unlimited capacity. However, later research suggested that sensory memory does have limits and that stored images are fuzzier than once thought (Goldstein, 2008; Grondin, Ouellet, & Roussel, 2004).

SHORT-TERM MEMORY: OUR "WORKING WITH" MEMORY

The second stage of memory processing, **short-term memory (STM)**, temporarily stores and processes sensory stimuli that has been encoded/attended to. If the information is meaningful, STM organizes and sends it along to relatively permanent storage, called long-term memory (LTM). Otherwise, it decays and is lost.

The *capacity* and *duration* of STM are limited (Best, 1999; Kareev, 2000). To extend the *capacity* of STM, you might use a memory technique called **chunking** (Boucher & Dienes, 2003; Miller, 1956). Have you noticed that credit card, social insurance, and telephone numbers are all grouped into three or four units separated by spaces? This is because it's easier to remember numbers in "chunks" rather than as a long string of single digits, as shown in *What a Psychologist Sees*.

You can extend the *duration* of your STM almost indefinitely by consciously repeating the information, a process called **maintenance rehearsal**. You are using maintenance rehearsal when you look up a

Chunking in Chess

What do you see when you observe the arrangement of pieces on a chessboard? To the novice, a chess game in progress looks like little more than a random assembly of black and white game pieces. Accordingly, inexperienced chess players can remember the positions of only a few pieces when a chess game is underway. But expert players generally can easily remember all the positions. To the experts, the scattered pieces form meaningful patterns—classic arrangements that recur often. Just as you group the letters of this sentence into meaningful words and remember them long enough to understand the meaning of the entire sentence, expert chess players group the chess pieces into easily recalled patterns (or chunks) (Huffman, Matthews, & Gagne, 2001; Waters & Gobet, 2003).

phone number and say it over and over again in your head until you dial the number. People who are good at remembering names also know to take advantage of maintenance rehearsal. They repeat the name of each person they meet, aloud or silently, to keep it active in STM.

"Working with" Memory Short-term memory is more than just a passive, temporary "holding area." Most current researchers (Baddeley, 1992; Baddeley & Jarrold, 2007; Jonides et al., 2008) realize that active processing of information occurs in STM. Because the short-term memory is active, and its contents are constantly being worked, we can think of STM as a three-part **working memory.** Let's look at each of these three parts (**FIGURE 7.4**).

Process Diagram

Working memory as a central executive FIGURE 7.4

The *central executive* supervises and coordinates two subsystems, the *phonological rehearsal loop* and the *visuospatial sketchpad*, while also sending and retrieving information to and from LTM. Picture yourself as a food server in a busy restaurant, and a couple has just given you a complicated food order.

Central executive
(Coordinates material phonologically and visuospatially along with long-term memory)

When you mentally rehearse the food order (the phonological loop) and combine it with a mental picture of the layout of plates on the customers' table (the visuospatial sketchpad), you're using your central executive.

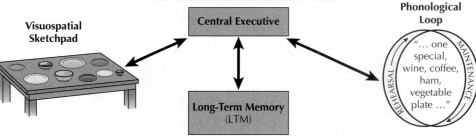

Visuospatial Sketchpad

Central Executive

Phonological Loop

REHEARSAL — MAINTENANCE

"… one special, wine, coffee, ham, vegetable plate …"

Long-Term Memory (LTM)

Visuospatial sketchpad
(Mentally imagines visual and spatial material)

Phonological loop
(Rehearses through speech, words, numbers)

The *visuospatial sketchpad* holds and manipulates visual images and spatial information (Baddeley & Jarrold, 2007; Lehnert & Zimmer, 2008). Again, imagine yourself as the food server who's delivering the food to the same customers. Using your mind's visuospatial sketchpad, you can mentally visualize where to fit all the entrees, side dishes, and dinnerware on their table.

The working memory's *phonological rehearsal loop* holds and manipulates verbal (phonological) information (Dasi et al., 2008; Jonides et al., 2008). Your phonological loop allows you to subvocally repeat all your customers' specific requests while you write a brief description on your order pad.

LONG-TERM MEMORY: GIVING CONTEXT TO THE PRESENT

Think back to the opening story of Henry Molaison. Although his surgery was successful in stopping his severe seizures, it also destroyed the mechanism that transfers information from short-term to long-term memory. That was why he could not remember the people he saw every day and didn't recognize photos of his own aging face.

> **long-term memory (LTM)** This third memory stage stores information for long periods. Its capacity is limitless; its duration is relatively permanent.

Once information is transferred from STM, it is organized and integrated with other information in **long-term memory (LTM)**. LTM serves as a storehouse of information that must be kept for long periods. When we need the information—perhaps to remember something—it is sent back to STM for our use. Compared with sensory memory and short-term memory, long-term memory has relatively unlimited *capacity* and *duration* (Klatzky, 1984).

How do we store the vast amount of information that we collect over our lifetime? Several types of LTM exist (see STUDY ORGANIZER 7.1). The two major systems are explicit/declarative memory and implicit/nondeclarative memory.

Explicit/declarative memory refers to intentional learning or conscious knowledge. If asked to remember your cell phone number or your mother's name, you can state (declare) the answers directly (explicitly). Explicit/declarative memory can be further subdivided into two parts. *Semantic* memory is memory for general knowledge, rules, public events, facts, and specific information. It is our mental encyclopedia.

In contrast, *episodic* memory is like a mental journal into which personal experiences are written. This subsystem records the major events (episodes) in our lives. Some of our episodic memories are short lived, such as where you had coffee this morning, while others can last a lifetime, such as remembering your first elementary school crush or first passionate kiss.

Have you ever wondered why most preschoolers can remember events that happened to them in the previous

> **explicit/ declarative memory** The subsystem within long-term memory that consciously stores facts, information, and personal life experiences.

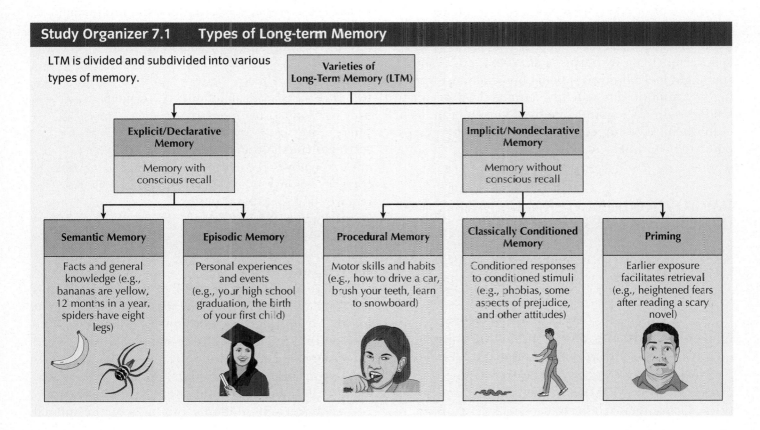

Study Organizer 7.1   Types of Long-term Memory

LTM is divided and subdivided into various types of memory.

Varieties of Long-Term Memory (LTM)

Explicit/Declarative Memory — Memory with conscious recall

Implicit/Nondeclarative Memory — Memory without conscious recall

Semantic Memory — Facts and general knowledge (e.g., bananas are yellow, 12 months in a year, spiders have eight legs)

Episodic Memory — Personal experiences and events (e.g., your high school graduation, the birth of your first child)

Procedural Memory — Motor skills and habits (e.g., how to drive a car, brush your teeth, learn to snowboard)

Classically Conditioned Memory — Conditioned responses to conditioned stimuli (e.g., phobias, some aspects of prejudice, and other attitudes)

Priming — Earlier exposure facilitates retrieval (e.g., heightened fears after reading a scary novel)

few months, yet most of us adults can recall almost nothing of those years before age 3? Not that you would want to, but why don't we remember our own birth? Research suggests that for us to encode these early events and recall them much later, the frontal lobes—along with other neural structures—need to be sufficiently mature (Leichtman, 2006; Morris, 2007; Prigatano & Gray, 2008; Suzuki & Amaral, 2004; Wang, 2008).

Implicit/nondeclarative memory refers to non-conscious learning or acquiring knowledge unintentionally. Try telling someone else how you tie shoelaces without demonstrating the actual behaviour. Because your memory of this skill is non-conscious and hard to describe (declare) in words, this type of memory is sometimes referred to as *nondeclarative*.

> **implicit/ nondeclarative memory** The subsystem within long-term memory that consists of non-conscious procedural skills, simple classically conditioned responses (Chapter 6), and priming.

Implicit/nondeclarative memory consists of *procedural* motor skills, like skateboarding, as well as *classically conditioned memory* responses, such as fears and phobias or taste aversions.

Implicit/nondeclarative memory also includes *priming*, where prior exposure to a stimulus facilitates or inhibits (primes) the processing of new information (Amir et al., 2008; Becker, 2008; Tulving, 2000; Tulving & Schacter, 1990; Woollams et al., 2008). For example, you might feel a little edgy being home alone after seeing a scary movie, and watching a romantic movie might kindle your own romantic feelings. Priming can occur even when we do not consciously remember being exposed to the prime.

IMPROVING LONG-TERM MEMORY: PRACTICE MAKES PERMANENT

Several processes can be employed to improve long-term memory. These include organization, rehearsal or repetition, and effective retrieval.

Organization
To successfully encode information for LTM, we need to *organize* material into hierarchies. This involves arranging a number of related items into broad categories that are further divided and subdivided. (This organization strategy for LTM is similar to the strategy of chunking material in STM.) Many textbooks are laid out using organization principles in the hope of improving long-term retention of the contents. Grouping small subsets of ideas together, as subheadings under larger, main headings, and within diagrams, tables, and so on, helps to make the material in the text more understandable and memorable.

Admittedly, organization takes time and effort. But you'll be happy to know that a little memory organization and filing is done automatically while you sleep (Mograss et al., 2008; Siccoli et al., 2008). Unfortunately, despite claims to the contrary, research shows that we can't recruit our sleeping hours to memorize new material, such as a foreign language.

Rehearsal
Like organization, *rehearsal* also improves encoding for both STM and LTM. If you need to hold information in STM for longer than 30 seconds, you can simply keep repeating it (maintenance rehearsal). But storage in LTM requires *deeper levels of processing* called **elaborative rehearsal** (FIGURE 7.5A).

> **elaborative rehearsal** The process of linking new information to previously stored material.

The immediate goal of elaborative rehearsal is to *understand the information better* and not to simply memorize it. Understanding is one of the best ways to encode new information into long-term memory.

Retrieval
Finally, effective *retrieval* is critical to improving long-term memory. There are two types of **retrieval cues**. *Specific cues* require you only to recognize the correct response. *General cues* require you to recall previously learned material by searching through all possible matches in LTM—a much more difficult task (FIGURE 7.5B and FIGURE 7.5C).

> **retrieval cue** A clue or prompt that helps stimulate recall and retrieval of a stored piece of information from long-term memory.

Whether cues require recall or only recognition is not all that matters. Imagine that while apartment hunting, you walk into a stranger's kitchen and are greeted with the unmistakable smell of freshly baked chocolate chip cookies. Instantly, the aroma transports you to your grandmother's kitchen, where you spent many childhood afternoons doing your homework. You find yourself suddenly thinking of the mental

A Elaborative rehearsal

To improve elaborative rehearsal, you can expand (or elaborate on) the information to try to understand it better, actively explore and question new information, and search for meaningfulness. For example, a student might compare what she reads in an anthropology or history textbook with what she knows about world geography. Can you see how this might deepen her understanding and memory for the subject?

B Recall versus recognition memory

Can you *recall* from memory the names of the eight planets in our solar system? Why is it so much easier to *recognize* the names if you're provided with the first three letters of each planet's name: Mer-, Ven-, Ear-, Mar-, Jup-, Sat-, Ura-, Nep-? *Recall*, like an essay question, requires you to retrieve previously learned material with only general (often vague), nonspecific cues. In contrast, *recognition* tasks, as in a multiple-choice question, offer specific cues that only require you to identify (recognize) the correct response. (Note that in 2006, Pluto was officially declassified as a planet.)

C Longevity and recognition memory

Both name recognition and picture recognition for high school classmates remain high even many years after graduation, whereas recall memory would be expected to drop significantly over time.

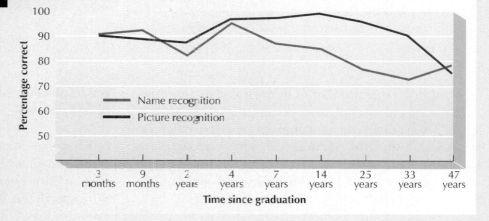

Time since graduation

- Name recognition
- Picture recognition

NATIONAL GEOGRAPHIC

shortcuts your grandmother taught you to help you learn your multiplication tables. You hadn't thought about these little tricks for years, but somehow a whiff of homemade cookies brought them back to you. Why?

In this imagined episode, you have stumbled on the **encoding specificity principle**, which states that retrieval of information will be better if conditions of recall are similar to conditions when encoded (Amir et al., 2008; Becker, 2008; Tulving & Thompson, 1973; Woollams et al., 2008). One important contextual cue for retrieval is *location*. In a clever, now classic study, Godden and Baddeley (1975) had underwater divers learn a list of 40 words either on land or underwater. The divers had better recall for lists that they had encoded underwater if they were also underwater at the time of retrieval; similarly, lists that were encoded above water were better recalled above water.

> **encoding specificity principle** Retrieval of information is improved when the conditions of recovery are similar to the conditions that existed when the information was first encoded.

People also remember information better if their moods during learning and retrieval match (Kenealy, 1997; Nouchi & Hyodo, 2007). This phenomenon, called *mood congruence*, occurs because a given mood tends to evoke memories that are consistent with that mood. When you're sad (or happy or angry), you're more likely to remember events and circumstances from other times when you were also sad (or happy or angry).

Finally, as generations of coffee-devouring university students have discovered, if you learn something while under the influence of a drug, such as caffeine, you will remember it a little more easily when you take that drug again than during other times (Ahmadi et al., 2008; Baddeley, 1998; Zarrindast et al., 2005; Zarrindast et al., 2007). This is called *state-dependent retrieval.*

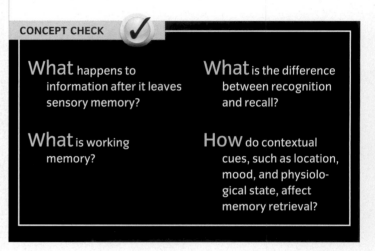

CONCEPT CHECK

What happens to information after it leaves sensory memory?

What is the difference between recognition and recall?

What is working memory?

How do contextual cues, such as location, mood, and physiological state, affect memory retrieval?

Biological Bases of Memory

LEARNING OBJECTIVES

Describe two kinds of biological changes that occur when we learn something new.

Identify the primary brain areas involved in memory.

Explain how injury and disease can affect memory.

A large number of biological changes occur when we learn something new. Among them are neuronal and synaptic changes. In this section we will discuss these changes, along with the research surrounding where memories are located in the brain and what might cause memory loss.

NEURONAL AND SYNAPTIC CHANGES IN MEMORY

We know that learning and new experiences modify the brain's neural architecture (Chapters 2 and 6). As you learn to snowboard, for example, repeated practice builds specific neural pathways in your brain that make

> **Long-term potentiation (LTP)**
> Long-lasting increase in neural excitability caused by repeated neural input. Believed to be the biological basis of learning and memory.

it easier and easier for you to get down the mountain without falling over and breaking your neck. Research has shown this **long-term potentiation (LTP)** happens in at least two ways.

First, as early research with rats raised in "enriched" environments showed (Rosenzweig, Bennett, & Diamond, 1972; Chapter 6), repeated stimulation of a synapse strengthened the synapse by causing the dendrites to grow more spines. Spines are knobby outcroppings on dendrites and more of them mean more synapses, more receptor sites, and more sensitivity. The neuron is said to be more sensitive because the action potential can now affect a greater number of downstream neurons.

Second, learning affects a particular neuron's ability to release its neurotransmitters. This has been shown in research with *Aplysia*, a rather pretty looking sea slug that can be classically conditioned to reflexively withdraw its gills when squirted with water. This change in *Aplysia* is mediated by an increase in neurotransmitter release at specific synapses (**FIGURE 7.6**).

Further evidence comes from research with genetically engineered "smart mice," which have extra neural receptors for a neurotransmitter named NMDA (N-methyl-d-aspartate). These mice performed significantly better on memory tasks than did normal mice (Tang et al., 2001; Tsien, 2000). Evidence of long-term potentiation (LTP) has also been documented in humans (Berger et al., 2008; Tecchio et al., 2008).

HORMONAL CHANGES AND MEMORY

When stressed or excited, we naturally produce hormones, such as epinephrine and cortisol (Chapter 3), that arouse and energize the body. These hormones in turn affect the amygdala (a brain structure involved in emotion), which then signals the hippocampus and cerebral cortex (parts of the brain that are important for memory storage). Research has shown that direct injections of epinephrine or cortisol or electrical stimulation of the amygdala increases the encoding and storage of new information (Hamilton & Gotlib, 2008; Jackson, 2008;

How does a sea slug learn and remember?
FIGURE 7.6

After repeated squirting with water, followed by a mild shock, the sea slug, *Aplysia*, releases more neurotransmitters at certain synapses. These synapses then become more efficient at transmitting signals that allow the slug to withdraw its gills when squirted. Why might this ability be evolutionarily advantageous?

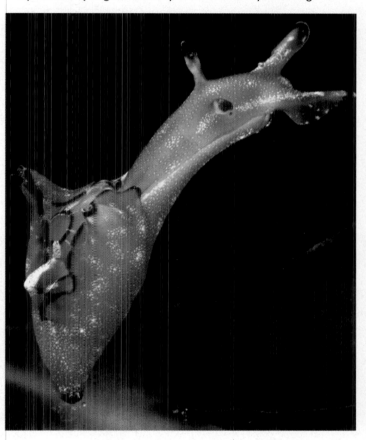

van Stegeren, 2008). Moreover, newer animal research has shown that a region of the amygdala can influence representations in the cortex, and this may be the mechanism by which long-term memories are strengthened (Chavez, McGaugh, & Weinberger, 2009). However, prolonged or excessive stress (and increased levels of cortisol) has been shown to interfere with memory (Al'absi, Hugdahl, & Lovallo, 2002; Heffelfinger & Newcomer, 2001; McAllister-Williams & Rugg, 2002).

The powerful effect of hormones on memory is evident in *flashbulb memories*—vivid images of circumstances associated with surprising or strongly emotional events (Brown & Kulik, 1977). In such situations, we secrete fight-or-flight hormones when the event occurs and then replay the event in our minds again and again, which makes for stronger memories. Despite their intensity, flashbulb memories are not as accurate as you might think (Cubelli & Della Sala, 2008; Talarico & Rubin, 2007). Even these types of memories, memories that feel crystal clear, are subject to errors; while we tend to remember the emotion and generalities of the event, many of the details are actually lost.

IT'S ALL IN YOUR HEAD: WHERE ARE MEMORIES LOCATED?

Early memory researchers believed that memory was localized, or stored in a particular discrete brain area. More recent research suggests that, in fact, memory tends not to be localized in a single region but stored in many separate areas throughout the brain.

Today, research techniques have advanced such that we can experimentally induce and measure memory-related brain changes as they occur. For example, James Brewer and his colleagues (1998) used functional magnetic resonance imaging (fMRI) to locate areas of the brain responsible for encoding memories of pictures. They showed 96 pictures of indoor and outdoor scenes to participants while scanning their brains, and then later tested participants' ability to recall the pictures. Brewer and his colleagues identified the *right prefrontal cortex* and the *parahippocampal cortex* as being the most active during the encoding of the pictures. These are only two of several brain regions involved in memory storage, however.

Ψ Psychological Science

Brain and Memory Formation

Damage to any one of these areas can affect the encoding, storage, and retrieval of memories.

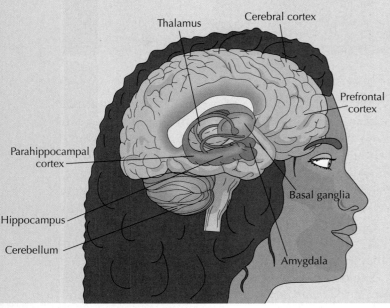

Amygdala	Emotional memory (Gerber et al., 2008; Hamilton & Gotlib, 2008; van Stegeren, 2008)
Basal Ganglia and Cerebellum	Creation and storage of the basic memory trace and implicit (nondeclarative) memories (such as skills, habits, and simple classically conditioned responses) (Chiricozzi et al., 2008; Gluck, 2008; Thompson, 2005)
Hippocampal Formation (hippocampus and surrounding area)	Memory recognition; implicit, explicit, spatial, episodic memory; declarative long-term memory; sequences of events (Hamilton & Gotlib, 2008; Yoo et al., 2007)
Thalamus	Formation of new memories and spatial and working memory (Hart & Kraut, 2007; Hofer et al., 2007; Ponzi, 2008)
Cortex	Encoding of explicit (declarative) memories; storage of episodic and semantic memories; skill learning; working memory (Davidson et al., 2008; Dougal et al., 2007; Thompson, 2005)

STOP Stop & Think
1. What effect might damage to the amygdala have on a person's relationships with others?
2. What effect do you think damage to the thalamus might have on a person's day-to-day functioning?

Two types of amnesia FIGURE 7.7

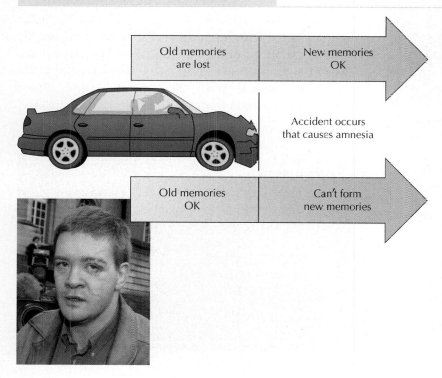

A In *retrograde amnesia*, the person loses memories of events that occurred *before* the accident yet has no trouble remembering things that happened afterward (old, "retro" memories are lost).

B In *anterograde amnesia*, the person cannot form new memories for events that occur *after* the accident. Anterograde amnesia also may result from a surgical injury (as in the case of Henry Molaison) or from diseases, such as chronic alcoholism.

Bodyguard Trevor Rees-Jones, the sole survivor of the car accident that killed Diana, Princess of Wales; Dodi Al-Fayed; and Henri Paul, experienced both anterograde and retrograde amnesia caused by his serious head injuries. He reports having no memory after getting into the black Mercedes and no memory of the accident or what happened soon after.

INJURY, DISEASE, AND MEMORY LOSS

Traumatic brain injury (TBI) occurs when the skull suddenly collides with another object. A closed TBI occurs when the skull is not penetrated and the brain is not exposed. A penetrating head injury damages or breaches the tough connective covering, which surrounds and protects the brain. Damage caused by compression, twisting, penetration, and distortion of the brain inside the skull all can cause serious and sometimes permanent damage to the brain. In an injury it is the frontal and temporal lobes that often take the heaviest hit because they directly collide with the bony ridges inside the skull.

Loss of memory as a result of brain injury is called *amnesia*. Two major types of amnesia are **retrograde amnesia** and **anterograde amnesia** (FIGURE 7.7). Usually, retrograde amnesia is temporary. Unfortunately, anterograde amnesia is usually permanent, but patients often show surprising abilities to learn and remember implicit/nondeclarative tasks (such as procedural motor skills). This type of memory was somewhat preserved for Henry Molaison.

Like traumatic brain injuries, disease can damage the physiology of the brain and nervous system and thereby affect memory processes. For example, **Alzheimer's disease (AD)** is a degenerative brain disease characterized by progressive mental deterioration that occurs most commonly in old age (FIGURE 7.8). The most noticeable early symptoms are minor disturbances in memory, which become progressively worse until in the final stages, the person fails to recognize loved ones, cannot take care of himself or herself, and needs total nursing care. The person ultimately dies from the advancing disease.

Alzheimer's does not attack all types of memory equally. A hallmark of the disease is an extreme decline in explicit/declarative memory (Haley, 2005; Libon et al., 2007; Salter et al., 2008). Alzheimer's patients fail to recall facts, information, and personal life experiences, yet they still retain some implicit/nondeclarative memories, such as simple classically conditioned responses and procedural tasks, like brushing their teeth and hair.

Brain autopsies of people with Alzheimer's show unusual tangles (structures formed from dead and dying

Alzheimer's disease (AD) Degenerative brain disease characterized by progressive mental deterioration and pathological memory loss.

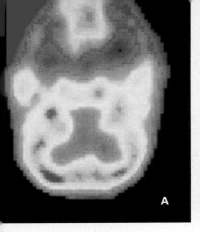
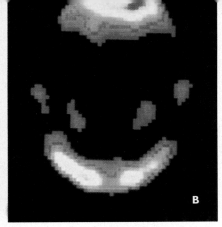

cell bodies) and plaques (structures formed from dead and dying axons and dendrites). Hereditary Alzheimer's generally strikes between the ages of 45 and 55. Some experts believe that the cause of Alzheimer's is primarily genetic, but others think that genetic makeup may make some people more susceptible to environmental influences (Diamond & Amso, 2008; Ertekin-Taner, 2007; Persson et al., 2008; Vickers et al., 2000; Weiner, 2008).

The effect of Alzheimer's disease on the brain
FIGURE 7.8

A Normal brain Note the large amount of red and yellow (signs of lots of brain activity) in the positron emission tomography (PET) scan of the normal brain.

B Brain of a patient with Alzheimer's disease The reduced activity in the brain of the Alzheimer's disease patient is evident. The loss is most significant in the temporal and parietal lobes. This suggests to researchers there is a strong link between these areas and memory storage.

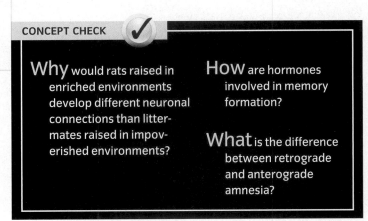

CONCEPT CHECK

Why would rats raised in enriched environments develop different neuronal connections than littermates raised in impoverished environments?

How are hormones involved in memory formation?

What is the difference between retrograde and anterograde amnesia?

Forgetting

LEARNING OBJECTIVES

Describe Ebbinghaus' research on learning and forgetting.

Outline the five key theories of why we forget.

Explain the factors that contribute to forgetting.

Psychologists have developed several theories to explain forgetting and have identified a number of factors that can interfere with the process of forming new memories. We examine these theories and factors in this section.

THEORIES OF FORGETTING

If you couldn't forget, your mind would be filled with meaningless data, such as every snack you've ever had in your life or every outfit you have ever worn. Similarly, think of the incredible pain you would continuously endure if memories of life's tragedies did not fade with time? The ability to forget is essential to the proper functioning of memory. Our annoyance with forgetting occurs when we forget things we did not intend to forget. These are the times when forgetting is an inconvenience, and we might fail to recognize how adaptive and useful it really is.

Five major theories attempt to explain why forgetting occurs (FIGURE 7.9): decay, interference, encoding failure, retrieval failure, and motivated forgetting. Each theory focuses on a different stage of the memory process or a particular type of problem in processing neural information.

FACTORS INVOLVED IN FORGETTING

Since Ebbinghaus' original research, scientists have discovered numerous factors that contribute to forgetting. Five of the most important are the misinformation

Process Diagram

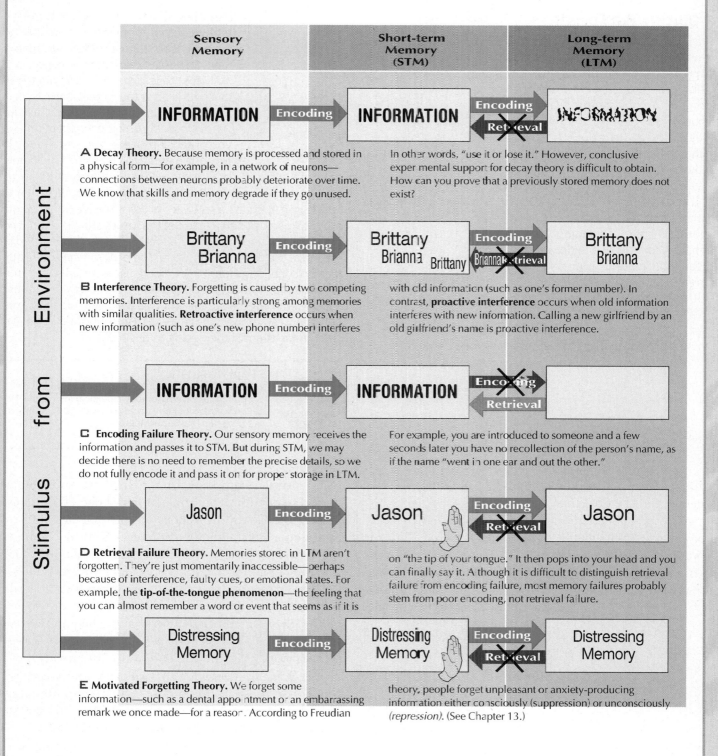

	Sensory Memory	Short-term Memory (STM)	Long-term Memory (LTM)

Stimulus from Environment

INFORMATION → Encoding → **INFORMATION** → Encoding / Retrieval ✗ → **INFORMATION**

A Decay Theory. Because memory is processed and stored in a physical form—for example, in a network of neurons—connections between neurons probably deteriorate over time. We know that skills and memory degrade if they go unused.

In other words, "use it or lose it." However, conclusive experimental support for decay theory is difficult to obtain. How can you prove that a previously stored memory does not exist?

Brittany Brianna → Encoding → Brittany Brianna *Brittany* → Encoding / Brianna ✗ Retrieval → Brittany Brianna

B Interference Theory. Forgetting is caused by two competing memories. Interference is particularly strong among memories with similar qualities. **Retroactive interference** occurs when new information (such as one's new phone number) interferes

with old information (such as one's former number). In contrast, **proactive interference** occurs when old information interferes with new information. Calling a new girlfriend by an old girlfriend's name is proactive interference.

INFORMATION → Encoding → **INFORMATION** → Enco✗ding / Retrieval → [ ]

C Encoding Failure Theory. Our sensory memory receives the information and passes it to STM. But during STM, we may decide there is no need to remember the precise details, so we do not fully encode it and pass it on for proper storage in LTM.

For example, you are introduced to someone and a few seconds later you have no recollection of the person's name, as if the name "went in one ear and out the other."

Jason → Encoding → Jason → Encoding / Retrieval ✗ → Jason

D Retrieval Failure Theory. Memories stored in LTM aren't forgotten. They're just momentarily inaccessible—perhaps because of interference, faulty cues, or emotional states. For example, the **tip-of-the-tongue phenomenon**—the feeling that you can almost remember a word or event that seems as if it is

on "the tip of your tongue." It then pops into your head and you can finally say it. Although it is difficult to distinguish retrieval failure from encoding failure, most memory failures probably stem from poor encoding, not retrieval failure.

Distressing Memory → Encoding → Distressing Memory → Encoding / Retrieval ✗ → Distressing Memory

E Motivated Forgetting Theory. We forget some information—such as a dental appointment or an embarrassing remark we once made—for a reason. According to Freudian

theory, people forget unpleasant or anxiety-producing information either consciously (suppression) or unconsciously (repression). (See Chapter 13.)

How Quickly We Forget

About a hundred and twenty years ago Hermann Ebbinghaus introduced the first experimental study on learning and forgetting. Using himself as a subject, he calculated how long it took to learn and remember a list of three-letter *nonsense syllables*, such as *SIB* and *RAL*. He then found that just one hour after learning a list perfectly, he remembered only 44 percent of the syllables. A day later, he recalled 35 percent, and a week later, only 21 percent. This figure shows his now famous "forgetting curve."

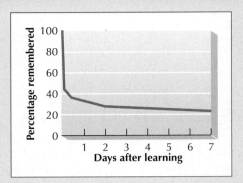

Depressing as these findings may seem (or the fact that Ebbinghaus had little else to do with his days), keep in mind that meaningful material is much more memorable than meaningless nonsense syllables. Even so, we all forget some of what we have learned.

On a more positive note, after some time passed and he believed he had forgotten the list, Ebbinghaus found that *relearning* a previously learned list took less time than the initial learning did. This research suggests that we retain some memory for things that we have learned, even when we seem to have forgotten them completely.

Most research based on Ebbinghaus' discoveries has found that there is an ideal time to practise something you have learned. Practising too soon is a waste of time, and if you practise too late, you will already have forgotten what you learned. The ideal time to practise is when you are about to forget.

Polish psychologist Piotr Wozniak used this insight to create a software program called SuperMemo. The program can be used to predict the future state of an individual's memory and help the person schedule reviews of learned information at the optimal time. So far the program has been applied mainly to language learning, helping users retain huge amounts of vocabulary. But Wozniak hopes that some day programs like SuperMemo will tell people when to wake and when to exercise, help them remember what they read and whom they have met, and remind them of their goals (Wolf, 2008).

Stop & Think
1. How do you think Ebbinghaus' findings might be applied to learning to play a musical instrument?
2. Can you think of any disadvantage of depending on a program like SuperMemo?

STOP

---

effect, the serial position effect, source amnesia, the sleeper effect, and spacing of practice.

Many people who haven't taken first-year psychology classes believe that when they are recalling an event, they're remembering it as if it were a video instant replay. However, as you know, our memories are re-creative and therefore highly fallible, filled with personal constructions and amendments that we create during encoding and storage. Research on the **misinformation effect** shows that information that occurs after an event may further alter and revise those constructions. Experimenters have created false memories in subjects by showing subjects doctored photos of themselves taking a fictitious hot-air balloon ride or by asking subjects to simply imagine an event, such as having a nurse remove a skin sample from their finger. In these and similar cases, a large number of subjects later believed that misleading information was correct and that fictitious or imagined events actually occurred (Allan & Gabbert, 2008; Garry & Gerrie, 2005; Mazzoni & Memon, 2003; Mazzoni & Vannucci, 2007; Pérez-Mata & Diges, 2007).

When research participants are given lists of words to learn and are allowed to recall them in any order they choose, they remember the words at the beginning (*primacy effect: STM is less crowded with information, so the words are more memorable*) and the end of the list (*recency effect: the most recent items put into STM and so are more memorable*) better than those in the middle, which are quite often forgotten (Azizian & Polich, 2007; Healy et al., 2008). This effect is known as the **serial position effect**.

The serial position effect has some interesting real-life implications. For example, a potential employer's memory for you might be enhanced if you are either the first or the last candidate interviewed.

misinformation effect Distortion of a memory by misleading post-event information.

Culture and memory FIGURE 7.10

In many societies, tribal leaders pass down important information by telling related stories. As a result, children living in these cultures have better memories for the information that is relayed to them through stories than do other children. Can you think of other ways in which culture might influence memory?

Each day we read, hear, and process an enormous amount of information, and it's easy to confuse who said what to whom, where, and in what context. Forgetting the true source of a memory is known as **source amnesia** (Kleider et al., 2008; Leichtman, 2006; Mitchell et al., 2005), and it has happened to all of us. While you know what city is Canada's capital, you probably don't remember where and when you learned it.

When we first hear something from an unreliable source, we tend to disregard the information in favour of a more reliable source. However, as the source of the information is forgotten (source amnesia), the unreliable information is less likely to be discounted. This is called the **sleeper effect** (Appel & Richter, 2007; Kumkale & Albarracín, 2004; Nabi, Moyer-Guse, & Byrne, 2007).

The sleeper effect can be a significant problem when reliable and unreliable information are intermixed—for example, when advertisements are disguised to look like more objective reports or newspaper articles. Can you see how, after a time, we may forget the source and no longer discount the information in the ad?

If we try to memorize too much information at once (as when students stay up and pull an all nighter cramming before an exam), we learn and remember less than when study sessions are divided up (Donovan & Radosevich, 1999). *Distributed practice* refers to spacing your learning periods, with rest periods between sessions. Cramming is an example of *massed practice* because the time spent learning is massed into a long, unbroken bout.

Finally, as illustrated in FIGURE 7.10, cultural factors can play a role in how well people remember what they have learned.

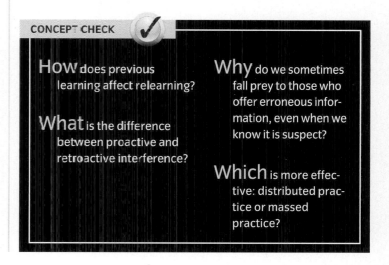

CONCEPT CHECK

How does previous learning affect relearning?

What is the difference between proactive and retroactive interference?

Why do we sometimes fall prey to those who offer erroneous information, even when we know it is suspect?

Which is more effective: distributed practice or massed practice?

Memory Distortions

 ne of my first memories would date, if it were true, from my second year. I can still see, most clearly, the following scene, in which I believed until I was about fifteen.

I was sitting in my pram, which my nurse was pushing in the Champs-Élysées, when a man tried to kidnap me. I was held in by the strap fastened round me while my nurse bravely tried to stand between the thief and me. She received various scratches, and I can still see vaguely those on her face. Then a crowd gathered, a policeman with a short cloak and a white baton came up, and the man took to his heels. I can still see the whole scene, and can even place it near the tube station. When I was about fifteen, my parents received a letter from my former nurse saying that she had been converted to the Salvation Army. She wanted to confess her past faults, and in

 ## Applying Psychology

A Memory Test

Carefully read through all the words in the columns below.

Bed	Drowse
Awake	Nurse
Tired	Sick
Dream	Lawyer
Wake	Medicine
Snooze	Health
Snore	Hospital
Rest	Dentist
Blanket	Physician
Doze	Patient
Slumber	Stethoscope
Nap	Curse
Peace	Clinic
Yawn	Surgeon

Now cover the list and write down all the words you remember.

Number of correctly recalled words:

21 to 28 words = excellent memory

16 to 20 words = better than most

12 to 15 words = average

8 to 11 words = below average

7 or fewer words = you might need a nap

How did you do? Do you have a good or excellent memory? Did you recall seeing the words *sleep* and *doctor*? Look back over the list. These words are not there. However, over 65 percent of students commonly report seeing these words. Why? Memory is not a faithful replication of an event; it is a *constructive* and *recreative process.* We actively shape and build on information as it is encoded and retrieved. Because *sleep* and *doctor* fit nicely and logically into the list, it is easy for us to conclude on recall that they were there all along.

 Stop & Think
1. Did you remember the words *bed* and *surgeon*? If so, why?
2. Can you see how this illustrates the serial position effect?

particular to return the watch she had been given as a reward on this occasion. She had made up the whole story, faking the scratches. I, therefore, must have heard, as a child, the account of this story, which my parents believed, and projected it into the past in the form of a visual memory, which was a memory of a memory, but false. (Piaget, 1962, pp. 187–188)

This is a self-reported childhood memory of Jean Piaget, a brilliant and world-famous cognitive and developmental psychologist (we discuss Piaget in Chapter 9). Why did Piaget create such a strange and elaborate memory for something that never happened?

We shape, rearrange, and distort our memories for several reasons. One of the most common is our need for logic and consistency. When we're initially forming new memories or sorting through the old ones, we fill in missing pieces, make "corrections," and rearrange information to make it logical, smooth, and consistent with our previous experiences. If Piaget's beloved nurse said someone attempted to kidnap him, it was only logical for the boy to "remember" the event as she said it had happened.

We also shape and construct our memories for the sake of efficiency. We summarize, augment, and tie new information in with related memories in LTM. Similarly, when we need to retrieve the stored information, we leave out seemingly unimportant elements or misremember the details.

Despite all their problems and biases, however, our memories are normally quite accurate and serve us well in most situations. Our memories have evolved to encode, store, and retrieve vital information. Even while sleeping we process and store important memories. However, when faced with such tasks as remembering precise details in a psychology text, the faces and names of potential clients, or where we left our house keys, our brains are simply not infallible.

"I SAW IT WITH MY OWN EYES": MEMORY AND EYEWITNESS TESTIMONY

When memory errors involve the criminal justice system, they can lead to wrongful judgements of guilt or innocence and occasionally life-or-death decisions.

In 1992 the small Saskatchewan community of Martensville was rocked by allegations of horrific child sexual abuse, animal mutilation, and satanic rituals in a home daycare run by Ron and Lynda Sterling. Along with the Sterlings, seven other people were charged with 180 sex-related offences against the children in their care. Ultimately, the Sterlings were tried and acquitted on all charges. After a thorough investigation it was discovered that the methods of police investigation—namely, using leading questions when interviewing the daycare children—caused the initial unfounded allegations. The Province of Saskatchewan ultimately paid out $1.3 million in compensation to those wrongly accused.

In the past, one of the best forms of trial evidence a lawyer could have was an *eyewitness* "I was there; I saw it with my own eyes." Unfortunately for lawyers, research has identified several problems with eyewitness testimony (Loftus, 2000, 2001, 2007; Ran, 2007; Rubinstein, 2008; Sharps et al., 2007; Yarmey, 2004). In fact, a number of researchers have demonstrated that it is relatively easy to create false memories (Allan & Gabbert, 2008; Howes, 2007; Loftus & Cahill, 2007; Pérez-Mata & Diges, 2007).

In a now classic study, participants watched a film of a car driving through the countryside. Later, those who were asked to estimate how fast the car was going when it passed the barn (actually nonexistent) were six times as likely to later report that they had seen a barn in the film than participants who hadn't been asked about a barn (Loftus, 1982).

Problems with eyewitness recollections are so well established and legally important that judges now allow expert testimony on the unreliability of eyewitness testimony and routinely instruct jurors on its limits (Durham & Dane, 1999; Ramirez, Zemba, & Geiselman, 1996). If you serve as a member of a jury or listen to accounts of crimes in the news, remind yourself of the problems surrounding eyewitness testimony. Also, keep in mind that research participants in eyewitness studies generally report their inaccurate memories with great self-assurance and strong personal conviction (Migueles & Garcia-Bajos, 1999). Eyewitnesses to an actual crime may similarly identify—with equally high confidence—an innocent person as the perpetrator (FIGURE 7.11).

Like eyewitness testimony, false memories can have serious legal and social implications. Consider this personal account:

When Elizabeth was 14 years old, her mother drowned in their backyard pool. As she grew older,

This is the true story of Elizabeth Loftus, who today is a well-known psychologist and influential memory researcher. Elizabeth's recovery of these gruesome childhood memories, although painful, initially brought great relief. It also seemed to explain why she had always been so fascinated by the topic of memory.

Then, years later her brother called to say there had been a mistake! The relative who told Elizabeth that she had been the one to discover her mother's body later remembered—and other relatives confirmed—that it had actually been Aunt Pearl and not Elizabeth Loftus. Loftus, a world-renowned expert on memory distortions, had unknowingly created her own false memory (FIGURE 7.12).

REPRESSED MEMORIES

Creating false memories may be somewhat common, but can we actually recover true memories that are buried from childhood? **Repression** is the supposed Freudian unconscious coping mechanism by which we prevent anxiety-provoking thoughts from reaching consciousness. According to some research, repressed memories are actively and consciously "forgotten" in an effort to avoid the pain of their retrieval (Anderson et al., 2004).

How often are eyewitnesses mistaken?

FIGURE 7.11

What do David Milgaard (left), Donald Marshall Jr. (right), and Thomas Sophonow have in common? They were all wrongfully convicted of sexual assault or murder or both in Canadian courts, and in each case eyewitness testimony contributed to their convictions. These men spent years in prison before their convictions were overturned based on DNA or newer, more reliable evidence. Witnessing or being the victim of a violent crime can be an extremely emotional event, and as mentioned, emotional events tend to make stronger, not weaker, memories. What memory processes might have contributed to the witnesses' errors in these cases?

the details surrounding her mother's death became increasingly vague for Elizabeth. Decades later, a relative told Elizabeth that she had been the one to find her mother's body. Despite her initial shock, the memories soon slowly started coming back to her.

> *I could see myself, a thin, dark-haired girl, looking into the flickering blue-and-white pool. My mother, dressed in her nightgown, is floating face down. I start screaming. I remember the police cars, their lights flashing, and the stretcher with the clean, white blanket tucked in around the edges of the body. The memory had been there all along, but I just couldn't reach it.* (Loftus & Ketcham, 1994, p. 45)

Elizabeth Loftus **FIGURE 7.12**

Mnemonic Devices

As you review the key points from this chapter you might want to revisit the SQ4R method discussed in Chapter 1. You can also think about how you might exploit basic principles of memory, using them to your own advantage. Another "trick" for giving your memory a boost is to use **mnemonic devices** to encode items in a special way. (But be warned—you may get more "bang for your buck" using the well-researched principles discussed throughout this chapter.)

Three popular mnemonic techniques are listed here.

A Method of loci Greek and Roman orators developed the *method of loci* to keep track of the many parts of their long speeches. Orators would imagine the parts of their speeches attached to places in a courtyard. For example, if an opening point in a speech was the concept of *justice*, they might visualize a courtroom placed in the first corner of their garden. As they mentally walked around their garden during their speech, they would encounter, in order, each of the points to be made. ▶

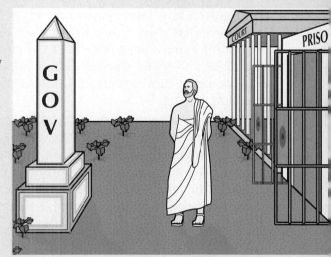

Grocery list

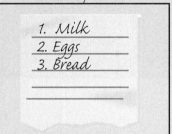

1. Milk
2. Eggs
3. Bread

One is a bun.

Two is a shoe.

Three is a tree.

◀ **B Peg words** To use the *peg-word* mnemonic, you first need to memorize a set of 10 images that you can use as "pegs" on which to hang ideas. For example, if you learn 10 items that rhyme with the numbers they stand for, you can then use the images as pegs to hold the items of any list. Try it with items you might want to buy on your next trip to the grocery store: milk, eggs, and bread.

C Acronyms To use the acronym method, create a new code ▶ word from the first letters of the items you want to remember. For example, to recall the names of the Great Lakes, think of *HOMES on a great lake* (Huron, Ontario, Michigan, Erie, Superior). Visualizing houses on each lake also helps you remember your code word *homes*.

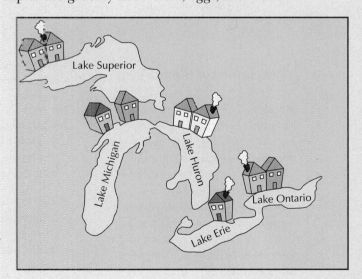

STOP

Stop & Think
1. How could you use the method of loci to remember the types of long-term memory described in Study Organizer 7.1?
2. How could you use the peg-word method to remember the five theories of forgetting in the previous *Applying Psychology* feature?

Others suggest that some memories are so painful that they exist only in an unconscious corner of the brain, making them inaccessible to the individual (Karon & Widener, 1998). In these cases, therapy would be necessary to unlock the hidden memories (Davies, 1996).

This is a complex and controversial topic in psychology. No one doubts that some memories are forgotten and later recovered. What is questioned, however, is the concept of *repressed memories* of painful experiences (especially of childhood sexual abuse) and their storage in the unconscious mind (Goodman et al., 2003; Kihlstrom, 2004; Loftus & Cahill, 2007).

Critics of repressed memories suggest that most people who have witnessed or experienced a violent crime, or are adult survivors of childhood sexual abuse, have intense, persistent memories. They have trouble forgetting the terrible memories, not remembering they happened in the first place. Some critics also wonder whether therapists sometimes inadvertently create false memories in their clients during therapy. Some worry that if a clinician even suggests the possibility of abuse, the client's own constructive memory processes may lead them to create a false memory. The client might start to incorporate portrayals of abuse from movies and books into their own memory, forgetting their original sources and eventually coming to see them as true, reliable, and real.

This is not to say that all psychotherapy clients who recover memories of sexual abuse (or other painful incidents) have invented those memories. Indeed, the repressed memory debate has grown increasingly bitter, and research on both sides is hotly contested. The stakes are high because some civil lawsuits and criminal prosecutions of sexual abuse have been based on recovered memories of childhood sexual abuse. As researchers continue exploring the mechanisms underlying memory systems, we must be careful not to chastise or condemn people who report recovering memories of abuse. In the same spirit, we must also protect the innocent from wrongful accusations that come from false memories. We look forward to a time when we can justly balance the interests and reputation of the victim with those of the accused.

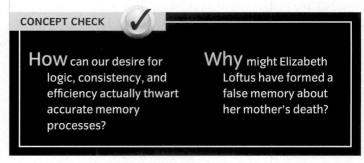

CONCEPT CHECK ✓

How can our desire for logic, consistency, and efficiency actually thwart accurate memory processes?

Why might Elizabeth Loftus have formed a false memory about her mother's death?

SUMMARY

1 The Nature of Memory

1. **Memory** is an internal representation of some prior event or experience. The two major perspectives on memory are the **information-processing model**—information enters memory in three stages: **encoding, storage,** and **retrieval;** and the three-stage memory model—information is stored and processed in **sensory memory, short-term memory (STM),** and **long-term memory (LTM).**

2. Information remains in sensory memory very briefly. Visual information is stored as an iconic memory and auditory information is stored as an echoic memory.

3. **Chunking** and **maintenance rehearsal** improve STM's duration and capacity. Researchers now think of STM as a three-part **working memory**.

4. LTM is an almost unlimited storehouse of information that is kept for long periods. The two major types of LTM are **explicit/declarative memory** and **implicit/nondeclarative memory**. Organization and **elaborative rehearsal** improve encoding for LTM. **Retrieval cues** help stimulate retrieval of

information from LTM. According to the **encoding specificity principle**, retrieval is improved when conditions of recovery are similar to encoding conditions.

2 Biological Bases of Memory

1. Learning modifies the brain's neural architecture through **long-term potentiation (LTP)**, strengthening particular synapses and affecting neurons' ability to release their neurotransmitters.

2. Stress hormones affect the amygdala, which activates brain areas that are important for memory storage.

Heightened arousal increases the encoding and storage of new information. Secretion of fight-or-flight hormones can contribute to "flashbulb" memories.

3. Research using advanced techniques has indicated that several brain regions are involved in memory storage.

4. Traumatic brain injuries and disease, such as **Alzheimer's disease (AD)**, can cause memory loss. Two major types of amnesia are **retrograde** and **anterograde amnesia**.

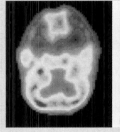

3 Forgetting

1. Researchers have proposed that we forget information through decay, retroactive and proactive interference, encoding failure, retrieval failure, and motivated forgetting.

2. Early research by Ebbinghaus showed that we tend to forget newly learned information quickly but that we relearn the information more readily the second time.

3. Five factors that contribute to forgetting are the **misinformation effect**, the **serial position effect** (primacy and recency effects), **source amnesia**, the **sleeper effect**, and spacing of practice (distributed versus massed practice).

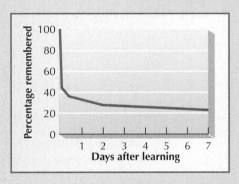

4 Memory Distortions

1. People shape, rearrange, and distort memories to create logical, consistent, and efficient thought processes. Despite all their problems and biases, our memories are normally quite accurate and usually serve us well.

2. When memory errors involve the criminal justice system, they can have serious legal and social consequences. Problems with eyewitness recollections are well established.

3. Memory **repression** (especially of childhood sexual abuse) is a complex and controversial topic in memory research. Critics note that most people who have witnessed or experienced a violent or traumatic event have intense, persistent memories. They also worry that if a clinician suggests the possibility of abuse, the client's *constructive memory processes* may lead them to create a false memory of being abused. Researchers continue to explore this aspect of memory.

4. **Mnemonic devices** help us remember lists and facts. Three popular mnemonic techniques are method of loci, the peg-word mnemonic, and the method of acronyms.

KEY TERMS

CRITICAL AND CREATIVE THINKING QUESTIONS

1. If you were forced to lose one type of memory—sensory, short-term, or long-term—which would you select? Why?

2. Why might students do better on a test if they take it in the same seat and classroom where they originally studied the material?

3. What might be the evolutionary advantage of heightened emotional arousal when a memory is being formed?

4. How might the serial position effect impact a person's ability to remember the names of a group of people when introduced at a party or other social gathering?

5. Why might advertisers of shoddy services or poor-quality products benefit from consumers "channel surfing" among news programs, talk shows, and infomercials?

6. As an eyewitness to a crime, how could you use information in this chapter to improve your memory for specific details? If you were a juror, what would you say to the other jurors about the reliability of eyewitness testimony?

7. Do you think scientific inquiry has the tools to test the presence of repressed memories? If you were a memory researcher what type of experiment would you design to evaluate this phenomenon? What would a behaviourist say about repression?

8. Can memory and remembering be influenced by culture? In North America, we rely heavily on electronic devices, such as cell phones and PDAs (personal digital assistants), to remind us to do things. How do you think this will affect our memories over time?

As adults we lack the ability look back into our childhood and remember important early milestones like learning to walk or drink from a cup. In fact, memories of events prior to age three or four are scant at best. One explanation for this *infantile amnesia* is a young child's brain is not neurologically mature enough to form long lasting episodic memories.

Based on what you have learned about the biology of memory, what brain regions do you think might still be maturing during early childhood?

SELF-TEST

(Check your answers in Appendix A.)

1. Label these terms on the following figure. In a computer model of memory, (a) _____ would happen at the keyboard, (b)_____ on the screen, and (c) _____ on the hard drive.

   a. _____
   b. _____
   c. _____

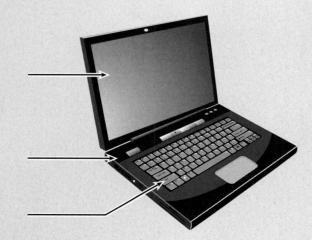

2. Label the three-stage memory model in the correct sequence on the following figure.

   a. _____
   b. _____
   c. _____

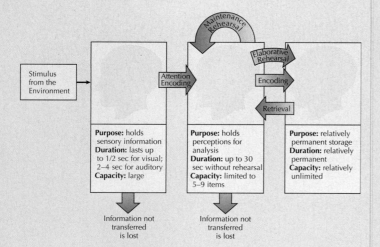

3. The following descriptions are characteristic of _____ : information lasts only a few seconds or less, and it has a relatively large (but not unlimited) storage capacity.
   a. perceptual processes
   b. short-term storage
   c. working memory
   d. sensory memory

4. _____ is the process of grouping separate pieces of information into a single unit.
   a. Chunking
   b. Cheating
   c. Method of loci
   d. Peg method

5. The two major systems of long-term memory are _____ .
   a. _____
   b. _____

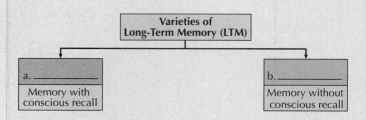

6. In answering this question, the correct multiple-choice option may serve as a _____ for recalling accurate information from your long-term memory.
   a. specificity code
   b. priming pump
   c. retrieval cue
   d. flashbulb stimulus

7. Although he knew how to skate since he was a young boy, Rian recently skated for the first time in many years. To his surprise, he did great and skated as he had as a child. What type of memory is Rian using in this situation?
   a. episodic (explicit/declarative)
   b. long-term memory
   c. motor memory
   d. procedural (implicit/nondeclarative)

8. Which type of memory ability is Mia using when she happily recalls her 13th birthday party?
   a. procedural (implicit/nondeclarative)
   b. episodic (explicit/declarative)
   c. motor memory
   d. flashbulb stimulus

9. The encoding specificity principle says that information retrieval is improved when _____.
   a. both maintenance and elaborative rehearsal are used
   b. reverberating circuits consolidate information
   c. conditions of recovery are similar to encoding conditions
   d. long-term potentiation is accessed

10. What is the name for the long-lasting increase in neural excitability caused by repeated neural input, which is believed to be the biological basis of learning and memory?
    a. maintenance rehearsal
    b. adrenaline activation
    c. long-term potentiation
    d. the reverberating response

11. A progressive mental deterioration characterized by severe memory loss that occurs most commonly old in age is called _____.
    a. retrieval loss
    b. prefrontal cortex deterioration
    c. Alzheimer's disease
    d. age-related amnesia

12. Label the two types of amnesia on the following.

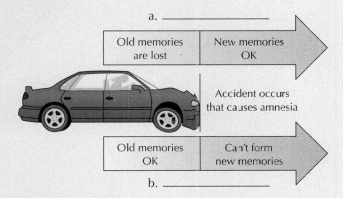

a. _____
Old memories are lost | New memories OK
Accident occurs that causes amnesia
Old memories OK | Can't form new memories
b. _____

13. Which of the following brain structures has not been implicated in memory formation?
    a. Pons
    b. Hippocampus
    c. Cerebral cortex
    d. Basal Ganglia and cerebellum

14. List the five major theories of forgetting:
    a. _____   d. _____
    b. _____   e. _____
    c. _____

15. Distributed practice is a learning technique in which _____.
    a. subjects are distributed across equally sized study groups
    b. learning periods alternate with non-learning rest periods
    c. learning decays faster than it can be distributed
    d. several students study together, distributing various subjects according to their individual strengths

16. Jill easily recalls knowing that her neighbour is an engineer, but she cannot remember exactly where she learned this information; she thinks it could be from another neighbour, her mother, or the woman at the post-office. What is Jill experiencing?
    a. the sleeper effect   c. sleeper amnesia
    b. source amnesia   d. repressed source

17. Researchers have demonstrated that it is _____ to create false memories.
    a. relatively easy
    b. moderately difficult
    c. rarely possible
    d. possible

18. _____ is a common mechanism by which anxiety-provoking thoughts or events are prevented from reaching consciousness.
    a. Suppression   c. Serial position
    b. Flashback   d. Repression

19. _____ devices improve memory by encoding items in a special way.
    a. Eidetic imagery
    b. Mnemonic
    c. Reverberating circuit
    d. ECS

20. Jessica meets Paulo, Shari, Yani, Cody, and Hugh at a party and remembers them by realizing that the first letters of their names spell the word PSYCH. Which memory technique is Jessica using?
    a. Peg words   c. Acronyms
    b. Mnemonic   d. Method of Loci

Thinking, Language, and Intelligence

On July 9, 2005, professional skateboarder Danny Way rocketed down a 36-metre ramp at almost 80 kilometres per hour and leapt an 18-metre gap across the Great Wall of China. He did it not once but five times. Do you think that this feat reflects merely athletic skill and daring, or does it also speak to Way's intelligence?

When we think of intelligence, many of us think of Nobel Prize winners, great inventors, or chess champions. But success as a professional skateboarder also requires intelligence—perhaps of a different kind than people generally associate with being "smart." Skateboarding enthusiasts admire the creativity and technical innovation that Way brings to the sport. He has broken many skateboarding records and has devised stunts—including a jump from a helicopter—that few others would try.

The three topics of this chapter—thinking, language, and intelligence—are often studied together under the broader umbrella of cognition: the mental activities involved in acquiring, storing, retrieving, and using knowledge. In a real sense, we discuss cognition throughout this text because psychology is "the scientific study of behaviour and *mental processes*" (Chapter 1). For example, the chapters on sensation and perception (Chapter 4), consciousness (Chapter 5), learning (Chapter 6), and memory (Chapter 7) all focus on cognition.

In this chapter, we emphasize thinking, language, and intelligence. As you will discover, each is a complex phenomenon that is greatly affected by numerous factors.

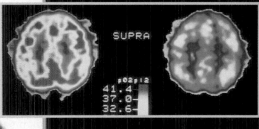

Thinking

LEARNING OBJECTIVES

Explain the role of the prefrontal cortex in thinking.

Describe how mental images, concepts, and prototypes enable thinking.

Identify the three steps involved in problem solving.

Summarize how biases and heuristics can hamper problem solving.

Explain Sternberg and Lubart's investment theory of creativity.

Thinking, language, and intelligence are closely related facets of **cognition**. Every time you take information and mentally act on it, you are thinking. Our thought processes are distributed throughout our brains in networks of neurons. However, they are also localized. For example, during problem solving or decision-making, our brains are active in the prefrontal cortex. This region associates complex ideas; makes plans; forms, initiates, and allocates attention; and supports multitasking. The **prefrontal cortex** also links to other areas of the brain, such as the limbic system (Chapter 2), to synthesize information from several senses (Carlson, 2008; Heyder, Suchan, & Daum, 2004; Sacchetti, Sacco, & Strata, 2007).

> **cognition** Mental activities involved in acquiring, storing, retrieving, and using knowledge.

COGNITIVE BUILDING BLOCKS

Imagine yourself lying relaxed on the warm, gritty sand of an ocean beach. Do you see palm trees swaying in the wind? Can you smell the salty sea and taste the dried salt on your lips? Can you hear children playing in the surf? What you've just created is a **mental image** (FIGURE 8.1), a mental representation of a previously stored sensory experience that includes visual, auditory, olfactory, tactile, motor, and gustatory imagery (McKellar, 1972). We all have a mental space in which we visualize and manipulate our sensory images (Hamm, Johnson, & Corballis, 2004).

In addition to mental images, our thinking also involves forming **concepts**, or mental representations of a group or category. We form concepts by grouping together objects, events, activities, or ideas that share similar characteristics (Smith, 1995). Concepts can be concrete (*car*, *concert*) or abstract (*intelligence*, *pornography*). They are

Mental imagery FIGURE 8.1

Some of our most creative and inspired moments come when we're forming and manipulating mental images. This mountain climber is probably visualizing her next move, and her ability to do so is critical to her success.

Some birds are "birdier" than others FIGURE 8.2

A Most of us have a *prototype,* or natural concept, for a bird that captures the essence of "birdness" and allows us to quickly classify flying animals correctly.

B When we encounter an example that doesn't quite fit our prototype, we need time to review our artificial concept. Because the penguin doesn't fly, it's harder to classify than a robin.

essential to thinking and communication because they simplify and organize information. Normally, when you see a new object or encounter a new situation, you relate it to the concepts you've already formed and categorize it according to where it fits. For example, if you see a metal box with four wheels being driven on the highway, you know it is a car, even if you've never seen that particular model before.

Some of our concepts are *artificial,* that is, created from logical rules or definitions. The concept of *triangle* is a good example. Triangles are defined as geometric forms with three sides and three angles. Any geometric form that contains these features would be included in the concept triangle, and if any feature were missing, we would not classify the form as a triangle. Such concepts are called *artificial* (or *formal*) because the rules for inclusion are sharply defined.

Artificial concepts are often found in science and other academic disciplines, but in everyday life, we seldom use precise, artificial definitions. When we see birds in the sky, we don't think *warm-blooded animals that fly, have wings, and lay eggs*—an artificial concept. Instead, we use *natural concepts,* or **prototypes,** which are based on a typical representative of that concept (Rosch, 1973) (**FIGURE 8.2**).

Some of our concepts also develop when we create **hierarchies,** that is, grouping specific concepts as subcategories within broader concepts. Note in the hierarchy depicted in **FIGURE 8.3** how the top (superordinate)

category of *animal* is very broad and includes many members, the midlevel categories of *bird* and *dog* are more specific but still rather general, and the lowest (subordinate) categories of *parakeet* and *poodle* are the most specific.

When we first learn something, we rely primarily on the middle or basic-level concepts (Rosch, 1978). Thus, children tend to learn *bird* or *dog* before they learn superordinate concepts like *animal* or subordinate concepts like *parakeet* or *poodle*. Even as adults, when shown a picture of a parakeet, we classify it as a *bird* first.

A concept hierarchy FIGURE 8.3

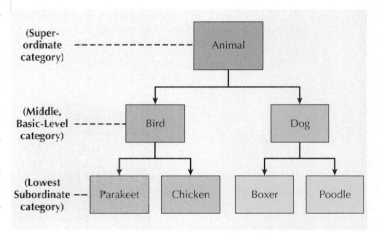

Three steps to the goal FIGURE 8.4

① PREPARATION

Imagine that you are determined to find a new home close to work. There are at least three separate components to successful preparation.

Must be able to walk to work.

I prefer a house to a large apartment building.

2. *Separating relevant from irrelevant facts.* What are your negotiable items? What do you consider irrelevant and easily compromised?

1. *Identifying given facts.* Decide what are your most basic, nonnegotiable limits and desires.

A fireplace would be a plus.

Must allow cats.

3. *Defining the ultimate goal.*

② PRODUCTION

During the *production step*, the problem solver produces possible solutions, called *hypotheses*. Two major approaches to generating hypotheses are *algorithms* and *heuristics*.

Algorithm:
Answers every ad.

An **algorithm** is a logical, step-by-step procedure (well suited for computers) that will always produce the solution. (For example, an algorithm for solving the problem 2×4 is $2 + 2 + 2 + 2$.) For complex problems, algorithms may take a long time.

A **heuristic** is a simple rule or shortcut that does not guarantee a solution. Heuristics include working backward from the solution (a known condition) and *creating subgoals*, stepping-stones to the original goal.

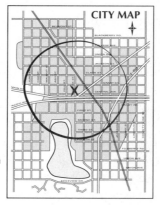

CITY MAP

Heuristic:
Works backward—start by drawing a 1-mile radius around work to narrow search.

algorithm A set of steps that, if followed correctly, will eventually solve the problem.

heuristic A simple rule used in problem solving and decision-making that does not guarantee a solution but offers a likely shortcut to it.

③ EVALUATION

1. Did your hypotheses (possible solutions) solve the problem? If not, then you must return to the production stage and produce more possible solutions.

2. Take action. Once you've identified the right home, sign the lease and start packing.

SOLVING PROBLEMS

Several years ago in Los Angeles, a 3.5-metre-high tractor-trailer got stuck under a bridge that was a few centimetres too low. After hours of towing, tugging, and pushing, the police and transportation workers were stumped. Then a young boy happened by and asked, "Why don't you let some air out of the tires?" It was a simple, creative suggestion—and it worked.

Our lives are filled with problems, some simple, some difficult. In all cases, **problem solving** requires moving from a given state (the problem) to a goal state (the solution), a process that usually involves three steps (Bourne, Dominowski, & Loftus, 1979) (**Figure 8.4**).

BARRIERS TO PROBLEM SOLVING

We all encounter barriers to solving problems. We stick to problem-solving strategies (**mental sets**) that worked in the past, rather than trying new, possibly more effective, ones (**Figure 8.5**). Or we fail to let our inventive instincts run free, thinking of objects as functioning only in their prescribed, customary way—a phenomenon called **functional fixedness** (**Figure 8.6**).

Other barriers to effective problem solving stem from our tendency to ignore important information. Have you

"Repurposing" as art FIGURE 8.6

Some people look at a pile of garbage and see only trash. Others see possibility. This photo shows how an artist recycled old hubcaps. Have you ever "repurposed" a discarded object, such as an old LP record for use as a wall decoration or even a bowl? If so, you have overcome *functional fixedness*.

ever caught yourself agreeing with friends who support your environmental opinions and discounting conflicting opinions? This inclination to seek confirmation of our existing beliefs and to overlook contradictory evidence is known as the **confirmation bias** (Jonas et al., 2008; Kerschreiter et al., 2008; Nickerson, 1998; Reich, 2004).

British researcher Peter Wason (1968) first demonstrated the confirmation bias. He asked participants to generate a list of numbers that conformed to the same rule that applied to this set of numbers:

$$2 \quad 4 \quad 6$$

Hypothesizing that the rule was "numbers increasing by two," most participants generated sets such as (4, 6, 8) or (1, 3, 5). Each time, Wason assured them that their sets of numbers conformed to the rule but that the rule "numbers increasing by two" was incorrect. The problem was that the participants were searching only for information that confirmed their hypothesis. Proposing a series such as (1, 3, 4) would have led them to reject their initial hypothesis and discover the correct rule: "numbers in increasing order of size."

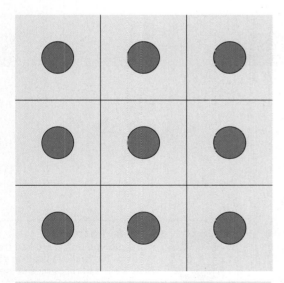

The nine-dot problem FIGURE 8.5

Draw no more than four lines that run through all nine dots on this page without lifting your pencil from the paper (the solution is provided at the end of this chapter, before the chapter summary).

Cognitive psychologists Amos Tversky and Daniel Kahneman found that heuristics, as handy as they can be, can lead us to ignore relevant information (Kahneman, 2003; Tversky & Kahneman, 1974, 1993). When we use the **availability heuristic**, we judge the likelihood of an event based on how easily recalled (or available) other instances of the event are (Buontempo & Brockner, 2008; Caruso, 2008; Oppenheimer, 2004). Shortly after the September 11, 2001, terrorist attacks, one study found that the average American believed that he or she had a 20.5 percent chance of being hurt in a terrorist attack within a year (Lerner et al., 2003). Can you see how intense media coverage of the attacks created this erroneously high perception of risk?

Tversky and Kahneman also demonstrated that the **representativeness heuristic** sometimes hinders problem solving. Using this heuristic, we estimate the probability of something based on how well the circumstances match (or represent) our prototype (Fisk, Bury, & Holden, 2006; Greene & Ellis, 2008). For example, if John is six feet, five inches tall, we may guess that he is a member of Canada's Olympic basketball team rather than, say, a physician. But in this case, the representative heuristic ignores *base rate information*—the probability of a characteristic occurring in the general population. In Canada, physicians outnumber members of the Olympic basketball team by more than 3,000 to 1.

So despite his height, John is much more likely to be a physician.

CREATIVITY: FINDING UNIQUE SOLUTIONS

What makes a person creative? Conceptions of creativity are subject to cultural relevance and to whether a solution or performance is considered useful at the time. In general, three characteristics are associated with **creativity**: originality, fluency, and flexibility.

Thomas Edison's invention of the light bulb offers a prime example of each of these characteristics (**TABLE 8.1**).

> **creativity**
> The ability to produce valued outcomes in a novel way.

Most tests of creativity focus on **divergent thinking**, a type of thinking in which many possibilities are developed from a single starting point (Baer, 1994). For example, in the Unusual Uses Test, people are asked to think of as many uses as possible for an object (such as "How many ways can you use a brick?"). In the Anagrams Test, people are asked to reorder the letters in a word to make as many new words as possible.

A classic example of divergent thinking is the decision of Xiang Yu, a Chinese general in the third century

---

 Applying Psychology

Are You Creative?

Everyone exhibits a certain amount of creativity in some aspects of life. Even when doing ordinary tasks, like planning an afternoon of errands, you are being somewhat creative. Similarly, if you've ever tightened a screw with a penny or used a telephone book on a chair as a booster seat for a child, you've found creative solutions to problems.

Would you like to test your own creativity?

- Find 10 coins and arrange them in the configuration shown here. By moving only 2 coins, form two rows that each contains 6 coins (the solution is provided at the end of this chapter, before the chapter summary).

- In five minutes, see how many words you can make by using the letters in the word *hippopotamus.*

- In five minutes, list all the things you can do with a paper clip.

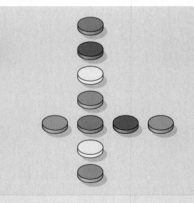

> **Stop & Think**
> STOP
> 1. How did you do? If you had trouble with any of these tasks, can you use the list of resources of creative people in Table 8.2 to identify the resources you lack? Is there anything you could do to increase your share of these resources?
> 2. Creativity is usually associated with art, poetry, and the like. Can you think of other areas in which creativity is highly valued?

Three elements of creative thinking TABLE 8.1

	Explanations	Thomas Edison Examples
Originality	Seeing unique or different solutions to a problem	After noting that electricity passing through a conductor produces a glowing red or white heat, Edison imagined using this light for practical uses.
Fluency	Generating a large number of possible solutions	Edison tried literally hundreds of different materials to find one that would heat to the point of glowing white heat without burning up.
Flexibility	Shifting with ease from one type of problem-solving strategy to another	When he couldn't find a long-lasting material, Edison tried heating it in a vacuum—thereby creating the first light bulb.

B.C., to crush his troops' cooking pots and burn their ships. You might think that no general in his right mind would make such a decision, but Xiang Yu explained that his purpose was to focus the troops on moving forward, as they had no hope of retreating. His divergent thinking was rewarded with victory on the battlefield.

One prominent theory of creativity is Robert J. Sternberg and Todd Lubart's **investment theory** (1992, 1996). According to this theory, creative people tend to "buy low" in the realm of ideas, championing ideas that others dismiss (much like a bold entrepreneur might invest in low-priced, unpopular stocks, believing that their value will rise). Once their creative ideas are highly valued, they "sell high" and move on to another unpopular but promising idea. Investment theory also suggests that creativity requires the coming together of six interrelated resources (Kaufman, 2002; Sternberg & Lubart, 1996). These resources are summarized in TABLE 8.2. One way to improve your personal creativity is to study this list and then strengthen those areas in which you think you need improvement.

Resources of creative people TABLE 8.2

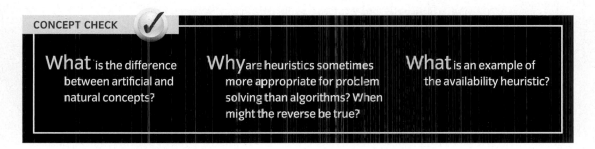

Intellectual Ability	Enough intelligence to see problems in a new light
Knowledge	Sufficient basic knowledge of the problem to effectively evaluate possible solutions
Thinking Style	Novel ideas and ability to distinguish between the worthy and worthless
Personality	Willingness to grow and change, take risks, and work to overcome obstacles
Motivation	Sufficient motivation to accomplish the task and more internal than external motivation
Environment	An environment that supports creativity

Which resources best explain Jim Carrey's phenomenal success?

CONCEPT CHECK

What is the difference between artificial and natural concepts?

Why are heuristics sometimes more appropriate for problem solving than algorithms? When might the reverse be true?

What is an example of the availability heuristic?

Language

LEARNING OBJECTIVES

Identify the building blocks of language.

Describe the prominent theories of how language and thought interact.

Describe the major stages of language development.

Review the evidence that non-human animals are able to learn and use language.

Language enables us to mentally manipulate symbols, thereby expanding our thinking, and to communicate our thoughts, ideas, and feelings. To produce language, we first build words using **phonemes** and **morphemes**. Then we string words into sentences using rules of **grammar** (syntax and semantics) (**FIGURE 8.7**).

■ **language** A form of communication that uses sounds and symbols combined according to specified rules.

■ **phoneme** [FO-neem] The smallest basic unit of speech or sound (the English language has about 40 phonemes).

LANGUAGE AND THOUGHT: A COMPLEX INTERACTION

Does the fact that you speak English instead of Spanish—or Chinese instead of Swahili—determine how you reason, think, and perceive the world? Linguist Benjamin Whorf (1956) believed so. As evidence for his **linguistic relativity hypothesis**,

■ **morpheme** [MOR-feem] The smallest meaningful unit of language, formed from a combination of phonemes.

■ **grammar** Rules that specify how phonemes, morphemes, words, and phrases should be combined to express thoughts; these rules include syntax and semantics.

Building blocks of language FIGURE 8.7

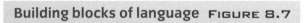

Grammar

A system of rules (syntax and semantics) used to generate acceptable language that enables us to communicate with and understand others.

They were in my psychology class.
versus
They was in my psychology class.

Syntax
A system of rules for putting words in order

I am happy.
versus
Happy I am.

Semantics
A system of using words to create meaning

I went out on a limb for you.
versus
Humans have several limbs.

Morphemes

The smallest units that carry meaning; they are created by combining phonemes. (*Function morphemes* are prefixes and suffixes. *Content morphemes* are root words.)

unthinkable = *un·think·able*
(prefix = *un*, root word = *think*, suffix = *able*)

Phonemes

The smallest units of sound that make up every language

p in pansy; *ng* in sting

Whorf offered a now classic example: because the Inuit have many words for snow (*apikak* for "first snow falling," *pukak* for "snow for drinking water," and so on), they can perceive and think about snow differently from English speakers, who have only one word—*snow*.

Although intriguing, Whorf's hypothesis has not fared well. He apparently exaggerated the number of Inuit words for snow (Pullum, 1991) and ignored the fact that English speakers have a number of terms to describe various forms of snow, such as *slush, sleet, hard pack,* and *powder.* Other research has directly contradicted Whorf's theory. For example, Eleanor Rosch (1973) found that although people of the Dani tribe in New Guinea possess only two colour names—one indicating cool, dark colours, and the other describing warm, bright colours—they discriminate among multiple hues as well as English speakers do.

Whorf apparently was mistaken in his belief that language determines thought. But there is no doubt that language *influences* thought (Hoff, 2009). People who speak both Chinese and English report that the language they're currently using affects their sense of self (Matsumoto & Juang, 2008). When using Chinese, they tend to conform to Chinese cultural norms; when speaking English, they tend to adopt Western norms.

Our words also influence the thinking of those who hear them. That's why companies avoid *firing* employees; instead, employees are *outplaced* or *non-renewed.* Similarly, the military uses terms such as *pre-emptive strike* to cover the fact that it attacked first and *tactical redeployment* to refer to a retreat. And research has shown that consumers who receive a *rebate* are less likely to spend the money than those who receive a *bonus* (Epley, 2008).

LANGUAGE DEVELOPMENT: FROM CRYING TO TALKING

From birth, a child communicates through facial expressions, eye contact, and body gestures (**FIGURE 8.8**). Babies who are only hours old begin to "teach" their caregivers when and how they want to be held, fed, and handled.

Eventually, children also communicate verbally, progressing through several distinct stages of language acquisition. These stages are summarized in **STUDY ORGANIZER 8.1**. By age 5, most children have mastered basic grammar and typically use about 2,000 words (a level of mastery considered adequate for getting by in any given culture). Past this point, vocabulary and grammar gradually improve throughout life.

Early non-verbal communication FIGURE 8.8

Even before they begin to communicate verbally, infants use non-verbal signals to "speak" to others. Infants as young as 2½ months express basic emotions, such as interest, joy, anger, and sadness. Children who are born blind and deaf exhibit the same emotional expressions as children who can see and hear, supporting the contention that these expressions are universal and innate. What emotions are each of these infants expressing?

Developmental Stage	Age	Language Features	Example
Prelinguistic stage	Birth to ~12 months	Crying (reflexive in newborns; soon, crying becomes more purposeful)	hunger cry anger cry pain cry
	2 to 3 months	**Cooing** (vowel-like sounds)	"ooooh" "aaaah"
	4 to 6 months	**Babbling** (consonants added)	"bahbahbah" "dahdahdah"
Linguistic stage	~12 months	Babbling begins to resemble language of the child's home. Child seems to understand that sounds relate to meaning.	
		At first, speech is limited to one-word utterances.	"Mama" "juice" "Daddy" "up"
		Expressive ability more than doubles once the child begins to join words into short phrases.	"Daddy, milk" "no night-night!"
	~ 2 years	Child sometimes **overextends** (using words to include objects that do not fit the word's meaning).	all men = "Daddy" all furry animals = doggy
	~2 years to ~5 years	Child links several words to create short but intelligible sentences. This speech is called **telegraphic speech** because (like telegrams) it omits nonessential connecting words.	"Me want cookie" "Grandma go bye-bye?"
		Vocabulary increases at a phenomenal rate.	
		Child acquires a wide variety of rules for grammar.	adding -ed for past tense adding s to form plurals
		Child sometimes **overregularizes** (applying the basic rules of grammar even to cases that are exceptions to the rule).	"I goed to the zoo" "Two mans"

Ψ Psychological Science

Baby Signing

Many babies and toddlers—beginning as young as 9 months of age—can learn to communicate by using a modified form of sign language, sometimes called baby sign lanuage. Symbolic gestures for basic ideas, such as *more*, *milk*, and *love* enhance parents' and caregivers' interactions with children who cannot yet talk. Many parents find that signing with their infant or toddler gives them a fascinating window into the baby's mind—and eliminates a lot of frustration for both them and the baby! Some researchers believe that teaching babies to sign helps foster better language comprehension and can speed up the process of learning to talk. In recent years, baby signing has become hugely popular in both Canada and the United States (Baby Signs Canada, 2006; CBC News Online, 2004).

STOP

Stop & Think
1. Would you teach your own child baby sign language? Why or why not?
2. How could signing be combined with a child's early attempts to talk to enhance language development?

Some theorists argue that the capability to acquire and use language is innate in humans. Noam Chomsky (1968, 1980) has argued that children are "prewired" with a set of cognitive and neurological abilities, labelled a **language acquisition device (LAD)**. This set of abilities enables children to analyze language and infer the basic rules of grammar. This mechanism needs only exposure to speech to unlock its potential. As evidence for this nativist position, Chomsky observes that children everywhere progress through the same stages of language development at about the same ages. He also notes that babbling is the same in all languages and that babies who are deaf initially babble just like hearing babies. Steven Pinker, an internationally acclaimed Canadian psychologist at Harvard University, agrees strongly with the nativist position (Pinker, 2007; Pinker & Jackendoff, 2005). Pinker has elaborated this view in his 1994 New York Times best-seller, *The Language Instinct*.

Nurturists argue that the nativist position doesn't fully explain individual differences in language development. They hold that children learn language through a complex system of rewards, punishments, and imitation. For example, parents smile and encourage any vocalizations from a very young infant. Later, they respond even more enthusiastically when the infant babbles "Mama" or "Dada." In this way, parents unknowingly use *shaping* (Chapter 6) to help babies learn language (**FIGURE 8.9**).

BILINGUALISM AND FRENCH IMMERSION

More than 6 million Canadians have a mother tongue other than English or French (Statistics Canada, 2007). Yet most children from such families readily acquire one of Canada's two official languages in addition to the heritage language spoken at home. Exposure to two languages does not present an unusually difficult challenge to young children. Moreover, as noted by Canadian researcher Ellen Bialystok (2007), the resultant bilingualism may even be associated with gains in some areas of cognition. Furthermore, some evidence suggests that bilingualism may also be associated with increased appreciation of both linguistic groups on the part of children (Genesee & Ganadara, 1999). Bilingualism, therefore, may be viewed as both a cognitive and social asset to many children.

An approach to bilingualism that is uniquely Canadian is the popular French immersion programs offered across the country. In these programs, children who speak English receive much of their school instruction in French. French immersion programs were initially developed in the 1960s by a group of English-speaking parents in a suburb of Montreal (Genesee & Gandara, 1999). Since then, French immersion programs have become popular across the country (**FIGURE 8.10**). In 2007, more than 314,000 students were enrolled in such programs in Canada (Canadian Parents for French, 2008).

Nature or nurture? FIGURE 8.9

Both sides of the nature-versus-nurture controversy have had staunch supporters. However, most psychologists nowadays believe that language acquisition is a combination of both biology (nature) and environment (nurture) (Hoff, 2009; Plomin, De Fries, & Fulker, 2007). Can you see how both might contribute to this child's pretend phone conversation?

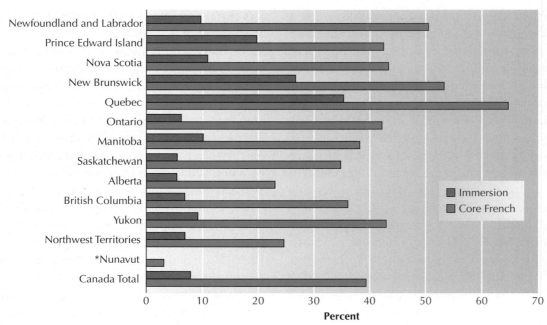

(*There is no immersion in Nunavut.)
Source: Canadian Parents for French, 2008.

Percentage of students enrolled in French immersion and core French programs in 2007 FIGURE 8.10

Why do you think participation in French immersion is highest in Quebec? What might explain the high participation in both immersion and core French programs in the Atlantic provinces?

French immersion programs take various forms. *Early immersion* begins in the lower elementary school grades, while *middle immersion* begins in grades 4 or 5, and *late immersion* begins at the end of elementary school or the beginning of high school (Canadian Council on Learning, 2007). Students who have participated in such programs usually show excellent French comprehension and high levels of speaking and writing abilities in French.

The majority of children in French immersion are in Quebec and eastern Canada. Many other English-speaking children across the country participate in core French programs, which offer up to one hour of instruction in French each day (Dicks & Christmanson, 2008). In 2007, more than 39 percent of Canadian children in junior kindergarten through grade 12 were enrolled in core French instruction (Canadian Parents for French, 2008). In general, research finds that the more exposure to French, whether through core French instruction, immersion, exchange programs, and so on, the better the students' proficiency (Genesee, 1987).

CAN HUMANS TALK TO NON-HUMAN ANIMALS?

Without question, non-human animals communicate, sending warnings, signalling sexual interest, sharing locations of food sources, and so on. But can non-human animals master the complexity of human language? Since the 1930s, many language studies have attempted to answer this question by probing the language abilities of chimpanzees and gorillas (e.g., Barner et al., 2008; Fields et al., 2007; Savage-Rumbaugh, 1990; Segerdahl, Fields, & Savage-Rumbaugh, 2006).

One of the most successful early studies was conducted by Beatrice and Allen Gardner (1969), who recognized chimpanzees' manual dexterity and ability to imitate gestures. The Gardners used American Sign Language (ASL) with a chimp named Washoe. By the time Washoe was 4 years old, she had learned 132 signs and was able to combine them into simple sentences, such as "Hurry, gimme toothbrush" and "Please tickle more." The famous gorilla Koko also uses ASL to communicate; she reportedly uses more than 1,000 words (**FIGURE 8.11**).

Signing FIGURE 8.11

According to her teacher, Penny Patterson, Koko has used ASL to converse with others, talk to herself, joke, express preferences, and even lie (Linden, 1993; Patterson, 2002).

In another well-known study, a chimp named Lana learned to use symbols on a computer to get things she wanted, such as food, a drink, a tickle from her trainers, and her curtains opened (Rumbaugh et al., 1974) (FIGURE 8.12).

Dolphins are also the subject of interesting language research. Communication with dolphins is done by means of hand signals or audible commands transmitted through an underwater speaker system. In one typical study, trainers gave dolphins commands made up of two- to five-word sentences, such as "Big ball—square— return," which meant that they should go get the big ball, put it in the floating square, and return to the trainer (Herman, Richards, & Woltz, 1984). By varying the syntax (for example, the order of the words) and specific content of the commands, the researchers showed that dolphins are sensitive to these aspects of language.

Psychologists disagree about how to interpret these findings about apes and dolphins. Most psychologists believe that non-human animals communicate but that their ideas are severely limited. Critics claim that apes and dolphins are unable to convey subtle meanings, use language creatively, or communicate at an abstract level (Jackendoff, 2003; Siegala & Varley, 2008).

Others claim that these animals do not truly understand language but are simply operantly conditioned (Chapter 6) to imitate symbols to receive rewards (Savage-Rumbaugh, 1990; Terrace, 1979). Finally, other critics have argued that data regarding animal language have not always been well documented (Lieberman, 1998; Willingham, 2001; Wynne, 2007).

Proponents of animal language respond that apes can use language creatively and have even coined some words of their own. For example, Koko signed "finger bracelet" to describe a ring and "eye hat" to describe a mask (Patterson & Linden, 1981). Proponents also argue that, as demonstrated by the dolphin studies, animals can be taught to understand basic rules of sentence structure.

Still, the gap between human and non-human animals' language is considerable. Current evidence suggests that, at best, non-human animal language is less complex, is less creative, and has fewer rules than any language used by humans.

Computer-aided communication FIGURE 8.12

Apes lack the necessary anatomical structures to vocalize the way humans do. For this reason, language research with chimps and gorillas has focused on teaching the animals to use sign language or to "speak" by pointing to symbols on a keyboard. Do you think this amounts to using language the same way humans do?

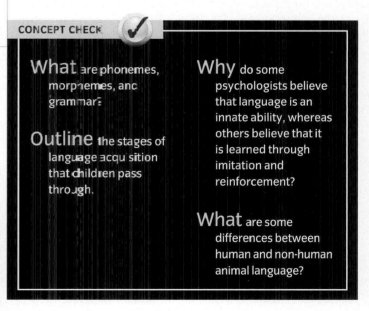

CONCEPT CHECK

What are phonemes, morphemes, and grammar?

Outline the stages of language acquisition that children pass through.

Why do some psychologists believe that language is an innate ability, whereas others believe that it is learned through imitation and reinforcement?

What are some differences between human and non-human animal language?

Intelligence

Many people equate intelligence with "book smarts." For others, what is intelligent depends on the characteristics and skills that are valued in a particular social group or culture (Matsumoto & Juang, 2008; Sternberg, 2008, 2009). For example, the Mandarin word that corresponds most closely to the word *intelligence* is a character meaning "good brain and talented" (Matsumoto, 2000). The word is associated with traits like imitation, effort, and social responsibility (Keats, 1982).

Even Western psychologists debate the definition of intelligence. In this discussion, we rely on a formal definition developed by psychologist David Wechsler (pronounced "WEX-ler") (1944, 1977). Wechsler defined **intelligence** as the global capacity to think rationally, act purposefully, and deal effectively with the environment.

intelligence
The global capacity to think rationally, act purposefully, and deal effectively with the environment.

DO WE HAVE ONE OR MANY INTELLIGENCES?

One of the central debates in research on intelligence concerns whether intelligence is a single ability or a collection of many specific abilities.

In the 1920s, British psychologist Charles Spearman first observed that high scores on separate tests of mental abilities tend to correlate with each other. Spearman (1923) thus proposed that intelligence is a single factor, which he termed **general intelligence (g)**. He believed that g underlies all intellectual behaviour, including reasoning, solving problems, and performing well in all areas of cognition. Spearman's work laid the foundations for today's standardized intelligence tests (Goldstein, 2008; Johnson et al., 2004).

About a decade later, L. L. Thurstone (1938) proposed seven primary mental abilities: verbal comprehension, word fluency, numerical fluency, spatial visualization, associative memory, perceptual speed, and reasoning. J. P. Guilford (1967) later expanded this number, proposing that as many as 120 factors were involved in the structure of intelligence.

Around the same time, Raymond Cattell (1963, 1971) reanalyzed Thurstone's data and argued against the idea of multiple intelligences. He believed that two subtypes of g exist:

- **Fluid intelligence (gf)** refers to innate, inherited reasoning abilities, memory, and speed of information processing. Fluid intelligence is relatively independent of education and experience, and like other biological capacities it declines with age (Bugg et al., 2006; Daniels et al., 2006; Rozencwajg et al., 2005).
- **Crystallized intelligence (gc)** refers to the store of knowledge and skills gained through experience and education (Goldstein, 2008). Crystallized intelligence tends to increase over the lifespan.

Today the concept of g as a measure of academic smarts has considerable support. However, many contemporary cognitive theorists believe that intelligence is not a single general factor but a collection of many separate specific abilities.

One of these cognitive theorists, Howard Gardner, believes that people have many kinds of intelligences. The fact that people with brain damage often lose some intellectual abilities while retaining others suggests to Gardner that different intelligences are located in discrete areas throughout the brain. According to Gardner's (1983, 1999, 2008) **theory of multiple intelligences**, people have different profiles of intelligence because they are stronger in some areas than others (**TABLE 8.3**). They also use their intelligences differently to learn new material, perform tasks, and solve problems.

Robert Sternberg's **triarchic theory of successful intelligence** also involves multiple abilities. As discussed

Visualizing

A modern intelligence test FIGURE 8.14

The most widely used intelligence test, the Wechsler Adult Intelligence Scale (WAIS), was developed by David Wechsler in the early twentieth century. He later created a similar test for school-age children, the Wechsler Intelligence Scale for Children (shown below), now in its fourth edition (WISC-IV), and one for preschool children, the Wechsler Preschool and Primary Scale of Intelligence (WPPSI).

Like the Stanford-Binet, Wechsler's tests yield an overall intelligence score. The most recent versions of both the Stanford-Binet and Wechsler tests also provide scores for a number of more specific intellectual abilities (Becker, 2003). The Wechsler scales provide separate scores for Verbal Reasoning (such as vocabulary and knowledge of general information), Perceptual Reasoning (such as arranging blocks to match a given pattern and indicating what's missing from a picture), Working Memory (such as short-term memory and mental arithmetic), and Processing Speed (such as pairing symbols with numbers and scanning for symbols in a list).

Verbal Comprehension

Information
How many wings does a bird have?
How many nickels make a dime?
What is pepper?

Vocabulary
What is a_____? What does_____ mean?
Hammer
Protect
Epidemic

Perceptual Reasoning

Block Design
Copy this design with blocks.

Picture Completion
What is missing from this ambulance?

Working Memory

Arithmetic
...n had three pieces of candy, and Joe gave him four more. How many pieces of candy did Sam have altogether?
...apples cost $0.15, what will be the cost of a dozen apples?

...n
following numbers:

Processing Speed

1	2	3	4	5						

in **TABLE 8.4**, Sternberg ... learned aspects of intelligen... gence, (2) creative intelligen... gence (Sternberg, 1985, 2007, 2...

Sternberg (1985, 1999) empha... lying thinking rather than just the pr...

than those published in popular magazines and foun on Internet websites? To be scientifically acceptable, all psychological tests must fulfill three basic requirements:

- **Standardization.** Intelligence tests (as well as personality, aptitude, and most other tests) must be standardized in two senses (Hogan, 2006). First, every test must have norms, or average scores, developed by giving the test to a representative sample of people (a diverse group of people who resemble those for whom the test is intended). Second, testing procedures must be standardized. All test takers must be given the same instructions, questions, and time limits, and all test administrators must follow the same objective score standards.

> ■ **standardization**
> Establishment of the norms and uniform procedures for giving and scoring a test.

- **Reliability.** To be trustworthy, a test must be consistent, or reliable, across time and situations. Reliability is usually determined by retesting subjects to see whether their test scores change significantly (Hogan, 2006, p. 142). Retesting can be done via the **test-retest method**, in which participants' scores on two separate administrations of the same test are compared, or via the **split-half method**, which involves splitting a test into two equivalent parts (e.g., odd and even questions) and determining the degree of similarity between the two halves.
- **Validity.** Validity is the ability of a test to mea-

> ■ **reliability**
> A measure of the consistency and stability of test scores when a test is re-administered.

> ■ **validity** The ability of a test to measure what it was designed to measure.

Psychological Science

Emotional Intelligence (EI): How Important Are "Emotional Smarts"?

Most people have heard of IQ, the intelligence quotient, but what about EI—emotional intelligence? Daniel Goleman's (1995, 2000) best-selling books have popularized the concept of **emotional intelligence (EI),** based on original work by Peter Salovey and John Mayer (1990).

According to the theory, emotional intelligence involves knowing and managing your emotions, empathizing with others, and maintaining satisfying relationships. In other words, an emotionally intelligent person successfully combines the three components of emotions (cognitive, physiological, and behavioural). Proponents of EI have suggested ways in which the close collaboration between emotion and reason may promote personal well-being and growth (Salovey et al., 2000).

Popular accounts, such as Goleman's, have suggested that traditional measures of human intelligence ignore a crucial range of abilities that characterize people who excel in real life: self-awareness, impulse control, persistence, zeal and self-motivation, empathy, and social deftness. Goleman also proposes that many societal problems, such as domestic abuse and youth violence, can be attributed to a low EI. Therefore, he argues, EI should be fostered in everyone.

Critics fear that a handy term like EI invites misuse, but their strongest reaction is to Goleman's proposals for teaching EI. For example, Paul McHugh, director of psychiatry at Johns Hopkins University, suggests that Goleman is "presuming that someone has the key to the right emotions to be taught to children. We don't even know the right emotions to be taught to adults" (cited in Gibbs, 1995, p. 68).

Stop & Think
1. Do you think you have high or low emotional intelligence? Why?
2. What value might EI have for a person's functioning in everyday life?

sure what it is designed to measure. The most important type of validity is **criterion-related validity**, or the accuracy with which test scores can be used to predict another variable of interest (known as the criterion). Criterion-related validity is expressed as the *correlation* (Chapter 1) between the test score and the criterion. If two variables are highly correlated, then one variable can be used to predict the other. Thus, if a test is valid, its scores will be useful in predicting people's behaviour in some other specified situation. One example of this is the use of intelligence test scores to predict grades at school.

Can you see why a test that is standardized and reliable but not valid is worthless? For example, a scale to measure weight is easy to standardize (the instructions specify exactly how to stand on the scale and accurately

measure your weight), and it is usually reliable (similar weight is obtained for the same individual on each retest). But it certainly would not be valid as a measure of intelligence.

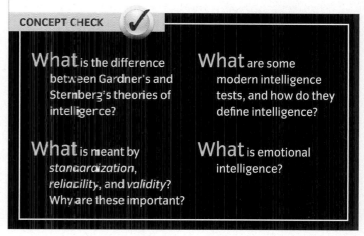

CONCEPT CHECK ✓

What is the difference between Gardner's and Sternberg's theories of intelligence?

What is meant by *standardization*, *reliability*, and *validity*? Why are these important?

What are some modern intelligence tests, and how do they define intelligence?

What is emotional intelligence?

The Intelligence Controversy

LEARNING OBJECTIVES

Explain why extremes in intelligence provide support for the validity of IQ testing.

Review research on how brain functioning is related to intelligence.

Describe how genetics and environment interact to shape intelligence.

Summarize the debate over ethnicity and intelligence.

P sychologists have long debated the two important questions related to intelligence: What causes some people to be more intelligent than others, and what factors—environmental or hereditary—influence an individual's intelligence? A related question is whether IQ tests are culturally biased. These questions, and the controversies surrounding them, are discussed in this section.

EXTREMES IN INTELLIGENCE: DEVELOPMENTAL DISABILITY AND GIFTEDNESS

One of the best methods for judging the validity of a test is to compare people who score at the extremes. Despite the uncertainties discussed in the previous section, intel-

ligence tests provide one of the major criteria for assessing mental ability at the extremes—specifically, for diagnosing **developmental disability** and **giftedness**.

The clinical label *developmentally disabled* (also referred to as *mentally retarded*) is applied when someone is significantly below average in intellectual functioning and has significant deficits in adaptive functioning (such as communicating, living independently, social or occupational functioning, or maintaining safety and health) (American Psychiatric Association, 2000; Phares, 2008).

Fewer than 3 percent of people are classified as having a developmental disability. Of this group, 85 percent have only a mild developmental disability and many become self-supporting, integrated members of society. Furthermore, people can score low on some measures of intelligence and still be average or even gifted in others.

The most dramatic examples are people with **savant syndrome** (FIGURE 8.15).

Some forms of developmental disability stem from genetic or chromosomal abnormalities, such as Down syndrome, fragile-X syndrome, and phenylketonuria (PKU). Other causes are environmental, including prenatal exposure to excessive alcohol and other drugs, extreme deprivation or neglect in early life, and brain damage from accidents. However, in many cases, there is no known cause of the developmental disability.

An unusual form of intelligence FIGURE 8.15

Although people with *savant syndrome* score very low on IQ tests (usually between 40 and 70), they demonstrate exceptional skills or brilliance in specific areas, such as rapid calculation, art, memory, or musical ability (Bor et al., 2007; Iavarone, 2007; Miller, 2005; Pring et al., 2008). Brittany Maier has autism and severe visual impairment; she's also a gifted composer and pianist who performs publicly and has recorded a CD. Her musical repertoire includes more than 15,000 songs.

At the other end of the intelligence spectrum are people with especially high IQs (typically defined as being in the top 1 or 2 percent).

In 1921, Lewis Terman identified 1,500 gifted children—affectionately nicknamed the "Termites"—with IQs of 140 or higher and tracked their progress through adulthood. The number who became highly successful professionals was many times the number a random group would have provided (Leslie, 2000; Terman, 1954). Those who were most successful tended to have extraordinary motivation, and they also had someone at home or school who was especially encouraging (Goleman, 1980). In other ways, however, many Termites were similar to their peers of average intelligence. Their rates of alcoholism, divorce, and suicide were close to the national rate (Leslie, 2000), and some of them were even quite unsuccessful. Thus, a high IQ is no guarantee of success in every endeavour; it offers only more intellectual opportunities.

THE BRAIN'S INFLUENCE ON INTELLIGENCE

A basic tenet of neuroscience is that all mental activity (including intelligence) results from neural activity in the brain. Most recent research on the biology of intelligence has focused on brain functioning. For example, neuroscientists have found that people who score highest on intelligence tests also respond more quickly on tasks involving perceptual judgements (Bowling & Mackenzie, 1996; Deary & Stough, 1996, 1997; Posthuma et al., 2001).

Other research using positron emission tomography (PET) to measure brain activity (Chapter 1) suggests that intelligent brains work smarter, or more efficiently, than less-intelligent brains (Jung & Haier, 2007; Neubauer et al., 2004; Posthuma et al., 2001) (FIGURE 8.16).

Does size matter? It makes logical sense that bigger brains would be smarter—after all, humans have larger brains than less-intelligent species, such as dogs. (Some animals, such as whales and dolphins, have larger brains than humans, but our brains are larger relative to our body size.) In fact, brain-imaging studies have found a significant correlation between brain size (adjusted for body size) and intelligence (Christensen et al., 2008; Deary et al., 2007; Ivanovic et al., 2004). However, Albert Einstein's brain was no larger than normal (Witelson, Kigar, & Harvey, 1999). In fact, some of Einstein's brain areas were actually smaller than average, but the area responsible for processing mathematical and spatial information was 15 percent larger than average.

Do intelligent brains work more efficiently?
FIGURE 8.16

When given problem-solving tasks, people of low intelligence (PET scans on the left) show more activity (red and yellow indicate more brain activity) in relevant brain areas than people of higher intelligence (PET scans on right).

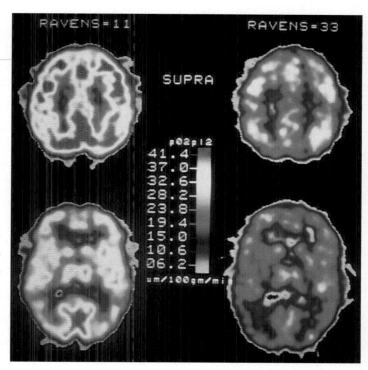

GENETIC AND ENVIRONMENTAL INFLUENCES ON INTELLIGENCE

Similarities in intelligence between family members are due to a combination of hereditary (shared genetic material) and environmental factors (similar living arrangements and experiences). Researchers who are interested in the role of heredity in intelligence often focus on identical (monozygotic) twins because they have 100 percent identical genetic material, as described in What a Psychologist Sees.

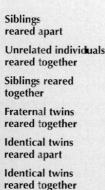

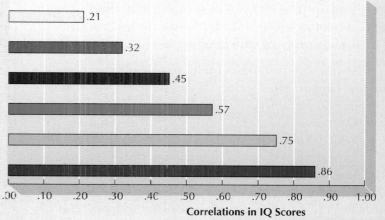

Correlations in IQ Scores

Group	Correlation
Siblings reared apart	.21
Unrelated individuals reared together	.32
Siblings reared together	.45
Fraternal twins reared together	.57
Identical twins reared apart	.75
Identical twins reared together	.86

Family Studies of Intelligence

Why are some people intellectually gifted while others struggle? As twin studies demonstrate, genetics play an important role. In the figure here, note the higher correlations between identical twins' IQ scores compared with the correlations between all other pairs (Bouchard & McGue, 1981; Bouchard et al., 1998; McGue et al., 1993). Although heredity equips each person with innate intellectual capabilities, the environment significantly influences whether a person will reach his or her full intellectual potential (Dickens & Flynn, 2001; Sangwan, 2001). For example, early malnutrition can retard a child's brain development, which in turn affects the child's curiosity, responsiveness to the environment, and motivation for learning—all of which can lower the child's IQ. The reverse is also true an enriching early environment can set the stage for intellectual growth.

The long-running Minnesota Study of Twins, an investigation of identical twins raised in different homes and reunited only as adults (Bouchard, 1994, 1999; Bouchard et al., 1998; Johnson et al., 2007), found that genetic factors appear to play a surprisingly large role in the IQ scores of identical twins.

However, such results are not conclusive. Adoption agencies tend to look for similar criteria in their choice of adoptive parents. Therefore, the homes of these "reared apart" twins were actually quite similar. In addition, these twins also shared the same nine-month prenatal environment, which also might have influenced their brain development and intelligence (White, Andreasen, & Nopoulos, 2002).

ETHNICITY AND INTELLIGENCE: ARE IQ TESTS CULTURALLY BIASED?

How would you answer the following questions?

1. A symphony is to a composer as a book is to a(n) _____. (a) musician; (b) editor; (c) novel; (d) author
2. If you throw a pair of dice and they land showing 7 on top, what is on the bottom? (a) snake eyes; (b) box cars; (c) little Joes; (d) 11

Can you see how the content and answers to these questions might reflect cultural bias? Which of these two questions do you think is most likely to appear on standard IQ tests?

One of the most controversial issues in psychology involves group differences in intelligence test scores and what they really mean. In 1969, Arthur Jensen began a heated debate when he argued that genetic factors are "strongly implicated" as the cause of ethnic differences in intelligence. Richard J. Herrnstein and Charles Murray's book *The Bell Curve: Intelligence and Class Structure in American Life* reignited this debate in 1994; in the book, the authors claimed that African Americans score below average in IQ because of their "genetic heritage."

Herrnstein and Murray's book provoked considerable discussion and research. Although the debate has no clear answer, psychologists have made several important points:

- Lack of cultural exposure to the concepts required on IQ tests can result in lowered test performance. Therefore, the tests may not be an accurate measure of true capability—they may be culturally biased (Manly et al., 2004; Naglieri & Ronning, 2000).

- Group differences in IQ may have more to do with socio-economic differences than with ethnicity. Minority children are disproportionately more likely to be living in poverty (Duncan & Magnuson, 2005), and the poorer medical and educational resources that accompany poverty have been found to hamper intellectual development (Sattler & Hoge, 2006; Solan & Mozlin, 2001).

- Differences in IQ scores may also reflect motivational and language factors. In some minority groups, a child who excels in school may be ridiculed for trying to be different from his or her classmates. Similarly, children from some groups may see little value in trying hard on a test or may even view such effort as negative, being associated with competitiveness (Sattler, 1988). Moreover, if children's own language and dialect do not match their education system or the IQ tests they take, they are obviously at a disadvantage (Cathers-Schiffman & Thompson, 2007; Rutter, 2007; Sternberg, 2007; Sternberg & Grigorenko, 2008; Sattler & Hoge, 2006).

- Members of every ethnic group can be found who have scores at all levels of the IQ scale. The distributions of IQ scores of different groups overlap considerably, and IQ scores and intelligence have their greatest relevance in terms of individuals, not groups (Garcia & Stafford, 2000; Myerson et al. 1998; Reifman, 2000). Many individual ethnic minority group members receive higher IQ scores than many individual Caucasians.

- Traditional IQ tests do not measure many of our multiple intelligences, tending to focus on school-related abilities (Manly et al., 2004; Naglieri & Ronning, 2000; Rutter, 2007; Sternberg, 2007, 2009; Sternberg & Grigorenko, 2008).

- People's performance on an IQ test may reflect, to some degree, their expectations of how well they will do. In particular, negative stereotypes about minority groups, referred to as **stereotype threat,** can significantly reduce the test scores of people in stereotyped groups (Bates, 2007; Keller & Bless, 2008; Steele, 2003).

> **stereotype threat** Negative stereotypes about minority groups cause some members to doubt their abilities.

- Intelligence (as measured by IQ tests) is not a fixed trait. Around the world, IQ scores have increased over the last half century, and this well-established phenomenon is known as the **Flynn effect**, in honour of New Zealand researcher James Flynn. Because these increases have occurred in a relatively short time, the cause or causes cannot be due to genetics or heredity. Other possible factors include improved nutrition, better public education, more proficient test-taking skills, and rising levels of education for a greater percentage of the world's population (Flynn, 1987, 2006, 2007; Huang & Hauser, 1998; Mingroni, 2004; Resing & Nijland, 2002). Further evidence for the lack of stability in IQ scores comes from even more recent international research. In the last decade this rise in scores has reversed itself, and several countries are now reporting a *decline* in IQ scores (Lynn & Harvey, 2008; Teasdale & Owen, 2008). Possible causes for this so-called *negative Flynn effect* are poorly understood. But whether IQ scores rise or fall, the important point is that *intelligence is not a fixed trait.*

Ψ Psychological Science

Stereotype Threat: Potential Pitfall for Minorities?

In the first study of stereotype threat, Claude Steele and Joshua Aronson (1995) asked African American and white Stanford University students to solve a series of challenging problems similar to those on the Graduate Record Exam (GRE), a standardized academic test used for graduate school admissions. In one condition, participants were told that the questions were a "performance exam" that supposedly measured intellectual abilities. In a second condition, they were told that the questions were simply part of a "laboratory task." Results showed that the African American students performed more poorly when they viewed the problems as a performance exam than as a laboratory task, an effect that was not seen in the white students' performance, which was the same under both conditions.

Subsequent research showed that this effect, which Steele labelled stereotype threat, occurs because members of stereotyped groups are anxious that they will fulfill their group's negative stereotype. This anxiety, in turn, hinders their performance on tests. Some people cope with stereotype threat by **disidentifying**, telling themselves they don't care about the test scores (Major et al., 1998). Unfortunately, this attitude lessens motivation, decreasing performance.

Barack Obama's election as U.S. president versus the stereotype threat Preliminary research has found a so-called "Obama effect," which may offset the performance gap between African Americans and whites (Dillon, 2009).

Stereotype threat affects the test performance of many social groups, including African Americans, women, Aboriginal people Latinos, people with low incomes, seniors, and even white male athletes (e.g., Bates, 2007; Ford et al., 2004; Keller & Bless, 2008; Klein et al., 2007; Steele, 2003; Steele, James, & Barnett, 2002). This research helps explain some group differences in intelligence and achievement tests. As such, it underscores why relying solely on such tests to make critical decisions affecting individual lives—for example, in hiring, college or university admissions, or clinical application—is unwarranted and possibly even unethical.

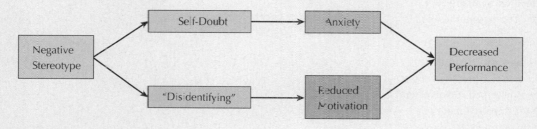

Stop & Think

1. Have you, or someone you know, experienced "stereotype threat"? If so, did it negatively affect your performance?
2. Apart from intelligence and achievement tests, what do you think might be some other areas where stereotype threat could affect performance?

The ongoing debate over the nature of intelligence and its measurement highlights the complexities of studying *cognition*. In this chapter, we've explored three cognitive processes: thinking, language, and intelligence. As you've seen, all three processes are greatly affected by numerous interacting factors.

Solution to the Nine-Dot Problem

People find this puzzle difficult because they see the arrangement of dots as a square—a *mental set* that limits possible solutions.

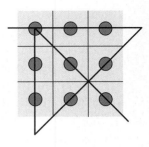

Solution to the Coin Problem

Stack one coin on top of the middle coin so that it shares both the row and the column.

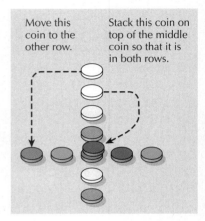

Move this coin to the other row.

Stack this coin on top of the middle coin so that it is in both rows.

CONCEPT CHECK ✓

Why might more-intelligent people show less activity in cognitive-processing areas of the brain than less-intelligent people?

How have twin studies improved researchers' understanding of intelligence?

What is stereotype threat, and why does it occur?

SUMMARY

1 Thinking

1. Thinking is a central aspect of **cognition**. Thought processes are distributed throughout the brain in neural networks. Mental images, concepts (both artificial and natural), and hierarchies aid our thought processes.

2. Problem solving usually involves three steps: preparation, production, and evaluation. **Algorithms** and **heuristics** help us produce solutions.

3. Barriers to problem solving include **mental sets**, **functional fixedness**, **confirmation bias**, **availability heuristic**, and **representativeness heuristic**.

4. **Creativity** is the ability to produce valued outcomes in a novel way. Tests of creativity usually focus on **divergent thinking**. One prominent theory of creativity is **investment theory**.

2 Language

1. **Language** supports thinking and enables us to communicate. To produce language, we use **phonemes, morphemes**, and **grammar** (syntax and semantics).

2. According to Whorf's **linguistic relativity hypothesis**, language determines thought. Generally, Whorf's hypothesis is not supported. However, language does strongly influence thought.

3. Children communicate non-verbally from birth. Their verbal communication proceeds in stages: prelinguistic (crying, cooing, babbling) and linguistic (single utterances, telegraphic speech, and acquisition of rules of grammar).

4. According to Chomsky, humans are "prewired" with a language acquisition device that enables language development. Nurturists hold that children learn language through rewards, punishments, and imitation. Most psychologists hold an intermediate view.

5. Many children in Canada and elsewhere learn more than one language quite easily. French immersion programs of various forms have been instituted in schools across Canada. The programs have been quite successful in developing French-language abilities in English-speaking children.

6. Research with apes and dolphins suggests that these animals can learn and use basic rules of language. However, non-human animal language is less complex, less creative, and not as rule-laden as human language.

3 Intelligence

1. There is considerable debate over the meaning of **intelligence**. Here it is defined as the global capacity to think rationally, act purposefully, and deal effectively with the environment.

2. Spearman proposed that intelligence is a single factor, which he termed **general intelligence** (g). Thurstone and Guilford argued that intelligence included distinct abilities. Cattell proposed two subtypes of g: **fluid intelligence** and **crystallized intelligence**. Many contemporary cognitive theorists, including Gardner and Sternberg, believe that intelligence is a collection of many separate specific abilities.

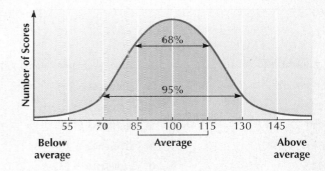

3. Early intelligence tests involved computing a person's mental age to arrive at an **intelligence quotient (IQ)**. Today, the most widely used intelligence tests are the Stanford-Binet Intelligence Scale, the Wechsler Adult Intelligence Scale (WAIS), and the Wechsler Intelligence Scale for Children (WISC).

4. To be scientifically acceptable, all psychological tests must fulfill three basic requirements: **standardization, reliability**, and **validity**.

5. **Emotional intelligence** involves knowing and managing your emotions, empathizing with others, and maintaining satisfying relationships.

4 The Intelligence Controversy

1. Intelligence tests provide one of the major criteria for assessing **developmental disability** and **giftedness.** Mental retardation exists on a continuum. In **savant syndrome,** a person who has a developmental disability is exceptional in some limited field. Studies of people who are intellectually gifted have found that they had more intellectual opportunities and tended to excel professionally. However, a high IQ is no guarantee of success in every endeavour.

2. Most recent research on the biology of intelligence has focused on brain functioning, not size. Research indicates that intelligent people's brains respond especially quickly and efficiently.

3. Both hereditary and environmental factors contribute to intelligence. Researchers interested in the role

of heredity on intelligence often focus on identical twins. Twin studies have found that genetics play an important role in intelligence. However, the environment significantly influences whether a person will reach his or her full intellectual potential.

4. Claims that genetic factors underlie ethnic differences in intelligence have caused heated debate and have

received intense scrutiny. Among other arguments, some psychologists argue that IQ tests may be culturally biased; that **stereotype threat** can significantly reduce test scores of people in stereotyped groups; that socio-economic factors may heavily influence intellectual development; and that traditional IQ tests do not measure many of our multiple intelligences.

KEY TERMS

CRITICAL AND CREATIVE THINKING QUESTIONS

1. During problem solving, do you use primarily algorithms or heuristics? What are the advantages of each?

2. Would you like to be more creative? Can you do anything to acquire more of the resources of creative people?

3. Do you believe that we are born with an innate "language acquisition device," or is language development a function of our environments?

4. Do you think apes and dolphins have true language? Why or why not?

5. Physicians, teachers, musicians, politicians, and people in many other occupations may become more successful with age and can continue working well into old age. Which kind of general intelligence might explain this phenomenon?

6. If Gardner's and Sternberg's theories of multiple intelligences are correct, what are the implications for intelligence testing and for education?

7. What are some areas where you feel you have higher intelligence? How do these fit with either Sternberg's or Gardner's theories of intelligence?

8. Have you listened to the speech of 2- to 3-year-old children? What sorts of language errors do they make?

What is happening in this picture ?

Jerry Levy and Mark Newman, twins separated at birth, first met as adults at a firefighters' convention.

■ **What factors might explain why they both became firefighters?**

■ **Does the brothers' choosing the same uncommon profession seem like a case of "telepathy"? How might *confirmation bias* contribute to this perception?**

SELF-TEST

(Check your answers in Appendix A.)

1. What is the term used for the mental activities involved in acquiring, storing, retrieving, and using knowledge?

   a. perception
   b. cognition
   c. consciousness
   d. awareness

2. Which of the following refer to mental representations of previously stored sensory experiences?

   a. illusions
   b. psychoses
   c. mental images
   d. mental propositions

3. Label the three stages of problem solving on the figure below:

a. _____

b. _____

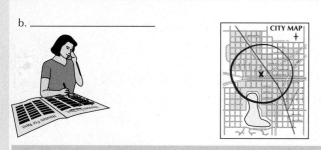

c. _____

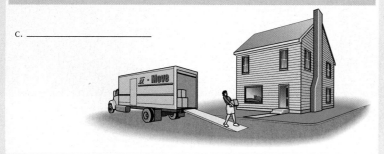

4. Which term describes a simple rule or shortcut that does not guarantee a solution, but that can be useful in problem solving?

   a. an algorithm
   b. a heuristic
   c. a problem-solving set
   d. brainstorming

5. Sarah and Richard mailed out 100 invitations to their wedding. They then took the number of replies they received and multiplied them by the price per plate provided by the caterer, to arrive at the cost of the reception dinner. What type of problem-solving strategy did they use?

   a. an algorithm
   b. a hierarchy
   c. a heuristic
   d. a prototype

6. When the fan belt broke on her car, Chantal pulled a pair of nylons out of her shopping bag and told Pierre: "We can use these to fix it!" Pierre couldn't imagine how you could use nylons for anything other than wearing. Which of the following describes Pierre's "problem"?

   a. the representativeness heuristic
   b. the availability heuristic
   c. functional fixedness
   d. confirmation bias

7. Dahlia sees an attractive man in the coffee shop and assumes he is a model at the nearby agency, when in fact he is a dentist with an office nearby. What is Dahlia demonstrating?

   a. the availability heuristic
   b. creativity
   c. the representativeness heuristic
   d. functional fixedness

8. What is the name for our ability to produce valuable outcomes in a novel way?

   a. problem solving
   b. incubation
   c. functional flexibility
   d. creativity

9. What is the term for the set of rules that specifies how phonemes, morphemes, words, and phrases should be combined to express meaningful thoughts?

   a. syntax
   b. pragmatics
   c. semantics
   d. grammar

10. Label the three building blocks of language on the figure below:

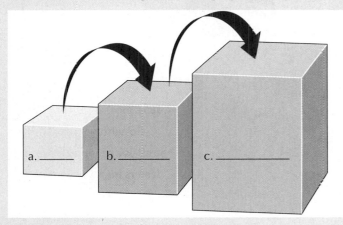

a. _____   b. _____   c. _____

11. According to Chomsky, what is the innate mechanism that enables a child to analyze language?

a. telegraphic understanding device (TUD)
b. language acquisition device (LAD)
c. language and grammar translator (LGT)
d. overgeneralized neural net (ONN)

12. Three-year-old Nika told her older sister that she and mommy "goed to the store." What is this an example of?

a. telegraphic speech
b. overregularizing
c. babbling
d. overextending

13. The definition of *intelligence* stated in your textbook stresses the global capacity to do which of the following?

a. perform in school and on the job
b. read, write, and make computations
c. perform verbally and physically
d. think rationally, act purposefully, and deal effectively with the environment

14. The IQ test sample in the figure below is from which intelligence scale?

a. Wechsler Intelligence Scale for Children
b. Wechsler Adult Intelligence Scale
c. Stanford-Binet Intelligence Scale
d. Binet-Terman Intelligence Scale

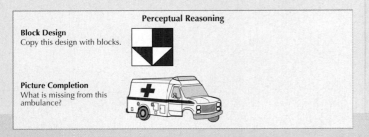

Perceptual Reasoning

Block Design
Copy this design with blocks.

Picture Completion
What is missing from this ambulance?

15. What do psychologists call the development of standard procedures for administering and scoring a test?

a. norming
b. standardization
c. procedural protocol
d. normalization

16. What term is used for people with developmental disability who demonstrate exceptional ability in specific areas?

a. savants
b. idiot geniuses
c. mildy retarded
d. connoisseurs

17. How is speed of response correlated with IQ scores?

a. negatively
b. positively
c. highly
d. there is no correlation between the two

18. Stereotype threat can affect the performance of which of the following groups?

a. women
b. white male athletes
c. seniors
d. all of these options

19. Jian helps his father in his auto repair shop and can fix many different types of vehicles, although he has never been formally trained in automotive repair. Which type of intelligence does Jian demonstrate?

a. Sternberg's analytical intelligence
b. Sternberg's practical intelligence
c. Gardner's naturalistic intelligence
d. Goleman's emotional intelligence

20. Dr. Hitchcock administered an intelligence test to a number of children throughout the Atlantic provinces. One year later he administered the test again to these same students, and found similar results. What does this test seem to have?

a. validity
b. standardization
c. reliability
d. a good split-half method

Lifespan Development I: Physical and Cognitive Development

If you have ever spent time at a daycare centre, you were probably struck by the sight of many exuberant children laughing, shrieking, and jostling for attention from those entrusted with their care. Yet amid this barely controlled chaos, babies learn to crawl, toddlers learn not to bite one another, and preschoolers learn their ABCs. Day by day, every child grows a little stronger, a little more independent.

Over a lifetime, every person undergoes many physical changes. These changes are most striking in early childhood because they happen so rapidly and are so visible. But everyone is in a state of constant change and development throughout his or her entire life. The typical human will be many different people in his or her lifetime—infant, child, teenager, adult, and senior citizen.

Would you like to know more about yourself at each of these ages? In the next two chapters, we will explore research in developmental psychology. We will begin this chapter by studying how developmental psychologists conduct their research. Then we will look at changes in our physical and cognitive development from conception to death. In Chapter 10, we will examine important aspects of our social, moral, and personality development across the lifespan. To emphasize that development is an ongoing, lifelong process, throughout the next two chapters we will trace physical, cognitive, social, moral, and personality development—one at a time—from conception to death. This topical approach will allow us to see how development affects an individual over the entire lifespan.

NATIONAL GEOGRAPHIC

Studying Development

LEARNING OBJECTIVES

Summarize the three most important debates or questions in developmental psychology.

Define *maturation* and *critical periods*.

Contrast the cross-sectional research method with the longitudinal research method.

Explain the advantages and limitations of cross-sectional and longitudinal research.

We begin our study of human development by focusing on some key theoretical issues and debates. We then discuss two basic research methods and their advantages and disadvantages.

THEORETICAL ISSUES: ONGOING DEBATES

The three most important debates or questions in **developmental psychology** are about nature versus nurture, continuity versus stages, and stability versus change.

> **developmental psychology**
> The study of age-related changes in behaviour and mental processes from conception to death.

Nature or Nurture

The issue of "nature versus nurture" has been with us since the beginning of psychology (Chapter 1). Even the ancient Greeks had the same debate—Plato argued that humans are born with innate knowledge and abilities, while Aristotle held that learning occurs through the five senses. Some early philosophers, the best known of whom is John Locke, proposed that at birth our minds are a *tabula rasa* (Latin for "blank slate") and that the environment determines what messages are written on that slate.

According to the nature position, human behaviour and development are governed by automatic, genetically predetermined signals in a process known as **maturation**. Just as a flower unfolds in accord with its genetic blueprint, we humans crawl before we walk and walk before we run. Furthermore, for many abili-

> **maturation**
> Development governed by automatic genetically predetermined signals.

ties, there are optimal periods during development, referred to as **critical periods**, when an organism is especially sensitive to certain experiences that shape the capacity for future development. On the other side of the debate, those who hold an extreme nurturist position argue that development occurs by learning through personal experience and observation of others.

> **critical period**
> A period of special sensitivity to specific types of learning that shapes the capacity for future development.

Continuity or Stages

Continuity proponents believe that development is continuous, with new abilities, skills, and knowledge being gradually added at a relatively uniform pace. Therefore, the continuity model suggests that an adult's thinking and intelligence differ quantitatively from those of a child. That is, adults simply have more math and verbal skills than do children. Stage theorists, conversely, believe that development occurs at different rates, alternating between periods of little change and periods of abrupt, rapid change. In this chapter, we discuss one such stage theory: Piaget's theory of cognitive development. In Chapter 10, we discuss two other stage theories: Erikson's psychosocial theory of personality development and Kohlberg's theory of moral development.

Stability or Change

Have you generally maintained your personal characteristics as you matured from infant to adult (stability)? Or does your current personality bear little resemblance to the personality you displayed as a young child (change)? Psychologists who emphasize stability in development hold that measurements of personality taken during childhood are

Deprivation and Development

What happens if a child is deprived of appropriate stimulation during critical periods of development? Consider the story of Genie, the so-called wild child. From the time she was 20 months old until authorities rescued her at age 13, Genie was locked alone in a tiny, windowless room. By day, she sat naked, tied to a chair with nothing to do and no one to talk to. At night, she was put in a kind of straitjacket and "caged" in a covered crib. Genie's abusive father forbade anyone to speak to her for those 13 years. If Genie made noise, her father beat her while he barked and growled like a dog.

Genie's tale is a heartbreaking account of the lasting scars from a disastrous childhood. In the years after her rescue, Genie spent thousands of hours receiving special training, and by age 19 she could use public transportation and was adapting well to her foster home and special classes at school (Rymer, 1993). Genie was far from normal, however. Her intelligence scores were still close to the cutoff for mental retardation. And although linguists and psychologists worked with her for many years, she never progressed beyond sentences like "Genie go" (Curtiss, 1977; Rymer, 1993). To make matters worse, she was also subjected to a series of foster home placements, one of which was abusive. At last report, Genie was living in a home for adults with developmental disabilities (Rymer, 1993).

Stop & Think
1. Does Genie's case prove that there is a critical period for language development? Why or why not?
2. Does Genie's case support either the nurture argument or the nature explanation of human development? Why or why not?

---

important predictors of adult personality. Of course, psychologists who emphasize change disagree.

Which of these positions is more correct? Most psychologists do not take a hard line either way. Rather, they prefer an **interactionist perspective**. For example, in the age-old nature versus nurture debate, psychologists generally agree that development emerges both from each individual's unique genetic predisposition and from individual experiences in the environment (Hartwell, 2008; Hudziak, 2008; Rutter, 2007). More recently, the interactionist position has evolved into the *biopsychosocial model* mentioned throughout this text. In this model, biological factors (genetics, brain functions,

biochemistry, and evolution), psychological influences (learning, thinking, emotion, personality, and motivation), and social forces (family, school, culture, ethnicity, social class, and politics) all affect and are affected by one another.

Like the nature versus nurture debate, the debates about continuity versus stages and stability versus change are not a matter of "either-or." Physical development and motor skills, for example, are believed to be primarily continuous in nature, whereas cognitive skills usually develop in discrete stages. Similarly, some traits are stable, whereas others vary greatly across the lifespan.

RESEARCH METHODS: TWO BASIC APPROACHES

cross-sectional method Research design that compares individuals of various ages at one point in time to provide information about age differences.

longitudinal method Research design that follows a single individual or a group of same-aged individuals over a period of time to provide information about age changes.

To study development, psychologists use either a cross-sectional or longitudinal method. The **cross-sectional method** examines individuals of various ages (e.g., 20, 40, 60, and 80 years old) at one point in time and gives information about age differences. The **longitudinal method,** in contrast, follows a single individual or a group of same-aged individuals over an extended period and gives information about age changes (**FIGURE 9.1**).

Imagine that you are a developmental psychologist interested in studying how intelligence changes with age in adults. Which method would you choose: cross-sectional or longitudinal? Before you decide, note the different research results shown in **FIGURE 9.2**.

Why do the two methods show such different results? Researchers suggest that the different results may reflect a central problem with cross-sectional studies. These studies often confuse genuine age differences with **cohort effects**, differences that result from specific histories of the age group studied (Elder, 1998). As Figure 9.2 shows, the 81-year-olds measured by the cross-sectional method have lower IQ scores than the 25-year-olds. But is this due to aging or to broad environmental differences, such as less formal education or poorer nutrition? Because the different age groups, called *cohorts,* grew up in different historical periods, their results may not apply to people growing up at other times. With the cross-sectional method, age effects and cohort effects are hopelessly entangled.

Longitudinal studies also have their limits. They are expensive in terms of time and money, and their results are restricted in generalizability. Because participants often drop out or move away during the extended test period, the experimenter may end up with a self-selected

Cross-sectional versus longitudinal research FIGURE 9.1

Note that cross-sectional research uses different participants and is interested in age-related differences, whereas longitudinal research studies the same participants over time to find age-related changes.

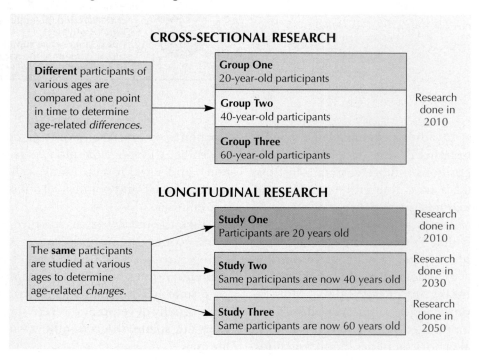

CROSS-SECTIONAL RESEARCH

Different participants of various ages are compared at one point in time to determine age-related *differences.*

Group One 20-year-old participants

Group Two 40-year-old participants

Group Three 60-year-old participants

Research done in 2010

LONGITUDINAL RESEARCH

The **same** participants are studied at various ages to determine age-related *changes.*

Study One Participants are 20 years old — Research done in 2010

Study Two Same participants are now 40 years old — Research done in 2030

Study Three Same participants are now 60 years old — Research done in 2050

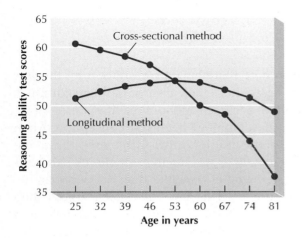

Cross-sectional studies have shown that reasoning and intelligence reach their peak in early adulthood and then gradually decline. In contrast, longitudinal studies have found that a marked decline does not begin until about age 60. (Adapted from Schaie, 1994, with permission.)

sample that differs from the general population in important ways. Each method of research has its own strengths and weaknesses (**TABLE 9.1**). Keep these differences in mind when you read the findings of developmental research.

Human development, like most areas of psychology, cannot be studied outside its sociocultural context. In fact, researchers have found that culture may be one of the most important determinants of development. If a child grows up in an individualistic/independent culture (such as North America or most of Western Europe), we can predict that this child will probably be competitive and question authority as an adult. If this same child were reared in a collectivist/interdependent culture (common in Africa, Asia, and Latin America), she or he would most likely grow up to be cooperative

and respectful of others (Berry et al., 2002; Delgado-Gaitan, 1994).

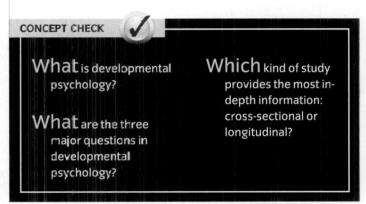

CONCEPT CHECK

What is developmental psychology?

What are the three major questions in developmental psychology?

Which kind of study provides the most in-depth information: cross-sectional or longitudinal?

	Cross-sectional	Longitudinal
Advantages and disadvantages of cross-sectional and longitudinal research design TABLE 9.1		
Advantages	Gives information about age differences	Gives information about age changes
	Quick	Increased reliability
	Less expensive	More in-depth information per participant
	Typically larger sample	
Disadvantages	Cohort effects are difficult to separate	More expensive
	Restricted generalizability (measures behaviours at only one point in time)	Time consuming
		Restricted generalizability (typically smaller sample and dropouts over time)

Physical Development

 n this section, we will explore the fascinating processes of physical development from conception through childhood, adolescence, and adulthood.

PRENATAL AND EARLY CHILDHOOD: A TIME OF RAPID CHANGE

The early years of development are characterized by rapid and unparalleled change. In fact, if you had continued to develop at the same rapid rate that marked your first two years of life, you would weigh several thousand kilograms and be more than four metres tall as an adult! Thankfully, physical development slows, yet it is important to note that change continues until the very moment of death. Let's look at some of the major physical changes that occur throughout the lifespan.

Prenatal development begins at conception, when an ovum from the mother unites with a sperm from the father (**FIGURE 9.3**), producing a single cell barely 0.1 millimetres in diameter—smaller than the period at the end of this sentence. This new cell, called a **zygote**, then begins a process of rapid cell division that results in a multimillion-celled infant some nine months later.

The vast changes that occur during the nine months of a full-term pregnancy are usually divided into three stages: the **germinal period**, the **embryonic period**, and the **fetal period** (**FIGURE 9.4**). Prenatal growth, as well as growth during the first few years after birth, is **cephalocaudal** (head to toe), with the head and upper body developing before the lower body.

During pregnancy, the **placenta** (the vascular life-support organ that unites the fetus to the mother's uterus) serves as the link for food and excretion of wastes. It also screens out some, but not all, harmful substances. Environmental hazards, such as X-rays or toxic waste, drugs, and diseases such as rubella (German measles) can cross the placental barrier. These influences generally have their most devastating effects during the first three months of pregnancy, making this a critical period in development.

Conception FIGURE 9.3

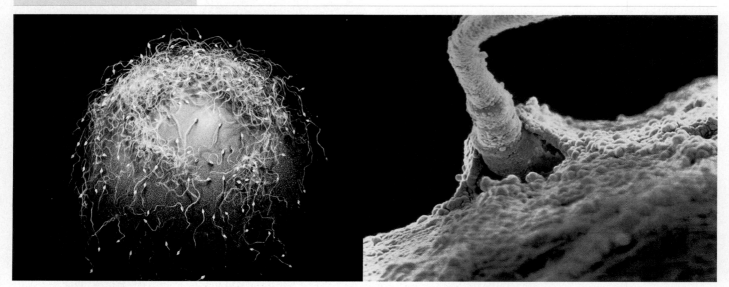

A Note the large number of sperm surrounding the ovum (egg).

B Although a joint effort is required to break through the outer coating, only one sperm will actually fertilize the egg.

Process Diagram

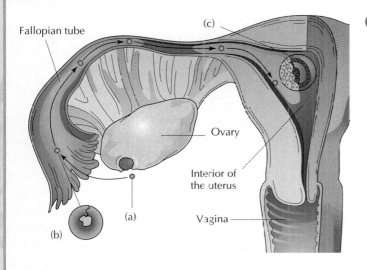

Fallopian tube
(c)
Ovary
Interior of the uterus
(a)
(b)
Vagina

1 **Germinal period**: From ovulation to implantation first two weeks. After discharge from either the left or right ovary (a) the ovum travels to the opening of the fallopian tube.

If fertilization occurs (b), it normally takes place in the first third of the fallopian tube. The fertilized ovum is referred to as a zygote.

When the zygote reaches the uterus, it implants itself in the wall of the uterus (c) and begins to grow tendril-like structures that intertwine with the rich supply of blood vessels located there. After implantation, the organism is known as an embryo.

VIEW THIS IN ACTION
in your WileyPLUS course

2 **Embryonic period.** This stage lasts from implantation ▶ to eight weeks. At eight weeks, the major organ systems have become well differentiated. Note that at this stage, the head grows at a faster rate than other parts of the body.

◀ **3** **Fetal period.** This is the period from the end of the second month to birth. At four months, all the actual body parts and organs are established. The fetal stage is primarily a time for increased growth and "fine detailing."

germinal period
The first stage of prenatal development, which begins with conception and ends with implantation in the uterus (the first two weeks).

embryonic period The second stage of prenatal development, which begins after uterine implantation and lasts through the eighth week.

fetal period
The third, and final, stage of prenatal development (eight weeks to birth), which is characterized by rapid weight gain in the fetus and the fine detailing of bodily organs and systems.

The pregnant mother plays a primary role in prenatal development because her health directly influences the child she is carrying (TABLE 9.2). Almost everything she ingests can cross the placental barrier. However, the father also plays a role (other than just fertilization). Environmentally, the father's smoking may pollute the air the mother breathes, and genetically, he may transmit heritable diseases. In addition, research suggests that alcohol, opiates, cocaine, various gases, lead, pesticides, and industrial chemicals can damage sperm (Baker & Nieuwenhuijsen, 2008; Bandstra et al., 2002; Ferretti et al., 2006).

Perhaps the most important—and generally avoidable—danger to the fetus comes from drugs, both legal and illegal. Nicotine and alcohol are major teratogens, environmental agents that cause damage during prenatal development.

Although the number of Canadian mothers who smoke while pregnant is on the decline, more than 5 percent of children born in Canada have been exposed prenatally to 10 or more cigarettes per day (Health Canada, 2003). Mothers who smoke tobacco during pregnancy have significantly higher rates of premature births, low-birth-weight infants, and fetal deaths (Bull, 2003; Health Canada, 2003; Oliver, 2002). Their children also show increased behavioural abnormalities and cognitive problems (Abadinsky, 2008; Fried, Watkinson, & Gray, 2003;

Fryer, Crocker, & Mattson, 2008; Howell et al., 2008; Hyde & DeLamater, 2008). To reduce such risks, the Public Health Agency of Canada (2008) advises expectant mothers to quit smoking completely—the sooner the better.

Alcohol also readily crosses the placenta, can affect fetal development, and can result in a neurotoxic syndrome called **fetal alcohol syndrome (FAS)** (FIGURE 9.5). Although, like those who smoke, the number of Canadian mothers who drink while pregnant is also on the decline, almost 15 percent of Canadian mothers report consuming some alcohol during their pregnancy (Health Canada, 2003). Between one and three out of a thousand babies in Canada and the United States are born with FAS (Chudley et al., 2005). Many others exposed prenatally to alcohol display some, although not all, of the features of FAS (National Organization on Fetal Alcohol Syndrome, 2008). Such children are said to have *fetal alcohol spectrum disorder* (*FASD*) (Chudley et al., 2005; Public Health Agency of Canada, 2007), which is more common than FAS (Streissguth & Connor, 2001). Indeed, an estimated 300,000 Canadians of all ages live with some negative effects of prenatal alcohol exposure (Public Health Agency of Canada, 2007).

The large majority of Canadians are aware that alcohol use is harmful to the fetus, although many are unsure whether there is a "safe" amount (Public Health

Sample environmental conditions that endanger the child TABLE 9.2

Maternal Factors	Possible effects on embryo, fetus, newborn, or young child
Malnutrition	Low birth weight, malformations, less developed brain, greater vulnerability to disease
Stress exposure	Low birth weight, hyperactivity, irritability, feeding difficulties
Exposure to X-rays	Malformations, cancer
Teratogens	**Possible effects on embryo, fetus, newborn, or young child**
Aspirin	In large quantities, miscarriage, bleeding, newborn respiratory problems
Thalidomide	Deformed limbs, sensory deficits, defects in internal organs, death
Cocaine and crack, heroin and methadone	Developmental disability, growth retardation, premature birth, irritableness in the newborn, withdrawal symptoms
Alcohol	Brain and heart damage, growth retardation, developmental disability, fetal alcohol syndrome (FAS)
Tobacco smoking	Low birth weight, prematurity, some evidence of behavioural and cognitive problems
Diseases	**Possible effects on embryo, fetus, newborn, or young child**
Rubella (German measles)	Developmental disability, eye damage, deafness, heart defects
Herpes	Developmental disability, eye damage, death
AIDS	Congenital malformations; makes infant vulnerable to infections of all types

Source: Abadinsky, 2008; Hyde & DeLamater, 2008; Howell, Coles, & Kable, 2008; Leventhal, 2008; Vasta, Younger, Adler, Miller, & Ellis, 2009.

Fetal alcohol syndrome FIGURE 9.5

Compare the healthy newborn infant brain (left) to the brain of a newborn (right) whose mother drank while pregnant. Prenatal exposure to alcohol can cause facial abnormalities and stunted growth. But the most disabling features of FAS are neurobehavioural problems, ranging from hyperactivity and learning disabilities to mental retardation, depression, and psychoses (Pellegrino & Pellegrino, 2008; Sowell et al., 2008; Wass, 2008). Prenatal alcohol exposure is the leading cause of developmental disability among Canadian children (Public Health Agency of Canada, 2006).

Agency of Canada, 2006). The answer to this question is not clear-cut. The Public Health Agency of Canada (2007) advises that there is no known safe amount and no known safe time to drink alcohol during pregnancy. The Canadian Pediatric Society (2009) likewise cautions that the more alcohol consumed while pregnant, the greater the risk, and advises that it is best to have none.

For many years, researchers have been aware of the harmful effects alcohol and tobacco can have on the developing fetus. In fact, for some time, Canadian health authorities have been attempting to educate the public, through the use of advertising in public places, pamphlets in doctors' offices and pharmacies, warnings on cigarette packages (see FIGURE 9.6), and so on.

Smoking and prenatal development FIGURE 9.6

WARNING
TOBACCO SMOKE HURTS BABIES

Tobacco use during pregnancy increases the risk of preterm birth. Babies born preterm are at an increased risk of infant death, illness and disability.

Health Canada

Do you think the Canadian public is aware of the risks to the fetus? If someone asked you what you should or should not do to have a healthy baby, how would you respond? Would you mention avoiding alcohol and cigarettes? What else would you mention? (See Table 9.3.)

Top 10 ways to increase the likelihood of having a healthy baby as mentioned by respondents in a Canada-wide survey TABLE 9.3	Total (%)	Women (%)	Men (%)
Eat well/good nutrition/vitamins	86	87	80
Cut down/stop alcohol use	52	51	54
Cut down/stop smoking	51	49	55
Increase/maintain exercise/physical activity	38	41	30
Visit doctor/health professional	18	20	10
Cut down/stop drug use (marijuana, crack, heroin, etc.)	17	17	14
Get rest/sleep	9	10	8
Avoid stress	6	6	3
Take prenatal class	4	4	3
Lifestyle/healthy living	3	3	4

Source: Public Health Agency of Canada (2006).

In 2006, the Public Health Agency of Canada reported the results of a nationwide survey in which 3,633 respondents (2,724 women and 909 men) were asked to name the important things women can do to increase the likelihood of having a healthy baby. As **TABLE 9.3** shows, the top three answers, mentioned by more than half the respondents, included getting proper nutrition, stopping/cutting down on alcohol use, and stopping/cutting down on smoking while pregnant.

Is the message getting across? What do you think health authorities could do to make their message even better known?

Like the prenatal period, early childhood is also a time of rapid physical development. Although Shakespeare described newborns as capable of only "mewling and puking in the nurse's arms," they are actually capable of much more. Let's explore three key areas of change in early childhood: brain, motor, and sensory and perceptual development.

Brain Development

The brain and other parts of the nervous system grow faster than any other part of the body during both prenatal development and the first two years of life. At birth, a healthy newborn's brain is one-fourth its full adult size, and it will grow to about 75 percent of its adult weight and size by the age of 2. At age 6, the child's brain is nine-tenths its full adult weight (**FIGURE 9.7**).

Body proportions FIGURE 9.7

As noted earlier in the chapter, a large part of human development results from the orderly sequence of genetically designed biological processes called *maturation*. Notice how our body proportions change as we grow older. At birth, an infant's head is one-fourth its total body's size, whereas in adulthood, the head is one-eighth.

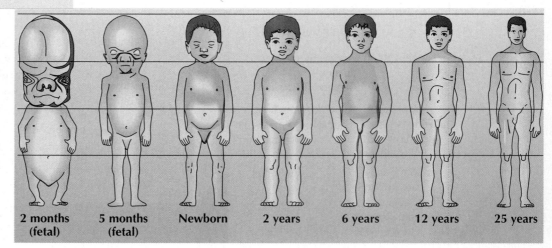

2 months (fetal)   5 months (fetal)   Newborn   2 years   6 years   12 years   25 years

Brain growth in the first two years FIGURE 9.8

As children learn and develop, synaptic connections between active neurons strengthen, and dendritic connections become more elaborate. *Synaptic pruning* (reduction of unused synapses) helps support this process. *Myelination,* the accumulation of fatty tissue coating the axons of neurons, continues until early adulthood. Myelin increases the speed of neural impulses, and the speed of information processing shows a corresponding increase (Chapter 2). In addition, synaptic connections in the frontal lobes and other parts of the brain continue growing and changing throughout the entire lifespan (Chapters 2 and 6).

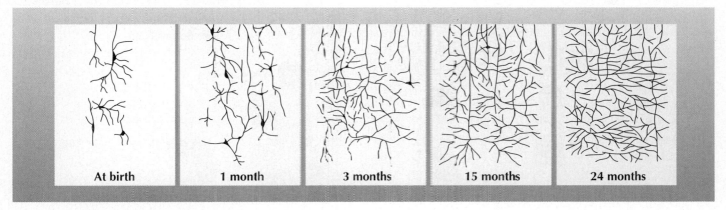

| At birth | 1 month | 3 months | 15 months | 24 months |

Rapid brain growth during infancy and early childhood slows down in later childhood. Further brain development and learning occur primarily because neurons grow in size and because the number of axons and dendrites, as well as the extent of their connections, increases (DiPietro, 2000) (**FIGURE 9.8**).

Motor Development Compared with the hidden, internal changes in brain development, the orderly emergence of active movement skills, known as motor development, is easily observed and measured. The newborn's first motor abilities are limited to *reflexes*, or involuntary responses to stimulation. For example, the rooting reflex occurs when something touches a baby's cheek: the infant will automatically turn its head, open its mouth, and "root" for a nipple.

In addition to simple reflexes, the infant soon begins to show voluntary control over the movement of various body parts (see **FIGURE 9.9**). Thus, a helpless newborn who cannot even lift her head is soon transformed into an active toddler capable of crawling, walking, and climbing. Keep in mind that motor development is largely due to natural maturation, but it can also be affected by environmental influences, such as disease and neglect.

Sensory and Perceptual Development
At birth, a newborn can smell most odours and distinguish among sweet, salty, and bitter tastes. Breast-fed newborns also very quickly recognize and show preference for the odour and taste of their mother's milk over that of another mother (DiPietro, 2000; Rattaz et al., 2005). In addition, the newborn's sense of touch and pain is highly developed, as evidenced by reactions to heel pricks for blood testing and to circumcision (Williamson, 1997).

The newborn's sense of vision, however, is poorly developed. At birth, an infant is estimated to have vision between 20/200 and 20/600 (Haith & Benson, 1998). Imagine what the infant's visual life is like: if you have 20/20 vision, the level of detail you see at 200 or 600 feet (about 60 metres or 180 metres) is what they see at 20 feet (6 metres). Within the first few months, vision quickly improves, and by 6 months it is 20/100 or better. At 2 years, visual acuity reaches a near-adult level of 20/20 (Courage & Adams, 1990).

One of the most interesting findings in infant sensory and perceptual research concerns hearing. Not only can the newborn hear quite well at birth (Matlin & Foley, 1997) but during the last few months in the womb, the fetus can also apparently hear sounds outside the mother's body (Kisilivesky, 2003; DeCasper et al., 1994). This raises the interesting possibility of fetal learning, and some have advocated special stimulation for the fetus as a way of increasing intelligence, creativity, and general alertness (e.g., Van de Carr & Lehrer, 1997). For more information, see *What a Psychologist Sees.*

Chin up

2.2 mo.

Rolls over

2.8 mo.

Sits with support

2.9 mo.

Sits alone

5.5 mo.

Stands holding furniture

5.8 mo.

A Milestones in motor development
In the typical progression of motor abilities, "chin up" occurs at 2.2 months. However, no two children are exactly alike; all follow their own individual timetables for physical development. (Adapted from Frankenburg et al., 1992, with permission.)

Walks holding on

9.2 mo.

Stands alone

11.5 mo.

Walks alone

12.1 mo.

Walks up steps

17.1 mo.

B Maturation and motor development
Infants around the world develop according to the same maturational sequence, despite wide variations in cultural beliefs and practices. For example, some Hopi Indian infants spend a great portion of their first year of life being carried in a cradleboard, rather than crawling and walking freely on the ground. Yet by age 1, their motor skills are very similar to those of infants who have not been restrained in this fashion (Dennis & Dennis, 1940).

Studies on possible fetal learning have found that newborn infants easily recognize their own mother's voice over that of a stranger (DeCasper & Fifer, 1980; Kisilevsky et al., 2003). They also show a preference for children's stories (such as *The Cat in the Hat* or *The King, the Mice, and the Cheese*) that were read to them while they were still in the womb (DeCasper & Spence, 1986; Karmiloff & Karmiloff-Smith, 2002). However, some experts caution that too much or the wrong kind of stimulation before birth can be stressful for both the mother and the fetus. They suggest that the fetus gets what it needs without any special stimulation.

ADOLESCENCE AND ADULTHOOD: A TIME OF BOTH DRAMATIC AND GRADUAL CHANGE

Think back for a moment to your teen years. Were you concerned about the physical changes you were going through? Did you worry about how you differed from

How an Infant Perceives the World

Because infants cannot talk or follow directions, researchers have had to create ingenious experiments to measure their perceptual abilities and preferences. One of the earliest experimenters, Robert Fantz (1956, 1963), designed a "looking chamber" to measure how long infants stared at stimuli. Research using this apparatus indicates that infants prefer complex rather than simple patterns and pictures of faces rather than nonfaces.

Researchers also use newborns' heart rates and innate abilities, such as the sucking reflex, to study learning and perceptual development (Bendersky & Sullivan, 2007). To study the sense of smell, researchers measure changes in the newborns' heart rates when odours are presented. Presumably, if they can smell one odour but not another, their heart rates will change in the presence of the first but not the second. Brain scans, such as fMRI, MRI, and CTs, also help scientists study changes in the infant's brain. From research such as this, we now know that the senses develop very early in life.

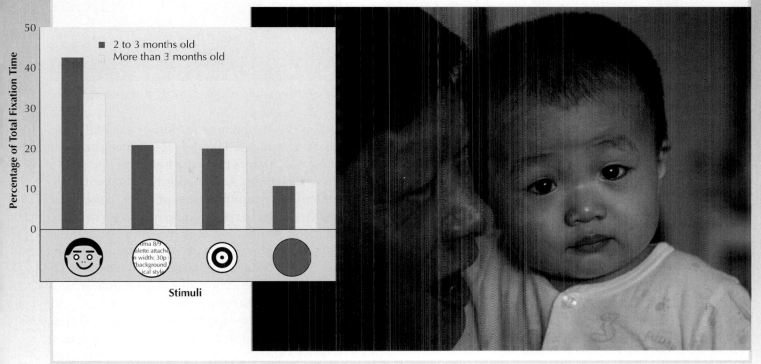

your classmates? Changes in height and weight, breast development and menstruation for girls, and a deepening voice and beard growth for boys, are important milestones for adolescents. **Puberty**, the period of adolescence when a person becomes capable of reproduction, is a major physical milestone for everyone. It is a clear biological signal of the end of childhood.

Although commonly associated with puberty, **adolescence** is the loosely defined psychological period of development between childhood and adulthood. In Canada and the United States, it roughly corresponds to the teenage years. The concept of adolescence and its meaning varies greatly across cultures (FIGURE 9.10).

The clearest and most dramatic physical sign of puberty is the **growth spurt**, which is characterized by rapid increases in height, weight, and skeletal growth (FIGURE 9.11), and by significant changes in reproductive structures and sexual characteristics. Maturation and hormone secretion cause rapid development of the ovaries and vagina and the onset of menstruation (**menarche**) in the adolescent female. In the adolescent male, the testes, scrotum, and penis develop, and he experiences his first ejaculation (**spermarche**). The ovaries and testes in turn produce hormones that lead to the development of secondary sex characteristics, such as the growth of pubic hair, deepening of the voice, and growth

Adolescence is not a universal concept. Unlike in Canada and other Western nations, some non-industrialized countries have no need for a slow transition from childhood to adulthood; children simply assume adult responsibilities as soon as possible. Can you see how this cultural difference is reflected in these two photos.

A Teenage girls in North America spend the day at a mall.

B A girl in Thailand hangs dyed silk skeins to dry outside a workshop.

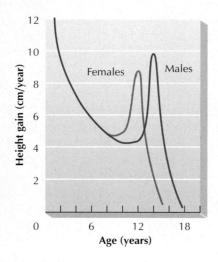

Adolescent growth spurt FIGURE 9.11

Note the sex differences in height gain during puberty. Most girls between the ages of 10 and 14 are about two years ahead of boys in their growth spurt and are therefore taller than most boys of the same age.

of facial hair in men, and the growth of breasts in women (FIGURE 9.12).

Age-related physical changes that occur after the obvious pubertal changes are less dramatic. Other than some modest increases in height and muscular development during the late teens and early twenties, most individuals experience only minor physical changes until middle age.

For women, **menopause**, the cessation of the menstrual cycle, which occurs somewhere between the ages of 45 and 55, is the second most important life milestone in physical development. The decreased production of estrogen (the dominant feminizing hormone) produces certain physical changes. Although some women experience troublesome symptoms, the popular belief that menopause (or "the change of life") causes serious psychological mood swings, loss of sexual interest, and depression is not supported by current research (Matlin, 2008; Tom, 2008). In fact, one large-scale study of postmenopausal American women found that almost two-thirds felt relief that their periods had stopped, and more than half did not experience hot flashes (Brim, 1999). When psychological problems do arise, they may in part reflect the social devaluation of aging women, not the physiological process of menopause. Given that in Western society women are highly valued for their youth and beauty, such a biological process as aging can be difficult for some women. Women in cultures that derogate aging tend to experience more anxiety and depression during menopause (Mingo, Herman, & Jasperse, 2000; Sampselle et al., 2002; Winterich, 2003).

For men, youthfulness is less important and the physical changes of middle age are less obvious. Beginning in middle adulthood, men experience a gradual decline in the production of sperm and testosterone (the dominant male hormone), although they remain capable of reproduction into their eighties or nineties. Physical changes, such as unexpected weight gain, decline in sexual responsiveness, loss of muscle strength, and greying or loss of hair, may lead some men (and women as well) to feel depressed and to question their life progress. They often see

Secondary sex characteristics FIGURE 9.12

Complex physical changes in puberty primarily result from hormones secreted from the ovaries and testes, the hypothalamus and the pituitary gland in the brain, and the adrenal glands on top of the kidneys.

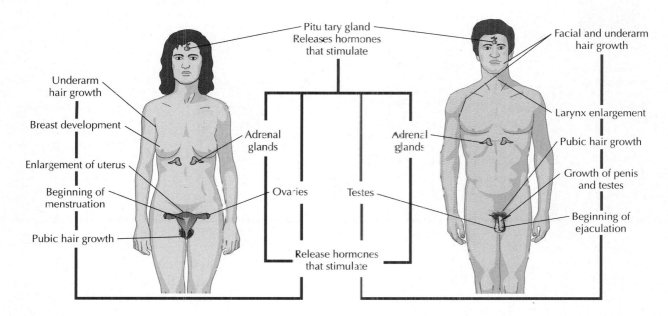

these alterations as a biological signal of aging and mortality. Such gradual physical and psychological changes in men are known as the **male climacteric**.

After middle age, most physical changes in development are gradual and occur in the heart and arteries and in the sensory receptors. For example, cardiac output (the volume of blood pumped by the heart each minute) decreases, whereas blood pressure increases because of the thickening and stiffening of arterial walls. Visual acuity and depth perception decline, hearing acuity lessens (especially for high-frequency sounds), and smell sensitivity decreases (Chung, 2006; Snyder & Alain, 2008; Whitbourne, 2009).

Television, magazines, movies, and advertisements generally portray aging as a time of balding and greying hair, sagging parts, poor vision, hearing loss, and, of course, no sex life. Such negative portrayals contribute to our society's widespread **ageism**—prejudice or discrimination based on physical age. However, as advertising companies pursue the revenue of the huge population of aging baby boomers, a shift has occurred toward a more accurate portrayal of aging as a time of vigour, interest, and productivity (FIGURE 9.13 and FIGURE 9.14).

What about memory problems and inherited genetic tendencies toward Alzheimer's disease and other serious diseases of old age? The public and most researchers have long thought that aging is accompa-

nied by widespread death of neurons in the brain. Although this decline does happen with degenerative disorders, like Alzheimer's disease, this is no longer believed to be a part of normal aging (Chapter 2). It is also important to remember that age-related memory problems are not on a continuum with Alzheimer's disease (Wilson et al., 2000). That is, normal forgetfulness does not mean that serious dementia is around the corner.

Use it or lose it? FIGURE 9.13

Contrary to the unfortunate (and untrue) stereotype that, "You can't teach an old dog new tricks," our cognitive abilities generally grow and improve throughout our lifespan.

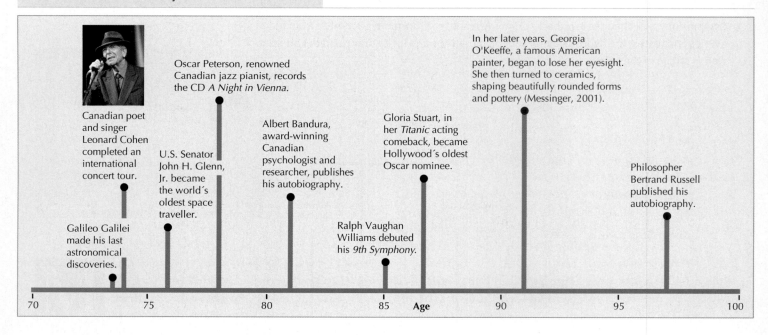

Canadian poet and singer Leonard Cohen completed an international concert tour.

Oscar Peterson, renowned Canadian jazz pianist, records the CD *A Night in Vienna*.

U.S. Senator John H. Glenn, Jr. became the world's oldest space traveller.

Galileo Galilei made his last astronomical discoveries.

Albert Bandura, award-winning Canadian psychologist and researcher, publishes his autobiography.

Ralph Vaughan Williams debuted his *9th Symphony*.

Gloria Stuart, in her *Titanic* acting comeback, became Hollywood's oldest Oscar nominee.

In her later years, Georgia O'Keeffe, a famous American painter, began to lose her eyesight. She then turned to ceramics, shaping beautifully rounded forms and pottery (Messinger, 2001).

Philosopher Bertrand Russell published his autobiography.

70   75   80   85   **Age**   90   95   100

Aging does seem to take its toll on the speed of information processing (Chapter 7). Decreased speed of processing may reflect problems with encoding (putting information into long-term storage) and retrieval (getting information out of storage). If memory is like a filing system, older people may have more filing cabinets, and it may take them longer to initially file and later retrieve information. Although mental speed declines with age, general information processing and memory ability is largely unaffected by the aging process (Lachman, 2004; Whitbourne, 2009).

What causes us to age and die? If we set aside contributions from **secondary aging** (changes resulting from disease, disuse, or neglect), we are left to consider **primary aging** (gradual, inevitable age-related changes in physical and mental processes). There are two main theories explaining primary aging and death: programmed theory and damage theory (Cristofalo, 1996; Medina, 1996; Wallace, 1997).

According to the **programmed theory**, aging is genetically controlled. Once the ovum is fertilized, the program for aging and death is set and begins to run. Researcher Leonard Hayflick (1977, 1996) found that human cells seem to have a built-in lifespan. He observed that after doubling about 50 times, laboratory-cultured cells ceased to divide—they reached the Hayflick limit.

The other explanation of primary aging is **damage theory**, which proposes that an accumulation of damage to cells and organs over the years ultimately causes death.

Whether aging is genetically controlled or caused by accumulated damage over the years, scientists generally agree that humans appear to have a maximum lifespan of about 110 to 120 years. Although we can try to control secondary aging in an attempt to reach that maximum, so far we have no means to postpone primary aging.

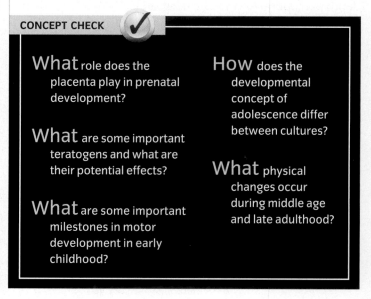

CONCEPT CHECK

What role does the placenta play in prenatal development?

What are some important teratogens and what are their potential effects?

What are some important milestones in motor development in early childhood?

How does the developmental concept of adolescence differ between cultures?

What physical changes occur during middle age and late adulthood?

Cognitive Development

LEARNING OBJECTIVES

Explain the role of schemas, assimilation, and accommodation in cognitive development.

Describe the major characteristics of Piaget's four stages of cognitive development.

Discuss two critiques of Piaget's theory.

The following fan letter was written to Shari Lewis (1963), a children's television performer, about her puppet Lamb Chop:

Dear Shari:
All my friends say Lamb Chop isn't really a little girl that talks. She is just a puppet you made out of a sock. I don't care even if it's true. I like the way Lamb Chop talks. If I send you one of my socks will you teach it how to talk and send it back?

Randi

Randi's understanding of fantasy and reality is certainly different from an adult's. Just as a child's body and physical abilities change, his or her way of knowing and perceiving the world also grows and changes. This seems intuitively obvious, but early psychologists—with one exception—focused on physical, emotional, language, and personality development. The one major exception was Jean Piaget (pronounced Pee–ah–ZHAY).

Piaget demonstrated that a child's intellect is fundamentally different from an adult's. He showed that an infant begins at a cognitively "primitive" level and that intellectual growth progresses in distinct stages, motivated by an innate need to know. Piaget's theory, developed in the 1920s and 1930s, has proven so comprehensive and insightful that it remains the major force in the cognitive area of developmental psychology today.

To appreciate Piaget's contributions, we need to consider three major concepts: schemas, assimilation, and accommodation. **Schemas** are the most basic units of intellect. They act as patterns of thought or action that organize our interactions with the environment. They serve as mental frameworks, similar to an architect's drawings or a builder's blueprints, that we use to understand our world.

In the first few weeks of life, for example, the infant apparently has several schemas based on the innate reflexes of sucking, grasping, and so on. These schemas are primarily motor and may be little more than stimulus-and-response mechanisms—the nipple is presented, and the baby sucks. Soon, other schemas emerge. The infant develops a more detailed schema for eating solid food, a different schema for the concepts of *mother* and *father*, and so on. Schemas, our tools for learning about the world, expand and change throughout our lives. For example, music lovers who were previously accustomed to LP records and cassette tapes have had to develop schemas for burning CDs and downloading MP3s.

Assimilation and accommodation are the two major processes by which schemas grow and change over time. **Assimilation** is the process of absorbing new information into existing schemas. For instance, infants use their sucking schema not only in sucking nipples but also in sucking blankets and fingers, and some toddlers use the word *dada* to refer to all men.

Accommodation occurs when new information or stimuli cannot easily be assimilated into existing schemas and new schemas are developed or old schemas are changed to better fit with the new information. An infant's first attempt to eat solid food with a spoon is a good example. When the spoon first enters her mouth, she attempts to assimilate it by using the previously successful sucking schema—shaping the lips and tongue around the spoon as if it were a nipple. After repeated attempts, she accommodates by adjusting her lips and tongue in a way that moves the food off the spoon and into her mouth. Similarly, if you meet someone through an online chat room and are later surprised when you talk face to face, it is because of the unexamined schemas you constructed. The awkwardness and discomfort you now feel are due, in part, to the work involved in readjusting, or accommodating, your earlier schemas to match the new reality.

schemas Cognitive structures or patterns consisting of a number of organized ideas that grow and differentiate with experience.

assimilation In Piaget's theory, the process of absorbing new information into existing schemas.

accommodation In Piaget's theory, the process of adjusting old schemas or developing new ones to better fit with new information.

STAGES OF COGNITIVE DEVELOPMENT: BIRTH TO ADOLESCENCE

According to Piaget, all children go through approximately the same four stages of cognitive development, regardless of the culture in which they live (STUDY ORGANIZER 9.1). Stages cannot be skipped because skills acquired at earlier stages are essential to mastery at later stages. Let's take a closer look at these four stages: sensorimotor, preoperational, concrete operational, and formal operational.

Piaget's four stages of cognitive development		Study Organizer 9.1
Stage	**Abilities**	**Limits**
① **Sensorimotor stage** (birth to age 2)	Uses senses and motor skills to explore and develop cognitively	Beginning of stage lacks object *permanence* (understanding that things continue to exist even when not seen, heard, or felt)
② **Preoperational stage** (ages 2 to 7)	Has significant language and thinks symbolically	Cannot perform "operations" *Egocentric* thinking (inability to consider another's point of view) *Animistic* thinking (believing all things are living)
③ **Concrete operational stage** (ages 7 to 11)	Can perform "operations" on concrete objects Understands conservation (realizing that changes in shape or appearance can be reversed)	Cannot think abstractly and hypothetically
④ **Formal operational stage** (age 11 and over)	Can think abstractly and hypothetically	Adolescent egocentrism at the beginning of this stage, with related problems of the *personal fable* and *imaginary audience*

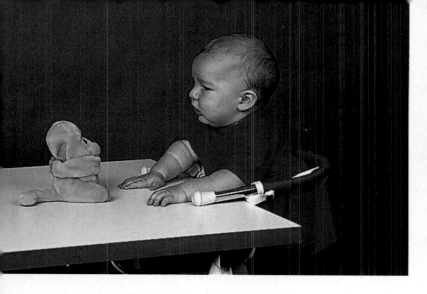
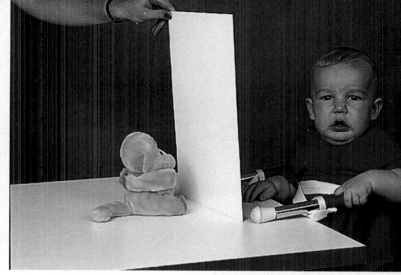

Object permanence FIGURE 9.15

At birth and for the next three or four months, children lack object permanence. They seem to have no schemas for objects they cannot see, hear, or touch—out of sight is truly out of mind. Why do you suppose this happens?

During the **sensorimotor stage**, which lasts from birth until "significant" language acquisition (about age 2), children explore the world and develop their schemas primarily through their senses and motor activities—hence the term *sensorimotor*. One important concept that infants acquire during the sensorimotor stage is **object permanence**, the understanding that objects continue to exist even when they cannot be seen, heard, or touched (**FIGURE 9.15**). Peekaboo becomes fabulously exciting for infants when they attain an understanding of object permanence. Because they know you are still there even though you are hidden, their anticipation is delightfully rewarded when you pop back into their sight.

During the **preoperational stage** (roughly ages 2 to 7), language advances significantly, and the child begins to think symbolically—using symbols, such as words, to represent concepts. Three other qualities characterize this stage.

Concepts Are Not Yet Operational

Piaget labelled this period "preoperational" because the child lacks **operations**, or reversible mental processes. For instance, if a preoperational boy who has a brother is asked, "Do you have a brother?" he will easily respond, "Yes." However, when

> **sensorimotor stage** Piaget's first stage (birth to approximately age 2) in which schemas are developed through sensory and motor activities.

> **preoperational stage** Piaget's second stage (roughly ages 2 to 7), which is characterized by the ability to employ significant language and to think symbolically though the child lacks operations (reversible mental processes) and thinking is egocentric and animistic.

asked, "Does your brother have a brother?" he will answer, "No!" To understand that his brother has a brother, he would have to be able to reverse the concept of "having a brother."

Thinking Is Egocentric

Children at this stage have difficulty understanding that there are points of view other than their own. **Egocentrism** refers to the preoperational child's limited ability to distinguish between his or her own perspective and that of someone else. (It does not mean "selfishness" in the ordinary sense of the word.) The preschooler who moves in front of you to get a better view of the TV or repeatedly asks questions while you are talking on the telephone is demonstrating egocentrism. Preoperational children assume that others see, hear, feel, and think exactly as they do. Consider the following telephone conversation between a 3-year-old, who is at home, and her mother, who is at work:

Mother: *Emma is that you?*

Emma: (Nods silently.)

Mother: *Emma, is Daddy there?*
May I speak to him?

Emma: (Twice nods silently.)

Egocentric preoperational children fail to understand that the phone caller cannot see their nodding head. Charming as this is, preoperational children's egocentrism also sometimes leads them to believe that their "bad thoughts" caused their sibling or parent to get sick or that their misbehaviour caused their parents' marital problems. Because they think the world centres on them, they often cannot separate reality from what goes on inside their own heads.

Thinking Is Animistic
Children in the preoperational stage believe that objects, such as the sun, trees, clouds, and bars of soap, have motives, feelings, and intentions (for example, "dark clouds are angry" and "soap sinks because it is tired"). **Animism** refers to the belief that all things are living (or animated). Our earlier example of Randi's letter asking puppeteer Shari Lewis to teach her sock to talk like Lamb Chop is also an example of animistic thinking.

Can preoperational children be taught how to use operations and to avoid egocentric and animistic thinking? Although some researchers have reported success in accelerating the preoperational stage, Piaget did not believe in pushing children ahead of their own developmental schedules. He believed that children should grow at their own pace, with minimal adult interference (Elkind, 2007). In fact, Piaget thought that Americans were particularly guilty of pushing their children, calling American childhood the "Great American Kid Race."

Following the preoperational stage, at approximately age 7, children enter the **concrete operational stage**. During this stage, many important thinking skills emerge. Unlike the preoperational stage, concrete operational children perform operations on concrete objects. Because they understand the concept of reversibility, they recognize that certain physical attributes (such as volume) remain unchanged when the outward appearance of an object is altered, a process known as **conservation** (FIGURE 9.16).

> **concrete operational stage** Piaget's third stage (roughly ages 7 to 11) in which the child can perform mental operations on concrete objects and understand reversibility and conservation though abstract thinking is not yet present.

Test for conservation FIGURE 9.16

A In the classic conservation of liquids test, the child is first shown two identical glasses with liquid at the same level.

B The liquid is poured from one of the short, wide glasses into the tall, thin one.

C When asked whether the two glasses have the same amount or if one has more, the preoperational child replies that the tall, thin glass has more. This demonstrates a failure to conserve volume.

Applying Psychology

Putting Piaget to the Test

If you have access to children in the preoperational or concrete operational stages, try some of the following experiments, which researchers use to test Piaget's various forms of conservation. The equipment is easily obtained, and you will find their responses fascinating. Keep in mind that this should be done as a game. The child should not feel that he or she is failing a test or making a mistake.

Type of Conservation Task (Average age at which concept is grasped)	Your task as experimenter . . .	Child is asked . . .
Length (ages 6–7)	**Step 1** Center two sticks of equal length. Child agrees that they are of equal length. **Step 2** Move one stick.	**Step 3** *"Which stick is longer?"* Preoperational child will say that one of the sticks is longer. Child in concrete stage will say that they are both the same length.
Substance amount (ages 6–7)	**Step 1** Center two identical clay balls. Child acknowledges that the two have equal amounts of clay. **Step 2** Flatten one of the balls.	**Step 3** *"Do the two pieces have the same amount of clay?"* Preoperational child will say that the flat piece has more clay. Child in concrete stage will say that the two pieces have the same amount of clay.
Area (ages 8–10)	**Step 1** Center two identical sheets of cardboard with wooden blocks placed on them in identical positions. Child acknowledges that the same amount of space is left open on each piece of cardboard. **Step 2** Scatter the blocks on one piece of the cardboard.	**Step 3** *"Do the two pieces of cardboard have the same amount of open space?"* Preoperational child will say that the cardboard with scattered blocks has less open space. Child in concrete stage will say that both pieces have the same amount of open space.

Stop & Think

1. Based on their responses, are the children you tested in the preoperational or concrete stage?
2. If you repeat the same tests with each child, do their answers change? Why or why not?

formal operational stage Piaget's fourth stage (around age 11 and beyond), which is characterized by abstract and hypothetical thinking.

The final stage in Piaget's theory is the **formal operational stage**, which typically begins around age 11. In this stage, children begin to be able to extend their operations beyond concrete objects, applying them to abstract concepts as well. They also become capable of hypothetical thinking ("What if?"), which allows systematic formulation and testing of concepts.

For example, before filling out applications for part-time jobs, adolescents may think about possible conflicts with school and friends, the number of hours they want to work, and the kind of work for which they are qualified. Formal operational thinking also allows the adolescent to construct a well-reasoned argument based on hypothetical concepts and logical processes. Consider the following argument:

1. If you hit a glass with a feather, the glass will break.
2. You hit the glass with a feather.

What is the logical conclusion? The correct answer, "The glass will break," is contrary to fact and direct experience. Therefore, the child in the concrete operational stage would have difficulty with this task, whereas the formal operational thinker understands that this problem is about abstractions that need not correspond to the real world.

Along with the benefits of this cognitive style come several problems. Adolescents in the early stages of the formal operational period demonstrate a type of egocentrism different from that of the preoperational child. Although adolescents recognize that others have unique thoughts and perspectives, they often fail to differentiate between what they are thinking and what others are thinking. This adolescent egocentrism has two characteristics that may affect social interactions as well as problem solving:

- *Personal fable.* Because of their unique form of egocentrism, adolescents may conclude that they alone are having insights or difficulties and that no one else understands or sympathizes with them. David Elkind (1967, 2007) described this as the formation of a **personal fable**, an intense investment in an adolescent's own thoughts and feelings and a belief that these thoughts are unique. For example, one young woman remembered being very upset in middle school when her mother tried to comfort her over the loss of an important relationship. "I felt like she couldn't possibly know how it felt—no one could. I couldn't believe that anyone had ever suffered like this or that things would ever get better."

Several forms of risk taking, such as engaging in sexual intercourse without contraception, driving dangerously, and experimenting with alcohol and illegal drugs, seem to arise from the personal fable (Alberts, Elkind, & Ginsburg, 2007; Flavell, Miller, & Miller, 2002; Greene et al., 2000). Adolescents have a sense of uniqueness, invulnerability, and immortality. They recognize the dangers of these activities but think the rules don't apply to them (FIGURE 9.17).

The personal fable FIGURE 9.17

Thanks to advances in brain imaging, scientists now know that the prefrontal cortex of the adolescent's brain is one of the later areas to develop (Giedd, 2008; Steinberg, 2008). How might this relatively slow development of the part of the brain responsible for higher processes, such as planning ahead and controlling emotions, provide a biological basis for the *personal fable* and risk taking during adolescence?

- *Imaginary audience.* Adolescents also tend to believe that they are the centre of others' thoughts and attentions, instead of considering that everyone is equally wrapped up in his or her own concerns and plans. In other words, adolescents feel that all eyes are focused on their behaviours. Elkind referred to this as the **imaginary audience**. This new form of egocentrism may explain what seems like extreme forms of self-consciousness and concern for physical appearance ("Everyone knows I don't know the answer"; or "They're all noticing this awful haircut").

If the imaginary audience results from an inability to differentiate the self from others, the personal fable is a product of differentiating too much. Thankfully, these two forms of adolescent egocentrism tend to decrease during later stages of the formal operational period.

ASSESSING PIAGET'S THEORY: CRITICISMS AND CONTRIBUTIONS

As influential as Piaget's account of cognitive development has been, it has received significant criticisms. Let's look briefly at two major areas of concern: underestimated abilities and underestimated genetic and cultural influences.

Research shows that Piaget may have underestimated young children's cognitive development (FIGURE 9.18 and FIGURE 9.19). For example, researchers report that very young infants have a basic concept of how objects move, have some awareness that objects continue to exist even when screened from view, and can recognize speech sounds (Baillargeon, 2000, 2008; Charles, 2007).

Non-egocentric responses also appear in the earliest days of life. For example, some newborn babies cry in response to the cry of another baby (Diego & Jones, 2007; Dondi, Simion, & Caltran, 1999). Also, preschoolers will adapt their speech by using shorter, simpler expressions when talking to 2-year-olds than when talking to adults.

Piaget's model, like other stage theories, has also been criticized for not sufficiently taking into account hereditary and cultural differences (Cole & Gajdamaschko, 2007; Matusov & Hayes, 2000; Maynard & Greenfield, 2003). During Piaget's time, hereditary influences on cognitive abilities were poorly understood, but there has been a rapid explosion of information in this field in recent years. In addition, formal education and specific cultural

Visualizing

Infant imitation FIGURE 9.18

In a series of well-known studies, Andrew Meltzoff and M. Keith Moore (1977, 1985, 1994) found that newborns could imitate such facial movements as tongue protrusion, mouth opening, and lip pursing. At 9 months, infants will imitate facial actions a full day after seeing them (Heimann & Meltzoff, 1996). Can you see how this early infant facial expression raises questions about Piaget's estimates of early infant abilities?

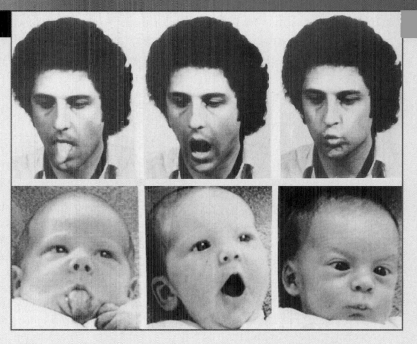

When an adult models a facial expression, even very young infants will respond with a similar expression. Is this true imitation or a simple stimulus-response reflex?

Are preoperational children always egocentric?

FIGURE 9.19

Some toddlers and preschoolers clearly demonstrate empathy for other people. How does this ability to take others' perspective contradict Piaget's beliefs about egocentrism in very young children?

experiences can also significantly affect cognitive development. Consider the following example from a researcher attempting to test the formal operational skills of a farmer in Liberia (Scribner, 1977):

> *Researcher:* All Kpelle men are rice farmers. Mr. Smith is not a rice farmer. Is he a Kpelle man?
>
> *Kpelle farmer:* I don't know the man. I have not laid eyes on the man myself.

Instead of reasoning in the "logical" way of Piaget's formal operational stage, the Kpelle farmer reasoned according to his specific cultural and educational training, which apparently emphasized personal knowledge. Not knowing Mr. Smith, the Kpelle farmer did not feel qualified to comment on him. Thus, Piaget's theory may have underestimated the effect of culture on a person's cognitive functioning.

Despite criticisms, Piaget's contributions to psychology are enormous. As one scholar put it, "assessing the impact of Piaget on developmental psychology is

like assessing the impact of Shakespeare on English literature or Aristotle on philosophy—impossible" (Beilin, 1992, p. 191).

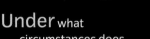

CONCEPT CHECK

Under what circumstances does accommodation occur?

How do egocentrism and animism limit children's thinking during the preoperational stage?

What are some important differences between the concrete operation and preoperational stages?

How might the personal fable explain risky behaviour among adolescents?

What are some criticisms of Piaget's theory?

SUMMARY

1 Studying Development

1. **Developmental psychology** is the study of age-related changes in behaviour and mental processes from conception to death. Development is an ongoing, lifelong process.

2. The three most important debates or questions in human development are about nature versus nurture (including studies of **maturation** and **critical periods**), continuity versus stages, and stability versus change.

For each question, most psychologists prefer an interactionist perspective.

3. Developmental psychologists use two research methods: the **cross-sectional method** and the **longitudinal method**. Although both have valuable attributes, each also has disadvantages. Cross-sectional studies can confuse true developmental effects with **cohort effects**. On the other hand, longitudinal studies are expensive and time-consuming, and their results are restricted in generalizability.

2 Physical Development

1. The early years of development are characterized by rapid change. Prenatal development begins at conception and is divided into three stages: the **germinal period**, the **embryonic period**, and the **fetal period**. During pregnancy, the **placenta** serves as the link for food and the excretion of wastes, and it screens out some harmful substances. However, some environmental hazards (**teratogens**), such as alcohol and nicotine, can cross the placental barrier and endanger prenatal development.

2. Early childhood is also a time of rapid physical development, including brain, motor, and sensory and perceptual development.

3. During **adolescence**, both boys and girls undergo dramatic changes in appearance and physical capacity. **Puberty** is the period of adolescence when a person becomes capable of reproduction. The clearest and most dramatic physical sign of puberty is the growth spurt, characterized by rapid increases in height, weight, and skeletal growth and by significant changes in reproductive structures and sexual characteristics.

4. During adulthood, most individuals experience only minor physical changes until middle age. Around age 45–55, women experience **menopause**, the cessation of the menstrual cycle. At the same time, men experience a gradual decline in the production of sperm and testosterone, as well as other physical changes, known as the **male climacteric**.

5. After middle age, most physical changes in development are gradual and occur in the heart and arteries and in the sensory receptors. Most researchers, as well as the public in general, have long thought that aging is accompanied by widespread death of neurons in the brain. Although this decline does happen with degenerative disorders, like Alzheimer's disease, this is no longer believed to be a part of normal aging. Although mental speed declines with age, general information processing and much of memory ability is largely unaffected by the aging process. There are two main theories explaining primary aging and death—**programmed theory** and **damage theory**.

3 Cognitive Development

1. In the 1920s and 1930s, Piaget conducted groundbreaking work on children's cognitive development. Piaget's theory remains a major force in the cognitive area of developmental psychology today.

2. Three major concepts are central to Piaget's theory: **schemas**, **assimilation**, and **accommodation**. According to Piaget, all children progress through four stages of cognitive development: the **sensorimotor stage**, the **preoperational stage**, the **concrete operational stage**, and the **formal operational stage**. As they progress through these stages, children acquire progressively more sophisticated ways of thinking.

3. Piaget's account of cognitive development has been enormously influential, but it has also received significant criticisms. In particular, research shows that Piaget may have underestimated infants' and young children's cognitive abilities, and he may have underestimated genetic and cultural influences on cognitive development.

KEY TERMS

CRITICAL AND CREATIVE THINKING QUESTIONS

1. Are there characteristics in you that seem to have been more influenced either by nature or by nurture? What are some ways to study how nature and nurture influence development?

2. Based on what you have learned about the advantages and disadvantages of cross-sectional and longitudinal methods, can you think of a circumstance when each might be preferable over the other?

3. If a mother knowingly ingests a quantity of alcohol that causes her child to develop fetal alcohol syndrome (FAS), is she guilty of child abuse? Why or why not?

4. From an evolutionary perspective, why might babies prefer looking at more complex patterns and at faces, rather than at simple patterns?

5. Based on what you have learned about development during late adulthood, do you think that this period is necessarily a time of physical and mental decline?

6. Piaget's theory states that all children progress through all of the discrete stages of cognitive development in order and without skipping any. Do you agree with this? Do you know any children who seem to contradict this notion?

7. Consider Piaget's concepts of assimilation and accommodation. Can you see examples of these processes in your own thinking? Are there times when one of these processes is better than the other?

8. Can you remember having thoughts consistent with the *personal fable* when you were an adolescent? Could such thoughts have contributed toward risky behaviour on your part?

What is happening in this picture ?

- What stage of cognitive development does this child's behaviour typify?

- What schemas might the child build by "exploring" her food in this way?

SELF-TEST

(Check your answers in Appendix A.)

1. What term is used to describe the study of age-related changes in behaviour and mental processes from conception to death?

   a. thanatology
   b. neo-gerontology
   c. developmental psychology
   d. longitudinal psychology

2. Which of the following is governed by automatic, genetically predetermined signals?

   a. growth
   b. natural progression
   c. maturation
   d. *tabula rasa*

3. Label the two basic types of research studies in the figure below:

   (a) _____

   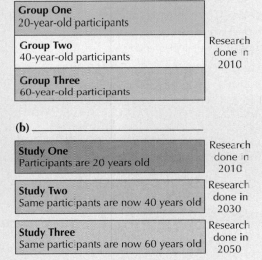

Group One 20-year-old participants	
Group Two 40-year-old participants	Research done in 2010
Group Three 60-year-old participants	

   (b) _____

Study One Participants are 20 years old	Research done in 2010
Study Two Same participants are now 40 years old	Research done in 2030
Study Three Same participants are now 60 years old	Research done in 2050

4. What is the first stage of prenatal development, which begins with conception and ends with implantation in the uterus?

   a. embryosis
   b. zygote stage
   c. critical period
   d. germinal period

5. At birth, an infant's head is _____ its body's size, whereas in adulthood, the head is _____ its body's size.

   a. 1/3; 1/4
   b. 1/3; 1/10
   c. 1/4; 1/10
   d. 1/4; 1/8

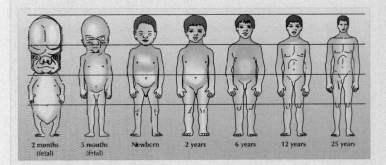

| 2 months (fetal) | 5 months (fetal) | Newborn | 2 years | 6 years | 12 years | 25 years |

6. Which of the following is **not** true regarding infant sensory and perceptual development?

   a. Vision is almost 20/20 at birth.
   b. A newborn's sense of pain is highly developed at birth.
   c. An infant can recognize, and prefers, its own mother's breast milk by smell.
   d. An infant can recognize, and prefers, its own mother's breast milk by taste.

7. Which of the following is the clearest and most physical sign of puberty, characterized by rapid increases in height, weight, and skeletal development?

   a. menses
   b. spermarche
   c. a growth spurt
   d. age of fertility

8. What do we call it when employers are reluctant to hire 50- to 60-year-old workers because of a generalized belief that they are sickly and will take too much time off?

   a. discrimination
   b. prejudice
   c. ageism
   d. all of these options

9. What is the term for changes in physical and mental processes throughout adulthood that are gradual, inevitable, and age-related?

a. ageism
b. primary aging
c. programmed theory
d. secondary aging

10. Who was one of the first scientists to demonstrate that a child's intellect is fundamentally different from that of an adult?

a. Baumrind
b. Beck
c. Piaget
d. Elkind

11. _____occurs when existing schemas are used to interpret new information, whereas_____ involves changing and adapting the schemas.

a. Adaptation; accommodation
b. Adaptation; reversibility
c. Egocentrism; post-schematization
d. Assimilation; accommodation

12. Label the four stages of Piaget's cognitive development model on the table below.

Piaget's four stages of cognitive development

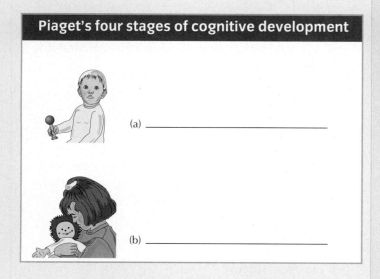

(a) _____

(b) _____

Piaget's four stages of cognitive development

(c) _____

(d) _____

13. What phenomenon do the photos below illustrate?

a. the lack of sensory permanence
b. the lack of perceptual constancy
c. the lack of perceptual permanence
d. the lack of object permanence

14. The ability to think abstractly or hypothetically occurs in which of Piaget's stages?

a. egocentric
b. postoperational
c. formal operational
d. concrete operational

15. Extreme forms of self-consciousness and concerns for physical appearance are common in adolescents. What is the term used for this early formal operational characteristic?

    a. the personal fable
    b. adolescent apprehension
    c. the imaginary audience
    d. the egocentric fable

16. What is one major criticism of Piaget's theory?

    a. Few of his findings have been replicated in subsequent studies.
    b. He placed far too much emphasis on the role of genetic influences in development.
    c. He ignored cognitive development in adolescents.
    d. He underestimated the cognitive abilities of infants and young children.

17. Which of the following is characteristic of children at the preoperational stage?

    a. realizing that changes in shape or appearance can be reversed
    b. being able to think in mildly abstract ways
    c. being able to use symbols in their thinking
    d. believing that they're at the centre of others' thoughts and attentions

18. Four year-old Johnny believes that others think, feel, and perceive things the same way as he does. What is the name for this way of thinking?

    a. animism
    b. egocentrism
    c. selfishness
    d. the personal fable

19. Which of the following is characteristic of Piaget's concrete operations stage?

    a. reversibility
    b. abstract thinking
    c. animism
    d. lack of object permanence

20. Alex is a teenager who feels unique and invulnerable. This perspective likely contributes to his tendency to engage in risky behaviours. What is the term for this type of thinking?

    a. the personal fable
    b. the imaginary audience
    c. secondary aging
    d. sensation seeking

Lifespan Development II: Social and Personality Development

Imagine that you are standing on a bridge over a railroad track when you see that a runaway train is about to kill five people. Coincidentally, you are standing next to a switching mechanism, and you realize that by simply throwing a switch, you can divert the train onto a spur, allowing the five to survive. But here is the catch: diverting the train will condemn *one* person, who is standing on the spur, to death. What would you do? Would you allow one person to die in order to save five others? Would your answer be different if that person were your mother, father, or some other much-loved person? What might lead different people to make different decisions?

It's unlikely that you will ever have to make such a gruesome choice. Yet everyone encounters moral dilemmas from time to time. Should you remind the cable company that they forgot to disconnect the cable after you discontinued the service? Should you give spare change to a friendly panhandler in your neighbourhood? Likewise, every one of us has personal relationships and particular character traits that colour our decisions. How we approach moral dilemmas—as well as many other events and circumstances throughout our lives—reflects several key facets of our personal growth: our social, moral, and personality development. In this chapter, we'll look at these aspects of development. We'll also examine how sex, gender, and culture influence our development. Finally, we'll explore several key developmental challenges during adulthood.

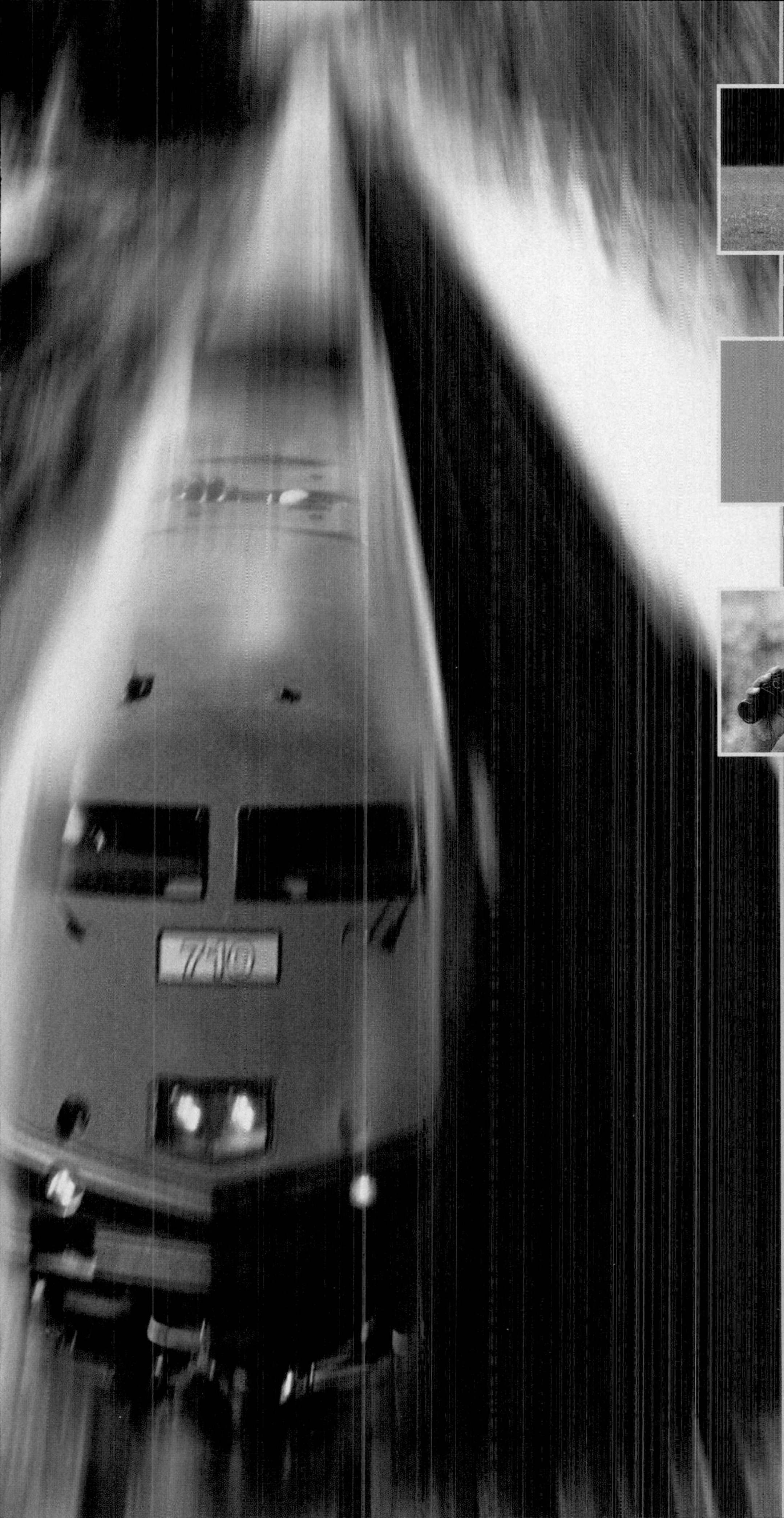

CHAPTER OUTLINE

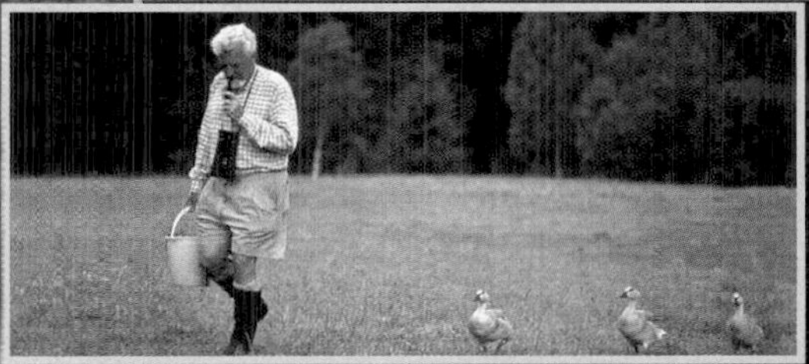

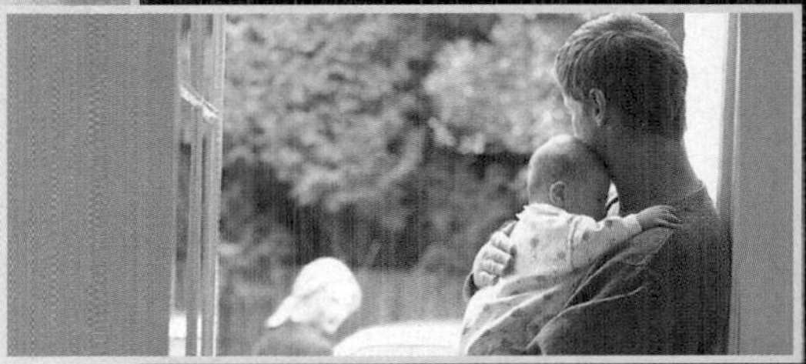

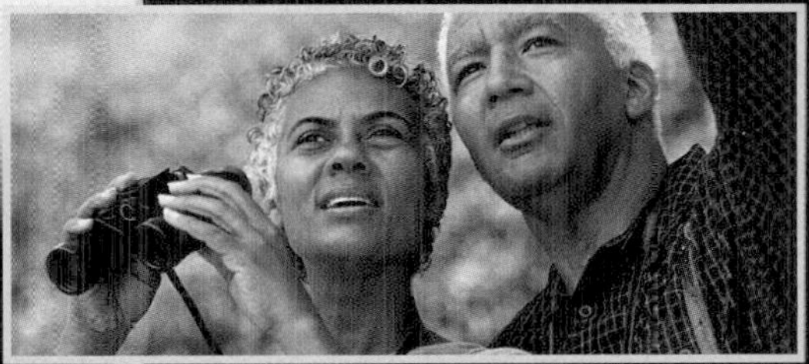

Social, Moral, and Personality Development

LEARNING OBJECTIVES

Describe the three types of attachment identified by Mary Ainsworth.

Explain how attachment influences social development.

Summarize the central characteristics of Kohlberg's theory of moral development.

Identify Erikson's eight stages of psychosocial development.

In addition to physical and cognitive development (Chapter 9), developmental psychologists study social, moral, and personality development by looking at how social forces and individual differences affect development over the lifespan. Poet John Donne wrote, "No man is an island, entire of itself." In this section, we focus on three major facets of development that shed light on how we affect one another: attachment, Kohlberg's stages of moral development, and Erikson's psychosocial stages.

SOCIAL DEVELOPMENT: THE IMPORTANCE OF ATTACHMENT

An infant arrives in the world with a multitude of behaviours that encourage a strong bond of **attachment** with primary caregivers. This bond provides a sense of security in which the infant can explore the physical and social environment.

attachment
A strong affectional bond with primary caregivers that endures over time.

In studying attachment behaviour, researchers are often divided along the lines of the nature–nurture issue. Those who advocate the nativist, or innate, position cite John Bowlby's work (1969, 1989, 2000). He proposed that newborn infants are biologically equipped with verbal and non-verbal behaviours (such as crying, clinging, and smiling) and with "following" behaviours (such as crawling and walking after the caregiver) that elicit instinctive nurturing responses from the caregiver. Konrad Lorenz's (1937) early studies of **imprinting** further support the biological argument for attachment (**FIGURE 10.1**). Attachment is discussed in more detail in *What a Psychologist Sees*.

What if a child does not form an attachment? Research shows that infants raised in impersonal surroundings (such as in institutions that do not provide the stimulation and love of a regular caregiver) or under abusive conditions suffer from a number of problems. They seldom cry, coo, or babble; they become rigid when picked up; and they have few language skills. They also tend to form shallow or anxious relationships. Some appear forlorn, withdrawn, and uninterested in their caretakers, whereas others seem insatiable in their need for affection (Zeanah, 2000). Finally, they also tend to show intellectual, physical, and perceptual retardation; increased susceptibility to infection; and neurotic "rocking" and isolation behaviours. In some cases, they die from lack of attachment (Bowlby, 1973, 1982, 2000; Combrink-Graham & McKenna, 2006; Nelson, Zeanah, & Fox, 2007; Spitz & Wolf, 1946; Zeanah, 2000).

Imprinting FIGURE 10.1

Lorenz's studies on imprinting demonstrated that baby geese attach to, and then follow, the first large moving object they see during a certain critical period shortly after hatching. What might be the advantages of this apparently instinctual pattern of behaviour?

Attachment: The Power of Touch

In a classic experiment involving infant rhesus monkeys, Harry Harlow and Robert Zimmerman (1959) investigated the variables that might affect attachment. They created two types of wire-framed surrogate (substitute) "mother" monkeys: one covered by soft terry cloth and one left uncovered (**A**). The infant monkeys were fed by either the cloth or the wire mother, but they otherwise had access to both mothers. The researchers found that monkeys "reared" by a cloth mother clung frequently to the soft material of their surrogate mother and developed greater emotional security and curiosity than did monkeys assigned to the wire mother.

In later research (Harlow & Harlow, 1966), monkey babies were exposed to rejection. Some of the "mothers" contained metal spikes that would suddenly protrude from the cloth covering and push the babies away; others had air jets that would sometimes blow the babies away. Nevertheless, the infant monkeys waited until the rejection was over and then clung to the cloth mothers as tightly as before. From these and related findings, Harlow concluded that **contact comfort**, the pleasurable tactile sensations provided by a soft and cuddly "parent," is a powerful contributor to attachment.

Maternal contact comfort

Several studies suggest that contact comfort between human infants and mothers is similarly important. For example, touching and massaging premature infants produces significant physical and emotional benefits (Field, 1998; Field et al., 2007; Feldman, 2007; Hernandez-Reif et al., 2007). Mothers around the world tend to kiss, nuzzle, nurse, comfort, clean, and respond to their children with lots of physical contact (**B**).

Although almost all research on attachment and contact comfort has focused on mothers and infants, recent research shows that the same results also apply to fathers and other caregivers (**C**) (Diener et al 2008; Grossmann et al., 2002; Lindberg et al. 2008; Martinelli, 2006).

Fathers matter too.

Most children, of course, are never exposed to such extreme institutional conditions. However, Mary Ainsworth (1967; Ainsworth et al., 1978), a world-renowned developmental psychologist who was educated at the University of Toronto, found significant differences in the typical levels of attachment between infants and their mothers. In addition, level of attachment affects long-term behaviours. Using a method called the **strange situation procedure**, in which she observed how infants responded to the presence or absence of their mother and a stranger, Ainsworth found that children could be divided into three groups: securely attached, avoidant, and anxious/ambivalent (**FIGURE 10.2**).

Ainsworth found that infants with a secure attachment style had caregivers who were sensitive and responsive to their signals of distress, happiness, and fatigue (Ainsworth, 1967; Ainsworth et al., 1978; Gini et al., 2007; Higley, 2008; Völker, 2007). Avoidant infants had caregivers who were aloof and distant, and anxious/ambivalent infants had inconsistent caregivers who alternated between strong affection and indifference.

Follow-up studies found that, over time, securely attached children were the most sociable, emotionally aware, enthusiastic, co-operative, persistent, curious, and competent (Bar-Haim et al., 2007; Brown & Whiteside, 2008; Johnson, Dweck, & Chen, 2007, Sroufe et al., 2005).

PARENTING STYLES: THEIR EFFECT ON DEVELOPMENT

How much of our personality comes from the way our parents treat us as we are growing up? Researchers since the 1920s have studied the effects of different methods of child rearing on children's behaviour, development, and mental health. Studies done by Diana Baumrind (1980, 1991, 1995) found that parenting styles could be reliably divided into three broad patterns: *permissive, authoritarian*, and *authoritative*, which could be identified by their degree of *control/demandingness* and *warmth/responsiveness* (**STUDY ORGANIZER 10.1**).

Types of attachment FIGURE 10.2

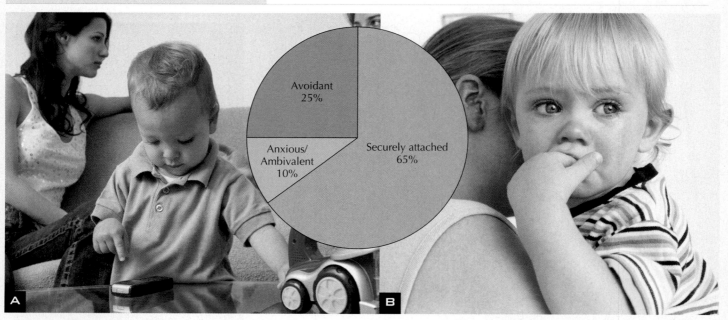

Ainsworth's research identified three different types of attachment.

- *Securely attached (65 percent).* When exposed to the stranger, the infant seeks closeness and contact with the mother, (**A**) uses the mother as a safe base from which to explore, (**B**) shows moderate distress on separation from the mother, and is happy when the mother returns.

- *Avoidant (25 percent).* The infant does not seek closeness or contact with the mother; treats the mother much like a stranger, and rarely cries when the mother leaves the room.
- *Anxious/ambivalent (10 percent).* The infant becomes very upset when the mother leaves the room. When she returns, the infant seeks close contact and then squirms angrily to get away.

Study Organizer 10.1 Parenting styles

Parenting Style	Description	Example	Effect on Children
Permissive-neglectful (permissive-indifferent) (low control, low warmth)	Parents make few demands, with little structure or monitoring, and show little interest or emotional support; may be actively rejecting.	"I don't care about you—or what you do."	Children tend to have poor social skills and little self-control (being overly demanding and disobedient).
Permissive-indulgent (low control, high warmth)	Parents set few limits or demands but are highly involved and emotionally connected.	"I care about you—and you're free to do what you like!"	Children often fail to learn respect for others and tend to be impulsive, immature, and out of control.
Authoritarian (high control, low warmth)	Parents are rigid and punitive while also being low on warmth and responsiveness.	"I don't care what you want. Just do it my way, or else!"	Children tend to be easily upset, moody, aggressive, and often fail to learn good communication skills.
Authoritative (high control, high warmth)	Parents generally set and enforce firm limits while also being highly involved, tender, and emotionally supportive.	"I really care about you, but there are rules and you need to be responsible."	Children become self-reliant, self-controlled, high achieving, and emotionally well-adjusted; also seem more content, goal oriented, friendly, and socially competent.

Sources: Coplan, Arbeau, & Armer, 2008; Driscoll, Russell, & Crockett, 2008; Martin & Fabes, 2009; McKinney, Donnelly, & Renk, 2008; Shields, 2008.

Ψ Psychological Science

Attachment across the Lifespan

If you've been around young children, you've probably noticed how they share toys and discoveries with a parent and seem much happier when a parent is nearby. You may also have thought how sweet it is when infants and parents share baby talk with each other. But have you noticed that similar behaviours often occur between adults in romantic relationships?

Intrigued by these parallels, researchers have studied the relationship between an infant's attachment to a parent and an adult's love for a romantic partner (Clulow, 2007; Duncan, 2007; Lele, 2008). Adults who report having an avoidant pattern in infancy often find it hard to trust others and to self-disclose, and they rarely report finding "true love". In short, it seems they block intimacy by being emotionally distant. Those who were anxious/ambivalent tend to be obsessed with their romantic partners as adults. As a result, they may smother intimacy by being possessive and emotionally demanding.

In contrast, individuals who were securely attached as infants easily become close to others, expect intimate relationships to endure, and perceive others as trustworthy. As you may expect, the securely attached lover has intimacy patterns that foster long-term relationships and is the most desired partner by most adults (Lele, 2008; Mikulincer & Goodman, 2006; Vorria et al., 2007).

Can attachment style in adults be changed? Canadian psychologist Sue Johnson (2004, 2008) has developed a therapy for couples that uses the attachment perspective to understand negative patterns of interaction and to guide couples into less distressed and more secure relationships. Her internationally-renowned *emotionally focused therapy* (EFT) argues that habitual

ways of dealing with attachment needs and fears often define adult love relationships. EFT attempts to foster feelings of security as a means to improve intimate relationships in couples.

As you consider the suggested relationship between attachment in infancy and adult romantic love, remember that it is always risky to infer causation from correlation. Accordingly, the relationship between romantic love and infant attachment is subject to several alternative explanations. Also, be aware that early attachment experiences may predict the future, but they do not determine it. Throughout life, we can learn new social skills and different attitudes toward relationships.

Stop & Think
1. What other factors might account for a romantic love style that does not reflect early infant attachment?
2. How do you think an anxious/ambivalent attachment style might affect an individual's relationship later in life?

MORAL DEVELOPMENT: KOHLBERG'S STAGES

Developing a sense of right and wrong, or morality, is a part of psychological development. Consider the following situation in terms of what you would do.

> *In Europe, a woman was near death from a special kind of cancer. There was one drug that doctors thought might save her. It was a form of radium that a druggist in the same town had recently discovered. The drug was expensive to make, but the druggist was charging 10 times what the drug cost him to make. He paid $200 for the radium and charged $2,000 for a small dose of the drug. The sick woman's husband, Heinz, went to everyone he knew to borrow the money, but he could gather together only about $1,000, half of what it cost. He told the druggist that his wife was dying and asked him to sell it cheaper or let him pay later. But the druggist said, "No, I discovered the drug, and I'm going to make money from it." So Heinz got desperate and broke into the man's store to steal the drug for his wife (Kohlberg, 1964, pp. 18–19).*

Was Heinz right to steal the drug? What do you consider moral behaviour? Is morality "in the eye of the beholder," or are there universal truths and principles? Whatever your answer, your ability to think, reason, and respond to Heinz's dilemma demonstrates another type of development that is very important to psychology: morality.

One of the most influential researchers in moral development was Lawrence Kohlberg (1927–1987). He presented what he called "moral stories," like the Heinz dilemma, to people of all ages, and on the basis of his findings, he developed a model of moral development (1964, 1984).

What is the right answer to Heinz's dilemma? Kohlberg was interested not in whether participants judged Heinz to be right or wrong but in the reasons they gave for their decisions. On the basis of participants' responses, Kohlberg proposed three broad levels in the evolution of moral reasoning, each composed of two distinct stages. Individuals at each stage and level may or may not support Heinz's stealing of the drug, but their reasoning changes from level to level.

Kohlberg believed that, like Piaget's stages of cognitive development (Chapter 9), his stages of moral development are universal and invariant. That is, they supposedly exist in all cultures, and everyone goes through each of the stages in a predictable fashion. The age trends tend to be rather broad.

Preconventional Level (Stages 1 and 2: Birth to Adolescence)

At the **preconventional level,** moral judgement is self-centred. What is right is what you can get away with or what is personally satisfying. Moral understanding is based on rewards, punishments, and the exchange of favours. This level is called "preconventional" because children have not yet accepted society's (conventional) rule-making processes.

> **preconventional level** Kohlberg's first level of moral development, in which morality is based on rewards, punishment, and the exchange of favours.

- *Stage 1 (punishment and obedience orientation).* Children at this stage focus on self-interest: obedience to authority and avoidance of punishment. Because they also have difficulty considering another's point of view, they ignore people's intentions in their moral judgements. Thus, a 5-year-old will often say that accidentally breaking 15 cups is "badder" and should receive more punishment than intentionally breaking 1 cup.

- *Stage 2 (instrumental-exchange orientation).* During this stage, children become aware of others' perspectives, but their morality is based on reciprocity: an equal exchange of favours. "I'll share my lunch with you because if I ever forget mine you'll share yours with me." The guiding philosophy is "You scratch my back and I'll scratch yours."

Conventional Level (Stages 3 and 4: Adolescence and Young Adulthood)
At the **conventional level**, moral reasoning advances from being self-centred to other-centred. The individual personally accepts conventional societal rules, because they help ensure social order, and judges morality in terms of compliance with these rules and values.

conventional level Kohlberg's second level of moral development, in which moral judgements are based on compliance with the rules and values of society.

- *Stage 3 ("good child" orientation).* At Stage 3, the primary moral concern is with being nice and gaining approval. People are also judged by their intentions and motives ("His heart was in the right place").

- *Stage 4 (law-and-order orientation).* During this stage, the individual takes into account a larger perspective: societal laws. Stage 4 individuals understand that if everyone violated laws, even with good intentions, there would be chaos. Thus, doing your duty and respecting law and order are highly valued. According to Kohlberg, Stage 4 is the highest level attained by most adolescents and adults.

Postconventional Level (Stages 5 and 6: Adulthood)
At the **postconventional level**, individuals develop personal standards for right and wrong. They also define morality in terms of abstract principles and values that apply to all situations and societies. A 20-year-old who judges the "discovery" and settlement of North America by Europeans as immoral because it involved the theft of land from native peoples is thinking in postconventional terms.

postconventional level Kohlberg's highest level of moral development, in which individuals develop personal standards for right and wrong, and they define morality in terms of abstract principles and values that apply to all situations and societies.

- *Stage 5 (social-contract orientation).* Individuals at Stage 5 appreciate the underlying purposes served by laws. When laws are consistent with interests of the majority, they are obeyed because of the "social contract." However laws can be morally disobeyed if they fail to express the will of the majority or fail to maximize social welfare (**FIGURE 10.3**).

Postconventional moral reasoning
FIGURE 10.3

Would you travel hundreds of kilometres to participate in a political demonstration? Would you be willing to be arrested for violating the law to express your moral convictions? How would Kohlberg's theory explain such actions?

Kohlberg's stages of moral development FIGURE 10.4

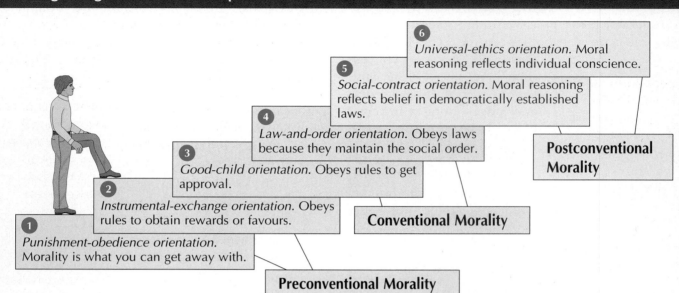

⑥ *Universal-ethics orientation.* Moral reasoning reflects individual conscience.

⑤ *Social-contract orientation.* Moral reasoning reflects belief in democratically established laws.

④ *Law-and-order orientation.* Obeys laws because they maintain the social order.

③ *Good-child orientation.* Obeys rules to get approval.

Postconventional Morality

② *Instrumental-exchange orientation.* Obeys rules to obtain rewards or favours.

Conventional Morality

① *Punishment-obedience orientation.* Morality is what you can get away with.

Preconventional Morality

Preconventional level (Stages 1 and 2—birth to adolescence) Moral judgement is *self-centred*. What is right is what one can get away with, or what is personally satisfying. Moral understanding is based on rewards, punishments, and the exchange of favours.

 ❶ Focus is on self-interest—obedience to authority and avoidance of punishment. Because children at this stage have difficulty considering another's point of view, they also ignore people's intentions.

❷ Children become aware of others' perspectives, but their morality is based on reciprocity—an equal exchange of favours.

Conventional level (Stages 3 and 4—adolescence and young adulthood) Moral reasoning is *other-centred*. Conventional societal rules are accepted because they help ensure the social order.

 ❸ Primary moral concern is being nice and gaining approval. The person judges others by their intentions—"His heart was in the right place."

 ❹ Morality is based on a larger perspective—societal laws. Understands that if everyone violated laws, even with good intentions, there would be chaos.

Postconventional level (Stages 5 and 6—adulthood) Moral judgements are based on *personal standards for right and wrong*. Morality is also defined in terms of abstract principles and values that apply to all situations and societies.

 ❺ Appreciates the underlying purposes served by laws. Societal laws are obeyed because of the "social contract," but they can be morally disobeyed if they fail to express the will of the majority or fail to maximize social welfare.

 ❻ "Right" is determined by universal ethical principles (e.g., non-violence, human dignity, freedom) that *all* religions or moral authorities might view as compelling or fair. These principles apply whether or not they conform to existing laws.

Sources: Adapted from Kohlberg, L. "Stage and Sequence: The Cognitive Developmental Approach to Socialization." In D. A. Goslin, *The Handbook of Socialization Theory and Research.* Chicago, IL: Rand McNally, 1969. p. 376 (Table 6.2).

- *Stage 6 (universal ethics orientation).* At this stage, "right" is determined by universal ethical principles that all religions or moral authorities might view as compelling or fair, such as non-violence, human dignity, freedom, and equality, whether or not they conform to existing laws. Thus, Mohandas Gandhi, Martin Luther King, Jr., and Nelson Mandela intentionally broke laws that violated universal principles, such as human dignity. Few individuals actually achieve Stage 6 (about 1 or 2 percent of those tested worldwide), and Kohlberg found it difficult to separate Stages 5 and 6. So, in time, he combined the two last stages (Kohlberg, 1981). See FIGURE 1 0.4.

Assessing Kohlberg's Theory

Kohlberg has been credited with enormous insights and contributions, but his theories have also been the focus of three major areas of criticism:

- *Moral reasoning versus behaviour.* Are people who achieve higher stages on Kohlberg's scale really more moral than others, or do they just "talk a good game"? Some studies show a positive correlation between higher stages of reasoning and higher levels of moral behaviour (Borba, 2001; Rest et al., 1999), but others have found that situational factors are better predictors of moral behaviour (FIGURE 1 0.5) (Bandura, 1986, 1991, 2008; Kaplan, 2006; Satcher, 2007; Slováčková & Slováček, 2007). For example, research participants are more likely to steal when they are told the money comes from a large company rather than from individuals (Greenberg, 2002). And both men and women will tell more sexual lies during casual relationships than during close relationships (Williams, 2001).

- *Possible gender bias.* Researcher Carol Gilligan criticized Kohlberg's model because on his scale, women tend to be classified at a lower level of moral reasoning than men. Gilligan suggested that this difference occurred because Kohlberg's theory emphasizes values more often held by men, such as rationality and independence, while de-emphasizing common female values,

such as concern for others and belonging (Gilligan, 1977, 1990, 1993; Kracher & Marble, 2008). Most follow-up studies of Gilligan's theory, however, have found few, if any, gender differences in level or type of moral reasoning (Hoffman, 2000; Hyde, 2007; Pratt, Skoe, & Arnold, 2004; Smith 2007).

- *Cultural differences.* Cross-cultural studies confirm that children from a variety of cultures generally follow Kohlberg's model and progress sequentially from his first level, the preconventional, to his second, the conventional (Rest et al., 1999; Snarey, 1985, 1995). At the same time, studies find differences among cultures. For example, cross-cultural comparisons of responses to Heinz's moral dilemma show that Europeans and North Americans tend to consider whether they like or identify with the victim in questions of morality. In contrast, Hindu Indians consider social responsibility and personal concerns to be separate issues (Miller & Bersoff, 1998). Researchers suggest that the difference reflects the Indians' broader sense of social responsibility.

Morality gap? FIGURE 1 0.5

What makes people who normally behave ethically willing to steal intellectual property, such as music or software?

"I swear I wasn't looking at smut—I was just stealing music."

Erikson's eight stages of psychosocial development FIGURE 10.6

Stage 1
Trust versus mistrust (birth–age 1)

Infants learn to *trust* or *mistrust* their caregivers and the world based on whether or not their needs—such as food, affection, safety—are met.

Stage 2
Autonomy versus shame and doubt (ages 1–3)

Toddlers start to assert their sense of independence (*autonomy*). If caregivers encourage this self-sufficiency, the toddler will learn to be independent versus feelings of *shame* and *doubt*.

Stage 3
Initiative versus guilt (ages 3–6)

Preschoolers learn to *initiate* activities and develop self-confidence and a sense of social responsibility. If not, they feel irresponsible, anxious, and *guilty*.

Stage 4
Industry versus inferiority (ages 6–12)

Elementary-school-age children who succeed in learning new, productive life skills develop a sense of pride and competence (*industry*). Those who fail to develop these skills feel inadequate and unproductive (*inferior*).

PERSONALITY DEVELOPMENT: ERIKSON'S PSYCHOSOCIAL THEORY

Like Piaget and Kohlberg, Erik Erikson (1902–1994) developed a stage theory of development. He identified eight **psychosocial stages** of social development (**FIGURE 10.6**), each marked by a "psychosocial" crisis or conflict related to a specific developmental task. The name given to each stage reflects the specific crisis encountered at that stage and the two possible outcomes. For example, the crisis or task of most young adults is intimacy versus isolation. This age group's developmental task is developing deep, meaningful relationships with others. Those who don't meet this developmental challenge risk social isolation.

Erikson believed that the more successfully we overcome each psychosocial crisis, the better chance we have to develop in a healthy manner (Erikson, 1950).

Many psychologists agree with Erikson's general idea that psychosocial crises contribute to personality development (Berzoff, 2008; Markstrom & Marshall, 2007; Torges, Stewart, & Duncan, 2008). However, some critics argue that his theory oversimplifies development. Others observe that the eight stages do not apply equally to all groups. For example, in some cultures, *autonomy* is highly

psychosocial stages In Erikson's theory, the eight developmental stages involving a crisis that must be successfully resolved.

Stage 5
Identity versus role confusion (ages 12–20)

Adolescents develop a coherent and stable self-definition (identity) by exploring many roles and deciding who or what they want to be in terms of career, attitudes, etc. Failure to resolve this **identity crisis** may lead to apathy, withdrawal and/or *role confusion*.

Stage 6
Intimacy versus isolation (young adulthood)

Young adults form lasting, meaningful relationships, which help them develop a sense of connectednesss and *intimacy* with others. If not, they become psychologically *isolated*.

Stage 7
Generativity versus stagnation (middle adulthood)

The challenge for middle-aged adults is to be nurturant of the younger generation. Failing to meet this challenge leads to self-indulgence and a sense of *stagnation*.

Stage 8
Ego integrity versus despair (late adulthood)

During this stage, older adults reflect on their past. If this reflection reveals a life well-spent, the person experiences self-acceptance and satisfaction (*ego integrity*). If not, he or she experiences regret and deep dissatisfaction (*despair*).

preferable to *shame and doubt,* but in others, the preferred resolution might be *dependence* or *merging relations* (Matsumoto & Juang, 2008).

During a period of serious questioning and intense soul-searching, adolescents develop a coherent sense of self and their role in society. Failure to resolve this **identity crisis** may be related to a lack of a stable identity, delinquency, and difficulty in maintaining close personal relationships in later life.

Despite their limits, Erikson's stages have greatly contributed to the study of North American and European psychosocial development. By suggesting that development continues past adolescence, Erikson's theory has encouraged further research.

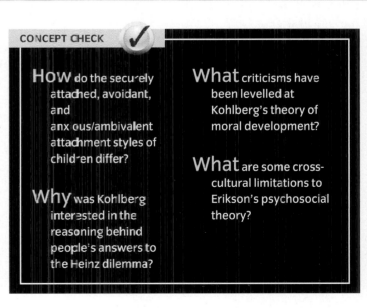

CONCEPT CHECK

How do the securely attached, avoidant, and anxious/ambivalent attachment styles of children differ?

Why was Kohlberg interested in the reasoning behind people's answers to the Heinz dilemma?

What criticisms have been levelled at Kohlberg's theory of moral development?

What are some cross-cultural limitations to Erikson's psychosocial theory?

How Sex, Gender, and Culture Affect Development

LEARNING OBJECTIVES

Identify biological sex differences in physical development.

Describe how gender differences are related to cognitive, personality, and social development.

Explain how individualistic versus collectivistic cultures shape personality development.

I magine for a moment what your life would be like if you were a member of the other sex. Would you think differently? Would you be more or less sociable and outgoing? Would your career plans or friendship patterns change? Most people believe that whether we are male or female has a strong impact on many facets of development. But why is that? Why is it that the first question most people ask after a baby is born is, "Is it a girl or a boy?"

SEX AND GENDER INFLUENCES ON DEVELOPMENT

In this section, we will explore how our development is affected by **sex** (a biological characteristic determined at the moment of conception) and by **gender** and **gender roles** (cultural meanings that accompany biological sex).

Sex Differences
Physical anatomy is the most obvious biological sex difference between men and women (**FIGURE 10.7**). Men and women also differ in secondary sex characteristics, such as facial hair and breast growth; signs of reproductive capability, such as menstruation and ejaculation of sperm; and physical responses to middle age or the end of reproduction, such as *menopause* and the *male climateric*. The brains of men and women also show several functional and structural differences. These result partly from the influence of prenatal sex hormones on the developing fetal brain.

sex Biological maleness and femaleness, including chromosomal sex. Also, activities related to sexual behaviours, such as masturbation and intercourse.

gender Psychological and sociocultural meanings added to biological maleness or femaleness.

gender roles Societal expectations for normal and appropriate male and female behaviour.

Gender Differences
In addition to biological sex differences, scientists have found numerous gender differences, which affect our cognitive, social, and personality development.

For example, on average females tend to score higher on tests of verbal skills, whereas males, on average, score higher on tests of visuospatial abilities and some aspects of math (Castelli, Corazzini, Geminiani, 2008; Kimura, 1999, 2004; Reynolds et al., 2008; van der Sluis et al., 2008).

Some researchers suggest that these differences in cognitive ability may reflect biological factors, including structural differences in the cerebral hemispheres, sex hormones, or the degree of hemispheric specialization. However, male–female differences in verbal abilities and math scores have declined in recent years, findings that raise questions concerning an explanation that is solely biological (Brown & Josephs, 1999; Halpern, 1997, 2000; Lizarraga & Ganuza, 2003).

Like cognitive ability, aggressive behaviour also differs slightly between the sexes. For example, boys are more likely to engage in mock fighting and rough-and-tumble play, and as adolescents and adults, they are somewhat more likely to commit violent crimes (Campbell & Muncer, 2008; Giancola & Parrott, 2008; Ostrov & Keating, 2004). Sex differences are clearer for physical aggression (like hitting) than for other forms of aggression. Early research suggested that females were more likely to engage in more indirect and relational forms of aggression, such as spreading rumours and ignoring or excluding someone (Bjorkqvist, 1994; Ostrov &

Body Size and Shape

The average man is 35 pounds heavier, has less body fat, and is 5 inches taller than the average woman. Men tend to have broader shoulders, slimmer hips and slightly longer legs in proportion to their height.

Brain

On average, men's brains are heavier and larger than women's (primarily because men have larger bodies). Women have larger speech and communication neural regions than men. The corpus callosum, the bridge joining the two halves of the brain, is larger in women. This size difference is interpreted by some to mean that women can more easily integrate information from the two halves of the brain and more easily perform more than one task simultaneously.

Sex Hormones

Although both men and women produce the sex hormones testosterone and estrogen, men have far more testosterone than women, and women have far more estrogen. Across the month, men have relatively constant levels of sex hormones, whereas women show cyclic sex hormone production that regulates the menstrual cycle.

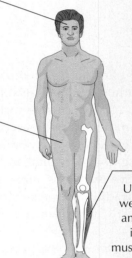

Muscular System

Until puberty, boys and girls are well matched in physical strength and ability. Once hormones kick in, the average man has more muscle mass and greater upper body strength than the average woman.

Source: Adapted from Le Vay, S., & Baldwin, J. (2009). *Human Sexuality* (3rd ed.). Sunderland, MA: Sinauer Associates Inc.

Keating, 2004). But more recent studies have not found such clear differences (Marsee, Weems, & Taylor, 2008; Shahim, 2008).

Some research has found that biological factors play an important role in male–female differences in aggression—a nativist position. Several studies have linked the masculinizing hormone testosterone to aggressive behaviour (Hermans, Ramsey, & van Honk, 2008; Popma et al., 2007; Trainor, Bird, & Marler,

2004). Other studies have found that aggressive men have disturbances in their levels of serotonin, a neurotransmitter that is inversely related to aggression (Berman, Tracy, & Coccaro, 1997; Holtzworth-Munroe, 2000; Nelson & Chiavegatto, 2001). In addition, studies of identical twins have found that genetic factors account for a considerable portion of aggressive behaviour (Bartels et al., 2007; Dodge et al., 2008; Jaffee et al., 2005; Moffitt, 2005).

Modelling gendered behaviour FIGURE 10.8

Some computer and video games include a great deal of violence and are often criticized for modelling and encouraging violence. In a new game called *Bully*, shown here, the main character ultimately takes on bullies rather than becoming one. The game includes plenty of fighting, but it also claims to show that actions have consequences. Do you think such an approach might encourage or discourage violent behaviour?

Other research has underscored the importance of nurture. This research suggests that male–female differences in aggressiveness may result from environmental experiences with social dominance and pressures that encourage "sex appropriate" behaviours and skills (Rowe et al., 2004) (FIGURE 10.8). TABLE 10.1 summarizes the gender differences between men and women.

Gender-Role Development

By age 2, children are well aware of gender roles. They recognize that boys "should" be strong, independent, aggressive, dominant, and achieving, whereas girls "should" be soft, dependent, passive, emotional, and "naturally" interested in children (Kimmel, 2000; Renzetti, Curran, & Kennedy-Bergen, 2006). The existence of similar gender roles in many cultures suggests that biology may play a role. However, most research emphasizes two major theories of gender role development: social learning and cognitive developmental.

Social learning theorists emphasize the power of the immediate situation and observable behaviours on gender role development. They suggest that girls learn how to be "feminine" and boys learn how to be "masculine" in two major ways: (1) They receive rewards or punishments for specific gender role behaviours, and (2) they watch and imitate the behaviour of others, particularly the same-sex parent (Bussey & Bandura, 2004; Fredricks &

Eccles, 2005; Kulik, 2005; Leaper & Friedman, 2007). A boy who puts on his father's tie or baseball cap wins big, indulgent smiles from his parents. But what would happen if he put on his mother's nightgown or lipstick? Parents, teachers, and friends generally reward or punish behaviours according to traditional gender role expectations. However they are much more accepting of girls' deviations from traditional roles than of boys'. Thus, a child "socially learns" what it means to be male or female.

According to the *cognitive developmental theory*, social learning is part of gender role development, but it's much more than a passive process of receiving rewards or punishments and modelling others. Instead, cognitive developmentalists argue that children actively observe, interpret, and judge the world around them (Bem, 1981, 1993; Cherney, 2005; Giles & Heyman, 2005; Ruble et al., 2006). As children process information about the world, they also create internal rules governing correct behaviours for boys versus girls. On the basis of these rules, they form **gender schemas** (mental images) of how they should act (FIGURE 10.9). Such gender schemas prompt the child to pay greater attention to information relevant to his or her own gender and also influence the child's choice of activities (Vasta, Younger, Adler, Miller, & Ellis, 2009).

Research-supported sex and gender differences   TABLE 10.1

Behaviour	More often shown by men	More often shown by women
Sexual	• Begin masturbating sooner in life cycle and have higher overall occurrence rates. • Start sexual life earlier and have first orgasm through masturbation. • Are more likely to recognize their own sexual arousal. • Experience more orgasm consistency in their sexual relations.	• Begin masturbating later in life cycle and have lower overall occurrence rates. • Start sexual life later and have first orgasm from partner stimulation. • Are less likely to recognize their own sexual arousal. • Experience less orgasm consistency in their sexual relations.
Touching	• Are touched, kissed, and cuddled less by parents. • Exchange less physical contact with other men and respond more negatively to being touched. • Are more likely to initiate both casual and intimate touch with sexual partner.	• Are touched, kissed, and cuddled more by parents. • Exchange more physical contact with other women and respond more positively to being touched. • Are less likely to initiate either casual or intimate touch with sexual partner.
Friendship	• Have a larger number of friends and express friendship by shared activities.	• Have a smaller number of friends and express friendship by shared communication about self.
Personality	• Are more self-confident of future success. • Attribute success to internal factors and failures to external factors. • Achievement is task oriented; motives are mastery and competition. • Are more self-validating. • Have higher self-esteem.	• Are less self-confident of future success. • Attribute success to external factors and failures to internal factors. • Achievement is socially directed with emphasis on self-improvement; have higher work motives. • Are more dependent on others for validation. • Have lower self-esteem.

Sources: Crooks & Baur, 2008; Hyde & DeLamater, 2008; King, 2009; Masters & Johnson, 1961, 1966, 1970; Matlin, 2008.

Developing gender schemas FIGURE 10.9

How would social learning theory and cognitive developmental theory explain why children tend to choose stereotypically "appropriate" toys?

Androgyny One way to overcome rigid or destructive gender role stereotypes is to express both the "masculine" and "feminine" traits found in each individual—for example, being assertive and aggressive when necessary but also gentle and nurturing. Combining characteristics in this way is known as **androgyny** [an-DRAW-juh-nee].

Using personality tests and other similar measures, researchers have found that masculine and androgynous individuals generally have higher self-esteem and creativity, are more socially competent and motivated to achieve, and exhibit better overall mental health than those with traditional feminine traits (Choi, 2004; Hittner & Daniels, 2002; Venkatesh et al., 2004). It seems that androgyny and masculinity are adaptive for both sexes.

How Sex, Gender, and Culture Affect Development   283

CULTURAL INFLUENCES ON DEVELOPMENT

Androgyny Figure 10.10

For both children and adults, it is generally more difficult for males to express so-called female traits, like nurturance and sensitivity, than it is for women to adopt such traditionally male traits as assertiveness and independence (Kimmel, 2000; Leaper, 2000; Wood et al., 1997). Can you see how being more androgynous can help many couples better meet the demands of modern life?

What makes androgyny and masculinity adaptive? Research has shown that traditional masculine characteristics (analytical thinking, independence) are more highly valued than traditional feminine traits (affectivity, cheerfulness) (Figure 10.10). For example, in business a good manager is still perceived as having predominantly masculine traits (Johnson et al., 2008). Also when college students in 14 different countries were asked to describe their "current self" and their "ideal self," the ideal self-descriptions for both men and women contained more masculine than feminine qualities (Williams & Best, 1990).

Our development is rooted in the concept of **self**—how we define and understand ourselves. Yet the very concept of *self* reflects our culture. In **individualistic cultures**, the needs and goals of the individual are emphasized over the needs and goals of the group.

> ■ **individualistic cultures** Cultures in which the needs and goals of the individual are emphasized over the needs and goals of the group.

When asked to complete the statement "I am . . . ," people from individualistic cultures tend to respond with personality traits ("I am shy"; "I am outgoing") or their occupation ("I am a teacher"; "I am a student").

In **collectivistic cultures**, however, the opposite is true. The person is defined and understood primarily by looking at his or her place in the social unit (Laungani, 2007; Matsumoto & Juang, 2008; McCrae, 2004). Relatedness, connectedness, and interdependence are valued, as opposed to separateness,

> ■ **collectivistic cultures** Cultures in which the needs and goals of the group are emphasized over the needs and goals of the individual.

independence, and individualism. When asked to complete the statement "I am . . . ," people from collectivistic cultures tend to mention their families or nationality ("I am a daughter"; "I am Chinese").

If you are North American or Western European, you are more likely to be individualistic than collectivistic (**Table 10.2**). And you may find the concept of a self that is defined in terms of others almost contradictory. A core selfhood probably seems intuitively obvious to you. Recognizing that more than 70 percent of the world's population lives in collectivistic cultures, however, may improve your cultural sensitivity and prevent misunderstandings (Singelis et al., 1995). For example, North Americans generally define *sincerity* as behaving in accordance with their inner feelings, whereas Japanese see it as behaviour that conforms to a person's role expectations (carrying out one's duties) (Yamada, 1997). Can you see how Japanese behaviour might appear insincere to a North American and vice versa?

A worldwide ranking of cultures TABLE 10.2

Individualistic cultures	Intermediate cultures	Collectivistic cultures
United States	Israel	Hong Kong
Australia	Spain	Chile
Great Britain	India	Singapore
Canada	Argentina	Thailand
Netherlands	Japan	West Africa region
New Zealand	Iran	El Salvador
Italy	Jamaica	Taiwan
Belgium	Arab region	South Korea
Denmark	Brazil	Peru
France	Turkey	Costa Rica
Sweden	Uruguay	Indonesia
Ireland	Greece	Pakistan
Norway	Philippines	Colombia
Switzerland	Mexico	Venezuela

How might these two groups differ in their physical, socioemotional, cognitive, and personality development?

CONCEPT CHECK

What is the difference between sex and gender?

How do people develop gender roles?

How is the concept of "self" different in individualistic versus collectivistic cultures?

Developmental Challenges through Adulthood

Describe the factors that ensure realistic expectations for marriage and long-term committed relationships.

Explain the factors that affect life satisfaction during the adult working years and retirement.

Describe the three basic concepts about death and dying that people learn to understand through the course of development.

In this section, we will explore three of the most important developmental tasks that people face during adulthood: developing a loving, committed relationship with another person; finding rewarding work and a satisfying retirement; and coping with death and dying.

COMMITTED RELATIONSHIPS: OVERCOMING UNREALISTIC EXPECTATIONS

One of the most important tasks faced during adulthood is that of establishing some kind of continuing, loving sexual relationship with another person. Yet navigating such partnerships is often very challenging. For example, about 38 percent of marriages in Canada end in divorce (Ambert, 2005; Statistics Canada, 2005), with serious implications for both adult and child development. Most divorces occur early in a marriage: The rate of divorce in Canada is highest three to four years into a marriage and then decreases slowly for each additional year (Statistics Canada, 2005). Following divorce, both spouses generally experience emotional as well as practical difficulties and are at high risk for depression and physical health problems. Often these problems were present even before the marital disruption.

It can be discouraging to realize that 38 percent of Canadian marriages end in divorce. However, it is important to understand that this figure also reveals that more than 60 percent of Canadian marriages do not end in divorce! Realistic expectations are a key ingredient in successful relationships (Gottman & Levenson, 2002; Waller & McLanahan, 2005). Yet many people harbour unrealistic expectations about marriage and the roles of husband and wife, opening the door to marital problems (FIGURE 10.11).

Did *The Cosby Show* set unrealistic expectations?
FIGURE 10.11

Where do unrealistic marital expectations originate? Women are more likely than men to try to model their family lives after what they have seen on TV programs and to expect their partners to act like the men they have seen on TV (Morrison & Westman, 2001). Men's expectations are more likely to be driven by certain myths about marriage, such as "Men are from Mars and women are from Venus" or "Affairs are the main cause of divorce."

Are Your Relationship Expectations Realistic?

To evaluate your own expectations, answer the following questions about traits and factors common to happy marriages and committed long-term relationships (Amato, 2007; Gottman & Levenson, 2002; Gottman & Notarius, 2000; Marks et al., 2008; Rauer, 2007):

1. Established "love maps"

Yes ___ No ___ *Do you believe that emotional closeness "naturally" develops when two people have the right chemistry?*

In successful relationships, both partners are willing to share their feelings and life goals. This sharing leads to detailed "love maps" of each other's inner emotional life and the creation of shared meaning in the relationship.

2. Shared power and mutual support

Yes ___ No ___ *Have you unconsciously accepted the imbalance of power promoted by many TV sitcoms, or are you willing to fully share power and to respect your partner's point of view, even if you disagree?*

The old ideas of husbands as "head of household" and wives as the "little women" who secretly wield the true power may help create unrealistic expectations for marriage.

3. Conflict management

Yes ___ No ___ *Do you expect to "change" your partner or to be able to resolve all your problems?*

Successful couples work hard (through negotiation and accommodation) to solve their solvable conflicts, to accept their unsolvable ones, and to know the difference.

4. Similarity

Yes ___ No ___ *Do you believe that "opposites attract?"*

Although we all know couples who are very different but are still happy, similarity (in values, beliefs, religion, and so on) is one of the best predictors of long-lasting relationships (Chapter 15).

5. Supportive social environment

Yes ___ No ___ *Do you believe that "love conquers all"?*

Unfortunately, several environmental factors can overpower or slowly erode even the strongest love. These include age (younger couples have higher divorce rates), money and employment (divorce is higher among the poor and unemployed), parents' marriages (divorce is higher for children of divorced parents), length of courtship (longer is better), and premarital pregnancy (no pregnancy is better, and waiting a while after marriage is even better).

6. Positive emphasis

Yes ___ No ___ *Do you believe that an intimate relationship is a place where you can indulge your bad moods and openly criticize one another?*

Think again. Positive emotions, positive mood, and positive behaviour toward one's partner are vitally important to a lasting, happy relationship.

WORK AND RETIREMENT: HOW THEY AFFECT US

Throughout most of our adult lives, work defines us in fundamental ways. It affects our health, our friendships, where we live, and even our leisure activities. Too often, however, career choices are made based on dreams of high income. In a 1995 survey conducted by the Higher Education Research Institute in the United States, nearly 74 percent of college freshmen said that being "very well-off financially" was "very important" or "essential." Seventy-one percent felt the same way about raising a family. These young people understandably hope to combine both family and work roles and "live the good life," but many will find themselves in unsatisfying jobs, having to work long hours just to pay the bills and keep ahead of inflation.

Choosing an occupation is one of the most important decisions in a person's life, and the task is becoming ever more complex. The *National Occupational Classification,* a government publication, currently lists more than 30,000 Canadian job titles (Human Resources and Social Development Canada, 2007). According to psychologist John Holland's **personality-job fit theory,** a match (or "good fit") between our individual personalities and our career choices is a major factor in determining job success and satisfaction. Holland's *self-directed search* questionnaire scores each person on six personality types and then matches their individual interests and abilities to the job demands of various occupations (Holland, 1985, 1994; see also Brkich, Jeffs, & Carless, 2002; Kieffer, Schinka, & Curtiss, 2004; Spokane, Meir, & Catalano, 2000; Tett & Murphy, 2002) (**TABLE 10.3**).

Work and career are a big part of adult life and self-identity, but the large majority of men and women in Canada and the United States choose to retire sometime in their sixties. What helps people successfully navigate this important life change? According to the **activity theory of aging**, successful aging appears to be most strongly related to

> ■ **activity theory of aging** Successful aging is fostered by a full and active commitment to life.

Are you in the right job? TABLE 10.3

Personality characteristics	Holland personality type	Matching/congruent occupation
Shy, genuine, persistent, stable, conforming, practical	1. *Realistic*: Prefers physical activities that require skill, strength, and coordination	Mechanic, drill press operator, assembly-line worker, farmer
Analytical, original, curious, independent	2. *Investigative*: Prefers activities that involve thinking, organizing, and understanding	Biologist, economist, mathematician, news reporter
Sociable, friendly, cooperative, understanding	3. *Social*: Prefers activities that involve helping and developing others	Social worker, counsellor, teacher, clinical psychologist
Conforming, efficient, practical, unimaginative, inflexible	4. *Conventional*: Prefers rule-regulated, orderly, and unambiguous activities	Accountant, bank teller, file clerk, corporate manager
Imaginative, disorderly, idealistic, emotional, impractical	5. *Artistic*: Prefers ambiguous and unsystematic activities that allow creative expression	Painter, musician, writer, interior decorator
Self-confident, ambitious, energetic, domineering	6. *Enterprising*: Prefers verbal activities with opportunities to influence others and attain power	Lawyer, real estate agent, public relations specialist, small business manager

Reproduced by special permission of the publisher, Psychological Assessment Resources, Inc., 16204 North Florida Avenue, Lutz, Florida 33549, from the Self-Directed Search Form R by John L. Holland, Ph.D, copyright 1985. Further reproduction is prohibited without permission from PAR, Inc.

Satisfaction after retirement FIGURE 10.12

Active involvement is a key ingredient to a fulfilling old age.

good health, control over one's life, social support, and participation in community services and social activities (Warr, Butcher, & Robertson, 2004; Yeh & Lo, 2004) (FIGURE 10.12).

The activity theory of aging has largely displaced the older notion that successful aging entails a natural and graceful withdrawal from life (Achenbaum & Bengtson, 1994; Cummings & Henry, 1961; Heckhausen, 2005; Lemus, 2008; Menec, 2003; Neugarten, Havighurst, & Tobin, 1968; Riebe et al., 2005; Sanchez, 2006). This **disengagement theory** has been seriously questioned and largely abandoned; we mention it because of its historical relevance and because of its connection to an influential modern theory,

disengagement theory Successful aging is characterized by mutual withdrawal between the aging person and society.

socioemotional selectivity theory. This perspective helps explain the predictable decline in social contact that almost everyone experiences as they move into their older years (Carstensen, 2006; Charles & Carstensen, 2007) (FIGURE 10.13). According to this theory, we don't naturally withdraw from society in our later years—we just become more selective with our time. We deliberately decrease our total number of social contacts in favour of familiar people who provide emotionally meaningful interactions.

socioemotional selectivity theory A natural decline in social contact as older adults become more selective with their time.

As we've seen, there are losses and stresses associated with the aging process—although much less than most people think. Perhaps the greatest challenge for older adults, at least in Canada and the United States, is the ageism they encounter. In societies that value older people as wise elders or keepers of valued traditions, the stress of aging is much less than in societies that view them as mentally slow and socially useless. In cultures like those in Canada and the United States in which youth, speed, and progress are strongly emphasized, a loss or decline in any of these qualities is deeply feared and denied (Powell, 1998).

Socioemotional selectivity FIGURE 10.13

During infancy, emotional connection is essential to our survival. During childhood, adolescence, and early adulthood, information gathering is critical and the need for emotional connection declines relative to knowledge needs. During late adulthood, emotional satisfaction is again more important—we tend to invest our time in those who can be counted on in times of need.

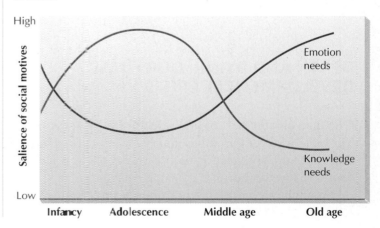

Myths of Development

A number of popular beliefs about age-related crises are not supported by research. The popular idea of a *midlife* crisis began largely as a result of Gail Sheehy's national best-seller *Passages* (1976). Sheehy drew on the theories of Daniel Levinson (1977, 1996) and psychiatrist Roger Gould (1975), as well as her own interviews. She popularized the idea that almost everyone experiences a "predictable crisis" at about age 35 for women and 40 for men. Middle age often *is* a time of re-examining values and lifetime goals. However, Sheehy's book led many people to automatically expect a midlife crisis with drastic changes in personality and behaviour. Research suggests that a severe reaction or crisis may actually be quite rare and not typical of what most people experience during middle age (Horton, 2002; Lachman, 2004).

Many people also believe that when the last child leaves home, most parents experience an *empty nest syndrome*: a painful separation and time of depression for the mother, the father, or both parents. Again, research suggests that the empty nest syndrome may be an exaggeration of the pain experienced by a few individuals and an effort to downplay positive reactions (White & Rogers, 1997; Whyte, 1992). For example, one major benefit of the empty nest is an increase in marital satisfaction. Data from Statistics Canada's *General Social Survey* indicate that many older couples whose children have grown up and left the home actually report higher levels of marital satisfaction than do those with adult children still living at home (Chalmers & Milan, 2005).

Of course, moving out of their parents' home does not imply that grown children have no further contact with their parents; most continue to maintain relationships with their parents. As one mother said, "The empty nest is surrounded by telephone wires" (Troll, Miller, & Atchley, 1979). Moreover, as children move out and establish their own relationships, the role played by their parents often expands to include that of grandparent. The majority of older Canadians have grandchildren, and, for some the role of grandparent is central in their lives (Rosenthal & Gladstone, 2007).

STOP

Stop & Think
1. Have you heard people saying that someone you know is "having a midlife crisis"? If so, do you think the crisis is genuine?
2. If your last child "left the nest," how do you think you would react?

DEATH AND DYING: OUR FINAL DEVELOPMENTAL CRISIS

One unavoidable part of life is death. In this section, we will look at developmental changes in how people understand and prepare for their own deaths and for the deaths of loved others.

As adults, we understand death in terms of three basic concepts: (1) *permanence*—once a living thing dies, it cannot be brought back to life; (2) *universality*—all living things eventually die; and (3) *non-functionality*—all living functions, including thought, movement, and vital signs, end at death.

Research has shown that permanence, the notion that death cannot be reversed, is the first and most easily understood concept (**FIGURE 10.14**). Understanding of universality comes slightly later, and by the age of 7, most children have mastered non-functionality and have an adult-like understanding of death.

How do children understand death?
FIGURE 10.14

Preschoolers seem to accept the fact that the dead person cannot get up again, perhaps because of their experiences with dead butterflies and beetles found while playing outside (Furman, 1990). Later, they begin to understand all that death entails and that they, too, will someday die.

Culture influences our response to death
FIGURE 10.15

In October 2006, a dairy truck driver took over a one-room Amish schoolhouse in Pennsylvania, killed and gravely injured several young girls, and then shot himself. Instead of responding in rage, his Amish neighbours attended his funeral. Amish leaders urged forgiveness for the killer and called for a fund to aid his wife and three children. Rather than creating an on-site memorial, the schoolhouse was torn down and replaced by a pasture. What do you think of this response? The fact that many people were offended, shocked, or simply surprised by the Amish reaction illustrates how strongly culture affects our emotion, beliefs, and values.

Although parents may fear that discussing death with children and adolescents will make them unduly anxious, those who are offered open, honest discussions of death have an easier time accepting it (Corr, Nabe, & Corr, 2009; Kastenbaum, 2007).

The same is true for adults—in fact, avoiding thoughts and discussion of death and associating aging with death contribute to ageism (Atchley, 1997). Moreover, the better we understand death and the more wisely we approach it, the more fully we can live. Since the late 1990s, right-to-die and death-with-dignity advocates have brought death out into the open, and mental health professionals have suggested that understanding the psychological processes of death and dying may play a significant role in good adjustment. Cultures around the world interpret and respond to death in widely different ways: "Funerals are the occasion for avoiding people or holding parties, for fighting or having sexual orgies, for weeping or laughter, in a thousand combinations" (Metcalf & Huntington, 1991) (FIGURE 10.15).

Confronting our own death is the last major crisis we face in life. What is it like? Is there a "best" way to prepare to die? Is there such a thing as a "good" death? After spending hundreds of hours at the bedsides of the terminally ill, Elisabeth Kübler-Ross developed her stage theory of the psychological processes surrounding death (1983, 1997, 1999). She proposed that most people go through five sequential stages when facing death:

- *Denial* of the terminal condition ("This can't be true; it's a mistake!")

- *Anger* ("Why me? It isn't fair!")

- *Bargaining* ("God, if you let me live, I'll dedicate my life to you!")

- *Depression* ("I'm losing everyone and everything I hold dear.")

- *Acceptance* ("I know that death is inevitable and my time is near.")

Psychological Science

Should Physician-Assisted Suicide Be Decriminalized?

In 1992, Sue Rodriguez, a Victoria, British Columbia, woman with Lou Gehrig's disease, a degenerative and fatal disease of the central nervous system, petitioned Parliament and the Supreme Court of Canada to legalize physician-assisted suicide. Her petition was ultimately denied. Two years later, however, she took her own life with the help of an anonymous doctor (CBC News, 2009b). More recently, Bloc Québécois MP Francine Lalonde introduced a bill in Parliament to legalize euthanasia and physician-assisted suicide. The bill has had a rough ride, however, having been defeated three times (Lewis, 2009). Physician-assisted suicide is a criminal offence in Canada, punishable by up to 14 years in prison, and many Canadians have serious questions about whether it should be legalized.

Is it morally wrong for doctors to assist patients who wish to end their lives in order to terminate their suffering? Although the answer depends on many factors, including personal ethics and religious beliefs, the majority of doctors are not in favour. In a survey of more than 2,000 Canadian physicians, 57 percent reported that they would not be willing to participate in an assisted suicide, even if it were legal (Kinsella & Verhoef, 1999). Patients, however, appear to hold a different view. The *Canadian National Palliative Care Survey* reported that of 379 terminally ill cancer patients, 63 percent believed that physician-assisted suicide should be legalized (Wilson et al., 2007). Interestingly, 40 percent of respondents in both surveys—whether physicians or patients—reported that they would consider making such a request for themselves.

Sue Rodriguez, who petitioned the Supreme Court of Canada to legalize physician-assisted suicide, ultimately took her own life in 1994 with the help of an anonymous physician.

Stop & Think
1. In cases of debilitating illness, where recovery is impossible and patients are suffering grievously, should doctors be allowed to end a patient's suffering?
2. Does it make a difference if the patient requests the doctor's help? What about someone who is too ill to communicate his or her desires?

Critics of the stage theory of dying stress that the five-stage sequence has not been scientifically validated and that each person's death is a unique experience (Kastenbaum, 2007). Others worry that popularizing such a stage theory will cause more avoidance and stereotyping of the dying ("He's just in the anger stage right now").

Kübler-Ross (1983, 1997, 1999) agrees that not all people go through the same stages in the same way and

regrets that anyone would use her theory as a model for a "good" death.

In spite of the potential abuses, Kübler-Ross' theory has provided valuable insights and spurred research into a long-neglected topic. **Thanatology**, the study of death and dying, has become a major topic in human development. Thanks in part to thanatology research, the dying are being helped to die with dignity by the hospice movement, which has created special facilities and trained staff and volunteers to provide loving support for the terminally ill and their families (McGrath, 2002; Parker-Oliver, 2002). Canadian health service providers have been among the leaders in the hospice movement in North America. Canadians have also been at the forefront in providing hospice care for homeless and marginalized individuals (Guirguis-Younger, Runnels, & Aubry, 2004).

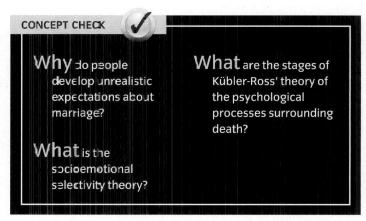

CONCEPT CHECK ✓

Why do people develop unrealistic expectations about marriage?

What is the socioemotional selectivity theory?

What are the stages of Kübler-Ross' theory of the psychological processes surrounding death?

SUMMARY

1 Social, Moral, and Personality Development

1. Konrad Lorenz's studies of imprinting support the nativist view of **attachment**. Harlow and Zimmerman's research with monkeys raised by cloth or wire "mothers" supports the nurturist view and indicates that **contact comfort** is an important contributor to attachment. Most infants are securely attached to their caregivers, but some exhibit either an avoidant or an anxious/ambivalent attachment style. These styles may carry over into adult relationships.

2. Parenting styles may be divided on the basis of degree of *control/demandingness* and *warmth/responsiveness* into three categories: *authoritative, authoritarian, and permissive* (either permissive-indulgent or permissive-neglectful).

3. Kohlberg proposed three levels in the development of moral reasoning: the **preconventional** level (Stages 1 and 2), the **conventional level** (Stages 3 and 4), and the **postconventional level** (Stages 5 and 6). According to Kohlberg, Stage 4 is the highest level attained by most individuals.

4. Erikson identified eight **psychosocial stages** of development, each marked by a crisis related to a specific developmental task. Although some critics argue that Erikson's theory oversimplifies development, many psychologists agree with Erikson's general idea that psychosocial crises do contribute to personality development.

2 How Sex, Gender, and Culture Affect Development

1. In addition to biological **sex** differences, scientists have found numerous **gender** differences relevant to cognitive, social, and personality development (for example, in cognitive ability and aggressive behaviour) and have proposed both biological and environmental explanations for these differences. Most research emphasizes two major theories of **gender role**

development: social learning and cognitive developmental. One way to overcome gender role stereotypes is to combine "masculine" and "feminine" traits (**androgyny**).

2. Our culture shapes how we define and understand ourselves. In **individualistic cultures**, the needs and goals of the individual are emphasized; in **collectivistic cultures**, the person is defined and understood primarily by looking at his or her place in the social unit.

3 Developmental Challenges through Adulthood

1. Having unrealistic expectations about marriage can open the door to marital problems. Developing realistic expectations is critical to a happy marriage.

2. Choosing an occupation is an important and complex decision. According to Holland's personality-job fit theory, a match between personality and career choice is a major factor in determining job success and satisfaction.

3. The **activity theory of aging** proposes that successful aging depends on having control over one's life, having social support, and participating in community services and social activities. **Disengagement theory** is an older approach to aging that has been largely abandoned. According to the **socioemotional selectivity theory**, people don't naturally withdraw from society in late adulthood but deliberately decrease the total number of their social contacts in favour of familiar people who provide emotionally meaningful interactions.

4. Adults understand death in terms of three basic concepts: permanence, universality, and non-functionality. Children most easily understand the concept of permanence; understanding of universality and non-functionality come later. For children, adolescents, and adults, understanding the psychological processes of death and dying are important to good adjustment. Kübler-Ross proposed that most people go through five sequential stages when facing death: denial, anger, bargaining, depression, and acceptance. But she has emphasized that her theory should not be interpreted as a model for a "good" death.

KEY TERMS

- activity theory of aging p. 288
- androgyny p. 283
- attachment p. 270
- collectivistic cultures p. 284
- contact comfort p. 271
- conventional level p. 275
- disengagement theory p. 289
- gender p. 280

- gender roles p. 280
- gender schemas p. 282
- hospice p. 293
- identity crisis p. 279
- imprinting p. 270
- individualistic cultures p. 284
- personality-job fit theory p. 288
- postconventional level p. 275

- preconventional level p. 274
- psychosocial stages p. 278
- self p. 284
- sex p. 280
- socioemotional selectivity theory p. 289
- strange situation procedure p. 272
- thanotology p. 292

CRITICAL AND CREATIVE THINKING QUESTIONS

1. Were Harlow and his colleagues acting ethically when they separated young rhesus monkeys from their mothers and raised them with either a wire or cloth "mother"? Why or why not?

2. Think of some current world events. Can you find examples of individuals reasoning at Kohlberg's postconventional level of moral development? Is it possible for world leaders to be guided by a universal ethics orientation (Stage 6) and also be effective leaders of their country?

3. According to Erikson's psychosocial theory, what developmental crisis are you now facing? What must you resolve in order to successfully move on to the next stage? Are there any earlier crises that you feel you may not have successfully resolved?

4. Research points to male-female differences in verbal and spatial abilities. Do the abilities of any of your male or female friends seem to contradict these findings? How could the environment in which a child is raised influence the development of these characteristics?

5. Can you think of instances where you have adopted traditional gender roles? What about times where you have expressed more androgyny?

6. According to Holland's personality-job fit theory, what occupations might be a good match for your personality?

7. Would you like to know ahead of time that you were dying? Or would you prefer to die suddenly with no warning? Briefly explain your choice.

8. Do you think *all* people would pass through Elizabeth Kübler-Ross' stages of dying, if given sufficient time? What could be some problems with assuming that all people *should* pass through this sequence of stages?

What is happening in this picture ?

Aboriginals generally revere and respect the elder members of their community. How might viewing old age as an honour and a blessing—rather than a dreaded process—affect the experience of aging?

SELF-TEST

(Check your answers in Appendix A.)

1. What term is used by developmental psychologists for a strong affectional bond with special others that endures over time?

   a. bonding
   b. love
   c. attachment
   d. intimacy

2. In Ainsworth's studies on infant attachment, which group of infants sought their mothers' comfort yet also squirmed to get away when the mother returned to the room?

   a. anxious/ambivalent
   b. avoidant
   c. securely attached
   d. dependently attached

3. Which parenting style is characterized by the combination of low control and high warmth?

   a. authoritative
   b. authoritarian
   c. permissive-indulgent
   d. permissive-neglectful

4. Kohlberg believed his stages of moral development to be which of the following?

   a. universal and invariant
   b. culturally bound, but invariable within a culture
   c. universal, but variable within each culture
   d. culturally bound and variable

5. Which level of moral development involves accepting and complying with the rules and values of society?

   a. preconventional
   b. unconventional
   c. conventional
   d. postconventional

6. After listening to the dilemma of Heinz and the druggist, an individual responds that Heinz should steal the drug, because the value of human life is far more important than obeying the law. This answer is consistent with which of Kohlberg's levels of moral development?

   a. preconventional
   b. postconventional
   c. unconventional
   d. conventional

7. According to Erikson, humans progress through eight stages of psychosocial development. Label the *correct* sequence on the figure below for the "successful" completion of the first four stages.

Stage 1 _____   Stage 2 _____

Stage 3 _____   Stage 4 _____

8. Label the *correct* sequence on the figure below for the "successful" completion of the last four stages of Erikson's psychosocial development.

Stage 5 _____   Stage 6 _____

Stage 7 _____   Stage 8 _____

9. Which of the following is related to societal expectations for normal and appropriate male or female behaviour?

   a. gender identity
   b. gender role
   c. sexual identity
   d. gender orientation

10. What is the term for mental images that prompt children to pay close attention to behaviours that are correct for their sex, and that influence their choice of activities?

   a. sexual identities
   b. gender identities
   c. gender schemas
   d. gender images

11. Which of the following is NOT true concerning differences between males and females?

   a. Males on average score higher on tests of visuospatial abilities.
   b. Females on average score higher on tests of verbal abilities.
   c. The hormone testosterone is produced only by males.
   d. The brains of males on average are heavier than those of females.

12. Which types of cultures emphasize the needs and goals of the group over the needs and goals of the individual?

    a. individualistic cultures
    b. collectivistic cultures
    c. worldwide cultures
    d. androgynous cultures

13. Which of the following has consistently been found to be a key factor in successful relationships?

    a. realistic expectations
    b. the ability to fight for equity
    c. satisfying sexual activity
    d. emotional stability

14. Which theory of aging suggests that successful adjustment is fostered by a full and active commitment to life?

    a. activity theory
    b. commitment theory
    c. engagement theory
    d. life-affirming theory

15. At age 83, Karine attends a twice-weekly morning yoga class, enjoys shopping for healthy foods, and is regularly involved in volunteer community work. What aging theory best describes Karine's lifestyle?

    a. Kübler-Ross' stage theory
    b. disengagement theory
    c. activity theory
    d. gender schema theory

16. Which theory of aging suggests that adjustment to retirement is fostered by mutual withdrawal between older adults and society?

    a. disengagement theory
    b. withdrawal theory
    c. disengagement theory
    d. death-preparation theory

17. Many couples whose children have grown up and recently left home

    a. experience emotional pain associated with the *empty nest syndrome*.
    b. find their lives now lacking in meaning.
    c. report an increase in marital satisfaction.
    d. experience loneliness and a deterioration of their marital relationship.

18. Which of the following concepts is considered permanent, universal, and non-functional?

    a. marriage
    b. taxes
    c. your grade on this test
    d. death

19. Which of the following is *true* about a child's understanding of death?

    a. Preschoolers understand that death is permanent.
    b. Preschoolers may not understand that death is universal.
    c. Children understand that death is non-functional by the age of 7.
    d. All of these options are true.

20. Which of the following is the correct sequence for Kübler-Ross' stage theory of dying?

    a. denial; anger; bargaining; depression; acceptance
    b. anger; denial; depression; bargaining; acceptance
    c. denial; bargaining; anger; depression; acceptance
    d. bargaining; denial; depression; anger; acceptance

Motivation and Emotion

11

In 1974, Bangladeshi economics professor Muhammad Yunus lent US$27 to a group of women weavers so they could buy their own materials rather than borrowing from an intermediary who charged exorbitant interest. Within a year, everyone had paid him back. Yunus then founded a bank that extends small loans to poor people. Since 1983, his Grameen Bank has lent billions of dollars to some 17 million people worldwide. In 2006, Yunus and the Grameen Bank were awarded the Nobel Peace Prize for their pioneering work.

In accepting the prize, Yunus said that he plans to use his share of the $1.4 million award to build an eye hospital and to establish a company to sell food to the poor for a nominal price. What motivates such generosity? When you read about philanthropists like Yunus, are you amazed, surprised, inspired, or annoyed? Why? Research on motivation and emotion attempts to answer these and a variety of related questions.

Motivation and emotion are inseparable. Consider the following example: if you saw your boyfriend or girlfriend passionately kissing someone else, you would probably experience a variety of emotions (jealousy, abandonment, sadness, anger, hurt), and your motives would determine how you would respond. Your anger might lead you to immediately end the relationship or to date someone else, but your need for love or sex might motivate you to not end it until after one last weekend together.

The words *motivation* and *emotion* are both derived from the same Latin root meaning "to move," and as you will see in this chapter, the psychology of motivation and emotion might better be described as the psychology of what moves us.

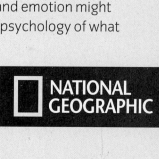

NATIONAL GEOGRAPHIC

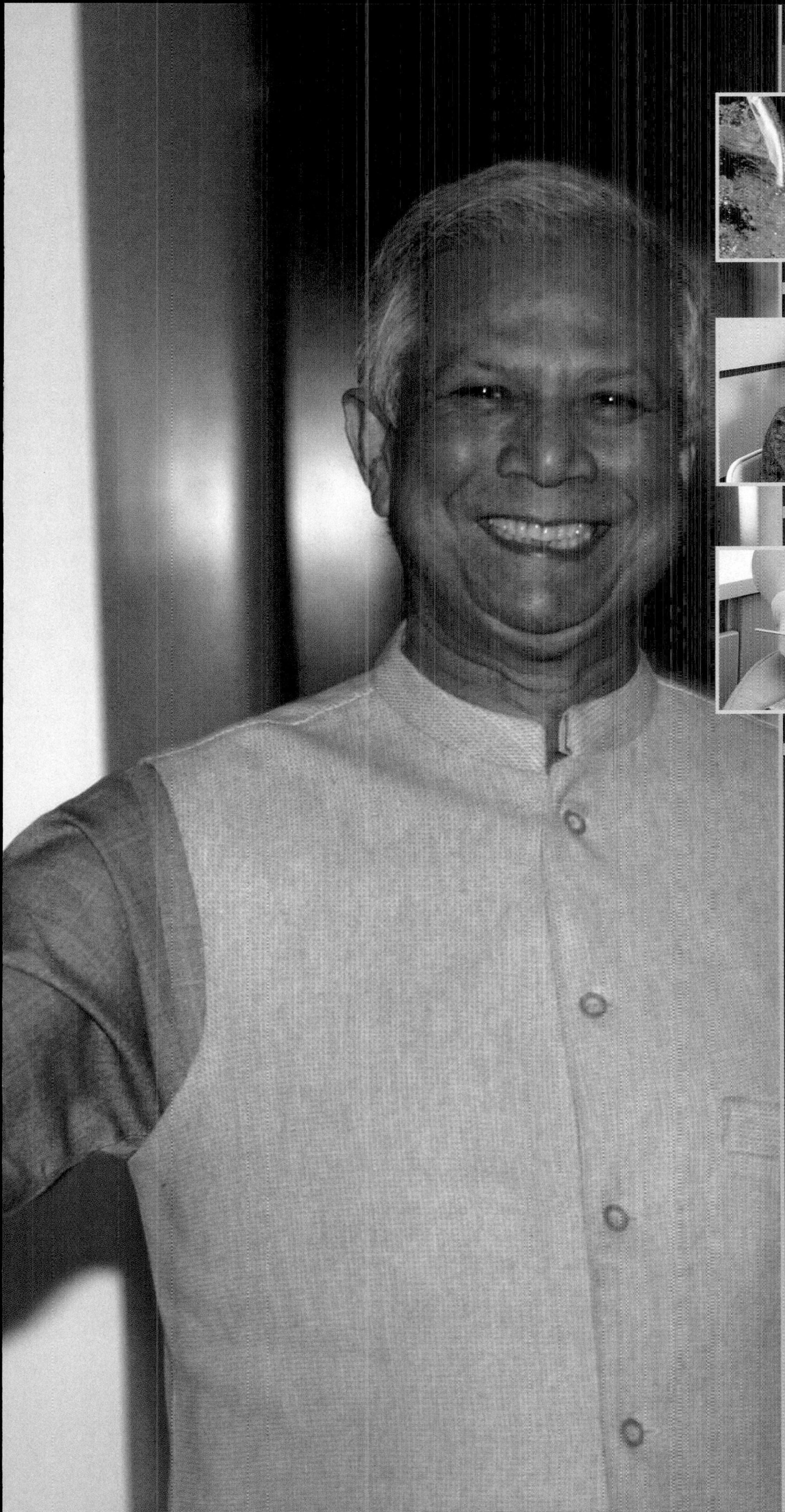

CHAPTER OUTLINE

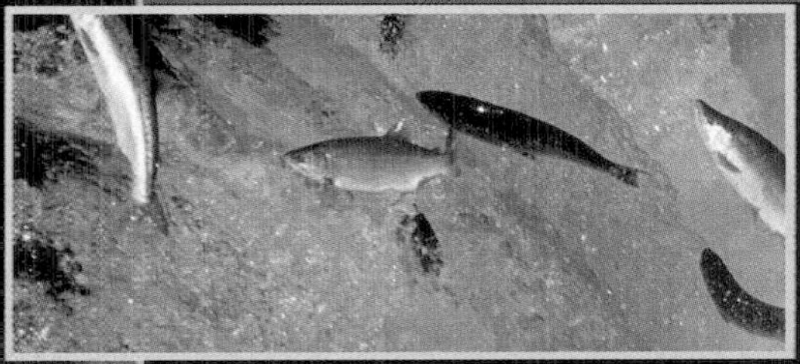

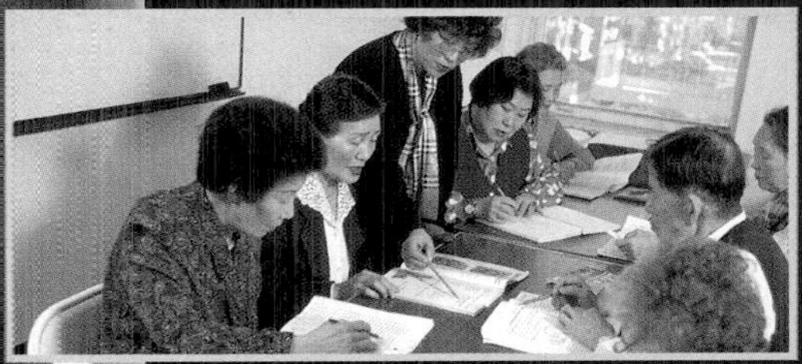

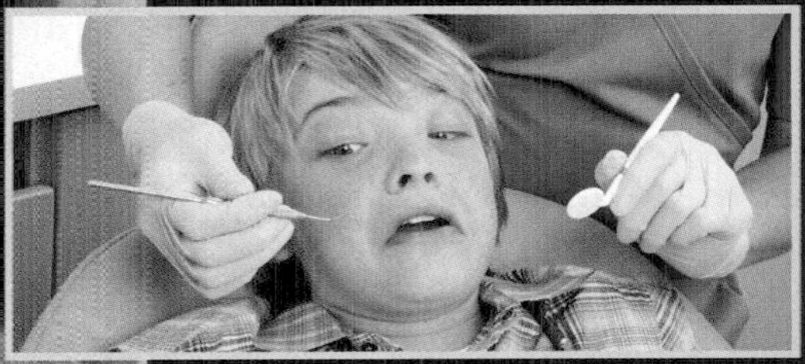

Understanding Motivation

Motivation can be described as an internal state that activates, directs, and maintains behaviour in a given direction, either toward a goal or away from an unfavourable situation.

EARLY IDEAS ABOUT MOTIVATION

Two early theories of **motivation** focused on the biological drives that seemed to control and direct behaviour. Researchers like William McDougall (1908) proposed that humans had numerous inborn "instincts," such as repulsion, curiosity, and self-assertiveness. Other researchers later added their favourite "instincts," and by the 1920s, the list of recognized instincts had become impossibly long. One researcher found listings for more than 10,000 human instincts (Bernard, 1924).

In addition to the problems with the growing list of instincts, the label *instinct* led to some very unscientific and circular explanations: "men are aggressive because they act aggressively" or "women are maternal because they act maternally." However, in recent years, a branch of biology called *sociobiology* has revived the case for human **instincts** when strictly defined in a specific way (**FIGURE 11.1**).

motivation An internal state that activates, directs, and maintains behaviour, usually toward a goal or away from an unfavourable situation.

instincts Behavioural patterns that are unlearned (inborn), always expressed in the same way, and are universal in a species.

Instincts FIGURE 11.1

▲ **A** Instinctual behaviours are generally unlearned and are universal in a species. They are obvious in many animals; for example, bears hibernate, birds build nests, and salmon swim upstream to spawn.

B Sociobiologists, such as Edward O. Wilson (1975, 1978), believe ▶ that humans also have instincts—such as competition and aggression—that are present in all of us to some degree and are genetically transmitted from one generation to the next.

In the 1930s, the concepts of drive and drive reduction began to replace the theory of instincts. According to *drive-reduction theory* (Hull, 1952), when biological needs (such as food, water, and oxygen) are unmet, a state of tension (known as a *drive*) is created, and the organism is motivated to reduce the tension. Drive-reduction theory is similar to the biological concept of **homeostasis**, a term that literally means "standing still." When an organism's normal state of equilibrium is disrupted (for example, when it needs food, water, or sex), the resulting tension creates a drive that motivates an urge to restore homeostasis: hungry—eat, thirsty—drink, aroused—have sex.

homeostasis

A body's tendency to maintain a relatively stable state, such as a constant internal temperature, blood sugar, oxygen level, or water balance.

The drive-reduction theory of motivation fell out of favour when it became clear that other factors must influence our motivations. That is, many drives are not always activated by a biological need and do not cease when the need is satisfied. For example, we eat when we are not hungry (recall the last time you ate dessert at a restaurant after a satisfying main course), and we often do not eat when we are hungry, such as when dieting or fasting. Moreover, many of us will drink beverages when we are not thirsty (often on a Friday or Saturday night for many college and university students). As you will see, a variety of factors other than biology also shape and influence our motivated behaviours.

CURIOSITY AND THE NEED FOR STIMULATION

Humans and other animals are innately curious and require a certain amount of novelty and complexity from the environment. This need for sensory stimulation begins shortly after birth and continues throughout the lifespan. Infants prefer complex versus simple visual stimuli, and adults pay more attention, for a longer time, to complex and changing stimuli. If it interests us, it captures our attention. Similarly, research shows that monkeys will work hard at tasks, such as opening latches, simply for the pleasure of satisfying their curiosity (**FIGURE 11.2**) (Butler, 1954; Harlow, Harlow, & Meyer, 1950).

It seems people vary considerably in their need for stimulation. Some people love to skydive from airplanes, extreme kayak, or race motorcycles, while merely the thought of these activities terrifies others. What might motivate people to engage in high-risk recreational activities? According to research, these

Arousal-seeking behaviour FIGURE 11.2

A Baby monkeys will persist at a task for a long time, apparently motivated by their own curiosity.

B The arousal motive is also apparent in the innate curiosity and exploration seen with baby humans.

"high-sensation seekers" may be biologically "prewired" to need more than the usual level of stimulation (Zuckerman, 1979, 1994, 2004). Research suggests that four distinct factors characterize sensation seeking (Legrand et al., 2007; Wallerstein, 2008; Zuckerman, 2004, 2008):

1. Thrill and adventure seeking (skydiving, driving fast, or trying to beat a train)

2. Experience seeking (travel, unusual friends, drug experimentation)

3. Disinhibition ("letting loose")

4. Susceptibility to boredom (lower tolerance for repetition and sameness)

Being very high or very low in sensation seeking could cause problems in relationships with partners who score towards opposite extremes. This is true not just in intimate relationships but also between parent and child and therapist and client. High-sensation seekers might also experience job difficulties if required to perform routine clerical or assembly line jobs, as will low-sensation seekers when faced with highly challenging and variable occupations.

However, the need for arousal is not limitless. According to *arousal theory*, organisms are motivated to achieve and maintain an optimal level of arousal that maximizes their performance. Either too much or too little arousal is associated with lowered performance (**FIGURE 11.3**).

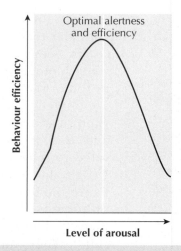

Optimal level of arousal FIGURE 11.3

Our need for stimulation suggests that behaviour efficiency increases as we move from low levels of arousal to increased alertness. However, once we pass the maximum level of arousal, our performance declines. Have you ever experienced a situation in which you were too aroused to function effectively? Think about exam performance. Being a little edgy going into an exam seems to sharpen your thinking; while being too edgy blocks your thought processes and not being edgy enough results in that "can't be bothered" feeling. *Applying Psychology* provides some strategies to deal with the all too common problem of exam nerves.

SOCIAL AND COGNITIVE ASPECTS OF NEEDS

Instinct and drive-reduction theories have been useful in explaining parts of some motivations but not all. For example, why does someone work overtime when his or her salary is sufficient to meet all basic biological needs? Why do we want bigger homes even though the ones we live in meet our needs? These questions are better answered by social and cognitive theories that emphasize incentives, attributions, and expectancies.

According to cognitive theories, motivation is directly affected by **attributions**, or how we interpret or think about our own and others' actions (Chapter 15). If you receive a high grade in this psychology course, for example, you can interpret that grade in several ways: You earned it because you really studied, you "lucked out," you have a very good instructor, or the textbook was exceptionally interesting and clear (our preference). People who attribute their successes to their personal ability and effort tend to work harder toward their goals than people who attribute their successes to external factors, such as luck (Hsieh, 2005; Houtz et al., 2007; Meltzer, 2004; Weiner, 1972, 1982).

Incentive theory holds that external stimuli motivate people to act to obtain desirable goals or to avoid undesirable events. People initially eat because their hunger "pushes" them toward the food, but they continue to eat because the sight of the chocolate or ice cream "pulls" them in.

Expectancies are what we believe will happen, and they are also important to motivation (Haugen, Ommundsen, & Lund, 2004; Schunk, 2008) (**FIGURE 11.4**). If

attribution
How we explain our own and others' actions.

Overcoming Test Anxiety

If you do become overly aroused on exam day, you may want to take a class in study skills or test anxiety. You can also try these basic study tips:

Step 1: *Prepare in advance.* The single most important cure for test anxiety is advance preparation and *hard work*. If you are well prepared, you will feel calmer and more in control.

- Read your textbook by using the SQ4R (**s**urvey, **q**uestion, **r**ead, **r**ecite, **r**eview, and **w**rite) method (see Chapter 1).

- Practise good time management and distribute your study time; don't cram the night before.

- Actively listen during lectures and take detailed, summarizing notes.

- Review the strategies for memory improvement (Chapter 7).

Step 2: *Learn to cope with the anxiety.* Performance is best at a moderate level of arousal, so a few butterflies before and during exams are okay and to be expected. However, too much anxiety can interfere with concentration and ruin your performance. To achieve the right amount of arousal, try these methods:

- Exercise regularly. This is a great stress reliever that also promotes deeper and more restful sleep.

- Replace anxiety with relaxed feelings. Practise deep breathing, which activates the parasympathetic nervous system.

- Create a 10-step test-taking hierarchy—starting with the least anxiety-arousing image (perhaps the day your instructor first mentions an upcoming exam) and ending with actually taking the exam.

- Begin with the least arousing image—hearing about the exam—and picture yourself at each stage. While maintaining a calm, relaxed state, work your way through all 10 steps. If you become anxious at any stage, stay there, repeating your relaxation technique until the anxiety diminishes.

Expectancies and psychosocial motivation FIGURE 11.4

How might the attributions and expectations of these learners affect their motivation to master a new language? Would you answer the same way if it were traditional-aged college or university students in a math, geography, or physics course?

you anticipate that you will receive a promotion at work, you're more likely to work late for no pay than if you expected no promotion. Likewise if you think that a final exam will be easy, you will likely study less.

THE HIERARCHY OF NEEDS

As in many areas of psychology, the best explanation is often the one that includes biological, social, and cognitive factors. Theories of motivation are no exception. One researcher who recognized this was Abraham Maslow (1954, 1970, 1999). Maslow believed that we all have numerous needs that compete for fulfillment but that some needs are more important than others. For

Maslow's hierarchy of needs FIGURE 11.5

As a humanistic psychologist, Maslow believed that we all have a compelling need to move up the hierarchy—to grow, belong, improve ourselves, and ultimately become self-actualized (chapters 12 and14).

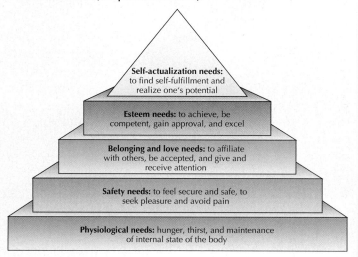

Self-actualization needs: to find self-fulfillment and realize one's potential

Esteem needs: to achieve, be competent, gain approval, and excel

Belonging and love needs: to affiliate with others, be accepted, and give and receive attention

Safety needs: to feel secure and safe, to seek pleasure and avoid pain

Physiological needs: hunger, thirst, and maintenance of internal state of the body

Bypassing basic needs FIGURE 11.6

What higher-level needs do these women seem to be trying to fulfill? Does it appear that their lower-level needs have been met? Is it possible to only partially satisfy lower-level needs and still pursue higher-level needs? What about the simultaneous pursuit of both higher- and lower-level needs?

hierarchy of needs Maslow's theory of motivation that some motives (such as physiological and safety needs) must be met before going on to higher needs (such as belonging and self-actualization).

example, your need for food and housing is generally more important than your college grades. Maslow's **hierarchy of needs** prioritizes our needs; survival needs are at the bottom (needs that must be met before others), and social and spiritual needs are at the top (**FIGURE 11.5**).

Maslow's hierarchy of needs seems intuitively correct—a starving person would look for food before love and friendship. This prioritizing and the concept of *self-actualization* (Chapter 12) are important ways to think about the study of motivation (Frick, 2000; Harper,

Harper, & Stills, 2003). But critics argue that parts of Maslow's theory are poorly researched and biased toward Western individualism. Critics also note that people sometimes seek to satisfy higher-level needs even when their lower-level needs have not been met (Cullen & Gotell, 2002; Hanley & Abell, 2002; Neher, 1991). For example, in some countries people live in war zones with little food, poor shelter, and the risk of injury and disease, yet they still seek the higher needs of strong social ties and self-esteem. Before the arrival of Europeans, Indigenous peoples of the Pacific Northwest Coast would host elaborate potlatches and give away abundant survival items, such as food and blankets—often at great cost—in return for earned prestige (**FIGURE 11.6**).

CONCEPT CHECK

Why are modern sociobiological theories of instincts more scientifically useful than older "instinct" theories?

What four factors are associated with sensation seeking?

What criticisms have been made of Maslow's hierarchy of needs theory?

Motivated Behaviours

LEARNING OBJECTIVES

Describe how internal and external factors regulate hunger and eating and how they affect eating disorders.

Summarize what happens to the human body during sexual arousal.

Discuss the evidence that suggests biology and genes are the dominant cause of sexual orientation.

Explain why some people are more highly achievement motivated than others.

Explain why providing extrinsic rewards can undermine intrinsic motivation.

Why do people put themselves in dangerous situations? Why do salmon swim upstream to spawn? Behaviour results from many motives. For example, we discuss the need for sleep in Chapter 5, and we look at aggression, altruism, and interpersonal attraction in Chapter 15. Here, we will focus on two basic motivations that are essential for species survival: eating and sex; we then discuss a motivation that is distinctly human: the motivation to achieve.

THE MOTIVATION TO EAT

What motivates hunger? Is it seeing someone else eating? Or is it your growling stomach? Or is it the sight of a juicy hamburger or the smell of a freshly baked cinnamon roll?

The Stomach
Early hunger researchers believed that it was the stomach that directly controlled hunger; when it was empty the contractions sent hunger signals to the brain. Today, we know that it's much more complicated than that; sensory input from the stomach is not essential for feeling hungry. Dieters learn this the hard way when they realize they cannot trick their stomachs into feeling full by drinking copious amounts of water. In fact, humans and non-human animals without stomachs continue to experience feelings of hunger.

A connection *does* exist, however, between the stomach and feeling hungry. Receptors in the stomach and intestines detect levels of nutrients, and specialized pressure receptors in the stomach walls signal feelings of emptiness or satiety (fullness or satiation). The stomach and other parts of the gastrointestinal tract also release chemical signals that play a role in hunger (Donini, Savina, & Cannella, 2003; Näslund & Hellström, 2007; Nogueiras & Tschöp, 2005).

BIOCHEMISTRY

Like the stomach, the brain and other parts of the body produce and are affected by numerous neurotransmitters, hormones, enzymes, and other chemicals that affect hunger and satiety (e.g., Arumugam et al., 2008; Cummings, 2006; Wardlaw & Hampl, 2007). It's unlikely that any one chemical completely controls our hunger and eating. Research in this area is complex because of the large number of known (and unknown) bodily chemicals that influence eating, and the interactions among them. Moreover, other internal factors, such as *thermogenesis* (the heat generated in response to food ingestion), also play an important role (Subramanian & Vollmer, 2002).

The Brain
In addition to its chemical signals, particular brain structures also influence hunger and eating. Primary among them is the hypothalamus, which regulates eating, drinking, and body temperature, among other functions.

Early research in this area suggested that one area of the hypothalamus, the lateral hypothalamus (LH), stimulates eating, while another area, the ventromedial hypothalamus (VMH), creates feelings of satiation, signalling the animal to stop eating. When the VMH area was destroyed in rats, researchers found that the rats overate to the point of extreme obesity

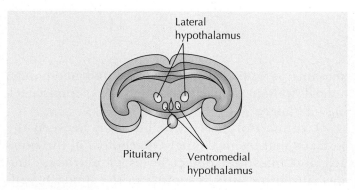

A This diagram shows a section of a rat's brain, including the ventromedial hypothalamus (VMH) and the lateral hypothalamus (LH). Notice that the rather complicated names are really just "neural landmarks." *Lateral* means "away from midline." *Ventromedial* means "toward the front (ventro) and toward the midline (medial)."

B The rat on the right is of normal weight. In contrast, the ventromedial area of the hypothalamus of the rat on the left was destroyed, which led to the tripling of its body weight.

How the hypothalamus affects eating FIGURE 11.7

(FIGURE 11.7). In contrast, when the LH area was destroyed, a starving animal would refuse to eat.

Later research, however, showed that the LH and VMH areas are not simply on-off switches for eating. For example, lesions (damage) to the VMH make animals picky eaters—they reject food that doesn't taste good to them. The lesions also increase insulin secretion, which may cause overeating (Challem et al., 2000). Today, researchers know that the hypothalamus plays an important role in hunger and eating, but it is not the brain's "eating centre" as was once thought. In fact, eating, like virtually all behaviours, is influenced by environmental factors and numerous neural circuits that run throughout the brain and body (Berthoud, 2002).

Psychosocial Factors

The internal physiological motivations for hunger we've discussed this far (stomach, biochemistry, the brain) are powerful. But psychosocial factors—for example, spotting a dessert tray in a restaurant or seeing a pizza commercial or even simply noticing that it's lunchtime—can be equally important triggers for hunger and eating.

Another important psychosocial influence on when, what, where, and why we eat is cultural conditioning. North Americans, for example, tend to eat dinner at around 6 p.m., whereas people in Spain and South America tend to eat around 10 p.m. When it comes to *what* we eat, have you ever eaten rat, dog, horsemeat, or seal heart? If you are a typical Canadian, this might sound distasteful to you, yet these are common meal items in many cultures. Most Hindus would feel similar revulsion to you about eating meat from a cow, something that is a fairly standard dinner fare in North America.

Eating Disorders

As you can see, hunger and eating are motivated by a variety of biological, psychological, and social factors, and these same biopsychosocial forces also play a role in three serious eating disorders: obesity, anorexia nervosa, and bulimia nervosa.

Obesity has reached epidemic proportions in Canada and many developed nations. More than a quarter of Canadians and half of all adults in the United States meet the current criteria for clinical **obesity** (having a body mass index, BMI,[1] of 30 or more). Each year, millions of dollars are spent treating serious and life-threatening medical problems related to obesity, such as diabetes, heart disease, and hypertension; and consumers spend millions more on largely ineffective weight-loss products and services.

[1] The formula for calculating BMI is weight (kg)/height (m)^2. Health Canada provides a BMI calculator at http://www.hc-sc.gc.ca/fn-an/nutrition/weights-poids/guide-ld-adult/bmi_chart_java-graph_imc_java-eng.php.

Given our culture's preference for thinness and dislike for fatness, why are so many Canadians and Americans overweight? The simple answer is we take in more food calories than we expend through exercise and daily activity (FIGURE 11.8). However, we all know some people who can eat anything they want and still not seem to gain weight. This may be a result of their ability to burn calories more effectively (thermogenesis), a higher metabolic rate, or other factors, such as moving more often and faster than most people. Adoption and twin studies indicate that genes also play a significant role. Heritability estimates for obesity ranges between 30 and 70 percent (Fernández et al., 2008; Lee et al., 2008; Schmidt, 2004). Unfortunately, identifying the genes for obesity is difficult. To date, researchers have isolated more than 2,000 genes that contribute in some way to normal and abnormal weight (Camarena et al., 2004; Costa, Brennen, & Hochgeschwender, 2002; Devlin, Yanovski, & Wilson, 2000).

As obesity has reached epidemic proportions, there has also been a similar rise in the rates of two other eating disorders: **anorexia nervosa** and **bulimia nervosa**. Both disorders are serious and chronic conditions that generally require some form of psychological and medical intervention.

anorexia nervosa An eating disorder characterized by a pathological drive to be thin and severe loss of weight resulting from self-imposed starvation.

bulimia nervosa An eating disorder characterized by the consumption of large quantities of food (bingeing), followed by vomiting, extreme exercise, or laxative use (purging).

Distorted body image FIGURE 11.9

In anorexia nervosa, body image is so distorted that even a skeletal, emaciated body (**A**) is perceived as fat. Many people with anorexia nervosa not only refuse to eat but also take up extreme exercise regimens—hours of cycling or running or constant walking to keep thin. One of the most famous victims of anorexia nervosa was Brazilian model Ana Carolina Reston (**B**) who died in 2006. At the time of her death this 173 cm (5′ 7″) model weighed just 40 kg (88 lb.).

A significant percentage of women, across all socioeconomic strata, in Western industrialized countries show some signs of an eating disorder, and approximately 2 percent meet the clinical criteria for anorexia nervosa or bulimia nervosa (Porzelius et al., 2001). Men also develop eating disorders, although the incidence is rarer (Raevuori et al., 2008; Jacobi et al., 2004).

Anorexia nervosa is characterized by an overwhelming fear of gaining weight, a distorted body image, a need for control, and the use of dangerous weight-loss strategies (**FIGURE 11.9**). The resulting extreme malnutrition often leads to emaciation, osteoporosis, bone fractures, interruption of menstruation, and the loss of neural tissue. A significant percentage of individuals with anorexia nervosa ultimately die of the disorder (Kaye, 2008; Wentz et al., 2007; Werth et al., 2003).

Occasionally, the person suffering from anorexia nervosa succumbs to the desire to eat, gorges on food, and then vomits or takes laxatives to rid the body of the calories. However, this type of bingeing and purging, which can occur independent of anorexia, is more characteristic of bulimia nervosa. Unlike anorexia, bulimia is exemplified by weight fluctuations within or above the normal range, which makes the illness easier to hide. The vomiting associated with bulimia nervosa causes dental damage, severe damage to the throat and stomach, heart problems, metabolic deficiencies, and serious digestive disorders.

There are many suspected causes of anorexia nervosa and bulimia nervosa but no known causes. Some theories focus on physical causes, such as hypothalamic disorders, low levels of various neurotransmitters, and genetic or hormonal disorders. Other theories emphasize psychosocial factors, such as a need for perfection, a perceived loss of control, being teased about body weight, destructive thought patterns, depression, dysfunctional families,

The pressure to be thin has many influences

FIGURE 11.10

A Can you explain why popular movie and television stars' extreme thinness may contribute to eating disorders?

B The drive to be thin is instilled into young girls from an early age. If a real woman standing 173 cm (5′ 7″) tall had the measurements of Barbie, she would have an 81 cm (32 inch) bust, a 40.5 cm (16 inch) waist, and 73.75 cm (29 inch) hips (Norton et al., 1996).

distorted body image, and sexual abuse (e.g., Behar, 2007; Fairburn et al., 2008; Kaye, 2008; Sachdev et al., 2008).

Cultural perceptions and stereotypes about weight and eating also play important roles in eating disorders (Eddy et al., 2007; Fairburn et al., 2008; Herman & Polivy, 2008). For instance, Asian Americans and African Americans report fewer eating and dieting disorders and greater body satisfaction than do European Americans (Ruffolo et al., 2006; Taylor et al., 2007), and Mexican students report less concern about their own weight and more acceptance of obese people than do other North American students (Crandall & Martinez, 1996). In Africa, where thinness can signal poverty, AIDS, and disease, plump is preferred, especially among the wealthy.

Although social pressures for thinness certainly contribute to eating disorders (FIGURE 11.10), anorexia nervosa has also been found in non-industrialized areas, like the Caribbean island of Curaçao (Hoek et al., 2005). On that island, being overweight is socially acceptable, and the average woman is considerably heavier than the average woman in North America. However, some women there still have anorexia nervosa. This research suggests that both culture and biology help explain eating disorders.

THE MOTIVATION TO HAVE SEX: PROBABLY RECREATION AS MUCH AS PROCREATION

Obviously, there is a strong motivation to have sex: it's essential for the survival of ours and many other species, and, for most, it's also extremely pleasurable. While sex evolved for reproductive purposes, it serves multiple other functions as well, such as intimacy, pleasure, and closeness. These and other qualities probably "piggybacked" along on the evolved reproduction adaptation. This is illustrated by the fact that most of the sex we have in our lives is for recreational and enjoyment purposes and not simply to procreate. Said more simply, if a person has just one sex partner in his or her entire life, most of the sex they will have will be for pleasure and not simply to make babies.

William Masters and Virginia Johnson (1966) were the first to conduct laboratory studies on what happens to the human body during sexual activity. Somewhat daring, even by today's standards, they achieved this by watching people having sex. By attaching recording devices to the genitalia of male and female volunteers and filming their physical responses while engaging in

| human sexual response cycle

Masters and Johnson's description of the four physiological stages of sexual arousal: excitement, plateau, orgasm, and resolution.

partnered sex or masturbating, Masters and Johnson could monitor people as they moved from non-arousal to orgasm and back to non-arousal. They labelled the bodily changes during this series of events the **human sexual response cycle** (FIGURE 11.11).

SEXUAL ORIENTATION

Of course, an essential part of any person's sexuality is the direction of their sexual attraction. For hundreds of years scientists and scholars have wondered what causes some people to be gay. Is it social factors, upbringing, or biology? What is missing from this age-old question is the assumption that heterosexuality needs no explanation. Therefore, a better question to ask is, What

Process Diagram

Masters and Johnson's sexual response cycle FIGURE 11.11

Note that sexual expression is extremely diverse and this simplified description does not account for all the individual variation seen in our species

2 During the **plateau phase**, physiological and sexual arousal continue at heightened levels. In men, the penis becomes more engorged and erect while the testes swell and pull up closer to the body. In the woman, the clitoris pulls up under the clitoral hood and the entrance to the vagina contracts while the uterus rises slightly. This movement of the uterus causes the upper two-thirds of the vagina to balloon, or expand. As arousal reaches its peak, both sexes may experience a feeling that orgasm is imminent and inevitable.

3 The **orgasm phase** involves a highly intense and pleasurable release of tension. In women, muscles around the vagina squeeze the vaginal walls in and out and the uterus pulsates. Muscles at the base of the penis contract in the man, causing ejaculation, the discharge of semen or seminal fluid.

1 The **excitement phase** can last for minutes or hours. Arousal is initiated through touching, fantasy, or erotic stimuli. Heart rate and respiration increase and increased blood flow to the region causes penile or clitoral erection, and vaginal lubrication in women. In both men and women, the nipples may become erect, and both may experience a sex flush (reddening of the upper torso and face).

4 Physiological responses gradually return to normal during the **resolution phase**. After one orgasm, most men enter a **refractory phase**, during which further excitement to orgasm is considered impossible. Many women (and some men), however, are capable of multiple orgasms in fairly rapid succession.

Plateau

Excitement

Orgasm

Resolution

A After orgasm men generally enter a refractory period. This can last from a few seconds to an entire day, depending on the age of the man. As men age, their refractory periods increase. ▼

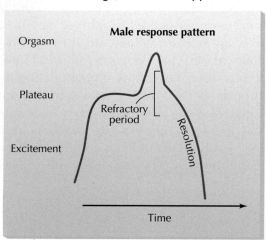

Male response pattern

Orgasm

Plateau

Refractory period

Resolution

Excitement

Time

B Sexual response in women is a little more variable and tends to follow one or more of three basic patterns. ▼

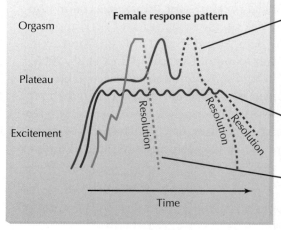

Female response pattern

Orgasm

Plateau

Resolution

Resolution

Resolution

Excitement

Time

This response is similar to the male pattern but allows the possibility of multiple orgasms without falling below the plateau level of arousal.

This response occurs when a woman is aroused but does not acheive an orgasm. In this case resolution takes longer.

In this response there is a rapid rise to orgasm without a definitive plateau and a quick resolution.

causes **sexual orientation**? To date, the direct or indirect causes are not well understood. However, most current studies suggest that genetics and biology play the dominant role (Bailey, Dunne, & Martin, 2000; Byne, 2007; Ellis et al., 2008; Gooren, 2006; Zucker, 2008).

Studies on identical (monozygotic) and fraternal (dizygotic) twins and adopted siblings found that if one identical twin was gay, 48 to 65 percent of the time so was the second twin (Hyde, 2005; Kirk et al., 2000). If the cause were totally genetic, the percentage would be 100, so clearly other factors are at play. The rate was 26 to 30 percent for fraternal twins and 6 to 11 percent for brothers and sisters who were adopted. Estimates of exclusive homosexuality in the general population are much lower than this, around 1 to 2 percent.

Research with rats and sheep and other animal species suggests that prenatal sex hormone levels (primarily the androgens, such as testosterone) affect fetal brain development and sexual orientation (Bagermihl, 1999), and some evidence exists for this in humans (Dittmann et al., 1992). However, the mechanism by which sex hormones have their effect on fetal development has not been clearly established as yet.

GAY FAMILIES

Canada was the fourth country to legalize same-sex marriage on July 20, 2005, with the enactment of the Civil Marriage Act. This Act redefined marriage from "the lawful union of a *man and woman* to the exclusion of all others" to "the lawful union of *two persons* to the exclusion of all others" (emphasis added). Earlier court decisions had already legalized same-sex marriage in eight out of the 10 provinces and one of the three territories, but it was this Act that made it universal across Canada. A number of polls and surveys have consistently shown that the majority of Canadians support the right of gay men and lesbians to marry.

As of the 2006 Canada census there were 45,345 same-sex cohabiting couples in Canada, of which 7,465 (16.5 percent) were married. Half of all same-sex couples live in the three largest metropolitan areas: Toronto (21.2 percent), Montreal (18.4 percent), and Vancouver (10.3 percent). A little more than half of same-sex married couples were men. About 9 percent of people in same-sex cohabiting relationships had children (defined as 24 years and under) living in the home. This was more common for women (16.3 percent) than for men (2.9 percent) (Statistics Canada, 2007).

According to the same Canadian census, approximately 4,000 same-sex Canadian households include children (**FIGURE 11.12**) (Statistics Canada, 2007). Some of these children are from prior heterosexual relationships, and some are either adopted or conceived by using assisted reproductive technologies. Because gay sex is not procreative sex, the children born in same-sex relationships are not accidentally conceived and are wanted and planned.

Various groups, including psychologists, have been interested in investigating how children raised in

Dispelling myths with empirical research
FIGURE 11.12

Research has investigated some long-held and widespread myths about homosexuality and has shown they are wrong (Bergstrom-Lynch, 2008; Boysen & Vogel, 2007; LeVay, 2003). Here are a few of the findings: Being raised by gay or lesbian (or cross-dressing) parents does not make a person gay. Nor is it true that gay men and lesbians were seduced as children by adults of their own sex. Sons do not become gay because of domineering mothers or weak fathers, and daughters do not become lesbians because their fathers were their primary role models. Finally, having unfruitful or unhappy heterosexual experiences does not "make" a person gay or lesbian.

same-sex families compare with children raised in opposite-sex families. The results of more than two dozen studies addressing this topic are clear. Children of same-sex families do not differ from those of opposite-sex families on a variety of dimensions, including general well-being, adjustment, self-esteem, gender roles, sexual identity, sexual orientation, psychiatric evaluations, behaviour problems, self-concept, moral judgement, school adjustment, and social relationships; see Patterson (2009) for a review. It seems that the traditional family structure that assumes heterosexual parents is not essential for healthy child development. Research has shown the most crucial ingredient in raising well-adjusted children appears to be the presence of at least one supportive and accepting caregiver (Strickland, 1995).

ACHIEVEMENT: THE NEED FOR SUCCESS

Do you wonder what motivates Olympic athletes to work so hard just for one shot at a gold medal? Or what about someone like Thomas Edison, who patented more than 1,000 inventions? What drives some people to high achievement?

The key to understanding what motivates high-achieving individuals lies in what psychologist Henry Murray (1938) identified as a high need for achievement (nAch), or **achievement motivation**.

> **achievement motivation**
>
> A desire to excel, especially when in competition with others.

Several traits distinguish people who have high achievement motivation (McClelland, 1958, 1987, 1993; Quintanilla, 2007; Senko et al., 2008):

- *Preference for moderately difficult tasks.* People high in nAch avoid tasks that are too easy because they offer little challenge or satisfaction. They also avoid extremely difficult tasks because the probability of success is too low.

- *Competitiveness.* High-achievement-oriented people are more attracted to careers and tasks that involve competition and an opportunity to excel.

- *Preference for clear goals with competent feedback.* High-achievement-oriented people tend to prefer tasks with a clear outcome and situations in which they can receive feedback on their performance. They also prefer criticism from a harsh but competent evaluator to that which comes from one who is friendlier but less competent.

- *Responsibility.* People with high nAch prefer being personally responsible for a project so that they can feel satisfied when the task is well done.

- *Persistence.* High-achievement-oriented people are more likely to persist at a task when it becomes difficult. In one study, 47 percent of high nAch individuals persisted on an "unsolvable task" until time was called, compared with only 2 percent of people with low nAch.

- *More accomplished.* People who have high nAch scores do better than others on exams, earn better grades in school, and excel in their chosen professions.

Achievement orientation appears to be largely learned in early childhood, primarily through interactions with parents, teachers, and the culture in which a person is raised (**FIGURE 11.13**).

Future high achiever? FIGURE 11.13

Highly motivated children tend to have parents who encourage independence and frequently reward successes (Maehr & Urdan, 2000). Cultural values also affect achievement needs (Lubinski & Benbow, 2000). Events and themes in children's literature, for example, often contain subtle messages about what the culture values. In North American and Western European cultures, many children's stories are about persistence and the value of hard work.

INTRINSIC VERSUS EXTRINSIC MOTIVATION: IS ONE BETTER THAN THE OTHER?

Should parents give their children money for getting good grades? Do pay raises improve work performance? Many psychologists are concerned about the widespread practice of giving external, or extrinsic, rewards to motivate and increase desirable behaviour (e.g., Deci & Moller, 2005; Markle, 2007; Prabhu et al., 2008; Reeve, 2005). They're concerned that providing such **extrinsic motivation** will significantly influence the individual's personal, **intrinsic motivation**. Participation in sports and hobbies, like swimming or playing Guitar Hero, is usually intrinsically motivated—we like to do it. Going to work is primarily extrinsically motivated—we do it for the paycheque.

Research has shown that people who are given extrinsic rewards (money, praise, or other incentives) for an intrinsically satisfying activity, such as watching TV, playing cards, or even engaging in sex, often lose enjoyment and interest and may decrease the time spent on the activity (Hennessey & Amabile, 1998; Kohn, 2000; Moneta & Siu, 2002).

One of the earliest experiments to demonstrate this effect was conducted with preschool children who liked to draw (Lepper, Greene, & Nisbett, 1973). Researchers found that children who were given paper and markers and promised a reward for their drawings were subsequently less interested in drawing than children who were not given a reward or who were given an unexpected reward when they were done (**FIGURE 11.14**).

Not all extrinsic motivation is bad, however (Banko, 2008; Konheim-Kalkstein & van den Broek, 2008; Moneta & Siu, 2002). Extrinsic rewards are motivating if they are used to inform a person of superior performance or as a special "no strings attached" treat (Deci, 1995). In fact, rewards may intensify the desire to do well again. Thus, getting a raise or an Olympic gold medal can inform us and provide valuable feedback about great performance, which may increase enjoyment. But if rewards are used to control behaviour—for example, when parents give children money or privileges as an incentive for good grades—they reduce intrinsic motivation (Eisenberger & Armeli, 1997; Eisenberger & Rhoades, 2002; Houlfort, 2006) (**FIGURE 11.15**).

extrinsic motivation
Motivation based on obvious external rewards or threats of punishment.

intrinsic motivation
Motivation resulting from personal enjoyment of a task or activity.

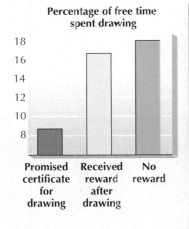

Extrinsic versus intrinsic rewards FIGURE 11.14

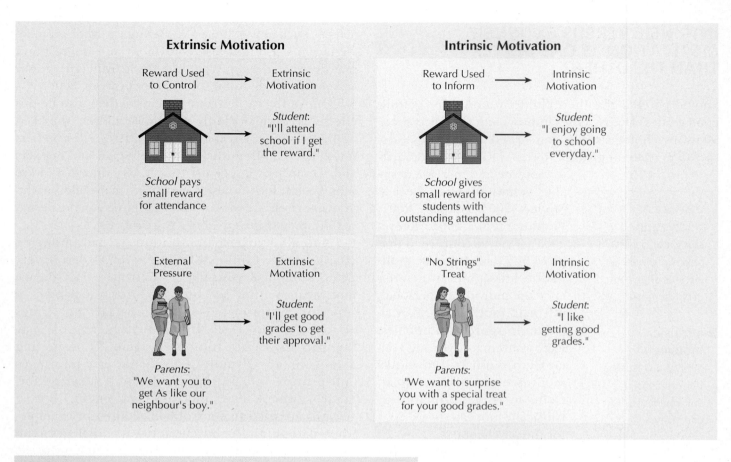

Extrinsic Motivation

Reward Used to Control → Extrinsic Motivation

Student: "I'll attend school if I get the reward."

School pays small reward for attendance

External Pressure → Extrinsic Motivation

Student: "I'll get good grades to get their approval."

Parents: "We want you to get As like our neighbour's boy."

Intrinsic Motivation

Reward Used to Inform → Intrinsic Motivation

Student: "I enjoy going to school everyday."

School gives small reward for students with outstanding attendance

"No Strings" Treat → Intrinsic Motivation

Student: "I like getting good grades."

Parents: "We want to surprise you with a special treat for your good grades."

Motivation is in the eye of the beholder FIGURE 11.15

Do rewards increase motivation, or are they seen as coercion or bribery? It depends. A controlling reward and external pressure can both lead to extrinsic motivation. However, an informing reward and a "no strings" treat produce intrinsic motivation.

CONCEPT CHECK ✓

What are the biological, psychological, and social factors that motivate hunger and eating?

What are the four stages of the human sexual response?

What traits characterize people with high achievement motivation?

What is the impact of using extrinsic motivation to reward behaviour?

What would motivate you to play a sport or participate in extracurricular activity?

How do you think employees could be motivated so they don't think of work as "just a job"?

Theories and Concepts of Emotion

LEARNING OBJECTIVE

Describe the physiological, cognitive, and behavioural components of emotion.

Outline the four major theories of emotion.

Explain the cultural similarities and differences in emotion.

Review the problems with relying on polygraph testing as a "lie detector."

THREE COMPONENTS OF EMOTION: MUCH MORE THAN JUST FEELINGS

Emotions play an essential role in our lives. They colour our memories, dreams, and perceptions. When disordered, they increase psychological problems and influence our key relationships. But what really are emotions, and how are they different from our subjective feelings? To answer this question, psychologists define and study **emotion** in three basic components: physiological, cognitive, and behavioural.

> **emotion** A state of physiological arousal and tendencies toward action involving changes in behaviour, cognitions, facial expressions, and subjective feelings.

The Physiological (Arousal) Component

Internal physical changes occur in our bodies whenever we experience an emotion. Imagine walking alone on a dark street when someone jumps out and starts running toward you. How would you respond? Like most people, you would undoubtedly interpret the situation as threatening and would either run or prepare to confront the intruder. Your predominant emotion, fear, would involve several physiological reactions, such as increased breathing, heart rate, and blood pressure; perspiration; and goose bumps (also known as piloerection). Such physiological reactions are controlled by certain brain structures and by the autonomic branch of the peripheral nervous system (ANS) (Chapter 2).

Our emotional experiences appear to result from important interactions between several areas of the brain, most particularly the *cerebral cortex* and the *limbic system* (Langenecker et al., 2005; LeDoux, 2002;

Panksepp, 2005). As we discussed in Chapter 2, the cerebral cortex serves as the body's ultimate control and information-processing centre and includes the ability to recognize and regulate our emotions.

The limbic system is also essential to our emotions. Electrical stimulation of specific parts of this brain region can produce an automatic rage that turns a docile cat into a hissing, slashing animal. Stimulating adjacent areas can cause the same animal to purr and lick your fingers. These dramatic changes in behaviour occur in the absence of provocation and disappear the moment the stimulus is removed. Several studies have shown that one area of the limbic system, the *amygdala*, plays a key role in emotion—especially fear. It sends signals to other areas of the brain, causing increased heart rate and all the other physiological reactions related to fear.

Interestingly, emotional arousal sometimes occurs without conscious awareness. According to psychologist Joseph LeDoux (1996a, 2002, 2007), when sensory inputs arrive in the *thalamus* (our brain's sensory switchboard), it sends separate messages up to the cortex (which "thinks" about the stimulus) and to the amygdala (which immediately activates the body's alarm system).

As important as the brain is to emotion, it is the *autonomic nervous system* (ANS, Chapter 2) that produces the obvious signs of arousal. These largely automatic responses result from interconnections between the ANS and the various glands and muscles of the body. (**FIGURE 11.16**).

The Cognitive (Thinking) Component

Our thoughts help determine the type and intensity of our emotional responses. Consequently, emotional reactions are very individual: what you experience as

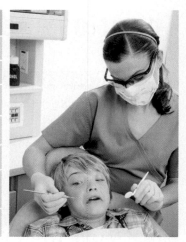

	Sympathetic		Parasympathetic
Pupils dilated	**Eyes**		Pupils constricted
Dry	**Mouth**		Salivating
Goose bumps (pilo-erection), perspiration	**Skin**		No goose bumps
Respiration increased	**Lungs**		Respiration normal
Increased rate	**Heart**		Decreased rate
Increased epinephrine and norepinephrine	**Adrenal glands**		Decreased epinephrine and norepinephrine
Decreased motility	**Digestion**		Increased motility

The autonomic nervous system FIGURE 11.16

During emotional arousal, the sympathetic branch of the autonomic nervous system prepares the organism for fight or flight. The hormones epinephrine and norepinephrine keep the system under sympathetic control until the emergency is over. The parasympathetic branch returns the body to a non-aroused state (remember homeostasis?), which is where it remains for most of the time. If sympathetic arousal is so good at mobilizing an organism to fight or flee, why do you think we need a parasympathetic system?

intensely pleasurable may be boring, annoying, or aversive to another. To study the cognitive (thought) component of emotions, psychologists typically use self-report techniques, such as paper-and-pencil tests, surveys, and interviews. However, people are sometimes unable or unwilling to accurately describe (or remember) their emotional states. For these reasons, our cognitions about our own and others' emotions are difficult to measure scientifically. This is why many researchers supplement participants' reports on their emotional experiences with methods that assess emotional experience indirectly (for example, by measuring physiological responses or behaviour).

The Behavioural (Expressive) Component

Emotional expression is a powerful form of communication, and while our bodily posture changes to reflect our emotions, facial expressions may be our most important form of emotional communication. Researchers have developed sensitive techniques to measure facial expressions of emotion and differentiate honest expressions from fake ones. Perhaps most interesting is the distinctive difference between the *social smile* and the *Duchenne smile* (named after French anatomist Duchenne de Boulogne,

who first described it in 1862) (FIGURE 11.17). In a false, social smile, our voluntary cheek muscles are pulled back, but our eyes are unsmiling. Smiles of real pleasure

The Duchenne smile: Which smile looks happier and more sincere? FIGURE 11.17

People who show a Duchenne smile (A) elicit more positive responses from strangers and enjoy better interpersonal relationships and personal adjustment than those who use social smiles (B) (Keltner, Kring, & Bonanno, 1999; Prkachin & Silverman, 2002).

(Duchenne smiles), conversely, use the muscles not only around the cheeks but also around the eyes.

The Duchenne smile illustrates the importance of non-verbal means of communicating emotion. We all know that people communicate in ways other than speaking or writing. However, few people recognize the full importance of non-verbal signals. Imagine yourself as an interviewer with two equally qualified applicants, both of whom are well spoken. Your first job applicant greets you with a big smile, full eye contact, a firm handshake, and an erect, open posture. The second applicant doesn't smile, looks down, offers a weak handshake, and slouches. Whom do you think you will hire?

Psychologist Albert Mehrabian would say that you're much less likely to hire the second applicant because of his or her "mixed messages." His research suggests that when we're communicating feelings or attitudes and the verbal and non-verbal dimensions don't match, the receiver trusts the predominant form of communication, which is about 93 percent non-verbal (the way the words are said and facial expression) versus the literal meaning of the words (Mehrabian, 1968, 1971, 2007).

Unfortunately, Mehrabian's research is often over-generalized, and many people misquote him as saying that more than 90 percent of communication is non-verbal. Clearly, if a police officer says, "Put your hands up," his or her verbal words might carry 100 percent of the meaning. However, when we're confronted with a mismatch between verbal and non-verbal, it is safe to say that we pay far more attention to the non-verbal because we believe it more often tells us what someone is really thinking or feeling. The importance of non-verbal communication, particularly facial expressions, is further illustrated by the popularity of "smileys," and other emoticon symbols, in our email and text messages.

FOUR MAJOR THEORIES OF EMOTION

Researchers generally agree on the three components of emotion (physiological, cognitive, and behavioural), but there is less agreement on *how* we become emotional. The four major theories in this area are the James-Lange, the Cannon-Bard, the facial-feedback,

and Schachter's two-factor. Each theory has its supporters and critics and each has flaws, but as shown in FIGURE 11.18 (on the next page), they all emphasize different sequences or aspects of the same three elements of emotion.

According to the **James-Lange theory** (originated by psychologist William James and later expanded on by physiologist Carl Lange), emotions depend on feedback from our physiological arousal and behavioural expression (FIGURE 11.18A). In other words, as James wrote: "We feel sorry because we cry, angry because we strike, afraid because we tremble" (James, 1890). In short, emotions are the result of physiological arousal. Without arousal or expression, there is no emotion.

In contrast, the **Cannon-Bard theory** holds that all emotions are physiologically similar and that arousal, cognitions, and expression all occur simultaneously. Important in this theory is the belief that arousal is not a necessary or even major factor in emotion. Walter Cannon (1927) and Philip Bard (1934) proposed that the thalamus sends simultaneous messages to both the ANS and the cerebral cortex (FIGURE 11.18B). Messages to the cortex produce the cognitive experience of emotion (such as fear), whereas messages to the autonomic nervous system produce physiological arousal and behavioural expressions (such as heart palpitations, running, and widening eyes).

Cannon supported his position with several experiments in which animals were surgically prevented from experiencing physiological arousal. His results showed these animals still exhibited emotion-like behaviours, such as growling and defensive postures (Cannon, Lewis, & Britton, 1927).

The third major theory of emotion focuses on the expressive component of emotions. According to the **facial-feedback hypothesis** (FIGURE 11.18C), facial changes not only correlate with and intensify emotions but also cause or reinforce the very emotions themselves (Adelmann & Zajonc, 1989; Ceschi & Scherer, 2001; Prkachin, 2005; Sigall & Johnson, 2006). Contractions of the various facial muscles send specific messages to the brain, identifying each of the basic emotions.

The facial-feedback hypothesis is consistent with Charles Darwin's (1872) theory, which states that freely expressing an emotion intensifies it, while suppressing

Four major theories of emotion FIGURE 11.18

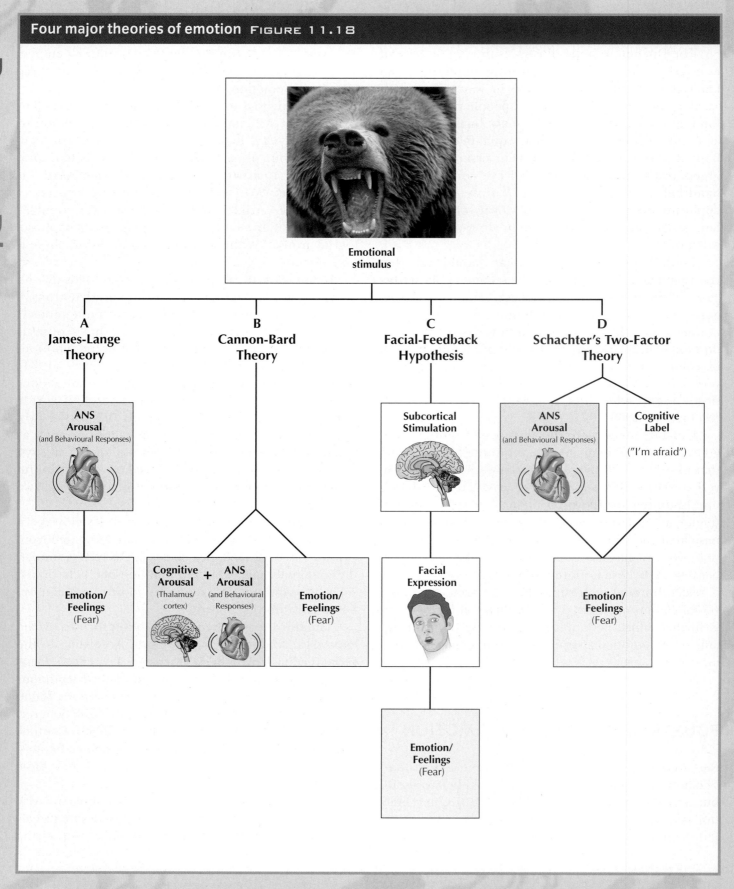

Emotional
stimulus

A
James-Lange
Theory

B
Cannon-Bard
Theory

C
Facial-Feedback
Hypothesis

D
Schachter's Two-Factor
Theory

**ANS
Arousal**
(and Behavioural Responses)

**Emotion/
Feelings**
(Fear)

**Cognitive
Arousal** + **ANS
Arousal**
(Thalamus/   (and Behavioural
cortex)   Responses)

**Emotion/
Feelings**
(Fear)

**Subcortical
Stimulation**

**Facial
Expression**

**Emotion/
Feelings**
(Fear)

**ANS
Arousal**
(and Behavioural Responses)

**Cognitive
Label**

("I'm afraid")

**Emotion/
Feelings**
(Fear)

Testing the facial-feedback hypothesis FIGURE 11.19

Hold a pen or pencil between your teeth with your mouth open. Spend about 30 seconds in this position. How do you feel? According to research, pleasant feelings are more likely when teeth are showing than when they are not. *Source:* Adapted from Strack, Martin, & Stepper, 1988.

outward expression diminishes it (FIGURE 11.19). A recent study involving recipients of Botox (Chapter 2) found that people who cannot frown because of cosmetic Botox injections report feeling happier and less anxious than those who received other cosmetic treatments. These results suggest that treatments that prevent frowning might influence negative moods (Lewis & Bowler, 2009). Interestingly, even watching another's facial expressions causes an automatic, reciprocal change in our own facial muscles (Dimberg & Thunberg, 1998). When people are exposed to pictures of angry faces, for example, the eyebrow muscles involved in frowning are activated. This automatic matching response can occur even without the participant's attention or conscious awareness (Dimberg, Thunberg, & Elmehed, 2000).

Finally, according to psychologist Stanley **Schachter's two-factor theory** (FIGURE 11.20 on the next page), emotions have two parts (or factors): physiological and cognitive. The cognitive factor is necessary to evaluate what in the situation has caused the physiological arousal. In other words, it is physical arousal and the cognitive label of the arousal that produces the subjective experience of emotion. If we cry at a wedding, we interpret our emotion as happiness, but if we cry at a funeral, we label our emotion sadness.

Which theory is correct? As said, each has its benefits and limitations to our understanding of emotion. For example, the James-Lange theory fails to acknowledge

that physical arousal can occur without emotional experience (e.g., when we work out). This theory also requires a distinctly different pattern of arousal for each emotion. Otherwise, how do we know whether we are sad, happy, disgusted, or mad? Although brain-imaging studies do show subtle differences among basic emotions (Levenson, 1992, 2007; Werner et al., 2007), most people are not aware of these slight variations. Thus, there must be other explanations for why we experience emotion.

The Cannon-Bard theory (that the cortex and autonomic nervous system receive simultaneous messages from the thalamus) has received some experimental support. Victims of spinal cord damage still experience emotions, often more intensely than before their injuries (Nicotra et al., 2006; Schopp et al., 2007). Instead of the thalamus, however, research shows that it is the limbic system, hypothalamus, and prefrontal cortex that are the most important in emotional experiences (LeDoux, 2007; Zillmer et al., 2008).

Research on the facial-feedback hypothesis has found that facial feedback does seem to contribute somewhat to the intensity of our subjective emotions and overall moods (Lewis & Bowler, 2009). Thus, if you want to change a bad mood or intensify a particularly good emotion, adopt the appropriate facial expression. In other words, "fake it 'til you make it."

Finally, Schachter's two-factor theory emphasizes the importance of cognitive processes in emotions, but

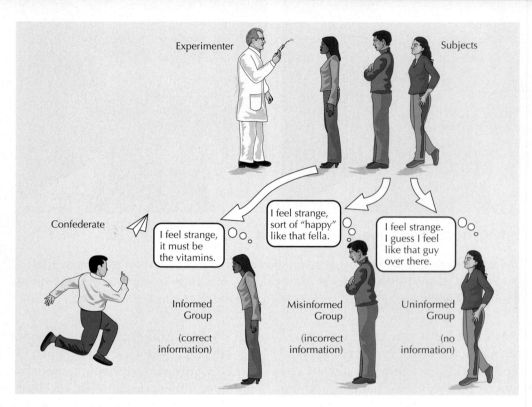

In Schachter and Singer's classic study (1962), participants were given injections of epinephrine and told it was a type of vitamin. One group of participants was correctly informed about the expected effects (hand tremors, excitement, and heart palpitations). A second group was misinformed and told to expect itching, numbness, and headache. A third group was told nothing about the possible effects.

Following the injection, each participant was placed in a room with a confederate (an assistant who was part of the experiment but who pretended to be a fellow volunteer) who acted either happy or unhappy.

The results showed that participants who lacked an appropriate cognitive label for their emotional arousal (the misinformed and uninformed groups) tended to look to the situation for an explanation. Thus, those placed with a happy confederate became happy, whereas those with an unhappy confederate became unhappy. Participants in the correctly informed group knew their physiological arousal was the result of the needle, so their emotions were generally unaffected by the confederate.

his findings have been criticized. For example, as mentioned earlier, some neural pathways involved in emotion bypass the cortex and go directly to the limbic system and we are not always accurate when labelling our emotions (see **FIGURE 11.21**). This and other evidence suggest that emotion is not simply the labelling of arousal (Dimberg, Thunberg, & Elmehed, 2000; LeDoux, 1996b, 2002; Mineka & Oehman, 2002).

CULTURE, EVOLUTION, AND EMOTION

Are emotions the same across all cultures? Given the seemingly vast array of emotions within Canadian culture, it may surprise you to learn that some researchers believe that all our feelings can be condensed into 7 to 10 universal emotions. Note the similarities in **TABLE 11.1**. These researchers hold that other

Does emotional arousal increase feelings of sexual attraction? Figure 11.21

In a classic study, psychologists at the University of British Columbia had an attractive female researcher interview men after they had just walked across the scary Capilano Suspension Bridge in North Vancouver (Dutton & Aron, 1974). Men who had just crossed the scary bridge were more inclined to telephone the researcher for further contact than were men who had just crossed a non-scary bridge. Could these participants have misinterpreted their high levels of emotional arousal as sexual attraction to the researcher?

emotions, such as love, are simply combinations of these primary emotions with variations in intensity (Figure 11.22).

Some research indicates that people in all cultures express and recognize the basic emotions in essentially the same way (Biehl et al., 1997; Ekman, 1993, 2004; Matsumoto & Juang, 2008).

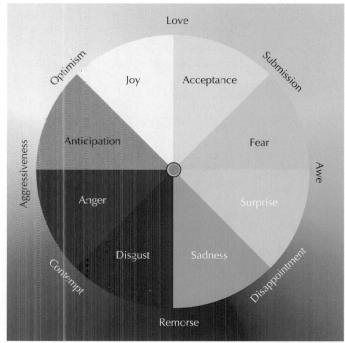

Plutchik's wheel of emotions Figure 11.22

Robert Plutchik (1984, 1994, 2000) suggested that the basic primary emotions (inner circle) combine to form secondary emotions (located outside the circle). Plutchik also found that emotions that lie next to each other are more alike than those that are farther apart. Can you provide examples of this phenomenon from your own life?

The basic human emotions as identified by different researchers TABLE 11.1

Carroll Izard	Paul Ekman and Wallace Friesen	Robert Plutchik	Silvan Tomkins
Fear	Fear	Fear	Fear
Anger	Anger	Anger	Anger
Disgust	Disgust	Disgust	Disgust
Surprise	Surprise	Surprise	Surprise
Joy	Happiness	Joy	Enjoyment
Shame	—	—	Shame
Contempt	Contempt	—	Contempt
Sadness	Sadness	Sadness	—
Interest	—	Anticipation	Interest
Guilt	—	—	—
—	—	Acceptance	—
—	—	—	Distress

Universal facial expressions of emotion

FIGURE 11.23

People everywhere can reliably identify at least six basic emotions: anger, happiness, disgust, surprise, sadness, and fear. Moreover, people from different cultures display similar facial expressions when experiencing particular emotions. Which emotions do you think are represented here?

From an evolutionary perspective, the idea of universal *facial* expressions makes adaptive sense because they signal others about our current emotional state (Ekman & Keltner, 1997) (FIGURE 11.23). Charles Darwin first advanced the evolutionary theory of emotion in 1872. He proposed that visible expressions of emotion evolved in different species because it increased survival value. For example, while fear helps animals avoid danger, visible expressions of anger and aggression are extremely adaptive when encountering a hostile intruder or fighting for mates or resources. Modern evolutionary theory suggests that basic emotions originate in the limbic system, which emerged evolutionarily much earlier than the higher brain areas responsible for thought (the cortex).

Studies with infants provide further support for an evolutionary basis for emotions. For example, infants only a few hours old show distinct expressions of emotion that closely match adult facial expressions (Field et al., 1982). And all infants, even those who are born deaf and blind, show similar facial expressions in similar situations (Field et al., 1982; Gelder et al., 2006). In addition, a recent study showed that families may have characteristic facial expressions, shared even by family members who have been blind from birth (Peleg et al., 2006). This collective evidence points to a strong biological evolutionary basis for emotional expression and interpretation.

How do we explain cultural differences in emotions? For example, in some cultures men greet one anther by hugging and kissing each another, but in others this expression is frowned on and men greet by shaking hands. Although we all seem to share similar facial expressions for some emotions, each culture has its own *display rules* governing how, when, and where to express emotions (Ekman, 1993, 2004; Fok et al., 2008). For instance, parents pass along their culture's specific display rules when they respond negatively to some emotions in their children, when they are sympathetic to some, and when they simply ignore others. Public physical contact is also governed by display rules. North Americans and Asians are less likely than people in other cultures to touch one another. For example, only the closest family and friends might hug in greeting or farewell. In contrast, Latin Americans and Middle Easterners often embrace and hold hands as a sign of casual friendship (Axtell, 1998, 2007).

THE POLYGRAPH AS A LIE DETECTOR: DOES IT WORK?

We've discussed the four major theories of emotion and how emotions are affected by culture and evolution. Now, we turn our attention to a topic of great interest to the general public and an important area of emotion research: the **polygraph**. This scientific instrument measures physiological responses, such as respiration, heart rate, and skin conductance (which increases during emotional arousal due to sweat gland activity). Given that we have less control over these physiological responses than over other behaviours, many people believe that when people lie, they feel guilty, fearful, and anxious. These feelings are then supposedly detected by the polygraph machine. *What a Psychologist Sees* describes how and if polygraphs work.

CONCEPT CHECK

How does the autonomic nervous system (ANS) respond to frightening or threatening stimuli?

What are the differences between the James-Lange theory and the Cannon-Bard theory of emotion?

Polygraph Testing

Do you believe that polygraph tests are a good way to determine if someone is lying? Some people believe the innocent have nothing to fear from a polygraph test. However, scientific research suggests otherwise (DeClue, 2003; Faigman et al., 1997; Iacono & Lykken, 1997). In fact, although proponents claim that polygraphs are 90 percent accurate or better, actual research findings report error rates ranging between 25 and 75 percent.

Traditional polygraph tests are based on the assumption that when people lie, they feel emotions—presumably anxiety and guilt. Special sensors supposedly detect these emotions by measuring sympathetic nervous system responses (**A** and **B**). Sounds good? The problem with the polygraph is that lying is only loosely related to anxiety and guilt, for a number of reasons. Some people become nervous even when they are telling the truth; certain words, such as *murder, slaughter,* and *cancer,* are emotionally arousing for most people; and some people can remain calm even when deliberately lying. A polygraph cannot tell which emotion is being felt (nervousness, excitement, sexual arousal, etc.) or whether a response is due to emotional arousal or something else. One study found that people could affect the outcome of a polygraph by about 50 percent simply by pressing their toes against the floor or biting their tongues (Honts & Kircher, 1994). For these reasons, polygraph results are not admissible in Canadian courts or in many jurisdictions of the United States.

Perhaps a more promising technique in evaluating lying is the use of brain scans, such as the functional magnetic resonance imaging (fMRI) (**C**). Unfortunately, this new lie-detection technique has some notable shortcomings and its own unique problems. So as far as accurately detecting lies is concerned, we are still quite a way from the truth in the matter.

A During a polygraph test, a band around the person's chest measures breathing rate, an arm cuff monitors blood pressure, and finger electrodes measure sweating, also called galvanic skin response (GSR).

B Note how the GSR rises sharply in response to the question, "Have you ever taken money from this bank?"

Measures of Autonomic Arousal

Respiration   GSR (Galvanic skin response)   Blood pressure/pulse

Have you ever falsified bank records?

Have you ever taken money from this bank?

Who is your supervisor?

What department do you work in?

C The three fMRI images show several research results suggesting specific areas of the cortex that appear to be most involved in lying versus telling the truth.

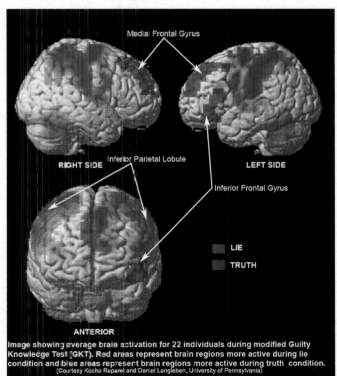

Medial Frontal Gyrus

RIGHT SIDE   Inferior Parietal Lobule   LEFT SIDE

Inferior Frontal Gyrus

LIE

TRUTH

ANTERIOR

Image showing average brain activation for 22 individuals during modified Guilty Knowledge Test (GKT). Red areas represent brain regions more active during lie condition and blue areas represent brain regions more active during truth condition.
(Courtesy Kosha Ruparel and Daniel Langleben, University of Pennsylvania)

1 Understanding Motivation

1. Because motivation and emotion are closely connected, they are often studied together.

2. Early theories of **motivation** focused on biological drives and **instincts**. The drive-reduction theory fell out of favour when it became clear that other factors must influence our motivations. A need for stimulation and novelty also motivates behaviour, as do social and cognitive factors, such as incentives, **attributions**, and expectations.

3. Maslow's **hierarchy of needs** theory takes a biopsychosocial approach. It prioritizes needs, with survival needs at the bottom and social and spiritual needs at the top. Although the theory has made important contributions and has intuitive appeal, some critics argue that it is poorly researched and biased toward Western individualism.

2 Motivated Behaviours

1. Hunger is a strong motivational drive, and both biological (stomach, biochemistry, the brain) and psychosocial (stimulus cues and cultural conditioning) factors affect hunger and eating. These same factors play a role in the pathological eating states of obesity, **anorexia nervosa**, and **bulimia nervosa**.

2. The human motivation for sex is evolutionarily powerful. Masters and Johnson first studied and described the **human sexual response cycle**: the series of physiological responses that occur during sexual arousal. Other sex research has focused on the roots of **sexual orientation**, and most studies suggest that genetics and biology play the dominant role.

3. The key to understanding what motivates high-achieving individuals lies in their high need for achievement (nAch), or **achievement motivation**, which is learned in early childhood, primarily through interactions with parents.

4. Providing **extrinsic motivation** (money, praise, or other incentives) for an intrinsically satisfying activity can undermine people's enjoyment and interest (**intrinsic motivation**) in the activity. This is especially true when extrinsic motivation is used to control—for example, when parents give children money or privileges for achieving good grades.

3 Theories and Concepts of Emotion

1. **Emotion** has physiological (brain and autonomic nervous system), cognitive (thoughts), and behavioural (expressive) components.

2. The four major theories of how the components of emotion interact are the **James-Lange, Cannon-Bard, facial-feedback,** and **Schachter's two-factor**. Each emphasizes different sequences or aspects of the three elements, and each has its limitations and makes specific contributions to our understanding of emotion.

3. Some researchers believe that there are 7 to 10 basic, universal emotions that are shared by people of all cultures. Research indicates that people around the world express and recognize these basic emotions in essentially the same way, supporting the evolutionary theory of emotion. Studies with infants add additional support. Although we all seem to share similar facial expressions for some emotions, display rules for emotions and for public physical contact vary across cultures.

4. **Polygraph** tests were originally designed to detect lying by measuring physiological signs of guilt and anxiety. As lying is only loosely related to these emotions, the results have been widely challenged and are not admissible in Canadian courts.

CRITICAL AND CREATIVE THINKING QUESTIONS

1. Do you think there are emotions that might be more a product of our evolved instincts (such as anger or fear), and other emotions that are more a product of our culture or society (such as guilt or embarrassment)? Is it possible to "learn" emotions from parents and elders?

2. In thinking about Maslow's hierarchy of needs, have you ever fulfilled certain higher-level needs without having sufficiently met lower-level needs?

3. Is obesity an eating disorder? Do you think it is more genetic than environmental, or more environmental than genetic? How do you think culture and historical time period influences eating and hunger?

4. Are intimate topics such as sexual pleasure, arousal, and orgasm the domain of psychological research? Does psychology go too far when it looks at such private and personal aspects of the human experience?

5. Same-sex marriage is legal in Canada. What do you think will be the long-term effects of these types of unions? Is Canada out-of-step or in-step with the rest of the world on this topic?

6. If you were going out on a date with someone or applying for an important job, how might you use the four theories of emotion to increase the chances that things will go well?

7. Have you ever felt depressed after listening to a friend complain about his or her problems? How might this be explained by the facial-feedback hypothesis?

8. Why do you think people around the world experience and express the same basic set of emotions? What evolutionary advantages might help explain these similarities?

What is happening in this picture ?

Curiosity is an important aspect of the human experience. Which of the six theories of motivation best explains this behaviour?

Why did curiosity evolve in ours and other species, and how might it be adaptive for an organism? Is it a limbic system or frontal lobe function?

(Check your answers in Appendix A.)

1. *Motivation* is **best** defined as _____ .
   a. an internal state that activates, directs, and maintains behaviour, usually toward a goal or away from an unfavourable situation
   b. the physiological and psychological arousal that occurs when a person really wants to achieve a goal
   c. being suitably stimulated to do something
   d. the conscious and unconscious thoughts that focus a person's behaviours and emotions toward a goal

2. What do we call the body's tendency to maintain a relatively stable state for internal processes?
   a. Homeostasis
   b. Heterogeneity
   c. Drive-induction
   d. Biostability

3. In which theory of motivation does need decrease once homeostasis occurs?
   a. drive-induction
   b. instinct
   c. drive-reduction
   d. achievement and satisfaction

4. The _____ theory says people are pulled by external stimuli to act a certain way.
   a. cognitive
   b. decentive
   c. hierarchy of needs (Maslow)
   d. incentive

5. After doing poorly on his psychology mid-term exam, Justin realized it was probably due to his lack of preparation and a very busy social life. Justin's thoughts reflect which type of cognitive process?
   a. an appraisal
   b. an attribution
   c. a cognition
   d. an incentive

6. The theory that lower motives must be satisfied before a person can advance to fulfilling higher motives is based on

   _____ .

   a. Freud's psychosexual stages of development
   b. Kohlberg's moral stages of development
   c. Erikson's psychosocial stages of development
   d. Maslow's hierarchy of needs

7. What term is used to describe the feelings of fullness after food has been ingested?
   a. homeostasis
   b. a belly full
   c. a bellyache
   d. satiety

8. A rat with a _____ lesion (damage) often refuses to eat, even to the point of starving.
   a. lateral hypothalamus (LH)
   b. distal hypothalamus (DH)
   c. ventromedial hypothalamus (VMH)
   d. hippocampal

9. _____ involves the consumption of large quantities of food followed by self-induced vomiting, the use of laxatives, or extreme exercise.
   a. Anorexia nervosa
   b. Binge-purge syndrome
   c. Bulimia nervosa
   d. Celebrity dieting

10. Label the **correct** sequence of events in Masters and Johnson's human sexual response cycle on the following figure.

b. _____

c. _____

a. _____   d. _____

11. _____ is the term used to describe the direction of a person's sexual attraction.
    a. Homosexuality
    b. Sexual orientation
    c. Human sexuality
    d. Heteroflexible

12. According to your textbook, the desire to excel, especially in competition with others, is known as _____.
    a. drive
    b. instincts
    c. achievement motivation
    d. all of the above

13. Extrinsic motivation is based on _____.
    a. the desire for rewards or threats of punishment
    b. the arousal motive
    c. the achievement motivation to please family and friends
    d. the satisfaction derived from personal enjoyment of a task

14. List the three components of emotion.
    a. positive, negative, and neutral
    b. perceiving, thinking, and acting
    c. cognitive, physiological, and behavioural
    d. active/passive, positive/negative, and direct/indirect

15. In a _____, as shown in the following figure, the cheek muscles are pulled back and the muscles around the eyes also contract.
    a. Madonna smile
    b. Duchenne smile
    c. Mona Lisa smile
    d. Da Vinci smile

16. While walking alone down a dark street, Jessica suddenly heard rapidly approaching footsteps from behind. Jessica's heart-rate immediately soared, her pulse quickened, and her breathing increased. She felt fear rising insider her. Which theory of emotion best captures Jessica's experience?
    a. the facial-feedback hypothesis
    b. Schachter's two-factor theory
    c. James-Lange's theory
    d. John Baird theory

17. Feeling mildly depressed for a few days, Jin decided to go for a walk. After being greeted by a few strangers with friendly smiles, to which she smiled back, Jin noticed a distinct improvement in her overall mood. What theory best explains the changes Jin experienced?
    a. The Duchenne smile effect
    b. Charles Darwin's theory of evolution
    c. Cannon-Bard's theory
    d. The facial-feedback hypothesis

18. According to _____, we look to external rather than internal cues to understand emotions.
    a. the Cannon-Bard theory
    b. the James-Lange theory
    c. the facial feedback hypothesis
    d. Schachter's two-factor theory

19. Researchers believe all our feelings can be condensed to _____ culturally universal emotions.
    a. 2 to 3
    b. 5 to 6
    c. 7 to 10
    d. 11 to 15

20. What is a polygraph test actually measuring?
    a. over-arousal
    b. guilt
    c. physiological responses
    d. lying

Personality

Consider the following personality description. How well does it describe you?

You have a strong need for other people to like and admire you. You tend to be critical of yourself. Although you have some personality weaknesses, you are generally able to compensate for them. At times, you have serious doubts about whether you have made the right decision or done the right thing. (Adapted from Ulrich, Stachnik, & Stainton, 1963.)

Does this sound like you? A high percentage of research participants who read a similar personality description reported that the description was "very accurate"—even after they were informed that it was a phony horoscope (Hyman, 1981). Other research shows that about three-quarters of adults read newspaper horoscopes and that many of them believe that these horoscopes were written especially for them (Halpern, 1998; Wyman & Vyse, 2008).

Why are such spurious personality assessments so popular? In part, it is because they seem to tap into our unique selves. However, the traits they supposedly reveal are characteristics that almost everyone shares. Do you know anyone who **doesn't** "have a strong need for other people to like and admire [them]"? The traits in horoscopes are also generally flattering, or at least neutral. In this chapter, rather than relying on these unscientific methods, we will focus on research-based methods used by psychologists to assess personality.

Unlike the pseudopsychologies offered in supermarket tabloids, newspaper horoscopes, and Chinese fortune cookies, the descriptions presented by personality researchers are based on empirical research. In this chapter, we examine the five most prominent theories and findings in personality research and discuss the techniques that psychologists use to assess personality.

NATIONAL GEOGRAPHIC

329

Trait Theories

Explain how early trait theorists approached the study of personality.

Identify the "Big Five" personality traits.

Summarize the major critiques of trait theory.

ersonality describes you as a person, how you are different from other people, and what patterns of behaviour are typical of you. You might qualify as an "extrovert," for example, if you are talkative and outgoing most of the time. Or you might be considered "conscientious" if you are responsible and self-disciplined most of the time.

The terms we use to describe other people (and ourselves) are called **traits**. Trait theorists are interested in discovering which traits best describe people and in measuring the degree of variation in traits within individuals and among people.

> ■ **personality**
> Relatively stable and enduring patterns of thoughts, feelings, and actions.

> ■ **traits** Relatively stable and consistent characteristics that can be used to describe someone.

EARLY TRAIT THEORISTS: ALLPORT, CATTELL, AND EYSENCK

An early study of dictionary terms found almost 4,500 words that described personality traits (Allport & Odbert, 1936). Faced with this enormous list, Gordon Allport (1937) believed that the best way to understand personality was to arrange a person's unique personality traits into a hierarchy, with the most pervasive or important traits at the top.

Later psychologists reduced the list of possible personality traits by using a statistical technique called **factor analysis**, in which large arrays of data are grouped into more basic units (factors). Raymond Cattell (1950, 1965, 1990) condensed the list of traits to between 30 and 35 basic characteristics. Hans Eysenck (1967, 1982, 1990) reduced the list even further: He described personality as a relationship among three basic types of traits: extroversion-introversion (E), neuroticism (N), and psychoticism (P).

THE FIVE-FACTOR MODEL: FIVE BASIC PERSONALITY TRAITS

Factor analysis was also used to develop the most promising modern trait theory, the **five-factor model (FFM)** (Costa, McCrae, & Martin, 2008; McCrae & Costa, 1990, 1999; McCrae & Sutin, 2007; Wood & Bell, 2008).

Combining previous research findings and the long list of possible personality traits, researchers discovered that five traits came up repeatedly, even when different tests were used.

These five major dimensions of personality are often dubbed the **Big Five**. As a handy way to remember the five factors, the first letters of each factor spell the word *ocean*. The Big Five are as follows:

> ■ **five-factor model (FFM)** The trait theory that explains personality in terms of the "Big Five" model, which is composed of openness, conscientiousness, extroversion, agreeableness, and neuroticism.

O *Openness.* People who score high in this factor are original, imaginative, curious, open to new ideas, artistic, and interested in cultural pursuits. Low scorers tend to be conventional, down-to-earth, narrower in their interests, and not artistic. Interestingly, critical thinkers tend to score higher than others on this factor (Clifford, Boufal, & Kurtz, 2004).

C *Conscientiousness.* This factor ranges from responsible, self-disciplined, organized, and achieving at the high end to irresponsible, careless, impulsive, lazy, and undependable at the other.

E *Extroversion.* This factor contrasts people who are sociable, outgoing, talkative, fun loving, and affectionate at the high end with introverted individuals who tend to be withdrawn, quiet, passive, and reserved at the low end.

A *Agreeableness.* Individuals who score high on this factor are good-natured, warm, gentle, cooperative, trusting, and helpful, whereas low scorers are irritable, argumentative, ruthless, suspicious, uncooperative, and vindictive.

N *Neuroticism* (or emotional stability). People who score high on neuroticism are emotionally unstable and prone to insecurity, anxiety, guilt, worry, and moodiness. People at the other end are emotionally stable, calm, even-tempered, easygoing, and relaxed.

Personality and your career FIGURE 12.1

Are some people better suited for certain jobs than others? According to psychologist John Holland's *personality–job fit theory,* a match (or "good fit") between our individual personality and our career choice is a major factor in determining job satisfaction (Holland, 1985, 1994). Research shows that a good fit between personality and occupation helps increase subjective well-being, job success, and job satisfaction. In other words, people tend to be happier and like their work when they're well matched to their jobs (Borchers, 2007; Donohue, 2006; Gottfredson & Duffy, 2008; Kieffer, Schinka, & Curtiss, 2004).

Love and the "Big Five"

Using the figure to the right, plot your personality profile by placing a dot on each line to indicate your degree of openness, conscientiousness, and so on. Do the same for a current, previous, or prospective boyfriend or girlfriend.

Now look at the two mate preferences lists below. David Buss and his colleagues (1989, 2003) surveyed more than 10,000 men and women from 37 countries and found a surprising level of agreement in the characteristics that men and women value in a mate. Moreover, most of the Big Five personality traits are found at the top of the list. Both men and women prefer dependability (conscientiousness), emotional stability (low neuroticism), pleasing disposition (agreeableness), and sociability (extroversion) to the alternatives. These findings may reflect an evolutionary advantage for people who are open, conscientious, extroverted, agreeable, and free of neuroses.

Big Five Traits	Low Scorers	High Scorers
1 **O**penness	Down-to-earth Uncreative Conventional Uncurious	Imaginative Creative Original Curious
2 **C**onscientiousness	Negligent Lazy Disorganized Late	Conscientious Hard-working Well-organized Punctual
3 **E**xtroversion	Loner Quiet Passive Reserved	Joiner Talkative Active Affectionate
4 **A**greeableness	Suspicious Critical Ruthless Irritable	Trusting Lenient Soft-hearted Good-natured
5 **N**euroticism	Calm Even-tempered Comfortable Unemotional	Worried Temperamental Self-conscious Emotional

Mate preferences around the world

In the two lists below, note how the top four desired traits are the same for both men and women, as well as how closely their desired traits match those of the five-factor model (FFM).

♂ What Men Want in a Mate

1. Mutual attraction—love
2. Dependable character
3. Emotional stability and maturity
4. Pleasing disposition
5. Good health
6. Education and intelligence
7. Sociability
8. Desire for home and children
9. Refinement, neatness
10. Good looks

♀ What Women Want in a Mate

1. Mutual attraction—love
2. Dependable character
3. Emotional stability and maturity
4. Pleasing disposition
5. Education and intelligence
6. Sociability
7. Good health
8. Desire for home and children
9. Ambition and industriousness
10. Refinement, neatness

Source: Buss et al., "International Preferences in Selecting Mates." *Journal of Cross-Cultural Psychology, 21*, pp. 5–47, 1990. Sage Publications, Inc.

Stop & Think

1. How do your personality traits compare with those of your boyfriend or girlfriend?
2. If your scores were noticeably different, what might explain the differences?

EVALUATING TRAIT THEORIES

The five-factor model is the first to achieve the major goal of trait theory—to describe and organize personality characteristics using the fewest number of traits. Critics argue, however, that the great variation seen in personalities cannot be accounted for by only five traits and that the Big Five model fails to offer causal explanations for these traits (Friedman & Schustack, 2006; Funder, 2000; Sollod, Monte, & Wilson, 2009).

Critics maintain that, in general, trait theories are good at describing personality, but they have difficulty explaining why people develop these traits or why personality traits differ across cultures. For example, trait theories do not explain why people in cultures that are geographically close tend to have similar personalities or why Europeans and North Americans tend to be higher in extroversion and openness to experience and lower in agreeableness than people in Asian and African cultures (Allik & McCrae, 2004).

In addition, some critics have faulted trait theories for their lack of specificity. Although trait theorists have documented a high level of personality stability after age 30 (**FIGURE 12.2**), they haven't identified which characteristics last a lifetime and which are most likely to change.

Finally, trait theorists have been criticized for ignoring the importance of situational and environmental effects on personality. In one example, psychologists Fred Rogosch and Dante Cicchetti (2004) found that abused and neglected children scored significantly lower in the traits of openness to experience, conscientiousness, and agreeableness and higher in the trait of neuroticism than did children who were not maltreated. Unfortunately, these maladaptive personality traits create significant liabilities that may trouble these children throughout their lifetimes.

Personality change over time FIGURE 12.2

Have you noticed how Madonna's public image and behaviour have changed over time? Cross-cultural research has found that neuroticism, extroversion, and openness to experience tend to decline from adolescence to adulthood, whereas agreeableness and conscientiousness increase (McCrae, Costa, Hrebíckova et al., 2004). How would you explain these changes? Do you think they're good or bad?

CONCEPT CHECK

What is the purpose of factor analysis?

What dimensions of personality are central to the five-factor model?

What are some weaknesses of trait theory?

Psychoanalytic/Psychodynamic Theories

LEARNING OBJECTIVES

Identify Freud's most basic and controversial contributions to the study of personality.

Explain how Adler's, Jung's, and Horney's theories differ from Freud's views.

Explore the major criticisms of Freud's psychoanalytic theories.

I n contrast to trait theories that describe personality as it exists, psychoanalytic (or psychodynamic) theories of personality attempt to explain individual differences by examining how unconscious mental forces interplay with thoughts, feelings, and actions. The founder of psychoanalytic theory is Sigmund Freud. We will examine Freud's theories in some detail and then briefly discuss three of his most influential followers.

FREUD'S PSYCHOANALYTIC THEORY: THE POWER OF THE UNCONSCIOUS

Who is the best-known figure in all of psychology? Most people immediately name Sigmund Freud, whose theories have been applied not only to psychology but also to anthropology, sociology, religion, medicine, art, and literature. Working from about 1890 until he died in 1939, Freud developed a theory of personality that has been one of the most influential—and most controversial—theories in all of science (Dufresne, 2007; Heller, 2005; Sollod et al., 2009). Let's examine some of Freud's most basic and debatable concepts.

Freud called the mind the "psyche" and asserted that it contains three **levels of consciousness**, or awareness: the **conscious**, the **preconscious**, and the **unconscious** (**FIGURE 12.3**).

conscious Freud's term for thoughts or motives that a person is currently aware of or is remembering.

preconscious Freud's term for thoughts or motives that can be easily brought to mind.

unconscious Freud's term for thoughts or motives that lie below a person's normal awareness but that can be made available through psychoanalysis.

Freud's three levels of consciousness FIGURE 12.3

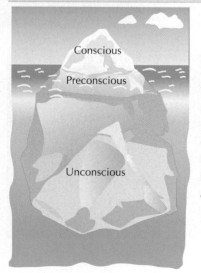

Freud compared people's conscious awareness—thoughts, feelings, and actions that we are actively aware of—to the tip of an iceberg, open to easy inspection. Beneath the conscious realm, and the water's surface, is the larger preconscious. It includes mental activities that we can access with little extra effort. The large, deeply submerged base of the iceberg is like the unconscious mind, hidden from personal inspection. According to Freud, the unconscious stores our primitive, instinctual motives and anxiety-laden memories and emotions, which are prevented from entering the conscious mind.

Freud believed that most psychological disorders originate from repressed memories and instincts (sexual and aggressive) that are hidden in the unconscious (**FIGURE 12.4**). To treat these disorders, Freud developed *psychoanalysis* (Chapter 14).

In addition to proposing that the mind functions at three levels of consciousness, Freud also thought that personality was composed of three mental structures: the id, the ego, and the superego (**FIGURE 12.5**).

According to Freud, the **id** is made up of innate, biological instincts and urges. It is immature, impulsive, and irrational. The id is also totally unconscious and serves as the reservoir of mental energy. When its primitive drives build up, the id seeks immediate gratification to relieve the tension—a concept known as the **pleasure principle**.

As a child grows older, the second part of the psyche—the ego—develops. The **ego** is responsible for planning, problem solving, reasoning, and controlling the potentially destructive energy of the id. In Freud's system, the ego corresponds to the *self*—our conscious identity of ourselves as persons.

One of the ego's tasks is to channel and release the id's energy in ways that are compatible with the external world. Thus, the ego is responsible for delaying gratification when necessary. Contrary to the id's pleasure principle, the ego operates according to the **reality principle** because it can understand and deal with objects and events in the "real world."

The final part of the psyche to develop is the **superego**, a set of ethical rules for behaviour. The superego develops from internalized parental and societal standards. It constantly strives for perfection and is therefore as unrealistic as the id. Some Freudian followers have suggested that the superego operates according to the **morality principle** because violating its rules results in feelings of guilt.

When the ego fails to satisfy both the id and the superego, anxiety slips into conscious awareness. Because anxiety is uncomfortable, people avoid it through **defence mechanisms**. For example, an alcoholic who uses his paycheque to buy drinks (a message from the id) may feel very guilty (a response from the superego). He may reduce this conflict by telling himself that he deserves a drink because he works so hard. This is an example of the defence mechanism **rationalization**.

defence mechanisms In Freudian theory, the ego's protective method of reducing anxiety by distorting reality.

Freudian slips FIGURE 12.4

Freud believed that a small slip of the tongue (known as a "Freudian slip") can reflect unconscious feelings that we normally keep hidden.

"Good morning, beheaded—uh, I mean beloved."

Freud's personality structure FIGURE 12.5

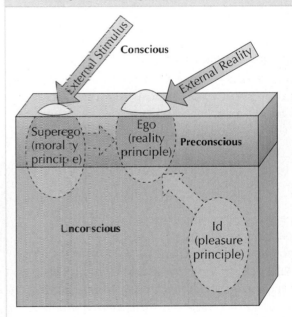

Defence Mechanism	Description	Example
Repression	Preventing painful or unacceptable thoughts from entering consciousness	Forgetting the details of your parent's painful death
Sublimation	Redirecting unmet desires or unacceptable impulses into acceptable activities	Rechannelling unacceptable desires into school, work, art, sports, or hobbies (e.g., joining a wrestling team, taking an art class to paint nude models)
Denial	Protecting oneself from an unpleasant reality by refusing to perceive it	Alcoholics refusing to admit their addiction
Rationalization	Substituting socially acceptable reasons for unacceptable ones	Justifying cheating on an exam by saying "everyone else does it"
Intellectualization	Ignoring the emotional aspects of a painful experience by focusing on abstract thoughts, words, or ideas	Emotionless discussion of your divorce while ignoring the underlying pain
Projection	Transferring unacceptable thoughts, motives, or impulses to others	Becoming unreasonably jealous of your mate while denying your own attraction to others
Reaction formation	Refusing to acknowledge unacceptable urges, thoughts, or feelings by exaggerating the opposite state	Promoting a petition against adults-only bookstores even though you are secretly aroused by pornography
Regression	Responding to a threatening situation in a way appropriate to an earlier age or level of development	Throwing a temper tantrum when a friend doesn't want to do what you'd like
Displacement	Redirecting impulses toward a less threatening person or object	Yelling at a co-worker after being criticized by your boss

Although Freud described many kinds of defence mechanisms (**STUDY ORGANIZER 12.1**), he believed that repression was the most important. **Repression** is the mechanism by which the ego prevents the most unacceptable, anxiety-provoking thoughts from entering consciousness (**FIGURE 12.6**).

The concept of defence mechanisms has generally withstood the test of time, and it is an accepted

Is it bad to use defence mechanisms?
FIGURE 12.6

Although defence mechanisms do distort reality, some misrepresentation seems to be necessary for our psychological well-being (Marshall & Brown, 2008; Wenger & Fowers, 2008). During a gruesome surgery, for example, physicians and nurses may **intellectualize** the procedure as an unconscious way of dealing with their personal anxieties. Can you see how focusing on highly objective technical aspects of the situation might help these people avoid becoming emotionally overwhelmed by the potentially tragic circumstances they often encounter?

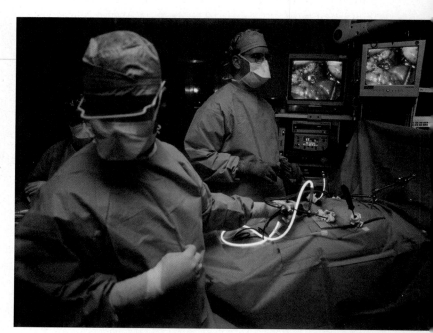

Freud's five psychosexual stages of development FIGURE 12.7

Name of Stage (Approximate Age)	Erogenous Zone (Key Conflict or Developmental Task)		Supposed Symptoms of Fixation and/or Regression
Oral (0–18 months)	**Mouth** (Weaning from breast or bottle)		Overindulgence reportedly contributes to gullibility ("swallowing" anything), dependence, and passivity. Underindulgence leads to aggressiveness, sadism, and a tendency to exploit others. Freud also believed orally fixated adults may orient their lives around their mouths—overeating, becoming alcoholic, smoking, or talking a great deal.
Anal (18 months–3 years)	**Anus** (Toilet training)		Fixation or regression supposedly leads to highly controlled and compulsively neat (anal-retentive) personality, or messy, disorderly, rebellious, and destructive (anal-expulsive) personality.
Phallic (3–6 years)	**Genitals** (Overcoming the Oedipus complex by identifying with same-sex parent)		According to Freud, unresolved, sexual longing for the opposite-sex parent can lead to long-term resentment and hostility toward the same-sex parent. Freud also believed that boys develop an **Oedipus complex,** or attraction to their mothers. He thought that young girls develop an attachment to their fathers and harbour hostile feelings toward their mothers, whom they blame for their lack of a penis. According to Freud most girls never overcome **penis envy** or give up their rivalry with their mothers, which leads to enduring moral inferiority.
Latency (6 years–puberty)	**None** (Interacting with same-sex peers)		The latency stage is a reported period of sexual "dormancy." Children do not have particular psychosexual conflicts that must be resolved during this period.
Genital (puberty–adult)	**Genitals** (Establishing intimate relationships with the opposite sex)		Unsuccessful outcomes at this stage supposedly may lead to sexual relationships based only on lustful desires, not on respect and commitment.

Psychosexual Development

psychosexual stages In Freudian theory, the five developmental periods (oral, anal, phallic, latency, and genital) during which particular kinds of pleasures must be gratified if personality development is to proceed normally.

part of modern psychology. However, this is not the case for Freud's theory of psychosexual stages of development.

According to Freud, strong biological urges residing within the id push all children through five universal **psychosexual stages** (FIGURE 12.7). The term *psychosexual* reflects Freud's

belief that children experience sexual feelings from birth (in different forms from those of adolescents or adults).

Freud held that if a child's needs are not met or are overindulged at one particular psychosexual stage, the child may become fixated, and a part of his or her personality will remain stuck at that stage. Furthermore, under stress, individuals may return (or regress) to a stage at which earlier needs were frustrated or overly gratified.

NEO-FREUDIAN/PSYCHODYNAMIC THEORIES: REVISING FREUD'S IDEAS

Some initial followers of Freud later rebelled and proposed theories of their own; they became known as **neo-Freudians**.

Alfred Adler (1870–1937) was the first to leave Freud's inner circle. Instead of seeing behaviour as motivated by unconscious forces, he believed that it is purposeful and goal-directed. According to Adler's **individual psychology**, we are motivated by our goals in life—especially our goals of obtaining security and overcoming feelings of inferiority.

Adler believed that almost everyone suffers from an **inferiority complex**, or deep feelings of inadequacy and incompetence that arise from our feelings of helplessness as infants. According to Adler, these early feelings result in a "will-to-power" that can take one of two paths. It can either cause children to strive to develop superiority over others through dominance, aggression, or expressions of envy, or—more positively—it can cause children to develop their full potential and creativity and to gain mastery and control in their lives (Adler, 1964, 1998) (FIGURE 12.8).

Another early Freud follower turned dissenter, Carl Jung (pronounced YOONG), developed **analytical psychology**. Like Freud, Jung (1875–1961) emphasized unconscious processes, but he believed that the unconscious contains positive and spiritual motives as well as sexual and aggressive forces.

Jung also believed that we have two forms of unconscious mind: the personal unconscious and the collective unconscious. The *personal unconscious* is created from our individual experiences, whereas the *collective unconscious* is identical in each person and is inherited (Jung, 1946, 1959, 1969). The collective unconscious consists of primitive images and patterns of thought, feeling, and behaviour that Jung called **archetypes** (FIGURE 12.9).

Because of archetypal patterns in the collective unconscious, we perceive and react in certain predictable ways. One set of archetypes refers to gender roles (Chapter 10). Jung claimed that both males and females have patterns for feminine aspects of personality (*anima*) and masculine aspects of personality (*animus*), which allow us to express both masculine and feminine personality traits and to understand the opposite sex.

An upside to feelings of inferiority? FIGURE 12.8

Adler suggested that the will-to-power could be positively expressed through social interest—identifying with others and cooperating with them for the social good. Can you explain how these volunteers might be fulfilling their will-to-power interest?

Archetypes in the collective unconscious
FIGURE 12.9

According to Jung, the collective unconscious is the ancestral memory of the human race, which explains the similarities in religion, art, symbolism, and dream imagery across cultures, such as the repeated symbol of the snake in ancient Egyptian tomb painting and early Australian aboriginal bark painting. Can you think of other such symbols?

Like Adler and Jung, psychoanalyst Karen Horney (pronounced HORN-eye) was an influential follower of Freud's who later came to reject major aspects of Freudian theory. She is remembered most for having developed a creative blend of Freudian, Adlerian, and Jungian theory, with added concepts of her own (Horney, 1939, 1945) (FIGURE 12.10).

Horney is also known for her theories of personality development. She believed that adult personality was shaped by the child's relationship to the parents—not by fixation at some stage of psychosexual development, as Freud argued. Horney believed that a child whose needs were not met by nurturing parents would experience extreme feelings of helplessness and insecurity. How people respond to this basic anxiety greatly determines emotional health.

According to Horney, everyone searches for security in one of three ways: We can move toward people (by seeking affection and acceptance from others); we can move away from people (by striving for independence, privacy, and self-reliance); or we can move against people (by trying to gain control and power over others). Emotional health requires a balance among these three styles.

Karen Horney (1885–1952) FIGURE 12.10

Horney argued that most of Freud's ideas about female personality reflected male biases and misunderstanding. She contended, for example, that Freud's concept of penis envy reflected women's feelings of cultural inferiority, not biological inferiority—*power envy*, not penis envy.

Evaluating psychoanalytic theories TABLE 12.1

Criticisms	• **Difficult to test.** From a scientific perspective, a major problem with psychoanalytic theory is that most of its concepts—such as the id or unconscious conflicts—cannot be empirically tested (Domhoff, 2004; Esterson, 2002; Friedman & Schustack, 2006). • **Overemphasizes biology and unconscious forces.** Modern psychologists believe that Freud did not give sufficient attention to learning and culture in shaping behaviour. • **Inadequate empirical support.** Freud based his theories almost exclusively on the subjective case histories of	his adult patients. Moreover, Freud's patients represented a small and selective sample of humanity: upper-class women in Vienna (Freud's home) who had serious adjustment problems. • **Sexism.** Many psychologists (beginning with Karen Horney) reject Freud's theories as derogatory toward women. • **Lack of cross-cultural support.** The Freudian concepts that ought to be most easily supported empirically—the biological determinants of personality—are generally not borne out by cross-cultural studies.
Enduring influences	• The emphasis on the unconscious and its influence on behaviour. • The conflict among the id, ego, and superego and the resulting defence mechanisms.	• Encouraging open talk about sex in Victorian times. • The development of psychoanalysis, an influential form of therapy. • The sheer magnitude of Freud's theory.

EVALUATING PSYCHOANALYTIC THEORIES: CRITICISMS AND ENDURING INFLUENCE

In this section, we look at major criticisms of Freud's psychoanalytic theories. In addition, we discuss the reasons that Freud has had enormous influence in the field of psychology. According to critics, Freud's theories are problematic for several reasons.

Today there are few Freudian purists. Instead, modern psychodynamic theorists and psychoanalysts use empirical methods and research findings to reformulate and refine traditional Freudian thinking (Knekt et al., 2008; Shaver & Mikulincer, 2005; Tryon, 2008; Westen, 1998).

But wrong as he was on many counts, Freud still ranks as one of the giants of psychology (Heller, 2005; Schülein, 2007; Sollod et al., 2009). Furthermore, Freud's impact on Western intellectual history cannot be overstated. He attempted to explain dreams, religion, social groupings, family dynamics, neurosis, psychosis, humour, the arts, and literature.

It's easy to criticize Freud if you forget that he began his work at the start of the twentieth century and lacked the benefit of modern research findings and technology. We can only imagine how our current theories will look 100 years from now. Right or wrong, Freud has a lasting place among the pioneers in psychology (**TABLE 12.1**).

CONCEPT CHECK

How do the conscious, preconscious, and unconscious shape personality, in Freud's view?

What is the collective unconscious?

What is an example of sexism in Freud's psychoanalytic theory?

Humanistic Theories

Explain the importance of the self in Rogers' theory of personality.

Describe how Maslow's hierarchy of needs affects personality.

Identify three criticisms of humanistic theories.

Humanistic theories of personality emphasize each person's internal feelings, thoughts, and sense of basic worth. In contrast to Freud, humanists believe that people are naturally good (or, at worst, neutral) and that they possess a positive drive toward self-fulfillment.

According to this view, our personality and behaviour depend on how we perceive and interpret the world, not on traits, unconscious impulses, or rewards and punishments. Humanistic psychology was developed largely by Carl Rogers and Abraham Maslow.

ROGERS' THEORY: THE IMPORTANCE OF THE SELF

To psychologist Carl Rogers (1902–1987), the most important component of personality is the **self**—what a person comes to identify as "I" or "me." Today, Rogerians (followers of Rogers) use the term **self-concept** to refer to all the information and beliefs you have regarding your own nature, unique qualities, and typical behaviours.

self-concept
Rogers' term for all the information and beliefs that individuals have about their own nature, qualities, and behaviour.

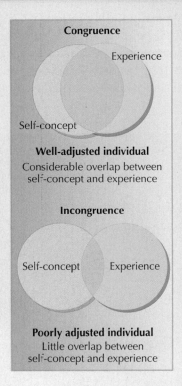

Congruence

Experience

Self-concept

Well-adjusted individual
Considerable overlap between self-concept and experience

Incongruence

Self-concept　　Experience

Poorly adjusted individual
Little overlap between self-concept and experience

Congruence, Mental Health, and Self-Esteem

According to Carl Rogers, mental health and adjustment are related to the degree of congruence between a person's self-concept and life experiences. He argued that self-esteem—how we feel about ourselves—is particularly dependent on this congruence. Can you see how an artistic child would likely have higher self-esteem if her family valued art highly than if they did not?

What a Psychologist Sees

Rogers was very concerned with the match between a person's self-concept and his or her actual experiences with life. He believed that poor mental health and maladjustment developed from a mismatch, or incongruence, between the self-concept and actual life experiences.

Rogers argued that mental health, congruence, and self-esteem are part of our innate, biological capacities. In his view, everyone naturally approaches and values people and experiences that enhance our growth and fulfillment and avoids those that do not. Therefore, Rogers believed that we should trust our feelings to guide us toward mental health and happiness. (See *What a Psychologist Sees*.)

Then why do some people have low self-esteem and poor mental health? Rogers believed that these outcomes generally result from early childhood experiences with parents and other adults who make their love conditional. That is, children learn that their acceptance is conditional on behaving in certain ways and expressing only certain feelings.

If children learn over time that their negative feelings and behaviours (which we all have) are unacceptable and unlovable, their self-concept and self-esteem may become distorted. They may always doubt the love and approval of others because others don't know "the real person hiding inside."

To help children develop to their fullest potential, adults need to create an atmosphere of **unconditional positive regard**—a setting in which children realize that they will be accepted no matter what they say or do.

Some people mistakenly believe that unconditional positive regard means that we should allow people to do whatever they please. But humanists separate the value of the person from his or her behaviours. They accept the person's positive nature while discouraging destructive or hostile behaviours. Humanistic psychologists believe in guiding children to control their behaviour so that they can develop a healthy self-concept and healthy relationships with others (**FIGURE 12.11**).

■ **unconditional positive regard** Rogers' term for positive behaviour toward a person with no contingencies attached.

MASLOW'S THEORY: IN PURSUIT OF SELF-ACTUALIZATION

Like Rogers, Abraham Maslow believed that there is a basic goodness to human nature and a natural tendency toward **self-actualization**. He saw personality as the quest to fulfill basic physiological needs (including safety, belonging and love, and esteem) and then move upward toward the highest level of self-actualization.

According to Maslow, self-actualization is the inborn drive to develop all one's talents and capacities. It involves understanding one's own potential, accepting oneself and others as unique individuals, and taking a problem centred approach to life situations (Maslow, 1970).

Conditional love? FIGURE 12.11

If a child is angry and hits his younger sister, some parents might punish the child or deny his anger, saying, "Nice children don't hit their sisters; they love them!" To gain parental approval, the child has to deny his true feelings of anger, but inside he secretly suspects he is not a "nice boy" because he did hit his sister and (at that moment) did not love her. How might repeated incidents of this type have a lasting effect on someone's self-esteem? What would be a more appropriate response to the child's behaviour that acknowledges that it is the behaviour that is unacceptable, not the child that is unacceptable?

Self-actualization is an ongoing process of growth rather than an end product or accomplishment.

Maslow believed that only a few, rare individuals, such as Albert Einstein, Mohandas Gandhi, and Eleanor Roosevelt, become fully self-actualized. However, he saw self-actualization as part of every person's basic hierarchy of needs. (See Chapter 11 for more information on Maslow's theory.)

EVALUATING HUMANISTIC THEORIES: THREE MAJOR CRITICISMS

Humanistic psychology was extremely popular during the 1960s and 1970s. It was seen as a refreshing new perspective on personality after the negative determinism of the psychoanalytic approach and the mechanical nature of learning theories (Chapter 6). Although this early popularity has declined, many humanistic ideas have been incorporated into approaches to counselling and psychotherapy.

At the same time, humanistic theories have also been criticized (e.g., Funder, 2000). Three of the most important criticisms are the following:

1. *Naïve assumptions.* Critics suggest that the humanists are unrealistic, romantic, and even naïve about human nature (**FIGURE 12.12**).

2. *Poor testability and inadequate evidence.* As is the case with many psychoanalytic terms and concepts, humanistic concepts (such as unconditional positive regard and self-actualization) are difficult to define operationally and to test scientifically.

3. *Narrowness.* Like trait theories, humanistic theories have been criticized for merely describing personality rather than explaining it. For example, where does the motivation for self-actualization come from? To say that it is an "inborn drive" doesn't satisfy those who favour using experimental research and hard data to learn about personality.

Are all people as inherently good as they say? FIGURE 12.12

Humankind's continuing history of murders, warfare, and other acts of aggression suggests otherwise.

CONCEPT CHECK ✓

How are self-concept and self-esteem linked in Rogers' theory?

What is self-actualization?

What criticism of humanistic theories is also a weakness of trait theories?

Social-Cognitive Theories

LEARNING OBJECTIVES

Explain Bandura's concepts of self-efficacy and reciprocal determinism and how they affect personality.

Describe the role that Rotter's concept of locus of control plays in personality.

Summarize the attractions and criticisms of the social-cognitive perspective on personality.

According to the social-cognitive perspective, each of us has a unique personality because we have individual histories of interactions with the environment (social) and because we think (cognitive) about the world and interpret what happens to us (Cervone & Shoda, 1999). Two of the most influential social-cognitive theorists are Albert Bandura and Julian Rotter.

BANDURA'S AND ROTTER'S APPROACHES: SOCIAL LEARNING PLUS COGNITIVE PROCESSES

Canadian-born Albert Bandura (also discussed in Chapter 6) has played a major role in reintroducing thought processes into personality theory. Cognition, or thought, is central to his concept of **self-efficacy** (Bandura, 1997, 2000, 2006, 2008).

self-efficacy Bandura's term for the learned belief that one is capable of producing desired results, such as mastering new skills and achieving personal goals.

According to Bandura, if you have a strong sense of self-efficacy, you believe you can generally succeed, regardless of past failures and current obstacles. Your self-efficacy will in turn affect which challenges you choose to accept and the effort you expend in reaching goals. However, Bandura emphasized that self-efficacy is always specific to the situation—it does not necessarily carry across situations. For example, self-defence training significantly improves women's belief that they could escape from or disable a potential assailant, but it does not lead them to feel more capable in all areas of their lives (Weitlauf et al., 2001). Finally, according to Bandura's concept of **reciprocal determinism**, self-efficacy beliefs will affect how others respond to you, influencing your chances for success (**FIGURE 12.13**). Thus, a cognition ("I can succeed") will affect behaviours ("I will work hard and ask for a promotion"), which in turn will affect the environment ("My employer recognized my efforts and promoted me").

reciprocal determinism Bandura's belief that cognitions, behaviours, and the environment interact to produce personality.

Julian Rotter's theory is similar to Bandura's in that it suggests that learning experiences create **cognitive expectancies** that guide behaviour and influence the environment (Rotter, 1954, 1990). According to Rotter, your behaviour or personality is determined by (1) what you expect to happen following a specific action and (2) the reinforcement value attached to specific outcomes.

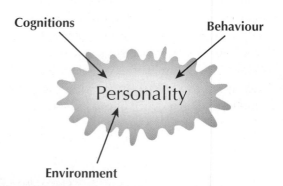

Albert Bandura's theory of reciprocal determinism FIGURE 12.13

According to Bandura, thoughts (or cognitions), behaviour, and the environment all interact to produce personality.

"We're encouraging people to become involved in their own rescue."

Locus of control and achievement
FIGURE 12.14

Research links possession of an internal locus of control with higher achievement and better mental health (Burns, 2008; Jones, 2008; Ruthig et al., 2007). What might this connection imply for human survival?

To understand your personality and behaviour, Rotter would want to know your expectancies and what you see as the source of life's rewards and punishments. To gain this information, Rotter would use personality tests that measure your internal versus external **locus of control** (Chapter 3). Rotter's tests ask people to respond to such statements as "People get ahead in this world primarily by luck and connections rather than by hard work and perseverance," and "When someone doesn't like you, there is little you can do about it." As you may suspect, people with an external locus of control think that environment and external forces have primary control over their lives, whereas people with an internal locus of control think that they can control events in their lives through their own efforts (**FIGURE 12.14**).

EVALUATING SOCIAL-COGNITIVE THEORY: THE PLUSES AND MINUSES

The social-cognitive perspective holds several attractions. First, it emphasizes how the environment affects and is affected by individuals. Second, it offers testable, objective hypotheses and operationally defined terms, and it relies on empirical data for its basic principles. However, critics note that social-cognitive theory ignores the unconscious and emotional aspects of personality (Mischel, Shoda, & Ayduk, 2008; Westen, 1998). For example, certain early experiences might have prompted a person to develop an external locus of control.

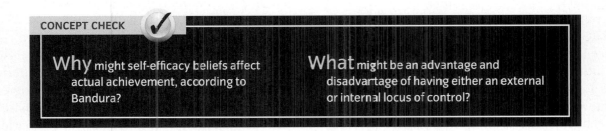

CONCEPT CHECK

Why might self-efficacy beliefs affect actual achievement, according to Bandura?

What might be an advantage and disadvantage of having either an external or internal locus of control?

Biological Theories

LEARNING OBJECTIVES

Summarize the roles that brain structures and neurochemistry play in personality.

Describe how researchers study genetic influences on personality.

Describe how the biopsychosocial model integrates different theories of personality.

In this section, we explore how inherited biological factors influence our personalities. We conclude with a discussion of how all theories of personality ultimately interact within the *biopsychosocial model*.

THREE MAJOR CONTRIBUTORS TO PERSONALITY: THE BRAIN, NEUROCHEMISTRY, AND GENETICS

Modern biological research suggests that certain brain areas may contribute to some personality traits. For instance, increased electroencephalographic (EEG) activity in the left frontal lobes of the brain is associated with sociability (or extroversion), whereas greater EEG activity in the right frontal lobes is associated with shyness (introversion) (Tellegen, 1985).

A major limitation of research on brain structures and personality is the difficulty in identifying which structures are uniquely connected with particular personality traits. Neurochemistry seems to offer more precise data on how biology influences personality (Kagan & Fox, 2006).

For example, sensation seeking (Chapter 11) has consistently been linked with levels of monoamine oxidase (MAO), an enzyme that regulates levels of neurotransmitters, such as dopamine (Ibáñez, Blanco, & Sáiz-Ruiz, 2002; Zuckerman, 1994, 2004). Dopamine also seems to be correlated with novelty seeking and extroversion (Dalley et al., 2007; Lang et al., 2007; Levinthal, 2008).

How can neurochemistry have such effects? Studies suggest that high-sensation seekers and extroverts tend to experience less physical arousal from the same stimulus than do introverts (Lissek & Powers, 2003). Extroverts' low arousal apparently motivates them to seek out situations that will elevate their arousal. Moreover, it is believed that a higher arousal threshold is genetically transmitted. In other words, personality traits like sensation seeking and extroversion may be inherited.

Finally, psychologists have recently recognized that genetic factors also have an important influence on personality (Johnson, McGue, et al., 2004; Murakami & Hayashi, 2002; Plomin & Crabbe, 2000; Sequeira et al., 2004). This relatively new area, called **behavioural genetics**, attempts to determine the extent to which behavioural differences among people are due to genetics as opposed to environment (Chapter 2).

One way to measure genetic influences is to compare similarities in personality between identical twins and fraternal twins. For example, studies of the heritability of the five-factor model personality traits suggest that genetic factors contribute about 40 to 50 percent of personality (Bouchard, 1997; Eysenck, 1967, 1990; Jang et al., 2006; McCrae, Costa, Martin, et al., 2004; Plomin, 1990; Weiss, Bates, & Luciano, 2008).

In addition to twin studies, researchers compare the personalities of parents with those of their biological children and their adopted children. Studies of extroversion and neuroticism have found that parents' traits correlate moderately with those of their biological children and hardly at all with those of their adopted children (Bouchard, 1997; McCrae et al., 2000).

At the same time, researchers are careful not to overemphasize genetic influences on personality (Deckers, 2005; Funder, 2001; Sollod et al., 2009). Some researchers believe that the importance of the nonshared environment (aspects of the environment that differ from one individual to another, even within a family) has been overlooked (Saudino, 1997). Others fear that research on "genetic determinism"—do our genes determine who we are?—could be misused to "prove" that an ethnic or racial group is inferior, that male dominance is natural, or that social progress is impossible. In short, they worry that an emphasis on genetic determinants of personality and behaviour may lead people to see themselves as merely "victims" of their genes. Clearly, genetics have produced exciting

Source: Bouchard, 1997, 2004; Eysenck, 1967, 1990; Jang et al., 2006; McCrae et al., 2004; Plomin, 1990; Weiss et al. 2008.

Multiple Influences on Personality

What gives a person certain personality characteristics, such as shyness or conscientiousness or aggressiveness? As shown in the figure here, research indicates that four major factors overlap to influence personality. These include genetic (inherited) factors; nonshared environmental factors, or how each individual's genetic factors react and adjust to his or her particular environment; shared environmental factors, involving parental patterns and shared family experiences; and error or unidentified factors or problems with testing.

For example, Hans Eysenck (1990) believed that certain traits (like introversion and extroversion) may reflect inherited patterns of cortical arousal, as well as social learning, cognitive processes, and the environment. Can you see how someone with an introverted personality (and therefore a higher level of cortical arousal) might try to avoid excessive stimulation by seeking friends and jobs with low stimulation levels? Eysenck's work exemplifies how trait, biological, and social-cognitive theories can be combined to provide better insight into personality—the *biopsychosocial model*.

 Stop & Think
1. Can you identify one key inherited influence and one major environmental influence on your personality?
2. What kind of jobs would an individual with an extroverted personality be most likely to choose?

and controversial results. However, more research is necessary before a cohesive biological theory of personality can be constructed.

THE BIOPSYCHOSOCIAL MODEL: PULLING THE PERSPECTIVES TOGETHER

No one personality theory explains everything we need to know about personality or the rich diversity seen across our species. Each theory offers different insights into how a person develops the distinctive set of characteristics we call "personality." That's why instead of adhering to any one theory, many psychologists believe in the biopsychosocial approach, or the idea that several factors—biological, psychological, and social—overlap in their contributions to personality (Mischel et al., 2008).

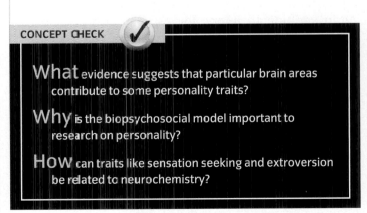

CONCEPT CHECK ✓

What evidence suggests that particular brain areas contribute to some personality traits?

Why is the biopsychosocial model important to research on personality?

How can traits like sensation seeking and extroversion be related to neurochemistry?

Personality Assessment

Identify the major methods that psychologists use to assess personality, and explore the benefits and limitations of each.

Summarize the major features of objective personality tests.

Explain why psychologists use projective tests to assess personality.

Numerous methods have been used over the decades to assess personality. Modern personality assessments are used by clinical and counselling psychologists, psychiatrists, and others for diagnosing psychotherapy patients and for assessing their progress in therapy. Personality assessment is also used for educational and vocational counselling and to aid businesses in making hiring decisions. Personality assessments can be grouped into a few broad categories: interviews, observations, objective tests, and projective tests.

INTERVIEWS AND OBSERVATION

We all use informal "interviews" to get to know other people. When first meeting someone, we usually ask about his or her job, academic interests, family, or hobbies. Psychologists also use interviews. Unstructured interviews are often used for job and college selection and for diagnosing psychological problems. In an unstructured format, interviewers get impressions and pursue hunches or let the interviewee expand on information that promises to disclose personality characteristics. In structured interviews, the interviewer asks specific questions so that the interviewee's responses can be evaluated more objectively (and compared with the responses of others).

In addition to interviews, psychologists also assess personality by directly and methodically observing behaviour. The psychologist looks for examples of specific behaviours and follows a careful set of evaluation guidelines. For instance, a psychologist might arrange to observe a troubled client's interactions with his or her family. Does the client become agitated by the presence of certain family members and not others? Does he or she become passive and withdrawn when asked a direct question? Through careful observation, the psychologist gains valuable insights into the client's personality as well as family dynamics (**FIGURE 12.15**).

Behavioural observation FIGURE 12.15

How might careful observation help a psychologist better understand a troubled client's personality and family dynamics?

OBJECTIVE TESTS

Objective personality tests, or inventories, are the most widely used method of assessing personality, for two reasons. They can be administered to a large number of people relatively quickly and the tests can be evaluated in a standardized fashion.

> **objective personality tests** Standardized questionnaires that require written responses, usually to multiple-choice or true-false questions.

An older and no longer used method of assessing personality is described in **FIGURE 12.16**.

Some objective tests measure one specific personality trait, such as sensation seeking (Chapter 11) or locus of control. However, psychologists in clinical, counselling, and industrial settings often wish to assess a range of personality traits. To do so, they generally use multitrait (or *multiphasic*) inventories.

The most widely studied and clinically used multitrait test is the **Minnesota Multiphasic Personality Inventory (MMPI)**—or its revision, the MMPI-2 (Butcher, 2000, 2005; Butcher & Perry, 2008). This test consists of over 500 statements that participants respond to with *true, false,* or *cannot say*. The following are examples of the kinds of statements found on the MMPI:

> My stomach frequently bothers me.
>
> I have enemies who really wish to harm me.
>
> I sometimes hear things that other people can't hear.
>
> I would like to be a mechanic.
>
> I have never indulged in any unusual sex practices.

Did you notice that some of these questions are about very unusual, abnormal behaviour? Although the full MMPI includes many "normal" questions, the test is designed primarily to help clinical and counselling psychologists diagnose psychological disorders. MMPI test items are grouped into 10 clinical scales, each measuring a different disorder (**TABLE 12.2**). There are also a number of validity scales designed to reflect the extent to which respondents (1) distort their answers (for example, to fake psychological disturbances or to appear more psychologically healthy than they really are), (2) do not understand the items, and (3) are being uncooperative. Another well-known and well-researched test that also focuses on

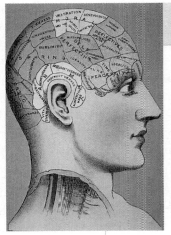

Personality and bumps on the head?
FIGURE 12.16

In the 1800s, if you wanted to have your personality assessed, you would go to a phrenologist, who would determine your personality by measuring bumps on your skull and by comparing the measurements with a chart that associated different areas of the skull with particular traits, such as *sublimity* (the ability to squelch natural impulses, especially sexual) and *ideality* (the ability to live by high ideals). What traits might be measured if we still believed in phrenology today?

psychological disorders is the Dimensional Assessment of Personality Pathology, developed by John Livesley and colleagues at the University of British Columbia. This measure assesses 18 personality traits, such as anxiety, suspiciousness, oppositionality, and so on (Livesley & Jackson, 2002).

There are many other objective personality measures that are less focused on psychological disorders. Some good examples include the NEO Personality Inventory-Revised (Costa & McRae, 1992), which assesses the dimensions comprising the five-factor model (discussed earlier in this chapter), and the Jackson Personality Inventory-Revised (Jackson, 1997), developed by Douglas N. Jackson at the University of Western Ontario.

One personality test with which you may be familiar is the Myers-Briggs Type Indicator (MBTI). This measure assesses four dimensions derived from Carl Jung's theory of personality: extroversion-introversion (EI), sensing-intuition (SI), thinking-feeling (TF), and

Subscales of the MMPI-2 TABLE 12.2

Clinical scales	Typical interpretations of high scores	Validity scales	Typical interpretations of high scores
1. Hypochondriasis	Numerous physical complaints	1. L (lie)	Denies common problems, projects a "saintly" or false picture
2. Depression	Seriously depressed and pessimistic		
3. Hysteria	Suggestible, immature, self-centred, demanding	2. F (confusion)	Answers are contradictory
4. Psychopathic deviate	Rebellious, nonconformist	3. K (defensiveness)	Minimizes social and emotional complaints
5. Masculinity–femininity	Interests like those of other sex		
6. Paranoia	Suspicious and resentful of others	4. ? (cannot say)	Many items left unanswered
7. Psychasthenia	Fearful, agitated, brooding		
8. Schizophrenia	Withdrawn, reclusive, bizarre thinking		
9. Hypomania	Distractible, impulsive, dramatic		
10. Social introversion	Shy, introverted, self-effacing		

judging-perceiving (JP). The MBTI has gained huge popularity among the general public and has been used in assessments as varied as career counselling, hiring executives, and even assigning college roommates (Flett, 2007). Despite its popular use, however, questions have been raised about the MBTI's test-retest reliability (i.e., whether an individual will obtain the same pattern of scores when taking the test a second time) and its validity for psychological assessments (Flett, 2007; Hunsley & Lee, 2010; Pittenger, 2005).

PROJECTIVE TESTS

> **projective tests**
> Psychological tests that use ambiguous stimuli, such as inkblots or drawings, which allow the test taker to project his or her unconscious thoughts onto the test material.

Unlike objective tests, **projective tests** use unstructured stimuli that can be perceived in many ways. As the name implies, projective tests supposedly allow each person to project his or her own unconscious conflicts, psychological defences, motives, and personality traits onto the test materials. Because

respondents may be unable (or unwilling) to express their true feelings if asked directly, the ambiguous stimuli purportedly provide an indirect "psychological X-ray" of important unconscious processes (Hogan, 2003). Two of the most widely used projective tests are the **Rorschach Inkblot Test** and the **Thematic Apperception Test (TAT)** (FIGURE 12.17).

ARE PERSONALITY MEASUREMENTS ACCURATE?

Let's evaluate the strengths and the challenges of each of the four methods of personality assessment: interviews, observation, objective tests, and projective tests.

Interviews and Observations Interviews and observations can provide valuable insights into personality, but they are time-consuming and expensive. Furthermore, raters of personality tests frequently disagree in their evaluations of the same individuals. Interviews and observations also involve unnatural settings, and, in fact, the very presence of an observer can alter a subject's behaviour.

Visualizing

Projective tests FIGURE 12.17

Responses to projective tests reportedly reflect unconscious parts of the personality that "project" onto the stimuli.

A The Rorschach Inkblot Test was ▶ introduced in 1921 by Swiss psychiatrist Hermann Rorschach. With this technique, individuals are shown 10 inkblots like this, one at a time, and are asked to report what figures or objects they see in each of them.

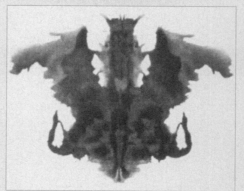

Reproduced with permission. This inkblot is not part of the Rorschach test.

B Created by personality researcher Henry Murray in 1938, the Thematic ▶ Apperception Test (TAT) consists of a series of ambiguous black-and-white pictures that are shown to the test taker, who is asked to create a story related to each. Can you think of two different stories that a person might create for the picture of two women here? How might a psychologist interpret each story?

Objective Tests Tests like the MMPI-2 provide specific, objective information about a broad range of personality traits in a relatively short period. However, they are also the subject of at least three major criticisms:

1. *Deliberate deception and social desirability bias.* Some items on personality inventories are easy to "see through," so respondents may intentionally, or unintentionally, fake particular personality traits. In addition, some respondents want to look good and will answer questions in ways that they perceive to be socially desirable. (The validity scales of the MMPI-2 are designed to help prevent these problems.)

2. *Diagnostic difficulties.* When inventories are used for diagnosis, overlapping items sometimes make it difficult to pinpoint a diagnosis (Graham, 1991). In addition, clients with severe disorders sometimes score within the normal range, and normal clients sometimes score within the elevated range (Gregory, 2007; Weiner, 2008).

3. *Cultural bias and inappropriate use.* Some critics think that the standards for "normalcy" on objective tests fail to recognize the impact of culture. For example, Latinos generally score higher than respondents from North American and Western European cultures on the masculinity-femininity scale of the MMPI-2 (Dana, 2005; Lucio et al., 2001; Lucio-Gómez et al., 1999). However, this tendency reflects traditional gender roles and cultural training more than any individual personality traits.

Projective Tests Although projective tests are extremely time-consuming to administer and interpret, their proponents suggest that because they are unstructured, respondents may be more willing to talk honestly about sensitive topics. Critics point out, however, that the reliability and validity (Chapter 8) of projective tests are among the lowest of all tests of personality (Garb et al., 2005; Gacono et al., 2008; Grove et al., 2002; Wood et al., 2001).

What would the effects be if the stimuli used in projective tests became widely known? In June 2009, an emergency room physician in Moose Jaw, Saskatchewan upset many psychologists around the world by posting all 10 Rorschach images on the Wikipedia website. Shortly thereafter, another individual posted the most common responses given for each image (CBC News, 2009b; Kyle, 2009). Critics claimed that publicizing the test and responses likely invalidates it for future use, by influencing how people will respond to the images. What do you think? Would revealing the content and common answers make the test less valid as a measure of personality?

As you can see, each of the four methods of personality assessment has its limits. Psychologists typically combine the results from various methods to create a full picture of an individual's personality.

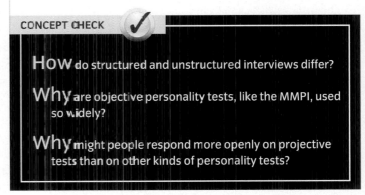

CONCEPT CHECK ✓

How do structured and unstructured interviews differ?

Why are objective personality tests, like the MMPI, used so widely?

Why might people respond more openly on projective tests than on other kinds of personality tests?

SUMMARY

1 Trait Theories

1. Psychologists define **personality** as an individual's relatively stable and enduring patterns of thoughts, feelings, and actions.

2. Allport believed that the best way to understand personality was to arrange a person's unique personality **traits** into a hierarchy. Cattell and Eysenck later reduced the list of possible personality traits by using **factor analysis**.

3. According to the **five-factor model (FFM)**, the five major dimensions of personality are openness, conscientiousness, extroversion, agreeableness, and neuroticism.

2 Psychoanalytic/ Psychodynamic Theories

1. Freud, the founder of psychodynamic theory, believed that the mind contained three levels of consciousness: the **conscious,** the **preconscious,** and the **unconscious.** He believed that most psychological disorders originate from unconscious memories and instincts. Freud also asserted that personality was composed of the **id,** the **ego,** and the **superego.** When the ego fails to satisfy both the id and the superego, anxiety slips into conscious awareness, which triggers **defence mechanisms.** Freud outlined a sequence of five **psychosexual stages:** oral, anal, phallic, latency, and genital.

2. **Neo-Freudians,** such as Adler, Jung, and Horney, were influential followers of Freud who later came to reject major aspects of Freudian theory and develop their own approaches. Today, few

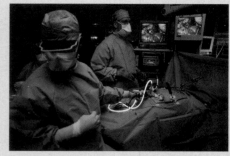

Freudian purists remain, but Freud's impact on psychology and on Western intellectual history cannot be overstated.

3 Humanistic Theories

1. According to Rogers, mental health and self-esteem are related to the degree of congruence between our **self-concept** and life experiences. He argued that poor mental health results when young children do not receive unconditional **positive regard** from caregivers.

2. Maslow saw personality as the quest to fulfill basic physiological needs and to move toward the highest level of **self-actualization.**

4 Social-Cognitive Theories

1. Cognition is central to Bandura's concept of self-efficacy. According to Bandura, **self-efficacy** affects the challenges we choose to accept and the effort we expend in reaching goals. His concept of **reciprocal determinism** holds that self-efficacy beliefs will also affect others' responses to us.

2. Rotter's theory suggests that learning experiences create cognitive expectancies that guide behaviour and influence the environment. Rotter believed that having an internal versus external locus of control affects personality and achievement.

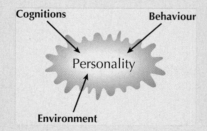

5 Biological Theories

1. There is evidence that certain brain areas may contribute to personality. However, neurochemistry seems to offer more precise data on how biology influences personality. Research in behavioural genetics indicates that genetic factors may also strongly influence personality.

2. Instead of adhering to any one theory of personality, many psychologists believe in the biopsychosocial approach—the idea that several factors overlap in their contributions to personality.

6 Personality Assessment

1. In an unstructured interview format, interviewers get impressions, pursue hunches, and let the interviewee expand on information that promises to disclose personality characteristics. In structured interviews, the interviewer asks specific questions so that the interviewee's responses can be evaluated more objectively.

Psychologists also assess personality by directly observing behaviour.

2. **Objective personality tests** are widely used because they can be administered broadly and relatively quickly, and because they can be evaluated in a standardized fashion. To assess a range of personality traits, psychologists use multitrait inventories, such as the MMPI.

3. **Projective tests** use unstructured stimuli that can be perceived in many ways. Projective tests are thought to allow individuals to project their own unconscious conflicts, psychological defences, motives, and personality traits onto the test materials.

KEY TERMS

- analytical psychology p. 338
- archetypes p. 338
- behavioural genetics p. 346
- Big Five p. 330
- cognitive expectancies p. 344
- conscious p. 334
- defence mechanisms p. 355
- ego p. 335
- factor analysis p. 330
- five-factor model (FFM) p. 330
- id p. 335

- individual psychology p. 338
- inferiority complex p. 338
- intellectualization p. 336
- levels of consciousness p. 334
- locus of control p. 345
- Minnesota Multiphasic Personality Inventory (MMPI) p. 349
- morality principle p. 335
- neo-Freudians p. 338
- objective personality tests p. 348

- Oedipus complex p. 337
- penis envy p. 337
- personality p. 330
- pleasure principle p. 335
- preconscious p. 334
- projective tests p. 350
- psychosexual stages p. 337
- rationalization p. 335
- reality principle p. 335
- reciprocal determinism p. 344
- repression p. 336

- Rorschach Inkblot Test p. 350
- self p. 341
- self-actualization p. 342
- self-concept p. 341
- self-efficacy p. 344
- superego p. 335
- Thematic Apperception Test (TAT) p. 350
- traits p. 330
- unconditional positive regard p. 342
- unconscious p. 334

CRITICAL AND CREATIVE THINKING QUESTIONS

1. How do you think you would score on each of the "Big Five" personality dimensions?

2. Think of Freud's defence mechanisms. Have you ever noticed any of these operating in your family members or friends?

3. If scientists have so many problems with Freud, why do you think his theories are still popular with the public? Should psychologists continue to discuss his theories (and include them in textbooks)? Why or why not?

4. In what ways is Adler's individual psychology more optimistic than Freud's theory?

5. What do you think of Rogers' notion of unconditional positive regard? How might parents discipline their children for misbehaving, yet still maintain unconditional positive regard toward them?

6. How do Bandura's and Rotter's social-cognitive theories differ from biological theories of personality?

7. Do you think that personality traits are consistent across time and situations?

8. Which method of personality assessment (interviews, behavioural observation, objective testing, or projective testing) do you think is likely to be most informative? Can you think of circumstances in which one type of assessment might be more effective than the others?

What is happening in this picture ?

- How would Freud interpret this woman's aggressive behaviour toward her "assailant"?

- How would Bandura's social cognitive concept of self-efficacy explain the benefits of taking a self-defence course?

- What biological factors might explain why some people choose activities that provide high levels of physiological arousal while others avoid such situations?

SELF-TEST

(Check your answers in Appendix A.)

1. A relatively stable and consistent characteristic that can be used to describe someone is known as _____ .

   a. character
   b. a trait
   c. temperament
   d. personality

2. Label the list of personality traits in the five-factor model on the figure below.

Big Five Traits	Low Scorers	High Scorers
1 _____	Down-to-earth Uncreative Conventional Uncurious	Imaginative Creative Original Curious
2 _____	Negligent Lazy Disorganized Late	Conscientious Hard-working Well-organized Punctual
3 _____	Loner Quiet Passive Reserved	Joiner Talkative Active Affectionate
4 _____	Suspicious Critical Ruthless Irritable	Trusting Lenient Soft-hearted Good-natured
5 _____	Calm Even-tempered Comfortable Unemotional	Worried Temperamental Self-conscious Emotional

3. Label Freud's three levels of consciousness on the figure below.

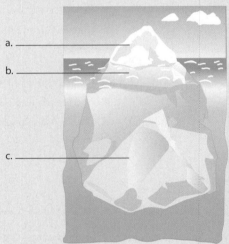

a. _____

b. _____

c. _____

4. According to Freud, what are the three mental structures that form personality?

   a. unconscious, preconscious, and conscious
   b. oral, anal, and phallic
   c. Oedipus, Rorschach, and TAT
   d. id, ego, and superego

5. While shopping, Jacqueline ran out of money and slipped some CDs from the record store into her bag. According to Freud, which part of her personality would likely produce feelings of guilt for this action?

   a. The preconscious   c. The ego
   b. The superego   d. The id

6. Used excessively, defence mechanisms can be dangerous because they _____.

    a. hide true feelings   c. distort reality

    b. become ineffective   d. become fixated

7. List Freud's psychosexual stages of development in the correct sequence.

8. Ten year-old Bianca spends her time interacting with and getting to know her female friends, and without any psychosexual conflicts. In which Freudian stage is Bianca?

    a. Genital stage   c. Oral stage

    b. Latency stage   d. Psychosexual stage

9. Which of the following were three of the most influential neo-Freudians?

    a. Plato, Aristotle, and Descartes

    b. Dr. Laura, Dr. Phil, and Dr. Ruth

    c. Rotter, Rogers, and Maslow

    d. Adler, Jung, and Horney

10. Many of Derrick's friends comment on how he shows qualities that seem stereotypically feminine (empathy, compassion, care). Jung would refer to this aspect of Derrick's personality as _____.

    a. the animus   c. self-efficacy

    b. the ego   d. the anima

11. Which of the following is **NOT** a criticism of Freud's psychoanalytic theory?

    a. Most of his concepts prove difficult to test.

    b. Most of his data show a lack of cross-cultural support.

    c. He underemphasized the role of biological determinants.

    d. Some of his views were sexist.

12. Justifying cheating on an exam by telling yourself "If I don't pass this course, my parents will be stuck paying my tuition for another whole year!" is an example of the defence mechanism of _____.

    a. denial   c. sublimation

    b. rationalization   d. projection

13. *Unconditional positive regard* is a Rogerian term for:

    a. accepting any and all behaviour as a positive manifestation of self-actualization

    b. positive behaviour toward a person without attaching any qualifications

    c. non-judgemental listening

    d. phenomenological congruence

14. Which personality theorist believed in the basic goodness of individuals and their natural tendency toward self-actualization?

    a. Karen Horney   c. Abraham Maslow

    b. Alfred Adler   d. Carl Jung

15. Bandura uses the term _____ to refer to an individual's belief about whether he or she can successfully engage in behaviours related to personal goals.

    a. self-actualization   c. self-efficacy

    b. self-esteem   d. self-congruence

16. Extroversion, neuroticism, and psychoticism are three types of personality traits identified by _____.

    a. Karen Horney   c. Alfred Adler

    b. Carl Rogers   d. Hans Eysenck

17. The study of the contribution of heredity to personality differences among people is referred to as _____.

    a. the biobehavioural approach

    b. the genetic-environmental perspective

    c. behavioural genetics

    d. the biopsychosocial model

18. Which of the following appear(s) to have the largest influence (40% to 50%) on personality?

    a. nonshared environment

    b. shared environments

    c. genetics

    d. unknown factors

19. Which of the following is the most widely researched and clinically used self-report personality test?

    a. MMPI-2   c. TAT

    b. Rorschach Inkblot Test   d. SVII

20. The Rorschach Inkblot Test is an example of:

    a. a career inventory

    b. a projective personality test

    c. the most reliable and valid personality test

    d. a culturally biased personalit

Psychological Disorders

*M*ary's troubles first began in adolescence. She was frequently truant, and her grades declined sharply. During family counselling sessions, it was discovered that Mary had prostituted herself for drug money. . . . She idealized new friends, but when they disappointed her, she angrily cast them aside. . . . Mary's problems, coupled with a preoccupation with inflicting pain on herself (by cutting and burning) and persistent thoughts of suicide, led to her admittance to a psychiatric hospital at age 26. (Kring et al., 2007, pp. 386–387)

Jim is a medical student. Over the last few weeks, he has been noticing that older men appear to be frightened of him when he passes them on the street. Recently, he has become convinced that he is actually the director of the Central Intelligence Agency and that these men are secret agents of a hostile nation. Jim has found confirmatory evidence in the fact that a helicopter flies over his house every day at 8:00 a.m. and at 4:30 p.m. Surely, this surveillance is part of the plot to assassinate him. (Bernheim & Lewine, 1979, p. 4)

Both Mary and Jim have severe psychological problems. Was there something in their early backgrounds to explain their later behaviours? Is there something medically wrong with them? What about less severe forms of abnormal behaviour?

In this chapter, we discuss how psychological disorders are identified, explained, and classified, and explore six major categories of psychological disorders. We also look at how gender and culture affect mental disorders.

Studying Psychological Disorders

NATIONAL GEOGRAPHIC

IDENTIFYING ABNORMAL BEHAVIOUR: FOUR BASIC STANDARDS

abnormal behaviour Patterns of emotion, thought, and action that are considered pathological (diseased or disordered) for one or more of these reasons: statistical infrequency, disability or dysfunction, personal distress, or violation of norms (Davison et al., 2008).

On the continuum ranging from normal to **abnormal behaviour**, people can show unusually healthy or extremely disturbed behaviour.

Mental health professionals generally agree on four criteria for abnormal behaviour: statistical infrequency, disability or dysfunction, personal distress, and violation of norms (**FIGURE 13.1**). However, as we consider these criteria, remember that no single criterion is adequate for identifying all forms of abnormal behaviour.

EXPLAINING ABNORMALITY: FROM SUPERSTITION TO SCIENCE

What causes abnormal behaviour? Historically, evil spirits and witchcraft have been blamed (Millon, 2004). Stone Age people, for example, believed that abnormal behaviour stemmed from demonic possession; the "therapy" was to bore a hole in the skull so that the evil spirit could escape. During the European Middle Ages, troubled people were sometimes treated with exorcism in an effort to drive the Devil out through prayer, fasting, noise making, beating, and drinking terrible-tasting brews. During the fifteenth century, many believed that some individuals chose to consort with the Devil. Many

of these supposed witches were tortured, imprisoned for life, or executed.

As the Middle Ages ended, special mental hospitals called *asylums* began to appear in Europe. Initially designed to provide quiet retreats from the world and to protect society (Millon, 2004), the asylums unfortunately became overcrowded, inhumane prisons.

Improvement came in 1792 when Philippe Pinel, a French physician in charge of a Parisian asylum, insisted that asylum inmates—whose behaviour he believed to be caused by underlying physical illness—be unshackled and removed from their unlighted, unheated cells. Many inmates improved so dramatically that they could be released. Pinel's **medical model** eventually gave rise to the modern medical specialty of **psychiatry**.

medical model The perspective that diseases (including mental illness) have physical causes that can be diagnosed, treated, and possibly cured.

psychiatry The branch of medicine that deals with the diagnosis, treatment, and prevention of mental disorders.

Unfortunately, when we label people "mentally ill," we may create new problems. One of the most outspoken critics of the medical model is psychiatrist Thomas Szasz (1960, 2000, 2004). Szasz believes that the medical model encourages people to believe that they have no responsibility for their actions. He contends that mental illness is a myth used to label individuals who are peculiar or offensive to others (Cresswell, 2008). Furthermore, labels can become self-perpetuating—that is, the person can begin to behave according to the diagnosed disorder.

Despite these potential dangers, the medical model—and the concept of mental illness—remains a founding principle of psychiatry. In contrast, psychology offers a multifaceted approach to explaining abnormal behaviour, as described in *What a Psychologist Sees*.

CLASSIFYING ABNORMAL BEHAVIOUR: *THE DIAGNOSTIC AND STATISTICAL MANUAL IV-TR*

Without a clear, reliable system for classifying the wide range of psychological disorders, scientific research on them would be almost impossible, and communication

Rather than fixed categories, both "abnormal" and "normal" behaviours exist along a continuum (Hansell & Damour, 2008).

(Rare)   (Common)

Statistical Infrequency
(e.g., believing others are plotting against you)

Normal   **Abnormal**

- A behaviour may be judged abnormal if it occurs infrequently in a given population. *Statistical infrequency* alone does not determine what is normal—for example, no one would classify Albert Einstein's great intelligence or Wayne Gretzky's exceptional athletic ability as abnormal.

(Low)   (High)

Personal Distress
(e.g., having thoughts of suicide)

Normal   **Abnormal**

- The *personal distress* criterion focuses on the individual's judgement of his or her level of functioning. Yet many people with psychological disorders deny they have a problem. Also, some serious psychological disorders (such as antisocial personality disorder) cause little or no emotional discomfort. The personal distress criterion by itself is not sufficient for identifying all forms of abnormal behaviour.

(Low)   (High)

Disability or Dysfunction
(e.g., being unable to go to work because of alcohol abuse)

Normal   **Abnormal**

- People who have psychological disorders may be so *disabled* or *dysfunctional* that they are unable to get along with others, hold a job, eat properly, or clean themselves. Their ability to think clearly and make rational decisions also may be impaired.

(Rare)   (Common)

Violation of Norms
(e.g., shouting at strangers)

Normal   **Abnormal**

- The fourth approach to identifying abnormal behaviour is *violation of norms*, or cultural rules that guide behaviour in particular situations. A major problem with this criterion, however, is that cultural diversity can affect what people consider a violation of norms (Lopez & Guarnaccia, 2000).

Seven Psychological Perspectives on Abnormal Behaviour

Each of the seven major perspectives in psychology emphasizes different factors believed to contribute to abnormal behaviour, but in practice they overlap. Consider the phenomenon of compulsive hoarding. Everyone sometimes makes an impulse purchase, and most people are reluctant to discard some possessions that are of questionable value. But when the acquisition of and inability to discard worthless items becomes extreme, it can interfere with basic aspects of living, such as cleaning, cooking, sleeping on a bed, and moving around one's home. This abnormal behaviour is associated with several psychological disorders, but it is most commonly found in people who have obsessive-compulsive disorder, or OCD (an anxiety disorder discussed later in this chapter). Can you imagine how each of the seven major perspectives might explain compulsive hoarding?

among mental health professionals would be difficult. Fortunately, mental health specialists share a uniform classification system: the text revision of the fourth edition of the *Diagnostic and Statistical Manual of Mental Disorders (DSM-IV-TR)* (American Psychiatric Association, 2000). The fifth edition of the *DSM* is expected in 2012.

Each revision of the *DSM* has expanded the list of disorders and changed the descriptions and categories to reflect both the latest in scientific research and the changes in the way abnormal behaviours are viewed within our social context (First & Tasman, 2004; Smart & Smart, 1997). For example, take the terms **neurosis** and **psychosis**. In previous editions, the term *neurosis* reflected Freud's belief that all neurotic conditions arise from unconscious conflicts (Chapter 12). Now, conditions that were previously grouped under the heading *neurosis* have been formally redistributed as anxiety disorders, somatoform disorders, and dissociative disorders.

Unlike neurosis, the term *psychosis* is still listed in the *DSM-IV-TR* because it is useful for distinguishing the most severe mental disorders, such as schizophrenia and some mood disorders.

> **Diagnostic and Statistical Manual of Mental Disorders (DSM-IV-TR)** The classification system developed by the American Psychiatric Association used to describe abnormal behaviours; the *IV-TR* indicates that it is the text revision (TR) of the fourth major edition (IV).

Applying Psychology

The Not Criminally Responsible Defence: Guilty of a Crime or Mentally Disordered?

On the night of July 30, 2008, 22-year-old Tim McLean was riding a Greyhound bus, heading home to Winnipeg after spending part of his summer working at a carnival. Seated at the rear of the bus, he fell asleep while listening to music near Portage la Prairie, Manitoba. According to reports, the passenger in the seat next to McLean suddenly pulled out a knife and, in front of horrified passengers, repeatedly stabbed McLean. With his knife, he then beheaded McLean, dismembered his body, and cannibalized some of the remains (McIntyre, 2009a). At his trial seven months later, it was learned that the accused, Vincent Li, suffered from schizophrenia and had been hearing voices telling him that McLean was an evil presence who must be killed (Lett, 2009; McIntyre, 2009b). Li was found not criminally responsible on account of mental disorder (formerly called the insanity plea) and was committed to a psychiatric institution, where he will remain until he is no longer considered a danger. Despite high-profile cases like this it is important to keep in mind that the not criminally responsible defence is used very rarely and is successful only when individuals are severely disturbed. Individuals found not criminally responsible on account of mental disorder are typically held for long periods in a psychiatric institution (Davison et al., 2008).

> **Stop & Think**
> 1. If you had been on the jury at Vincent Li's trial, what would have been your verdict, and why?
> 2. Do you think the not criminally responsible defence lets guilty people off the hook?

Understanding the *DSM-IV-TR* The *DSM-IV-TR* is organized according to five major dimensions called *axes*, which serve as guidelines for making decisions about symptoms (**FIGURE 13.2**). Axis I describes **state disorders** (the patient's current condition, or "state"), such as anxiety, substance abuse, and depression. Axis II describes **trait disorders** (enduring problems that seem to be an integral part of the self), including long-running personality disorders and developmental disability (mental retardation).

The other three axes are used to record important supplemental information. Medical conditions (Axis III) and psychosocial and environmental stressors (Axis IV) can contribute to moods and mental health problems. Finally, Axis V evaluates a person's overall level of functioning, on a scale from 1 (serious attempt at suicide) to 100 (happy and productive).

The *DSM-IV-TR* contains more than 200 diagnostic categories grouped into 17 subcategories (**STUDY ORGANIZER 13.1**).

In this chapter, we focus on only the first 6 of the 17 categories shown in Study Organizer 13.1. Before we go on, note that the *DSM-IV-TR* classifies disorders, not people. Accordingly, we use such terms as *a person with schizophrenia*, rather than describing people as *schizophrenic*.

Evaluating the *DSM-IV-TR* The *DSM-IV-TR* has been praised for carefully and completely describing symptoms, standardizing diagnoses and treatments, facilitating communication, and serving as a valuable educational tool. Critics, however, suggest that it relies too heavily on the medical model and unfairly labels people (Cooper, 2004; Horwitz, 2007; Mitchell, 2003; Zalaquett et al., 2008). The *DSM-IV-TR* has also been criticized for its possible cultural bias. The manual does provide a culture-specific section and a glossary of culture-bound syndromes, such as *amok* (Indonesia), *genital retraction syndrome* (Asia), and *windigo psychosis* (First Nations cultures), which we discuss later in this chapter. However, the classification of most disorders still reflects a Western European and North American perspective (Ancis, Chen, & Schultz, 2004; Borra, 2008; Smart & Smart, 1997).

Axis V:
Global Assessment of Functioning
The individual's overall level of functioning in social, occupational, and leisure activities

Axis I:
Clinical Disorders
Symptoms that cause distress or significantly impair social or occupational functioning (such as anxiety disorders, depression)

Axis IV:
Psychosocial and Environmental Problems
Problems (such as interpersonal stressors and negative life events) that may affect the diagnosis, treatment, and prognosis (expected cause and outcome) of psychological disorders

Axis II:
Personality Disorders and Mental Retardation
Chronic and enduring problems that generally persist throughout life and impair interpersonal or occupational functioning

Axis III:
General Medical Condition
Physical disorders that may be relevant to understanding or treating a psychological disorder

Five axes of the *DSM-IV-TR* **FIGURE 13.2**

Each axis serves as a broad category that helps organize the wide variety of mental disorders and acts as a guideline for making decisions. However, the *DSM* does not suggest therapies or treatment. Reprinted with permission from the *Diagnostic and Statistical Manual of Mental Disorders*, copyright 2000, American Psychiatric Association.

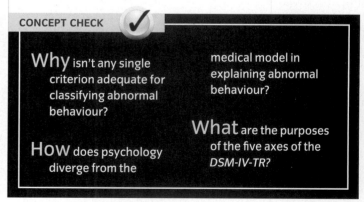

CONCEPT CHECK

Why isn't any single criterion adequate for classifying abnormal behaviour?

How does psychology diverge from the medical model in explaining abnormal behaviour?

What are the purposes of the five axes of the *DSM-IV-TR*?

Category	Description	Examples
Anxiety Disorders	Problems associated with severe anxiety	phobias, obsessive-compulsive disorder, post-traumatic stress disorder
Mood Disorders	Problems associated with severe disturbances of mood (affect)	depression, mania, bipolar disorder
Schizophrenia and Other Psychotic Disorders	A group of disorders characterized by major disturbances in perception, language and thought, emotion, and behaviour	schizophrenia, brief psychotic disorder
Dissociative Disorders	Disorders in which the normal integration of consciousness, memory, or identity is suddenly and temporarily altered	amnesia, dissociative identity disorders
Personality Disorders	Problems related to lifelong maladaptive personality traits	antisocial personality disorders, borderline personality disorders
Substance-Related Disorders	Problems caused by alcohol, cocaine, tobacco, and other drugs	substance dependence, substance abuse
Somatoform Disorders	Problems related to unusual preoccupation with physical health or physical symptoms with no physical cause	pain disorder, hypochondriasis
Factitious Disorders	Disorders that the individual adopts to satisfy some economic or psychological need	factitious disorder
Sexual and Gender Identity Disorders	Problems related to unsatisfactory sexual activity, finding unusual objects or situations arousing, or gender identity problems	sexual dysfunctions, sexual desire disorders
Eating Disorders	Problems related to eating behaviour	anorexia nervosa, bulimia
Sleep Disorders	Serious disturbances of sleep	insomnia, sleep terrors, hypersomnia
Impulse Control Disorders (not elsewhere classified)	Disorders involving failure to resist an impulse or temptation to perform an act that is harmful to the person or others	kleptomania, pyromania, pathological gambling
Adjustment Disorders	Problems involving excessive emotional reaction to specific stressors	excessive emotional reaction to divorce, family discord, or unemployment
Disorders usually first diagnosed in infancy, childhood, or early adolescence	Problems that appear before adulthood	mental retardation (developmental disability), language development disorders
Delirium, Dementia, Amnestic, and Other Cognitive Disorders	Problems caused by known damage to the brain	Alzheimer's disease, strokes
Mental disorders caused by a general medical condition (not elsewhere classified)	Problems caused by physical deterioration of the brain caused by disease, drugs, etc.	personality change caused by a general medical condition
Other conditions that may be a focus of clinical attention	Symptoms that may or may not be related to mental disorders but are severe enough to warrant clinical attention	medication-induced movement disorders

Anxiety disorders

Mood disorders

Substance-related disorders

Eating disorders

Anxiety Disorders

Anxiety disorders—which are diagnosed twice as often in women as in men—are the most frequently occurring mental disorders in the general population (National Institute of Mental Health, 2008; Swartz & Margolis, 2004). Fortunately, they are also among the easiest disorders to treat and have one of the best chances for recovery (Chapter 14).

> **anxiety disorder**
> A type of abnormal behaviour characterized by unrealistic, irrational fear.

this section, we consider four anxiety disorders: generalized anxiety disorder, panic disorder, phobias, and obsessive-compulsive disorder (**FIGURE 13.3**). (Post-traumatic stress disorder, another major anxiety disorder, is discussed in Chapter 3.) Although we discuss these disorders separately, people often have more than one anxiety disorder (Halgin & Whitbourne, 2008).

FOUR MAJOR ANXIETY DISORDERS: THE PROBLEM OF FEAR

Symptoms of anxiety, such as rapid breathing, dry mouth, and increased heart rate, plague all of us during stressful moments. But some people experience anxiety that is so intense and chronic it seriously disrupts their lives. They feel threatened, unable to cope, unhappy, and insecure in a world that seems dangerous and hostile. In

Generalized Anxiety Disorder This disorder affects twice as many women as it does men (Brown, O'Leary, & Barlow, 2001). **Generalized anxiety disorder** is characterized by chronic, uncontrollable, and excessive fear and worry that lasts at least six months and that is not focused on any particular object or situation. Because of persistent muscle tension and autonomic fear reactions, people with this disorder may develop headaches, heart palpitations, dizziness, and insomnia, making it even harder to cope with normal daily activities.

Major anxiety disorders FIGURE 13.3

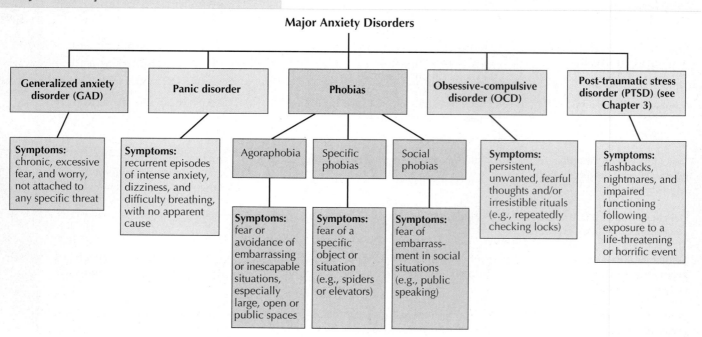

Panic Disorder

Sudden, but brief, attacks of intense apprehension that cause trembling, dizziness, and difficulty breathing are symptoms of **panic disorder**. Panic attacks generally happen after frightening experiences or prolonged stress (and sometimes even after exercise). Panic disorder is diagnosed when several apparently spontaneous panic attacks lead to a persistent concern about future attacks. A common complication of panic disorder is agoraphobia (Cully & Stanley, 2008; Roberge et al., 2008).

Phobias

Phobias involve strong, irrational fear and avoidance of objects or situations that are usually considered harmless (fear of elevators or fear of going to the dentist, for example). Although the person recognizes that the fear is irrational, the experience is still one of overwhelming anxiety, and a full-blown panic attack may follow. The *DSM-IV-TR* divides phobic disorders into three broad categories: agoraphobia, specific phobias, and social phobias.

People with *agoraphobia* restrict their normal activities because they fear having a panic attack in crowded, enclosed, or wide-open places where they would be trapped—unable to escape easily or to receive help. In severe cases, people with agoraphobia may even refuse to leave the safety of their homes.

A *specific phobia* is a fear of a specific object or situation, such as needles, heights, rats, or spiders. Claustrophobia (fear of closed spaces) and acrophobia (fear of heights) are the specific phobias most often treated by therapists. People with specific phobias generally recognize that their fears are excessive and unreasonable, but they are unable to control their anxiety and will go to great lengths to avoid the feared stimulus (FIGURE 13.4).

People with *social phobias* are irrationally fearful of embarrassing themselves in social situations. Fear of public speaking and of eating in public are the most common social phobias. The fear of public scrutiny and potential humiliation may become so pervasive that normal life is impossible (Acarturk et al., 2008; Swartz, 2008).

Obsessive-Compulsive Disorder (OCD)

Obsessive-compulsive disorder involves persistent, unwanted fearful thoughts (obsessions) or irresistible urges to perform an act or repeated ritual (compulsions), which help relieve the anxiety created by the obsession. In adults, this disorder is equally common in men and women. However, it is more prevalent among boys when the onset is in childhood (American Psychiatric Association, 2000).

Imagine what it would be like to worry so obsessively about germs that you compulsively wash your hands hundreds of times a day until they are raw and bleeding.

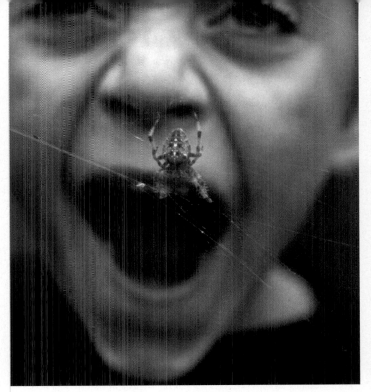

Spider phobia FIGURE 13.4

Can you imagine how it would feel to be so frightened by a spider that you would try to jump out of a speeding car to get away from it? That is how a person suffering from a phobia might feel.

Most sufferers of OCD realize that their actions are senseless. But when they try to stop the behaviour, they experience mounting anxiety, which is relieved only by giving in to the urges.

CAUSES OF ANXIETY DISORDERS

The causes of anxiety disorders have been debated by the experts; however, research has focused on the roles of psychological, biological, and sociocultural processes (the *biopsychosocial model*).

Psychological Causes of Anxiety Disorders

Psychological contributions to anxiety disorders are primarily in the form of faulty cognitive processes and maladaptive learning.

Faulty cognitions People with anxiety disorders have habits of thinking, or cognitive habits, that make them prone to fear. They tend to be hypervigilant—they constantly scan their environment for signs of danger and ignore signs of safety. They also tend to magnify ordinary threats and failures and to be hypersensitive to others' opinions of them (FIGURE 13.5).

Faulty thinking patterns FIGURE 13.5

People who suffer from social phobia are excessively concerned about others' evaluations, hypersensitive to any criticism, and obsessively worried about potential mistakes. This intense self-preoccupation leads these people to perpetually believe they have failed. What changes in thinking patterns might lessen this anxiety?

Maladaptive learning According to learning theorists, anxiety disorders generally result from conditioning and social learning (Chapter 6) (Cully & Stanley, 2008; Mineka & Oehlberg, 2008; Swartz, 2008). During classical conditioning, for example, a stimulus that is originally neutral (e.g., a harmless spider) becomes paired with a frightening event (a sudden panic attack) so that it becomes a conditioned stimulus that elicits anxiety. The person then begins to avoid spiders in order to reduce anxiety (an operant conditioning process known as negative reinforcement).

Most people with phobias, however, cannot remember specific instances that led to their fear. Moreover, such frightening experiences do not trigger the development of phobias in everyone. In other words, conditioning may not be the only explanation.

Social learning theorists propose that some phobias are the result of modelling and imitation. Parents who are fearful and overprotective, for example, may create family environments where such anxiety is easily learned. Phobias may also be learned vicariously (indirectly). In one study, rhesus monkeys viewed videos showing another monkey apparently experiencing extreme fear of a toy snake, a toy rabbit, a toy crocodile, and flowers (Cook & Mineka, 1989). The "viewing" monkeys were later afraid of the snake and crocodile but not of the rabbit or flowers, suggesting that phobias have both learned and biological components.

Biological Causes of Anxiety Disorders

Some researchers believe that phobias reflect an evolutionary predisposition to fear things that were dangerous to our ancestors (Mineka & Oehlberg, 2008; Walker et al., 2008). Such "preparedness" (Seligman, 1971) to develop fears to certain stimuli might account for selective fears learned vicariously by rhesus monkeys in the study discussed previously.

Anxiety disorders may also have a biological basis. Some people with panic disorder seem to be genetically predisposed toward an overreaction of the autonomic nervous system, responding more readily than other people to anxiety-producing stimulation. In addition, stress and arousal seem to play a role in panic attacks, and drugs, such as caffeine or nicotine, and even hyperventilation can trigger an attack, all suggesting a biochemical disturbance.

Factors that may contribute to anxiety FIGURE 13.6

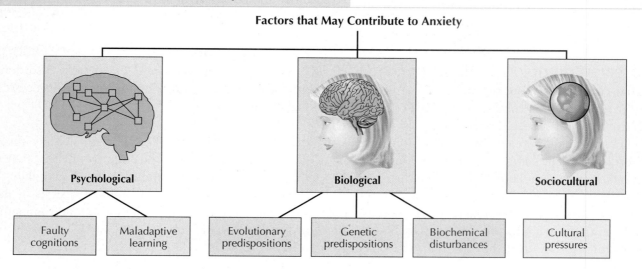

Sociocultural Causes of Anxiety Disorders

In addition to psychological and biological components, sociocultural factors can contribute to anxiety. The number of people diagnosed with anxiety disorders has risen sharply in the past 50 years, particularly in Western industrialized countries. Can you see how our increasingly fast-paced lives—along with our increased mobility, decreased job and financial security, and decreased family support—might contribute to anxiety? Unlike the dangers that humans may have faced in our evolutionary history, today's threats are less identifiable and immediate, which may lead some people to become hypervigilant and predisposed to anxiety disorders (FIGURE 13.6).

Anxiety disorders can have dramatically different forms in other cultures, further supporting the influence of sociocultural factors. For example, in a collectivist twist on anxiety, the Japanese have a type of social phobia called *taijin kyofusho* (TKS), which involves morbid dread of doing something to embarrass others. This disorder is quite different from the Western version of social phobia, which centres on a fear of criticism.

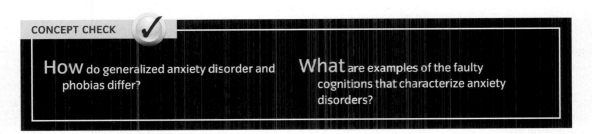

CONCEPT CHECK

How do generalized anxiety disorder and phobias differ?

What are examples of the faulty cognitions that characterize anxiety disorders?

Mood Disorders

LEARNING OBJECTIVES

Explain how major depressive disorder and bipolar disorder differ.

Summarize research on the biological and psychological factors that contribute to mood disorders.

UNDERSTANDING MOOD DISORDERS: MAJOR DEPRESSIVE DISORDER AND BIPOLAR DISORDER

As the name implies, **mood disorders** (also known as affective disorders) are characterized by extreme disturbances in emotional states. There are two main types of mood disorders: major depressive disorder and bipolar disorder.

We all feel sad sometimes, especially following the loss of a job, end of a relationship, or death of a loved one. People suffering from **major depressive disorder**, however, may experience a lasting and continuously depressed mood without a clear trigger or precipitating event.

> **major depressive disorder** Long-lasting depressed mood that interferes with the ability to function, feel pleasure, or maintain interest in life.

> **bipolar disorder** Repeated episodes of mania (unreasonable elation and hyperactivity) and depression.

People with clinical depression are so deeply sad and discouraged that they often have trouble sleeping, are likely to lose (or gain) weight, and may feel so fatigued that they cannot go to work or school or even comb their hair and brush their teeth. They may sleep both day and night, have problems concentrating, and feel so profoundly sad and guilty that they consider suicide. These feelings have no apparent cause and may be so severe that the individual loses contact with reality.

When depression is *unipolar*, the depressive episode eventually ends, and the person returns to a "normal" emotional level. People with **bipolar disorder**, however, rebound to the opposite state, known as *mania* (FIGURE 13.7).

During a manic episode, the person is overly excited, extremely active, and easily

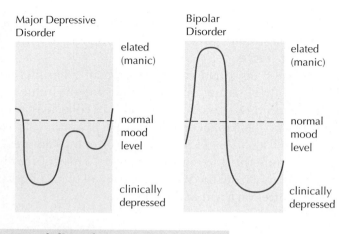

Mood disorders FIGURE 13.7

If major depressive disorders and bipolar disorders were depicted on a graph, they might look something like this.

No limits FIGURE 13.8

Poor judgement is common during manic episodes. A person may give away valuable possessions, go on wild spending sprees, or make elaborate plans for becoming rich and famous. Why do you think such behaviour could contribute to or trigger major depression?

distracted. The person exhibits unrealistically high self-esteem, an inflated sense of importance, and poor judgement (FIGURE 13.8). The person may not sleep for days at a time yet does not become fatigued. Thinking is speeded up and can change abruptly to new topics, showing "rapid flight of ideas." Speech is also rapid ("pressured speech"), and it is difficult for others to get a word in edgewise.

A manic episode may last a few days or a few months, and it generally ends abruptly. The ensuing depressive episode generally lasts three times as long as the manic episode. The lifetime risk for bipolar disorder is low—somewhere between 0.5 and 1.6 percent—but it can be one of the most debilitating and lethal disorders, with a suicide rate between 10 and 20 percent among sufferers (Carballo et al., 2008; Kinder et al., 2008; Klimes-Dougan et al., 2008).

EXPLAINING MOOD DISORDERS: BIOLOGICAL AND PSYCHOSOCIAL FACTORS

Biological factors appear to play a significant role in both major depression and bipolar disorder. Recent research suggests that structural brain changes may contribute to these mood disorders (Almeida et al., 2003; Lyoo et al., 2004; Steffens et al., 2003). Other research points to imbalances of the neurotransmitters serotonin, norepinephrine, and dopamine (Barton et al., 2008; Delgado, 2004; Lyoo et al., 2004; Montgomery, 2008; Wiste et al., 2008). Indeed, drugs that alter the activity of these neurotransmitters also decrease the symptoms of depression (and are therefore called antidepressants) (Chuang, 1998).

As Canadian researchers Hymie Anisman, Zul Merali, and John Stead (2008) point out, mood disorders may have an inherited component (see also Baldessarini & Hennen, 2004; Horiuchi et al., 2004; Sequeira et al., 2004). For example, when one identical twin has a mood disorder, there is about a 50 percent chance that the other twin will also develop the illness (Brent & Melhem, 2008; Faraone, 2008; Swartz, 2008). It is important to remember, however, that relatives generally have similar environments, as well as similar genes.

Finally, the evolutionary perspective suggests that moderate depression may be a normal and healthy adaptive response to a very real loss (such as the death of a loved one). The depression helps us to step back and reassess our goals (Nesse, 2000; Nesse & Jackson, 2006). Consistent with this theory is the observation that primates also show signs of depression when they suffer a significant loss (Suomi, 1991). Clinical, severe depression may just be an extreme version of this generally adaptive response.

Psychosocial theories of depression focus on environmental stressors and disturbances in the person's interpersonal relationships, thought processes, self-concept, and history of learned behaviours (Cheung, Gilbert, & Irons, 2004; Hammen, 2005; Mathews & McLeod, 2005). The psychoanalytic explanation sees depression as anger turned inward against oneself when an important relationship or attachment is lost. The anger is assumed to result from feelings of rejection or

A Psychologist's Struggle with Bipolar Disorder

In his early 40s, Dr. Norman Endler was at the pinnacle of his career. The eminent Canadian researcher was chair of the psychology department of York University in Toronto, was a clinical consultant to a major hospital, and was an international expert in the areas of anxiety, stress, and coping. His energy level seemed limitless, as he not only took care of his numerous professional responsibilities but also filled his days with many athletic, cultural, and family activities. He was always on the go. But then things began to change. What had once seemed easy became insurmountable. He became troubled by anxiety and self-doubt. His work and relationships began to suffer as he sank into a deep depression. Realizing the seriousness of his condition, he sought psychiatric help where it was discovered that he had been experiencing the highs and lows of bipolar disorder. Dr. Endler wrote of his experiences, his symptoms, and the treatments he received, with the goal of de-stigmatizing mental illness and offering help to the public. His 1982 book, *Holiday of Darkness: A Psychologist's Journey Out of His Depression*, chronicled his struggle and his eventual recovery, offering guidance and reassurance to those suffering from mood disorders.

withdrawal from rejection, especially when a loved one dies. The humanistic school says that depression results when a person demands perfection of himself or herself or when positive growth is blocked.

The **learned helplessness** theory of depression (Seligman, 1975, 1994, 2007) maintains that when people (and other animals) are subjected to pain that they cannot escape, they develop a sense of helplessness or resignation and thereafter do not attempt to escape painful experiences. The perception that one is unable to change things for the better leads to depression. Learned helplessness may be particularly likely to trigger depression if the person attributes failure to causes that are internal ("my own weakness"), stable ("this weakness is long-standing and unchanging"), and global ("this weakness is a problem in lots of settings") (Ball, McGuffin, & Farmer, 2008; Chaney et al., 2004; Gotlieb & Abramson, 1999; Wise & Rosqvist, 2006).

Whatever the causes of depression, one of the major dangers associated with the condition is the increased risk of suicide. Because of the shame and secrecy associated with suicide, many fail to get or give help. If you believe someone is contemplating suicide, there are some things that you can do. Stay with the person if he or she is in any immediate danger. Encourage him or her to talk to you rather than to withdraw. Show the person that you care, but try not to give false reassurances that "everything will be OK." Instead, you could openly ask if the person is feeling hopeless and suicidal. Do not be afraid to ask about suicide with people who are depressed or hopeless, fearing that you will just put ideas into their heads. The reality is that people who are left alone or who are told they can't be serious about suicide are more likely to attempt it.

If you do suspect someone is suicidal, it is vitally important that you do your best to help the person obtain counselling. Most cities have suicide prevention centres with 24-hour hotlines or walk-in centres that provide emergency counselling. Hospital emergency rooms are also well-equipped to deal with potentially suicidal persons. In addition, it is valuable to inform the person's family doctor and to also share your suspicions with parents, friends, or others who can help in a suicidal crisis. To save a life, you may have to betray a secret when someone confides in you. (See Finding a Therapist in Chapter 14.)

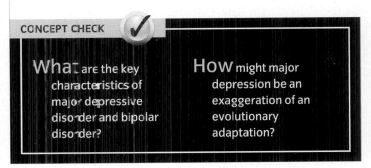

CONCEPT CHECK

What are the key characteristics of major depressive disorder and bipolar disorder?

How might major depression be an exaggeration of an evolutionary adaptation?

Schizophrenia

LEARNING OBJECTIVES

Describe some common symptoms of schizophrenia.

Compare the traditional (four-group) system for classifying different types of schizophrenia with the (two-group) system that has recently emerged.

Summarize the biological and psychosocial factors that contribute to schizophrenia.

I magine that your daughter has just left for college and that you hear voices inside your head shouting, "You'll never see her again! You have been a bad mother! She'll die." Or what if you saw live animals in your refrigerator? These experiences have plagued Mrs. T for decades (Gershon & Rieder, 1993).

schizophrenia
A group of psychotic disorders involving major disturbances in perception, language, thought, emotion, and behaviour. The individual withdraws from people and reality, often into a fantasy life of delusions and hallucinations.

Mrs. T suffers from **schizophrenia** [skit-so-FREE-nee-uh]. Schizophrenia is often so severe that it is considered a psychosis, meaning that the person is out of touch with reality. People with schizophrenia have serious problems caring for themselves, relating to others, and holding a job. In extreme cases, people with schizophrenia require institutional or custodial care.

Schizophrenia is one of the most widespread and devastating mental disorders. Approximately 1 out of every 100 people will develop schizophrenia in his or her lifetime, and approximately half of all people who are admitted to psychiatric hospitals are diagnosed with this disorder (Gottesman, 1991; Kendler et al., 1996; Kessler et al., 1994; Regier et al., 1993). Schizophrenia usually emerges between the late teens and the mid-30s. It seems to be equally prevalent in men and women, but it's generally more severe and strikes earlier in men than in women (Combs et al., 2008; Faraone, 2008; Gottesman, 1991; Mueser & Jeste, 2008; Tsuang, Stone, & Faraone, 2001).

Many people confuse schizophrenia with dissociative identity disorder, which is sometimes referred to as *split* or *multiple personality disorder*. Schizophrenia means "split mind," but when Eugen Bleuler coined the term in 1911, he was referring to the fragmenting of thought processes and emotions, not personalities (Neale, Oltmanns, &

Winters, 1983). As we discuss later in this chapter, dissociative identity disorder is the rare condition of having more than one distinct personality.

SYMPTOMS OF SCHIZOPHRENIA: FIVE AREAS OF DISTURBANCE

Schizophrenia is a group of disorders characterized by a disturbance in one or more of the following areas: perception, language, thought, affect (emotions), and behaviour.

Perceptual Symptoms The senses of people with schizophrenia may be either enhanced or blunted. That is, the filtering and selection processes that allow most people to concentrate on whatever they choose are impaired, and their sensory and perceptual experiences are jumbled and distorted. These disruptions may explain why people with schizophrenia experience **hallucinations,** which can occur in all the senses but are most commonly auditory (hearing voices and sounds).

hallucinations
Imaginary sensory perceptions that occur without an external stimulus.

On rare occasions, people with schizophrenia will hurt others in response to their distorted perceptions. But a person with schizophrenia is more likely to be self-destructive and suicidal than violent toward others.

Language and Thought Disturbances For people with schizophrenia, words lose their usual meanings and associations, logic is impaired, and thoughts are disorganized and bizarre. When language and thought disturbances are mild, the individual jumps from topic to topic. With more severe disturbances, the person jumbles phrases and words together (into a *word salad*) or creates artificial words.

The most common—and frightening—thought disturbance experienced by people with schizophrenia is the lack of contact with reality (psychosis).

delusions Mistaken beliefs based on misrepresentations of reality.

Delusions are also common in people with schizophrenia. We all experience exaggerated thoughts from time to time, such as thinking a friend is trying to avoid us, but the delusions of schizophrenia are much more extreme. For example, Jim (the med student in the chapter opener) was completely convinced that others were trying to assassinate him (a *delusion of persecution*). In *delusions of grandeur*, people believe that they are someone very important, perhaps Jesus Christ or the queen of England. In *delusions of reference*, unrelated events are given special significance, as when a person believes that a radio station is giving him or her a special message. (See FIGURE 13.9 and FIGURE 13.10.)

A recent trend among individuals coping with various psychological disorders is to join Internet groups where they can share their experiences with others. For example, people with schizophrenia and other psychotic disorders can now share with fellow sufferers their belief that they are being stalked or that their minds are being controlled by technology. Some experts consider Internet groups that offer peer support to be helpful to those with mental illnesses, but others believe that they may reinforce troubled thinking and impede treatment. People who use the sites report feeling relieved that they are not alone in their suffering, but it should be noted that these sites are not moderated by professionals and pose

the danger of actually amplifying the symptoms of individuals with mental illness (Kershaw, 2008).

Affect (Emotional) Disturbances
Changes in emotion usually occur in people with schizophrenia. In some cases, emotions are exaggerated and fluctuate rapidly. At other times, emotions become blunted. Some people with schizophrenia have *flattened affect*—almost no emotional response of any kind.

Behavioural Disturbances
Disturbances in behaviour may take the form of unusual actions that have special meaning. For example, one patient massaged his head repeatedly to "clear it" of unwanted thoughts. People with schizophrenia may become *cataleptic* and assume a nearly immobile stance for an extended period.

TYPES OF SCHIZOPHRENIA: RECENT METHODS OF CLASSIFICATION

For many years, researchers divided schizophrenia into five subtypes: paranoid, catatonic, disorganized, undifferentiated, and residual (**TABLE 13.1**). Although these terms are still included in the *DSM-IV-TR*, critics contend that this system does not differentiate in terms of prognosis, cause, or response to treatment, and that the undifferentiated type is merely a catchall for cases that are difficult to diagnose (American Psychiatric Association, 2000).

Subtypes of schizophrenia TABLE 13.1

Paranoid	Dominated by delusions (persecution and grandeur) and hallucinations (hearing voices)
Catatonic	Marked by motor disturbances (immobility or wild activity) and echo speech (repeating the speech of others)
Disorganized	Characterized by incoherent speech, flat or exaggerated emotions, and social withdrawal
Undifferentiated	Meets the criteria for schizophrenia but is not any of the above subtypes
Residual	No longer meets the full criteria for schizophrenia but still shows some symptoms

For these reasons, researchers have proposed an alternative classification system of two groups of symptoms:

1. **Positive schizophrenia symptoms** involve *additions* to or exaggerations of normal thought processes and behaviours, including bizarre delusions and hallucinations.

2. **Negative schizophrenia symptoms** involve the *loss* or absence of normal thought processes and behaviours, including impaired attention, limited or toneless speech, flattened affect (or emotions), and social withdrawal.

Positive symptoms are more common when schizophrenia develops rapidly, whereas negative symptoms are more often found in slow-developing schizophrenia. Positive symptoms are associated with better adjustment before the onset and a better prognosis for recovery.

In addition to these two groups, the latest *DSM* suggests adding another dimension to reflect *disorganization of behaviour,* including rambling speech, erratic behaviour, and inappropriate affect.

CAUSES OF SCHIZOPHRENIA: NATURE AND NURTURE THEORIES

Because schizophrenia comes in many different forms, it probably has multiple biological and psychosocial bases (Walker et al., 2004). Let's look at biological contributions first.

Prenatal viral infections, birth complications, immune responses, maternal malnutrition, and advanced paternal age all may contribute to the development of schizophrenia (Ellman & Cannon, 2008; Meyer et al., 2008; Tandon, Keshavan, & Nasrallah, 2008; Zuckerman & Weiner, 2005). However, most biological theories of schizophrenia focus on genetics, neurotransmitters, and brain abnormalities.

- *Genetics.* Although researchers are beginning to identify specific genes related to schizophrenia, most genetic studies have focused on twins and adoptions (Elkin, Kalidindi, & McGuffin, 2004; Faraone, 2008; Hall et al., 2007). This research indicates that the risk for schizophrenia increases with genetic similarity; that is, people who share more genes with a person who has schizophrenia are more likely to develop the disorder (**FIGURE 13.11**).

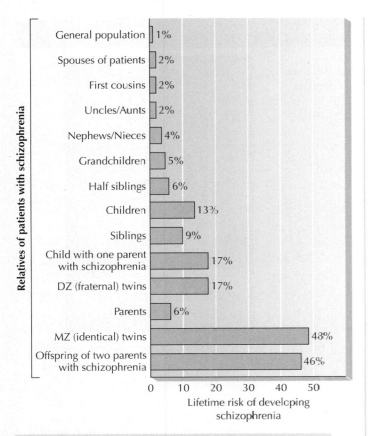

Genetics and schizophrenia FIGURE 13.11

Your lifetime risk of developing schizophrenia depends, in part, on how closely you are genetically related to someone with schizophrenia. *Source:* Gottesman, "Schizophrenia Genesis," 1991, W. H. Freeman and Company/Worth Publishers.

- *Neurotransmitters.* Precisely how genetic inheritance produces schizophrenia is unclear. According to the **dopamine hypothesis**, overactivity of certain dopamine neurons in the brain causes schizophrenia (Ikemoto, 2004; Paquet et al., 2004). This hypothesis is based on two observations. First, large doses of amphetamines increase the amount of dopamine and can produce *positive* symptoms of schizophrenia even in people with no history of schizophrenia. Such effects are even more likely to occur in people with a genetic predisposition to the disorder. Second, drugs that reduce dopamine activity in the brain reduce or eliminate some symptoms of schizophrenia.

- *Brain abnormalities.* The third major biological theory for schizophrenia involves abnormalities in brain function and structure. Researchers have found larger cerebral ventricles (fluid-filled spaces in the brain) in some people with schizophrenia (Galderisi et al., 2008; Gaser et al., 2004).

Also, some people with chronic schizophrenia have a lower level of activity in their frontal and temporal lobes—areas that are involved in language, attention, and memory (FIGURE 13.12). Damage in these regions might explain the thought and language disturbances that characterize schizophrenia. This lower level of brain activity, and schizophrenia itself, may also result from an overall loss of grey matter (neurons in the cerebral cortex) (Crespo-Facorro et al., 2007; Gogtay et al., 2004).

Clearly biological factors play a key role in schizophrenia. But even in identical twins—who share identical genes—if one twin has schizophrenia, the chance of the other also having schizophrenia is only 48 percent. This tells us that non-genetic factors must contribute the remaining percentage. Most psychologists believe that there are at least two possible psychosocial contributors.

According to the **diathesis-stress model** of schizophrenia, stress plays an essential role in triggering schizophrenic episodes in people with an inherited predisposition (or

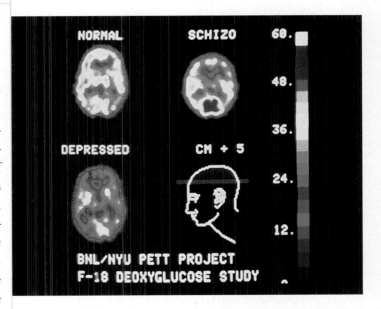

Brain activity in schizophrenia FIGURE 13.12

These positron emission tomography (PET) scans show variations in the brain activity of individuals without a disorder, people with major depressive disorder, and individuals with schizophrenia. Warmer colours (red, yellow) indicate increased activity.

The biopsychosocial model and schizophrenia FIGURE 13.13

Biological Factors

- Malfunctioning neurotransmitters
- Metabolic and anatomical abnormalities of the brain
- Genetic predisposition
- Possible other *unknown* factors

Psychological and Social Factors

- Stress
- Family communication deviance
- Possible other *unknown* factors

Schizophrenia

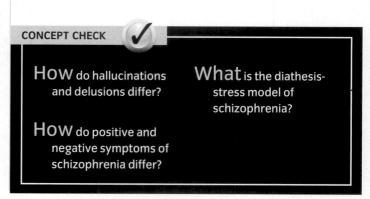

In his portrayal of the homeless musical prodigy Nathaniel Ayers, actor Jamie Foxx demonstrated several classic symptoms of schizophrenia, including disturbances in perception, language, thought, behaviour, and emotion. For Ayers, as with others with schizophrenia, no single factor led to his illness.

There is strong evidence linking schizophrenia to biological, psychological, and social factors—the *biopsychosocial model*.

Source: Reprinted from *Biological Psychiatry*, Meltzer, "Genetics and Etiology of Schizophrenia and Bipolar Disorder," pp. 171–178, 2000, with permission from Society of Biological Psychiatry.

---

diathesis) toward the disease (see Figure 13.11) (Jones & Fernyhough, 2007; Reulbach et al., 2007).

Some investigators suggest that communication disorders in family members may also be a predisposing factor for schizophrenia. Such disorders include using unintelligible speech, having fragmented communication, and frequently sending severely contradictory messages to children. Several studies have also shown greater rates of relapse and worsening of symptoms among hospitalized patients who went home to families that were critical and hostile toward them or overly involved in their lives emotionally (Hooley & Hiller, 2001; McFarlane, 2006).

How should we evaluate the different theories about the causes of schizophrenia? Critics of the dopamine hypothesis and the brain damage theory argue that those theories fit only some cases of schizophrenia. Moreover,

with both theories, it is difficult to determine cause and effect. The disturbed-communication theories are also hotly debated, and research is inconclusive. Schizophrenia is probably the result of a combination of known and unknown interacting factors (**FIGURE 13.13**).

CONCEPT CHECK ✓

HOW do hallucinations and delusions differ?

HOW do positive and negative symptoms of schizophrenia differ?

What is the diathesis-stress model of schizophrenia?

Other Disorders

SUBSTANCE-RELATED DISORDERS

substance-related disorders
Abuse of or dependence on a mood- or behaviour-altering drug.

The category of **substance-related disorders** is subdivided into two general groups: substance abuse and substance dependence (**TABLE 13.2**). When alcohol or other drug use interferes with a person's social or occupational functioning, it is called *substance abuse*. Drug use becomes *substance dependence* when it causes physical reactions, including *tolerance* (requiring more of the drug to get the desired effect) and *withdrawal* (negative physical effects when the drug is removed) (see Chapter 5).

Some people can use alcohol and other drugs and not develop a problem. Unfortunately, researchers have not been able to definitively identify ahead of time those who can use drugs without developing problems and those who are likely to become abusers. Complicating diagnosis and treatment is the fact that substance-related disorders commonly coexist with other mental disorders, including anxiety disorders, mood disorders, schizophrenia, and personality disorders (Cornelius & Clark, 2008; Green et al., 2004; Munro & Edward, 2008; Thomas et al., 2008). This co-occurrence of disorders is called **comorbidity** (**FIGURE 13.14**).

What causes comorbidity? Perhaps the most influential hypothesis is **self-medication**: individuals drink or use drugs to reduce their painful and frightening symptoms (Robinson, 2008). Regardless of the causes, it is critical that patients, family members, and clinicians recognize and deal with comorbidity if treatment is to be effective.

Comorbidity complicates treatment

FIGURE 13.14

Can you see how comorbidity can cause serious problems? What difficulties could there be in identifying the appropriate cause, progression, or treatment of someone dealing with a combination of disorders?

DSM-IV-TR substance abuse and substance dependence TABLE 13.2	
Criteria for substance abuse (alcohol and other drugs)	**Criteria for substance dependence (alcohol and other drugs)**
Maladaptive use of a substance shown by one of the following: • Failure to meet obligations • Repeated use in situations where it is physically dangerous • Continued use despite problems caused by the substance • Repeated substance-related legal problems	*Three or more of the following:* • Tolerance • Withdrawal • Substance taken for a longer time or greater amount than intended • Lack of desire or effort to reduce or control use • Social, recreational, or occupational activities given up or reduced • Much time spent in activities to obtain the substance • Use continued despite knowing that psychological or physical problems are worsened by it

DISSOCIATIVE DISORDERS: WHEN THE PERSONALITY SPLITS APART

The most dramatic and controversial psychological disorders are **dissociative disorders**. There are several types of dissociative disorders, but all involve a splitting apart (a *disassociation*) of significant aspects of experience from memory or consciousness. Individuals dissociate from the core of their personality by failing to remember past experiences (*dissociative amnesia*) (**FIGURE 13.15**), by leaving home and wandering off (*dissociative fugue*), by losing their sense of reality and feeling estranged from the self (*depersonalization disorder*), or by developing completely separate personalities (*dissociative identity disorder*).

> **dissociative disorders** Amnesia, fugue, or multiple personalities resulting from avoidance of painful memories or situations.

Unlike most other psychological disorders, the primary cause of dissociative disorders appears to be environmental variables, with little or no genetic influence (Waller & Ross, 1997).

Dissociation as an escape FIGURE 13.15

The major force behind all dissociative disorders is the need to escape from anxiety. Imagine witnessing a loved one's death in a horrible car accident. Can you see how your mind might cope by blocking out all memory of the event?

The most severe dissociative disorder is **dissociative identity disorder (DID)**—previously known as multiple personality disorder—in which at least two separate and distinct personalities exist within a person at the same time. Each personality has unique memories, behaviours, and social relationships. Transition from one personality to another occurs suddenly and is often triggered by psychological stress. Usually, the original personality has no knowledge or awareness of the other personalities, but all the personalities may be aware of lost periods of time. The disorder is diagnosed more among women than among men. Women with DID also tend to have more identities, averaging 15 or more, compared with men, who average 8 (American Psychiatric Association, 2000).

DID is a controversial diagnosis. Some experts suggest that many cases are faked or result from false memories and an unconscious need to please the therapist (Kihlstrom, 2005; Lawrence, 2008; Pope et al., 2007; Stafford & Lynn, 2002). Other psychologists accept the validity of multiple personality and contend that the condition is underdiagnosed (Dalenberg et al., 2007; Lipsanen et al., 2004; Spiegel & Maldonado, 1999).

PERSONALITY DISORDERS: ANTISOCIAL AND BORDERLINE

What would happen if the characteristics of a personality were so inflexible and maladaptive that they significantly impaired someone's ability to function? This is what happens with **personality disorders**. Several types of personality disorders are included in this category in the *DSM-IV-TR*, but here we will focus on antisocial personality disorder and borderline personality disorder.

> **personality disorders** Inflexible, maladaptive personality traits that cause significant impairment of social and occupational functioning.

Antisocial Personality Disorder The term **antisocial personality disorder** is used interchangeably with the terms *sociopath* and *psychopath*. These labels describe behaviour so far outside the ethical and legal standards of society that many consider it the most serious of all mental disorders. Unlike the situation with anxiety, mood disorders, and schizophrenia, people with this diagnosis feel little personal distress (and may not be motivated to change). Yet their maladaptive traits generally bring considerable harm and suffering to others (Hervé et al., 2004; Kirkman, 2002; Nathan et al., 2003). Although serial killers are often seen as classic examples of those with antisocial personality disorder (FIGURE 13.16), many sociopaths harm people in less dramatic ways—for example, as ruthless businesspeople and crooked politicians.

The four hallmarks of antisocial personality disorder are egocentrism (preoccupation with oneself and insensitivity to the needs of others), lack of conscience, impulsive behaviour, and superficial charm (American Psychiatric Association, 2000).

Unlike most adults, individuals with antisocial personality disorder act impulsively, without giving thought to the consequences. They are usually poised when confronted with their destructive behaviour and feel contempt for anyone they are able to manipulate. They also change jobs and relationships suddenly, and they often have a history of truancy from school and of being expelled for destructive behaviour. People with antisocial personalities can be charming and persuasive, and they have remarkably good insight into the needs and weaknesses of other people.

Serial killer Paul Bernardo FIGURE 13.16

In 1995, Paul Bernardo was convicted of the kidnapping, sexual assault, and murder of two teenagers in southern Ontario. Bernardo had been well-liked, and many people were shocked that someone who appeared so charming could display such cruelty with no apparent signs of remorse (Offman, 2008). Such egocentrism and lack of conscience are primary characteristics of antisocial personality disorder.

Twin and adoption studies suggest a possible genetic predisposition to antisocial personality disorder (Bock & Goode, 1996; Jang et al., 2003). Biological contributions are also suggested by studies that have found abnormally low autonomic activity during stress, right hemisphere abnormalities, and reduced grey matter in the frontal lobes (De Oliveira-Souza et al., 2008; Huesmann & Kirwil, 2007; Kendler & Prescott, 2006; Lyons-Ruth et al., 2007; Raine & Yang, 2006).

Evidence also exists for environmental or psychological causes. Antisocial personality disorder is highly correlated with abusive parenting styles and inappropriate modelling (Barnow et al., 2007; De Oliveira-Souza et al., 2008; Grover et al., 2007; Lyons-Ruth et al., 2007). People with antisocial personality disorder often come from homes characterized by emotional deprivation, harsh and inconsistent disciplinary practices, and antisocial parental behaviour. Still other studies show a strong interaction between both heredity and environment (Gabbard, 2006; Hudziak, 2008).

Borderline Personality Disorder Borderline personality disorder (BPD) is among the most commonly diagnosed personality disorders (Ansell & Grilo, 2007; Bradley, Conklin, & Westen, 2007). The core features of this disorder are impulsivity and instability in mood, relationships, and self-image. Originally, the term implied that the person was on the borderline between neurosis and schizophrenia (Davison et al., 2008). The modern conceptualization no longer has this connotation, but BPD remains one of the most complex and debilitating of all the personality disorders.

Mary's story of chronic, lifelong dysfunction, described in the chapter opener, illustrates the serious problems associated with this disorder. People with borderline personality disorder experience extreme difficulties in relationships. They are subject to chronic feelings of depression, emptiness, and intense fear of abandonment, and engage in destructive, impulsive behaviours, such as sexual promiscuity, drinking, gambling, and eating sprees (Chabrol et al., 2004; Trull et al., 2000). They may attempt suicide and sometimes engage in self-mutilating behaviour (Chapman, Leung, & Lynch, 2008; Crowell et al., 2008; Links et al., 2008).

People with BPD tend to see themselves and everyone else in absolute terms—perfect or worthless (Mason & Kreger, 1998). They constantly seek reassurance from others and may quickly erupt in anger at the slightest sign of disapproval. The disorder is also typically marked by a long history of broken friendships, divorces, and lost jobs.

People with borderline personality disorder frequently have a childhood history of neglect; emotional deprivation; and physical, sexual, or emotional abuse (Christopher et al., 2007; Minzenberg, Poole, & Vinogradov, 2008). Borderline personality disorder also tends to run in families, and some data suggest it is a result of impaired functioning of the brain's frontal lobes and limbic system, areas that regulate impulsive behaviours (Schmahl et al., 2004; Tebartz van Elst et al., 2003).

Although some therapists have had success treating BPD with drug therapy and behaviour therapy (Bohus et al., 2004; Markovitz, 2004), the general prognosis is not favourable. In one study, seven years after treatment, about 50 percent of the original group still had the disorder (Links, Heslegrave, & van Reekum, 1998).

CONCEPT CHECK ✓

Why does the presence of comorbid disorders complicate the diagnosis and treatment of substance-related disorders?

How do personality disorders differ from the other psychological disorders discussed in this chapter?

Why is the diagnosis of dissociative identity disorder considered controversial?

How Gender and Culture Affect Abnormal Behaviour

NATIONAL GEOGRAPHIC

LEARNING OBJECTIVES

Identify the biological, psychological, and social factors that might explain gender differences in depression.

Explain why it is difficult to directly compare mental disorders across cultures.

Explain why recognizing the difference between culture-general and culture-bound disorders and symptoms can help prevent ethnocentrism in the diagnosis and treatment of psychological disorders.

Among the Ojibwa, Cree, and Montagnais-Naskapi First Nations in Canada, there is a disorder called *windigo*—or *wiitiko*—*psychosis*, which is characterized by delusions and cannibalistic impulses. Believing that they have been possessed by the spirit of a windigo (**FIGURE 13.17**), a cannibal giant with a heart and entrails of ice, victims become severely depressed (Faddiman, 1997). As the malady begins, the individual typically experiences loss of appetite, diarrhea, vomiting, and insomnia, and he or she may see people turning into beavers and other edible animals.

In later stages, the victim becomes obsessed with cannibalistic thoughts and may even attack and kill loved ones in order to devour their flesh (Berreman, 1971), sometimes begging to be killed to end the obsession.

If you were a therapist, how would you treat this disorder? Does it fit neatly into any of the categories of psychological disorders that you have learned about?

We began this chapter discussing the complexities and problems with defining, identifying, and classifying abnormal behaviour. Before we close, we need to add two additional confounding factors: sex and culture. In this section, we explore a few of the many ways in which men and women differ in how they experience abnormal behaviour. We also look at cultural variations in abnormal behaviour.

SEX DIFFERENCES AND DEPRESSION: WHY ARE WOMEN MORE PRONE TO DEPRESSION?

In Canada, the United States, and other countries, the rate of severe depression for women is two to three times the rate for men (Barry et al., 2008; Nicholson et al., 2008; Nolen-Hoeksema, Larson, & Grayson, 2000).

A *windigo* cannibalizing humans, whom it sees as beavers or other animals FIGURE 13.17

Why do you think some disorders, such as *windigo* psychosis, are limited to a particular group or culture?

Why is there such a disparity between the rates for men and women? Research explanations can be grouped under biological influences (hormones, biochemistry, and genetic predisposition), psychological processes (ruminative thought processes), and social factors (greater poverty, work-life conflicts, unhappy marriages, and sexual or physical abuse) (Cooper et al., 2008; Jackson & Williams, 2006; Shear et al., 2007).

According to the *biopsychosocial model,* some women inherit a genetic or hormonal predisposition toward depression. This biological predisposition may combine with society's socialization processes to help reinforce behaviours—such as greater emotional expression, passivity, and dependence—that increase the chances for depression (Alloy et al., 1999; Nolen-Hoeksema, Larson, & Grayson, 2000). At the same time, males are socialized to suppress their emotions or at least not to report them. Focusing only on traditionally identified symptoms of depression (sadness, low energy, and feelings of helplessness) may cause us to overlook large numbers of depressed men, who may show their distress in other ways (e.g., aggression or substance abuse) (FIGURE 13.18).

Depression in disguise? FIGURE 13.18

In our society, men are typically socialized to suppress their emotions and to show their distress by acting out (showing aggression), acting impulsively (driving recklessly and committing petty crimes), and engaging in substance abuse. How might such societal pressures lead us to underestimate male depression?

CULTURE AND SCHIZOPHRENIA: DIFFERENCES AROUND THE WORLD

Peoples of different cultures experience mental disorders in a variety of ways. For example, the reported incidence of schizophrenia varies for different cultures around the world. It is unclear whether these differences result from actual differences in prevalence of the disorder or from differences in definition, diagnosis, or reporting (Hoye et al., 2006).

The symptoms of schizophrenia also vary across cultures (Stompe et al., 2003), as do the particular stresses that may trigger its onset (**FIGURE 13.19**). In Western nations, the major symptom is auditory hallucinations (e.g., hearing voices). Interestingly, the perceived sources of these auditory hallucinations have changed with technological advances, with voices coming from the radio in the 1920s, from the television in the 1950s, from satellites in the 1960s, and from microwave ovens in the 1970s and 1980s (Brislin, 2000).

Finally, despite the advanced treatment facilities and methods in industrialized nations, the prognosis for people with schizophrenia is actually better in non-industrialized societies. This may be because the core symptoms of schizophrenia (poor rapport with others, incoherent speech, etc.) make it more difficult to survive in highly industrialized countries. In addition, in most industrialized nations, families and other support groups are less likely to feel responsible for relatives and friends with schizophrenia (Brislin, 2000; Lefley, 2000).

AVOIDING ETHNOCENTRISM

Most research on psychological disorders originates and is conducted primarily in Western cultures. Such a restricted sampling can limit our understanding of disorders in general and lead to an ethnocentric view of mental disorders.

Fortunately, cross-cultural researchers have devised ways to overcome these difficulties (Matsumoto & Juang, 2008; Triandis, 2007). For example, Robert Nishimoto (1988) has found several **culture-general symptoms** that are useful in diagnosing disorders across cultures (**TABLE 13.3**).

In addition, Nishimoto found several **culture-bound symptoms**. For example, the Vietnamese Chinese reported "fullness in head," the Mexican respondents had "problems with [their] memory," and the Anglo-Americans reported "shortness of breath" and "headaches." Apparently, people learn to express their problems in ways that are acceptable to others in the same culture (Brislin, 1997, 2000; Dhikav et al., 2008; Laungani, 2007; Tolin et al., 2007). This division between culture-general and culture-bound symptoms also helps us understand depression. Certain symptoms

What is stressful? FIGURE 13.19

A Some stressors are culturally specific, such as feeling possessed by evil forces or being the victim of witchcraft.

B Other stressors are shared by many cultures, such as the death of a spouse or the unexpected loss of a job (Al-Issa, 2000; Browne, 2001; Neria et al., 2002; Torrey & Yolken, 1998).

Twelve culture-general symptoms of mental health difficulties		TABLE 13.3
Nervous	Trouble sleeping	Low spirits
Weak all over	Personal worries	Restless
Feel apart, alone	Can't get along	Hot all over
Worry all the time	Can't do anything worthwhile	Nothing turns out right

Source: From *Understanding Culture's Influence on Behavior*, 2nd edition by Brislin. ©2000. Reprinted with permission of Wadsworth, a division of Thomson Learning.

of depression (such as intense sadness, poor concentration, and low energy) seem to exist across all cultures (World Health Organization, 2007, 2008), but some are culture-bound. For example, feelings of guilt are found more often in North America and Europe. And in China, *somatization* (the conversion of depression into bodily complaints) occurs more frequently than it does in other parts of the world (Helms & Cook, 1999).

Just as there are culture-bound and culture-general symptoms, researchers have found that mental disorders are themselves sometimes culturally bound (**FIGURE 13.20**) The earlier example of *windigo* psychosis, a disorder limited to certain groups of First Nations Canadians, illustrates just such a case.

As you can see, culture has a strong effect on mental disorders. Studying the similarities and differences across cultures can lead to better diagnosis and understanding. It also helps mental health professionals who work with culturally diverse populations understand both cultural-general and cultural-bound symptoms.

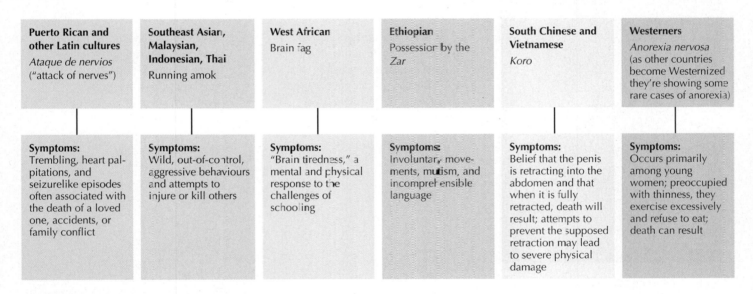

Puerto Rican and other Latin cultures *Ataque de nervios* ("attack of nerves")	**Southeast Asian, Malaysian, Indonesian, Thai** Running amok	**West African** Brain fag	**Ethiopian** Possession by the Zar	**South Chinese and Vietnamese** *Koro*	**Westerners** *Anorexia nervosa* (as other countries become Westernized they're showing some rare cases of anorexia)
Symptoms: Trembling, heart palpitations, and seizurelike episodes often associated with the death of a loved one, accidents, or family conflict	**Symptoms:** Wild, out-of-control, aggressive behaviours and attempts to injure or kill others	**Symptoms:** "Brain tiredness," a mental and physical response to the challenges of schooling	**Symptoms:** Involuntary movements, mutism, and incomprehensible language	**Symptoms:** Belief that the penis is retracting into the abdomen and that when it is fully retracted, death will result; attempts to prevent the supposed retraction may lead to severe physical damage	**Symptoms:** Occurs primarily among young women; preoccupied with thinness, they exercise excessively and refuse to eat; death can result

Culture-bound disorders FIGURE 13.20

Some disorders are fading as remote areas become more Westernized, whereas other disorders (such as anorexia nervosa) are spreading as other countries adopt Western values. *Sources:* Barlow & Durand, 2009; Dhikav et al., 2008; Gaw, 2001; Kring et al., 2007; Laungani, 2007; Sue & Sue, 2008; Tolin et al., 2007.

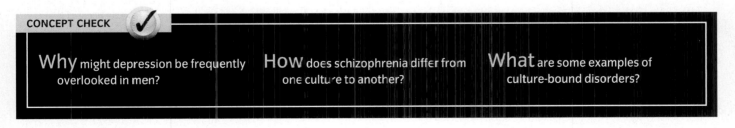

CONCEPT CHECK

Why might depression be frequently overlooked in men?

How does schizophrenia differ from one culture to another?

What are some examples of culture-bound disorders?

SUMMARY

1 Studying Psychological Disorders

1. Criteria for **abnormal behaviour** include statistical infrequency, disability or dysfunction, personal distress, and violation of norms. None of these criteria alone is adequate for classifying abnormal behaviour.

2. Superstitious explanations for abnormal behaviour were replaced by the **medical model**, which eventually gave rise to the modern specialty of psychiatry. In contrast to the medical model, psychology offers a multi-faceted approach to explaining abnormal behaviour.

3. The *Diagnostic and Statistical Manual of Mental Disorders,* fourth edition, text revision (*DSM-IV-TR*) is organized according to five major axes, which serve as guidelines for making decisions about symptoms.

2 Anxiety Disorders

1. Major **anxiety disorders** include **generalized anxiety disorder, panic disorder, phobias** (including agoraphobia, specific phobias, and social phobias), and **obsessive-compulsive disorder** (OCD).

2. Psychological (faulty cognitions and maladaptive learning), biological (evolutionary and genetic predispositions, biochemical disturbances), and sociocultural (cultural pressures toward hypervigilance) factors likely all contribute to anxiety.

3 Mood Disorders

1. **Mood disorders** are characterized by extreme disturbances in emotional states. People suffering from **major depressive disorder** may experience a lasting depressed mood without a clear trigger. In contrast, people with **bipolar disorder** alternate between periods of depression and mania (hyperactivity and poor judgement).

2. Biological factors play a significant role in mood disorders. Psychosocial theories of depression focus on environmental stressors and disturbances in interpersonal relationships, thought processes, self-concept, and learning history (including **learned helplessness**).

4 Schizophrenia

1. **Schizophrenia** is a group of disorders, each characterized by a disturbance in perception (including **hallucinations**), language, thought (including **delusions**), emotions, and/or behaviour.

2. In the past, researchers divided schizophrenia into multiple subtypes. More recently, researchers have proposed focusing instead on **positive** versus **negative** symptoms. *DSM-IV-TR* also suggests adding another dimension to reflect disorganization of behaviour.

3. Most biological theories of schizophrenia focus on genetics, neurotransmitters, and brain abnormalities. Psychologists believe that there are also at least two possible psychosocial contributors: stress and communication disorders in families.

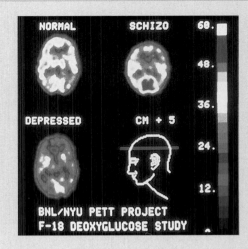

5 Other Disorders

1. **Substance-related disorders** fall into two general groups: substance abuse and substance dependence. Substance-related disorders commonly coexist with other mental disorders (**comorbidity**), which complicates their diagnosis and treatment.

2. **Dissociative disorders** include dissociative amnesia, dissociative fugue, depersonalization disorder, and **dissociative identity disorder (DID)**. Environmental variables appear to be the primary cause of dissociative disorders.

3. **Personality disorders** occur when inflexible, maladaptive personality traits cause significant impairment of social and occupational functioning. The best-known type of personality disorder is **antisocial personality disorder**, characterized by egocentrism, lack of conscience, impulsive behaviour, and superficial charm. The most common personality disorder is **borderline personality disorder (BPD)**. Its core features are impulsivity and instability in mood, relationships, and self-image. Although some therapists have success with drug therapy and behaviour therapy, prognosis is not favourable.

6 How Gender and Culture Affect Abnormal Behaviour

1. Men and women differ in how they experience and express abnormal behaviour. For example, in North America severe depression is much more common in women than in men. Biological, psychological, and social factors probably combine to explain this phenomenon.

2. Peoples of different cultures experience mental disorders in a variety of ways. For example, the reported incidence of schizophrenia varies within different cultures around the world, as do the disorder's symptoms, triggers, and prognosis.

3. Some symptoms of psychological disorders, as well as some disorders themselves, are **culture general**, whereas others are **culture-bound**.

KEY TERMS

- abnormal behaviour p. 358
- antisocial personality disorder p. 376
- anxiety disorder p. 364
- bipolar disorder p. 367
- borderline personality disorder (BPD) p. 377
- comorbidity p. 375
- culture-bound symptoms p. 380
- culture-general symptoms p. 380
- delusions p. 371
- *Diagnostic and Statistical Manual of Mental Disorders (DSM-IV-TR)* p. 361
- diathesis-stress model p. 373
- dissociative disorders p. 376
- dissociative identity disorder (DID) p. 376
- dopamine hypothesis p. 373
- generalized anxiety disorder p. 364
- hallucinations p. 370
- learned helplessness p. 369

- major depressive disorder p. 367
- medical model p. 358
- mood disorders p. 367
- negative schizophrenia symptoms p. 372
- neurosis p. 361
- obsessive-compulsive disorder (OCD) p. 365
- panic disorder p. 365
- personality disorders p. 376
- phobias p. 365
- positive schizophrenia symptoms p. 372
- psychiatry p. 358
- psychosis p. 361
- schizophrenia p. 370
- self-medication p. 375
- state disorders p. 362
- substance-related disorders p. 375
- trait disorders p. 362

CRITICAL AND CREATIVE THINKING QUESTIONS

1. Can you think of cases in which each of the four criteria for abnormal behaviour might *not* be suitable for classifying a person's behaviour as abnormal?

2. Do you think the not criminally responsible defence, as it is currently structured, should be abolished? Why or why not?

3. Why do you suppose that anxiety disorders are among the easiest to treat?

4. Most people have felt "depressed" from time to time. How would you distinguish between "normal" depression and a major depressive disorder?

5. Culture clearly can have strong effects on mental disorders. How does culture influence the way you think about what is normal or abnormal?

6. What are some social and cultural reasons why women may talk about their depression or anxiety more easily than do men?

7. For many of the disorders discussed in this chapter there is some evidence for a genetic predisposition. If someone had a family member with one of these disorders, what might be his or her chances of developing the same disorder?

What is happening in this picture ?

- Is this man's behaviour abnormal? Which criteria for abnormal behaviour do his piercings and tattoos meet? Which do they not?

- Can you think of any behaviour you exhibit that might be considered abnormal if your own cultural norms were not taken into account?

SELF-TEST

(Check answers in Appendix A.)

1. *Abnormal behaviour* can be defined as _____.

   a. a statistically infrequent pattern of pathological emotion, thought, or action

   b. patterns of emotion, thought, and action that are considered pathological

   c. a pattern of pathological emotion, thought, or action that causes personal distress, or violates social norms

   d. all of these options

2. Which of the following is the branch of medicine that deals with the diagnosis, treatment, and prevention of mental disorders?

   a. psychological medicine

   b. psychiatry

   c. psychobiology

   d. psychodiagnostics

3. Label the five axes of the *Diagnostic and Statistical Manual of Mental Disorders* (*DSM-IV-TR*) on the figure below.

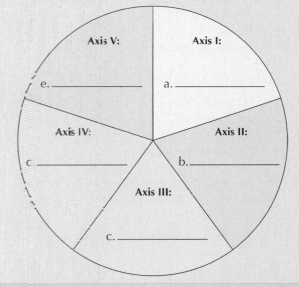

Axis V:
e. _____

Axis I:
a. _____

Axis IV:
c. _____

Axis II:
b. _____

Axis III:
c. _____

4. Anxiety disorders are _____.

   a. characterized by unrealistic, irrational fear
   b. the least frequent of the mental disorders
   c. twice as common in men as in women
   d. all of these options

5. Label the five major anxiety disorders on the figure below.

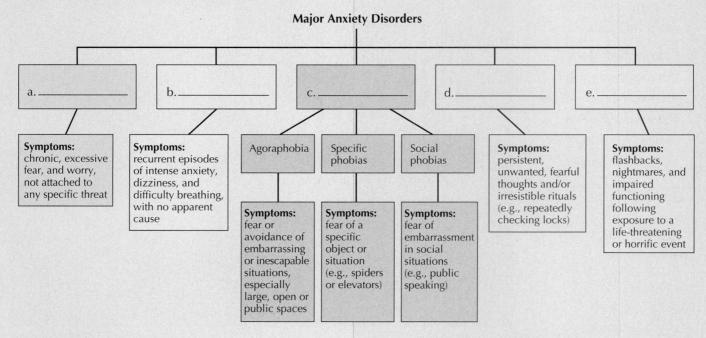

Major Anxiety Disorders

a. _____

Symptoms: chronic, excessive fear, and worry, not attached to any specific threat

b. _____

Symptoms: recurrent episodes of intense anxiety, dizziness, and difficulty breathing, with no apparent cause

c. _____

Agoraphobia — **Symptoms:** fear or avoidance of embarrassing or inescapable situations, especially large, open or public spaces

Specific phobias — **Symptoms:** fear of a specific object or situation (e.g., spiders or elevators)

Social phobias — **Symptoms:** fear of embarrassment in social situations (e.g., public speaking)

d. _____

Symptoms: persistent, unwanted, fearful thoughts and/or irresistible rituals (e.g., repeatedly checking locks)

e. _____

Symptoms: flashbacks, nightmares, and impaired functioning following exposure to a life-threatening or horrific event

6. For the past nine months, Nura has been experiencing intense fear and worry that just won't go away. She's been having trouble sleeping and finds it hard to cope with her daily activities. What is the most likely label for her problems?

   a. bipolar disorder
   b. a phobic disorder
   c. panic disorder
   d. generalized anxiety disorder

7. What are the two main types of mood disorders?

   a. major depression and bipolar disorder
   b. mania and depression
   c. GAD and OCD
   d. learned helplessness and suicide

8. Someone who experiences repeated episodes of mania, or alternates between mania and depression, has which of the following disorders?

   a. disruption of circadian rhythms
   b. bipolar disorder

   c. manic-depressive personality disorder
   d. post-traumatic stress disorder

9. When faced with a painful situation from which there is no escape, animals and people enter a state of helplessness and resignation. What is the term for this condition?

   a. autonomic resignation
   b. helpless resignation
   c. resigned helplessness
   d. learned helplessness

10. Which of the following is a psychotic disorder characterized by major disturbances in perception, language, thought, emotion, and behaviour?

   a. schizophrenia
   b. multiple personality disorder
   c. borderline psychosis
   d. neurotic psychosis

11. Perceptions for which there are no appropriate external stimuli are called _____, and the most common type among people suffering from schizophrenia is _____.

    a. hallucinations; auditory
    b. hallucinations; visual
    c. delusions; auditory
    d. delusions; visual

12. An individual is firmly convinced that he is Michael Jackson, even though he has never been a singer or a songwriter and is actually of Asian descent. What is this symptom called?

    a. severe schizophrenia
    b. a hallucination
    c. a compulsion
    d. a delusion

13. Label the five subtypes of schizophrenia on the table below.

Subtypes of schizophrenia	
_____	Dominated by delusions (persecution and grandeur) and hallucinations (hearing voices)
_____	Marked by motor disturbances (immobility or wild activity) and echo speech (repeating the speech of others)
_____	Characterized by incoherent speech, flat or exaggerated emotions, and social withdrawal
_____	Meets the criteria for schizophrenia but is not any of the above subtypes
_____	No longer meets the full criteria for schizophrenia but still shows some symptoms

14. The neurotransmitter that seems to be involved in schizophrenia is

    a. dopamine
    b. GABA
    c. norepinephrine
    d. acetylcholine

15. A patient believes that people are secretly talking to him, sending him "special" important messages. What is the term for this symptom?

    a. a delusion of grandeur
    b. a delusion of persecution
    c. a delusion of reference
    d. a delusion of control

16. Failure to meet obligations may be indicative of alcohol or drug _____, whereas tolerance and withdrawal may be indicative of alcohol or drug _____.

    a. use; abuse
    b. abuse; dependence
    c. abuse; abuse
    d. dependence; abuse

17. Which disorder is an attempt to avoid painful memories or situations, and is characterized by amnesia, fugue, or multiple personalities?

    a. dissociative disorder
    b. displacement disorder
    c. disoriented disorder
    d. identity disorder

18. Which of the following are characterized by inflexible, maladaptive personality traits that cause significant impairment of social and occupational functioning?

    a. nearly all mental disorders
    b. the psychotic and dissociative disorders
    c. personality disorders
    d. anxiety disorders

19. A patient who grew up in a severely abusive family reports serious difficulties in her relationships. She often feels "empty" and depressed, and constantly worries about abandonment by others. What might be a likely diagnosis for these symptoms?

    a. post-traumatic stress disorder
    b. antisocial personality disorder
    c. borderline personality disorder
    d. dissociative identity disorder

20. Which of the following are examples of culture-general symptoms of mental health difficulties, useful in diagnosing disorders across cultures?

    a. trouble sleeping
    b. can't get along
    c. worry all the time
    d. all of the above

Since the beginning of the movie age, people who have mental illness and the treatment they receive have been the subject of some of Hollywood's most popular and influential films. But consider how people with mental illness are generally portrayed in the movies. They are either cruel, sociopathic criminals (Anthony Hopkins in *Silence of the Lambs*) or helpless, incompetent victims (Jack Nicholson in *One Flew Over the Cuckoo's Nest* and Winona Ryder in *Girl Interrupted*). Likewise, popular films about mental illness often feature mad doctors, heartless nurses, and brutal treatment methods. Although these portrayals may boost movie ticket sales, they also perpetuate harmful stereotypes.

In this chapter, we offer a balanced, factual presentation of the latest research on psychotherapy and mental illness. As you will see, modern psychotherapy can be very effective and prevent much needless suffering, not only for people with serious psychological disorders but also for those seeking help with everyday problems in living.

In addition to psychologists, professionals involved in psychotherapy include psychiatrists, psychiatric nurses, social workers, counsellors, and clergy with training in pastoral counselling (Hunsley & Lee, 2010). Psychotherapy can take numerous forms. According to one expert (Kazdin, 1994), there may be over 400 approaches to treatment. To organize our discussion, we have grouped treatments into three categories: insight therapies, behaviour therapies, and biomedical therapies. After exploring these approaches, we conclude with a discussion of issues that are common to all major forms of psychotherapy.

Insight Therapies

We begin our discussion of professional **psychotherapy** with traditional psychoanalysis and its modern counterpart: psychodynamic therapy. Then we explore cognitive, humanistic, group, and family therapies. Although these therapies differ significantly, they're often grouped together as **insight therapies** because they seek to increase clients' insight into their difficulties. The general goal is to help people gain greater control over and improve their thoughts, feelings, and behaviours. (See STUDY ORGANIZER 14.1.)

> **psychotherapy**
> Techniques employed to improve psychological functioning and promote adjustment to life.

PSYCHOANALYSIS AND PSYCHODYNAMIC THERAPIES: UNLOCKING THE SECRETS OF THE UNCONSCIOUS

> **psychoanalysis**
> Freudian therapy designed to bring unconscious conflicts, which usually date back to early childhood experiences, into consciousness. Also refers to Freud's theoretical school of thought, which emphasizes unconscious processes.

In **psychoanalysis**, a person's *psyche* (or mind) is analyzed. In traditional psychoanalysis, the patient lies on a couch, with the therapist out of the patient's view. The process involves three to five hourly sessions per week, over a period of several years. Psychoanalysis is based on Sigmund Freud's central belief that abnormal behaviour is caused by unconscious conflicts among the three parts of the psyche: the id, ego, and superego (Chapter 12).

During psychoanalysis, these conflicts are brought to consciousness. The patient comes to understand the reasons for his or her behaviour and realizes that the childhood conditions under which the conflicts developed no longer exist. Once this realization (or insight) occurs, the conflicts can be resolved and the patient can develop more adaptive behaviour patterns.

How can gaining insight into one's unconscious change behaviour? Freud explained that becoming aware of previously hidden conflicts permits a release of tension and anxiety called **catharsis**. He observed that when his patients relived a traumatic incident, the conflict seemed to lose its power to control the person's behaviour.

According to Freud, the ego has strong defence mechanisms that block unconscious thoughts from coming to light. Thus, to gain insight into the unconscious, the ego must be "tricked" into relaxing its guard. With that goal, psychoanalysts employ five major methods: free association, dream analysis, analyzing resistance, analyzing transference, and interpretation.

Free Association
According to Freud, when you let your mind wander and remove conscious censorship over thoughts—a process called **free association**—interesting and even bizarre connections seem to spring into awareness. Freud believed that the first thing to come to a patient's mind is often an important clue to what the person's unconscious wants to conceal. Having the patient recline on a couch, with only the ceiling to look at, is believed to encourage free association.

Dream Analysis
According to Freud, defences are lowered during sleep, and forbidden desires and unconscious conflicts can be freely expressed. Even while dreaming, however, these feelings and conflicts are recognized as being unacceptable and must be disguised as images that have deeper symbolic meaning. Thus, according to Freudian dream theory, a therapist might interpret a dream of riding a horse or driving a car (the surface description or **manifest content**) as a desire for, or concern about, sexual intercourse (the underlying meaning or **latent content**).

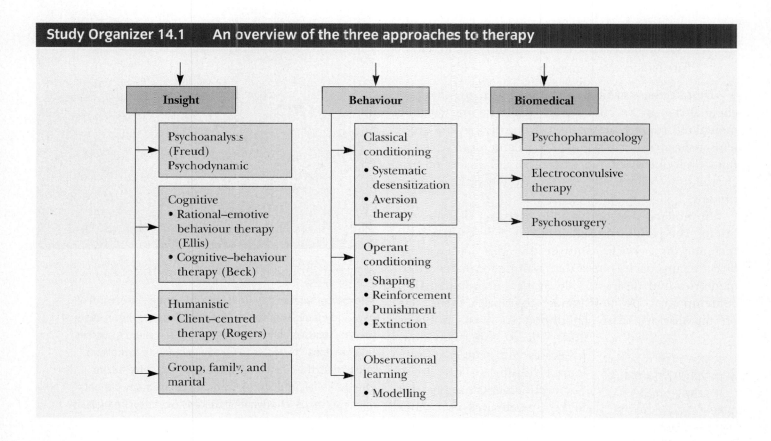

Analyzing Resistance

During free association or dream analysis, Freud found that patients often show **resistance**—the inability or unwillingness to discuss or reveal certain memories, thoughts, motives, or experiences. For example, patients may suddenly "forget" what they were saying or completely change the subject. It is the therapist's job to identify these cases of resistance and help patients face their problems and learn to deal with them realistically.

Analyzing Transference

During psychoanalysis, patients disclose intimate feelings and memories, and the relationship between the therapist and patient may become complex and emotionally charged. As a result, patients often unconsciously apply (or *transfer*) some of their unresolved emotions and attitudes from past relationships onto the therapist. The therapist uses this process of **transference** to help patients "relive" painful past relationships in a safe, therapeutic setting so that they can move on to healthier relationships.

Interpretation

The core of all psychoanalytic therapy is **interpretation**. During free association, dream analysis, resistance, and transference, the analyst listens closely and tries to find patterns and hidden conflicts. At the right time, the therapist explains (or *interprets*) the underlying meanings to the client.

As you can see, most of psychoanalysis rests on the assumption that repressed memories and unconscious conflicts actually exist. But, as noted in Chapters 7 and 12, this assumption is questioned by some modern scientists and has become the subject of a heated, ongoing debate. In addition to questioning the validity of repressed memories, critics also point to two other problems with psychoanalysis:

- *Limited applicability.* Critics argue that psychoanalysis seems to suit only a select group of highly motivated, articulate individuals with less severe disorders. Psychoanalysis is also time consuming (often lasting several years, with four to five sessions a week) and expensive, and it seldom works well with severe mental disorders, such as schizophrenia, in which verbalization and rationality are significantly disrupted. Finally, critics suggest that spending years chasing unconscious conflicts from the past allows patients to escape from the responsibilities and problems of adult life.

- *Lack of scientific credibility.* Another problem with psychoanalysis is that its "insights" (and therefore its success) cannot be proven or disproven.

Despite these criticisms, there is evidence that psychoanalysis can be effective in treating some chronic mental disorders (Carey, 2008). Nevertheless, the problems associated with this form of treatment have led to the development of more streamlined forms of psychotherapy, collectively referred to as psychodynamic therapy.

In modern **psychodynamic therapy**, treatment is briefer, the patient is treated face to face (rather than reclining on a couch), and the therapist takes a more directive approach (rather than waiting for unconscious memories and desires to slowly be uncovered). Also, contemporary psychodynamic therapists focus less on unconscious, early childhood roots of problems and more on conscious processes and current problems (Hunsley & Lee, 2010). Such refinements have helped make psychoanalysis more available and more effective for an increasing number of people (Knekt et al., 2008; Lehto et al., 2008; Lerner, 2008) (**FIGURE 14.1**).

> **psychodynamic therapy** A modern form of psychoanalysis that emphasizes internal conflicts, motives, and unconscious forces.

Interpersonal therapy (IPT) FIGURE 14.1

Interpersonal therapy (IPT) is an influential, brief form of psychodynamic therapy. As the name implies, interpersonal therapy focuses almost exclusively on the client's current relationships. Its goal is to relieve immediate symptoms and to help the client learn better ways to solve future interpersonal problems. Why do you think many patients might prefer psychodynamic therapy over psychoanalysis?

COGNITIVE THERAPIES: A FOCUS ON FAULTY THOUGHTS AND BELIEFS

> **cognitive therapy** Therapy that focuses on changing faulty thought processes and beliefs to treat problem behaviours.

Cognitive therapy assumes that faulty thought processes—beliefs that are irrational, that are overly demanding, or that fail to match reality—create problem behaviours and emotions (Barlow, 2008; Corey, 2009; Davies, 2008; Ellis, 1996, 2003b, 2004; Kellogg & Young, 2008).

Like psychoanalysts, cognitive therapists believe that exploring unexamined beliefs can produce insight into the reasons for disturbed behaviours. However, instead of believing that a change in behaviour occurs because of insight and catharsis, cognitive therapists believe that insight into negative self-talk (the unrealistic things a

person tells himself or herself) is most important. Through a process called **cognitive restructuring**, cognitive therapists help clients to challenge their thoughts, change how they interpret events, and change maladaptive behaviours (**FIGURE 14.2**).

In addition, whereas psychoanalysts focus primarily on childhood family relationships, cognitive therapists assume that a broad range of events and people—both inside and outside the family—influence beliefs.

One of the best-known cognitive therapists was Albert Ellis (1913–2007), who developed an approach known as rational-emotive therapy (RET) (1961, 2003a, 2003b, 2004). Ellis called RET an A-B-C-D approach, referring to the four steps involved in creating and dealing with maladaptive thinking: an activating event, the person's belief system, the emotional and behavioural consequences that the person experiences, and disputing (or challenging) erroneous beliefs (**FIGURE 14.3**).

According to Ellis, when people demand certain "musts" ("I must get into graduate school") and "shoulds" ("He should love me") from themselves and others, they create emotional distress and behavioural dysfunction (David, Schnur, & Belloiu, 2002; Ellis, 1997, 2003a, 2003b, 2004).

Cognitive restructuring FIGURE 14.2

By changing the way a person interprets events, cognitive restructuring helps alter his or her behaviour.

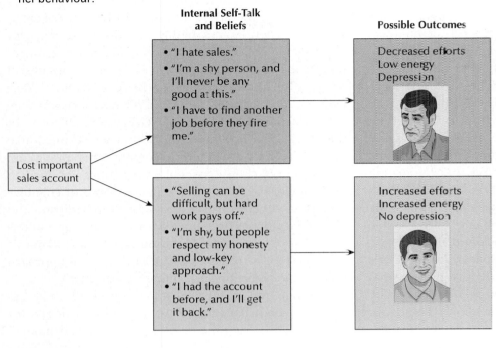

Internal Self-Talk and Beliefs

- "I hate sales."
- "I'm a shy person, and I'll never be any good at this."
- "I have to find another job before they fire me."

Possible Outcomes

Decreased efforts
Low energy
Depression

A Note how the negative interpretation and dysfunctional self-talk lead to dysfunctional and self-defeating outcomes.

Lost important sales account

- "Selling can be difficult, but hard work pays off."
- "I'm shy, but people respect my honesty and low-key approach."
- "I had the account before, and I'll get it back."

Increased efforts
Increased energy
No depression

B Cognitive therapy teaches clients to challenge and change their negative beliefs and negative self-talk into positive ones, which, in turn, leads to more positive outcomes. Can you think of other situations in which such reinterpretation could be helpful?

The development and treatment of irrational misconceptions FIGURE 14.3

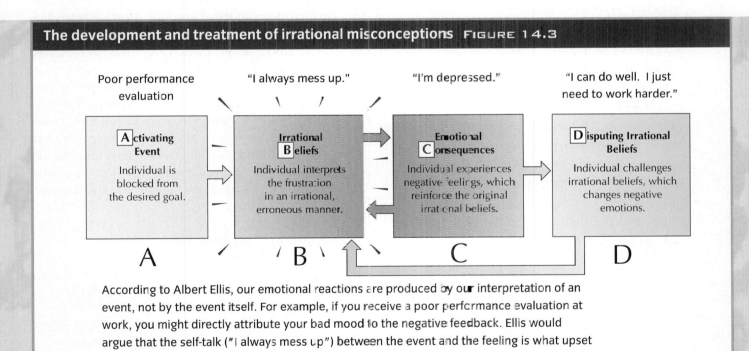

Poor performance evaluation

"I always mess up."

"I'm depressed."

"I can do well. I just need to work harder."

Activating Event

Individual is blocked from the desired goal.

B Irrational Beliefs

Individual interprets the frustration in an irrational, erroneous manner.

C Emotional Consequences

Individual experiences negative feelings, which reinforce the original irrational beliefs.

Disputing Irrational Beliefs

Individual challenges irrational beliefs, which changes negative emotions.

A   B   C   D

According to Albert Ellis, our emotional reactions are produced by our interpretation of an event, not by the event itself. For example, if you receive a poor performance evaluation at work, you might directly attribute your bad mood to the negative feedback. Ellis would argue that the self-talk ("I always mess up") between the event and the feeling is what upset you. Furthermore, ruminating on all the other bad things in your life maintains your negative emotional state. Ellis' therapy emphasizes disputing, or challenging, these irrational beliefs, which, in turn, causes changes in maladaptive emotions—it breaks the vicious cycle.

Process Diagram

Rational-emotive therapists believe that such unrealistic, unproductive self-talk generally goes unexamined unless the client is confronted directly. In therapy, Ellis would often argue with clients, cajoling and teasing them, sometimes in very blunt language. Once clients recognized their self-defeating thoughts, he would begin working with them on how to behave differently—to test out new beliefs and to learn better coping skills. Reflecting this increased attention to behavioural change, Ellis renamed his therapy **rational-emotive behaviour therapy (REBT)** (Crosby, 2003).

Another well-known cognitive therapist is Aaron Beck (1976, 2000). Like Ellis, Beck believes that psychological problems result from illogical thinking and negative self-talk. But Beck seeks to directly confront and change the behaviours associated with negative cognitions by providing clients with experiences, both inside and outside the therapy session, that will alter their self-talk in a favourable way—hence the term **cognitive-behaviour therapy**.

One of the most successful applications of Beck's theory has been in the treatment of depression. Beck has identified several maladaptive thinking patterns that he believes are associated with depression. These are among the most important:

- *Selective perception.* Depression-prone people tend to focus selectively on negative events while ignoring positive events.

- *Overgeneralization.* Depressed people overgeneralize and draw negative conclusions about their self-worth—for example, believing that they are completely worthless because they lost a promotion or failed an exam.

- *Magnification.* Depressed people tend to exaggerate the importance of undesirable events or personal shortcomings, seeing them as catastrophic and unchangeable.

- *All-or-nothing thinking.* Depressed people see things as black or white: totally good or bad, right or wrong, a success or a failure.

In Beck's cognitive-behaviour therapy, clients are first taught to recognize and keep track of their thoughts. Next, the therapist trains the client to develop ways to test these automatic thoughts against reality. This approach helps depressed people discover that negative attitudes are largely a product of unrealistic or faulty thought processes (**FIGURE 14.4**).

At this point, Beck introduces the second phase of therapy—persuading the client to actively pursue pleasurable activities. Depressed individuals often lose motivation, even for experiences they used to find enjoyable. Simultaneously taking an active rather than a passive role and reconnecting with enjoyable experiences help in recovering from depression.

Cognitive therapies, whether REBT or cognitive-behaviour therapy, are highly effective treatments for depression, anxiety disorders, bulimia nervosa, anger management, addiction, and even some symptoms of schizophrenia and insomnia (Beck & Grant, 2008; Dobson, 2008; Ellis, 2003a, 2003b, 2004; Kellogg & Young, 2008; Neenan, 2008; Palmer & Gyllensten, 2008). Over the past 25 years, cognitive therapies have become quite popular in Canada. Training in cognitive therapy is a core component of clinical psychology programs in Canadian universities, and many clinicians make use of cognitive therapy techniques. Toronto's Centre for Addiction and Mental Health has developed a specialized centre in this approach: Its Cognitive-Behavioural Therapy Clinic is renowned for its research and training in this approach (Centre for Addiction and Mental Health, 2008).

Despite the popularity and efficacy of their approaches, both Beck and Ellis have been criticized for ignoring or denying the client's unconscious dynamics, overemphasizing rationality, and minimizing the importance of the client's past (Hammack, 2003). Other critics suggest that cognitive therapies are successful because they employ behaviour techniques, not because they change the underlying cognitive structure (Bandura, 1969, 1997, 2006, 2008; Laidlaw & Thompson, 2008; Wright & Beck, 1999). Imagine that you sought treatment for depression and learned to construe events more positively and to curb your all-or-nothing thinking. Imagine that your therapist also helped you identify activities and behaviours that would promote greater fulfillment. If you found your depression lessening, would you attribute the improvement to your changing thought patterns or to changes in your overt behaviour?

HUMANISTIC THERAPIES: BLOCKED PERSONAL GROWTH

Humanistic therapy assumes that people with problems are suffering from a disruption of their normal growth potential and, hence, their self-concept (Chapter 12). When obstacles are removed, the individual is

> ■ **humanistic therapy** Therapy that seeks to maximize personal growth through affective restructuring (emotional readjustment).

In cognitive-behaviour therapy, clients often record their thoughts in thought journals so that, together with the therapist, they can compare their thoughts with reality, detecting and correcting faulty thinking.

Name: ___Jordan Holley___   Date: ___November 11___

DYSFUNCTIONAL THOUGHT RECORD

Directions: When you notice your mood getting worse, ask yourself, **"What's going through my mind right now?"** and as soon as possible jot down the thought or mental image in the Automatic Thought Column.

DATE/TIME	SITUATION	AUTOMATIC THOUGHT(S)	EMOTION(S)	ALTERNATIVE RESPONSE	OUTCOME
	1. What actual event or stream of thoughts, or day-dreams, or recollection led to the unpleasant emotion? 2. What (if any) distressing physical sensations did you have?	1. What thought(s) and/or image(s) went through your mind? 2. How much did you believe each one at the time?	1. What emotion(s) (sad, anxious, angry, etc.) did you feel at the time? 2. How intense (0–100%) was the emotion?	1. (optional) What cognitive distortion did you make (e.g., all-or-nothing thinking, mind-reading, catastrophizing)? 2. Use questions at the bottom to compose a response to the automatic thought(s). 3. How much do you believe each response?	1. How much do you now believe each automatic thought? 2. What emotion(s) do you feel now? How intense (0–100%) is the emotion? 3. What will you do? (or did you do?)
Nov. 10, 9 P.M.	My mom called last night. When I saw her number on the caller I.D., I felt my jaw clench and my heart rate go up. 	She's going to nag me again to spend the whole Thanksgiving weekend there to make me feel guilty. I was 90% this was it, so I didn't pick up.	I felt angry and frustrated. Intensity = about 80%	Cognitive distortion was mind-reading or maybe all-or-nothing thinking. The evidence that the automatic thoughts were true is from my past talks with my mom. Maybe she was calling for another reason, not to make me feel guilty about Thanksgiving. The worst that could happen is that she'd make me feel guilty again... if so, I could refuse to feel that way. I could also say I didn't like the repeated pressure — it makes me guilty and sad. Maybe she'd understand and we'd break this pattern, or she'd stop nagging me so much. Now, I feel angry whenever she calls and often don't pick up the phone. If I changed my thinking, maybe I'll feel better about her calls, at least sometimes. So, I should work on not expecting the worst when she calls.	1. 50% 2. Now I feel more optimistic, anger is decreased to about 20% 3. Next time I will remind myself of the alternative response before picking up the phone.

Questions to help compose an alternative response:

1. What is the evidence that the automatic thought is true? Not true?
2. Is there an alternative explanation?
3. What's the worst that could happen? If it did happen, how could I cope? What's the best that could happen? What's the most realistic outcome?
4. What's the effect of my believing the automatic thought? What could be the effect of changing my thinking?
5. What should I do about it?
6. If_____ (friend's name) was in this situation and had this thought, what would I tell him/her?

free to become the self-accepting, genuine person everyone is capable of being.

One of the best-known humanistic therapists is Carl Rogers (Rogers, 1961, 1980), who developed an approach that encourages people to actualize their potential and to relate to others in genuine ways. His approach is referred to as **client-centred therapy** (Rogers used the term *client* because he believed the label *patient* implied that the person was sick or mentally ill, rather than being responsible and competent) (**FIGURE 14.5**).

Client-centred therapy, like psychoanalysis and cognitive therapies, explores thoughts and feelings as a way for clients to obtain insight into the causes of their behaviours. For Rogerian therapists, however, the focus is on providing an accepting atmosphere and encouraging healthy emotional experiences. Clients are responsible for discovering their own maladaptive patterns.

Rogerian therapists create a therapeutic relationship by focusing on four important qualities of communication: empathy, unconditional positive regard, genuineness, and active listening.

Nurturing growth FIGURE 14.5

Imagine how you feel when you are with someone who believes that you are a good person with unlimited potential, a person who believes that your "real self" is unique and valuable. These are the feelings that are nurtured in humanistic therapy.

Applying Psychology

Client-Centred Therapy in Action

This is an excerpt from an actual session. As you can see, humour and informality can be an important part of the therapeutic process.

THERAPIST (TH): What has it been like coming down to the emergency room today?

CLIENT (CL): Unsettling, to say the least. I feel very awkward here, sort of like I'm vulnerable. To be honest, I've had some horrible experiences with doctors. I don't like them.

TH: I see. Well, they scare the hell out of me, too (smiles, indicating the humour in his comment).

CL: (Chuckles) I thought you were a doctor.

TH: I am (pauses, smiles)—that's what's so scary.

CL: (Smiles and laughs)

TH: Tell me a little more about some of your unpleasant experiences with doctors, because I want to make sure I'm not doing anything that is upsetting to you. I don't want that to happen.

CL: Well, that's very nice to hear. My last doctor didn't give a hoot about what I said, and he only spoke in huge words. (Shea, 1988, pp. 32–33).

Stop & Think
1. What techniques of client-centred therapy are being used in this excerpt?
2. If you were the client in this case, would you find this exchange helpful?

Empathy

Empathy is a sensitive understanding and sharing of another person's inner experience, putting yourself into another's shoes. Therapists pay attention to body language and listen for subtle cues to help them understand the emotional experiences of clients. To help clients explore their feelings, therapists use open-ended statements, such as "You found that upsetting" or "You haven't been able to decide what to do about this," rather than asking questions or offering explanations.

Unconditional Positive Regard

Unconditional positive regard is genuine caring for people based on their innate value as individuals. Because humanists believe human nature is positive and each person is unique, clients can be respected and cherished without having to prove themselves worthy of the therapist's esteem. The therapist avoids judging the client and his or her actions. Humanists believe that when people receive unconditional caring from others, they become better able to value themselves in a similar way.

Genuineness

Genuineness, or *authenticity*, is being aware of our true inner thoughts and feelings, and sharing them honestly with others. Humanists believe that when therapists are genuine with their clients, their clients will, in turn, develop self-trust and honest self-expression.

Active Listening

Active listening involves reflecting, paraphrasing, and clarifying what the client says and means. By being an active listener, the clinician communicates that he or she is genuinely interested in what the client is saying (**FIGURE 14.6**).

Supporters say that there is empirical evidence for the efficacy of client-centred therapy (Hardcastle et al., 2008; Kirschenbaum & Jourdan, 2005; Lein & Wills, 2007; Stiles et al., 2008), but critics argue that such outcomes as self-actualization and self-awareness are difficult to test scientifically. In addition, research on specific therapeutic techniques, such as "empathy" and "active listening" has had mixed results (Clark, 2007; Hodges & Biswas-Diener, 2007; Rosenthal, 2007).

GROUP, FAMILY, AND MARITAL THERAPIES: HEALING INTERPERSONAL RELATIONSHIPS

In contrast to the therapies described so far, group, marital, and family therapies treat multiple individuals simultaneously. During sessions, therapists often apply psychoanalytic, cognitive, and humanistic techniques.

Active listening FIGURE 14.6

Noticing a client's brow furrowing and hands clenching while he is discussing his marital problems, a clinician might respond, "It sounds as if you're angry with your wife and feeling pretty miserable right now." Can you see how this statement reflects the client's anger, paraphrases his complaint, and gives feedback to clarify the communication?

In **group therapy**, multiple people meet together to work toward therapeutic goals. Typically, a group of 8 to 10 people meet with a therapist on a regular basis to talk about problems in their lives.

A variation on group therapy is the **self-help group**. Unlike other group therapy approaches, a professional does not guide these groups. They are simply groups of people who share a common problem (such as alcoholism, single parenthood, or breast cancer) and who meet to give and receive support. Such programs as Alcoholics Anonymous,

group therapy
A form of therapy in which a number of people meet together to work toward therapeutic goals.

Narcotics Anonymous, and Spenders Anonymous are good examples of self-help groups.

Although group members don't get the same level of individual attention found in one-on-one therapies, group and self-help therapies provide their own unique advantages (Corey, 2009; Minuchin, Lee, & Simon, 2007; Qualls, 2008). Compared with one-on-one therapies, they are less expensive and provide a broader base of social support. Group members can learn from one another's mistakes, share insights and coping strategies, and role-play social interactions together.

Therapists often refer their patients to group therapy and self-help groups to supplement individual therapy. Research on self-help groups for alcoholism, obesity, and other disorders suggests that they can be very effective, either alone or in addition to individual psychotherapy (McEvoy, 2007; Oei & Dingle, 2008; Silverman et al., 2008).

Because a family or marriage is a system of interdependent parts, the problem of any one individual unavoidably affects all the others, and therapy can help everyone involved (Minuchin, et al., 2007; Qualls, 2008). The line between marital (or couples) therapy and family therapy is often blurred. Here, our discussion will focus on **family therapy**, in which the primary aim is to change maladaptive family interaction patterns (**FIGURE 14.7**). All members of the family attend therapy sessions, though at times the therapist may see family members individually or in twos or threes.

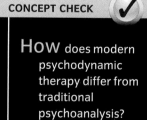

family therapy
Treatment to change maladaptive interaction patterns within a family.

Family therapy is also useful in treating a number of disorders and clinical problems. As we discuss in Chapter 13, schizophrenic patients are more likely to relapse if their family members express emotions, attitudes, and behaviours that involve criticism, hostility, or emotional overinvolvement (Hooley & Hiller, 2001; Lefley, 2000; Quinn, Barrowclough, & Tarrier, 2003). Family therapy can help family members modify their behaviour toward the patient. Family therapy can also be the most favourable setting for the treatment of adolescent drug abuse (Minuchin et al., 2007; Ng et al., 2008; O'Farrell et al., 2008; Sim & Wong, 2008).

Family therapy FIGURE 14.7

Many families initially come into therapy believing that one member is the cause of all their problems. However, family therapists generally find that this "identified patient" is a scapegoat for deeper disturbances. For example, instead of confronting their own problems with intimacy, a couple may focus all their attention and frustration on a delinquent child (Hanna & Brown, 1999). How could changing ways of interacting within the family system promote the health of individual family members and the family as a whole?

CONCEPT CHECK ✓

How does modern psychodynamic therapy differ from traditional psychoanalysis?

What are the four steps of Ellis' RET?

What is the significance of the term *client-centred therapy*?

When might family therapy be more successful than individual psychotherapy?

Behaviour Therapies

Sometimes having insight into a problem does not automatically solve it. In **behaviour therapy**, the focus is on the problem behaviour itself, rather than on any underlying causes. Although the person's feelings and interpretations are not disregarded, they are also not emphasized. The therapist diagnoses the problem by listing maladaptive behaviours that occur and adaptive behaviours that are absent. The therapist then attempts to shift the balance of the two, drawing on the learning principles of classical conditioning, operant conditioning, and observational learning (Chapter 6).

> **behaviour therapy** A group of techniques based on learning principles that is used to change malacaptive behaviours.

© Sidney Harris

CLASSICAL CONDITIONING TECHNIQUES

Behaviour therapists use the principles of classical conditioning to decrease maladaptive behaviours by creating new associations to replace the faulty ones. We will explore two techniques based on these principles: aversion therapy and systematic desensitization.

Aversion therapy uses principles of classical conditioning to create anxiety rather than extinguish it (**FIGURE 14.8**). People who engage in excessive drinking, for example, build up a number of pleasurable associations. Because these pleasurable associations cannot always be prevented, aversion therapy provides negative associations to compete with the pleasurable ones. Someone who wants to stop drinking, for example, could take a drug called Antabuse, which causes nausea whenever alcohol is consumed. When the new connection between alcohol and nausea has been classically conditioned, engaging in the once-desirable behaviour will cause an immediate negative response: Alcohol has now become a conditioned stimulus for nausea.

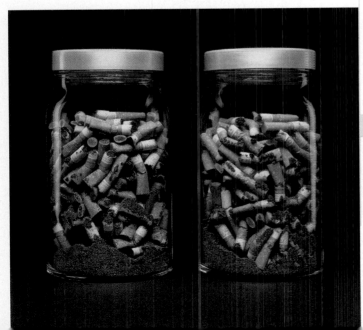

Making a nasty habit nastier FIGURE 14.8

A person who wants to quit smoking could collect a jar full of (smelly) cigarette butts or smoke several cigarettes at once to create an aversion to smoking. Can you see how this aversion therapy uses classical conditioning?

Rather than using mental imaging or actual physical experiences of a fearful situation, modern therapy can use the latest in computer technology—virtual reality headsets and data gloves. A Canadian researcher, Stéphane Bouchard of the Université du Québec en Outaouais, is among the leading researchers in the use of computer-generated environments to treat phobias. What kind of "virtual" experiences do you think a therapist might provide for a client with a fear of spiders?

Aversion therapy is controversial. First, some researchers question whether it is ethical to hurt someone (even when the person has given permission). The treatment also has been criticized because it does not provide lasting relief (Seligman, 1994). One reason is that (in the case of the aversion therapy for alcoholism) people understand that the nausea is produced by the Antabuse and do not generalize their learning to the alcohol.

In contrast to aversion therapy, **systematic desensitization** (Wolpe & Plaud, 1997) begins with relaxation training, followed by imagining or directly experiencing various versions of a feared object or situation while remaining deeply relaxed. The goal is to replace an anxiety response with a relaxation response when confronting the feared stimulus (Heriot & Pritchard, 2004). Recently, some therapists have been using advanced technologies to aid in the desensitization process (**FIGURE 14.9**).

Desensitization is a three-step process. First, a client is taught how to maintain a state of deep relaxation that is physiologically incompatible with an anxiety response. Next, the therapist and client construct a hierarchy, or ranked listing, of anxiety-arousing images (**FIGURE 14.10**). In the final step, the relaxed client mentally visualizes or physically experiences items in the hierarchy, starting at the bottom and working his or her way to the most anxiety-producing images at the top. If any image or situation begins to create anxiety, the client stops momentarily and returns to a state of complete relaxation. Eventually, the fear response is extinguished.

OPERANT CONDITIONING TECHNIQUES

As we learned in Chapter 6, operant conditioning involves learning to associate a behaviour with its consequences. One operant conditioning technique for eventually bringing about a desired (or target) behaviour is **shaping**—providing rewards for successive approximations of the target behaviour. One of the most successful applications of shaping and reinforcement has been with developing language skills in children with autism. First, the child is rewarded for making any sounds, and later, only for forming words and sentences.

Shaping can also help people acquire social skills and greater assertiveness. If you are painfully shy, for example, a clinician might first ask you to role-play simply saying hello to someone you find attractive. Then you might practise behaviours that gradually lead you to suggest a date. During such role-playing, or behaviour rehearsal, the clinician would give you feedback and reinforcement.

Adaptive behaviours can also be taught or increased with techniques that provide immediate reinforcement in the form of tokens (Kazdin, 2008; Tarbox, Ghezzi, & Wilson, 2006). For example, patients in an inpatient treatment facility might at first be given tokens (to be exchanged for primary rewards, such as food, treats, TV time, a private room, or outings) for merely attending group therapy sessions. Later they will be rewarded only for actually participating in the sessions. Eventually, the tokens can be discontinued when the patient receives the reinforcement of being helped by participation in the therapy sessions.

OBSERVATIONAL LEARNING TECHNIQUES

We all learn many things by observing others. Therapists use this principle in **modelling therapy**, in which clients are asked to observe and imitate appropriate models as they perform desired behaviours. For example, Albert Bandura (1969) asked clients with snake phobias to watch other (non-phobic) people handle snakes. After only two hours of exposure, more than 92 percent of the phobic observers allowed a snake to crawl over their hands, arms, and necks.

modelling therapy A learning technique in which the subject watches and imitates models who demonstrate desirable behaviours.

Made eine, a college student, has been offered a lucrative summer job painting commercial buildings. She is deathly afraid of heights, but she needs the money. She goes to see a therapist, who tells her that she can be treated in a relatively brief period of time through systematic desensitization. To understand how this works, look at the six behavioural steps depicted on the continuum. Can you see how this technique might help Madeleine gradually overcome her fear of heights?

Least   1   3   Amount of anxiety   5   Most

2   4   6

NATIONAL GEOGRAPHIC

Modelling is also part of social skills training and assertiveness training. Clients learn how to interview for a job by first watching the therapist role-play the part of the interviewee. The therapist models the appropriate language (assertively asking for a job), body posture, and so forth, and then asks the client to imitate the behaviour and play the same role. Over several sessions, the client gradually becomes desensitized to the anxiety of interviews and learns interview skills.

EVALUATING BEHAVIOUR THERAPIES

Behaviour therapy has been effective in treating various problems, including phobias, obsessive-compulsive disorder (OCD), eating disorders, autism, development disability, and delinquency (Ekers, Richards, & Gilbody, 2008; Miltenberger, 2008). Critics of behaviour therapy, however, raise important questions that fall into two major categories:

- *Generalizability.* What happens after the treatment stops? Critics argue that in the "real world," patients are not consistently reinforced, and their newly acquired behaviours may

disappear. To deal with this possibility, behaviour therapists work to gradually shape clients toward rewards that are typical of life outside the clinic setting.

- *Ethics.* Critics contend that it can be unethical for one person to control another's behaviour. Behaviourists, however, argue that rewards and punishments already control our behaviours and that behaviour therapy actually increases a person's freedom by making these controls overt and by teaching people how to change their own behaviour.

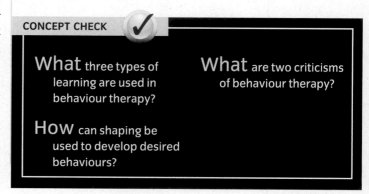

CONCEPT CHECK

What three types of learning are used in behaviour therapy?

How can shaping be used to develop desired behaviours?

What are two criticisms of behaviour therapy?

Biomedical Therapies

Biomedical therapies are based on the premise that problem behaviours are caused, at least in part, by chemical imbalances or disordered nervous system functioning. A physician, rather than a psychologist, must prescribe biomedical therapies, but psychologists do work with patients receiving biomedical therapies and are frequently involved in research programs to evaluate their effectiveness. In this section, we will discuss three aspects of biomedical therapies: psychopharmacology, electroconvulsive therapy (ECT), and psychosurgery.

biomedical therapy The use of physiological interventions (drugs, electroconvulsive therapy, and psychosurgery) to reduce or alleviate symptoms of psychological disorders.

PSYCHOPHARMACOLOGY: TREATING PSYCHOLOGICAL DISORDERS WITH DRUGS

psychopharmacology The study of drug effects on the brain and behaviour.

Since the 1950s, drug companies have developed an amazing variety of chemicals to treat abnormal behaviours. In some cases, discoveries from **psychopharmacology** have helped correct chemical imbalances. In other cases, drugs have been used to relieve or suppress the symptoms of psychological disturbances even when the underlying cause was not thought to be biological. Canadian researchers have been at the forefront of this field. The first North American research on the use of drugs to control the symptoms of psychosis was published in 1954 by Dr. Hans Lehmann of Montreal (Davison et al., 2008). Moreover, for the last 15 years, a nationwide network of researchers in hospitals and universities—the Canadian Network for Mood and Anxiety Treatments (CANMAT)—has promoted innovative research and education in pharmaceutical treatment of mental disorders (Canadian Network for Mood and Anxiety Treatments, 2009). As shown in TABLE 14.1, psychiatric drugs are classified into four major categories: antianxiety, antipsychotic, mood stabilizer, and antidepressant.

- **Antianxiety drugs** (also known as "minor tranquilizers" or anxiolytics) lower the sympathetic activity of the brain—the crisis mode of operation—so that anxious responses are diminished or

"Before Prozac, she loathed company."

© The New Yorker Collection 1993. Lee Lorenz from cartoonbank.com. All Rights Reserved.

Common drug treatments for psychological disorders TABLE 14.1

Type of Drug (Chemical Group)	Psychological Disorder	Generic Name	Brand Name
Antianxiety drugs (Benzodiazepines)	Anxiety disorders	alprazolam	Xanax
		diazepam	Valium
		lorazepam	Ativan
Antipsychotic drugs (Phenothiazines Butyrophenones Atypical antipsychotics)	Schizophrenia and bipolar disorders	chlorpromazine	Thorazine
		fluphenazine	Prolixin
		thioridazine	Mellaril
		haloperidol	Haldol
		clozapine	Clozaril
		resperidone	Risperdal
		quetiapine	Seroquel
Mood stabilizer drugs (Antimanic)	Bipolar disorder	lithium carbonate	Eskalith CR
		carbamazepine	Lithobid
			Tegretol
Antidepressant drugs Tricyclic antidepressants Monoamine oxidase inhibitors (MAOIs) Selective serotonin reuptake inhibitors (SSRIs) Serotonin and norepinephrine reuptake inhibitors (SNRIs) Atypical antidepressants	Depressive disorders	imipramine	Tofranil
		amitriptyline	Elavil
		phenelzine	Nardil
		paroxetine	Paxil
		fluoxetine	Prozac
		venlafaxine	Effexor
		duloxetine	Cymbalta
		bupropion	Wellbutrin
		mirtazapine	Remeron

prevented and are replaced by feelings of tranquility and calmness (Barlow, 2008; Swartz, 2008).

- **Antipsychotic drugs,** or neuroleptics, are used to treat schizophrenia and other acute psychotic states. They are often referred to as "major tranquilizers," creating the mistaken impression that they invariably have a strong sedating effect. However, the main effect of antipsychotic drugs is to diminish or eliminate psychotic symptoms, including hallucinations, delusions, withdrawal, and apathy. They are not designed to sedate the patient. Traditional antipsychotics work by decreasing activity at the dopamine synapses in the brain. A large majority of patients show marked improvement when treated with antipsychotic drugs.

- **Mood-stabilizer drugs,** such as lithium, can help relieve manic episodes and depression for people with bipolar disorder. Because lithium acts relatively slowly—it can be three or four weeks before it takes effect—its primary use is in preventing future episodes and helping to break the manic-depressive cycle.

- **Antidepressant drugs** are used to treat people with depression. There are five types of antidepressant drugs: tricyclics, monoamine oxidase inhibitors (MAOIs), selective serotonin reuptake inhibitors (SSRIs), serotonin and norepinephrine reuptake inhibitors (SNRIs), and atypical antidepressants. Each class of drugs affects neurochemical pathways in the brain in slightly different ways, increasing or decreasing the availability of certain neurochemicals. SSRIs (such as Paxil and Prozac) are by far the most commonly prescribed antidepressants. The atypical antidepressants are a miscellaneous group of drugs used for patients who fail to respond to the other drugs or for people who experience side effects common to other antidepressants.

ELECTROCONVULSIVE THERAPY AND PSYCHOSURGERY

In **electroconvulsive therapy (ECT)**, also known as electroshock therapy (EST), a moderate electrical current is passed through the brain between two electrodes placed on the outside of the head. The current triggers a widespread firing of neurons, resulting in a convulsion or seizure. The convulsions produce many changes in the central and peripheral nervous systems, including activation of the autonomic nervous system, increased secretion of various hormones and neurotransmitters, and changes in the blood-brain barrier.

> **electroconvulsive therapy (ECT)** Biomedical therapy in which electrical current is passed through the brain.

During the early years of ECT, some patients received hundreds of treatments (Fink, 1999), but today most receive 12 or fewer treatments. Sometimes the electrical current is applied only to the right hemisphere, which causes less interference with verbal memories and left hemisphere functioning.

Modern ECT is used primarily on patients with severe depression who do not respond to antidepressant drugs or psychotherapy and on suicidal patients because it works much faster than antidepressant drugs (Birkenhäger, Renes, & Pluijms, 2004; Goforth & Holsinger, 2007). In his account of his personal struggle with bipolar disorder (Chapter 13), Dr. Norman Endler (1982) of York University provided a well-balanced discussion of the pros and cons of ECT, cogently describing its rapid and positive effects on his depression. (ECT is described further in *What a Psychologist Sees.*)

Although clinical studies of ECT conclude that it is effective for very severe depression (Jain et al., 2008; Khalid et al., 2008), its use remains controversial because it triggers massive changes in the brain—and because we do not fully understand why it works (Baldwin & Oxlad, 2000; Cloud, 2001; Pearlman, 2002).

The most extreme, and least used, biomedical therapy is **psychosurgery**—brain surgery performed to reduce serious, debilitating psychological problems.

You may have heard of lobotomy, a form of psychosurgery that is no longer practised. This technique originated in 1936, when Portuguese neurologist Egaz Moniz first treated uncontrollable psychoses by cutting the nerve fibres between the frontal lobes (where association areas for monitoring and planning behaviour are found) and the thalamus and hypothalamus.

> **psychosurgery** Operative procedures on the brain designed to relieve severe mental symptoms that have not responded to other forms of treatment.

Electroconvulsive Therapy (ECT)

Although electroconvulsive therapy may seem cruel, for some severely depressed people it is their only hope for lifting the depression. Unlike portrayals of ECT in movies like *One Flew Over the Cuckoo's Nest* and *The Snake Pit*, patients show few, if any, visible reactions to the treatment, because patients are now sedated and given muscle-relaxant drugs that dramatically reduce muscle contractions during the seizure. Most ECT patients are also given an anaesthetic to block their memories of the treatment, but some patients still find the treatment extremely uncomfortable (Jain et al., 2008; Khalid et al., 2008). However, for many others, it is lifesaving.

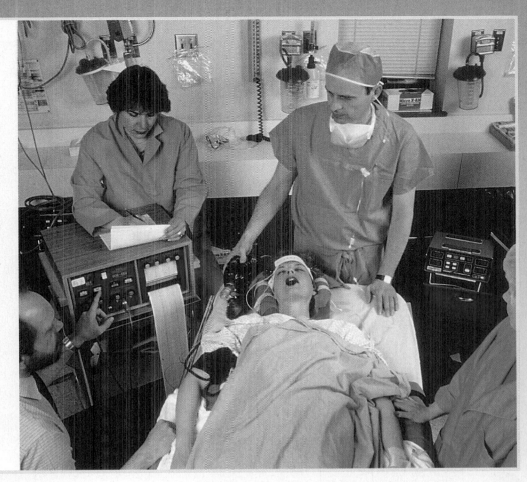

Although these surgeries did reduce emotional outbursts and aggressiveness, many patients were left with permanent brain damage. In the mid-1950s, when antipsychotic drugs came into use, psychosurgery virtually stopped. Recently, however, psychiatrists have been experimenting with a much more limited and precise surgical procedure called *cingulotomy*, in which the cingulum (a small structure in the brain's limbic system known to be involved in emotionality) is partially destroyed. On rare occasions, it is used in the treatment of severely debilitating cases of obsessive-compulsive disorder; severe depression; and chronic, intractable pain (Cohen et al., 2001; Dougherty et al., 2002; Sotres-Bayón & Pellicer, 2000).

EVALUATING BIOMEDICAL THERAPIES

Like all forms of therapy, biomedical therapies have both proponents and critics.

Pitfalls of Psychopharmacology Drug therapy poses several potential problems. First, although drugs may relieve symptoms for some people, they seldom provide cures. We can easily treat an anxiety disorder with a drug, but the symptoms return when the medication stops. To cure the disorder the patient needs some form of psychotherapy. In addition, some patients become physically dependent on the drugs. Also, researchers are still learning about the long-term effects and potential interactions of these medications. Furthermore, psychiatric medications can cause a variety of side effects, ranging from mild fatigue to severe impairments in memory and movement.

A final potential problem with drug treatment is that its relative inexpensiveness and generally fast results have led to its overuse in some cases. One report found that antidepressants are prescribed roughly 50 percent of the time a patient walks into a psychiatrist's office (Olfson et al., 1998).

What about Herbal Remedies?

Some recent research suggests that the herbal supplement St. John's Wort may be an effective treatment for mild to moderate depression, with fewer side effects than traditional medications (Butterweck, 2003; Lecrubier et al., 2002; Mayers et al., 2003). However, other studies have found the drug to be ineffective for people with major depression (Hypericum Depression Trial Study Group, 2002). Herbal supplements, like kava, valerian, and gingko biloba, also have been used in the treatment of anxiety, insomnia, and memory problems (e.g., Connor & Davidson, 2002; Parrott et al., 2004). Although many people assume that these products are safe because they are "natural," they can produce a number of potentially serious side effects. Since 2004, the Natural Health Products Directorate (NHPD) branch of Health Canada has regulated the quality, importing, and labelling of, as well as claims that manufacturers can make about herbal supplements (Health Canada, 2009b). However, because they are not considered drugs, natural remedies do not typically undergo the same rigorous research trials as do pharmaceuticals. For these reasons, researchers advise a wait-and-see approach (Crone & Gabriel, 2002; Swartz, 2008).

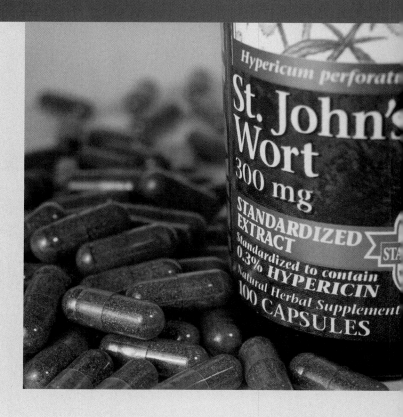

Stop & Think
1. Do you think herbal remedies should be regulated by the government in the same way as drugs?
2. Do you think these products should carry labels warning that they can produce potentially serious side effects?

Despite the problems associated with them, psychotherapeutic drugs have led to revolutionary changes in mental health. Before the use of drugs, some patients were destined to spend a lifetime in psychiatric institutions. Today, most patients improve enough to return to their homes and live successful lives if they continue to take their medications to prevent relapse.

Challenges to ECT and Psychosurgery
As we mentioned, ECT is a controversial treatment for several reasons. However, problems with ECT may become obsolete thanks to **repetitive transcranial magnetic stimulation (rTMS),** which delivers a brief (but powerful) electrical current through a coil of wire placed close to the head. Unlike ECT, which passes a strong electrical current directly through the brain, the rTMS coil creates a strong magnetic field that is applied to certain areas in the brain. When used to treat depression, the coil is usually placed over the prefrontal cortex, a region linked to deeper parts of the brain that regulate mood. Currently, the benefits of rTMS over ECT remain uncertain (Bloch et al., 2008; Knapp et al., 2008; Wasserman, Epstein, & Ziemann, 2008).

Because all forms of psychosurgery have potentially serious or fatal side effects and complications, some critics suggest that they should be banned altogether. Furthermore, the consequences are irreversible. For these reasons, psychosurgery is considered experimental and remains a highly controversial treatment of last resort.

CONCEPT CHECK ✓

When are drug therapies used?

How does modern ECT differ from the therapy's early use?

Why is psychosurgery a rarely used and controversial treatment?

Therapy Essentials

Earlier, we mentioned that there may be more than 400 forms of therapy. How would you choose one for yourself or someone you know? In this section, we help you to synthesize the material in this chapter and to put what you have learned about each of the major forms of therapy into a broader context.

THERAPY GOALS AND EFFECTIVENESS

All major forms of therapy are designed to help the client in five specific areas (**FIGURE 14.11**).

Although most therapists work with clients in several of these areas, the emphasis varies according to the therapist's training (psychodynamic, cognitive, humanistic, behaviourist, or biomedical). Clinicians who regularly borrow freely from various theories are said to take an **eclectic approach**.

Does therapy work? After many years of controlled research and *meta-analysis* (a method of statistically combining and analyzing data from many studies), we have fairly clear evidence that it does. Forty to 90 percent of people who receive treatment are better off than people who do not. Furthermore, some short-term treatments can be as effective as long-term treatments (Castonguay & Hill, 2007; Cleaves & Latner, 2008; Knekt et al., 2008; Loewental & Winter, 2006; Stiles et al., 2008; Wachtel, 2008).

The five most common goals of therapy FIGURE 14.11

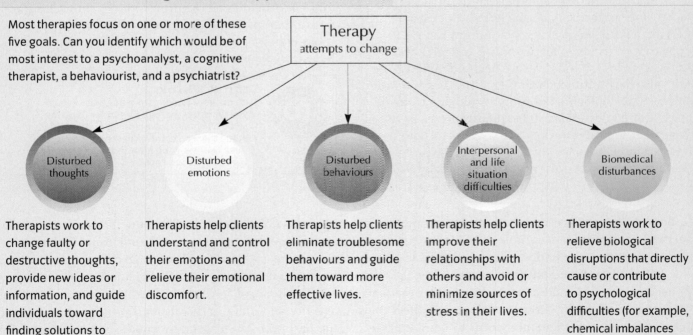

Most therapies focus on one or more of these five goals. Can you identify which would be of most interest to a psychoanalyst, a cognitive therapist, a behaviourist, and a psychiatrist?

Therapy attempts to change

| Disturbed thoughts | Disturbed emotions | Disturbed behaviours | Interpersonal and life situation difficulties | Biomedical disturbances |

Therapists work to change faulty or destructive thoughts, provide new ideas or information, and guide individuals toward finding solutions to problems.

Therapists help clients understand and control their emotions and relieve their emotional discomfort.

Therapists help clients eliminate troublesome behaviours and guide them toward more effective lives.

Therapists help clients improve their relationships with others and avoid or minimize sources of stress in their lives.

Therapists work to relieve biological disruptions that directly cause or contribute to psychological difficulties (for example, chemical imbalances that lead to depression).

Finding a Therapist

When stresses overwhelm our natural coping mechanisms, professional therapy can provide invaluable relief. But how do we find a good therapist for our specific needs? If you have the time (and the money) to explore options, search for a therapist who is best suited to your specific goals. Often your own physician can provide you with a recommendation and a referral. However, if you are in a crisis—you have suicidal thoughts or are the victim of abuse—get help fast (see Chapter 13). Most communities have telephone hotlines that provide counselling on a 24-hour basis. In addition, most colleges and universities have counselling centres that provide immediate, short-term therapy to students free of charge. If you are encouraging someone else to get therapy, you might offer to help locate a therapist and to accompany him or her to the first visit. If he or she refuses help and the problem affects you, it is often a good idea to seek therapy yourself. You will gain insights and skills that will help you deal with the situation more effectively.

In Canada, a variety of therapists are able to offer counselling or psychological help, including psychologists, psychiatrists, social workers, and psychotherapists. *Psychologists* most often have doctoral degrees in psychology with advanced training in the diagnosis and treatment of psychological disorders. Psychologists must be licensed by the province or territory in which they practise (see the Canadian Psychological Association's website at www.cpa.ca for a listing of all provincial and territorial licensing agencies.) *Psychiatrists* are licensed medical doctors who also have advanced training in the diagnosis and treatment of psychological disorders. In addition to providing psychotherapy, psychiatrists frequently prescribe drugs to treat psychological disorders. *Social workers* usually have a master's degree in social work, with expertise in working with families and community agencies, and many also

provide counselling. In the majority of provinces, social workers are licensed (see the Canadian Association of Social Workers website at www.casw-acts.ca). The terms *counsellor* or *psychotherapist* refer to professionals who, although not psychologists or psychiatrists, have advanced training (usually a master's degree) in counselling. In some provinces, counsellors and psychotherapists are licensed by the province. The Canadian Counselling and Psychotherapy Association website, www.ccpa-accp.ca, provides more information on the professions of counselling and psychotherapy. Depending on your situation, goals, and preferences, a professional from one of these groups may be helpful for your needs.

 Stop & Think
1. If you were looking for a therapist, would you want the therapist's gender to be the same as yours, or wouldn't it matter? Why?
2. Some therapists treat clients online. Do you think this is a good idea and would be effective? Why or why not?

Some therapies are more effective than others for specific problems. For example, phobias seem to respond best to systematic desensitization, and OCD can be significantly relieved with cognitive-behaviour therapy accompanied by medication. Most studies that have compared medication alone versus medication plus therapy have found the combination to be more effective (e.g., Doyle & Pollack, 2004).

Who are the people who benefit from psychotherapy? Data from the National Population Health Survey conducted by Statistics Canada reveal some interesting findings (Hunsley & Lee, 2010; Hunsley, Lee, & Aubry, 1999). The survey revealed that 2.2 percent of Canadians aged 12 and older had consulted with a psychologist in the past year. Twice as many women as men sought psychological help. Teenagers and adults between 30 and

50 years of age were most likely to consult a psychologist, as were those with higher education and higher income. Canadians living in urban settings were three times more likely than those in rural settings to consult a psychologist. Those seeking psychological help reported poorer health, higher stress levels, and more distress in their lives, and were more likely to be using medication for their distress. However, despite the documented effectiveness of psychological interventions for many disorders, the study revealed that a large number of Canadians are not receiving treatment. The authors conclude that the Canadian public would benefit from being made more aware of psychotherapeutic interventions and their effectiveness (Hunsley et al., 1999).

CULTURAL ISSUES IN THERAPY

The therapies described in this chapter are based on Western European and North American culture. Does this mean they are unique? Or do our psychotherapists do some of the same things that, say, a native healer or shaman does? Are there similarities in therapies across cultures? Conversely, are there fundamental therapeutic differences among cultures?

When we look at therapies in all cultures, we find that they have certain key features in common (Laungani, 2007; Lee, 2002; Sue & Sue, 2008). Richard Brislin (2000) has summarized some of these features:

- *Naming the problem.* People often feel better just by knowing that others experience the same problem and that the therapist has had experience with their particular problem.

- *Qualities of the therapist.* Clients must feel that the therapist is caring, competent, approachable, and concerned with finding solutions to their problem.

- *Establishing credibility.* Word-of-mouth testimonials and status symbols (such as diplomas on the wall) establish the therapist's credibility. Among native healers, in lieu of diplomas, credibility may be established by having served as an apprentice to a revered healer.

- *Placing the problem in a familiar framework.* If the client believes that evil spirits cause psychological disorders, the therapist will direct treatment toward eliminating these spirits. Similarly, if the client believes in the importance of early childhood experiences and the unconscious mind, psychoanalysis will be the likely treatment of choice.

- *Applying techniques to bring relief.* In all cultures, therapy involves action. Either the client or the therapist must do something. Moreover, what they do must fit the client's expectations—whether it is performing a ceremony to expel demons or talking with the client about his or her thoughts and feelings.

- *A special time and place.* The fact that therapy occurs outside the client's everyday experiences seems to be an important feature of all therapies.

Although there are basic similarities in therapies across cultures, there are also important differences. In the traditional Western European and North American model, the emphasis is on the self and on independence and control over one's life—qualities that are highly valued in individualistic cultures. In collectivist cultures, however, the focus of therapy is on interdependence and accepting the realities of one's life (Sue & Sue, 2008) (FIGURE 14.12).

Emphasizing interdependence FIGURE 14.12

In Japanese Naikan therapy, the patient sits quietly from 5:30 a.m. to 9:00 p.m. for seven days and is visited by an interviewer every 90 minutes. During this time, the patient reflects on his or her relationships with others, with the goals of discovering personal guilt for having been ungrateful and troublesome to others and developing gratitude toward those who have helped (Nakamura, 2006; Ozawa-de Silva, 2007; Ryback, Ikerni, & Miki, 2001). How do these goals and methods differ from those of the therapies we have described in this chapter? Do you think this approach would work with Westerners? Why or why not?

Not only does culture affect the types of therapy that are developed, it also influences the perceptions of the therapist. What one culture considers abnormal behaviour may be quite common—and even healthy—in others. For this reason, recognizing cultural differences is very important for building trust between therapists and clients and for effecting behavioural change (Laungani, 2007; Sue & Sue, 2008; Tseng, 2004).

GENDER AND THERAPY

Within our individualistic Western culture, men and women present different needs and problems to therapists. For example, compared with men, women are more comfortable and familiar with their emotions and have fewer negative attitudes toward therapy (Komiya, Good, & Sherrod, 2000). In contrast, as discussed in Chapter 13, men are more likely to suppress their emotions and to show their distress through being aggressive, acting impulsively, or engaging in substance abuse. Moreover, Canadian women are twice as likely as men to seek psychological help (Hunsley & Lee, 2010).

Research has identified five major concerns related to gender and psychotherapy (Halbreich & Kahn, 2007; Hall, 2007; Hyde, 2007; Matlin, 2008; Russo & Tartaro, 2008).

1. *Rates of diagnosis and treatment of mental disorders.* Women are diagnosed and treated for mental illness at a much higher rate than men. Is this because women experience more mental health problems than men, or are they just more willing to admit their problems? Or perhaps the categories for illness are biased against women. More research is needed to answer this question.

2. *Stresses of poverty.* Women are disproportionately likely to be poor. Poverty contributes to stress, which is directly related to many psychological disorders.

3. *Stresses of multiple roles.* Women today are mothers, wives, homemakers, professionals, wage earners, students, and so on, whereas men are less likely to occupy such multiple roles. The conflicting demands of their multiple roles often create special stresses (**FIGURE 14.13**).

4. *Stresses of aging.* In contrast to men, aging brings additional concerns for women. Women, on average, live longer than men. Older women, primarily those with age-related dementia, account

Paying attention to gender-specific needs
FIGURE 14.13

Therapists must be sensitive to possible connections between clients' problems and their gender. Rather than prescribing drugs to relieve depression in women, for example, it may be more appropriate for therapists to explore ways to relieve the stresses of multiple roles or poverty. Can you see how helping a single mother identify parenting resources, such as play groups, parent support groups, and high-quality child care, might be just as effective at relieving depression as prescribing drugs? In the case of men, can you see how relieving loneliness or depression might alleviate issues with alcohol abuse or aggression?

for more than 70 percent of those with chronic mental illnesses who live in nursing homes.

5. *Violence against women.* Sexual assault, incest, and sexual harassment—which are much more likely to happen to women than to men—may lead to depression, insomnia, post-traumatic stress disorders, eating disorders, and other problems.

INSTITUTIONALIZATION

Despite Hollywood film portrayals, forced institutionalization of people with mental illness poses serious ethical problems and is generally reserved for only the most serious and life-threatening situations or when no reasonable, less restrictive alternative is available.

In emergencies, mental health professionals can authorize temporary commitment for 24 to 72 hours—time enough for laboratory tests to be performed to rule out medical illnesses that could be causing the symptoms. The patient can also receive psychological testing, medication, and short-term therapy during this time.

Today, many provinces have a policy of **deinstitutionalization**—discharging patients from mental hospitals as soon as possible and discouraging admissions (Davison et al., 2008). As an alternative to institutionalizing people in public mental institutions, most clinicians suggest expanding and improving community care (Duckworth & Borus, 1999; Lamb, 2000). They recommend that general hospitals be equipped with special psychiatric units where acutely ill patients can receive in-patient care. For less disturbed individuals and chronically ill patients, they recommend walk-in clinics, crisis intervention services, improved residential treatment facilities, and psychosocial and vocational rehabilitation. Public mental institutions would be reserved for the most unmanageable patients.

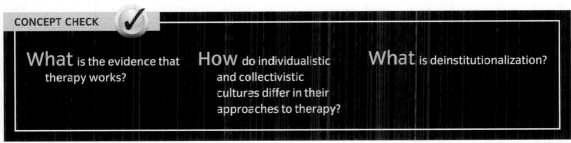

CONCEPT CHECK ✓

What is the evidence that therapy works?

How do individualistic and collectivistic cultures differ in their approaches to therapy?

What is deinstitutionalization?

SUMMARY

1 Insight Therapies

1. **Insight therapies** are forms of **psychotherapy** that seek to increase clients' insight into their difficulties.

2. In **psychoanalysis**, the therapist seeks to identify the patient's unconscious conflicts and to help the patient resolve them through **catharsis**. In modern **psychodynamic therapy**, treatment is briefer and the therapist takes a more directive approach (and puts less emphasis on unconscious childhood memories) than in traditional psychoanalysis.

3. **Cognitive therapy** seeks to help clients challenge faulty thought processes and adjust maladaptive behaviours. Ellis' **rational-emotive behaviour therapy (REBT)** and Beck's **cognitive-behaviour therapy** are important examples of cognitive therapy.

4. **Humanistic therapy**, such as Rogers' **client-centred therapy**, seeks to maximize personal growth, encouraging people to actualize their potential and relate to others in genuine ways.

5. In **group therapy**, multiple people meet together to work toward therapeutic goals. A variation is the **self-help group**, which is not guided by a professional. Therapists often refer their patients to group therapy and self-help groups to supplement individual therapy.

6. In **family therapy**, the aim is to change maladaptive family interaction patterns. All members of the family attend therapy sessions, though at times the therapist may see family members individually or in twos or threes.

2 Behaviour Therapies

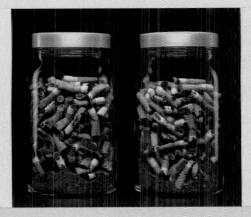

1. In **behaviour therapy**, the focus is on the problem behaviour itself, rather than on any underlying causes. The therapist uses learning principles to change behaviour.

2. Classical conditioning techniques include **aversion therapy** and **systematic desensitization**.

3. Operant conditioning techniques used to increase adaptive behaviours include shaping and reinforcement.

4. In **modelling therapy**, clients observe and imitate others who are performing the desired behaviours.

3 Biomedical Therapies

1. **Biomedical therapies** are based on the premise that chemical imbalances or disturbed nervous system functioning contribute to problem behaviours.

2. **Psychopharmacology** is the most common form of biomedical therapy. Major classes of drugs used to treat psychological disorders are **antianxiety drugs**, **antipsychotic drugs**, **mood-stabilizer drugs**, and **antidepressant drugs**.

3. In **electroconvulsive therapy (ECT)**, an electrical current is passed through the brain, stimulating convulsions that produce changes in the central and peripheral nervous systems. ECT is used primarily in cases of severe depression that do not respond to other treatments.

4. The most extreme biomedical therapy is **psychosurgery**. Lobotomy, an older form of psychosurgery, is now outmoded. Recently, psychiatrists have been experimenting with a more limited and precise surgical procedure called cingulotomy.

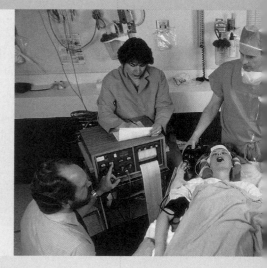

4 Therapy Essentials

1. All major forms of therapy are designed to address disturbed thoughts, disturbed emotions, disturbed behaviours, interpersonal and life situation difficulties, and biomedical disturbances. Research indicates that, overall, therapy does work.

2. Therapies in all cultures have certain key features in common; however, there are also important differences among cultures. Therapists must

recognize cultural differences in order to build trust with clients and effect behavioural change.

3. Therapists must also be sensitive to possible gender issues in therapy.

4. Forced institutionalization of people with mental illnesses is generally reserved for only the most serious and life-threatening situations. Many provinces have a policy of **deinstitutionalization,** and most clinicians suggest expanding and improving community care to ensure that people with mental health problems receive appropriate care.

KEY TERMS

CRITICAL AND CREATIVE THINKING QUESTIONS

1. You undoubtedly had certain beliefs and ideas about therapy before reading this chapter. Has studying this chapter changed these beliefs and ideas? Explain.

2. Which form of therapy do you personally find most appealing? Why?

3. What do you consider the most important commonalities among the major forms of therapy described in this chapter? What are the most important differences?

4. Do you think dreams can really reveal unconscious conflicts and desires? Why would such desires or conflicts be more likely to emerge while we're sleeping than when we're awake?

5. Imagine that you were going to use the principles of cognitive-behavioural therapy to change some aspect of your own thinking and behaviour. (Maybe you'd like to quit smoking, or be more organized, or overcome your fear of riding in elevators.) How would you identify faulty thinking? What could you do to change your thinking patterns and behaviour?

6. Cognitive therapists believe that negative thoughts or "self-talk" can lead to negative feelings. Have you ever noticed that your own thoughts about a situation can lead to negative emotions? Does changing these thoughts affect your feelings?

7. Client-centred therapy emphasizes the techniques of empathy and active listening. Could these be used outside the therapy situation? Could using these skills improve your relations with family and friends?

8. Why do you think some therapists make use of an *eclectic* approach? What could be the advantages and/or disadvantages of employing different types of therapies with different clients?

What is happening in this picture ?

In the 2008 movie, *The Changeling*, Angelina Jolie portrays a grief-stricken mother (Christine) who loudly and publicly challenges the police and press who try to force her to accept an impostor as her abducted son. The authorities try everything to silence her, including involuntary commitment to the county hospital's "psychopathic ward." While confined, she is forced to take mood-altering drugs and is told that her only chance for release is to admit she was mistaken about the identity of her son.

■ How might this film contribute to the negative stereotypes of psychotherapy? Given that this movie was based on real life events in 1928, what special danger does this "true story" pose?

■ Can you think of a Hollywood film that offers a positive portrayal of psychotherapy?

SELF-TEST

(Check your answers in Appendix A.)

1. Psychoanalysis, cognitive, humanistic, group, and family therapy are often grouped together as _____.
   a. insight therapies
   b. behaviour therapies
   c. humanistic and operant conditioning
   d. cognitive restructuring

2. The type of psychotherapy developed by Freud that seeks to bring unconscious conflicts into conscious awareness is referred to as _____.
   a. transference
   b. cognitive restructuring
   c. psychoanalysis
   d. the "hot seat" technique

3. Which modern form of therapy emphasizes internal conflicts, motives, and unconscious forces?
   a. self-talk therapy
   b. belief-behaviour therapy
   c. psychodynamic therapy
   d. thought analysis

4. Jessica's therapist has been drawing attention to how her close friends and family members can either negatively or positively affect Jessica's overall well-being. What type of therapy is being used in this situation?
   a. cognitive restructuring
   b. interpersonal therapy (IPT)
   c. psychodynamic therapy
   d. interpretation

5. The following figure illustrates the process by which the therapist and client work to change dysfunctional ways of thinking. What is this process called?
   a. problem-solving
   b. self-talk
   c. cognitive restructuring
   d. rational recovery

Internal Self-Talk and Beliefs

- "I hate sales."
- "I'm a shy person, and I'll never be any good at this."
- "I have to find another job before they fire me."

Possible Outcomes

Decreased efforts
Low energy
Depression

- "Selling can be difficult, but hard work pays off."
- "I'm shy, but people respect my honesty and low-key approach."
- "I had the account before, and I'll get it back."

Increased efforts
Increased energy
No depression

6. Antipsychotic medications are also sometimes called _____.
   a. benzodiazepines
   b. selective serotonin reuptake inhibitors (SSRIs)
   c. major tranquilizers
   d. monoamine oxidase (MAO) inhibitors

7. Beck practises _____, which attempts to change not only dysfunctional thoughts and beliefs, but the associated behaviours as well.
   a. psycho-behaviour therapy
   b. cognitive-behaviour therapy
   c. thinking-acting therapy
   d. belief-behaviour therapy

8. _____ therapy seeks to maximize personal growth through affective restructuring.
   a. Cognitive-emotive
   b. Emotive
   c. Humanistic
   d. Actualization

9. In Rogerian therapy, the _____ is responsible for discovering maladaptive patterns.
   a. therapist
   b. analyst
   c. patient
   d. client

10. This type of group does not have a professional leader, and members assist each other in coping with a specific problem.
    a. self-help group
    b. encounter group
    c. peer group
    d. behaviour group

11. The main focus in behaviour therapy is to increase _____ and decrease _____.
    a. positive thoughts and feelings; negative thoughts and feelings
    b. adaptive behaviours; maladaptive behaviours
    c. coping resources; coping deficits
    d. all of these options

12. A therapist devises a treatment in which smokers receive a mild shock whenever they reach for a cigarette. What type of therapy is the therapist using?
    a. systematic desensitization
    b. virtual reality therapy
    c. operant conditioning
    d. aversion therapy

13. The three steps in systematic desensitization include all of the following **EXCEPT** _____.
    a. learning to become deeply relaxed
    b. arranging anxiety-arousing stimuli into a hierarchy from least to worst arousing
    c. practising relaxation to anxiety-arousing stimuli, starting at the top of the hierarchy
    d. all of these options are included

14. Which form of therapy involves watching and imitating appropriate models who demonstrate desirable behaviours.
    a. shaping
    b. spectatoring
    c. modelling
    d. systematic desensitization

15. Label the four major categories of psychiatric drugs on the following table.

Common drug treatments for psychological disorders	
Type of drug	**Psychological disorder**
a. _____	Anxiety disorders
b. _____	Schizophrenia
c. _____	Bipolar disorder
d. _____	Depressive disorders

16. In Canada, both _____ and _____ usually have doctorate degrees, with advanced training in diagnosis of psychological disorders.
    a. social workers and counsellors
    b. social workers and psychotherapists
    c. psychiatrists and psychologists
    d. all of the above

17. In electroconvulsive therapy (ECT), _____.
    a. current is never applied to the left hemisphere
    b. convulsions activate the ANS, stimulate hormone and neurotransmitter release, and change the blood-brain barrier
    c. electrical current passes through the brain for up to one minute
    d. most patients today receive hundreds of treatments because it is safer than in the past

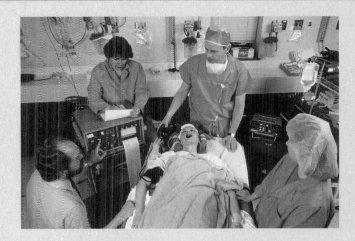

18. Label the five most common goals of therapies on the following figure.

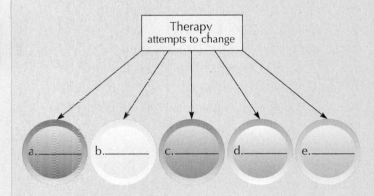

19. Transference refers to _____.
    a. how selective serotonin reuptake inhibitors (SSRIs) affect chemical pathways in the brain
    b. the replacement of a conditioned fear response with relaxation in the process of systematic desensitization
    c. the process whereby people apply some of their unresolved emotions and attitudes from past relationships onto the therapist
    d. the process by which the therapist models a behaviour and then gradually encourages the patient to engage in the same behaviour

20. Psychiatric professionals may authorize temporary commitment for assessment and treatment of a dangerous or incompetent individual for up to _____.
    a. 12 to 24 hours
    b. 24 to 72 hours
    c. 3 to 4 days
    d. 3 to 4 weeks

Social Psychology  15

In May 2009, *Maclean's* magazine published the results of a nationwide poll surveying the attitudes Canadians hold concerning major religious groups. The results were surprising, as they showed that Canadians are not as tolerant as many people believe. Although a majority of those surveyed reported generally favourable views of Christianity, Buddhism, and Judaism, the view of Islam and Sikhism was considerably less favourable. These findings were a concern for religious leaders, many of whom had been trying for some time to foster positive public opinion. Why do people hold positive or negative views of certain groups, sometimes without even knowing a member of that group? The authors of the *Maclean's* article argued that the respondents' views may have been influenced by current world events and may shift in accordance with such events.

Understanding why we admire, like, love, or dislike and even hate some people or groups of people is essential to understanding ourselves and the world around us. Social psychologists study both the negative aspects of social behaviour, such as prejudice and aggression, and the more positive aspects, such as interpersonal attraction and helping behaviours. Because almost everything we do is social, the subject matter is enormous and varied.

We will approach our study by looking at the three major components of social psychology: thoughts, feelings, and actions toward others. We'll conclude with a discussion of how social psychology can help reduce prejudice, discrimination, and destructive behaviour.

Our Thoughts about Others

Explain how attributions and attitudes affect the way we perceive and judge others.

Summarize the three components of attitudes.

Describe cultural differences in how people explain behaviour.

ATTRIBUTION: EXPLAINING BEHAVIOUR

social psychology The study of how other people influence a person's thoughts, feelings, and actions.

attributions How we explain our own and others' actions.

One critical aspect of **social psychology** is the search for reasons and explanations for our own and others' behaviour. It's natural to want to understand and explain why people behave as they do and why events occur as they do. Many social psychologists believe that developing logical **attributions** for people's behaviour makes us feel safer and more in control (Chiou, 2007; Heider, 1958; Krueger, 2007). To do so, most people begin with the basic question of whether a given action stems mainly from the person's internal disposition or from the external situation.

Mistaken Attributions Making the correct choice between disposition and situation is central to accurately judging why people do what they do. Unfortunately, our attributions are frequently marred by two major errors: the fundamental attribution error and the self-serving bias. Let's explore each of these.

Our attributions as to the reasons for people's actions are generally accurate when we take into account situational influences on behaviour. However, given that people have enduring personality traits (Chapter 12) and a tendency to take cognitive shortcuts (Chapter 8), we more often choose *dispositional* attributions—that is, we blame the person rather than the circumstance. For example, suppose a new student joins your class and seems distant, cold, and uninterested in interaction. It is easy to conclude that she is an unfriendly, and maybe even stuck-up, person—a dispositional attribution. You might be surprised to find that in one-on-one interactions with familiar, close friends, she is actually much more outgoing and warmer. In other words, her behaviour depends on the situation.

This bias toward personal, dispositional factors rather than situational factors in our explanations for others' behaviour is so common that it is called the **fundamental attribution error (FAE)** (Gebauer, Krempl, & Fleisch, 2008; Tal-Or & Papirman, 2007).

Why do we so often jump to internal, personal explanations? Social psychologists suggest that one reason is that human personalities and behaviours are more *salient* (or noticeable) than situational factors, the **saliency bias** (FIGURE 15.1). We also tend to focus on people and "blame the victim" because of our need to believe that the world is just and fair. This **just-world phenomenon** suggests that people generally deserve what they get, while also allowing us to feel safer in an uncontrollable world.

When judging others, we often blame the person rather than the situation. However, when explaining our own behaviour, we favour internal attributions for our successes and external attributions for our failures. This **self-serving bias** is motivated by a desire to maintain positive self-esteem and a good public image (Gobbo & Raccanello, 2007; Krusemark, Campbell, & Clementz, 2008; Shepperd, Malone, & Sweeny, 2008). For example, students often take personal credit for doing well on an exam. If they fail the test, however, they tend to blame the instructor, the textbook, or the "tricky" questions.

fundamental attribution error (FAE) Attributing people's behaviour to internal (dispositional) causes rather than external (situational) factors.

Culture and Attributional Biases Both the fundamental attribution error and the self-serving bias may depend in part on cultural factors (Kudo & Numazaki, 2003; Matsumoto, 2000) (FIGURE 15.2). In highly individualistic cultures, like those of Canada and the United States, people are defined and understood as individual selves—largely responsible for their successes and failures. But in collectivistic cultures, like that in

Saliency bias FIGURE 15.1

How would you explain this situation? According to the *saliency bias*, we're likely to blame homeless individuals for their condition because human personalities and behaviours (dispositional factors) are more conspicuous and "salient" than the situational factors that lead to poverty and homelessness. How would the *just-world phenomenon* explain this same situation?

Culture and attributional biases FIGURE 15.2

Westerners watching a baseball game in Japan who saw the umpire make a bad call would probably make a dispositional attribution ("He's a lousy umpire"), whereas Japanese spectators would tend to make a situational attribution ("He's under pressure") . What accounts for this difference?

China, people are primarily defined as members of their social network—responsible for doing as others expect. Accordingly, they tend to be more aware of situational constraints on behaviour, making the FAE less likely (Bozkurt & Aydin, 2004; Norenzayan, 2006).

The self-serving bias is also much less common in Eastern nations. In Japan, for instance, the ideal person is someone who is aware of his or her shortcomings and continually works to overcome them—not someone who thinks highly of himself or herself (Heine & Renshaw, 2002). In the East (as well as in other collectivistic cultures), self-esteem is not related to doing better than others but to fitting in with the group (Markus & Kitayama, 2003).

ATTITUDES: LEARNED PREDISPOSITIONS TOWARD OTHERS

When we observe and respond to the world around us, we are seldom completely neutral. Rather, our responses toward subjects as diverse as pizza, people, AIDS, and abortion reflect our **attitudes**. We learn our attitudes both from direct experience and from watching others.

> **attitudes** Learned predispositions to respond cognitively, affectively, and behaviourally to particular objects in a particular way.

Social psychologists generally agree that most attitudes have three components (**FIGURE 15.3**): cognitive (thoughts and beliefs), affective (feelings), and behavioural

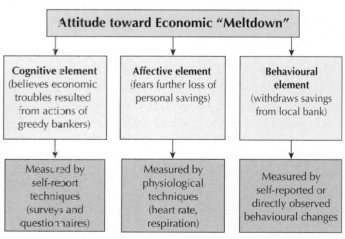

Attitude toward Economic "Meltdown"		
Cognitive element (believes economic troubles resulted from actions of greedy bankers)	**Affective element** (fears further loss of personal savings)	**Behavioural element** (withdraws savings from local bank)
Measured by self-report techniques (surveys and questionnaires)	Measured by physiological techniques (heart rate, respiration)	Measured by self-reported or directly observed behavioural changes

Three components of attitudes FIGURE 15.3

When social psychologists study attitudes, they measure each of the three components: cognitive, affective, and behavioural.

Cognitive dissonance theory FIGURE 15.4

Cognitive Dissonance Theory

People are motivated to maintain consistency in their thoughts, feelings, and actions. → When inconsistencies or conflicts exist among our thoughts, feelings, and actions, they can lead to... → Strong tension and discomfort (cognitive dissonance). → To reduce this cognitive dissonance, we are motivated to change our attitude or behaviour.

How would health professionals, who obviously know the dangers of smoking, deal with their cognitive dissonance? They could quit smoking, but, like most people, they probably take the easier route. They change their attitudes about the dangers of smoking by reassuring themselves with examples of people who smoke and live to be 100, or they simply ignore or discount contradictory information.

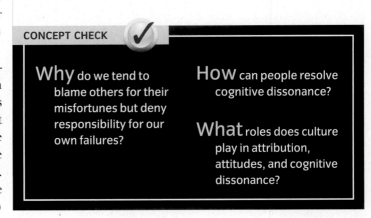

REGIONAL CANCER CENTER

SMOKING INSIDE PATIO ONLY

(predisposition to act in a certain way toward an object or a situation, or **attitude object**). Figure 15.3 illustrates these three components with reference to one's attitude to the 2008–2009 economic crisis.

Although attitudes begin to form in early childhood, they are not permanent (a fact that advertisers and politicians know and exploit). One way to change attitudes is to make direct, persuasive appeals. But an even more efficient strategy is to create **cognitive dissonance** (Cooper & Hogg, 2007; Gringart, Helmes, & Speelman, 2008). Contradictions between our attitudes and behaviours can motivate us to change our attitudes to agree with our behaviours (Festinger, 1957) (FIGURE 15.4).

cognitive dissonance A feeling of discomfort caused by a discrepancy between an attitude and a behaviour or between two attitudes.

In one of the best-known tests of cognitive dissonance theory, Leon Festinger & J. Merrill Carlsmith (1959) paid participants either $1 or $20 to tell others that a boring experimental task in which they had just participated was actually very enjoyable and fun. Those who were paid $1 subsequently held more positive attitudes toward the task than those who were paid $20. Why? All participants presumably recognized the discrepancy between their attitude (the task was boring)

and their behaviour (saying it was enjoyable and fun). In participants' minds, a $20 payment might justify the lie, resolving cognitive dissonance, but a $1 payment could not. Those who were paid $1 had only one way to reduce cognitive dissonance: by changing their attitude.

The experience of cognitive dissonance may depend on a distinctly Western way of thinking about and evaluating the self. As we mentioned earlier, people in Eastern cultures tend not to define themselves in terms of their individual accomplishments. For this reason, making a bad decision may not pose the same threat to self-esteem that it would in more individualistic cultures, such as those in Canada or the United States (Choi & Nisbett, 2000; Markus & Kitayama, 1998, 2003).

CONCEPT CHECK

Why do we tend to blame others for their misfortunes but deny responsibility for our own failures?

How can people resolve cognitive dissonance?

What roles does culture play in attribution, attitudes, and cognitive dissonance?

Our Feelings about Others

LEARNING OBJECTIVES

Explain the difference between prejudice and discrimination.

Identify four explanations for why prejudice develops.

Summarize the factors that influence interpersonal attraction.

Explain how loving is different from liking.

Having explored our thoughts about others (attributions and attitudes), we now focus on our feelings about others. First we will examine the negative feelings (and thoughts and actions) associated with prejudice and discrimination. Then we'll explore the generally positive feelings of interpersonal attraction (liking and loving).

PREJUDICE AND DISCRIMINATION

Prejudice, which literally means "prejudgement," creates enormous problems for its victims and also limits the perpetrator's ability to accurately judge others and to process information.

> **prejudice**
> A learned, generally negative attitude directed toward specific people solely because of their membership in an identified group.

Like all attitudes, prejudice is composed of three elements: cognitive (stereotypical beliefs about people in a group), affective (emotions about the learned, generally negative attitude directed toward specific people solely because of their membership in an identified group), and behavioural (predisposition to discriminate against members of the group). Although the terms *prejudice* and *discrimination* are often used interchangeably, they are not the same. Prejudice refers to an attitude, whereas **discrimination** refers to action (Fiske, 1998). The two often coincide, but not always (**FIGURE 15.5**).

> **discrimination**
> Negative behaviour directed at members of a group.

How do prejudice and discrimination originate? Why do they persist? Four commonly cited sources of prejudice are learning, mental shortcuts, economic and political competition, and displaced aggression.

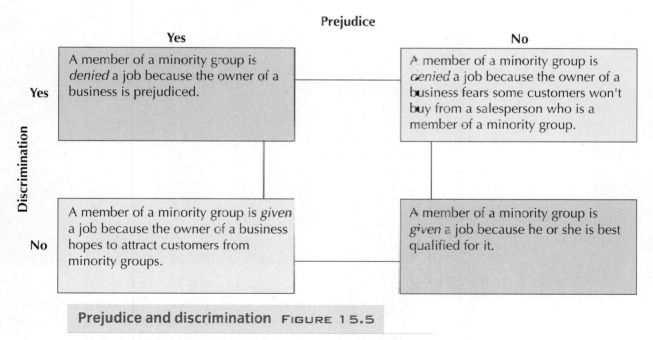

Prejudice

	Yes	No
Discrimination Yes	A member of a minority group is *denied* a job because the owner of a business is prejudiced.	A member of a minority group is *denied* a job because the owner of a business fears some customers won't buy from a salesperson who is a member of a minority group.
No	A member of a minority group is *given* a job because the owner of a business hopes to attract customers from minority groups.	A member of a minority group is *given* a job because he or she is best qualified for it.

Prejudice and discrimination FIGURE 15.5

Note how prejudice can exist without discrimination, and vice versa.

Learning

People learn prejudice the same way they learn all attitudes—through classical and operant conditioning and social learning (Chapter 6). For example, repeated exposure to stereotypical portrayals of minorities and women on television, in movies, and in books and magazines teach children that such images are correct. Hearing parents, friends, and teachers express prejudice also initiates and reinforces prejudice (Anderson & Hamilton, 2005; Bennett et al., 2004; Kassin, Fein, & Markus, 2008; Levitan, 2008; Livingston & Drwecki, 2007; Neto & Furnham, 2005). People also learn prejudice through direct experience. For example, derogating others or receiving attention for expressing racist or sexist remarks can boost a person's self-esteem (Fein & Spencer, 1997; Plummer, 2001). Generalizing a single negative experience with a specific member of a group also creates prejudice (Vidmar, 1997).

Mental Shortcuts

Prejudice may stem from normal attempts to simplify a complex social world (Kulik, 2005; Sternberg, 2007, 2009). Stereotypes allow people to make quick judgements about others, thereby freeing up their mental resources for other activities (FIGURE 15.6A). In fact, stereotypes and prejudice can occur even without a person's conscious awareness or control. This process is known as "automatic" or "implicit" bias (Greenwald et al., 2009; Hofmann, Gschwendner, Castelli, & Schmitt, 2008; von Hippel, Brener, & von Hippel, 2008).

People use stereotypes to classify others in terms of their membership in a group. Given that people generally classify themselves as part of the preferred group, they also create ingroups and outgroups. An *ingroup* is any category that people see themselves as belonging to; an *outgroup* is any other category (FIGURE 15.6B).

Visualizing

The cost of prejudice FIGURE 15.6

A Harmless stereotypes?
Even seemingly positive forms of prejudice can be destructive. For example, the stereotype that "Asian Canadians are good at math" might lead Asian Canadians to see few other routes to success. ▼

B Prejudice and war ▲
This group supports Osama Bin Laden and is demonstrating against the United States. How would you explain their loyalty to Bin Laden and prejudice against Americans?

Compared with how they see outgroup members, people tend to see ingroup members as being more attractive, having better personalities, and so on—a phenomenon known as **ingroup favouritism** (Ahmed, 2007; Dunham, 2007; Harth, Kessler, & Leach, 2008). People also tend to recognize greater diversity among members of their ingroup than they do among members of outgroups (Cehajic, Brown, & Castano, 2008; Wegener, Clark, & Petty, 2006). This "they all look alike to me" tendency is termed the **outgroup homogeneity effect**. A danger with such outgroup homogeneity bias is that when members of minority groups are not recognized as varied and complex individuals, it is easier to perceive them as faceless objects and treat them in discriminatory ways. A good example is war: viewing the people on the other side as simply faceless enemies makes it easier to kill large numbers of soldiers and civilians. This type of dehumanization and facelessness also helps to perpetuate the high levels of fear and anxiety associated with terrorism (Haslam et al., 2007; Hodson & Costello, 2007; Zimbardo, 2004, 2007).

Competition for Limited Resources Some theorists think that prejudice develops and is maintained because it offers significant economic and political advantages to the dominant group (Esses et al., 2001; Mays, Cochran, & Barnes, 2007; Schaefer, 2008) (**FIGURE 15.6C**).

Displaced Aggression As we discuss in the next section, frustration often leads people to attack the source of frustration. As history has shown, when the cause of frustration is too powerful and capable of retaliation or is ambiguous, people often redirect their aggression toward an alternative, innocent target, or a scapegoat (**FIGURE 15.6D**).

C Immigration and competition
The immigration question is complex; what roles might competition for limited resources play in anti-immigrant prejudice? ▼

D **Prejudice and genocide** ▲
Prejudice can lead to atrocities. These skulls are from the recent acts of genocide in Sudan, where thousands of black Africans have died from starvation, disease, and violence.

Understanding the causes of prejudice is just a first step toward overcoming it. Later in this chapter, we consider several methods that psychologists have developed to reduce prejudice. In the next section, we examine the positive side of our feelings about others.

INTERPERSONAL ATTRACTION

What causes us to feel admiration, liking, friendship, intimacy, lust, or love? All of these social experiences are reflections of **interpersonal attraction**. Psychologists have found three compelling factors in interpersonal attraction: physical attractiveness, proximity, and similarity. Each influences our attraction in different ways.

interpersonal attraction Positive feelings toward another.

Physical attractiveness (size, shape, facial characteristics, and manner of dress) is one of the most important factors in our initial liking or loving of others (Andreoni & Petrie, 2008; Buss, 2003, 2005, 2007, 2008; Cunningham, Fink, & Kenix, 2008; Lippa, 2007; Maner et al., 2008). Attractive individuals are seen as more poised, interesting, cooperative, achieving, sociable, independent, intelligent, healthy, and sexually warm than unattractive people (Fink & Penton-Voak, 2002; Swami & Furnham, 2008; Willis, Esqueda, & Schacht, 2008).

Many cultures around the world share similar standards of attractiveness, especially for women—for example, youthful appearance and facial and body symmetry (Fink et al., 2004; Jones, DeBruine, & Little, 2007). From an evolutionary perspective, these findings may reflect the fact that good looks generally indicate good health, sound genes, and high fertility. However, what is considered beautiful also varies from era to era and from culture to culture (**FIGURE 15.7**).

How do those of us who are not "superstar beautiful" manage to find mates? The good news is that people usually do not hold out for partners who are "ideally attractive." Instead, both men and women tend to select partners whose physical attractiveness approximately matches their own (Regan, 1998; Sprecher & Regan, 2002). Also, people use non-verbal flirting behaviour to increase their attractiveness and signal interest to a potential romantic partner (Lott, 2000; Moore, 1998). Although both men and women flirt, in heterosexual couples women generally initiate courtship.

Culture and attraction FIGURE 15.7

Which of these women do you find most attractive? Can you see how your cultural background might train you to prefer one look to the others?

We even like ourselves better when we see ourselves in a familiar way. People presented with pictures of themselves and reversed images of themselves strongly prefer the reversed images, which they are used to seeing in the mirror. Close friends prefer the unreversed images (Mita, Dermer, & Knight, 1977).

Attraction also depends on two people being in the same place at the same time. Such proximity promotes attraction, largely because of **mere exposure**—that is, repeated exposure increases liking (Monin, 2003; Rhodes, Halberstadt, & Brajkovich, 2001) (**FIGURE 15.8**).

The major cementing factor for both liking and loving relationships is similarity in social background and values (Caprara et al., 2007; Smithson & Baker, 2008). In other words, "Birds of a feather flock together." However, what about the old saying "Opposites attract"? This adage probably refers to personality traits. That is, attraction to seemingly opposite people is most often based on the recognition that those people offer us something we lack (Dryer & Horowitz, 1997).

We can think of interpersonal attraction as a fundamental building block of how we feel about others. But how do we make sense of love? Many people find the subject to be alternately mysterious, exhilarating, comforting—and even maddening. In this section, we explore three perspectives on love: liking versus loving, romantic love, and companionate love.

Love often develops from initial feelings of friendship and liking. Using a paper-and-pencil test of liking and loving, Zick Rubin (1970) found that liking involves a favourable evaluation reflected in greater feelings of admiration and respect. Love, a more intense experience, involves caring, attachment to the other person, and intimacy (**TABLE 15.1**). For more about love over the life span, see *What a Psychologist Sees*.

Couples who scored highest on Rubin's love scale spent more time looking into one another's eyes. Although both partners tended to match each other on their love scores, women liked their dating partners significantly more than they were liked in return (Rubin, 1970).

Sample items from Rubin's liking and loving test TABLE 15.1

Love scale	*Liking scale*
1. I feel that I can confide in _____ about virtually everything.	1. I think that _____ is unusually well adjusted.
2. I would do almost anything for _____.	2. I would highly recommend _____ for a responsible job.
3. If I could never be with _____, I would feel miserable.	3. In my opinion, _____ is an exceptionally mature person.

Source: Rubin, Z. (1970). "Measurement of romantic love," *Journal of Personality and Social Psychology, 16,* 265–273.
Copyright © 1970 by the American Psychological Association. Reprinted by permission of the author.

Love over the Lifespan

Even in the most devoted couples, the intense attraction and excitement of **romantic love** generally begin to fade 6 to 30 months after the relationship begins (Hatfield & Rapson, 1996; Livingston, 1999). This is because romantic love is largely based on mystery and fantasy—people often fall in love with what they want another person to be (Fletcher & Simpson, 2000; Levine, 2001). These illusions usually fade with the realities of everyday living.

Companionate love is a strong, lasting attraction based on admiration, respect, trust, deep caring, and commitment. Studies of close friendships show that satisfaction grows with time as we come to recognize the value of companionship and intimacy (Kim & Hatfield, 2004). One tip for maintaining companionate love is to overlook each other's faults. People are more satisfied with relationships when they have a somewhat idealized perception of their partner (Campbell et al., 2001; Fletcher & Simpson, 2000). This makes sense in light of research on cognitive dissonance: idealizing our mates allows us to believe we have a good deal.

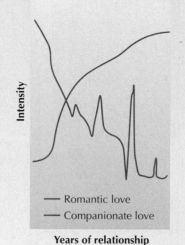

Intensity

— Romantic love
— Companionate love

Years of relationship

CONCEPT CHECK ✓

What factors contribute to the development of prejudice?

What process accounts for someone saying that members of another ethnic group "all look alike"?

What are the major factors that affect our attraction to others?

Our Actions toward Others

urt Lewin (1890–1947), often considered the "father of social psychology," was among the first to suggest that all behaviour results from interactions between the individual and the environment. In this section we consider several examples of such interaction, including social influence, group processes, and aggression.

SOCIAL INFLUENCE: CONFORMITY AND OBEDIENCE

Our society and culture teach us to believe certain things, feel certain ways, and act in accordance with these beliefs and feelings. These influences are so strong and so much a part of who we are that we rarely recognize them. In this section, we discuss two kinds of social influence: conformity and obedience.

Solomon Asch's study of conformity

FIGURE 15.9

Which line (A, B, or C) is most like line X in the bottom box? Could anyone convince you otherwise?

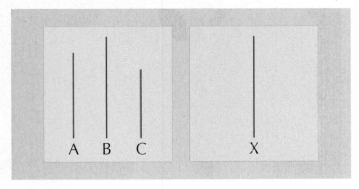

Conformity: Going Along with Others

Imagine that you have volunteered for a psychology experiment on perception. You are seated around a table with six other students. You are all shown a card with three lines labelled A, B, and C, as in **FIGURE 15.9**. You are then asked to select the line that is closest in length to a fourth line, X.

At first, everyone agrees on the correct line. On the third trial, however, the first participant selects line A, obviously a wrong answer. When the second, third, fourth, and fifth participants also say line A, you really start to wonder: "What's going on here? Are they blind? Or am I?"

What do you think you would do at this point in the experiment? Would you stick with your convictions and say line B, regardless of what the others have answered? Or would you go along with the group? In the original version of this experiment, conducted by Solomon Asch (1951), six of the seven participants were actually *confederates* of the experimenter (that is, they were working with the experimenter and purposely gave wrong answers). Their incorrect responses were designed to test the participant's degree of **conformity**.

> **conformity** The act of changing behaviour as a result of real or imagined group pressure.

More than one-third of Asch's participants conformed—they agreed with the group's obviously incorrect choice. (Participants in a control group experienced no group pressure and almost always chose correctly.) Asch's study has been conducted dozens of times, in at least 17 countries, and always with similar results (Bond & Smith, 1996; Jung, 2006; Takano & Sogon, 2008).

Why would so many people conform? To the onlooker, conformity is often difficult to understand. Even the conformer sometimes has a hard time explaining his or her behaviour. Let's look at three factors that drive conformity:

- *Normative social influence.* Often, people conform to group pressure out of a need for approval and acceptance by the group. **Norms** are expected behaviours that are adhered to by members of a group. Most often, norms are quite subtle and implicit. Have you ever asked what others are wearing to a party, or watched the person seated next to you at dinner to be sure you pick up the right fork? Such behaviour reflects your desire to conform and the power of normative social influence.

- *Informational social influence.* Have you ever bought a specific product simply because of a friend's recommendation? You conform not to gain their approval (normative social influence) but because you assume they have more information than you do. Given that participants in Asch's experiment observed all the other participants give unanimous decisions on the length of the lines, they also may have conformed because they believed the others had more information.

- *Reference groups.* The third major factor in conformity is the power of **reference groups**—people we most admire, like, and want to resemble. Attractive actors and popular sports stars are paid millions of dollars to endorse products because advertisers know that we want to be as cool as Canadian mixed martial arts champion Georges "Rush" St. Pierre or as beautiful as Canadian film star Elisha Cuthbert. Of course, we also have more important reference groups in our lives—parents, friends, family members, teachers, religious leaders, and so on.

Ψ Psychological Science

Cultural Norms for Personal Space

Culture and socialization have a lot to do with shaping norms for personal space. If someone invades the invisible "personal bubble" around our bodies, we generally feel very uncomfortable. People from Mediterranean, Muslim, and Latin American countries tend to maintain smaller interpersonal distances than do North Americans and Northern Europeans (Axtell, 2007; Steinhart, 1986). Children also tend to stand very close to others until they are socialized to recognize and maintain a greater personal distance. Furthermore, friends stand closer than strangers, women tend to stand closer than men, and violent prisoners prefer approximately three times the personal space of non-violent prisoners (Axtell, 1998, 2007; Gilmour & Walkey, 1981; Lawrence & Andrews, 2004).

Stop & Think
1. Does it bother you when someone stands "too close" to you?
2. If this happens in a crowded bus or an elevator, does it make a difference?
3. If men and women have different norms for personal space, what effect might this have on their relationships?

The advantages of conformity and obedience FIGURE 15.10

These people willingly obey the firefighters who order them to evacuate a building, and many lives are saved. What would happen to our everyday functioning if people did not go along with the crowd or generally did not obey orders?

Obedience: Following Orders

As we've seen, conformity involves going along with the group. A second form of social influence, **obedience**, involves going along with a direct command, usually from someone in a position of authority.

Conformity and obedience aren't always bad (**FIGURE 15.10**). In fact, most people conform and obey most of the time because it is in their own best interest (and everyone else's) to do so. Like most North Americans, you stand in line at the movie theatre instead of pushing ahead of others. This allows an orderly purchasing of tickets. Conformity and obedience allow social life to proceed with safety, order, and predictability.

However, on some occasions it is important not to conform or obey. We don't want teenagers (or adults)

obedience The act of following a direct command, usually from an authority figure.

engaging in risky sex or drug use just to be part of the crowd. And we don't want soldiers (or anyone else) mindlessly following orders just because they were told to do so by an authority figure. Because recognizing and resisting destructive forms of obedience are particularly important to our society, we'll explore this material in greater depth at the end of this chapter.

Imagine that you have responded to a newspaper ad that is seeking volunteers for a study on memory. At the Yale University laboratory, an experimenter explains to you and another participant that he is studying the effects of punishment on learning and memory. You are selected to play the role of the "teacher." The experimenter leads you into a room where he straps the other participant—the "learner"—into a chair. He applies electrode paste to the learner's wrist "to avoid blisters and burns" and attaches an electrode that is connected to a shock generator.

What Influences Obedience?

Milgram conducted a series of studies to discover the specific conditions that either increased or decreased obedience to authority.

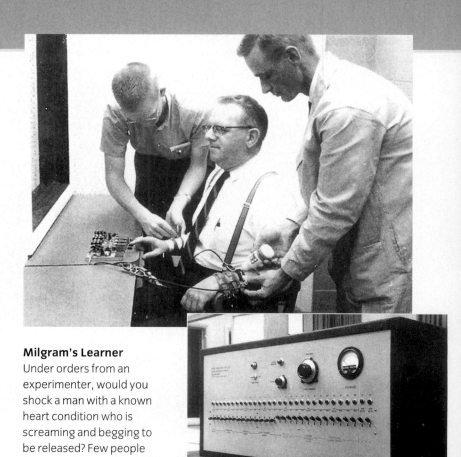

Milgram's Learner
Under orders from an experimenter, would you shock a man with a known heart condition who is screaming and begging to be released? Few people believe they would. But research shows otherwise.

Milgram's Shock Generator

You are shown into an adjacent room and told to sit in front of this same shock generator, which is wired through the wall to the chair of the learner. The shock machine consists of 30 switches representing successively higher levels of shock, from 15 volts to 450 volts. Written labels appear below each group of switches, ranging from "Slight Shock" to "Danger: Severe Shock," all the way to "XXX." The experimenter explains that it is your job to teach the learner a list of word pairs and to punish any errors by administering a shock. With each wrong answer, you are to increase the shock by one level. The setup for the experiment is illustrated in *What a Psychologist Sees.*

You begin teaching the word pairs, but the learner's responses are often wrong. Before long, you are inflicting shocks that you can only assume must be extremely painful. After you administer 150 volts, the learner begins to protest: "Get me out of here. . . . I refuse to go on."

You hesitate, and the experimenter tells you to continue. He insists that even if the learner refuses to answer, you must keep increasing the shock levels. But the other person is obviously in pain. What should you do?

Actual participants in this research—the "teachers"—suffered real conflict and distress when confronted with this problem. They sweated, trembled, stuttered, laughed nervously, and repeatedly protested that they did not want to hurt the learner. But still they obeyed.

The psychologist who designed this study, Stanley Milgram, was actually investigating not punishment and learning but obedience to authority: would participants obey the experimenter's prompts and commands to shock another human being? In Milgram's public survey, fewer than 25 percent thought they would go beyond 150 volts. And no respondents

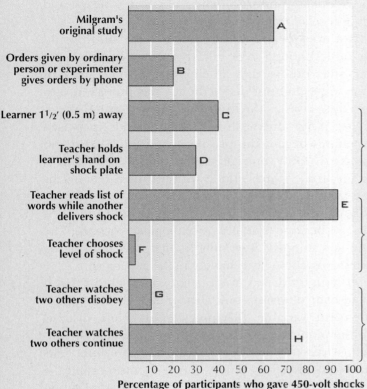

Milgram's original study — A

Orders given by ordinary person or experimenter gives orders by phone — B

Learner 1½' (0.5 m) away — C

Teacher holds learner's hand on shock plate — D

Teacher reads list of words while another delivers shock — E

Teacher chooses level of shock — F

Teacher watches two others disobey — G

Teacher watches two others continue — H

10 20 30 40 50 60 70 80 90 100

Percentage of participants who gave 450-volt shocks

As you can see in the first bar on the graph (A), 65 percent of the participants in Milgram's original study gave the learner the full 450-volt level of shocks.

In the second bar (B), when orders came from an ordinary person, or from the experimenter by phone (versus in person), obedience dropped to 20 percent.

Now look at the third and fourth bars (C and D). Note how the physical closeness of the victim affected obedience. In the original experiment, the learner was seated behind a wall in another room, and 65 percent of the teachers gave the full 450-volt level of shocks. But obedience dropped to 40 percent when the learner was only 1 1/2 feet (0.5 m) away, and dropped even further to 30 percent when the teacher was required to hold the learner's hand on the shock plate.

Looking at bars (E) and (F), how does the teacher's level of responsibility affect obedience? In the original experiment, the teacher was required to actually pull the lever that supposedly delivered shocks to the learner. When the teacher only read the list of words, while another person delivered the shock, obedience increased to 92 percent. In contrast, when the teacher was allowed to choose the level of shock, obedience dropped to 2 percent.

Finally, looking at bars (G) and (H), note how modelling and imitation affected obedience. When teachers watched two other supposed teachers disobey the experimenter's orders, their own obedience dropped to 10 percent. However, when they watched other teachers follow the experimenter's orders, their obedience increased to more than 70 percent (Milgram 1963, 1974).

predicted they would go past the 300-volt level. Yet 65 percent of the teacher-participants in this series of studies obeyed completely—going all the way to the end of the scale, even beyond the point when the "learner" (Milgram's confederate, who actually received no shocks at all) stopped responding altogether.

Even Milgram was surprised by his results. Before the study began, he polled a group of psychiatrists, and they predicted that most people would refuse to go beyond 150 volts and that fewer than 1 percent of those tested would "go all the way." But, as Milgram discovered, most of his participants—men and women, of all ages, and from all walks of life—administered the highest voltage. The study was replicated many times and in many other countries, with similarly high levels of obedience.

In a series of follow-up studies, Milgram found several important factors that influenced obedience: (1) legitimacy and physical closeness of the authority figure, (2) remoteness of the victim, (3) assignment of responsibility, and (4) modelling or imitating others (Blass, 1991, 2000; Meeus & Raaijmakers, 1989; Snyder, 2003). These are summarized in *What a Psychologist Sees*.

Many people are upset both by Milgram's findings and by the treatment of the participants in his research. Although deception is a necessary part of some research, the degree of deception and discomfort of participants in Milgram's research is now viewed as highly unethical. His study would never be undertaken today. However, Milgram did carefully debrief every subject after the study and followed up with the participants for several months. Most of his "teachers" reported the experience as being personally informative and valuable.

GROUP PROCESSES

Although we seldom recognize the power of group membership, social psychologists have identified several important ways that groups affect us.

Group Membership

How do the roles that we play within groups affect our behaviour? This question fascinated social psychologist Philip Zimbardo. In his famous study at Stanford University, 24 carefully screened, well-adjusted young college men were paid $15 a day for participating in a two-week simulation of prison life (Haney, Banks, & Zimbardo, 1978; Zimbardo, 1993).

The students were randomly assigned to the role of either prisoner or guard. Prisoners were "arrested," frisked, photographed, fingerprinted, and booked at the police station. They were then blindfolded and driven to the "Stanford Prison." There, they were given ID numbers, deloused, issued prison clothing (tight nylon caps, shapeless gowns, and no underwear), and locked in cells. Participants assigned to be guards were outfitted with official-looking uniforms, billy clubs, and whistles, and they were given complete control.

Not even Zimbardo foresaw how the study would turn out. Although some guards were nicer to the prisoners than others, they all engaged in some abuse of power. The slightest disobedience was punished with degrading tasks or the loss of "privileges" (such as eating, sleeping, and washing). As demands increased and abuses began, the prisoners became passive and depressed. Only one prisoner fought back with a hunger strike, which ended with a forced feeding by the guards.

Four prisoners had to be released within the first four days because of severe psychological reactions. The study was stopped after only six days because of the alarming psychological changes in the participants.

Although this was not a true experiment in that it lacked control groups and clear measurements of the dependent variable (Chapter 1), it offers insights into the potential effects of roles on individual behaviour (**FIGURE 15.11**). According to interviews conducted after the study, the students became so absorbed in their roles that they forgot they were volunteers in a university study (Zimbardo, Ebbeson, & Maslach, 1977).

Zimbardo's study also demonstrates **deindividuation**. To be deindividuated means that you feel less self-conscious, less inhibited, and less personally responsible as a member of a group than when you're alone. Although deindividuation can sometimes be positive, it also helps explain angry mobs, rioters, gang rapes, lynchings, and hate crimes (Rodrigues, Assmar, & Jablonski, 2005; Zimbardo, 2007). Groups sometimes actively promote deindividuation by requiring their members to wear uniforms, for example, as a way to increase allegiance and conformity (**FIGURE 15.12**).

> **deindividuation** Increased arousal, and reduced self-consciousness, inhibition, and personal responsibility that may occur in a group.

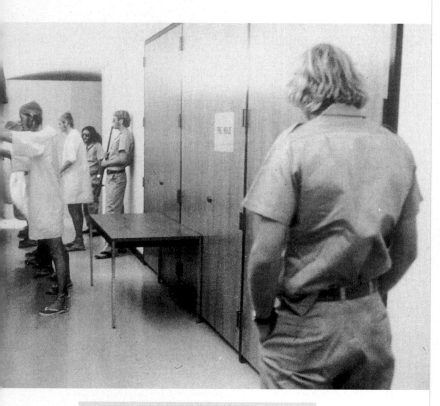

Power corrupts FIGURE 15.11

Zimbardo's prison study showed how the demands of roles and situations could produce dramatic changes in behaviour in just a few days. Can you imagine what happens to prisoners during life imprisonment, six-year sentences, or even a few nights in jail?

Group Decision-Making

We have seen that the groups we belong to and the roles that we play within them influence how we think about ourselves. How do groups affect our decisions? Are two heads truly better than one?

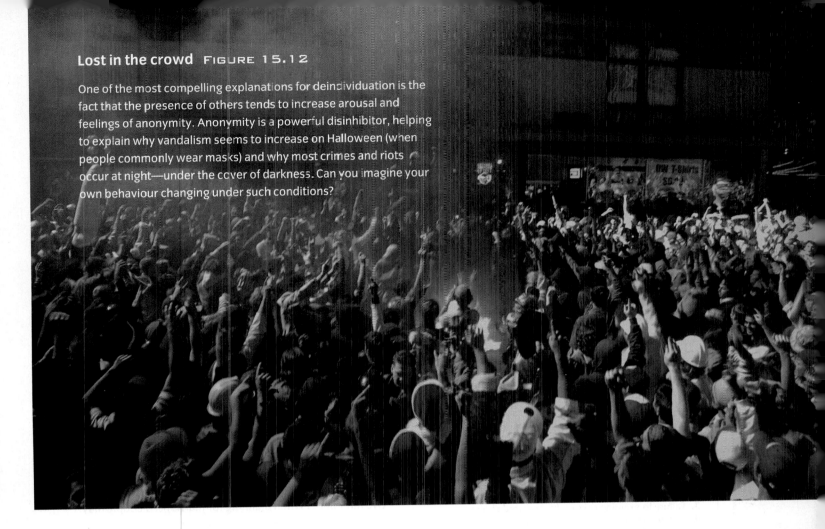

Lost in the crowd FIGURE 15.12

One of the most compelling explanations for deindividuation is the fact that the presence of others tends to increase arousal and feelings of anonymity. Anonymity is a powerful disinhibitor, helping to explain why vandalism seems to increase on Halloween (when people commonly wear masks) and why most crimes and riots occur at night—under the cover of darkness. Can you imagine your own behaviour changing under such conditions?

Most people assume that group decisions are more conservative, cautious, and middle-of-the-road than individual decisions. But is this true? Initial investigations indicated that after discussing an issue, groups actually support riskier decisions than decisions the members made as individuals before the discussion (Stoner, 1961).

Subsequent research on this *risky-shift* phenomenon, however, shows that some groups support riskier decisions while others support conservative decisions (Liu & Latané, 1998). How can we tell if a given group's decision will be risky or conservative? The final decision (risky or conservative) depends primarily on the dominant pre-existing tendencies of the group. That is, as individuals interact and discuss their opinions, their initial positions become more exaggerated (or polarized).

Why are group decisions more exaggerated? This tendency toward **group polarization** stems from increased exposure to persuasive arguments that reinforce the group's original opinion (Liu & Latané, 1998).

A related phenomenon is **groupthink** (FIGURE 15.13). When a group is highly cohesive (a couple, a family, a panel of military advisers, an athletic team), the members' desire for agreement may lead them to ignore important information or points of view held by outsiders or critics (Hergovich & Olbrich, 2003; Vaughn, 1996). During the discussion process, the members

- come to believe that they are invulnerable

- tend to develop common rationalizations and stereotypes of the outgroup

- exert considerable pressure on anyone who dares to offer a dissenting opinion

group polarization

A group's movement toward either riskier or more conservative behaviour, depending on the members' initial dominant tendencies.

groupthink Faulty decision-making that occurs when a highly cohesive group strives for agreement and avoids inconsistent information.

Our Actions toward Others 433

create empathy—a subjective grasp of that person's feelings or experiences. When we feel empathic toward another, we are motivated to help that person for his or her own sake. The ability to empathize may even be innate. Research with infants in the first few hours of life shows that some become distressed and cry at the sound of another infant's cries (Hay, 1994; Hoffman, 1993).

Many theories have been proposed to explain why people help, but few explain why we do not. One of the most comprehensive explanations for helping or not helping comes from the research of Bibb Latané and John Darley (1970) (see FIGURE 15.16B). They found that whether or not someone helps depends on a series of interconnected events and decisions: the potential helper must first notice what is happening, interpret the event as an emergency, accept personal responsibility for helping, decide how to help, and then actually initiate the helping behaviour.

How does this sequence explain television programs and "caught on tape" situations in which people are robbed or attacked and no one comes to their aid? In follow-up interviews most onlookers report that they failed to intervene because they were certain that someone must have called the police already. Latané and Darley called this the **diffusion of responsibility** phenomenon—the dilution (or diffusion) of personal responsibility for acting by spreading it among all other group members.

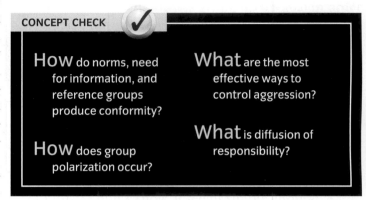

CONCEPT CHECK ✓

How do norms, need for information, and reference groups produce conformity?

How does group polarization occur?

What are the most effective ways to control aggression?

What is diffusion of responsibility?

Applying Social Psychology to Social Problems

LEARNING OBJECTIVES

Describe four major approaches to reducing prejudice and discrimination.

Explain how social changes might create cognitive dissonance and eventually promote a reduction in prejudice.

Summarize the principles that explain destructive obedience to authority.

Every day we're confronted with social problems—from noisy neighbours to freeway congestion to terrorism. Unfortunately, social psychology has been more successful in describing, explaining, and predicting social problems than in changing them. However, researchers have found several helpful techniques. In this section, we first explore what scientists have discovered about methods to reduce prejudice, and then we discuss effective ways to cope with destructive forms of obedience.

REDUCING PREJUDICE AND DISCRIMINATION

What can be done to combat prejudice? Four major approaches can be used.

Cooperation and Common Goals One of the best ways to combat prejudice is to encourage cooperation rather than competition (Cunningham, 2002; Sassenberg et al., 2007). In a classic study, Muzafer Sherif and his colleagues (1966, 1998) created strong feelings of ingroup loyalty at a summer camp by physically separating two groups of boys into different cabins and assigning different projects to each group.

Once each group developed strong feelings of group identity and allegiance, the researchers set up a series of competitive games and awarded desirable prizes to the winning teams. The groups soon began to pick fights, call each other names, and raid each other's camps.

After using competition to create prejudice between the two groups, the researchers created "mini-crises" (such as a non-functioning water supply on a hot day) and tasks that required expertise, labour, and cooperation from both groups. The prejudice between the groups slowly began to dissipate, and by the end of camp, the earlier hostilities and ingroup favouritism had vanished. Sherif's study showed not only the importance of cooperation as opposed to competition but also the importance of *common goals* (resolving the mini-crises) in reducing prejudice (Der-Karabetian, Stephenson, & Poggi, 1996).

Increased Contact A second approach to reducing prejudice is increasing contact between groups (Cameron, Rutland, & Brown, 2007; Gómez & Huici, 2008; Wagner, Christ, & Pettigrew, 2008). But as you just saw in Sherif's study of the boys at the summer camp, contact can sometimes increase prejudice. Increasing contact works only under conditions that provide for close interaction, interdependence (common goals that require cooperation), and equal status. When people have positive experiences with one group, they tend to generalize to other groups (Pettigrew, 1998).

Cognitive Retraining One of the most recent strategies for prejudice reduction requires taking another's perspective or undoing associations of negative stereotypical traits (Buswell, 2006; Galinsky & Ku, 2004; Galinsky & Moskowitz, 2000). People can also learn to be unprejudiced if they are taught to selectively pay attention to similarities between groups, rather than differences (Phillips & Ziller, 1997).

Cognitive Dissonance One of the most efficient methods of changing an attitude uses the principle of cognitive dissonance discussed earlier in the chapter (Cook, 2000; D'Alessio & Allen, 2002). Each time we meet someone who does not conform to our prejudiced views, we experience dissonance—"I thought all gay men were effeminate. This guy is a deep-voiced professional athlete. I'm confused." To resolve the dissonance, we can maintain our stereotypes by saying, "This gay man is an exception to the rule." However, if we continue to come into contact with a variety of gay men, this "exception to the rule" defence eventually breaks down, and attitude change occurs (FIGURE 15.17).

Creating cognitive dissonance FIGURE 15.17

How might social changes, such as increasing numbers of minority group students in schools, and integration of visible minorities into the workforce and into positions of governance and leadership, initially create cognitive dissonance and then eventually lead to a reduction in prejudice? What other principle of attitude change is illustrated in this photo?

OVERCOMING DESTRUCTIVE OBEDIENCE: WHEN IS IT OKAY TO SAY NO?

Obedience to authority is an important part of our lives. If we routinely refused to obey police officers, firefighters, and other official personnel, our individual safety and social world would collapse. However, there are also many times when obedience may be unnecessary and even destructive—such as obedience to someone who is abusing military power or to a religious cult leader—and should be reduced.

How do we explain (and reduce) destructive obedience? Let's re-examine some of the major points discussed in this chapter while also introducing a few new ones.

Socialization Society and culture have a tremendous influence on all our thoughts, feelings, and actions. Obedience is no exception. From very early childhood, we're taught to respect and obey our parents, teachers, and other authority figures, and without this obedience we would have social chaos. Unfortunately, this early (and lifelong) socialization often becomes so deeply ingrained that we no longer recognize it, which helps explain many instances of mindless obedience to immoral requests from people in positions of authority (similar to what was found in Milgram's study on obedience). History is replete with instances in which atrocities were committed because people were "just following orders."

Power of the Situation

Situational factors also have a strong impact on obedience. For example, the roles of police officer or public citizen, teacher or student, and parent or child all have built-in guidelines for appropriate behaviour. One person is ultimately "in charge," and the other person is supposed to follow along. Because these roles are so well socialized, we mindlessly play them and find it difficult to recognize the point where they become maladaptive. As we discovered in the Zimbardo prison study, when well-adjusted and well-screened college students were suddenly given the roles of prisoners and guards, their behaviours were dramatically affected.

Groupthink

When discussing Milgram's study and other instances of destructive obedience, most people believe that they and their friends would never do such a thing. Can you see how this might be a form of groupthink, a type of faulty thinking discussed earlier in the chapter that occurs when group members strive for agreement and avoid inconsistent information? When we proclaim that Canadians would never follow the orders that some German people did during the holocaust, we're demonstrating several symptoms of groupthink—stereotypes of the outgroup, illusion of unanimity, belief in the morality of the group, and so on. We're also missing one of the most important lessons from Milgram's studies and the cross-cultural follow-ups: as philosopher

Hannah Arendt has suggested, the horrifying thing about the Nazis was not that they were so deviant but that they were so "terrifyingly normal."

Foot-in-the-Door

The gradual nature of many situations involving obedience may also help explain why so many people were willing to give the maximum shocks in Milgram's studies. The initial mild level of shocks may have worked as a **foot-in-the-door technique**, in which a first, small request is used as a setup for later, larger requests. Once Milgram's participants complied with the initial request, they might have felt obliged to continue (Chartrand, Pinckert, & Burger, 1999; Sabini & Silver, 1993). Can you see how this technique helps explain other forms of destructive obedience?

Relaxed Moral Guard

One common intellectual illusion that hinders critical thinking about obedience is the belief that only evil people do evil things, or that evil announces itself. For example, the experimenter in Milgram's study looked and acted like a reasonable person who was simply carrying out a research project. Because he was not seen as personally corrupt and evil, the participants' normal moral guard was down, which can maximize obedience. This relaxed moral guard might similarly explain obedience to a highly respected military officer or the leader of a religious cult.

These forces toward obedience are powerful. It's important to remember that each of us must be personally alert to immoral forms of obedience. On occasion, we also need the courage to stand up and say "No!"

CONCEPT CHECK

What is cognitive retraining?

How might groupthink contribute to destructive obedience?

SUMMARY

1 Our Thoughts about Others

1. **Social psychology** is the study of how other people influence our thoughts, feelings, and actions. Our attributions are frequently marred by the **fundamental attribution error** and the **self-serving bias**. Both biases may depend in part on cultural factors.

2. **Attitudes** have three components: cognitive, affective, and behavioural. An efficient strategy for changing attitudes is to create **cognitive dissonance**. Like attributional biases, the experience of cognitive dissonance may depend on culture.

2 Our Feelings about Others

1. Like all attitudes, **prejudice** involves cognitive, affective, and behavioural components. Although the terms prejudice and **discrimination** are often used interchangeably, they are not the same. Four commonly cited sources of prejudice are learning, mental shortcuts, economic and political competition, and displaced aggression.

2. Psychologists have found three compelling factors in interpersonal attraction: physical attractiveness, proximity, and similarity. Love often develops from initial feelings of friendship and liking. **Romantic love** is an intense but generally short-lived attraction based on mystery and fantasy, whereas **companionate love** is a strong, lasting attraction based on admiration, respect, trust, deep caring, and commitment.

3 Our Actions toward Others

1. Three factors drive **conformity**: normative social influence, informational social influence, and the role of **reference groups**. Conformity involves going along with the group, while **obedience** involves going along with a direct command, usually from someone in a position of authority. Milgram's research demonstrated the startling power of social situations to create obedience. The degree of deception and discomfort that Milgram's participants were subjected to raises serious ethical questions, and the same study would never be done today.

2. The roles that we play within groups strongly affect our behaviour, as Zimbardo's Stanford Prison experiment showed. Zimbardo's study also demonstrated **deindividuation**. In addition, groups affect our decisions. As individuals interact and discuss their opinions, **group polarization** (a group's movement toward more extreme decisions) and **groupthink** (a group's tendency to strive for agreement and to avoid inconsistent information) tend to occur. Both processes may hinder effective decision-making.

3. Several biological factors may help explain **aggression**, including instincts, genetic predisposition, aggression circuits in the brain and nervous system, mental disorders, and hormones and neurotransmitters.

(Continued on the following page)

Researchers have also proposed several psychosocial explanations for aggression, including aversive stimuli, culture and learning, and media influences. Catharsis does not appear to help release aggressive impulses; more effective ways to control aggression are to introduce incompatible responses and to improve social and communication skills.

4. Evolutionary theory suggests that **altruism** is an evolved, instinctual behaviour. Other research suggests that helping may actually be self-interest in disguise (**egoistic model**). The **empathy-altruism hypothesis** proposes that although altruism is sometimes based in selfish motivations, it is sometimes truly

selfless and motivated by concern for others (empathy). Latané and Darley found that for helping to occur, the potential helper must notice what is happening, interpret the event as an emergency, take personal responsibility for helping, decide how to help, and then actually initiate the helping behaviour.

4 Applying Social Psychology to Social Problems

1. Four major approaches can be used to combat prejudice: cooperation and superordinate goals, increased contact, cognitive retraining, and cognitive dissonance.

2. There are many times when obedience is unnecessary and destructive. Reducing destructive obedience requires an understanding of several social psychological principles, including socialization, the power of the situation, groupthink, the **foot-in-the-door technique,** and relaxed moral guard.

KEY TERMS

CRITICAL AND CREATIVE THINKING QUESTIONS

1. Have you ever changed a strongly held attitude? What caused the change for you?

2. Do you believe that you are free of prejudice? After reading this chapter, which of the many factors that cause prejudice do you think is most important to change?

3. How do Milgram's results—particularly the finding that the remoteness of the victim affected obedience—relate to some aspects of modern warfare?

4. Have you ever witnessed an episode of bullying? Did you try to intervene? What thoughts went through your head as you thought about intervening?

5. Have you ever done something in a group that you would not have done if you were alone? What happened? How did you feel? What have you learned from this chapter that might help you avoid this behaviour in the future?

6. Have you ever gone along with decisions simply because you were in a group? Can you see how groupthink can influence people's thinking?

7. Can you think of situations in which the egoistic model of altruism seems most likely correct? What about the empathy-altruism hypothesis?

8. Has anyone ever used the *foot-in-the-door* technique on you? Can you see how this technique can influence people to go along with an unpleasant request?

What is happening in this picture ?

From a very early age, Andrew Golden was taught how to fire hunting rifles. At age 11, he and a friend killed four classmates and a teacher in a school shooting. What factors might have contributed to Golden's tragically aggressive act?

What if a genetic study were somehow able to show that the boy was biologically predisposed to engage in hostile acts? Does this mean he was doomed to behave aggressively? Why or why not?

SELF-TEST

(Check your answers in Appendix A.)

1. The study of how other people influence our thoughts, feelings, and actions is called _____.

   a. sociology
   b. social science
   c. social psychology
   d. sociobehavioural psychology

2. Which of the following are two major attribution mistakes?

   a. the fundamental attribution error and the self-serving bias
   b. situational attributions and dispositional attributions
   c. the actor bias and the observer bias
   d. stereotypes and biases

3. When some people see homeless individuals, they think of them as lazy and unmotivated, failing to take into account the environments or situations that may have led to their condition. What explains people's tendency to focus on only this one aspect of the situation?

   a. self-serving bias
   b. cognitive dissonance
   c. groupthink
   d. saliency bias

4. Gaston thought his excellent qualifications and pleasant interpersonal style were the reasons he was hired for his new job. He then thought back to his recent firing from his previous job and how the boss was a miserable man who did not recognize his many talents. Which form of bias underlies Gaston's feelings?

   a. self-attribution bias
   b. self-serving bias
   c. actor bias
   d. saliency bias

5. Label the three components of attitudes on the figure below.

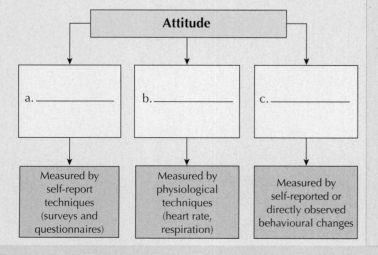

6. This theory says that contradictions between our attitudes and behaviour can motivate us to change our attitudes to agree with our behaviour.

   a. Social learning theory
   b. Cognitive dissonance theory
   c. Defence mechanisms theory
   d. Power of inconsistencies theory

7. _____ is a learned, generally negative, attitude toward specific people solely because of their membership in an identified group.

   a. Discrimination
   b. Stereotyping
   c. Cognitive biasing
   d. Prejudice

8. A number of studies have suggested that low levels of _____ may be associated with aggressive behaviour.

   a. frustration
   b. serotonin and GABA
   c. adrenaline
   d. blood sugar

9. The degree of positive feelings you have toward others is called _____.

   a. affective relations
   b. interpersonal attraction
   c. interpersonal attitudes
   d. affective connections

10. A strong and lasting attraction characterized by trust, caring, tolerance, and friendship is called _____.

    a. companionate love
    b. intimate love
    c. passionate love
    d. all of these options

11. This is the act of changing behaviour as a result of real or imagined group pressure.

    a. Norm compliance
    b. Obedience
    c. Conformity
    d. Mob rule

12. What was Stanley Milgram investigating in his classic teacher-learner shock study?

    a. the effects of punishment on learning
    b. the effects of reinforcement on learning
    c. obedience to authority
    d. all of these options

13. During _____ a person who feels anonymous within a group or crowd experiences an increase in arousal and a decrease in self-consciousness, inhibitions, and personal responsibility.

    a. groupthink
    b. group polarization
    c. authoritarianism
    d. deindividuation

14. Faulty decision-making that is the result of a highly cohesive group striving for agreement to the point of avoiding inconsistent information is known as _____.

    a. the risky shift
    b. group polarization
    c. groupthink
    d. destructive conformity

15. Zimbardo's research in which students played roles of prison inmates and guards showed that:

    a. roles can influence social behaviour.
    b. because the roles were hypothetical, the students did not take them seriously.
    c. roles have little influence on social behaviour.
    d. social behaviour likely affects the roles people choose.

16. Actions that are designed to help others with no obvious benefit to the helper are referred to as _____.

    a. empathy
    b. sympathy
    c. altruism
    d. egoism

17. Cézar came upon the scene of a serious car accident and found a number of people standing around, yet no one had called 911. What is a likely reason why no one had yet called for help?

    a. altruism
    b. diffusion of responsibility
    c. egoistic model
    d. antisocial behaviour

18. Label the three major explanations for helping on the figure below.

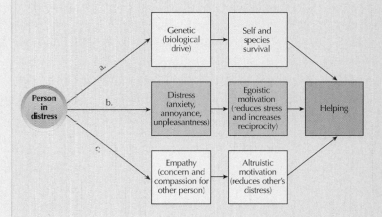

19. Research suggests that one of the best ways to decrease prejudice is to encourage _____.

    a. cooperation
    b. friendly competition
    c. reciprocity of liking
    d. conformity

20. Which of the following is most **UNLIKELY** to increase obedience?

    a. power of the situation
    b. foot-in-the-door
    c. socialization
    d. None of the above, as these are all ways to increase obedience.

Statistics and Psychology Module: Using Numbers to Describe and Interpret Research Results

We are constantly bombarded with numbers: "Save 30 percent," "70 percent chance of rain," "9 out of 10 dentists recommend it." Politicians use numbers to try to convince us that the economy is healthy (or unhealthy). Advertisers use numbers to convince us of the effectiveness of their products. Charitable organizations use numbers to convince us how badly they need our money. Psychologists and other scientists use numbers to summarize their results and support or refute their research findings. When people use numbers in these ways, they are using statistics. **Statistics** is a branch of applied mathematics that uses numbers to describe, analyze, interpret, and present information on a subject.

> **statistics**
> A branch of applied mathematics that uses numbers to describe, analyze, interpret, and present information.

Statistics make it possible for psychologists to quantify the information they obtain from their studies. They can then critically analyze and evaluate their results. Statistical analysis is imperative for researchers to describe, predict, or explain behaviour. For instance, Canadian psychologist Albert Bandura proposed that watching violence on television causes aggressive behaviour in children (Bandura & Walters, 1963). In carefully controlled experiments, he gathered numerical information and analyzed it according to specific statistical methods. The statistical analysis helped him demonstrate that the aggression of his subjects and the aggressive acts they had seen on television were related and that the relationship was causal and not mere coincidence (Chapter 6).

You don't have to be a math whiz to use statistics. Simple arithmetic is all you need to do most of the calculations and for more complex statistics computer programs are now readily available. A basic understanding of statistics is essential to critical thinking and real-world applications. Although the mathematical computations and formulas are important, what is more important is the development of an understanding of when and why each type of statistic is used. The purpose of this section, then, is to help you understand the significance of the most commonly used statistics.

Organizing and Summarizing Research Results

Psychologists design their studies to gather information in order to answer research questions. The information they obtain from subjects in their studies is known as *data* (*data* is plural; its singular is *datum*). When the data are gathered, they are generally in the form of numbers; if they aren't, they are converted to numbers. After they are gathered, the data must be organized in such a way that statistical analysis is possible.

Variables

A **variable** is simply a factor or a thing that varies. In effect, a variable is anything that can assume more than one value. Height, weight, sex, eye colour, and scores on an IQ test or video game are all factors that can assume more than one value in a population and are therefore variables. The number of noses is not considered a variable as it typically does not vary in a population. Anything that does not vary is called a **constant**. If researchers use only francophone Canadians in a study, then linguistic background is a

> **variable** Anything that can assume more than one value.

> **constant** Anything that does not vary.

constant and not a variable. Some variables will vary between people, such as sex (generally, a person is either male or female but not both at the same time). Some may vary within one person, such as scores on an on-line game; the same person might get 10,000 points on one try and only 800 on another.

In non-experimental studies, variables can be factors that are merely observed and recorded through naturalistic observation or case studies, or they can be factors about which people are questioned in a test or survey. In experimental studies, the two variables of interest are the independent variable and the dependent variable. In correlational research, the variables are the linked (or related) things the researcher is studying. Beware here: do not confuse the independent variable and dependent variable of experimental designs with the related variables of correlational research. These are two completely different designs and the terms are not interchangeable. Consider this similar to the lack of interchangeability between say a spoon and a toaster.

Frequency Distributions

After conducting a study and obtaining measures of the variable(s) being studied, psychologists need to organize the data in a meaningful way. **TABLE A.1** presents test scores from a statistics aptitude test collected from 50 college students. We use the letter n to represent the sample size. In this case $n = 50$. This information is called *raw data* because there is no order to the numbers and it has not been summarized in any way. The data are presented as they were collected.

The lack of order in raw data makes them very difficult to assess directly. Thus, the first step in understanding the results of an experiment is to impose some order on the raw data. This can be done in several ways. One of the

■ **frequency distribution**
A summary of the number of times each score in a data set occurs.

simplest is to create a **frequency distribution**, which allows us to look at the number of times (or frequency) a score or an event occurs. The simplest way to make a frequency distribution is to list all the possible test scores and then tally the number of people who received those scores. **TABLE A.2** presents a frequency distribution using the raw data from Table A.1. As you can see, the data are now easier to read. From looking at the frequency distribution, you can see that most of the test scores lie in the middle, with only a few at the very high or very low ends of the distribution. This was not at all evident when looking at the raw data and neither were the test marks that no one scored, such as 71, 69, 55, and 53.

This type of frequency distribution is practical when the number of possible scores is 20 or fewer. However, when there are more than 20 possible scores, it can be very difficult to make sense of. This difficulty can be seen

Statistics Aptitude Test scores for 50 college students TABLE A.1

73	57	63	59	50
72	66	50	67	51
63	59	65	62	65
62	72	64	73	66
61	68	62	68	63
59	61	72	63	52
59	58	57	68	57
64	56	65	59	60
50	62	68	54	63
52	62	70	60	68

Frequency distribution of 50 students on Statistics Aptitude Test TABLE A.2

Score	Frequency
73	2
72	3
71	0
70	1
69	0
68	5
67	1
66	2
65	3
64	2
63	5
62	5
61	2
60	2
59	5
58	1
57	3
56	1
55	0
54	1
53	0
52	2
51	1
50	3
Total = 3,100*	$n = 50$

*Each score is multiplied by its frequency, e.g. 73 × 2 = 146, and all of these scores are added up to total 3,100.

Personality test scores for 50 college students TABLE A.3

1350	750	530	540	750
1120	410	780	1020	430
720	1080	1110	770	610
1130	620	510	1160	630
640	1220	920	650	870
930	660	480	940	670
1070	950	680	450	990
690	1010	800	660	500
860	520	540	880	1090
530	730	570	560	740

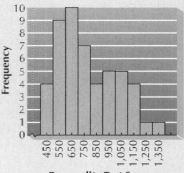

Personality Test Scores

in **TABLE A.3**, which presents the scores of 50 students who completed a hypothetical personality test. Notice that if we were to include all the test marks, including the marks that no one scored—that is, *all* the values between the highest score of 1,350 and the lowest score of 410—we would have 940 entries in the frequency distribution, making it extremely difficult to read, let alone interpret. So, when there are more than 20 possible scores, a group frequency distribution is normally used.

In a *group frequency distribution*, individual scores are clustered together in a range of scores (see **TABLE A.4**). These groups are called *class intervals*. Grouping scores like this makes it much easier to make sense out of the distribution. As you can see, it is far easier to understand Table A.4 than Table A.3. Group frequency distributions are also easier to represent in a graph.

Information can be presented in the form of a bar graph, called a *histogram,* or in the form of a point or line graph, called a *polygon*. Both frequency histograms and frequency polygons allow us to picture the data and look

at the shape of the distribution. **FIGURE A.1** shows a histogram presenting the data from Table A.4. Note that the class intervals are represented along the bottom line of the graph (the *x*-axis). The width of the bar stands for the width of the class interval, and the height of the bar stands for the frequency in that interval. Look at the third bar from the left in Figure A.1. This bar represents the interval "600 to 690 personality scores," which has a frequency of 10. You can see that this directly corresponds to the same class interval in Table A.4, since graphs and tables are merely alternative ways to illustrate the same information. Now look at **FIGURE A.2**. The information presented here is exactly the same as that in Figure A.1 but is represented in the form of a polygon rather than a histogram. Notice that each point represents a class interval and is placed at the centre of the interval and at the height corresponding to the frequency of that interval. To make the graph easier to read, straight lines connect the points. Can you see how both histograms and polygon graphs illustrate the same information? In fact, if we were to imagine a curve that touches the top of each histogram bar, it would look exactly the same as the polygon.

Group frequency distribution of personality test scores for 50 college students TABLE A.4

Class Interval	Frequency
1300–1390	1
1200–1290	1
1100–1190	4
1000–1090	5
900–990	5
800–890	4
700–790	7
600–690	10
500–590	9
400–490	4
Total	50

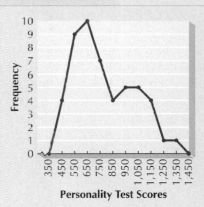

Personality Test Scores

Graphs and Misrepresenting Data

As you have just learned, every graph has several major parts, including labels; axes; and points, lines, or bars. Find these parts in Figure A.1 and Figure A.2.

An important thing to notice when interpreting a graph are the axes, labels, and values because they tell what the data are portraying. Labels should be clear, short, and easily understood. For example, in Figure A.1 the horizontal axis is clearly labelled "Personality test scores," and the vertical axis is labelled "Frequency." If a graph is not labelled, as we sometimes see in TV commercials or magazine ads, it is impossible to interpret and should be ignored. Even when a graph *is* labelled, the labels can be misleading. For example, if graph designers want to distort the information, they can elongate one of the two axes. Thus, it is important to pay careful attention to the graph axes. Do not be misled by a graph that has been drawn to prove a point or sell a product.

Displaying the data in a frequency distribution or in a graph can be especially helpful when researchers are trying to find relationships between certain variables. However, as we explained earlier, if psychologists want to make predictions or explanations about behaviour, they need to perform mathematical computations on the data.

Numerically Describing the Data in a Distribution

Once the study has been completed and the data have been collected, the researcher must then organize the data. Along with collapsing data into meaningful graphs, the researcher must also condense them into meaningful summary numbers. This process of describing the data is formally known as **descriptive statistics**.

> **descriptive statistics** The summary numbers used to describe the results of a study.

Descriptive statistics are the numbers used to describe the data set. They can be used to describe the characteristics of a population (an entire group, such as all people living in Canada) or a sample (a part of a group, such as a randomly selected group of 250 students from McGill University). The major descriptive statistics include the measures of central tendency and the measures of spread.

Measures of Central Tendency

Descriptive statistics indicating the centre or middle of the distribution are called **measures of central tendency** and include the mean, median, and mode. They are all scores that are typical of the centre of the distribution. The *mean* is what most of us think of when we hear the word "average." The *median* is the middle value when the data set is rank ordered. The *mode* is the score that occurs most often.

> **measures of central tendency** Descriptive statistics used to indicate the centre or middle of the distribution.

Mean

Each measure of central tendency has different advantages, but in psychological research, the mean is used most often. The mean or arithmetic average is obtained by adding all the raw scores and then dividing this number by the total number of scores in the sample (n). The mean is represented by an x with a bar above it ($\overline{X}$, pronounced "x bar"). If we wanted to compute the $\overline{X}$ of the raw statistics test scores in Table A.2, we would sum all the x's and divide by n. In Table A.2, the sum of all the scores is 3,100 and there are 50 scores. Therefore, the mean of these scores is 62.

$$\overline{X} = \frac{3,100}{50} = 62$$

Although the mean is probably the most widely used measure of central tendency, it has one important problem: it is exquisitely sensitive to extreme scores or outliers. Take a look at the example in **TABLE A.5**. The values represent household incomes in 2009 for three small Toronto streets. Notice how the means differ among the streets. What accounts for the difference you see between street A and C compared with B? If you did not have access to the raw data, you might wrongly conclude that Street B was far more affluent than A and C. It turns out that one extreme score is artificially inflating the mean in Street B. Without this score the mean for this street would be much closer to the means of the other two streets; calculate it and see. In such cases, when the data set contains extreme scores, the mean is tricky as a measure of central tendency and can properly be considered only with the measures of spread and the other measures of central tendency.

Mean household income for streets A, B, and C TABLE A.5		
Street A	**Street B**	**Street C**
66,000	65,000	63,000
72,000	80,000	69,000
78,000	79,000	82,000
67,000	3,000,000	71,000
79,000	58,000	73,000
65,000	77,000	65,000
80,000	71,000	68,000
$\overline{X}=$ 72,428	490,000	70,142

Median

The median is the middle score in the distribution once all the scores have been ranked from lowest to highest. If the total number of scores is odd, then there actually is a middle score and that middle score is the median. When n is an even number, the median is the mean of the two middle scores. TABLE A.6 shows the computation of the median for two different sets of scores, one set with an odd number of scores (15) and one with an even number of scores (10).

Mode

Of all the measures of central tendency, the easiest to compute is the mode, which is the most frequent score or the score that occurs most often.

Computation of median for odd and even numbers of IQ scores TABLE A.6	
IQ	**IQ**
139	137
130	135
121	121
116	116
107	108 ← middle score
101	106 ← middle score
98	105
96 ← middle score	101
84	98
83	97
82	$n = 10$
75	n is even
75	
68	
65	Median $= \dfrac{106 + 108}{2} = 107$
$n = 15$	
n is odd	
Median $= 96$	

Measures of Spread

When describing a distribution, it is not sufficient to give only the measures of central tendency; it is also necessary to give a **measure of spread**, which is a measure of the variation of the scores in the distribution. By examining the spread, we can determine whether the scores are bunched tightly around the middle value or tend to extend far from the middle value. FIGURE A.3 shows three different distributions, all with the same mean but with different spreads of scores. Notice that different spreads correspond to different distribution shapes. To measure spread, we use one of three calculations.

> **measures of spread** Measures of the amount of variation of the scores in the distribution.

Range

The simplest measure of spread is the range. It is calculated by subtracting the highest score in the data set from the lowest score. The range gives a measure of total spread, but its biggest limitation is that it is extremely sensitive to outliers. This sensitivity occurs because the formula for calculating the range requires that the two most extreme scores be used—the biggest and the smallest value. Because extreme scores are often not representative values in the data set, the range has limited usefulness and is not widely used as a measure of spread.

Variance

So, as we have just seen, using extreme scores to calculate a measure of spread is problematic. A better spread measure—the variance—calculates how far each and every score in the data set deviates (or differs) from the

Squished together or spread out? Measure of spread FIGURE A.3

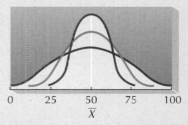

Three distributions with the same mean but a different variability or measure of spread. Notice that the mean of 50 is the same for all three distributions.

middle score (usually the mean). Both the variance and the standard deviation are calculated by using these deviation scores.

$$s^2 = \frac{\sum (X - \overline{X})^2}{N}$$

Dismantling the sample variance formula: Explaining it in words

Step 1: Subtract the mean from each score in the data set. This provides a set of deviation scores.
Step 2: Square each deviation score.
Step 3: Add all the squared deviation scores to get one overall total deviation score.
Step 4: Divide the total deviation score by the sample size.

The result is an average squared deviation score or the sample variance, which is represented by s^2. After you have calculated the variance, the standard deviation is very easy.

Standard Deviation

You might notice that the standard deviation is simply the square root of the variance. The standard deviation is the most widely used measure of variation and is represented

by a lowercase s. The standard deviation is a standard measurement of how much the scores in a distribution deviate from the mean. The formula for the standard deviation is shown below. Also, **TABLE A.7** shows how to compute standard deviation and a variance.

$$s = \sqrt{\frac{\sum (X - \overline{X})^2}{N}}$$

Most distributions of psychological data are bell shaped. That is, most of the scores are grouped around the mean, and the farther the scores are from the mean in either direction, the fewer the scores. Notice the bell shape of the distribution in **FIGURE A.4**. Distributions such as this are called *normal* distributions. In normal distributions, approximately two-thirds of the scores fall within a range that is one standard deviation below the mean to one standard deviation above the mean. For example, the Wechsler IQ tests (Chapter 8) have a mean of 100 and a standard deviation of 15. This means that approximately two-thirds of the people taking these tests will have scores between 85 and 115.

Computation of the standard deviation for 10 IQ scores TABLE A.7

Mean = 110; n = 10

IQ Scores X	X − X̄	(X − X̄)²
Score	Score − mean = deviation score	Deviation score squared
143	143 − 110 = 33	1089
127	17	289
116	6	36
98	−12	144
85	−25	625
107	−3	9
106	−4	16
98	−12	144
104	−6	36
116	6	36
$\sum X = 1100$		$\sum (X - \overline{X})^2 = 2424$

Standard Deviation = s

$$= \sqrt{\frac{\sum (X - \overline{X})^2}{N}} = \sqrt{\frac{2424}{10}}$$

$$= \sqrt{242.4} = 15.569$$

variance = 242.4

Inferential Statistics: Using the Sample to Generalize to the Larger Population

Descriptive statistics do just that—describe the data obtained from the study. Although descriptive statistics have many uses in numerically summarizing the results, they do not allow a researcher to make conclusions about the larger population. After all, who really cares about the results of a study of 50 people when the

Normal distributions FIGURE A.4

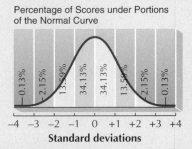

Percentage of Scores under Portions of the Normal Curve

0.13% | 2.15% | 13.59% | 34.13% | 34.13% | 13.59% | 2.15% | 0.13%

−4 −3 −2 −1 0 +1 +2 +3 +4
Standard deviations

The normal distribution forms a symmetrical bell-shaped curve. In a normal distribution, two-thirds of the scores lie between one standard deviation above and one standard deviation below the mean.

inferential statistics The use of sample statistics to make reliable claims about the larger population.

population might be a million or more? The use of **inferential statistics** allows psychologists and scientists to take a sample result and draw reliable conclusions about the larger population. Using a variety of different statistical tools a researcher can say with some degree of certainty what the results would have been if they had tested the entire population (which they can obviously never do). Inferential statistics also allow researchers to assess the probability of random or chance findings in their study and make comparisons between different study groups. As you can imagine this is a very valuable statistical tool that provides the ability to draw powerful conclusions from study results.

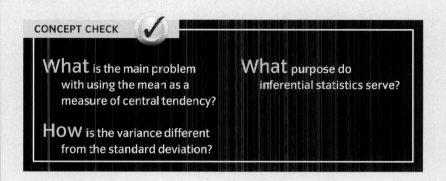

CONCEPT CHECK ✓

What is the main problem with using the mean as a measure of central tendency?

What purpose do inferential statistics serve?

How is the variance different from the standard deviation?

SUMMARY

1 Organizing and Summarizing Research Results

1. **Statistics** make it possible for psychologists to quantify the information they gather from their studies. Research results are obtained by measuring **variables** of interest. These are then numerically organized for statistical analysis and interpretation by using **frequency distributions**. Frequency polygons and frequency histograms allow us to look

at the shape of the research results and draw conclusions. Care must be taken in interpreting graphs as they can be used to misrepresent data.

2 Numerically Describing the Data in a Distribution

1. Descriptive statistics (which are not the same as descriptive studies) are used to numerically organize and summarize research results. The **measures of central tendency** provide information

about the middle values. The **measures of spread** numerically quantify the shape of the distribution.

3 Inferential Statistics: Using the Sample to Generalize to the Larger Population

1. **Inferential statistics** allow us to generalize sample results to the larger population.

KEY TERMS

- constant p. 447
- descriptive statistics p. 450
- frequency distribution p. 448
- inferential statistics p. 453
- measures of central tendency p. 450
- measures of spread p. 451
- statistics p. 447
- variable p. 447

SELF-TEST

(Check your answers in Appendix A.)

1. The measure of central tendency that requires adding all the values and dividing by *n* is the _____
   a. median. b. mode.
   c. mean. d. middle value.

2. The primary problem with the mean is it _____
   a. is sensitive to outliers.
   b. is not sensitive to outliers.
   c. is complicated and difficult to calculate.
   d. does not include all the values in the data set.

3. One measure of spread is the _____
   a. independent variable.
   b. mode.
   c. standard deviation.
   d. standard median.

4. The standard deviation is the _____
   a. square of the variance.
   b. middle value in an ordered data set.
   c. square root of the variance.
   d. least commonly used measure of spread.

5. _____ allow(s) us to take a sample result and draw research conclusions about the larger population.
   a. Descriptive statistics
   b. Inferential statistics
   c. Correlational research
   d. Experimental research

Appendix A
Answers to Self-Tests

Chapter 1: 1d; 2d; 3c; 4c; 5b; 6a, 7b; 8d; 9: Step 1: Literature review; Step 2: Operationally defined hypothesis; Step 3: Research design; Step 4: Statistical analysis; Step 5: Peer-reviewed scientific journal; Step 6: Theory; 10b; 11d; 12a; 13d; 14b; 15c; 16b; 17b; 18d; 19: Survey, Question, Read, Recite, Review, wRite; 20b

Chapter 2: 1b; 2d; 3a; 4a; 5 see Figure 2.6; 6c; 7b; 8d; 9b; 10c; 11 see Figure 2.8; 12a; 13d; 14c; 15a; 16 see Figure 2.16; 17 see Figure 2.18; 18a; 19a. left, b. right, c. right, d. left, 20b

Chapter 3: 1c; 2c; 3d; 4b; 5d; 6c; 7b; 8 see Figure 3.3; 9d; 10a; 11b; 12d; 13c; 14c; 15b; 16c; 17a; 18b; 19d; 20b

Chapter 4: 1c; 2c; 3d, 4b; 5 see Figure 4.6; 6c; 7d; 8 see Figure 4.7; 9c; 10a; 11b; 12a; 13a. photo 1, b. photo 2; 14c; 15b; 16a; 17b; 18c; 19b; 20d.

Chapter 5: Critical and creative thinking question 8: the drug is alcohol 1b; 2c; 3b; 4c; 5d; 6a; 7 see Figure 5.2; 8d; 9c; 10c; 11c; 12d; 13a; 14c; 15 a-2, b-1, c-4, d-3; 16c; 17b; 18d; 19d; 20c

Chapter 6: 1c; 2c; 3d; 4d; 5d; 6c; 7c; 8 a-2, b-1; 9a; 10c; 11d; 12a; 13c; 14b; 15d; 16c; 17d; 18c; 19c; 20d.

Chapter 7: 1: a, encoding, b, retrieval, c, storage; 2: a. sensory memory, b. short-term memory (STM), c. long-term memory (LTM)]; 3d; 4a; 5: a, explicit and declarative, b, implicit and nondeclarative; 6c; 7d; 8b; 9c; 10c; 11c; 12: a. retrograde amnesia, b. anterograde amnesia (bottom); 13a; 14: a. decay, b. interference, c. encoding failure, d. retrieval failure, e. motivated forgetting; 15b; 16b; 17a; 18d; 19b; 20c

Chapter 8: 1b; 2c; 3: a. preparation, b. identify given facts, c. separate relevant from irrelevant facts; 4b; 5a; 6c; 7c; 8d; 9d; 10: a. phonemes, b. morphemes, c. grammar; 11b; 12b; 13d; 14a; 15b; 16a; 17b; 18d; 19b; 20c.

Chapter 9: 1c; 2c; 3: a. cross-sectional research, b. longitudinal research; 4d; 5d; 6a; 7c; 8c; 9b; 10c; 11d; 12: a. sensorimotor, b. preoperational, c. concrete operations, d, formal operations; 13d; 14c; 15c; 16d; 17c; 18b; 19a; 20a.

Chapter 10: 1c; 2a; 3c; 4a; 5c; 6b; 7: a. trust → b. autonomy → c. initiative → d. industry; 8: a. identity → b. intimacy → c. generativity → d. ego integrity; 9b; 10c; 11c; 12b; 13a; 14a; 15c; 16a; 17c; 18d; 19d; 20a

Chapter 11: 1a; 2a; 3c; 4d; 5b; 6d; 7d; 8a; 9c; 10: a. excitement → b. plateau → c. orgasm → d. resolution; 11b; 12c; 13a; 14c; 15b; 16c; 17d; 18d 19c; 20c

Chapter 12: 1b; 2: a. openness, b. conscientiousness, c. extroversion, d. agreeableness, e. neuroticism (OCEAN); 3: a. conscious, b. preconscious, c. unconscious; 4d; 5b; 6c; 7: a. oral → b. anal → c. phallic → d. latency → e. genital; 8b; 9d; 10d; 11c; 12b; 13b; 14c; 15c; 16d; 17c; 18c; 19a; 20b

Chapter 13: 1d; 2b; 3: Axis I. clinical disorders, Axis II. personality disorders and mental retardation, Axis III. General medical conditions, Axis IV. psychosocial and environmental problems, Axis V. global assessment of functioning; 4a; 5: a. generalized anxiety disorder, b. panic disorder, c. phobias, d. obsessive-compulsive disorder, e. post-traumatic stress disorder; 6d; 7a; 8b; 9d; 10a; 11a; 12d; 13 a. paranoid, b. catatonic, c. disorganized, d. undifferentiated, e. residual; 14a; 15c; 16b; 17a; 18c; 19c; 20d

Chapter 14: 1a; 2c; 3c; 4b; 5c; 6c; 7b; 8c; 9d; 10a; 11b; 12d; 13c; 14c; 15: a. antianxiety drugs, b. antipsychotic drugs, c. mood stabilizer drugs, d. antidepressant drugs; 16c; 17b; 18; a. disturbed thoughts, b. disturbed emotions, c. disturbed behaviours, d. interpersonal and life situation difficulties, e. biomedical disturbances; 19c; 20b

Chapter 15: 1c; 2a; 3d; 4b; 5 a. cognitive, b. affective, c. behavioural ; 6b; 7d; 8b; 9b; 10a; 11c; 12c; 13d; 14c; 15a; 16c; 17b; 18 a. evolutionary model, b. egoistic model, c. empathy-altruism model; 19a; 20d

Statistics Module: 1c, 2a, 3c, 4c, 5b

GLOSSARY

abnormal behaviour   Patterns of emotion, thought, and action that are considered pathological (diseased or disordered) for one, or more of these reasons: statistical infrequency, disability or dysfunction, personal distress, or violation of norms (Davison et al., 2008).

accommodation   In Piaget's theory, the process of adjusting old schemas or developing new ones to better fit with new information.

achievement motivation   A desire to excel, especially when in competition with others.

action potential   The voltage change across an axon membrane when an impulse is transmitted.

activity theory of aging   Successful aging is fostered by a full and active commitment to life.

addiction   A broad term referring to a condition in which a person has an overwhelming commitment to the drug of choice that supplants all other activities.

aggression   Any behaviour intended to harm someone.

agonistic drug   A drug that mimics or enhances the activity of neurotransmitters.

algorithm   A set of steps that, if followed correctly, will eventually solve the problem.

altered state of consciousness (ASC)   Mental states found generally during sleep, dreaming, psychoactive drug use, and hypnosis.

altruism   Actions designed to help others with no obvious benefit to the helper.

Alzheimer's disease (AD)   Degenerative brain disease characterized by progressive mental deterioration and pathological memory loss.

anorexia nervosa   An eating disorder characterized by a pathological drive to be thin and severe loss of weight resulting from self-imposed starvation.

antagonistic drug   A drug that blocks or inhibits the activity of neurotransmitters.

anxiety disorder   A type of abnormal behaviour characterized by unrealistic, irrational fear.

applied research   Research designed to solve practical real-world problems.

assimilation   In Piaget's theory, the process of absorbing new information into existing schemas.

assumption   Something taken for granted to be true.

attachment   A strong affectional bond with primary caretakers that endures over time.

attitudes   Learned predispositions to respond cognitively, affectively, and behaviourally to particular objects in a particular way.

attributions   How we explain our own and others' actions.

autonomic nervous system (ANS)   Subdivision of the peripheral nervous system (PNS) that controls involuntary functions of tissues, organs, and glands. It is subdivided into the *sympathetic* nervous system and the *parasympathetic* nervous system.

basic research   Research conducted to advance scientific knowledge rather than for practical application.

behaviour therapy   A group of techniques based on learning principles that is used to change maladaptive behaviours.

behavioural genetics   The study of the relative contributions of genetic influences and environment factors on behaviour and mental processes.

bias   When a belief prevents fair judgement.

binge drinking   When a man consumes five or more drinks in a row, or a woman consumes four or more drinks in a row on at least three occasions during the previous two weeks.

biological preparedness   Built-in (innate) readiness to form associations between certain stimuli and responses.

biological research   Scientific studies of the brain and other parts of the nervous system.

biomedical therapy   The use of physiological interventions (drugs, electroconvulsive therapy, and psychosurgery) to reduce or alleviate symptoms of psychological disorders.

biopsychosocial model   A unifying theme of modern psychology that considers biological, psychological, and social processes.

bipolar disorder   Repeated episodes of mania (unreasonable elation and hyperactivity) and depression.

bulimia nervosa   An eating disorder characterized by the consumption of large quantities of food (bingeing), followed by vomiting, extreme exercise, or laxative use (purging).

central nervous system (CNS)   The brain and spinal cord.

cerebral cortex   The thin surface layer on the cerebral hemispheres that regulates most complex behaviour, including processing sensations, motor control, and higher mental processes.

chunking   The act of grouping separate pieces of information into a single unit (or chunk).

circadian [ser-KAY-dee-an] **rhythms**   Biological, biochemical, and behavioural changes that occur in living organisms on a 24-hour cycle (in Latin, *circa* means "about," and *dies* means "day").

classical conditioning   Learning that occurs when a neutral stimulus (NS) becomes paired (associated) with an unconditioned stimulus (UCS) to elicit a conditioned response (CR).

cognition   Mental activities involved in acquiring, storing, retrieving, and using knowledge.

cognitive dissonance   A feeling of discomfort caused by a discrepancy between an attitude and a behaviour or between two attitudes.

cognitive therapy   Therapy that focuses on changing faulty thought processes and beliefs to treat problem behaviours.

cognitive-social theory   A perspective that emphasizes the roles of thinking and social learning in behaviour.

collectivistic cultures   Cultures in which the needs and goals of the group are emphasized over the needs and goals of the individual.

concrete operational stage   Piaget's third stage (roughly ages 7 to 11) in which the child can perform mental operations on concrete objects and understand reversibility and conservation though abstract thinking is not yet present.

conditioning The process of learning associations between environmental stimuli and behavioural responses.

conduction deafness (middle-ear deafness) Deafness resulting from problems with the mechanical system that conducts sound waves to the inner ear.

conformity The act of changing behaviour as a result of real or imagined group pressure.

confound variables Nuisance variables that can affect the outcome of the study and lead to erroneous conclusions about the effects of the independent variable on the dependent variable.

conscious Freud's term for thoughts or motives that a person is currently aware of or is remembering.

consciousness An organism's awareness of its own self and surroundings (Damasio, 1999).

control group The group that does not receive the experimental manipulations but is treated in the same way as the experimental group in all other areas.

conventional level Kohlberg's second level of moral development, in which moral judgements are based on compliance with the rules and values of society.

coping Adaptive or compensatory strategies designed to reduce the effects of a stressor.

correlational research A research method in which variables are observed or measured (without directly manipulating) to identify possible relationships between them.

creativity The ability to produce valued outcomes in a novel way.

critical period A period of special sensitivity to specific types of learning that shapes the capacity for future development.

critical thinking The ability to accurately analyze information and be able to draw rational, fact-based conclusions based on the empirical evidence provided.

cross-sectional method Research design that compares individuals of various ages at one point in time to provide information about age differences.

debriefing Informing participants after a study about the purpose of the study, the nature of the anticipated results, and any deception used.

defence mechanisms In Freudian theory, the ego's protective method of reducing anxiety by distorting reality.

deindividuation Increased arousal and reduced self-consciousness, inhibition, and personal responsibility that may occur in a group.

delusions Mistaken beliefs based on misrepresentations of reality.

dependent variable (DV) A variable that is measured; it is affected by (or dependent on) the independent variable and is the outcome or effect variable.

depressants Drugs that slow or depress nervous system activity.

descriptive research Research methods used to observe, record, and describe behaviour (without producing cause–effect explanations).

developmental psychology The study of age-related changes in behaviour and mental processes from conception to death.

Diagnostic and Statistical Manual of Mental Disorders (DSM-IV-TR) The classification system developed by the American Psychiatric Association used to describe abnormal behaviours; the *IV-TR* indicates that it is the text revision (*TR*) of the fourth major edition (*IV*).

discrimination Negative behaviour directed at members of a group.

disengagement theory Successful aging is characterized by mutual withdrawal between the aging person and society.

dissociative disorders Amnesia, fugue, or multiple personalities resulting from avoidance of painful memories or situations.

drug abuse Drug use that is necessary for feelings of continued well-being; use continues despite adverse consequence.

dyssomnias Problems in the amount, timing, and quality of sleep, including insomnia, sleep apnea, and narcolepsy.

elaborative rehearsal The process of linking new information to previously stored material.

electroconvulsive therapy (ECT) Biomedical therapy in which electrical current is passed through the brain.

embryonic period The second stage of prenatal development which begins after uterine implantation and lasts through the eighth week.

emotion A state of physiological arousal and tendencies toward action involving changes in behaviour, cognitions, facial expressions, and subjective feelings.

emotion-focused forms of coping Coping strategies based on changing one's perceptions of stressful situations.

empirical evidence Information acquired by formal observation, experimentation, and measurement by using systematic scientific methods.

encoding Processing information into the memory system.

encoding specificity principle Retrieval of information is improved when the conditions of recovery are similar to the conditions that existed when the information was first encoded.

eustress Pleasant, beneficial, or curative stress.

evolutionary psychology A branch of psychology that studies the ways in which natural selection and evolution can help to explain behaviour and mental processes.

evolutionary/circadian theory As a part of circadian rhythms, sleep evolved to conserve energy and to serve as protection from predators.

experiment A carefully controlled scientific procedure that determines whether variables manipulated by the experimenter have a causal effect on the experiment result.

experimental group The group that receives the experimental manipulation.

explicit/declarative memory The subsystem within long-term memory that consciously stores facts, information, and personal life experiences.

extrinsic motivation Motivation based on obvious external rewards or threats of punishment.

family therapy Treatment to change maladaptive interaction patterns within a family.

feature detectors Specialized brain cells that respond only to certain sensory information.

fetal period The third, and final, stage of prenatal development (eight weeks to birth), which is characterized by rapid weight gain in the fetus and the fine detailing of bodily organs and systems.

five-factor model (FFM) The trait theory that explains personality in terms of the "Big Five" model, which is composed of openness, conscientiousness, extroversion, agreeableness, and neuroticism.

formal operational stage Piaget's fourth stage (around age 11 and beyond), which is characterized by abstract and hypothetical thinking.

fundamental attribution error (FAE) Attributing people's behaviour to internal (dispositional) causes rather than external (situational) factors.

gate-control theory The theory that pain sensations are processed and altered by mechanisms within the spinal cord.

gender Psychological and socio-cultural meanings added to biological maleness or femaleness.

gender roles Societal expectations for normal and appropriate male and female behaviour.

general adaptation syndrome (GAS) Selye's three-part model of how organisms characteristically react to stressors.

germinal period The first stage of prenatal development, which begins with conception and ends with implantation in the uterus (the first two weeks).

glial cell A nervous system cell that supports, nourishes, insulates, and protects neurons.

grammar Rules that specify how phonemes, morphemes, words, and phrases should be combined to express thoughts; these rules include syntax and semantics.

group polarization A group's movement toward either riskier or more conservative behaviour, depending on the members' initial dominant tendencies.

group therapy A form of therapy in which a number of people meet together to work toward therapeutic goals.

groupthink Faulty decision-making that occurs when a highly cohesive group strives for agreement and avoids inconsistent information.

habituation The tendency of the brain to ignore environmental factors that remain constant.

hallucinations Imaginary sensory perceptions that occur without an external stimulus.

hardiness Resilient personality with a strong commitment to personal goals, control over life, and viewing change as a challenge rather than a threat.

health psychology The study of how biological, psychological, and social factors interact in health and illness.

heuristic A simple rule used in problem solving and decision-making that does not guarantee a solution but offers a likely shortcut to it.

hierarchy of needs Maslow's theory of motivation that some motives (such as physiological and safety needs) must be met before going on to higher needs (such as belonging and self-actualization).

homeostasis A body's tendency to maintain a relatively stable state, such as a constant internal temperature, blood sugar, oxygen level, or water balance.

hormones Chemicals synthesized by endocrine glands that are released into the bloodstream to bind to target tissues and organs, producing bodily changes or maintaining normal function.

humanistic therapy Therapy that seeks to maximize personal growth through affective restructuring (emotional readjustment).

human sexual response cycle Masters and Johnson's description of the four physiological stages of sexual arousal: excitement, plateau, orgasm, and resolution.

hypnosis A trance-like state of heightened suggestibility, deep relaxation, and intense focus.

implicit/nondeclarative memory The subsystem within long-term memory that consists of nonconscious procedural skills, simple classically conditioned responses, and priming.

independent variable (IV) A variable that is manipulated by the researcher to determine its effect on the dependent variable. The IV is the cause variable.

individualistic cultures Cultures in which the needs and goals of the individual are emphasized over the needs and goals of the group.

informed consent A participant's agreement to take part in a study after being told what to expect.

ingroup favouritism Viewing members of the ingroup more positively than members of an outgroup.

insight Sudden understanding of a problem that implies the solution.

instinctive drift The tendency of some conditioned responses to shift (or drift) back toward innate response pattern.

instincts Behavioural patterns that are unlearned (inborn), always expressed in the same way, and are universal in a species.

intelligence quotient (IQ) An individual's mental age divided by his or her chronological age and multiplied by 100.

intelligence The global capacity to think rationally, act purposefully, and deal effectively with the environment.

internal locus of control The belief that one controls one's own fate.

interpersonal attraction Positive feelings toward another.

intrinsic motivation Motivation resulting from personal enjoyment of a task or activity.

labelled lines The way the brain interprets the type of sensory information based on its neural origin in the body and its destination location in the brain.

language A form of communication that uses sounds and symbols combined according to specified rules.

latent learning Hidden learning that exists without behavioural signs.

law of effect Thorndike's rule that the probability of an action being repeated is strengthened when followed by a pleasant or satisfying consequence.

learning A relatively permanent change in behaviour or mental processes because of practice or experience.

localization of function Specialization of various parts of the brain for particular functions.

longitudinal method Research design that follows a single individual or a group of same-aged individuals over a period of time to provide information about age changes.

long-term memory (LTM) This third memory stage stores information for long periods. Its capacity is limitless; its duration is relatively permanent.

long-term potentiation (LTP) Long-lasting increase in neural excitability caused by repeated neural input. Believed to be the biological basis of learning and memory.

maintenance rehearsal Repeating information to keep it active in short-term memory.

major depressive disorder Long-lasting depressed mood that interferes with the ability to function, feel pleasure, or maintain interest in life (Swartz & Margolis, 2004).

maturation Development governed by automatic, genetically predetermined signals.

medical model The perspective that diseases (including mental illness) have physical causes that can be diagnosed, treated, and possibly cured.

meditation A group of techniques designed to refocus attention, block out all distractions, and produce an altered state of consciousness.

memory An internal record or representation of some prior event or experience.

misinformation effect Distortion of a memory by misleading post-event information.

modelling therapy A learning technique in which the subject watches and imitates models who demonstrate desirable behaviours.

morpheme [MOR-feem] The smallest meaningful unit of language, formed from a combination of phonemes.

motivation An internal state that activates, directs, and maintains behaviour, usually toward a goal or away from an unfavourable situation.

myelin sheath The fatty insulation that segmentally wraps an axon and serves to speed neural transmission.

natural selection The process by which across a wide range of inherited trait variation, those traits that confer a survival or reproductive advantage will increase in the population.

nature-nurture controversy Dispute over the relative contributors of nature (heredity) and nurture (environment) in the development of behaviour and mental processes.

nerve deafness (inner-ear deafness) Damage to the cochlea, hair cells, or auditory nerve.

neurogenesis The division and differentiation of non-neuronal cells to produce neurons.

neuron A nervous system cell that receives and conducts electrochemical impulses.

neuroplasticity The brain's remarkable malleability to reorganize and change its structure and function across the lifespan.

neuroscience An interdisciplinary field that studies how biological processes interact with behaviour and mental processes.

neurotransmitters Chemicals that neurons release in response to the arrival of an action potential, which affect other cells, including other neurons.

non-rapid-eye-movement (NREM) sleep Stages 1 to 4 of sleep.

obedience The act of following a direct command, usually from an authority figure.

objective personality tests Standardized questionnaires that require written responses, usually to multiple-choice or true-false questions.

observational learning Learning new behaviour or information by watching others (also known as social learning or modelling).

operant conditioning Learning in which voluntary responses are controlled by their consequences (also known as instrumental or Skinnerian conditioning).

opiates Drugs derived from opium or synthetically derived and molecularly similar to opium that relieve pain and induce sleep.

opponent-process theory The theory that colour perception is based on three systems of colour receptors, each of which responds in an on-off fashion to opposite-colour stimuli: blue-yellow, red-green, and black-white.

outgroup homogeneity effect Judging members of an outgroup as more alike and less diverse than members of the ingroup.

parasomnias Abnormal disturbances occurring during sleep, including nightmares, night terrors, sleepwalking, and sleep talking.

perception The higher-level process of selecting, organizing, and interpreting sensory data into useful mental representations of the world.

perceptual constancy Tendency for the environment to be perceived as remaining the same, even with changes in sensory input.

peripheral nervous system (PNS) All other nerves and neurons connecting the CNS to the rest of the body.

personality Relatively stable and enduring patterns of thoughts, feelings, and actions.

personality disorders Inflexible, maladaptive personality traits that cause significant impairment of social and occupational functioning.

phoneme [FO-neem] The smallest basic unit of speech or sound (the English language has about 40 phonemes).

physical dependence Changes in physical or bodily processes that make the drug necessary for daily functioning.

plagiarism A form of academic dishonesty in which a person takes credit for the work or ideas of another person.

pleasure principle In Freud's theory, the principle on which the id operates—seeking immediate gratification.

postconventional level Kohlberg's highest level of moral development, in which individuals develop personal standards for right and wrong, and they define morality in terms of abstract principles and values that apply to all situations and societies.

post-traumatic stress disorder (PTSD) An anxiety disorder that develops following exposure to a life-threatening or other extreme event that evoked great horror or helplessness. It is characterized by flashbacks, nightmares, and impaired daily functioning.

preconscious Freud's term for thoughts or motives that can be easily brought to mind.

preconventional level Kohlberg's first level of moral development, in which morality is based on rewards, punishment, and the exchange of favours.

prejudice A learned, generally negative attitude directed toward specific people solely because of their membership in an identified group.

preoperational stage Piaget's second stage (roughly ages 2 to 7 years), which is characterized by the ability to employ significant language and to think symbolically though the child lacks operations (reversible mental processes) and thinking is egocentric and animistic.

problem-focused forms of coping Coping strategies that use problem-solving strategies to decrease or eliminate the source of stress.

projective tests Psychological tests that use ambiguous stimuli, such as inkblots or drawings, which allow the test taker to project his or her unconscious thoughts onto the test material.

psychiatry The branch of medicine that deals with the diagnosis, treatment, and prevention of mental disorders.

psychoactive drugs Chemicals that alter perception, conscious awareness, or mood.

psychoanalysis Freudian therapy designed to bring unconscious conflicts, which usually date back to early childhood experiences, into consciousness. Also refers to Freud's theoretical school of thought, which emphasizes unconscious processes.

psychodynamic therapy A modern form of psychoanalysis that emphasizes internal conflicts, motives, and unconscious forces.

psychology The scientific study of behaviour and mental processes.

psychoneuroimmunology The interdisciplinary field that studies the interaction among the mind, the nervous system, and the immune system.

psychopharmacology The study of drug effects on the brain and behaviour.

psychosexual stages In Freudian theory, the five developmental periods (oral, anal, phallic, latency, and genital) during which particular kinds of pleasures must be gratified if personality development is to proceed normally.

psychosocial stages In Erikson's theory, the eight developmental stages involving a crisis that must be successfully resolved.

psychosurgery Operative procedures on the brain designed to relieve severe mental symptoms that have not responded to other forms of treatment.

psychotherapy Techniques employed to improve psychological functioning and promote adjustment to life.

punishment A consequence that weakens a response and makes it less likely to recur.

random assignment Everyone selected to be in the study has an equal chance of being put in either the control group or the experimental group.

random selection Everyone in the population of interest has an equal chance of being in the sample.

rapid-eye-movement (REM) sleep Stage of sleep marked by rapid eye movements, high-frequency brain waves, paralysis of large muscles, and dreaming.

reciprocal determinism Bandura's belief that cognitions, behaviours, and the environment interact to produce personality.

reflexes or **reflex arcs** Involuntary, automatic behaviour initiated by the spinal cord in response to some stimulus.

reinforcement A consequence that strengthens a response and makes it more likely to recur.

reliability A measure of the consistency and stability of test scores when a test is re-administered.

repair/restoration theory Sleep serves a recuperative function, allowing organisms to repair or replenish key cognitive and physiological factors.

retrieval Recovering information from memory storage.

retrieval cue A clue or prompt that helps stimulate recall and retrieval of a stored piece of information from long-term memory.

savant syndrome A condition in which a person who has a developmental disability exhibits exceptional skill or brilliance in some limited field.

schemas Cognitive structures or patterns consisting of a number of organized ideas that grow and differentiate with experience.

schizophrenia A group of psychotic disorders involving major disturbances in perception, language, thought, emotion, and behaviour. The individual withdraws from people and reality, often into a fantasy life of delusions and hallucinations.

scientific method A systematic and orderly procedure for understanding and learning about the world.

selective attention Filtering out and attending only to important sensory messages.

self-concept   Rogers' term for all the information and beliefs that individuals have about their own nature, qualities, and behaviour.

self-efficacy   Bandura's term for the learned belief that one is capable of producing desired results, such as mastering new skills and achieving personal goals.

sensation   The process of receiving, translating, and transmitting raw sensory data from the external and internal environments to the brain.

sensorimotor stage   Piaget's first stage (birth to approximately age 2), in which schemas are developed through sensory and motor activities.

sensory adaptation   Repeated or constant stimulation decreases the number of sensory messages sent to the brain from the sense receptors.

sensory memory   This first memory stage holds sensory information and has a relatively large capacity but the duration is only a few seconds.

sensory transduction   The process by which a physical stimulus is converted into neural impulses.

sex   Biological maleness and femaleness, including chromosomal sex. Also, activities related to sexual behaviours, such as masturbation and intercourse.

sexual orientation   The direction of a person's sexual attraction toward persons of the same sex (gay or lesbian), the other sex (heterosexual), or both sexes (bisexual).

shaping   Reinforcing successively closer and closer approximations to the desired response.

short-term memory (STM)   This second memory stage temporarily stores encoded sensory information and decides whether to send it on to long-term memory (LTM). Its capacity is limited to five to nine items, and its duration is about 30 seconds.

social psychology   The study of how other people influence a person's thoughts, feelings, and actions.

socio-emotional selectivity theory   A natural decline in social contact as older adults become more selective with their time.

somatic nervous system (SNS)   Subdivision of the peripheral nervous system (PNS). The SNS receives incoming sensory information and controls the skeletal muscles.

standardization   Establishment of the norms and uniform procedures for giving and scoring a test.

stem cells   Precursor (immature) cells that can develop into any type of new specialized cells; a stem cell holds all information it needs to make bone, blood, brain—any part of a human body—and can also copy itself to maintain a stock of stem cells.

stereotype threat   Negative stereotypes about minority groups cause some members to doubt their abilities.

stimulants   Drugs that speed up nervous system activity.

storage   Retaining information over time.

stress   The body's non-specific response to any demand made on it; the physical and mental arousal to circumstances that we perceive as threatening or challenging.

stressor   An event that places demands on an organism that tax its resources.

substance-related disorders   Abuse of or dependence on a mood- or behaviour-altering drug.

tolerance   A state reached when the physiological reaction to the drug decreases, such that increasing doses are necessary for the same effect.

traits   Relatively stable and consistent characteristics that can be used to describe someone.

trichromatic theory   The theory that colour perception results from mixing three distinct colour systems: red, green, and blue.

unconditional positive regard   Rogers' term for positive behaviour toward a person with no contingencies attached.

unconscious   Freud's term for thoughts or motives that lie beyond a person's normal awareness but that can be made available through psychoanalysis.

validity   The ability of a test to measure what it was designed to measure.

withdrawal   Characteristic signs that appear in a person when a drug is discontinued after prolonged use.

Chapter 1

Pages 2–3: (inset top) Alaska Stock Images/National Geographic Stock, (inset bottom) Alaska Stock Images/National Geographic Stock, Katherine Feng/National Geographic Stock; Page 3: images repeated, see individual pages; Page 5: (top) AP/The Canadian Press/Alan DiazHenry Groskinsky; Page 6: From xkcd.com, used with permission; Page 7: Stuart Pearce/Age Fotostock; Page 9: Bettmann/Corbis Images; Page 10: Nina Leen/Time Life Pictures/Getty Images; Page 11: Tim Mantoani/Masterfile; Page 15 (left) © Image Source/Corbis, (right) © Understanding Animal Research; Page 21: (top) © A & J Visage/Alamy, (bottom) Jeffrey Greenberg/Photo Researchers; Page 22: Jeffrey Greenberg/Photo Researchers, Inc.; Page 23: (right) From Damasio H., Grabowski T., Frank R., Galaburda A.M., Damasio A.R.: The return of Phineas Gage: Clues about the brain from a famous patient. Science, 264:1102–1105, 1994, Department of Neurology & Image Analysis Facility, University, (left) ©The Image Works; Page 24: (right) © Chris Carroll/Corbis, (left) Superstock RF/Superstock; Page 25: (1) Science Pictures Ltd./Photo Researchers, (2) Kopf Model 962 Dual Ultra Precise Small Animal Stereotaxic Instrument designed and manufactured by David Kopf Instruments, Tujunga, CA, (3) Reproduced from "A case of self-inflicted craniocerebral penetrating injury," Figure 1, *Emergency Medicine Journal, 23 (5)*, James, G., et al., © 2006, with permission from BMJ Publishing Group Ltd." (4) Gary D. Landsman/© Corbis, (5) Time & Life Pictures/Getty Images; Page 26: (1) Mehau Kulyk/Photo Researchers, (2) N.I.H./Photo Researchers, (3) Scott Camazine/Photo Researchers, (4) Science Photo Library/Photo Researchers, Inc., (5) ©AP/Wide World Photos; Page 28: PhotoDisc/Getty Images; Page 29: Lynsey Addario/National Geographic Stock; Pages 30–32: images repeated, see individual pages; Page 33: Jonathan Selig/Getty Images.

Chapter 2

Pages 36–37: AP/The Canadian Press/Paul Sancya; Page 37: images repeated, see individual pages; Page 39: W.E. Garrett/National Geographic Stock, (centre) NHLI via Getty Images; (bottom) FilmMagic; Page 40: David Young-Wolff/Stone/Getty Images, Inc; Page 41: (left), Popperfoto/Getty Images, (centre) Mark Moffett/Minden Pictures/National Geographic Stock, (right) Frans Lanting/National Geographic Stock; Page 42: (right) Courtesy E.R. Lewis, Berkeley; Page 43: Reuters New Media Inc./Corbis Images; Page 45: Courtesy E.R. Lewis, Berkeley; Page 46: (1) PhotoDisc, Inc., (2) PhotoDisc, (3) Digital Vision, (4) Digital Vision, (5) Purestock, (6) PhotoDisc, Inc., (7) Purestock; Page 50: Courtesy of McGill University; Page 52: PhotoDisc/Getty Images; Page 53: (left) Woogies1/Dreamstime.com/GetStock.com, (right) Alaska Stock Images/National Geographic Stock; Page 54: Getty Images News and Sport Services; Page 56: (centre right) Alaska Stock Images/National Geographic Stock, (right) Adrian Weinbrecht/Stone/Getty Images, (centre left) Corbis Images, (left) Justin Guariglia/National Geographic Stock; Page 58: (left and right) Associated Press; Page 59: (right and left) © Natural History Museum, London; Page 65: Everett Collection, Inc./The Canadian Press/Rob McEwan.

Chapter 3

Pages 68–69: Ira Block/National Geographic Stock; Page 69: images repeated, see individual pages; Page 71: (left) Corbis Digital Stock, (right) Toronto Star/GetStock.com; Page 72: Photofest Inc.; Page 74: (top) Time & Life Pictures/Getty Images, (bottom) A. Operti/American Museum of Natural History Library; Page 76: (top) Bonnier Alba, (bottom left) Media Bakery, (bottom right) Rick Gomez/Corbis/First Light; Page 77: Digital Vision/SuperStock; Page 78: The Canadian Press/Fred Chartland; Page 80: Comstock/SuperStock; Page 81: Health Canada. Licensed

under Health Canada copyright.; Page 82: Rayman/Digital Vision/Getty Images; Page 83: (top) Purestock, (bottom) McComb Photography/Photonica/Getty Images; Page 84: Gusto/Photo Researchers; Page 86: (top and bottom) ©AP/Wide World Photos; Page 87: (1) Purestock, (2) © Remi Ochlik/IP3/MAXPPP, (3) Digital Vision, (4) iStockphoto, (5) PhotoDisc/Getty Images, (6) Purestock, (7) PhotoDisc/Getty Images, (8) Purestock; Pages 88–89: images repeated, see individual pages; Page 90: © Dion Ogust/The Image Works.

Chapter 4

Pages 92–93: Superstock, (woman) Corbis/Superstock; Page 93: images repeated, see individual pages; Page 95 (top) Canada Border Service Agency, (bottom) Phanie/Photo Researchers, Inc.; Page 96: Getty Images; Page 97: Wolcott Henry/National Geographic Stock; Page 101: (top) Stock 4B, (bottom) Getty Images; Page 105: (left) Roy Toft/National Geographic Stock, (centre) John Dominis/Time Life Pictures/Getty Images, (right) AP/The Canadian Press/Amy Sancetta; Page 106: (top left) Ryan McVay/Photodisc Green/Getty, (top right) Medford Taylor/National Geographic Stock, (bottom) Cleo Photo/Alamy; Page 107: Tourism Moncton; Page 109: (top) © SSPL/The Image Works, (bottom left) © The M.C. Escher Company, (bottom right) Mark Richard/PhotoEdit Inc.; Page 110: (top) Medford Taylor/National Geographic Stock, (centre) New Line/Saul Zaentz/Wing Nut/The Kobal Collection/Vinet, Pierre, (bottom left) Baaron Wolman/Woodfin Camp, (bottom right) Mark Raycroft/Minden Pictures/Getty Images; Page 112: Ed George/National Geographic Stock; Page 114: Time & Life Pictures/Getty Images; Page 115: Trinity Mirror/Mirrorpix/Alamy; Page 116: STRGSW/The Canadian Press/Steve White; Pages 116 (bottom) and 117, images repeated, see individual pages; Page 119: Lindsey Hebberd/Corbis; Pages 120–121: images repeated, see individual pages.

Chapter 5

Pages 122–123: *Stream of Consciousness* by Jason Zuckerman. Reproduced with permission.; Page 123: images repeated, see individual pages; Page 117: (top) David Evans/National Geographic Stock, (just below top, left) Walter Hodges/Stone/Getty Images, (top centre) Joel Sartore/National Geographic Stock, (bottom right) Photodisc/Getty Images, (bottom right) The Canadian Press/ Darcy Hordichuk, George Parros; Page 129: (top) Hank Morgan/Rainbow; Page 133: (top left and right) Louis Psihoyos; (centre) Courtesy Stephen David Smith, D.M.D., (bottom) Photo Researchers, Inc.; Page 134: Urban Zone/Alamy; Page 135: Richard Levine/Alamy; Page 138: (1) PhotoDisc/Getty Images, (2) Taylor S. Kennedy/National Geographic Stock, (3) PhotoDisc, Inc., (4) Aj Wilhelm/National Geographic Stock, (5) ©AP/Wide World Photos; Page 139: Zefa/SuperStock; Page 140: Jim Varney/Science Photo Library/Photo Researchers, Inc.; Page 142: (left) Emme Lee/Photographer's Choice RF/Getty Images, (right) Terry Vine/Blend/Getty Images; Page 143: Justin Guariglia®/National Geographic Stock; Page 144: (left) Bill Bridges/Getty Images, (right) Michael Newman/PhotoEdit; Page 147: (left) Dorling Kindersley/Getty Images, Inc., (right) Neo Vision/Getty Images, Inc; Pages 149: images repeated, see individual pages.

Chapter 6

Pages 150–151: The Canadian Press/Richard Lam; Page 151: images repeated, see individual pages; Page 154: Courtesy Benjamin Harris; Page 155: (top right) ©The New Yorker Collection 1998 Sam Gross from the cartoonbank.com. All Rights Reserved; Page 158: Blend Images/SuperStock; Page 160: (top) RK Studio/Monashee Frantz/Getty Images, (centre)

Age Fotostock/SuperStock; Page 161: (top) Kaku Kurita, (bottom) DAJ/Getty Images; Page 163: Joel Sartore/National Geographic Stock; Page 164: Courtesy American Philosophical Society; Page 165: Age Fotostock/ SuperStock; Page 166: Albert Bandura; Page 168: (left) Alamy/ GetStock.com, (right) Jodi Cobb/National Geographic Stock; Page 170: ©James Balog Photography; Page 171: Corbis; Page 172: Jodi Cobb/ National Geographic Stock; Page 173: (left) Jim Lo Scalzo for U.S.News & World Report, (top right) Index Source Limited/Index Stock, (bottom right) Associated Press; Page 174: AP/The Canadian Press/Ariana Cubullos; Pages 175–176: images repeated, see individual pages; Page 177: The Canadian Press/Adrian Wyld; Pages 178–179: images repeated, see individual pages.

Chapter 7

Pages 180–181: The Brain Observatory; Page 181: images repeated, see individual pages; Page 183: PhotoDisc/Getty Images; Page 184 (left) iStockphoto, (right) Blue Jean Images/Getty Images; Page 185: Dean Conger/National Geographic Stock; Page 189: (top) Ted Tamburo/ National Geographic Stock, (centre) Antonio M. Rosario/Photographers Choice/Getty Images; Page 191: . Bill Rudman/Australian Museum; Page 193: AP Photo/Michel Euler; Page 194: (left and right) Science Source/Photo Researchers; Page 197: M. & E. Bernheim/Woodfin Camp & Associates; Page 200: (top) Rick Eglinton/GetStock.com, (bottom) Associated Press; Pages 202–203: images repeated, see individual pages; Page 205: Purestock.

Chapter 8

Pages 208–209: Associated Press; Page 181: images repeated, see individual pages; Page 210: Blend Images/SuperStock; Page 211: (left) Stephen St. John/National Geographic Stock, (right) Gordon Wiltsie/National Geographic Stock; Page 213: Hubcapcreatures/Photo Researchers; Page 215: (top) Courtesy U. S. Department of the Interior, National Parks Service, Edison National Historic Site, (bottom) Film Magic/Getty Images; Page 217: (right) Stacy Gold/National Geographic Stock; Page 218 (small photos: top, centre, bottom) iStockphoto, (bottom) David Young-Wolff/PhotoEdit; Page 219: iStockphoto; Page 221: (top) Courtesy Georgia State University Language Research Center, (bottom) Michael Nichols/ National Geographic Stock; Page 223: Peter Kramer/Getty Images News and Sport Services, (center) Harry How/Getty Images News and Sport Services, (right) Associated Press; 226: Digital Vision/Getty Images; Page 228: Timothy Fadek/©Polaris Images; Page 229: PhotoDisc, Inc./Getty Images; Page 231: Reuters/Larry Dowring/Landov; Pages 232–234: images repeated, see individual pages; Page 235: T.K. Wanstal/The Image Works.

Chapter 9

Pages 238–239: Banana Stock; Page 239: images repeated, see individual pages; Page 241: Patricia McDonough/Photonica/Getty Images; Page 244: (left) Francis Leroy, Biocosmos/Photo Researchers, (right) Bonnier Alba; Page 245: (right) Bonnier Alba, (left) Petit Format/Nestle/ Photo Researchers; Page 247: (top left) Streissguth, A.P., & Little, R.E. (1994). Unit 5: Alcohol, Pregnancy, and the Fetal Alcohol Syndrome: Second Edition of the Project Cork Institute Medical School Cirriculum (slide lecture series) on Biomedical Education: Alcohol Use and Its Medical Consequences, produced by Dartmouth Medical School, (top right) David H. Wells/Corbis, (bottom) Health Canada. Licensed under Health Canada copyright.; Page 250: Victor Englebert/Photo Researchers, Inc.; Page 251: Randy Olson/National Geographic Stock; Page 252 (left) Purestock, (right) Robert Moore/National Geographic Stock; Page 253: Willie B. Thomas/iStockphoto; Page 254: STRPA/The

Canadian Press/Anthongy Devlin; Page 257: (left and right) Doug Goodman/Photo Researchers; Page 258 (all three photos) Ellen Senisi/The Image Works; Page 260: Gordon Wilsie/National Geographic Stock; Page 261: A.N. Meltzoff & M.K. Moore, Imitation of facial and manual gestures by human neonates. Science, 1977, 198, 75–78; Page 262: (top) Ellen Senisi/The Image Works; Pages (bottom) 262–263: images repeated, see individual pages; Page 264: George F. Mobley/National Geographic Stock; Page 266: image repeated, see individual page.

Chapter 10

Pages 268–269: image100/SuperStock; Page 268: images repeated, see individual pages; Page 270: Nina Leen/Getty Images/Time Life Pictures; 271: (top) Nina Leen/Time Life Pictures/Getty Images, (bottom left) James L. Stanfield/ National Geographic Stock, (bottom right) Jodi Cobb/National Geographic Stock; Page 272: left) Image Source/Getty Images, (right) Banana Stock/AgeFotostock; Page 273: (left) Rich Reid/National Geographic Stock, (right) Purestock; Page 275: The Canadian Press/Tom Hanson; Page 277: © The New Yorker Collection 2002 Alex Gregory from cartoonbank. com. All Rights Reserved; Pages 278: (1) Gordon Wiltsie/National Geographic Stock, (2) Rich Reid/ National Geographic Stock, (3) Dynamic Graphics, Inc./Creatas, (4) PhotoDisc/Getty Images, Inc.; Page 279: (1) Joel Sartore/National Geographic Stock, (2) Scott Barrow/SuperStock, (3) Kate Thompson/National Geographic Stock, (4) Pete Oxford/National Geographic Stock; Page 281: Jon Feingersh/Iconica/Getty Images; Page 282: Associated Press; Page 283: (top) Comstock/SuperStock, (bottom) © Romell/ Masterfile; Page 284: Ranald Mackechnie/Stone/Getty Images; Page 285: (top) Associated Press, (bottom) Michael Nichols/ National Geographic Stock; Page 286: NBC-TV / The Kobal Collection; Page 287: iStockphoto; Page 288 (left) Courtesy of CBC Still Photo Collection, (centre) iStockphoto, (right) STREVT/The Canadian Press; Page 389: Blend Images/SuperStock, Inc.; Page 290: Ron Levine/Getty Images; Page 291: (left) Susan Van Etten/PhotoEdit, (right) Associated Press; Page 292: The Canadian Press/Chuck Stoddy; Pages 293–294: images repeated, see individual pages; Page 295: John Eastcott and Yva Momatiuk/National Geographic Stock; Page 296: images repeated, see individual pages.

Chapter 11

Pages 298–299: ©PHOTOPQR/Nice Matin/Eric Duliere/NewsCom; Page 299: images repeated, see individual pages; Page 300: (left) Alaska Stock Images/National Geographic Stock, Associated Press (right); (left) Tim Laman/National Geographic Stock, (right) Stacy Gold/National Geographic Stock; Page 303 (top) PhotoDisc/Getty Images (bottom) Don Smetzer/PhotoEdit; Page 304: James A. Sugar/ National Geographic Stock; Page 306: Philip Teitelbaum; Page 307: Christian Thomas/Getty Images; Page 308 (left) STRREX/The Canadian Press/ Peter Lawson/Rex Features, (right) REUTERS/L'Equipe Agence/Handout; Page 309 (left) WireImage/Getty Images, (right) © Christian Charisius/ Reuters/Corbis; Page 311: Sunday's Child Photography; Page 312: Courtesy of Claire Vanston; Page 313: Courtesy of Claire Vanston; Page 316: (top left) Time & Life Pictures/Getty Images, (top right) Upper Cut Images/SuperStock, Inc, (bottom left and right) Courtesy Karen Huffman; Page 318: Alaska Stock Images/National Geographic Stock; Page 319: (left and right) Mark Owens/John Wiley & Sons, Inc.; Page 321: GetStock.com; Page 322: Simon Gerzina Photography; Page 323: (top) Michael L. Abramson/Woodfin Camp & Associates, (bottom) Courtesy of Daniel Langleben, MD and Kosha Ruparel, MS, University of Pennsylvania; Page 324: images repeated, see individual pages; Page 325: Courtesy of Claire Vanston; Page 327: images repeated, see individual page.

Chapter 12

Pages 328–329: Colin Hawkins/The Image Bank/Getty Images; Page 329: images repeated, see individual pages; Page 331: Page 317: (top right) © Larry Kolvoord/The Image Works, (centre right) © AP/Wide World Photos, (bottom right) Jen Siska/Photonica/ Getty Images, Inc., (left) Tim Matsui/Getty Images; Page 332: Purestock; Page 333: (left and right) Associated Press; Page 335: © The New Yorker Collection 1979 Dana Fradon from cartoonbank.com. All Rights Reserved; Page 336: Karen Kasmauski/ National Geographic Stock; Page 338: Sam Bell/National Geographic Stock; Page 339: (top left) Roger Wood/Corbis, (top right) Charles & Josette Lenars/Corbis, (bottom) Corbis Images; Page 340: PEANUTS reprinted by permission of United Features Syndicate, Inc.; Page 341: © Masterfile; Page 342: PhotoAlto/Getty Images; Page 343: David Pluth/National Geographic Stock; Page 345: © The New Yorker Collection 1997 Mike Twohy from cartoonbank.com. All Rights Reserved; Page 347: Taylor S. Kennedy/ National Geographic Stock; Page 348: Joel Sartore/ National Geographic Stock; Page 350: (left) © Index Stock Imagery, (right) Courtesy Harvard University Press; Pages 351–353: images repeated, see individual pages; Page 354: William Thomas Gain/Getty Images.

Chapter 13

Pages 356–357: Michael Blann/Digital Vision; Page 357: images repeated, see individual pages; 359: (top left) zefa/Corbis Images, (top right) Digital Vision/SuperStock, Inc., (bottom left) ThinkStock, LLC/Index Stock, (bottom right) Digital Vision/Getty Images; Page 360: Lego/ Getty Images; Page 361: The Canadian Press/John Woods; Associated Press; Page 363: (1) Corbis Images, (2) Bobby Model/NGS Image Sales, (3) Blair Seitz/Photo Researchers, (4) David Young-Wolff/PhotoEdit; Page 365: Mark Clarke/Photo Researchers; Page 366: Image Source/ Getty Images; Page 368: Big Cheese Photo/SuperStock, Inc.; Page 369: Courtesy of York University; Page 371: (top) Stephanie Yao, (bottom) Associated Press; Page 373: Photo Researchers; Page 374: Dreamworks/ The Kobal Collection®; Page 375: Frank Siteman/Index Stock; Page 376: Associated Press; Page 377: Keith Beaty/GetStock.com; Page 379: (left) art work by Norval Morrisseau, "Windingo," no date, tempera on heavy light brown building paper, Collection of Glenbow Museum, Calgary, Canada, 64.37.9 (right) Pixland/Index Stock; 380: (left) David

Alan Harvey/National Geographic Stock, (right) Benelux/Zefa/Corbis; Pages 382–384: images repeated, see individual pages; Page 385: Jodi Cobb/National Geographic Stock.

Chapter 14

Pages 388–389: Mauritius/SuperStock; Page 389: images repeated, see individual pages; Page 392: PhotoDisc/Getty Images; Page 395: © John Wiley & Sons Inc.; Page 396: (top) Comstock/SuperStock, (bottom) Don Hammond/AgeFotostock; Page 397: © David Young Wolff/PhotoEdit; Page 398: © David Young Wolff/PhotoEdit; Page 399: (top) Sidney Harris, (bottom) Kevin Curtis/Photo Researchers; Page 400: James King-Holmes/Photo Researchers; Page 401: Stephen Mallon/The Image Bank/Getty Images; Page 403: ©The New Yorker Collection 1993 Lee Lorenz from cartoonbank.com. All Rights Reserved; Page 405: James D. Wilson/Woodfin Camp & Associates; Page 406: Cordelia Molloy/Photo Researchers; Page 408: iStockphoto; Page 409: Sky Bonillo/PhotoEdit; Page 410: iStockphoto; Pages 411–412: images repeated, see individual pages; Page 413: Photos 12/Alamy; Page415: image repeated, see individual page.

Chapter 15

Pages 416–417: STRGSW/The Canadian Press; Page 417: images repeated, see individual pages; Page 419: (top) Gerd Ludwig/NG Image Collection, (bottom) Associated Press; Page 422: (left) Justin Guariglia/ National Geographic Stock, (right) Getty Images News and Sport Services; Page 423: (left) Earl S. Cryer/UPI /Landov, (right) Anthony Njuguna/Reuters/ Corbis; Page 424: (left) Corbis/SuperStock, (centre) Arat Wolfe/Stone/ Getty Images, (right) William Albert Allard/ National Geographic Stock; Page 425: (left and right) Bernhard Kuhmsted/Retna; Page 426: (left) iStockphoto, (centre) Purestock, (right) Alaska Stock Images/National Geographic Stock; Page 428: Associated Press; Page 429: Associated Press; Page 430: ©1965 by Stanley Milgram. From the film OBEDIENCE, distributed by the New York University Film Library; Page 432: Philip G. Zimbardo, Inc.; Page 433: Associated Press; Page 434: Joel Satore/ National Geographic Stock; Page 435: Getty Images; Page 436: Courtesy of Andrew Brash; Page 437: (top) SuperStock, (bottom) Marcelo Santos/Getty Images, Inc.; Page 439: Bob Daemmrich/PhotoEdit; Pages 441–442: images repeated, see individual pages; Page 443: Najlah Feanny-Hicks/Corbis.

TEXT, TABLE, AND ILLUSTRATION CREDITS

Chapter 1

Table 1.2: From Huffman, Karen. *Psychology in Action, 9e*. Reprinted with permission of John Wiley & Sons, Inc.; Study Organizer 1.1: From Huffman, Karen. *Psychology in Action, 9e*. Reprinted with permission of John Wiley & Sons, Inc.

Chapter 2

Figure 2.1: From Huffman, Karen. *Psychology in Action, 8e*. Reprinted with permission of John Wiley & Sons, Inc.; Figure 2.6: From Tortora and Derrickson; *Principles of Anatomy and Physiology, 12e*. Reprinted with permission of John Wiley & Sons, Inc.; What a Psychologist Sees A–D (page 43), from *Psychology in Action, 8e*. Reprinted with permission of John Wiley & Sons, Inc.; Psychological Science (page 52) Adapted from Fig. 4.9 in Le Vay, S., & Baldwin, J. (2009). *Human Sexuality* (3rd ed.). Sunderland, MA: Sinauer Associates Inc., p103; Figure 2.7, Figure 2.8, Figure 2.10, Figure 2.12, Figure 2.13, Figure 2.14, Figure 2.16, Figure 2.17, Figure 2.18, Figure 2.20 (illustrations), Figure 2.21, Figure 2.22: From Huffman, Karen. *Psychology in Action, 9e*. Reprinted with permission of John Wiley & Sons, Inc.

Chapter 3

Figure 3.1: From Huffman, Karen. *Psychology in Action, 9e*. Reprinted with permission of John Wiley & Sons, Inc.; Table 3.1: Hobson, C. J., Kamen, J., Szostek, J., Nethercut, C. M., Tiedmann, J. W., & Wojnarowicz, S. (1998). Stressful life events: A revision and update of the Social Readjustment Rating Scale. *International Journal of Stress Management, 5*(1), 1–23.; Figure 3.3, Figure 3.4, Figure 3.12, from Huffman, Karen. *Psychology in Action, 9e*. Reprinted with permission of John Wiley & Sons, Inc.

Chapter 4

Figure 4.1, Figure 4.3, Figure 4.6, Figure 4.7, Figure 4.10, What a Psychologist Sees drawings of coins and Ames room (page 103): From Huffman, Karen. *Psychology in Action, 9e*. Reprinted with permission of John Wiley & Sons, Inc.

Chapter 5

Figure 5.2: From Huffman, Karen. *Psychology in Action, 9e*. Reprinted with permission of John Wiley & Sons, Inc. Applying Psychology—quiz (page 127): From POWER SLEEP by James B. Maas and M L Wherry, copyright © 1999 by James Maas. Used by permission of Villard Books, a division of Random House, Inc. Figure 5.12: From Adlaf, E. M., & Paglia-Boak, A. (2007). Drug use among Ontario students 1977–2007: OSDUHS Highlights, p. 3. Centre for Addiction and Mental Health.; What a Psychologist Sees, drawings of the brain (page 143): From Huffman, Karen. *Psychology in Action, 9e*. Reprinted with permission of John Wiley & Sons, Inc.

Chapter 6

Figure 6.1, Figure 6.4, Figure 6.12: From Huffman, Karen. *Psychology in Action, 9e*. Reprinted with permission of John Wiley & Sons, Inc.

Chapter 7

Figure 7.1, Figure 7.2, Figure 7.3, Figure 7.4, Figure 7.5, Study Organizer 7.1—drawings (page 187), Figure 7.5c, Psychological Science—drawing (page 192), Figure 7.7, Figure 7.8: From Huffman, Karen. *Psychology in Action, 9e*. Reprinted with permission of John Wiley & Sons, Inc. Psychological Science-graph, (page 196): Bahrick, H. P., Bahrick, P. O.,

& Wittlinger, R. P. (1974). Long-term memory: Those unforgettable high-school days. *Psychology Today*, 8, 50–56. Reprinted with permission from Psychology Today Magazine, Copyright © 1978 Sussex Publishers, LLC. Figure 7.9, Applying Psychology—drawings A–C (page 201): From Huffman, Karen. *Psychology in Action, 9e*. Reprinted with permission of John Wiley & Sons, Inc.

Chapter 8

Figure 8.3, Figure 8.5, Applying Psychology-drawing (page 214), Figure 8.7, Study Organizer 8.1, Table 8.3: From Huffman, Karen. *Psychology in Action, 9e*. Reprinted with permission of John Wiley & Sons, Inc. Table 8.4: From Sternberg: Beyond IQ. ©1985 Cambridge University Press. Reprinted with permission of the Cambridge University Press. Figure 8.13, What a Psychologist Sees—graph (page 229), Psychological Science—drawing (page 231), Solution to the nine-dot problem (page 220), Coin problem solution (page 220): From Huffman, Karen. *Psychology in Action, 9e*. Reprinted with permission of John Wiley & Sons, Inc.

Chapter 9

Figure 9.1: From Huffman, Karen. *Psychology in Action, 9e*. Reprinted with permission of John Wiley & Sons, Inc. Figure 9.2: From Schaie: *The life course of Adult intellectual abilities, American Psychologist*, American Psychological Association. Reprinted with permission. Figure 9.41 (1): From Huffman, Karen. *Psychology in Action, 9e*. Reprinted with permission of John Wiley & Sons, Inc. Figure 9.7: Reproduced with permission from *Pediatrics*, Vol 89, Issue 1, pages 91–97, Copyright 1992. Figure 9.9a, Graph in What a Psychologist Sees (page 250): From Huffman, Karen. *Psychology in Action, 9e*. Reprinted with permission of John Wiley & Sons, Inc. Figure 9.11: Reproduced from Tanner J.M. Whitehouse, R.N. and Takaislu, M. "Male/female growth spurt." Archives of Diseases in childhood, 41, 454–471, 1996 with permission from BMJ Publishing Group Ltd. Figure 9.12: From Huffman, Karen. *Psychology in Action, 9e*. Reprinted with permission of John Wiley & Sons, Inc. Figure 9.14: From the chart of Elderly Achievers in, "The Brain—A User's Manual." 1982: Reprinted with permission by Diagram Visual Information. Study Organizer 9.1, Applying Psychology: From Huffman, Karen. *Psychology in Action, 9e* Reprinted with permission of John Wiley & Sons, Inc.

Chapter 10

What a Psychologist Sees, Figure 10.2: From Huffman, Karen. *Psychology in Action, 9e*. Reprinted with permission of John Wiley & Sons, Inc. Figure 10.4: Kohlberg's Stages of Moral Development: Original Sketch: Adapted from Kohlberg, L. "Stage and Sequence: The Cognitive Developmental Approach to Socialization." in D.A. Goslin, *The Handbook of Socialization Theory and Research*. Chicago: Rand McNally, 1969. P 376 (Table 6.2). Table 10.3: Adapted and reproduced with special permission of the Publisher, Psychological Assessment Resources, Inc., 16204 North Florida Avenue, Lutz, Florida, 33549, from the Dictionary of Holland Occupational Codes, Third Edition, by Gary D. Gottfredson, Ph.D., and John L. Holland, Ph.D., Copyright 1982, 1989, 1996. Further reproduction is prohibited without permission from PAR, Inc. Figure 10.7, Adapted from Le Vay, S., & Baldwin, J. (2009). *Human Sexuality* (3rd ed.). Sunderland, MA: Sinauer Associates Inc.; Figure 10.13: *The Social Context of Emotional Experience*, Annual Review of Geriatrics & Gerontology, From Laura L. Carstensen, James J. Gross, and Helen H. Fung, Reproduced with the permission of Springer Publishing Company, LLC, New York, NY 10036.

Chapter 11

Figure 11.3, Applying Psychology 303: From Huffman, Karen. *Psychology in Action, 9e.* Reprinted with permission of John Wiley & Sons, Inc.; Figure 11.5: From Maslow, A.H./Frager, R.D./Fadiman, J., MOTIVATION AND PERSONALITY, © 1987. Adapted by permission of Pearson Education, Inc., Upper Saddle River, New Jersey. Figure 11.7a: From Huffman, Karen. *Psychology in Action, 9e.* Reprinted with permission of John Wiley & Sons, Inc. Figure 11.12ab: From Masters, W. H., & Johnson, V. E. (1966). *Human sexual response.* Boston: Little, Brown. Reprinted with permission of Geraldine B. Masters. Psychological Science—graph: Extrinsic versus intrinsic rewards (page 313): Copyright © 1973 by the American Psychological Association. Adapted with permission. Lepper, Mark R; Greene, David; Nisbett, Richard E. "Undermining children's intrinsic interest with intrinsic reward: A Test of the 'Overjustification' Hypothesis." *Journal of Personality and Social Psychology.* No further reproduction or distribution is permitted without written permission from the American Psychological Association. Figure 11.15, Figure 11.18, Figure 11.20: From Huffman, Karen. *Psychology in Action, 9e.* Reprinted with permission of John Wiley & Sons, Inc. Figure 11.22 Plutchik, EMOTION: PSYCHOEVOLUTIONARY SYNTHESIS, "Plutchick's Wheel of Emotion", © 1979 Individual Dynamics Inc Reproduced by permission of Pearson Education, Inc.; What a Psychologist Sees: (page 323): From Huffman, Karen. *Psychology in Action, 9e.* Reprinted with permission of John Wiley & Sons, Inc.

Chapter 12

Applying Psychology-"Mate selection around the world" (page 332): From Buss et al., "*International Preferences in Selecting Mates,*" Journal of Cross-Cultural Psychology, 21, pp. 5–47 © 1990. Reprinted by permission of SAGE Publications, Inc. Figure 12.3, Figure 12.5, Figure 12.7, What a Psychologist Sees—drawing (page 341), Figure 12.13, Psychological Science-pie chart (page 347): From Huffman, Karen. *Psychology in Action, 9e.* Reprinted with permission of John Wiley & Sons, Inc. Figure 12.17b, TAT Harvard University Press.

Chapter 13

Figure 13.1: From Huffman, Karen. *Psychology in Action, 9e.* Reprinted with permission of John Wiley & Sons, Inc. Study Organizer 13.1 (page 349), Figure 13.2, Figure 13.3, Table 13.1: From the Diagnostic and Statistical Manual of Mental Disorders, fourth edition text revision, Washington, DC, © 2000 American Psychiatric Association. Reprinted with permission from the Diagnostic and Statistical Manual of Mental Disorders, Text Revision, Fourth Edition, (Copyright 2000). American Psychiatric Association. Figure 13.6, Figure 13.7: From Huffman, Karen. *Psychology in Action, 9e.* Reprinted with permission of John Wiley & Sons, Inc. Figure 13.11: "Graph: 'Genetics and schizophrenia' from the book, SCHIZOPHRENIA GENESIS by I. I. Gottesman. Copyright © 1991 by W. H. Freeman and Company. Reprinted by arrangement with Henry Holt and Company, LLC. Figure 13.13 Reprinted from *Biological Science*, Volume 47, Meltzer, "Genetics and Etiology of Schizophrenia and Bipolar Disorder" Pages 171–173, 2000 with permission from Elsevier; Table 13.3, Reprinted with permission of Wadsworth, a division of Thomson Learning; Figure 13.19: From Huffman, Karen. *Psychology in Action, 9e.* Reprinted with permission of John Wiley & Sons, Inc.

Chapter 14

Figure 14.2, Figure 14.3: From Huffman, Karen. *Psychology in Action, 9e.* Reprinted with permission of John Wiley & Sons, Inc. Figure 14.4: From Beck, Judith S. *Cognitive Therapy: Basics and Beyond* © 1993. Dysfunctional Thought Record, Figure 9.1, page 126. Reprinted with permission of Guilford Publications, Inc. Applying Psychology (page 396) from Shea, S.C., (1988) *Psychiatric Interviewing: the art of understanding,* Philadelphia: PA, Saunders (publisher), p.32–33; Figure 14.11: From Huffman, Karen. *Psychology in Action, 9e.* Reprinted with permission of John Wiley & Sons, Inc.

Chapter 15

Figure 15.3, Figure 15.4, Figure 15.5: From Huffman, Karen. *Psychology in Action, 9e.* Reprinted with permission of John Wiley & Sons, Inc. Table 15.1: From Rubin, Z. (1970). "Measurement of romantic love," *Journal of Personality and Social Psychology, 16,* 265–273. Copyright © 1970 by Zick Rubin. Reprinted by permission of the author; Graph in What a Psychologist Sees (page 426), Figure 15.9, What a Psychologist Sees (page 430) Figure 15.16: From Huffman, Karen. *Psychology in Action, 9e.* Reprinted with permission of John Wiley & Sons, Inc.

Aarts, H. (2007). Unconscious authorship ascription: The effects of success and effect-specific information priming on experienced authorship. *Journal of Experimental Social Psychology, 43*, 119–126.

Abadinsky, H. (2008). *Drug use and abuse: A comprehensive introduction* (6th ed.). Belmont, CA: Cengage.

Abbott, A. (2004). Striking back. *Nature, 429* (6990), 338–339.

Aboa-Éboulé, C. (2008). Job strain and recurrent coronary heart disease events—Reply. *Journal of the American Medical Association, 299*, 520–521.

Aboa-Éboulé, C., Brisson, C., Maunsell, E., Benoît, M., Bourbonnais, R., Vézina, M., Milot, A., Théroux, P., & Dagenais, G. R. (2008). Job strain and risk of acute recurrent coronary heart disease events. *Journal of the American Medical Association, 298*, 1652–1660.

About James Randi. (2002). *Detail biography*. Retrieved from http://www.randi.org/jr/bio.html

Acarturk, C., de Graaf, R., van Straten, A., ten Have, M., & Cuijpers, P. (2008). Social phobia and number of social fears, and their association with comorbidity, health-related quality of life and help seeking: A population-based study. *Social Psychiatry and Psychiatric Epidemiology, 43*, 273–279.

Achenbaum, W. A., & Bengtson, V. L. (1994). Reengaging the disengagement theory of aging: On the history and assessment of theory development in gerontology. *Gerontologist, 34*, 756–763.

Adelmann, P. K., & Zajonc, R. B. (1989). Facial efference and the experience of emotion. *Annual Review of Psychology, 40*, 249–280.

Adlaf, E. M., & Paglia-Boak, A. (2007). *Drug use among Ontario students 1977–2007: OSDUHS highlights*. Centre for Addiction and Mental Health. Retrieved from http://www.camh.net/Research/Areas_of_research/Population_Life_Course_Studies/OSDUS/OSDUHS2007_DrugHighlights_final.pdf

Adler, A. (1964). The individual psychology of Alfred Adler. In H. L. Ansbacher & R. R. Ansbacher (Eds.), *The individual psychology of Alfred Adler*. New York, NY: Harper & Row.

Adler, A. (1998). *Understanding human nature*. Center City, MN: Hazelden Information Education.

Advertising Age. (1958, February 10). "Phone now," said CBC subliminally—but nobody did.

Aftanas, L. I., & Golosheikin, S. A. (2003). Changes in cortical activity in altered states of consciousness: The study of meditation by high-resolution EEG. *Human Physiology, 29*, 143–151.

Ahlsén, E. (2008). Embodiment in communication– Aphasia, apraxia, and the possible role of mirroring and imitation. *Clinical Linguistics & Phonetics, 22*, 311–315.

Ahmadi, S., Sarrindast, M. R., Nouri, M., Haeri-Rohini, A., & Rezayof, A. (2007). N-Methyl-D-aspartate receptors in the ventral tegmental area are involved in retrieval of inhibitory avoidance memory of nicotine. *Neurobiology of Learning and Memory, 88*, 352–358.

Ahmed, A. M. (2007). Group identity social distance, and intergroup bias. *Journal of Economic Psychology, 28*, 324–337.

Ainsworth, M. D. S. (1967). *Infancy in Uganda: Infant care and the growth of love*. Baltimore: Johns Hopkins University Press.

Ainsworth, M. D. S., Blehar, M., Waters, E., & Wall, S. (1978). *Patterns of attachment: Observations in the strange situation and at home*. Hillsdale, NJ: Erlbaum.

Al'absi, M., Hugdahl, K., & Lovallo, W. R. (2002). Adrenocortical stress responses and altered working memory performance. *Psychophysiology, 39*(1), 95–99.

Alberts, A., Elkind, D., & Ginsberg, S. (2007). The personal fable and risk-taking in early adolescence. *Journal of Youth and Adolescence, 36*, 71–76.

Alexander, B. K. (1990). *Peaceful measures: Canada's way out of the "war on drugs."* Toronto, ON: University of Toronto Press.

Alexander, B. K. (1997). *Peaceful measures: Canada's way out of the war on drugs* (2nd ed.). Toronto, ON: University of Toronto Press.

Al-Issa, I. (2000). Culture and mental illness in Algeria. In I. Al-Issa (Ed.), *Al-Junun: Mental illness in the Islamic world* (pp. 101–119). Madison, CT: International Universities Press.

Allan, K., & Gabbert, F. (2008). I still think it was a banana: Memorable "lies" and forgettable "truths." *Acta Psychologica, 127*, 299–308.

Allik, J., & McCrae, R. R. (2004). Toward a geography of personality traits: Patterns of profiles across 36 cultures. *Journal of Cross-Cultural Psychology, 35*(1), 13–28.

Alloy, L. B., Abramson, L. Y., Whitehouse, W. G., Hogan, M. E., Tashman, N. A., Steinberg, D. L., Rose, D. T., & Donovan, P. (1999). Depressogenic cognitive styles: Predictive validity, information processing and personality characteristics, and developmental origins. *Behavior Research and Therapy, 37*, 503–531.

Allport, G. W. (1937). *Personality: A psychological interpretation*. New York, NY: Holt Rinehart and Winston.

Allport, G. W., & Odbert, H. S. (1936). Trait-names: A psycho-lexical study. *Psychological Monographs: General and Applied, 47*, 1–21.

Almeida, O. P., Burton, E. J., Ferrier, N., McKeith, I. G., & O'Brien, J. T. (2003). Depression with late onset is associated with right frontal lobe atrophy. *Psychological Medicine, 33*(4), 675–681.

Amato, P. R. (2007). Transformative processes in marriage: Some thoughts from a sociologist. *Journal of Marriage and Family, 69*, 305–309.

Ambert, A-M. (2005). *Divorce: Facts, causes, and consequences*. Ottawa, ON: The Vanier Institute of the Family. Retrieved from http://www.vifamily.ca/library/publications/divorce.html

American Counseling Association. (2006). *Crisis fact sheet: 10 ways to recognize post-traumatic stress disorder*. Retrieved from http://www.counseling.org/zPressRoom/PressReleases.aspx?AGuid=69c6fad2-c05e-4be3-af4e-3a1771414044.

American Medical Association. (2008). *Alcohol and other drug abuse*. Retrieved from http://www.ama-assn.org/ama/pub/category/3337.html

American Psychiatric Association. (2000). *Diagnostic and statistical manual of mental disorders* (4th ed. TR). Washington, DC: American Psychiatric Press.

American Psychiatric Association. (2002). *APA Let's talk facts about posttraumatic stress disorder*. Retrieved from http://www.psych.org/disasterpsych/fs/ptsd.cfm.

American Psychological Association. (1984). *Behavioral research with animals*. Washington, DC: Author.

Amir, N., Cobb, M., & Morrison, A. S. (2008). Threat processing in obsessive-compulsive disorder: Evidence from a modified negative priming task. *Behaviour Research and Therapy, 46*, 728–736.

Amundson, J. K., & Nuttgens, S. A. (2008). Strategic eclecticism in hypnotherapy: Effectiveness research considerations. *American Journal of Clinical Hypnosis, 50*, 233–245.

Ancis, J. R., Chen, Y., & Schultz, D. (2004). Diagnostic challenges and the so-called culture bound syndromes. In J. R. Ancis (Ed.), *Culturally responsive interventions: Innovative approaches to working with diverse populations* (pp. 197–209). New York, NY: Brunner-Routledge.

Anderson, C. A. (2001). Heat and violence. *Current Directions in Psychological Science, 10*(1), 33–38.

Anderson, C. A. (2004). An update on the effects of playing violent video games. *Journal of Adolescence, 27*(1), 113–122.

Anderson, C. A., & Hamilton, M. (2005). Gender role stereotyping of parents in children's picture books: The invisible father. *Sex Roles, 52,* 145–151.

Anderson, C. A., Buckley, K. E., & Carnegey, N. L. (2008). Creating your own hostile environment: A laboratory examination of trait aggressiveness and the violence escalation cycle. *Personality and Social Psychology Bulletin, 34,* 462–473.

Anderson, C. A., Carnagey, N. L., Flanagan, M., Benjamin, A. J., Eubanks, J., & Valentine, J. C. (2004). Violent video games: Effects of violent content on aggressive thoughts and behavior. *Advances in Experimental Social Psychology, 36,* 199–249.

Anderson, C. A., Gentile, D. A., & Buckley, K. E. (2007). *Violent video game effects on children and adolescents: Theory, research, and public policy.* New York, NY: Oxford University Press.

Anderson, L. E., & Silver, J. M. (2008). Neurological and medical disorders. In R. I. Simon & K. Tardiff (Eds.), *Textbook of violence assessment and management* (pp. 185–209). Arlington, VA: American Psychiatric Publishing.

Anderson, M. C., Ochsner, K. N., Kuhl, B., Cooper, J., Robertson, E., Gabrieli, S. W., Glover, G. H., & Gabrieli, J. D. E. (2004). Neural systems underlying the suppression of unwanted memories. *Science, 303*(5655), 232–235.

Andrade, T. G. C. S., & Graeff, F. G. (2001). Effect of electrolytic and neurotoxic lesions of the median raphe nucleus on anxiety and stress. *Pharmacology, Biochemistry & Behavior, 70*(1), 1–14.

Andrasik, F. (2006). Psychophysiological disorders: Headache as a case in point. In F. Andrasik (Ed.), *Comprehensive handbook of personality and psychopathology: Vol. 2: Adult Psychopathology* (pp. 409–422). Hoboken, NJ: Wiley.

Andreasen, N. C., Calage, C. A., & O'Leary, D. S. (2008). Theory of mind and schizophrenia: A positron emission tomography study of medication-free patients. *Schizophrenia Bulletin, 34*(4), 708–719.

Andreoni, J., & Petrie, R. (2008). Beauty, gender and stereotypes: Evidence from laboratory experiments. *Journal of Economic Psychology, 29,* 73–93.

Anisman, H., Merali, Z., & Stead, J. D. H. (2008). Experiential and genetic contributions to depressive- and anxiety-like disorders: Clinical and experimental studies. *Neuroscience & Biobehavioral Reviews, 32,* 1185–1206.

Ansell, E. B., & Grilo, C. M. (2007). Personality disorders. In M. Hersen, S. M. Turner, &

D. C. Beidel (Eds.), *Adult psychopathology and diagnosis* (5th ed.) (pp. 633–678). Hoboken, NJ: Wiley.

Aou, S. (2006). Role of medial hypothalamus on peptic ulcer and depression. In C. Kubo & T. Kuboki (Eds.), *Psychosomatic medicine: Proceedings of the 18th World Congress on Psychosomatic Medicine.* New York, NY: Elsevier Science.

Appel, M., & Richter, T. (2007). Persuasive effects of fictional narratives increase over time. *Media Psychology, 10,* 113–134.

Appiah, K. A. (2008). *Experiments in ethics.* Cambridge, MA: Harvard University Press.

Arbib, M. A., & Mundhenk, T. N. (2005). Schizophrenia and the mirror system: An essay. *Neuropsychologia, 43,* 268–280.

Arriagada, O., Constandil, L., Hernández, A., Barra, R., Soto-Moyano, R., & Laurido, C. (2007). Brief communication: Effects of interleukin-1B on spinal cord nociceptive transmission in intact and propentofylline-treated rats. *International Journal of Neuroscience, 117,* 617–625.

Arumugam, V., Lee, J-S., Nowak, J. K., Pohle, R. J., Nyrop, J. E., Leddy, J. J., & Pelkman, C. L. (2008). A high-glycemic meal pattern elicited increased subjective appetite sensations in overweight and obese women. *Appetite, 50,* 215–222.

Asch, S. E. (1951). Effects of group pressure upon the modification and distortion of judgment. In H. Guetzkow (Ed.), *Groups, leadership, and men.* Pittsburgh: Carnegie Press.

Asghar, A. U. R., Chiu, Y-C., Hallam, G., Liu, S., Mole, H., Wright, H., & Young, A. W. (2008). An amygdala response to fearful faces with covered eyes. *Neuropsychologia, 46,* 2364–2370.

Atchley, R. C. (1997). *Social forces and aging* (8th ed.). Belmont, CA: Wadsworth.

Atkinson, R. C., & Shiffrin, R. M. (1968). Human memory: A proposed system and its control processes. In K. W. Spence & J. T. Spence (Eds.), *The psychology of learning and motivation* (Vol. 2). New York, NY: Academic Press.

Atlas, R. S., & Pepler, D. J. (1998). Observations of bullying in the classroom. *Journal of Educational Research, 92,* 86–99.

Aubert, A., & Dantzer, R. (2005). The taste of sickness: Lipopolysaccharide-induced finickiness in rats. *Physiology & Behavior, 84*(3), 437–444.

Axtell, R. E. (1998). *Gestures: The do's and taboos of body language around the world,* revised and expanded ed. New York, NY: Wiley.

Axtell, R. E. (2007). *Essential do's and taboos: The complete guide to international business and leisure travel.* Hoboken, NJ: Wiley.

Ayers, S., Baum, A., McManus, C., Newman, S., Wallston, K., Weinman, J., & West, R. (Eds.). (2007). *Cambridge handbook of psychology, health, and medicine.* New York, NY: Cambridge University Press.

Azizian, A., & Polich, J. (2007). Evidence for attentional gradient in the serial position memory curve from event-related potentials. *Journal of Cognitive Neuroscience, 19,* 2071–2081.

Baby Signs Canada. (2006). Retrieved from http://www.babysigns.ca

Bachman, G., & Zakahi, W. R. (2000). Adult attachment and strategic relational communication: Love schemas and affinity-seeking. *Communication Reports, 13*(1), 11–19.

Baddeley, A. D. (1992). Working memory. *Science, 255,* 556–559.

Baddeley, A. D. (1998). Recent developments in working memory. *Current Opinion in Neurobiology, 8,* 234-238.

Baddeley, A., & Jarrold, C. (2007). Working memory and Down syndrome. *Journal of Intellectual Disability Research, 51,* 925–931.

Badge, J. L., Cann, A. J., & Scott, J. (2007). To cheat or not to cheat? A trial of the JISC plagiarism detection service with biological science students. *Assessment and Evaluation in Higher Education, 32*(4), 1–7.

Baer, J. (1994). Divergent thinking is not a general trait: A multi-domain training experiment. *Creativity Research Journal, 7,* 35–36.

Bagermihl, B. (1999). *Biological exuberance: Animal homosexuality and natural diversity.* New York, NY: St Martins Press.

Bailey, J. M., Dunne, M. P., & Martin, N. G. (2000). Genetic and environmental influences on sexual orientation and its correlates in an Australian twin sample. *Journal of Personality and Social Psychology, 78*(3), 524–536.

Bailey, K. R., & Mair, R. G. (2005). Lesions of specific and nonspecific thalamic nuclei affect prefrontal cortex-dependent aspects of spatial working memory. *Behavioral Neuroscience, 119*(2), 410–419.

Baillargeon, R. (2000). Reply to Bogartz, Shinskey, and Schilling; Schilling; and Cashon and Cohen. *Infancy, 1,* 447–462.

Baillargeon, R. (2008). Innate ideas revisited: For a principle of persistence in infants' physical reasoning. *Perspectives on Psychological Science, 3,* 2–13.

Baker, D., & Nieuwenhuijsen, M. J. (Eds.) (2008). *Environmental epidemiology: Study methods and application.* New York, NY: Oxford University Press.

Baker, R. R., & Pickren, W. E. (2007). *Psychology and the Department of Veterans Affairs: A historical analysis of training, research, practice, and advocacy.* Washington, DC: American Psychological Association.

Baldessarini, R. J., & Hennen, J. (2004). Genetics of suicide: An overview. *Harvard Review of Psychiatry, 12*(1), 1–13.

Baldwin, S., & Oxlad, M. (2000). *Electroshock and minors: A fifty year review.* New York, NY: Greenwood Publishing Group.

Ball, H. A., McGuffin, P., & Farmer, A. E. (2008). Attributional style and depression. *British Journal of Psychiatry, 192,* 275–278.

Bandstra, E. S., Morrow, C. E., Vogel, A. L., Fifer, R. C., Ofir, A. Y., Dausa, A. T., Xue, L., & Anthony, J. C. (2002). Longitudinal influence of prenatal cocaine exposure on child language functioning. *Neurotoxicology & Teratology, 24*(3), 297–308.

Bandura, A. (1969). *Principles of behavior modification.* New York, NY: Holt, Rinehart and Winston.

Bandura, A. (1986). *Social foundations of thought and action: A social cognitive theory.* Englewood Cliffs, NJ: Prentice Hall.

Bandura, A. (1991). Social cognitive theory of moral thought and action. In W. M. Kurtines & J. L. Gewirtz (Eds.), *Handbook of moral behavior and development: Vol. 1. Theory.* Hillsdale, NJ: Erlbaum.

Bandura, A. (1997). *Self-efficacy: The exercise of control.* New York, NY: Freeman.

Bandura, A. (2000). Exercise of human agency through collective efficacy. *Current Directions in Psychological Science, 9*(3), 75–83.

Bandura, A. (2003). On the psychosocial impact and mechanisms of spiritual modeling: Comment. *International Journal of Psychology of Religion, 13*(3), 167–173.

Bandura, A. (2006). Going global with social cognitive theory: From prospect to paydirt. In D. E. Berger & K. Pezdek (Eds.), *The rise of applied psychology: New frontiers and rewarding careers.* Mahwah, NJ: Erlbaum.

Bandura, A. (2008). Reconstrual of "free will" from the agentic perspective of social cognitive theory. In J. Baer, J. C. Kaufman, & R. F. Baumeister (Eds.), *Are we free? Psychology and free will.* New York, NY: Oxford University Press.

Bandura, A., & Walters, R. H. (1963). *Social learning and personality development.* New York, NY: Holt, Rinehart and Winston.

Bandura, A., Ross, D., & Ross, S. (1961). Transmission of aggression through imitation of aggressive models. *Journal of Abnormal & Social Psychology, 63,* 575–582.

Banko, K. M. (2008). Increasing intrinsic motivation using rewards: The role of the social context. *Dissertation Abstracts International: Section B: The Sciences and Engineering, 68*(10-B), 7005.

Banks, M. S., & Salapatek, P. (1983). Infant visual perception. In M. M. Haith & J. J. Campos (Eds.), *Handbook of child psychology.* New York, NY: Wiley.

Bard, C. (1934). On emotional expression after decortication with some remarks on certain theoretical views. *Psychological Review, 41,* 309–329.

Bargai, N., Ben-Shakar, G., & Shalev, A. Y. (2007). Posttraumatic stress disorder and depression in battered women: The mediating role of learned helplessness. *Journal of Family Violence, 22*(5), 267–275.

Bar-Haim, Y., Dan, O., Eshel, Y., & Sagi-Schwartz, A. (2007). Predicting children's anxiety from early attachment relationships. *Journal of Anxiety Disorders, 21,* 1061–1068.

Barlett, C. P., Harris, R. J., & Bruey, C. (2008). The effect of the amount of blood in a violent video game on aggression, hostility, and arousal. *Journal of Experimental Social Psychology, 44,* 539–546.

Barlow, D. H. (Ed.). (2008). *Clinical handbook of psychological disorders: A step-by-step treatment manual* (4th ed.). New York, NY: Guilford Press.

Barlow, D. H., & Durand, V. M. (2009). *Abnormal psychology: An integrative approach* (5th ed.). Belmont, CA: Cengage.

Barner, D., Wood, J., Hauser, M., & Carey, S. (2008). Evidence for a non-linguistic distinction between singular and plural sets in rhesus monkeys. *Cognition, 107,* 603–622.

Barnow, S., Ulrich, I., Grabe, H-J, Freyberger, H. J., & Spitzer, C. (2007). The influence of parental drinking behaviour and antisocial personality disorder on adolescent behavioural problems: Results of the Greifswalder family study. *Alcohol and Alcoholism, 42,* 623–628.

Barry, L. C., Allore, H. G., Guo, Z., Bruce, M. L., & Gill, T. M. (2008). Higher burden of depression among older women: The effect of onset, persistence, and mortality over time. *Archives of General Psychiatry, 65,* 172–178.

Bartels, M., van Beijsterveldt, C. E. M., Derks, E. M., Stroet, T. M., Polderman, T. J. C., Hudziak, J. J., & Boomsma, D. I. (2007). Young Netherlands Twin Register (Y-NTR): A longitudinal multiple informant study of problem behavior. *Twin Research and Human Genetics, 10,* 3–11.

Bartholow, B. D., & Anderson, C. A. (2002). Effects of violent video games on aggressive behavior: Potential sex differences. *Journal of Experimental Social Psychology, 38*(3), 283–290.

Barton, D. A., Esler, M. D., Dawood, T., Lambert, E. A., Haikerwal, D., Brenchley, C., Socratous, F., Hastings, J., Guo, L., Wiesner, G., Kaye, D. M., Bayles, R., Schlaich, M. P., Lambert, G. W. (2008). Elevated brain serotonin turnover in patients with depression: Effect of genotype and therapy. *Archives of General Psychiatry, 65,* 38–46.

Barton, J. J. S. (2008). Prosopagnosia associated with left occipitotemporal lesion. *Neuropsychologia, 46,* 2214–2224.

Batacharya, S. (2004). Racism, "girl violence," and the murder of Reena Virk. In C. Alder & A. Worrall (Eds.), *Girls' Violence* (pp. 61–80). Albany, NY: SUNY Press.

Bates, A. L. (2007). How did you get in? Attributions of preferential selection in college admissions. *Dissertation Abstracts International: Section B: The Sciences and Engineering, 68*(4-B), 2694.

Batson, C. D. (1991). *The altruism question: Toward a social-psychological answer.* Hillsdale, NJ: Erlbaum.

Batson, C. D. (1998). Altruism and prosocial behavior. In D. T. Gilbert, S. T. Fiske, & G. Lindzey (Eds.), *The handbook of social psychology, Vol. 2* (4th ed., pp. 282–316). Boston, MA: McGraw-Hill.

Batson, C. D. (2006). "Not all self-interest after all": Economics of empathy-induced altruism. In D. De Cremer, M. Zeelenberg, & J. K. Murnighan (Eds.), *Social psychology and economics* (pp. 281–299). Mahwah, NJ: Erlbaum.

Batson, C. D., & Ahmad, N. (2001). Empathy-induced altruism in a prisoner's dilemma II: What if the target of empathy has defected? *European Journal of Social Psychology, 31*(1), 25–36.

Baumrind, D. (1980). New directions in socialization research. *American Psychologist, 35,* 639–652.

Baumrind, D. (1991). Effective parenting during the early adolescent transition. In P. A. Cowan & E. M. Hetherington (Eds.), *Family transition* (pp. 111–163). Hillsdale, NJ: Erlbaum.

Baumrind, D. (1995). *Child maltreatment and optimal caregiving in social contexts.* New York, NY: Garland.

Bearer, C. F., Stoler, J. M., Cook, J. D., & Carpenter, S. J. (2004–2005). Biomarkers of alcohol use in pregnancy. *Alcohol Research & Health, 28*(1), 38–43.

Beck, A. T. (1976). *Cognitive therapy and the emotional disorders.* New York, NY: International Universities Press.

Beck, A. T. (2000). *Prisoners of hate.* New York, NY: Harper Perennial.

Beck, A. T., & Grant, P. M. (2008). Negative self-defeating attitudes: Factors that influence everyday impairment in individuals with schizophrenia. *American Journal of Psychiatry, 165*, 772.

Becker, A. J., McCulloch, E. A., & Till, J. E. (1963). Cytological demonstration of the clonal nature of spleen colonies derived from transplanted mouse marrow cells. *Nature, 197*, 452–454.

Becker, K. A. (2003). *History of the Stanford-Binet intelligence scales: Content and psychometrics* (5th ed., Stanford-Binet Intelligence Scales, Assessment Service Bulletin No. 1). Itasca, IL: Riverside Publishing.

Becker, S. I. (2008). The mechanism of priming: Episodic retrieval or priming of popout? *Acta Psychologica, 127*, 324–339.

Begg, I. M., Needham, D. R., & Bookbinder, M. (1993). Do backward messages unconsciously affect listeners? No. *Canadian Journal of Experimental Psychology, 47*, 1–14.

Behar, R. (2007). Gender related aspects of eating disorders: A psychosocial view. In J. S. Rubin (Ed.), *Eating disorders and weight loss research* (pp. 39–65). Hauppauge, NY: Nova Science Publishers.

Beilin, H. (1992). Piaget's enduring contribution to developmental psychology. *Developmental Psychology, 28*, 191–204.

Bem, S. L. (1981). Gender schema theory: A cognitive account of sex typing. *Psychological Review, 88*, 354–364.

Bem, S. L. (1993). *The lenses of gender: Transforming the debate on sexual inequality.* New Haven, CT: Yale University Press.

Ben-Eliyahu, S., Page, G. G., & Schleifer, S. J. (2007). Stress, NK cells, and cancer: Still a promissory note. *Brain, Behavior, & Immunity, 21*, 881–887.

Bennett, M., Barrett, M., Karakozov, R., Kipiani, G., Lyons, E., Pavlenko, V., & Riazanova, T. (2004). Young children's evaluations of the ingroup and of outgroups: A multi-national study. *Social Development, 13*(1), 124–141.

Berenbaum, S. A., Martin, C. L., & Ruble, D. N. (2008). Gender development. In W. Damon & R. M. Lerner (Eds.), *Child and adolescent development: An advanced course* (pp. 647–695). Hoboken, NJ: Wiley.

Berger, M., Speckmann, E.-J., Pape, H. C., & Gorji, A. (2008). Spreading depression enhances human neocortical excitability in vitro. *Cephalalgia, 28*, 558–562.

Bergstrom-Lynch, C. A. (2008). Becoming parents, remaining childfree: How same-sex couples are creating families and confronting social inequalities. *Dissertation Abstracts International Section A: Humanities and Social Sciences, 68*(8-A), 3608.

Berman, M. E., Tracy, J. I., & Coccaro, E. F. (1997). The serotonin hypothesis of aggression revisited. *Clinical Psychology Review, 17*(6), 651–665.

Bernard, L. L. (1924). *Instinct.* New York, NY: Holt.

Bernheim, K. F., & Lewine, R. R. J. (1979). *Schizophrenia: Symptoms, causes, and treatments.* New York, NY: Norton.

Berreman, G. (1971). *Anthropology today.* Del Mar, CA: CRM Books.

Berry, J. W., Poortinga, Y. H., Segall, M. H., & Dasen, P. R. (2002). *Cross-cultural psychology: Research and applications* (2nd ed.). New York, NY: Cambridge University Press.

Berthoud, H. (2002). Multiple neural systems controlling food intake and body weight. *Neuroscience & Biobehavioral Reviews, 26*(4), 393–428.

Berzoff, J. (2008). Psychosocial ego development: The theory of Erik Erikson. In J. Berzoff, L. M. Flanagan, & P. Hertz (Eds.), *Inside out and outside in: Psychodynamic clinical theory and psychopathology in contemporary multicultural contexts* (2nd ed., pp. 99–120). Lanham, MD: Jason Aronson.

Best, J. B. (1999). *Cognitive psychology* (5th ed.). Belmont, CA: Wadsworth.

Bhattacharya, S. K., & Muruganandam, A. V. (2003). Adaptogenic activity of Withania somnifera: An experimental study using a rat model of chronic stress. *Pharmacology, Biochemistry & Behavior, 75*(3), 547–555.

Bialystok, E. (2007). Cognitive effects of bilingualism: How linguistic experience leads to cognitive change. *International Journal of Bilingual Education and Bilingualism, 10*, 210–223.

Biehl, M., Matsumoto, D., Ekman, P., Hearn, V., Heider, K., Kudoh, T., & Ton, V. (1997). Matsumoto and Ekman's Japanese and Caucasian facial expressions of emotion (JACFEE): Reliability data and cross-national differences. *Journal of Nonverbal Behavior, 21*, 3–21.

Billiard, M. (2007). Sleep disorders. In L. Candelise, R. Hughes, A. Liberati, B. M. J. Uitdehaag, & C. Warlow (Eds.), Evidence-based neurology: Management of neurological disorders (pp. 70–78). *Evidence-based medicine.* Malden, MA: Blackwell Publishing.

Binks, G. (2008, November 19). *Student binge drinking: A problem well past the tipping point.* CBC News. Retrieved from http://www.cbc.ca/canada/story/2008/11/19/f-student-drinking.html

Birkenhäger, T. K., Renes, J., & Pluijms, E. M. (2004). One-year follow-up after successful ECT: A naturalistic study in depressed inpatients. *Journal of Clinical Psychiatry, 65*(1), 87–91.

Bjorkqvist, K. (1994). Sex differences in physical, verbal, and indirect aggression: A review of recent research. *Sex Roles, 30*, 177–188.

Blakemore, C., & Cooper, G. F. (1970). Development of the brain depends on the visual environment. *Nature, 228*, 477–478.

Blanco, C., Schneier, F. R., Schmidt, A., Blanco-Jerez, C. R., Marshall, R. D., Sanchez-Lacay, A., & Liebowitz, M. R. (2003). Pharmacological treatment of social anxiety disorder: A meta-analysis. *Depression & Anxiety, 18*(1), 29–40.

Blass, T. (1991). Understanding behavior in the Milgram obedience experiment: The role of personality, situations, and their interactions. *Journal of Personality and Social Psychology, 60*(3), 398–413.

Blass, T. (2000). Stanley Milgram. In A. E. Kazdin (Ed.), *Encyclopedia of psychology* (Vol. 5) (pp. 248–250). Washington, DC: American Psychological Association.

Bob, P. (2008). Pain, dissociation and subliminal self-representations. *Consciousness and Cognition: An International Journal, 17*, 355–369.

Boccato, G., Capozza, D., Falvo, R., & Durante, F. (2008). Capture of the eyes by relevant and irrelevant onsets. *Social Cognition, 26*, 224–234.

Bock, G. R., & Goode, J. A. (Eds.). (1996). *Genetics of criminal and antisocial behavior.* Chichester, England: Wiley.

Bohm-Starke, N., Brodda-Jansen, G., Linder, J., & Danielsson, I. (2007). The result of treatment on vestibular and general pain thresholds in women with provoked vestibulodynia. *Clinical Journal of Pain, 23*(7), 598–604.

Bohus, M., Haaf, B., Simms, T., Limberger, M. F., Schmahl, C., Unckel, C., Lieb, K., & Linehan, M. M. (2004). Effectiveness of inpatient dialectical behavioral therapy for borderline personality disorder: A controlled trial. *Behaviour Research & Therapy, 42*(5), 487–499.

Bond, F. W., & Bunce, D. (2000). Mediators of change in emotion-focused and problem-focused worksite stress management intervention. *Journal of Occupational Health Psychology, 5*, 153–163.

Bond, M. H., & Smith, P. B. (1996). Crosscultural social and organizational psychology. *Annual Review of Psychology, 47*, 205–235.

Bor, D., Billington, J., & Baron-Cohen, S. (2007). Savant memory for digits in a case of synaesthesia and Asberger Syndrome is related to hyperactivity in the lateral prefrontal cortex. *Neurocase, 13*, 311–319.

Borba, M. (2001). *Building moral intelligence: The seven essential virtues that teach kids to do the right thing.* San Francisco, CA: Jossey-Bass.

Borbely, A. A. (1982). Circadian and sleep-dependent processes in sleep regulation. In J. Aschoff, S. Daan, & G. A. Groos (Eds.), *Vertebrate circadian rhythms* (pp. 237–242). Berlin, Germany: Springer/Verlag.

Borchers, B. J. (2007). Workplace environment fit, commitment, and job satisfaction in a nonprofit association. *Dissertation Abstracts International: Section B: The Sciences and Engineering, 67*(7-B), 4139.

Borenstein, A. R., Copenhaver, C. I., & Mortimer, J. A. (2006). Early-life risk factors for Alzheimer disease. *Alzheimer Disease and Associated Disorders, 20*(1), 63–72.

Borra, R. (2008). Working with the cultural formulation in therapy. *European Psychiatry, 23,* S43–S48.

Borrego, J., Ibanez, E. S., Spendlove, S. J., & Pemberton, J. R. (2007). Treatment acceptability among Mexican American parents. *Behavior Therapy, 38*(3), 218–227.

Bosacki, S. L., Marini, Z. A., & Dane, A. V. (2006). Voices from the classroom: Pictorial and narrative representations of children's bullying experiences. *Journal of Moral Education, 35,* 231–245.

Bouchard, T. J., Jr. (1994). Genes, environment, and personality. *Science, 264,* 1700–1701.

Bouchard, T. J., Jr. (1997). The genetics of personality. In K. Blum & E. P. Noble (Eds.), *Handbook of psychiatric genetics.* Boca Raton, FL: CRC Press.

Bouchard, T. J., Jr. (1999). The search for intelligence. *Science, 284,* 922–923.

Bouchard, T. J., Jr. (2004). Genetic influence on human psychological traits: A survey. *Current Directions in Psychological Science, 13*(4), 148–151.

Bouchard, T. J., Jr., & McGue, M. (1981). Familial studies of intelligence: A review. *Science, 212*(4498), 1055–1059.

Bouchard, T. J., Jr., McGue, M., Hur, Y., & Horn, J. M. (1998). A genetic and environmental analysis of the California Psychological Inventory using adult twins reared apart and together. *European Journal of Personality, 12,* 307–320.

Boucher, L., & Dienes, Z. (2003). Two ways of learning associations. *Cognitive Science, 27*(6), 807–842.

Bourne, L. E., Dominowski, R. L., & Loftus, E. F. (1979). *Cognitive processes.* Englewood Cliffs, NJ: Prentice Hall.

Bouton, M. E. (1994). Context, ambiguity, and classical conditioning. *Current Directions in Psychological Science, 2,* 49–53.

Bowers, K. S., & Woody, E. Z. (1996). Hypnotic amnesia and the paradox of intentional forgetting. *Journal of Abnormal Psychology, 105,* 381–390.

Bowlby, J. (1969). *Attachment and loss: Vol. 1. Attachment.* New York, NY: Basic Books.

Bowlby, J. (1973). *Attachment and loss: Vol. 2. Separation and anxiety.* New York, NY: Basic Books.

Bowlby, J. (1982). Attachment and loss: Retrospect and prospect. *American Journal of Orthopsychiatry, 52,* 664–678

Bowlby, J. (1989). *Secure attachment.* New York, NY: Basic Books.

Bowlby, J. (2000). *Attachment.* New York, NY: Basic Books.

Bowling, A. C., & Mackenzie, B. D. (1996). The relationship between speed of information processing and cognitive ability. *Personality & Individual Differences, 20*(6), 775–800.

Boyle, S. H., Williams, R. B., Mark, D. B., Brummett, B. H., Siegler, I. C., Helms, M. J., & Brady, S. S. (2007). Young adults' media use and attitudes toward interpersonal and institutional forms of aggression. *Aggressive Behavior, 33*(6), 519–525.

Boysen, G. A., & Vogel, D. L. (2007). Biased assimilation and attitude polarization in response to learning about biological explanations of homosexuality. *Sex Roles, 56,* 755–762.

Bozkurt, A. S., & Aydin, O. (2004). Temel yükleme hatasinin degisik yas ve iki alt kültürde incelenmesi [A developmental investigation of fundamental attribution error in two subcultures]. *Türk Psikoloji Dergisi, 19,* 91–104.

Bradley, R., Conklin, C. Z., & Westen, D. (2007). Borderline personality disorder. In W. O'Donohue, K. A. Fowler, S. O. Lilienfeld (Eds.), *Personality disorders: Toward the DSM-V* (pp. 167–201). Thousand Oaks, CA: Sage.

Brady, I. (2004). *Illustrating nature: Right-brain art in a left-brain world.* Talent, OR: Nature Works Press.

Bragdon, A. D., & Gamon, D. (1999). *Building left-brain power: Left-brain conditioning exercises and tips to strengthen language, math, and uniquely human skills.* Thousand Oaks, CA: Brainwaves Books.

Brandon, T. H., Collins, B. N., Juliano, L. M., & Lazev, A. B. (2000). Preventing relapse among former smokers: A comparison of minimal interventions through telephone and mail. *Journal of Consulting and Clinical Psychology, 68*(1), 103–113.

Breland, K., & Breland, M. (1961). The misbehavior of organisms. *American Psychologist, 16,* 681–684.

Bremner, J. D., Vythilingam, M., Vermetten, E., Anderson, G., Newcomer, J. W. & Charney, D. S. (2004). Effects of glucocorticoids on declarative memory function in major depression. *Biological Psychiatry, 55*(8), 811–815.

Brent, D. A., Melhem, N. (2008). Familial transmission of suicidal behavior. *Psychiatric Clinics of North America, 31,* 157–177.

Brett, M. A., Roberts, L. F., Johnson, T. W., & Wassersug, R. J. (2007). Eunuchs in contemporary society: Expectations, consequences, and adjustments to castration (part II). *Journal of Sexual Medicine, 4*(1), 946–955.

Brewer, J. B., Zhao, Z., Desmond, J. E., Glover, G. H., & Gabrieli, J. D. (1998). Making memories: Brain activity that predicts how well visual experience will be remembered. *Science, 281,* 1185–1187.

Brim, O. (1999). *The MacArthur Foundation study of midlife development.* Vero Beach, FL: MacArthur Foundation.

Brislin, R. W. (1997). *Understanding culture's influence on behavior* (2nd ed.). San Diego: Harcourt Brace.

Brislin, R. W. (2000). *Understanding culture's influence on behavior.* Ft. Worth, TX: Harcourt.

Brkich, M., Jeffs, D., & Carless, S. A. (2002). A global self-report measure of person-job fit. *European Journal of Psychological Assessment, 18*(1), 43–51.

Brody, A., Olmstead, R. E., London, E. D., Farahi, J., Meyer, J. H., Grossman, P., Lee, G. S., Huang, J., Hahn, E. L., & Mandelkern, M. A. (2004). Smoking-induced ventral striatum dopamine release. *American Journal of Psychiatry, 161*(7), 1211–1218.

Brown, A., & Whiteside, S. P. (2008). Relations among perceived parental rearing behaviors, attachment style, and worry in anxious children. *Journal of Anxiety Disorders, 22,* 263–272.

Brown, E., Deffenbacher, K., & Sturgill, K. (1977). Memory for faces and the circumstances of encounter. *Journal of Applied Psychology, 62,* 311–318.

Brown, P. K., & Wald, G. (1964). Visual pigments in single rods and cones of the human retina. Direct measurements reveal mechanisms of human night and color vision. *Science, 144,* 45–52.

Brown, R. P., & Josephs, R. A. (1999). A burden of proof: Stereotype relevance and gender differences in math performance. *Journal of Personality and Social Psychology, 76*(2), 246–257.

Brown, R., & Kulik, J. (1977). Flashbulb memories. *Cognition, 5,* 73–99.

Brown, T. A., O'Leary, T. A., & Barlow, D. H. (2001). Generalized anxiety disorder. In D. H. Barlow (Ed.), *Clinical handbook of psychological disorders: A step-by-step treatment manual* (3rd ed.) (pp. 154–208). New York, NY: Guilford Press.

Browne, K. O. (2001). Cultural formulation of psychiatric diagnoses. *Culture, Medicine & Psychiatry, 25*(4), 411–425.

Bugg, J. M., Zook, N. A., DeLosh, E. L., Davalos, D. B., & Davis, H. P. (2006). Age differences in fluid intelligence: Contributions of general slowing and frontal decline. *Brain and Cognition, 62*, 9–16.

Bull, L. (2003). What can be done to prevent smoking in pregnancy? A literature review. *Early Child Development & Care, 173*(6), 661–667.

Bunde, J., & Suls, J. (2006). A quantitative analysis of the relationship between the Cook-Medley Hostility Scale and traditional coronary artery disease risk factors. *Health Psychology, 25*, 493–500.

Buontempo, G., & Brockner, J. (2008). Emotional intelligence and the ease of recall judgment bias: The mediating effect of private self-focused attention. *Journal of Applied Social Psychology, 38*, 159–172.

Burgdorf, J., Knutson, B., & Panksepp, J. (2000). Anticipation of rewarding electrical brain stimulation evokes ultrasonic vocalization in rats. *Behavioural Neuroscience, 114(2)*, 320–327.

Burns, S. M. (2008). Unique and interactive predictors of mental health quality of life among men living with prostate cancer. *Dissertation Abstracts International: Section B: The Sciences and Engineering, 68*(10-B), 6953.

Bushman, B. J. (2002). Does venting anger feed or extinguish the flame? Catharsis, rumination, distraction, anger and aggressive responding. *Personality & Social Psychology Bulletin, 28*(6), 724–731.

Buss, D. M. (1989). Sex differences in human mate preferences: Evolutionary hypotheses tested in 37 cultures. *Behavioral and Brain Sciences, 12*, 1–49.

Buss, D. M. (2003). *The evolution of desire: Strategies of human mating.* New York, NY: Basic Books.

Buss, D. M. (2005). *The handbook of evolutionary psychology.* Hoboken, NJ: Wiley.

Buss, D. M. (2007). The evolution of human mating. *Acta Psychologica Sinica, 39*, 502–512.

Buss, D. M. (2008). *Evolutionary psychology: The new science of the mind* (3rd ed.). Boston, MA: Allyn & Bacon.

Buss, D. M. and 40 colleagues. (1990). International preferences in selecting mates: A study of 37 cultures. *Journal of Cross-Cultural Psychology, 21*, 5–47.

Bussey, K., & Bandura, A. (2004). Social cognitive theory of gender development and functioning. In A. H. Eagly, A. E. Beall, & R. J. Sternberg (Eds.) *The psychology of gender* (2nd ed., pp. 92–119). New York, NY: Guilford Press.

Buswell, B. N. (2006). The role of empathy, responsibility, and motivations to respond without prejudice in reducing prejudice. *Dissertation Abstracts International: Section B: The Sciences and Engineering, 66*, 6968.

Butcher, J. N. (2000). Revising psychological tests: Lessons learned from the revision of the MMPI. *Psychological Assessment, 12*(3), 263–271.

Butcher, J. N. (2005). *A beginner's guide to the MMPI-2* (2nd ed.). Washington, DC: American Psychological Association.

Butcher, J. N., & Perry, J. N. (2008). *Personality assessment in treatment planning: Use of the MMPI-2 and BTPI.* New York, NY: Oxford University Press.

Butler, R. A. (1954, February). Curiosity in monkeys. *Scientific American, 190*, 70–75.

Butterweck, V. (2003). Mechanism of action of St John's Wort in depression: What is known? *CNS Drugs, 17*(8), 539–562.

Byne, W. (2007). Biology and sexual minority status. In I. H. Meyer & M. E. Northridge (Eds.), *The health of sexual minorities: Public health perspectives on lesbian, gay, bisexual, and transgender populations* (pp. 65–90). New York, NY: Springer Science + Business Media.

Byne, W., Dracheva, S., Chin, B., Schmeidler, J. M., Davis, K. L., & Haroutunian, V. (2008). Schizophrenia and sex associated differences in the neuronal and oligodendrocyte specific genes in individual thalamic nuclei. *Schizophrenia Research, 98*, 118–128.

Cai, W-H., Blundell, J., Han, J., Greene, R. W., & Powell, C. M. (2006). Postreactivation glucocorticoids impair recall of established fear memory. *Journal of Neuroscience, 26*(37), 9560–9566.

Cairns, R. B., & Cairns, B. D. (2006). The making of developmental psychology. In R. M. Lerner (Ed.), *Handbook of child psychology, volume one: Theoretical models of human development* (6th ed., pp. 89–65). Hoboken, NJ: Wiley.

Camarena, B., Santiago, H., Aguilar, A., Ruvinskis, E., González-Barranco, J., & Nicolini, H. (2004). Family-based association study between the monoamine oxidase A gene and obesity: Implications for psychopharmacogenetic studies. *Neuropsychobiology, 49*(3), 126–129.

Cameron, L., Rutland, A. & Brown, R. (2007). Promoting children's positive intergroup attitudes towards stigmatized groups: Extended contact and multiple classification skills training. *International Journal of Behavioral Development, 31*, 454–466.

Campbell, A., & Muncer, S. (2008). Intent to harm or injure? Gender and the expression of anger. *Aggressive Behavior, 34*, 282–293.

Campbell, L., Simpson, J. A., Kashy, D. A., & Fletcher, G. J. O. (2001). Ideal standards, the self, and flexibility of ideals in close relationships. *Personality & Social Psychology Bulletin, 27*(4), 447–462.

Canadian Centre on Substance Abuse. (2007). *Reducing alcohol-related harm in Canada: Toward a culture of moderation.* Retrieved from http://www.ccsa.ca/2007%20CCSA%20Documents/ccsa-023876-2007.pdf

Canadian Council on Animal Care. (2005). Guidelines for the treatment of animals in behavioural research and teaching. (2005). *Animal Behaviour, 69*(1), i–vi.

Canadian Council on Learning. (2007). *Lessons in Learning: French Immersion Education in Canada.* Ottawa, ON: Author. Retrieved from http://www.ccl-cca.ca/CCL/Reports/LessonsInLearning/LinL20070517_French_Immersion_programs.htm

Canadian Institute of Health Research & Institute of Population and Public Health. (2002). *Sleepiness and the health and performance of adolescent students.* Retrieved from http://www.css.to/pdf/sleep/Workshop_CIHR.pdf

Canadian Lung Association. (2008). *Smoking and tobacco: Facts about smoking.* Retrieved from http://www.lung.ca/protect-protegez/tobacco-tabagisme/facts-faits/index_e.php

Canadian Network for Mood and Anxiety Treatments. (2009). Retrieved from http://www.canmat.org

Canadian Parents for French. (2008). *Enrolment trends 2006–2007.* Ottawa, ON: Author. Retrieved from http://www.cpf.ca/eng/resources-reports-enrolment-0607.html

Canadian Pediatric Society. (2009). *Fetal alcohol spectrum disorder: What you should know about drinking during pregnancy.* Retrieved from http://www.caringforkids.cps.ca/pregnancy&babies/FASpregnancy.htm

Cannon, W. B. (1927). The James-Lange theory of emotions: A critical examination and an alternative theory. *American Journal of Psychology, 39*, 106–124.

Cannon, W. B., Lewis, J. T., & Britton, S. W. (1927). The dispensability of the sympathetic division of the autonomic nervous system. *Boston Medical Surgery Journal, 197*, 514.

Caprara, G. V., Vecchione, M., Barbaranelli, C., & Fraley, R. C. (2007). When likeness goes with liking: The case of political preference. *Political Psychology, 28*, 609–632.

Carballo, J. J., Harkavy-Friedman, J., Burke, A. K., Sher, L., Baca-Garcia, E., Sullivan, G. M., Gruneman, M. F., Parsey, R. V., Mann, J. J., & Oquendo, M. A. (2008). Family history of suicidal behavior and early traumatic experiences: Addictive effect on suicidality and course of bipolar illness? *Journal of Affective Disorders, 109*, 57–63.

Carels, R. A., Konrad, K., Young, K. M., Darby, L. A., Coit, C., Clayton, A. M., & Oemig, C. K. (2008). Taking control of your personal eating and exercise environment: A weight maintenance program. *Eating Behaviors, 9,* 228–237.

Carey, B. (2008, October 1). Psychoanalytic therapy wins backing. *New York Times.* [Online]. Retrieved from http://www.nytimes.com/2008/10/01/health/01psych.html

Carlson, L. E., Speca, M., Faris, P., & Patel, K. D. (2007). One year pre-post intervention follow-up of psychological, immune, endocrine and blood pressure outcomes of mindfulness-based stress reduction (MBSR) in breast and prostate cancer outpatient. *Brain, Behavior, and Immunity, 21,* 1038–1049.

Carlson, N. R. (2008). *Foundations of physiological psychology* (international ed.). Boston, MA: Allyn & Bacon.

Carnagey, N. L., Anderson, C. A., & Bartholow, B. D. (2007). Media violence and social neuroscience: New questions and new opportunities. *Current Directions in Psychological Science, 16,* 178–182.

Carnagey, N. L., Anderson, C. A., & Bushman, B. J. (2007). The effect of video game violence on physiological desensitization to real-life violence. *Journal of Experimental Social Psychology, 43,* 489–496.

Carstensen, L. L. (2006). The influence of a sense of time on human development. *Science, 312,* 1913–1915.

Caruso, E. M. (2008). Use of experienced retrieval ease in self and social judgments. *Journal of Experimental Social Psychology, 44,* 148–155.

Carvalho, C., Mazzoni, G., Kirsch, I., Meo, M., & Santandrea, M. (2008). The effect of posthypnotic suggestion, hypnotic suggestibility, and goal intentions on adherence to medical instructions. *International Journal of Clinical and Experimental Hypnosis, 56,* 143–155.

Castelli, L., Corazzini, L. L., & Geminiani, G. C. (2008). Spatial navigation in large-scale virtual environments: Gender differences in survey tasks. *Computers in Human Behavior, 24,* 1643–1667.

Castillo, R. J. (2003). Trance, functional psychosis, and culture. *Psychiatry: Interpersonal & Biological Processes, 66*(1), 9–21.

Castonguay, L. G., & Hill, C. (Eds.) (2007). *Insight in psychotherapy.* Washington, DC: American Psychological Association.

Cathers-Schiffman, T. A., & Thompson, M. S. (2007). Assessment of English-and Spanish-speaking students with the WISC-III and Leiter-R. *Journal of Psychoeducational Assessment, 25,* 41–52.

Cattell, R. B. (1950). *Personality: A systematic, theoretical, and factual study.* New York, NY: McGraw-Hill.

Cattell, R. B. (1963). Theory of fluid and crystallized intelligence: A critical experiment. *Journal of Educational Psychology, 54,* 1–22.

Cattell, R. B. (1965). *The scientific analysis of personality.* Baltimore: Penguin.

Cattell, R. B. (1971). *Abilities: Their structure, growth, and action.* Boston, MA: Houghton Mifflin.

Cattell, R. B. (1990). Advances in Cattellian personality theory. In L. A. Pervin (Ed.), *Handbook of personality: Theory and research.* New York, NY: Guilford Press.

CBC News. (2007). *The fight for the right to die.* Retrieved from http://www.cbc.ca/news/background/assistedsuicide/

CBC News. (2009a). *Girl watched skinhead videos and talked of how to kill, hearing told.* Retrieved from http://www.cbc.ca/canada/manitoba/story/2009/05/25/mb-swastika-parents-winnipeg.html

CBC News. (2009b). *Sask. MD's Wikipedia posting of ink blots angers psychologists.* Retrieved from http://www.cbc.ca/canada/saskatchewan/story/2009/07/31/rorschach-test.html#socialcomments

CBC News. (2009c). *The fight for the right to die.* Retrieved from http://www.cbc.ca/canada/story/2009/02/09/f-assisted-suicide.html

Cehajic, S., Brown, R., & Castano, E. (2008). Forgive and forget? Antecedents and consequences of intergroup forgiveness in Bosnia and Herzegovina. *Political Psychology, 29,* 351–367.

Centre for Addiction and Mental Health. (2008). *Cognitive behavioural therapy (CBT) clinic.* Retrieved from http://www.camh.net/About_CAMH/Guide_to_CAMH/Mental_Health_Programs/Mood_and_Anxiety_Program/guide_cognitive_behavtherapy.html

Cervone, D., & Shoda, Y. (1999). Beyond traits in the study of personality coherence. *Current Directions in Psychological Science, 8*(a), 27–32.

Cesaro, P, & Ollat, H. (1997). Pain and its treatments. *European Neurology, 38,* 209–215.

Ceschi, G., & Scherer, K. R. (2001). Contrôler l'expression faciale et changer l'émotion: Une approche développementale [The role of facial expression in emotion: A developmental perspective]. *Enfance, 53*(3), 257–269.

Chabrol, H., Montovany, A., Duvonge, E., Kallmeyer, A., Mullet, E., & Leichsenring, F. (2004). Factor structure of the borderline personality inventory in adolescents. *European Journal of Psychological Assessment, 20*(1), 59–65.

Challem, J., Berkson, B., Smith, M. D., & Berkson, B. (2000). *Syndrome X: The complete program to prevent and reverse insulin resistance.* New York, NY: Wiley.

Chalmers, L., & Milan, A. (2005). *Marital satisfaction during the retirement years.* Statistics Canada. Cat. No. 11-008. Retrieved from http://www.statcan.gc.ca/pub/11-008-x/2004004/article/7776-eng.pdf

Chandrashekar, J., Hoon, M. A., Ryba, N. J. P., & Zuker, C. S. (2006). The receptors and cells for mammalian taste. *Nature, 444,* 288–294.

Chaney, J. M., Mullins, L. L., Wagner, J. L., Hommel, K. A., Page, M. C., Doppler, & Matthew, J. (2004). A longitudinal examination of causal attributions and depression symptomatology in rheumatoid arthritis. *Rehabilitation Psychology, 49*(2), 126–133.

Chang, G., Orav, J., McNamara, T. K., Tong, M. Y., & Antin, J. H. (2005). Psychosocial function after hematopoietic stem cell transplantation. *Psychosomatics: Journal of Consultation Liaison Psychiatry, 46*(1), 34–40.

Chapman, A. L., Leung, D. W., & Lynch, T. R. (2008). Impulsivity and emotion dysregulation in borderline personality disorder. *Journal of Personality Disorders, 22,* 148–164.

Charach, A., Pepler, D., & Ziegler, S. (1995). Bullying at school. *Education Canada, 37,* 12–18.

Charles, E. P. (2007). Object permanence, an ecological approach. *Dissertation Abstracts International: Section B: The Sciences and Engineering, 67*(8-B), 4737.

Charles, S. T., & Carstensen, L. L. (2007). Emotion regulation and aging. In J. J. Gross (Ed.), *Handbook of emotion regulation.* New York, NY: Guilford Press.

Chartrand, T., Pinckert, S., & Burger, J. M. (1999). When manipulation backfires: The effects of time delay and requester on the foot-in-the-door technique. *Journal of Applied Social Psychology, 29,* 211–221.

Chavez, C. M., McGaugh, J. L., & Weinberger, N. M. (2009). The basolateral amygdala modulates specific sensory memory representations in the cerebral cortex. *Neurobiology of Learning and Memory, 91*(4), 382–392.

Cherney, I. D. (2005). Children's and adults' recall of sex-stereotyped toy pictures: Effects of presentation and memory task. *Infant & Child Development, 14*(1), 11–27.

Cheung, M. S., Gilbert, P., & Irons, C. (2004). An exploration of shame, social rank, and rumination in relation to depression. *Personality & Individual Differences, 36*(5), 1143–1153.

Chiou, W-B. (2007). Customers' attributional judgments towards complaint handling in airline service: A confirmatory study based on attribution theory. *Psychological Reports, 100*, 1141–1150.

Chiricozzi, F. R., Clausi, S., Molinari, M., & Leggio, M. G. (2008). Phonological shortterm store impairment after cerebellar lesion: A single case study. *Neuropsychologia, 46*, 1940–1953.

Choi, I., & Nisbett, R. E. (2000). Cultural psychology of surprise: Holistic theories and recognition of contradiction. *Journal of Personality and Social Psychology, 79*(6), 890–905.

Choi, N. (2004). Sex role group differences in specific, academic, and general selfefficacy. *Journal of Psychology: Interdisciplinary & Applied, 138*(2), 149–159.

Chomsky, N. (1968). *Language and mind.* New York, NY: Harcourt, Brace, World.

Chomsky, N. (1980). *Rules and representations.* New York, NY: Columbia University Press.

Christensen, D. (2000). Is snoring a diZZZease? Nighttime noises may serve as a wake-up call for future illness. *Science News, 157*, 172–173.

Christensen, H., Anstey, K. J., Leach, L. S., & Mackinnon, A. J. (2008). Intelligence, education, and the brain reserve hypothesis. In F. I. M. Craik & T. A. Salthouse (Eds.), *The handbook of aging and cognition* (3rd ed.) (pp. 133–188). New York, NY: Psychology Press.

Christopher, K., Lutz-Zois, C. J., & Reinhardt, A. R. (2007). Female sexual-offenders: Personality pathology as a mediator of the relationship between childhood sexual abuse history and sexual abuse. *Child Abuse & Neglect, 31*, 871–883.

Chuang, D. (1998). Cited in J. Travis, Stimulating clue hints how lithium works. *Science News, 153*, 165.

Chudley, A., Conry, J., Cook, J., Loock, C., Rosales, T., & Leblanc, N. (2005). Fetal alcohol spectrum disorder: Canadian guidelines for diagnosis. *Canadian Medical Association Journal, 172*(5 supp), S3–S21.

Chung, J. C. C. (2006). Measuring sensory processing patterns of older Chinese people: Psychometric validation of the adult sensory profile. *Aging & Mental Health, 10*, 648–655.

Cialdini, R. B. (2009). *Influence: Science and practice* (5th ed.). Boston, MA: Allyn & Bacon.

Clark, A. J. (2007). *Empathy in counseling and psychotherapy: Perspectives and practices.* Mahwah, NJ: Erlbaum.

Clark, K. B., & Clark, M. P. (1939). The development of consciousness of self and the emergence of racial identification in Negro preschool children. *Journal of Social Psychology, 10*, 591–599.

Cleaves, D. H., & Latner, J. D. (2008). Evidence-based therapies for children and adolescents with eating disorders. In R. G. Steele, D. T. Elkin, & M. C. Roberts (Eds.), *Handbook of evidence-based therapies for children and adolescents: Bridging science and practice* (pp. 335–353). *Issues in clinical child psychology.* New York, NY: Springer Science + Business Media.

Cleeremans, A., & Sarrazin, J. C. (2007). Time, action, and consciousness. *Human Movement Science, 26*, 180–202.

Clifford, J. S., Boufal, M. M., & Kurtz, J. E. (2004). Personality traits and critical thinking: Skills in college students empirical tests of a two-factor theory. *Assessment, 11*(2), 169–176.

Clinton, S. M., & Meador-Woodruff, J H. (2004). Thalamic dysfunction in schizophrenia: Neurochemical, neuropathological, and in vivo imaging abnormalities. *Schizophrenia Research, 69*(2–3), 237–253.

Cloud, J. (2001, February 26). New sparks over electroshock. *Time*, 60–62.

Clulow, C. (2007). John Bowlby and couple psychotherapy. *Attachment & Human Development, 9*, 343–353.

Cohen, D., Mason, K., & Farley, T. A. (2004). Beer consumption and premature mortality in Louisiana: An ecologic analysis. *Journal of Studies on Alcohol, 65*(3), 398–403.

Cohen, R. A., Paul, R., Zawacki, T. M., Moser, D. J., Sweet, L., & Wilkinson, H. (2001). Emotional and personality changes following cingulotomy. *Emotion, 1*(1), 38–50.

Cohen, S., & Lemay, E. P. (2007). Why would social networks be linked to affect and health practices? *Health Psychology, 26*, 410–417.

Cohen, S., Hamrick, N., Rodriguez, M. S., Feldman, P. J., Rabin, B. S., & Manuck, S. B. (2002). Reactivity and vulnerability to stress associated risk for upper respiratory illness. *Psychosomatic Medicine, 64*(2), 302–310.

Cole, M., & Gajdamaschko, N. (2007). Vygotsky and culture. In H. Daniels, J. Wertsch, & M. Cole (Eds.), *The Cambridge companion to Vygotsky* (pp. 193–211). New York, NY: Cambridge University Press.

Combrink-Graham, L., & McKenna, S. B. (2006). Families with children with disrupted attachments. In L. Combrinck-Graham (Ed.), *Children in family contexts: Perspectives on treatment* (pp. 242–264). New York, NY: Guilford Press.

Combs, D. R., Basso, M. R., Wanner, J. L., & Ledet, S. N. (2008). Schizophrenia. In M. Hersen & J. Rosqvist (Eds.), *Handbook of psychological assessment, case conceptualization, and treatment, Vol 1: Adults* (pp. 352–402). Hoboken, NJ: Wiley.

Connolly, S. (2000). *LSD (just the facts).* Baltimore: Heinemann Library.

Connor, K. M., & Davidson, J. R. T. (2002). A placebo-controlled study of Kava kava in generalized anxiety disorder. *International Clinical Psychopharmacology, 17*(4), 185–188.

Constantino, M. J., Manber, R., Ong, J., Kuo, T. F., Huang, J. S., & Arnow, B. A. (2007). Patient expectations and therapeutic alliance as predictors of outcome in group cognitive-behavioral therapy for insomnia. *Behavioral Sleep Medicine, 5*, 210–228.

Cook, M., & Mineka, S. (1989). Observational conditioning of fear to fear-relevant versus fear-irrelevant stimuli in rhesus monkeys. *Journal of Abnormal Psychology, 98*, 448–459.

Cook, P. F. (2000). Effects of counselors' etiology attributions on college students' procrastination. *Journal of Counseling Psychology, 47*(3), 352–361.

Cooper, C., Bebbington, P. E., Meltzer, H., Bhugra, D., Brugha, T., Jenkins, R., Farrell, M., & King, M. (2008). Depression and common mental disoders in lone parents: Results of the 2000 National Psychiatric Morbidity Survey. *Psychological Medicine, 38*, 335–342.

Cooper, R. (2004). What is wrong with the DSM? *History of Psychiatry, 15*(1), 5–25.

Cooper, W. E. Jr., Pérez-Mellado, V., Vitt, L. J., & Budzinsky, B. (2002). Behavioral responses to plant toxins in two omnivorous lizard species. *Physiology & Behavior, 76*(2), 297–303.

Coplan, R. J., Arbeau, K. A., & Armer, M. (2008). Don't fret, be supportive! Maternal characteristics linking child shyness to psychosocial and school adjustment in kindergarten. *Journal of Abnormal Child Psychology, 36*, 359–371.

Coren, S. (1996). *Sleep thieves: An eye opening exploration into the science and mysteries of sleep.* New York, NY: Freeman.

Corey, G. (2009). *Theory and practice of counseling and psychotherapy* (8th ed.). Belmont, CA: Cengage.

Corkin, S. (2002). What's new with the amnesic patient H. M.? *Nature Reviews Neuroscience, 3*, 153–160.

Cornelius, J. R., & Clark, D. B. (2008). Depressive disorders and adolescent substance use disorders. In Y. Kaminer & O. G. Bukstein (Eds.), *Adolescent substance abuse: Psychiatric comorbidity and high-risk behaviors* (pp. 221–242). New York, NY: Routledge/Taylor & Francis Group.

Corr, C. A., Nabe, C. M., & Corr, D. M. (2009). *Death and dying: Life and living* (6th ed.). Belmont, CA: Wadsworth.

Costa, J. L., Brennen, M. B., & Hochgeschwender, U. (2002). The human genetics of eating disorders: Lessons from the leptin/melanocortin system. *Child & Adolescent Psychiatric Clinics of North America, 11*(2), 387–397.

Costa, P. T. Jr., & McCrae, R. R. (1992). *NEO PI-R professional manual*. Odessa, FL: Psychological Assessment Resources.

Costa, P. T. Jr., McCrae, R. R., & Martin, T. A. (2008). Incipient adult personality: The NEO-PI-3 in middle-school-aged children. *British Journal of Developmental Psychology, 26*, 71–89.

Courage, M. L., & Adams, R. J. (1990). Visual acuity assessment from birth to three years using the acuity card procedures: Cross-sectional and longitudinal samples. *Optometry and Vision Science, 67*, 713–718.

Coyne, S. M., Archer, J., & Eslea, M. (2004). Cruel intentions on television and in real life: Can viewing indirect aggression increase viewers' subsequent indirect aggression? *Journal of Experimental Child Psychology, 88*(3), 234–253.

Coyne, S. M., Archer, J., & Eslea, M. (2004). Cruel intentions on television and in real life: Can viewing indirect aggression increase viewers' subsequent indirect aggression? *Journal of Experimental Child Psychology, 88*(3), 234–253.

Craig, A. D., & Bushnell, M. C. (1994). The thermal grill illusion: Unmasking the burn of cold pain. *Science, 265*, 252–255.

Craig, C. L., Russell, S. J., Cameron, C., & Beaulieu, A. (1999). *Foundation for joint action: Reducing physical inactivity*. Ottawa, ON: Canadian Fitness and Lifestyle Research Institute.

Craig, W., & Pepler, D. (1995). Peer processes in bullying and victimization: An observational study. *Exceptionality Education Canada, 5*, 81–95.

Craig, W., & Pepler, D. (2000). *Making a difference in bullying*. LaMarsh Research Programme, Report Series, Report # 60. Toronto, ON: LaMarsh Centre for Research on Violence and Conflict Resolution.

Craig, W., & Pepler, D. (2003). Identifying and targeting risk for involvement in bullying and victimization. *Canadian Journal of Psychiatry, 48*, 577–582.

Craig, W., Pepler, D., & Blais, J. (2007). Responding to bullying: What works. *School Psychology International, 28*, 465–477.

Crandall, C. S., & Martinez, R. (1996). Culture, ideology, and antifat attitudes. *Personality and Social Psychology Bulletin, 22*, 1165–1176.

Crawford, C. S. (2008). Ghost in the machine: A genealogy of phantom-prosthetic relations (amputation, dismemberment, prosthetic). *Dissertation Abstracts International Section A: Humanities and Social Sciences, 68*(7-A), 3173.

Crespo-Facorro, B., Barbadillo, L., Pelayo-Terán, J., Rodríguez-Sánchez, J. M., & Terán, J. M. (2007). Neuropsychological functioning and brain structure in schizophrenia. *International Review of Psychiatry, 19*, 325–336.

Cresswell, M. (2008). Szasz and his interlocutors: Reconsidering Thomas Szasz's "Myth of mental illness" thesis. *Journal for the Theory of Social Behaviour, 38*, 23–44.

Crews, F. T., Collins, M. A., Dlugos, C., Littleton, J., Wilkins, L., Neafsey, E. J., Pentney, R., Snell, L. D., Tabakoff, B., Zou, J., & Noronha, A. (2004). Alcohol-induced neurodegeneration: When, where and why? *Alcoholism: Clinical & Experimental Research, 28*(2), 350–364.

Cristofalo, V. J. (1996). Ten years later: What have we learned about human aging from studies of cell cultures? *Gerontologist, 36*, 737–741.

Crone, C. C., & Gabriel, G. (2002). Herbal and nonherbal supplements in medical-psychiatric patient populations. *Psychiatric Clinics of North America, 25*(1), 211–230.

Crooks, R., & Bauer, K. (2008). *Our sexuality* (10th ed.). Belmont, CA: Cengage.

Crosby, B. (2003). Case studies in rational emotive behavior therapy with children and adolescents. *Journal of Cognitive Psychotherapy, 17*(3), 289–291.

Crowell, S. E., Beauchaine, T. P., & Lenzenweger, M. F. (2008). The development of borderline personality disorder and self-injurious behavior. In T. P. Beauchaine & S. P. Hinshaw (Eds.), *Child and adolescent psychopathology* (pp. 510–539). Hoboken, NJ: Wiley.

CTV. (2008). *Calgary man makes it to top of Everest on 3rd try*. Retrieved from http://www.ctv.ca/servlet/ArticleNews/story/CTVNews/20080523/everest_brash_080523?s_name=&no_ads

Cubelli, R., & Della Sala, S. (2008) Flashbulb memories: Special but not iconic. *Cortex, 44*, 908–909.

Cullen, D., & Gotell, L. (2002). From orgasms to organizations: Maslow, women's sexuality and the gendered foundations of the needs hierarchy. *Gender, Work & Organization, 9*(5), 537–555.

Cully, J. A., & Stanley, M. A. (2008). Assessment and treatment of anxiety in later life. In K. Laidlaw & B. Knight (Eds.), *Handbook of emotional disorders in later life: Assessment and treatment*. New York, NY: Oxford University Press.

Cummings, D. E. (2006). Ghrelin and the short- and long-term regulation of appetite and body weight. *Physiology & Behavior, 89*, 71–84.

Cummings, E., & Henry, W. E. (1961). *Growing old: The process of disengagement*. New York, NY: Basic Books.

Cunningham, G. B. (2002). Diversity and recategorization: Examining the effects of cooperation on bias and work outcomes. *Dissertation Abstracts International Section A: Humanities and Social Sciences, 63*, 1288.

Cunningham, G. B., Fink, J. S., & Kenix, L. J. (2008). Choosing an endorser for a women's sporting event: The interaction of attractiveness and expertise. *Sex Roles, 58*, 371–378.

Curtiss, S. (1977). *Genie: A psycholinguistic study of a modern-day "wild child."* New York, NY: Academic Press.

D'Alessio, D., & Allen, M. (2002). Selective exposure and dissonance after decisions. *Psychological Reports, 91*(2), 527–532.

Dackis, C. A., & O'Brien, C. P. (2001). Cocaine dependence: A disease of the brain's reward centers. *Journal of Substance Abuse Treatment, 21*(3), 111–117.

Dalenberg, C., Loewenstein, R., Spiegel, D., Brewin, C., Lanius, R., Frankel, S., Gold, S., Van der Kolk, B., Simeon, D., Vermetten, E., Butler, L., Koopman, C., Courtois, C., Dell, P., Nijenhuis, E., Chu, J., Sar, V., Palesh, O., Cuevas, C., & Paulson, K. (2007). Scientific study of the dissociative disorders. *Psychotherapy and Psychosomatics, 76*, 400–401.

Dalley, J. W., Fryer, T. D., Brichard, L., Robinson, E. S. J., Theobald, D. E. H., Lääne, K., Peña, Y., Murphy, E. R., Shah, Y., Probst, K., Abakumova, I., Aigbirhio, F. I., Richards, H. K., Hong, Y., Baron, J-C., Everitt, B. J., & Robbins, T. W. (2007). Nucleus accumbens D2/3 receptors predict trait impulsivity and cocaine reinforcement. *Science, 315*, 1267–1270.

Damasio, A. R. (1999). *The feeling of what happens: Body and emotion in the making of consciousness*. New York, NY: Harcourt Brace.

Damasio, A. R. (2006). From Descartes' error: Emotion, reason, and the human brain. In G. Marcus (Ed.), *The Norton Psychology Reader* (pp. 58–69). New York, NY: Norton.

Dana, R. H. (2005). *Multicultural assessment: Principles, applications, and examples*. Mahwah, NJ: Erlbaum.

Daniels, K., Toth, J., & Jacoby, J. (2006). The aging of executive functions. In E. Bialystok & F. I. M. Craik (Eds.), *Lifespan cognition: Mechanisms of change*. New York, NY: Oxford University Press.

Dantzer, R., O'Connor, J. C., Freund, G. C., Johnson, R. W., & Kelley, K. W. (2008). From inflammation to sickness and depression: When the immune system subjugates the brain. *Nature Reviews Neuroscience, 9*, 46–57.

Danziger, K. (1994). Does the history of psychology have a future? *Theory and Psychology, 4*(4), 467–484.

Dapretto, M., Davies, M. S., Pfeifer, J. H., Scott, A. A., Sigman, M., Bookheimer, S. Y., & Iacoboni,

M. (2006). Understanding emotions in others: Mirror neuron dysfunction in children with autism spectrum disorders. *Nature Neuroscience, 9*, 28–30.

Darmani, N. A., & Crim, J. L. (2005) Delta9-tetrahydrocannabinol prevents emesis more potently than enhanced locomotor activity produced by chemically diverse dopamine D2/D3 receptor agonists in the least shrew (Cryptotis parva). *Pharmacology Biochemistry and Behavior, 80*, 35–44.

Darwin, C. (1859). *On the origin of species.* London, UK: Murray.

Darwin, C. (1872). *The expression of the emotions in man and animals.* London: Murray.

Dasi, C., Soler, M. J., Cervera, T., & Ruiz, J. C. (2008). Influence of articulation rate on two memory tasks in young and older adults. *Perceptual and Motor Skills, 106*, 579–589.

David, D., Schnur, J. E., & Belloiu, A. (2002). Another search for the "hot" cognitions: Appraisal, irrational beliefs, attributions, and their relation to emotion. *Journal of Rational-Emotive & Cognitive Behavior Therapy, 20*(2), 93–132.

Davidson, P. S. R., Anaki, D., Ciaramelli, E., Cohn, M., Kim, A. S. N., Murphy, K. J., Troyer, A. K., Moscovitch, M., & Levine, B. (2008). Does lateral parietal cortex support episodic memory? Evidence from focal lesion patients. *Neuropsychologia, 46*, 1743–1755.

Davies, I. (1998). A study of colour grouping in three languages: A test of the linguistic relativity hypothesis. *British Journal of Psychology, 89*, 433–452.

Davies, J. M. (1996). Dissociation, repression and reality testing in the countertransference: the controversey over memory and false memory in the psychoanalytic treatment of adult survivors of childhood sexual abuse. *Psychoanalytic Dialogues, 6*, 189–218.

Davies, M. F. (2008). Irrational beliefs and unconditional self-acceptance. III. The relative importance of different types of irrational belief. *Journal of Rational-Emotive & Cognitive Behavior Therapy, 26*, 102–118.

Davison, G., Blankstein, K.,, Flett, G., & Neale, J. (2008). *Abnormal psychology* (3rd Cdn ed.). Etobicoke, ON: Wiley.

Dawson, K. A. (2004). Temporal organization of the brain: Neurocognitive mechanisms and clinical implications. *Brain & Cognition, 54*(1), 75–94.

De Coteau, T. J., Hope, D. A., & Anderson, J. (2003). Anxiety, stress, and health in northern plains Native Americans. *Behavior Therapy, 34*(3), 365–380.

de Oliveira-Souza, R., Moll, J., Ignácio, F. A., & Hare, R. D. (2008). Psychopathy in a civil psychiatric outpatient sample. *Criminal Justice and Behavior, 35*, 427–437.

de Pinho, R. S. N., da Silva-Júnior, F. P., Bastos, J. P. C., Maia, W. S., de Mello, M. T., de Bruin, V. M. S., & de Bruin, P. F. C. (2006). Hypersomnolence and accidents in truck drivers: A cross-sectional study. *Chronobiology International, 23*(5), 963–971.

de Waal, F. B. M. (2008). Putting the altruism back into altruism: The evolution of empathy. *Annual Review of Psychology, 59*, 279–300.

Deary, I. J., & Stough, C. (1996). Intelligence and inspection time: Achievements, prospects, and problems. *American Psychologist, 51*, 599–608.

Deary, I. J., & Stough, C. (1997). Looking down on human intelligence. *American Psychologist, 52*, 1148–1149.

Deary, I. J., Ferguson, K. J., Bastin, M. E., Barrow, G. W. S., Reid, L. M., Seckl, J. R., Wardlaw, J. M., & MacLullich, A. M. J. (2007). Skull size and intelligence, and King Robert Bruce's IQ. *Intelligence, 35*, 519–528.

DeCasper, A. J., & Fifer, W. D. (1980). Of human bonding: Newborns prefer their mother's voices. *Science, 208*, 1174–1176.

Deci, E. L. (1995). *Why we do what we do: The dynamics of personal autonomy.* New York, NY: Putnam's Sons.

Deci, E. L., & Moller, A. C. (2005). The concept of competence: A starting place for understanding intrinsic motivation and selfdetermined extrinsic motivation. In A. J. Elliot & C. S. Dweck (Eds.), *Handbook of competence and motivation* (pp. 579–597). New York, NY: Guilford.

Deckers, L. (2005). *Motivation: Biological, psychological, and environmental* (2nd ed.). Boston, MA: Allyn & Bacon/Longman.

DeClue, G. (2003). The polygraph and lie detection. *Journal of Psychiatry & Law, 31*(3), 361–368.

Delgado, J. M. R. (1960). Emotional behavior in animals and humans. *Psychiatric Research Report, 12*, 259–271.

Delgado, P. L. (2004). How antidepressants help depression: Mechanisms of action and clinical response. *Journal of Clinical Psychiatry, 65*, 25–30.

Delgado-Gaitan, C. (1994). Socializing young children in Mexican-American families: An intergenerational perspective. In P. M. Greenfield & R. R. Cocking (Eds.), *Crosscultural roots of minority child development* (pp. 55–86). Hillsdale, NJ: Erlbaum.

Deller, T., Haas, C. A., Freiman, T. M., Phinney, A., Jucker, M., & Frotscher, M. (2006). Lesion induced axonal sprouting in the central nervous system. *Advances in Experimental Medicine and Biology, 557*, 101–121.

Delville, Y., Mansour, K. M., & Ferris, C. F. (1996). Testosterone facilitates aggression by modulating vasopressin receptors in the hypothalamus. *Physiology and Behavior, 60*, 25–29.

Dembe, A. E., Erickson, J. B., Delbos, R. G., & Banks, S. M. (2006). Nonstandard shift schedules and the risk of job-related injuries. *Scandinavian Journal of Work, Environment, & Health, 32*, 232–240.

Dement, W. (1997). *Sleepless at Stanford: What all undergraduates should know about how their sleeping lives affect their waking lives.* Retrieved from http//www.stanford.edu/~dement/sleepless.html

Dement, W. C., & Vaughan, C. (1999). *The promise of sleep.* New York, NY: Delacorte Press.

Dennis, W., & Dennis, M. G. (1940). Cradles and cradling customs of the Pueblo Indians. *American Anthropologist, 42*, 107–115.

Der-Karabetian, A., Stephenson, K., & Poggi, T. (1996). Environmental risk perception, activism and world-mindedness among samples of British and U. S. college students. *Perceptual and Motor Skills, 83*(2), 451–462.

DeValois, R. L. (1965). Behavioral and electrophysiological studies of primate vision. In W. D. Neff (Ed). *Contributions to sensory physiology* (Vol. 1). New York, NY: Academic Press.

Devlin, M. J., Yanovski, S. Z., & Wilson, G. T. (2000). Obesity: What mental health professionals need to know. *American Journal of Psychiatry, 157*(6), 854–866.

Dhikav, V., Aggarwal, N., Gupta, S., Jadhavi, R., & Singh, K. (2008). Depression in Dhat syndrome. *Journal of Sexual Medicine, 5*, 841–844.

Diamond, A., & Amso, D. (2008). Contributions of neuroscience to our understanding of cognitive development. *Current Directions in Psychological Science, 17*, 136–141.

Diamond, L. M. (2004). Emerging perspectives on distinctions between romantic love and sexual desire. *Current Directions in Psychological Science, 13*(3), 116–119.

Diaz-Berciano, C., de Vicente, F., & Fontecha, E. (2008). Modulating effects in learned helplessness of dyadic dominance-submission relations. *Aggressive Behavior, 34*(3), 273–281.

Dickens, W. T., & Flynn, J. R. (2001). Heritability estimates versus large environmental effects: The IQ paradox resolved. *Psychological Review, 108*(2), 346–369.

Dickinson, D. J., O'Connell, D. Q., & Dunn, J. S. (1996). Distributed study, cognitive study strategies and aptitude on student learning. *Psychology: A Journal of Human Behavior, 33*(3), 31–39.

Dicks, J., & Christmanson, P. (2008). French immersion: when and why? In *The State of French Second-Language Education in Canada 2008* (p. 16). Ottawa, ON: Canadian Parents for French. Retrieved from http://www.cpf.ca/eng/pdf/resources/reports/fsl/2008/FSL2008.pdf

Diego, M. A., & Jones, N. A. (2007). Neonatal antecedents for empathy. In T. Farrow & P. Woodruff (Eds.), *Empathy in mental illness* (pp. 145–167). New York, NY: Cambridge University Press.

Diener, M. L., Isabella, R. A., Behunin, M. G., & Wong, M. S. (2008). Attachment to mothers and fathers during middle childhood: Associations with child gender, grade, and competence. *Social Development, 7*, 84–101.

Diener, M. L., Mangelsdorf, S. C., McHale, J. L., & Frosch, C. A. (2002). Infants' behavioral strategies for emotion regulation with fathers and mothers: Associations with emotional expressions and attachment quality. *Infancy, 3*(2), 153–174.

Dijksterhuis, A., Aarts, H., & Smith, P. K. (2005). The power of the subliminal: On subliminal persuasion and other potential applications. In R. R. Hassin, J. S. Uleman, & J. A. Bargh (Eds.), The new unconscious (pp. 77–106). *Oxford series in social cognition and social neuroscience*. New York, NY: Oxford University Press.

DiLauro, M. D. (2004). Psychosocial factors associated with types of child maltreatment. *Child Welfare, 83*(1), 69–99.

Dill, K. E., & Thill, K. P. (2007). Video game characters and the socialization of gender roles: Young people's perceptions mirror sexist media depictions. *Sex Roles, 57*, 851–864.

Dillon, S. (2009). Study sees an Obama effect as lifting black test-takers. *The New York Times*. [Online]. Retrieved from http://www.nytimes.com/2009/01/23/education/23gap.html

Dimberg, U., & Thunberg, M. (1998). Rapid facial reactions to emotion facial expressions. *Scandinavian Journal of Psychology, 39*(1), 39–46.

Dimberg, U., Thunberg, M., & Elmehed, K. (2000). Unconscious facial reactions to emotional facial expressions. *Psychological Science, 11*(1), 86–89.

DiPietro, J. A. (2000). Baby and the brain: Advances in child development. *Annual Review of Public Health, 21*, 455–71.

Dittmann, R. W., Kappes, M. E., & Kappes, M. H. (1992). Sexual behavior in adolescent and adult females with congenital adrenal hyperplasia. *Psychoneuroendocrinology, 17*, 153–170.

Dobson, K. S. (2008). Cognitive therapy for depression. In M. A. Whisman (Ed.), *Adapting cognitive therapy for depression: Managing complexity and comorbidity* (pp. 3–35). New York, NY: Guilford.

Dodge, K. A., Coie, J. D., & Lynam, D. (2008). Aggression and antisocial behaviour in youth. In W. Damon & R. M. Lerner (Eds.), *Child and adolescent development* (pp. 437–472). Hoboken, NJ: Wiley.

Dollard, J., Doob, L., Miller, N., Mowrer, O. H., & Sears, R. R. (1939). *Frustration and aggression*. New Haven, CT: Yale University Press.

Domhoff, G. W. (2004). Why did empirical dream researchers reject Freud? A critique of historical claims by Mark Solms. *Dreaming, 14*(1), 3–17.

Domhoff, G. W. (2005). A reply to Hobson (2005). *Dreaming, 15*(1), 30–32.

Domhoff, G. W. (2007). Realistic simulation and bizarreness in dream content: Past findings and suggestions for future research. In D. Barrett & P. McNamara (Eds.), *The new science of dreaming Volume 2. Content, recall, and personality correlates* (pp. 1–27). Praeger perspectives. Westport, CT: Praeger.

Domjan, M. (2005). Pavlovian conditioning: A functional perspective. *Annual Review of Psychology, 56*, 179–206.

Dondi, M., Simion, F., & Caltran, G. (1999). Can newborns discriminate between their own cry and the cry of another newborn infant? *Developmental Psychology, 35*, 418–426.

Donini, L. M., Savina, C., & Cannella, C. (2003). Eating habits and appetite control in the elderly: The anorexia of aging. *International Psychogeriatrics, 15*(1), 73–87.

Donohue, R. (2006). Person-environment congruence in relation to career change and career persistence. *Journal of Vocational Behavior, 68*, 504–515.

Donovan, J. J., & Radosevich, D. J. (1999). A meta-analytic review of the distribution of practice effect: Now you see it, now you don't. *Journal of Applied Psychology, 84*, 795–805.

Dougal, S., Phelps, E. A., & Davachi, L. (2007). The role of medial temporal lobe in item recognition and source recollection of emotional stimuli. *Cognitive, Affective & Behavioral Neuroscience, 7*, 233–242.

Dougherty, D. D., Baer, L., Cosgrove, G. R., Cassem, E. H., Price, B. H., Nierenberg, A. A., Jenike, M. A., & Rauch, S. L. (2002). Prospective long-term follow-up of 44 patients who received cingulotomy for treatment-refractory obsessive-compulsive disorder. *American Journal of Psychiatry, 159*(2), 269–275.

Doyle, A., & Pollack, M. H. (2004). Long-term management of panic disorder. *Journal of Clinical Psychiatry. 65*(Suppl5), 24–28.

Driscoll, A. K., Russell, S. T., & Crockett, L. J. (2008). Parenting styles and youth wellbeing across immigrant generations. *Journal of Family Issues, 29*, 185–209.

Dryer, D. C., & Horowitz, L. M. (1997). When do opposites attract? Interpersonal complementarity versus similarity. *Journal of Personality and Social Psychology, 72*, 592–603.

Duckworth, K., & Borus, J. F. (1999). Population-based psychiatry in the public sector and managed care. In A. M. Nicholi (Ed.), *The Harvard guide to psychiatry*. Cambridge, MA: Harvard University Press.

Dufresne, T. (2007). *Against Freud: Critics talk back*. Palo Alto, CA: Stanford University Press.

Duncan, G. J., & Magnuson, K.A. (2005). Can family socioeconomical resources account for racial and ethnic test score gaps? *The Future of Children, 15*, 35–54.

Duncan, T. B. (2007). Adult attachment and value orientation in marriage. *Dissertation Abstracts International: Section B: The Sciences and Engineering, 68*, 3447.

Dunham, Y. C. (2007). Assessing the automaticity of intergroup bias. *Dissertation Abstracts International: Section B: The Sciences and Engineering, 68*(6-B), 4153.

Durham, M. D., & Dane, F. C. (1999). Juror knowledge of eyewitness behavior: Evidence for the necessity of expert testimony. *Journal of Social Behavior & Personality, 14*, 299–308.

Dutton, D. G., & Aron, A. P. (1974). Some evidence for heightened sexual attraction under conditions of high anxiety. *Journal of Personality and Social Psychology, 30*, 510–517.

Eaker, E. D., Sullivan, L. M., Kelly-Hayes, M., D'Agostino, R. B., & Benajmin, E. J. (2007). Marital status, marital strain, and risk of coronary heart disease or total mortality: The Framingham offspring study. *Psychosomatic Medicine, 69*, 509–513.

Ebbinghaus, H. (1913). *Memory: A contribution to experimental psychology* (H. A. Ruger & C. E. Bussenius, Trans.). New York, NY: Teachers College, Columbia University. (Original work published in 1885)

Eddy, K. T., Hennessey, M., & Thompson-Brenner, H. (2007). Eating pathology in East African women: The role of media exposure and globalization. *Journal of Nervous and Mental Disease, 195*, 196–202.

Edwards, B. (1999). *The new drawing on the right side of the brain*. Baltimore: J P Tarcher.

Ehrenreich, B. (2004, July 15). *All together now*. Retrieved from http://select.nytimes.com/gst/abstract.html?res=F00E16FA3C5E0C768DDDAE0894DC404482

Eisen, S. A., Chantarujikapong, S., Xian, H., Lyons, M. J., Toomey, R., True, W. R., Scherrer, J. F., Goldberg, J., & Tsuang, M. T. (2002). Does marijuana use have residual adverse effects on self-reported health measures, sociodemographics and quality of life? A monozygotic co-twin control study in men. *Addiction, 97*(9), 1137–1144.

Eisenberger, R., & Armeli, S. (1997). Can salient reward increase creative performance without reducing intrinsic creative interest? *Journal of Personality and Social Psychology, 72,* 652–663.

Eisenberger, R., & Rhoades, L. (2002). Incremental effects of reward on creativity. *Journal of Personality and Social Psychology, 81*(4), 728–741.

Ekers, D., Richards, D., & Gilbody, S. (2008). A meta-analysis of randomized trials of behavioural treatment of depression. *Psychological Medicine, 38,* 611–623.

Ekman, P. (1993). Facial expression and emotion. *American Psychologist, 48,* 384–392.

Ekman, P. (2004). *Emotions revealed: Recognizing faces and feelings to improve communication and emotional life.* Thousand Oaks, CA: Owl Books.

Ekman, P., & Keltner, D. (1997). Universal facial expressions of emotion: An old controversy and new findings. In U. C. Segerstrale & P. Molnar (Eds.), *Nonverbal communication: Where nature meets culture.* Mahwah, NJ: Erlbaum.

Elder, G. (1998). The life course as developmental theory. *Current Directions in Psychological Science, 69,* 1–12.

Elkin, A., Kalidindi, S., & McGuffin, P. (2004). Have schizophrenia genes been found? *Current Opinion in Psychiatry, 17*(2), 107–113.

Elkind, D. (1967). Egocentrism in adolescence. *Child Development, 38,* 1025–1034.

Elkind, D. (2007). *The hurried child: Growing up too fast, too soon* (25th anniversary ed.). Cambridge, MA: De Capo Press.

Ellis, A. (1961). *A guide to rational living.* Englewood Cliffs, NJ: Prentice-Hall.

Ellis, A. (1996). *Better, deeper, and more enduring brief therapy.* New York, NY: Institute for Rational Emotive Therapy.

Ellis, A. (1997). Using rational emotive behavior therapy techniques to cope with disability. *Professional Psychology: Research and Practice, 28,* 17–22.

Ellis, A. (2003a). Early theories and practices of rational emotive behavior therapy and how they have been augmented and revised during the last three decades. *Journal of Rational-Emotive & Cognitive Behavior Therapy, 21*(3–4), 219–243.

Ellis, A. (2003b). Similarities and differences between rational emotive behavior therapy and cognitive therapy. *Journal of Cognitive Psychotherapy, 17*(3), 225–240.

Ellis, A. (2004). Why rational emotive behavior therapy is the most comprehensive and effective form of behavior therapy. *Journal of Rational Emotive & Cognitive Behavior Therapy, 22*(2), 85–92.

Ellis, L., Ficek, C., Burke, D., & Das, S. (2008). Eye color, hair color, blood type, and the rhesus factor: Exploring possible genetic links to sexual orientation. *Archives of Sexual Behavior, 37,* 145–149.

Ellman, L. M., & Cannon, T. D. (2008). Environmental pre- and perinatal influences in etiology. In K. T. Mueser & D. V. Jeste (Eds.), *Clinical handbook of schizophrenia* (pp. 65–73). New York, NY: Guilford.

Endler, N. (1982). *Holiday of darkness: A psychologist's personal journey out of depression.* Toronto, ON: Wiley.

Epley, N. (2008, January 31). Rebate psychology. *The New York Times.* Retrieved from http://select.nytimes.com/mem/tnt.html?tntget=2008/01/31/opinion/31epley.html

Erikson, E. (1950). *Childhood and society.* New York, NY: Norton.

Erlacher, D., & Schredl, M. (2004). Dreams reflecting waking sport activities: A comparison of sport and psychology students. *International Journal of Sport Psychology, 35*(4), 301–308.

Ertekin-Taner, N. (2007). Genetics of Alzheimer's disease: A centennial review. *Neurologic Clinics, 25,* 611–667.

Esses, V. M., Dovidio, J. F., Jackson, L. M., & Armstrong, T. L. (2001). The immigration dilemma: The role of perceived group competition, ethnic prejudice, and national identity. *Journal of Social Issues, 57*(3), 389–412.

Evans, J. S. B. T. (2003). In two minds: Dual-process accounts of reasoning. *Trends in Cognitive Sciences, 7*(10), 454–459.

Evans, M. A. (2001). Shyness in the classroom and at home. In W. R. Crozier & L. E. Alden (Eds.), *International Handbook of Social Anxiety* (pp. 159–183). New York, NY: Wiley.

Evans, S., Ferrando, S., Findler, M., Stowell, C., Smart, C., & Haglin, D. (2008). Mindfulness-based cognitive therapy for generalized anxiety disorder. *Journal of Anxiety Disorders, 22,* 716–721.

Eysenck, H. J. (1967). *The biological basis of personality.* Springfield, IL: Charles C Thomas.

Eysenck, H. J. (1982). *Personality, genetics, and behavior: Selected papers.* New York, NY: Prager.

Eysenck, H. J. (1990). Biological dimensions of personality. In L. A. Pervin (Ed.), *Handbook of personality: Theory and research.* New York, NY: Guilford Press.

Faddiman, A. (1997). *The spirit catches you and you fall down.* New York, NY: Straus & Giroux.

Faigman, D. L., Kaye, D., Saks, M. J., & Sanders, J. (1997). *Modern scientific evidence: The law and science of expert testimony.* St. Paul, MN: West.

Fairburn, C. G., Cooper, Z., Shafran, R., & Wilson, G. T. (2008). Eating disorders: A transdiagnostic protocol. In D. H. Barlow (Ed.), *Clinical handbook of psychological disorders: A step-by-step treatment manual* (4th ed., pp. 578–614). New York, NY: Guilford Press.

Fang, X., & Corso, P. S. (2007). Child maltreatment, youth violence, and intimate partner violence: Developmental relationships. *American Journal of Preventive Medicine, 33,* 281–290.

Fantz, R. L. (1956). A method for studying early visual development. *Perceptual and Motor Skills, 6,* 13–15.

Fantz, R. L. (1963). Pattern vision in newborn infants. *Science, 140,* 296–297.

Faraone, S. V. (2008). Statistical and molecular genetic approaches to developmental psychopathology: The pathway forward. In J. J. Hudziak (Ed.), *Developmental psychopathology and wellness: Genetic and environmental influences* (pp. 245–265). Arlington, VA: American Psychiatric Publishing.

Fassler, O., Lynn, S. J., & Knox, J. (2008). Is hypnotic suggestibility a stable trait? *Consciousness and Cognition: An International Journal, 17,* 240–253.

Fehr, C., Yakushev, I., Hohmann, N., Buchholz, H-G., Landvogt, C., Deckers, H., Eberhardt, A., Kläger, M., Smolka, M. N., Scheurich, A., Dielentheis, T., Schmidt, L. G., Rösch, F., Bartehstein, P., Gründer, G., & Schreckenberger, M. (2008). Association of low striatal dopamine D-sub-2 receptor availability with nicotine dependence similar to that seen with other drugs of abuse. *American Journal of Psychiatry, 165,* 507–514.

Fein, S. & Spencer, S. J. (1997). Prejudice as self image maintenance: Affirming the self through derogating others. *Journal of Personality and Social Psychology, 73*(1), 31–44.

Feng, S. Q., Zhou, X. F., Rush, R. A., & Ferguson, I. A. (2008). Graft of pre-injured sural nerve promotes regeneration of corticospinal tract and functional recovery in rats with chronic spinal cord injury. *Brain Research, 1209,* 40–48.

Fernández, J. R., Casazza, K., Divers, J., & López-Alarcón, M. (2008). Disruptions in energy balance: Does nature overcome nurture? *Physiology & Behavior, 94,* 105–112.

Fernández, M. I., Bowen, G. S., Varga, L. M., Collazo, J. B., Hernandez, N., Perrino, T., & Rehbein, A.

(2005). High rates of club drug use and risky sexual practices among Hispanic men who have sex with men in Miami, Florida. *Substance Use & Misuse, 40*(9–10), 1347–1362.

Ferrari, P. F., Rozzi, S., & Fogassi, L. (2005). Mirror neurons responding to observation of actions made with tools in monkey ventral premotor cortex. *Journal of Cognitive Neuroscience, 17*, 212–226.

Ferretti, P., Copp, A., Tickle, C., & Moore, G. (Eds.) (2006). *Embryos, genes, and birth defects* (2nd ed.). Hoboken, NJ: Wiley.

Festinger, L. A. (1957). *A theory of cognitive dissonance.* Palo Alto, CA: Stanford University Press.

Festinger, L. A., & Carlsmith, L. M. (1959). Cognitive consequences of forced compliance. *Journal of Abnormal and Social Psychology, 58*, 203–210.

Field, A. P. (2006). Is conditioning a useful framework for understanding the development and treatment of phobias? *Clinical Psychology Review, 26*, 857–875.

Field, K. M., Woodson, R., Greenberg, R., & Cohen, D. (1982). Discrimination and imitation of facial expressions by neonates. *Science, 218*, 179–181.

Field, T., & Hernandez-Reif, M. (2001). Sleep problems in infants decrease following massage therapy. *Early Child Development & Care, 168*, 95–104.

Fields, R. (2007). *Drugs in perspective* (6th ed.). New York, NY: McGraw-Hill.

Fields, W. M., Segerdahl, P., & Savage-Rumbaugh, S. (2007). The material practices of ape language research. In J. Valsiner & A. Rosa (Eds.), *The Cambridge handbook of sociocultural psychology* (pp. 164–186). New York, NY: Cambridge University Press.

Fink, B., & Penton-Voak, I. (2002). Evolutionary psychology of facial attractiveness. *Current Directions in Psychological Science, 11*(5), 154–158.

Fink, B., Manning, J. T., Neave, N., & Grammer, K. (2004). Second to fourth digit ratio and facial asymmetry. *Evolution and Human Behavior, 25*(2), 125–132.

Fink, M. (1999). *Electroshock: Restoring the mind.* London: Oxford University Press.

First, M., & Tasman, A. (2004). *DSM-IV-TR mental disorders: Diagnosis, etiology, and treatment.* Hoboken, NJ: Wiley.

Fisher, J. O. & Kral, T. V. E. (2008). Super-size me: Portion size effects on young children's eating. *Physiology & Behavior, 94*, 39–47.

Fisk, J. E., Bury, A. S., & Holden, R. (2006). Reasoning about complex probabilistic concepts in childhood. *Scandinavian Journal of Psychology, 47*, 497–504.

Fiske, S. T. (1998). Stereotyping, prejudice, and discrimination. In D. T. Gilbert, S. T. Fiske, and G. Lindzey (Eds.), *The handbook of social psychology* (4th ed., Vol. 2, pp. 357–411). New York, NY: Oxford University Press.

Flavell, J. H., Miller, P. H., & Miller, S. A. (2002). *Cognitive development* (4th ed.). Upper Saddle River, NJ: Prentice-Hall.

Fleischmann, B. K., & Welz, A. (2008). Cardiovascular regeneration and stem cell therapy. *Journal of the American Medical Association, 299*(6), 700–701.

Fletcher, G. J. O., & Simpson, J. A. (2000). Ideal standards in close relationships: Their structure and functions. *Current Directions in Psychological Science, 9*, 102–105.

Flett, G. (2007). *Personality theory and research.* Toronto, ON: Wiley.

Flynn, J. R. (1987). Massive IQ gains in 14 nations: What IQ tests really measure. *Psychological Bulletin, 101*, 171–191.

Flynn, J. R. (2006). The history of the American mind in the 20th century: A scenario to explain gains over time and a case for the irrelevance of g. In P. C. Kyllonen, R. D. Roberts, & L. Stankov (Eds.), *Extending intelligence.* Mahwah, NJ: Erlbaum.

Flynn, J. R. (2007). *What is intelligence? Beyond the Flynn Effect.* New York, NY: Cambridge University Press.

Foer, J. (2008). The unspeakable odyssey of the motionless boy. *Esquire,* October 2. Retrieved from http://www.esquire.com/features/unspeakable-odyssey-motionless-boy-1008?click=main_sr

Fogarty, A., Rawstorne, P., Prestage, G., Crawford, J., Grierson, J., & Kippax, S. (2007). Marijuana as therapy for people living with HIV/AIDS: Social and health aspects. *AIDS Care, 19*, 295–301.

Fogassi, L., Ferrari, P. F., Gesierich, B., Rozzi, S., Chersi, F., & Rizzolatti, G. (2005). Parietal lobe: From action understanding to intention understanding. *Science, 308*, 662–667.

Fok, H. K., Hui, C. M., Bond, M. H., Matsumoto, D., & Yoo, S. H. (2008). Integrating personality, context, relationship, and emotion type into a model of display rules. *Journal of Research in Personality, 42*, 133–150.

Folk, C. L., & Remington, R. W. (1998). Selectivity in distraction by irrelevant featural singletons: Evidence for two forms of attentional capture. *Journal of Experimental Psychology: Human Perception and Performance, 24*, 1–12.

Ford, T. E., Ferguson, M. A., Brooks, J. L., & Hagadone, K. M. (2004). Coping sense of humor reduces effects of stereotype threat on women's math performance. *Personality & Social Psychology Bulletin, 30*(5), 643–653.

Frankenburg, W., Dodds, J., Archer, P., Shapiro, H., & Bresnick, B. (1992). The Denver II: A major revision and restandardization of the Denver Developmental Screening Test. *Pediatrics, 89*, 91–97.

Fredricks, J. A., & Eccles, J. S. (2005). Family socialization, gender, and sport motivation and involvement. *Journal of Sport & Exercise Psychology, 27*(1), 3–31.

Frick, W. B. (2000). Remembering Maslow: Reflections on a 1968 interview. *Journal of Humanistic Psychology, 40*(2), 128–147.

Fried, P., Watkinson, B., & Gray, R. (2003). Differential effects on cognitive functioning in 13- to 16-year-olds prenatally exposed to cigarettes and marijuana. *Neurotoxicology and Teratology, 25*, 427–436.

Friedman, H., & Schustack, M. (2006). *Personality: Classic theories and modern research* (3rd ed.). Boston, MA: Allyn & Bacon/Longman.

Fryer, S. L., Crocker, N. A., & Mattson, S. N. (2008). Exposure to teratogenic agents as a risk factor for psychopathology. In T. P. Beauchaine & S. P. Hinshaw (Eds.), *Child and adolescent psychopathology* (pp. 180–207). Hoboken, NJ: Wiley.

Funder, D. C. (2000). Personality. *Annual Review of Psychology, 52*, 197–221.

Funder, D. C. (2001). The really, really fundamental attribution error. *Psychological Inquiry, 12*(1), 21–23.

Funk, J. B., Baldacci, H. B., Pasold, T., & Baumgardner, J. (2004). Violence exposure in real-life, video games, television, movies, and the internet: Is there desensitization? *Journal of Adolescence, 27*, 23–39.

Furman, E. (1990, November). Plant a potato, learn about life (and death). *Young Children, 46*(1), 15–20.

Gabbard, G. O. (2006). Mente, cervello e disturbi di personalita [Mind, brain, and personality disorders]. *Psicoterapia e scienze umane, 40*, 9–26.

Gabry, K. E., Chrousos, G. P., Rice, K. C., Mostafa, R. M., Sternberg, E., Negrao, A. B., Webster, E. L., McCann, S. M., & Gold, P. W. (2002). Marked suppression of gastric ulcerogenesis and intestinal responses to stress by a novel class of drugs. *Molecular Psychiatry, 7*(5), 474–483.

Gacono, C. B., Evans, F. B., & Viglione, D. J. (2008). Essential issues in the forensic use of the Rorschach. In C. B. Gacono (Ed.), F. B. Evans (Ed.), N. Kaser-Boyd (Col.), & L. A. Gacono (Col.), *The handbook of forensic Rorschach assessment* (pp. 3–20). *The LEA series in personality and clinical psychology.* New York, NY: Routledge/Taylor & Francis Group.

Galderisi, S., Quarantelli, M., Volpe, U., Mucci, A., Cassano, G. B., Invernizzi, G., Rossi, A., Vita, A., Pini, S., Cassano, P., Daneluzzo, E., De Peri, L., Stratta, P., Brunetti, A., & Maj, M. (2008). Patterns of structural MRI abnormalities in deficit and nondeficit schizophrenia. *Schizophrenia Bulletin, 34,* 393–401.

Galinsky, A. D., & Ku, G. (2004). The effects of perspective-taking on prejudice: The moderating role of self-evaluation. *Personality & Social Psychology Bulletin, 30*(5), 594–604.

Galinsky, A. D., & Moskowitz, G. B. (2000). Perspective-taking: Decreasing stereotype expression, stereotype accessibility, and in-group favoritism. *Journal of Personality and Social Psychology, 78*(4), 708–724.

Garb, H. N., Wood, J. M., Lilienfeld, S. O., & Nezworski, M. T. (2005). Roots of the Rorschach controversy. *Clinical Psychology Review, 25,* 97–118.

Garcia, G. M., & Stafford, M. E. (2000). Prediction of reading by Ga and Gc specific cognitive abilities for low-SES White and Hispanic English-speaking children. *Psychology in the Schools, 37*(3), 227–235.

Garcia, J. (2003). Psychology is not an enclave. In R. Sternberg (Ed.), *Psychologists defying the crowd: Stories of those who battled the establishment and won* (pp. 67–77). Washington, DC: American Psychological Association.

Garcia, J., & Koelling, R. S. (1966). Relation of cue to consequence in avoidance learning. *Psychonomic Science, 4,* 123–124.

Gardiner, H., & Kosmitzki, G. (2005). *Lives across cultures: Cross-cultural human development* (3rd ed.). Boston: Allyn & Bacon/Longman.

Gardner, H. (1983). *Frames of mind.* New York: Basic Books.

Gardner, H. (1999, February). Who owns intelligence? *Atlantic Monthly, 283*(2), 67–76.

Gardner, H. (2008). Who owns intelligence? In M. H. Immordino-Yang (Ed.), *Jossey-Bass Education Team. The Jossey-Bass reader on the brain and learning* (pp. 120–132). San Francisco, CA: Jossey-Bass.

Gardner, R. A., & Gardner, B. T. (1969). Teaching sign language to a chimpanzee. *Science, 165,* 664–672.

Garno, J. L., Gunawardane, N., & Goldberg, J. F. (2008). Predictors of trait aggression in bipolar disorder. *Bipolar Disorders, 10,* 285–292.

Garrick, J. (2006). The humor of trauma survivors: Its application in a therapeutic milieu. *Journal of Aggression, Maltreatment & Trauma, 12,* 169–182.

Garry, M., & Gerrie, M. P. (2005). When photographs create false memories. *Current Directions in Psychological Science, 14,* 321–324.

Gaser, C., Nenadic, I., Buchsbaum, B. R., Hazeltt, E. A., & Buchsbaum, M. S. (2004). Ventricular enlargement in schizophrenia related to volume reduction of the thalamus, striatum, and superior temporal cortex. *American Journal of Psychiatry, 161*(1), 154–156.

Gasser, S., & Raulet, D. H. (2006). Activation and self-tolerance of natural killer cells. *Immunology Review, 214,* 130–142.

Gaw, A. C. (2001). *Concise guide to cross-cultural psychiatry. Concise guides.* Washington, DC: American Psychiatric Association.

Gay, P. (2000). *Freud for historians.* Boston, MA: Replica Books.

Gebauer, H., Krempl, R., & Fleisch, E. (2008). Exploring the effect of cognitive biases on customer support services. *Creativity and Innovation Management, 17,* 58–70.

Gelder, B. D., Meeren, H. K., Righart, R., Stock, J. V., van de Riet, W. A., & Tamietto, M. (2006). Beyond the face: Exploring rapid influences of context on face processing. *Progress in Brain Research, 155,* 37–48.

Genesee, F. (1987). *Learning through two languages: Studies of immersion and bilingual education.* Cambridge, MA: Newbury House.

Genesee, F., & Gandara, P. (1999). Bilingual education programs: A cross-national perspective. *Journal of Social Issues, 55,* 665–685.

Gentile, D. A., Lynch, P. J., Linder, J. R., & Walsh, D. A. (2004). The effects of violent video game habits on adolescent hostility, aggressive behaviors, and school performance. *Journal of Adolescence, 27,* 5–22.

Gerber, A. J., Posner, J., Gorman, D., Colibazzi, T., Yu, S., Wang, Z., Kangarlu, A., Zhu, H., Russell, J., & Peterson, B. S. (2008). An affective circumplex model of neural systems subserving valence, arousal, and cognitive overlay during the appraisal of emotional faces. *Neuropsychologia, 46,* 2129–2139.

Gershon, E. S., & Rieder, R. O. (1993). Major disorders of mind and brain. *Mind and brain: Readings from Scientific American Magazine* (pp. 91–100). New York, NY: Freeman.

Giacobbi, P. Jr., Foore, B., & Weinberg, R. S. (2004). Broken clubs and expletives: The sources of stress and coping responses of skilled and moderately skilled golfers. *Journal of Applied Sport Psychology, 16*(2), 166–182.

Giancola, P. R., & Parrott, D. J. (2008). Further evidence for the validity of the Taylor aggression paradigm. *Aggressive Behavior, 34,* 214–229.

Gibbs, N. (1995, October 2). The EQ factor. *Time, 146*(14), 60–68.

Gibson, E. J., & Walk, R. D. (1960). The visual cliff. *Scientific American, 202*(2), 67–71.

Giedd, J. N. (2008). The teen brain: Insights from neuroimaging. *Journal of Adolescent Health, 42,* 335–343.

Giles, J. W., & Heyman, G. D. (2005). Young children's beliefs about the relationship between gender and aggressive behavior. *Child Development, 76*(1), 107–121.

Gilligan, C. (1977). In a different voice: Women's conception of morality. *Harvard Educational Review, 47*(4), 481–517.

Gilligan, C. (1990). Teaching Shakespeare's sister. In C. Gilligan, N. Lyons, & T. Hanmer (Eds.), *Mapping the moral domain* (pp. 73–86). Cambridge, MA: Harvard University Press.

Gilligan, C. (1993). Adolescent development reconsidered. In A. Garrod (Ed.), *Approaches to moral development: New research and emerging themes.* New York, NY: Teachers College Press.

Gilmour, D. R., & Walkey, F. H. (1981). Identifying violent offenders using a video measure of interpersonal distance. *Journal of Consulting and Clinical Psychology, 49,* 287–291.

Gini, M., Oppenheim, D., & Sagi-Schwartz, A. (2007). Negotiation styles in mother-child narrative co-construction in middle childhood: Associations with early attachment. *International Journal of Behavioral Development, 31,* 149–160.

Girardi, P., Monaco, E., Prestigiacomo, C., Talamo, A., Ruberto, A., & Tatarelli, R. (2007). Personality and psychopathological profiles in individuals exposed to mobbing. *Violence & Victims, 22,* 172–188.

Gitau, R., Modi, N., Gianakoulopoulos, X., Bond, C., Glover, V., & Stevenson, J. (2002). Acute effects of maternal skin-to-skin contact and massage on saliva cortisol in preterm babies. *Journal of Reproductive & Infant Psychology, 20*(2), 83–88.

Giumetti, G. W., & Markey, P. M. (2007). Violent video games and anger as predictors of aggression. *Journal of Research in Personality, 41,* 1234–1243.

Gluck, M. A. (2008). Behavioral and neural correlates of error correction in classical conditioning and human category learning. In M. A. Gluck, J. R. Anderson, & S. M. Kosslyn (Eds.), *Memory and mind: A festschrift for Gordon H. Bower* (pp. 281–305). Mahwah, NJ: Lawrence Erlbaum.

Gobbo, C., & Raccanello, D. (2007). How children narrate happy and sad events: Does affective state count? *Applied Cognitive Psychology, 21,* 1173–1190.

Godden, D. R., & Baddeley, A. D. (1975). Context-dependent memory in two natural environments: On land and underwater. *British Journal of Psychology, 66,* 325–331.

Godfrey, R. (2005). *Under the bridge: The true story of the murder of Reena Virk*. Toronto, ON: Harper-Collins.

Goforth, H. W., & Holsinger, T. (2007). Response to effect of the first ECT in a series by C. Kellner, MD. *Journal of ECT, 23*, 209.

Gogtay, N., Sporn, A., Clasen, L. S., Nugent, T. F. III, Greenstein, D., Nicolson, R., Giedd, J. N., Lenane, M., Gochman, P., Evans, A., & Rapoport, J. L. (2004). Comparison of progressive cortical gray matter loss in childhood-onset schizophrenia with that in childhood-onset atypical psychoses. *Archives of General Psychiatry, 61*(1), 17–22.

Golden, W. L. (2006). Hypnotherapy for anxiety, phobias and psychophysiological disorders. In R. A. Chapman (Ed.), *The clinical use of hypnosis in cognitive behavior therapy: A practitioner's casebook* (pp. 101–137). New York, NY: Springer.

Goldstein, E. G. (2008). *Cognitive psychology: Connecting mind, research, and everyday experience* (2nd ed.). Belmont, CA: Cengage.

Goleman, D. (1980, February). 1,528 little geniuses and how they grew. *Psychology Today, 13*(9), 28–53.

Goleman, D. (1995). *Emotional intelligence: Why it can matter more than IQ*. New York, NY: Bantam.

Goleman, D. (2000). *Working with emotional intelligence*. New York, NY: Bantam Doubleday.

Gómez, Á., & Huici, C. (2008). Vicarious intergroup contact and role of authorities in prejudice reduction. *The Spanish Journal of Psychology, 11*, 103–114.

Goodman, G. S., Ghetti, S., Quas, J. A., Edelstein, R. S., Alexander, K. W., Redlich, A. D., Cordon, I. M., & Jones, D. P. H. (2003). A prospective study of memory for child sexual abuse: New findings relevant to the repressed memory controversy. *Psychological Science, 14*(2), 113–118.

Goodwin, C. J. (2009). *A history of modern psychology* (3rd ed.). Hoboken, NJ: Wiley.

Gooren, L. (2006). The biology of human psychosexual differentiation. *Hormones and Behavior, 50*, 589–601.

Gotlieb, I. H., & Abramson, L. Y. (1999). Attributional theories of emotion. In T. Dalgleish & M. Power (Eds.), *Handbook of cognition and emotion*. New York, NY: Wiley.

Gottesman, I. I. (1991). *Schizophrenia genesis: The origins of madness*. New York, NY: Freeman.

Gottfredson, G. D., & Duffy, R. D. (2008). Using a theory of vocational personalities and work environments to explore subjective well-being. *Journal of Career Assessment, 16*, 44–59.

Gottman, J. M., & Levenson, R. W. (2002). A two-factor model for predicting when a couple will divorce: Exploratory analyses using 14-year longitudinal data. *Family Process, 41*(1), 83–96.

Gottman, J. M., & Notarius, C. I. (2000). Decade review: Observing marital interaction. *Journal of Marriage & the Family, 62*(4) 927–947.

Gould, R. L. (1975, August). Adult life stages: Growth toward self-tolerance. *Psychology Today*, pp. 74–78.

Gracely, R. H., Farrell, M. J., & Grant, M. A. (2002). Temperature and pain perception. In H. Pashler & S. Yantis (Eds.), *Steven's handbook of experimental psychology: Vol. 1. Sensation and perception* (3rd ed.). Hoboken, NJ: Wiley.

Graham, J. R. (1991). Comments on Duckworth's review of the Minnesota Multiphasic Personality Inventory-2. *Journal of Counseling and Development, 69*, 570–571.

Graziano, M. (2006). The organization of behavioral repertoire in motor cortex. *Annual Review of Neuroscience, 29*, 105–134.

Green, A. I., Tohen, M. F., Hamer, R. M., Strakowski, S. M., Lieberman, J. A., Glick, I., Clark, W. S., & HGDH Research Group. (2004). First episode schizophrenia-related psychosis and substance use disorders: Acute response to olanzapine and haloperidol. *Schizophrenia Research, 66*(2–3), 125–135.

Greenberg, J. (2002). Who stole the money, and when? Individual and situational determinants of employee theft. *Organizational Behavior and Human Decision Processes, 89*(1), 985–1003.

Greenberg, L., & Johnson, S. (1988). *Emotionally focused therapy for couples*. New York, NY: Guilford Press.

Greene, E., & Ellis, L. (2008). *Decision making in criminal justice*. In D. Carson, R. Milne, F. Pakes, K. Shalev, & A. Shawyer (Eds.), *Applying psychology to criminal justice* (pp. 183–200). New York, NY: Wiley.

Greene, K., Kremar, M., Walters, L. H., Rubin, D. L., Hale, J., & Hale, L. (2000). Targeting adolescent risk-taking behaviors: The contributions of egocentrism and sensation seeking. *Journal of Adolescence, 23*, 439–461.

Greenwald, A. G., Poehlman, T. A., Uhlmann, E. L., & Banaji, M. R. (2008). Understanding and using the Implicit Association Test III: Meta-analysis of predictive validity. *Journal of Personality and Social Psychology, 97*(1), 17–41.

Gregory, R. J. (2007). *Psychological testing: History, principles, and applications* (5th ed.). Needham Heights, MA: Allyn and Bacon.

Gresack, J. E., Kerr, K. M., & Frick, K. M. (2007). Life-long environmental enrichment differentially affects the mnemonic response to estrogen in young, middle-aged, and aged female mice. *Neurobiology of Learning & Memory, 88*, 393–408.

Grondin, S., Ouellet, B., & Roussel, M. (2004). Benefits and limits of explicit counting for discriminating temporal intervals. *Canadian Journal of Experimental Psychology, 58*(1), 1–12.

Grossmann, K., Grossmann, K. E., Fremmer-Bombik, E., Kindler, H., Scheuerer-Englisch, H., & Zimmermann, P. (2002). The uniqueness of the child-father attachment relationship: Fathers' sensitive and challenging play as a pivotal variable in a 16-year longitudinal study. *Social Development, 11*(3), 307–331.

Grove, W. M., Barden, R. C, Garb, H. N., & Lilienfeld, S. O. (2002). Failure of Rorschach-Comprehensive-System-based testimony to be admissible under the Daubert-Joiner-Kumho standard. *Psychology, Public Policy, & Law, 8*(2), 216–234.

Grover, K. E., Carpenter, L. L., Price, L. H., Gagne, G. G., Mello, A. F., Mello, M. F., & Tyra, A. R. (2007). The relationship between childhood abuse and adult personality disorder symptoms. *Journal of Personality Disorders, 21*, 442–447.

Guidelines for Ethical Conduct in the Care and Use of Animals. (2008). Retrieved from http://www.apa.org/science/anguide.html

Guilford, J. P. (1967). *The nature of human intelligence*. New York, NY: McGraw-Hill.

Guirguis-Younger, M., Runnels, V., & Aubry, T. (2004). *Conceptual models for end-of-life care in persons who are homeless*. A Community Forum on Homelessness: Linking Ottawa Research with Action and Policy. Ottawa, ON: The Alliance to End Homelessness.

Gunzerath, L., Faden, V., Zakhari, S., & Warren, K. (2004). National Institute on Alcohol Abuse and Alcoholism report on moderate drinking. *Alcoholism: Clinical & Experimental Research, 28*(6), 829–847.

Gustavson, C. R., & Garcia, J. (1974, August). Pulling a gag on the wily coyote. *Psychology Today*, pp. 68–72.

Haberstick, B. C., Schmitz, S., Young, S. E., & Hewitt, J. K. (2006). Genes and developmental stability of aggressive behavior problems at home and school in a community sample of twins aged 7–12. *Behavior Genetics, 36*, 809–819.

Haddock, G., & Shaw, J. J. (2008). Understanding and working with aggression, violence, and psychosis. In K. T. Mueser & D. V. Jeste (Eds.), *Clinical handbook of schizophrenia* (pp. 398–410). New York, NY: Guilford Press.

Haith, M. M., & Benson, J. B. (1998). Infant cognition. In W. Damon & R. M. Lerner (Eds.), *Handbook of child psychology* (Vol. 1). New York, NY: Wiley.

Halbreich, U., & Kahn, L. S. (2007). Atypical depression, somatic depression and anxious depression in women: Are they gender preferred phenotypes? *Journal of Affective Disorders, 102,* 245–258.

Haley, A. P. (2005). Effects of orally administered glucose on hippocampal metabolites and cognition in Alzheimer's disease. *Dissertation Abstracts International: Section B: The Sciences and Engineering, 66*(3-B), 1719.

Halgin, R. P., & Whitbourne, S. K. (2008). *Abnormal psychology: Clinical perspectives on psychological disorders.* New York, NY: McGraw-Hill.

Hall, K. (2007). Sexual dysfunction and childhood sexual abuse: Gender differences and treatment implications. In S. R. Leiblum (Ed.), *Principles and practice of sex therapy* (4th ed., pp. 350–378). New York, NY: Guilford.

Hall, M.-H., Rijsdijk, F., Picchioni, M., Schulze, K., Ettinger, U., Toulopoulou, T., Bramon, E., Murray, R. M., & Sham, P. (2007). Substantial shared genetic influences on schizophrenia and event-related potentials. *American Journal of Psychiatry, 164,* 804–812.

Haller, S., Radue, E. W., Erb, M., Grodd, W., & Kircher, T. (2005). Overt sentence production in event-related fMRI. *Neuropsychologia, 43*(5), 807–814.

Halpern, D. F. (1997). Sex differences in intelligence: Implications for education. *American Psychologist, 52,* 1091–1102.

Halpern, D. F. (1998). Teaching critical thinking for transfer across domains. *American Psychologist, 53,* 449–455.

Halpern, D. F. (2000). *Sex differences in cognitive abilities.* Hillsdale, NJ: Erlbaum.

Hamilton, J. P., & Gotlib, I. H. (2008). Neural substrates of increased memory sensitivity for negative stimuli in major depression. *Biological Psychiatry, 63,* 1155–1162.

Hamm, J. P., Johnson, B. W., & Corballis, M. C. (2004). One good turn deserves another: An event-related brain potential study of rotated mirror-normal letter discriminations. *Neuropsychologia, 42*(6), 810–820.

Hammack, P. L. (2003). The question of cognitive therapy in a postmodern world. *Ethical Human Sciences & Services, 5*(3), 209–224.

Hammen, C. (2005). Stress and depression. *Annual Review of Clinical Psychology, 1,* 293–319.

Hammond, D. C. (2005). Neurofeedback with anxiety and affective disorders. *Child & Adolescent Psychiatric Clinics of North America, 14*(1), 105–123.

Hammond, D. C. (2007). What is neurofeedback? *Journal of Neurotherapy, 10,* 25–36.

Hampton, T. (2006). Stem cells probed as diabetes treatment. *Journal of American Medical Association, 296,* 2785–2786.

Hampton, T. (2007). Stem cells ease Parkinson symptoms in monkeys. *Journal of American Medical Association, 298,* 165.

Haney, C., Banks, C., & Zimbardo, P. (1978). Interpersonal dynamics in a simulated prison. *International Journal of Criminology and Penology, 1,* 69–97.

Hanley, S. J., & Abell, S. C. (2002). Maslow and relatedness: Creating an interpersonal model of self-actualization. *Journal of Humanistic Psychology, 42*(4), 37–56.

Hanna, S. M., & Brown, J. H. (1999). *The practice of family therapy: Key elements across models* (2nd ed.). Belmont, CA: Brooks/Cole.

Hansell, J. H., & Damour, L. K. (2008). *Abnormal psychology* (2nd ed.). Hoboken, NJ: Wiley.

Hardcastle, S., Taylor, A., Bailey, M., & Castle, R. (2008). A randomized controlled trial on the effectiveness of a primary health care based counseling intervention on physical activity, diet and CHD risk. *Patient Education and Counseling, 70,* 31–39.

Harlow, H. F., & Harlow, M. K. (1966). Learning to love. *American Scientist, 54,* 244–272.

Harlow, H. F., & Zimmerman, R. R. (1959). Affectional responses in the infant monkey. *Science, 130,* 421–432.

Harlow, H. F., Harlow, M. K., & Meyer, D. R. (1950). Learning motivated by a manipulation drive. *Journal of Experimental Psychology, 40,* 228–234.

Harper, F. D., Harper, J. A., & Stills, A. B. (2003). Counseling children in crisis based on Maslow's hierarchy of basic needs. *International Journal for the Advancement of Counseling, 25*(1), 10–25.

Harrison, E. (2005). *How meditation heals: Scientific evidence and practical applications* (2nd ed.). Berkeley, CA: Ulysses Press.

Hart, J. Jr., & Kraut, M. A. (2007). Neural hybrid model of semantic object memory (version 1.1). In J. Hart Jr. & M. A. Kraut (Eds.), *Neural basis of semantic memory* (pp. 331–359). New York, NY: Cambridge University Press.

Hartenbaum, N., Collop, N., Rosen, I. M., Phillips, B., George, C. F. P., Rowley, J. A., Freedman, N., Weaver, T. E., Gurubhagavatula, I., Strohl, K., Leaman, H. M., Moffitt, G. L., & Rosekind, M. R. (2006). Sleep apnea and commercial motor vehicle operators: Statement from the joint task force of the American College of Chest Physicians, American College of Occupational and Environmental Medicine, and the National Sleep Foundation. *Journal of Occupational & Environmental Medicine, 48,* S4-S37.

Harth, N. S., Kessler, T., & Leach, C. W. (2008). Advantaged group's emotional reactions to intergroup inequality: The dynamics of pride, guilt, and sympathy. *Personality and Social Psychology Bulletin, 34,* 115–129.

Hartwell, L. (2008). *Genetics* (3rd ed.). New York, NY: McGraw-Hill.

Haslam, N., Loughnan, S., Reynolds, C., & Wilson, S. (2007). Dehumanization: A new perspective. *Social and Personality Psychology Compass, 1,* 409–422.

Hatfield, E., & Rapson, R. L. (1996). *Love and sex: Cross-cultural perspectives.* Needham Heights, MA: Allyn & Bacon.

Hatsukami, D. K. (2008). Nicotine addiction: Past, present and future. *Drug and Alcohol Dependence, 92,* 312–316.

Haugen, R., Ommundsen, Y., & Lund, T. (2004). The concept of expectancy: A central factor in various personality dispositions. *Educational Psychology, 24*(1), 43–55.

Hawkins, D. L., Pepler, D. J., & Craig, W. M. (2001). Naturalistic observations of peer interventions in bullying. *Social Development, 10*(5), 512–527.

Hay, D. F. (1994). Prosocial development. *Journal of Child Psychology and Psychiatry, 35,* 29–71.

Hayflick, L. (1977). The cellular basis for biological aging. In C. E. Finch & L. Hayflick (Eds.), *Handbook of the biology of aging* (pp. 159–186). New York, NY: Van Nostrand Reinhold.

Hayflick, L. (1996). *How and why we age.* New York, NY: Ballantine Books.

Hays, W. S. T. (2003). Human pheromones: Have they been demonstrated? *Behavioral Ecology & Sociobiology, 54*(2), 89–97.

Hazan, C., & Shaver, P. (1987). Romantic love conceptualized as an attachment process. *Journal of Personality and Social Psychology, 52,* 511–524.

Hazan, C., & Shaver, P. R. (1994). Attachment as an organizational framework for research on close relationships. *Psychological Inquiry, 5,* 1–22.

Health Canada. (2008). *Summary of results of the 2006–07 Youth Smoking Survey.* Retrieved from http://www.hc-sc.gc.ca/hc-ps/tobac-tabac/research-recherche/stat/_survey-sondage_2006-2007/result-eng.php

Health Canada. (2003). *Canadian perinatal health report* (Catalogue no. H49-142/2003E). Ottawa: Minister of Public Works and Government Services Canada.

Health Canada. (2006a). *Safe use of energy drinks.* Retrieved from http://www.hc-sc.gc.ca/hl-vs/iyh-vsv/prod/energy-energie-eng.php

Health Canada. (2006b). *Drug and health products: Medical use of marihuana.* Retrieved from http://www.hc-sc.gc.ca/dhp-mps/marihuana/

Health Canada. (2009a). *Healthy living.* Retrieved from http://www.hc-sc.gc.ca/hl-vs/index-eng.php

Health Canada. (2009b). *Drugs and health products: Natural health products.* Retrieved from http://www.hc-sc.gc.ca/dhp-mps/prodnatur/index-eng.php

Healy, A. F., Shea, K. M., Kole, J. A., & Cunningham, T. F. (2008). Position distinctiveness, item familiarity, and presentation frequency affect reconstruction of order in immediate episodic memory. *Journal of Memory and Language, 58,* 746–764.

Hebb, D. O. (1949). *The organization of behaviour: A neuropsychological theory.* New York, NY: Wiley.

Heckhausen, J. (2005). Competence and motivation in adulthood and old age: Making the most of changing capacities and resources. In A. J. Elliot & C. S. Dweck (Eds.), *Handbook of competence and motivation* (pp. 240–256). New York, NY: Guilford.

Hedges, D., & Burchfield, C. (2006). *Mind, brain, and drug: An introduction to psychopharmacology.* Boston, MA: Allyn & Bacon/Longman.

Heffelfinger, A. K., & Newcomer, J. W. (2001). Glucocorticoid effects on memory function over the human life span. *Development & Psychopathology, 13*(3), 491–513.

Heider, F. (1958). *The psychology of interpersonal relations.* New York, NY: Wiley.

Heimann, M., & Meltzoff, A. N. (1996). Deferred imitation in 9- and 14-month-old infants. *British Journal of Developmental Psychology, 14,* 55–64.

Heine, S. J., & Renshaw, K. (2002). Inter-judge agreement, self-enhancement, and liking: Cross-cultural divergences. *Personality & Social Psychology Bulletin, 28*(5), 578–587.

Heller, S. (2005). *Freud A to Z.* Hoboken, NJ: Wiley.

Helms, J. E., & Cook, D. A. (1999). *Using race and culture in counseling and psychotherapy: Theory and process.* Boston, MA: Allyn & Bacon.

Hennessey, B. A., & Amabile, T. M. (1998). Reward, intrinsic motivation, and creativity. *American Psychologist, 53,* 674–675.

Hergovich, A., & Olbrich, A. (2003). The impact of the Northern Ireland conflict on social identity, groupthink and integrative complexity in Great Britain. *Review of Psychology, 10*(2), 95–106.

Heriot, S. A., & Pritchard, M. (2004). Test of time: Reciprocal inhibition as the main basis of psychotherapeutic effects' by Joseph Wolpe (1954) [Book review]. *Clinical Child Psychology and Psychiatry, 9*(2), 297–307.

Herman, C. P., & Polivy, J. (2008). External cues in the control of food intake in humans: The sensory-normative distinction. *Physiology & Behavior, 94,* 722–728.

Herman, L. M., Richards, D. G., & Woltz, J. P. (1984). Comprehension of sentences by bottlenosed dolphins. *Cognition, 16,* 129–139.

Hermans, E. J., Ramsey, N. F., & van Honk, J. (2008). Exogenous testosterone enhances responsiveness to social threat in the neural circuitry of social aggression in humans. *Biological Psychiatry, 63*(3), 263–270.

Herrnstein, R. J., & Murray, C. (1994). *The bell curve: Intelligence and class structure in American life.* New York, NY: Free Press.

Hervé, H., Mitchell, D., Cooper, B. S., Spidel, A., & Hare, R. D. (2004). Psychopathy and unlawful confinement: An examination of perpetrator and event characteristics. *Canadian Journal of Behavioural Science, 36*(2), 137–145.

Heyder, K., Suchan, B., & Daum, I. (2004). Cortico-subcortical contributions to executive control. *Acta Psychologica, 115*(2–3), 271–289.

Higley, E. R. (2008). Nighttime interactions and mother-infant attachment at one year. *Dissertation Abstracts International. Section B: The Sciences and Engineering, 68,* 5575.

Hilgard, E. R. (1978). Hypnosis and consciousness. *Human Nature, 1,* 42–51.

Hilgard, E. R. (1992). Divided consciousness and dissociation. *Consciousness and Cognition, 1,* 16–31.

Hill, E. L. (2004). Evaluating the theory of executive dysfunction in autism. *Developmental Review, 24*(2), 189–233.

Hinton, E. C., Parkinson, J. A., Holland, A. J., Arana, F. S., Roberts, A. C., & Owen, A. M. (2004). Neural contributions to the motivational control of appetite in humans. *European Journal of Neuroscience, 20*(5), 1411–1418.

Hittner, J. B., & Daniels, J. R. (2002). Gender-role orientation, creative accomplishments and cognitive styles. *Journal of Creative Behavior, 36*(1), 62–75.

Hobson, C. J., Kamen, J., Szostek, J., Nethercut, C. M., Tiedmann, J. W., & Wojnarowicz, S. (1998). Stressful life events: A revision and update of the Social Readjustment Rating Scale. *International Journal of Stress Management, 5*(1), 1–23.

Hobson, J. A. (1988). *The dreaming brain.* New York, NY: Basic Books.

Hobson, J. A. (1999). *Dreaming as delirium: How the brain goes out of its mind.* Cambridge, MA: MIT Press.

Hobson, J. A. (2002). *Dreaming: An introduction to the science of sleep.* New York, NY: Oxford University Press.

Hobson, J. A. (2005). In bed with Mark Solms? What a nightmare! A reply to Domhoff. *Dreaming, 15*(1), 21–29.

Hobson, J. A., & McCarley, R. W. (1977). The brain as a dream-state generator: An activation-synthesis hypothesis of the dream process. *American Journal of Psychiatry, 134,* 1335–1348.

Hobson, J. A., & Silvestri, L. (1999). Parasomnias. *The Harvard Mental Health Letter, 15*(8), 3–5.

Hodges, S. D., & Biswas-Diener, R. (2007). Balancing the empathy expense account: Strategies for regulating empathic response. In T. Farrow & P. Woodruff (Eds.), *Empathy in mental illness* (pp. 389–407). New York, NY: Cambridge University Press.

Hodson, G., & Costello, K. (2007). Interpersonal disgust, ideological orientations, and dehumanization as predictors of intergroup attitudes. *Psychological Science, 18,* 691–698.

Hoek, H. W., van Harten, P. N., Hermans, K. M. E., Katzman, M. A., Matroos, G. E., & Susser, E. S. (2005). The incidence of anorexia nervosa on Curacao. *American Journal of Psychiatry, 162,* 748–752.

Hofer, A., Siedentopf, C. M., Ischebeck, A., Rettenbacher, M. A., Verius, M., Golaszewski, S. M., Felber, S., & Fleischhacker, W. W. (2007). Neural substrates for episodic encoding and recognition of unfamiliar faces. *Brain and Cognition, 63,* 174–181.

Hoff, E. (2009). *Language development* (4th ed.). Belmont, CA: Wadsworth.

Hoffman, M. L. (1993). Empathy, social cognition, and moral education. In A. Garrod (Ed.), *Approaches to moral development: New research and emerging themes.* New York, NY: Teachers College Press.

Hoffman, M. L. (2000). *Empathy and moral development: Implications for caring and justice.* New York, NY: Cambridge University Press.

Hofmann, W., Gschwendner, T., Castelli, L., & Schmitt, M. (2008). Implicit and explicit attitudes and interracial interaction: The moderating role of situationally available control resources. *Group Processes & Intergroup Relations, 11,* 69–87.

Hogan, T. P. (2003). *Psychological testing: A practical introduction.* New York: Wiley.

Hogan, T. P. (2006). *Psychological testing: A practical Introduction* (2nd ed.). Hoboken, NJ: Wiley.

Holland, J. L. (1985). *Making vocational choices: A theory of vocational personalities and work environments* (2nd ed.). Englewood Cliffs, NJ: Prentice Hall.

Holland, J. L. (1994). *Self-directed search form R.* Lutz, FL: Psychological Assessment Resources.

Holmes, T. H., & Rahe, R. H. (1967). The social readjustment rating scale. *Journal of Psychosomatic Research, 11,* 213–218.

Holtzworth-Munroe, A. (2000). A typology of men who are violent toward their female partners: Making sense of the heterogeneity in husband violence. *Current Directions in Psychological Science, 9*(4), 140–143.

Honts, C. R., & Kircher, J. C. (1994). Mental and physical countermeasures reduce the accuracy of polygraph tests. *Journal of Applied Psychology, 79*(2), 252–259.

Hooley, J. M., & Hiller, J. B. (2001). Family relationships and major mental disorder: Risk factors and preventive strategies. In B. R. Sarason & S. Duck (Eds.), *Personal relationships: implications for clinical and community psychology.* New York, NY: Wiley.

Horiuchi, Y., Nakayama, K., Ishiguro, H., Ohtsuki, T., Detera-Wadleigh, S. D., Toyota, T., Yamada, K., Nankai, M., Shibuya, H., Yoshikawa, T., & Arinami, T. (2004). Possible association between a haplotype of the GABA-A receptor alpha 1 subunit gene (GABRA1) and mood disorders. *Biological Psychiatry, 55*(1), 40–45.

Horney, K. (1939). *New ways in psychoanalysis.* New York, NY: International Universities Press.

Horney, K. (1945). *Our inner conflicts: A constructive theory of neurosis.* New York, NY: Norton.

Horton, S. L. (2002). Conceptualizing transition: The role of metaphor in describing the experience of change at midlife. *Journal of Adult Development, 9*(4), 277–290.

Horwitz, A. V. (2007). Transforming normality into pathology: The *DSM* and the outcomes of stressful social arrangements. *Journal of Health and Social Behavior, 48*, 211–222.

Houlfort, N. (2006). The impact of performance-contingent rewards on perceived autonomy and intrinsic motivation. *Dissertation Abstracts International Section A: Humanities and Social Sciences, 67*(2-A), 460.

Houtz, J. C., Matos, H., Park, M-K. S., Scheinholtz, J., & Selby, E. (2007). Problem-solving style and motivational attributions. *Psychological Reports, 101*, 823–830.

Hovland, C. I. (1937). The generalization of conditioned responses: II. The sensory generalization of conditioned responses with varying intensities of tone. *Journal of Genetic Psychology, 51*, 279–291.

Howell, K. K., Coles, C. D., & Kable, J. A. (2008). The medical and developmental consequences of prenatal drug exposure. In J. Brick (Ed.), *Handbook of the medical consequences of alcohol and drug abuse* (2nd ed.) (pp. 219–249). The Haworth Press series in neuropharmacology. New York, NY: Haworth Press/Taylor and Francis Group.

Howes, M. B. (2007). *Human memory: Structures and images.* Thousand Oaks, CA: Sage Publications.

Hoye, A., Rezvy, G., Hansen, V., & Olstad, R. (2006). The effect of gender in diagnosing early schizophrenia: An experimental case simulation study. *Social Psychiatry and Psychiatric Epidemiology, 41*, 549–555.

Hsieh, P.-H. (2005). How college students explain their grades in a foreign language course: The interrelationship of attributions, self-efficacy, language learning beliefs, and achievement. *Dissertation Abstracts International Section A: Humanities and Social Sciences, 65*(10-A), 3691.

Huang, M., & Hauser, R. M. (1998). Trends in Black–White test-score differentials: II. The WORDSUM Vocabulary Test. In U. Neisser (Ed.), *The rising curve: Long-term gains in IQ and related measures* (pp. 303–334). Washington, DC: American Psychological Association.

Hubel, D. H., & Wiesel, T. N. (1965). Receptive fields and the functional architecture in two nonstriate visual areas (18 and 19) of the cat. *Journal of Neurophysiology, 28*, 229–289.

Hubel, D. H., & Wiesel, T. N. (1979). Brain mechanisms of vision. *Scientific American, 241*, 150–162.

Hudziak, J. J. (Ed). (2008). *Developmental psychopathology and wellness: Genetic and environmental influences.* Arlington, VA: American Psychiatric Publishing.

Huesmann, L. R., & Kirwil, L. (2007). Why observing violence increases the risk of violent behavior by the observer. In D. J. Flannery, A. T. Vazsonyi, & I. D. Waldman (Eds.), *The Cambridge handbook of violent behavior and aggression* (pp. 545–570). New York, NY: Cambridge University Press.

Huffman, C. J., Matthews, T. D., & Gagne, P. E. (2001). The role of part-set cuing in the recall of chess positions: Influence of chunking in memory. *North American Journal of Psychology, 3*(3), 535–542.

Hull, C. (1952). *A behavior system.* New Haven, CT: Yale University Press.

Human Resources and Social Development Canada. (2007). *National occupational classification.* Cat. no. MP53-25/2006E. Ottawa, ON: Government of Canada.

Hunsley, J., & Lee, C. M. (2010). *Introduction to clinical psychology* (2nd ed.). Toronto, ON: Wiley.

Hunsley, J., Lee, C. M., & Aubrey, T. (1999). Who uses psychological services in Canada? *Canadian Psychology, 40*, 232–240.

Hurley, S. (2008). The shared circuits model (SCM): How control, mirroring, and simulation can enable imitation, and deliberation, and mindreading. *Behavioral and Brain Sciences, 31*, 1–22.

Hutchinson-Phillips, S., Gow, K., & Jamieson, G. A. (2007). Hypnotizability, eating behaviors, attitudes, and concerns: A literature survey. *International Journal of Clinical and Experimental Hypnosis, 55*, 84–113.

Hyde, J. S. (2005). The genetics of sexual orientation. In J. S. Hyde (Ed.), *Biological substrates of human sexuality.* Washington, DC: American Psychological Association.

Hyde, J. S. (2007). *Half the human experience: The psychology of women* (7th ed.). Boston, MA: Houghton Mifflin.

Hyde, J. S., & DeLamater, J. D. (2008). *Understanding human sexuality* (10th ed.). New York, NY: McGraw-Hill.

Hyman, R. (1981). Cold reading: How to convince strangers that you know all about them. In K. Fraizer (Ed.), *Paranormal borderlands of science* (pp. 232–244). Buffalo, NY: Prometheus.

Hyman, R. (1996). The evidence for psychic functioning: Claims vs. reality. *Skeptical Inquirer, 20*, 24–26.

Hypericum Depression Trial Study Group. (2002). Effect of Hypericum performatum (St John's wort) in major depressive disorder: A randomized controlled trial. *JAMA: Journal of the American Medical Association, 287*(14), 1807–1814.

Iacono, W. G., & Lykken, D. T. (1997). The validity of the lie detector: Two surveys of scientific opinion. *Journal of Applied Psychology, 82*(3), 426–433.

Iavarone, A., Patruno, M., Galeone, F., Chieffi, S., & Carlomagno, S. (2007). Brief report: Error pattern in an autistic savant calendar calculator. *Journal of Autism and Developmental Disorders, 37*, 775–779.

Ibáñez, A., Blanco, C., & Sáiz-Ruiz, J. (2002). Neurobiology and genetics of pathological gambling. *Psychiatric Annals, 32*(3), 181–185.

Ikemoto, K. (2004). Significance of human striatal D-neurons: Implications in neuropsychiatric functions. *Neuropsychopharmacology, 29*(4), 429–434.

International Human Genome Sequencing Consortium. (2004). Finishing the euchromatic sequence of the human genome. *Nature, 431*(7011), 931–945.

Irwin, M., Mascovich, A., Gillin, J. C., Willoughby, R., Pike, J., & Smith, T. L. (1994). Partial sleep deprivation reduced natural killer cell activity in humans. *Psychosomatic Medicine, 56*(6), 493–498.

Ivanovic, D. M., Leiva, B. P., Pérez, H. T., Olivares, M. G., Díaz, N. S., Urrutia, M. S. C., Almagià, A. F., Toro, T. D., Miller, P. T., Bosch, E. O., & Larraín, C. G. (2004). Head size and intelligence, learning, nutritional status and brain development: Head, IQ, learning, nutrition and brain. *Neuropsychologia, 42*(8), 1118–1131.

Jackendoff, R. (2003). Foundations of language, brain, meaning, grammar, evolution. *Applied Cognitive Psychology, 17*(1), 121–122.

Jackson, D. N. (1997). *Jackson Personality Inventory-Revised.* London, ON: Research Psychologists' Press.

Jackson, E. D. (2008). Cortisol effects on emotional memory: Independent of stress effects. *Dissertation Abstracts International: Section B: The Sciences and Engineering, 68*(11-B), 7666.

Jackson, P. B., & Williams, D. R. (2006). Culture, race/ethnicity, and depression. In C. L. M. Keyes & S. H. Goodman (Eds), *Women and depression: A handbook for the social, behavioral, and biomedical sciences* (pp. 328–359). New York, NY: Cambridge University Press.

Jacob, P. (2008). What do mirror neurons contribute to human social cognition? *Mind & Language, 23,* 90–223.

Jacobi, C., Hayward, C., de Zwaan, M., Kraemer, H. C., & Agras, W. S. (2004). Coming to terms with risk factors for eating disorders: Application of risk terminology and suggestions for a general taxonomy. *Psychological Bulletin, 130*(1), 19–65.

Jaffee, S. R., Caspi, A., Moffitt, T. E., Dodge, K. A., Rutter, M., Taylor, A. & Tully, L. A. (2005). Nature x nurture: Genetic vulnerabilities interact with physical maltreatment to promote conduct problems. *Development and Psychopathology, 17,* 67–84.

Jain, G., Kumar, V., Chakrabarti, S., & Grover, S. (2008). The use of electroconvulsive therapy in the elderly: A study from the psychiatric unit of a North Indian teaching hospital. *Journal of ECT, 24,* 122–127.

James Randi Educational Foundation. (2008). Retrieved from http://www.randi.org/joom/challenge-info.html

James, F. O., Cermakian, N., & Boivin, D. B. (2007). Circadian rhythms of melatonin, cortisol, and clock gene expression during simulated night shift work. *Sleep: Journal of Sleep and Sleep Disorders Research, 30*(11), 1427–1436.

James, G., Blakeley, C. J., Hashemi, K., Channing, K. & Duff, M. (2006). A case of self-inflicted craniocerebral penetrating injury. *Emergency Medicine Journal, 23,* e32.

James, W. (1890). *The principles of psychology* (Vol. 2). New York, NY: Holt.

Jamieson, G. A., & Hasegawa, H. (2007). New paradigms of hypnosis research. In G. A. Jamieson (Ed.), *Hypnosis and conscious states: The cognitive neuroscience perspective* (pp. 133–144). New York, NY: Oxford University Press.

Jang, K. L., Livesley, W. J., Anso, J., Yamagata, S., Suzuki, A., Angleitner, A., Ostendorf, F., Riemann, R., & Spinath, F. (2006). Behavioral genetics of the higher-order factors of the Big Five. *Personality and Individual Differences, 41,* 261–272.

Jang, K. L., Stein, M. B., Taylor, S., Asmundson, G. J. G., & Livesley, W. J. (2003). Exposure to traumatic events and experiences: Aetiological relationships with personality function. *Psychiatry Research, 120*(1), 61–69.

Jensen, M. P., Hakimian, S., Sherlin, L. H., & Fregni, F. (2008). New insights into neuromodulatory approaches for the treatment of pain. *The Journal of Pain, 9,* 193–199.

Johnson, D. M., Delahanty, D. L., & Pinna, K. (2008). The cortisol awakening response as a function of PTSD severity and abuse chronicity in sheltered battered women. *Journal of Anxiety Disorders, 22,* 793–800.

Johnson, N. J. (2008). Leadership styles and passive-aggressive behavior in organizations. *Dissertation Abstracts International: Section B: The Sciences and Engineering, 68*(7-3), 4828.

Johnson, S. (2004). *The practice of emotionally focused couple therapy* (2nd ed.). New York, NY: Brunner-Routledge.

Johnson, S. (2008). *Hold me tight: Seven conversations for a lifetime of love.* New York, NY: Little, Brown, & Co.

Johnson, S. C., Dweck, C. S., & Chen, F. S. (2007). Evidence for infants' internal working methods of attachment. *Psychological Science, 18,* 501–502.

Johnson, S. K., Murphy, S. E., Zewdie, S., & Reichard, R. J. (2008). The strong, sensitive type: Effects of gender stereotypes and leadership prototypes on the evaluation of male and female leaders. *Organizational Behaviour and Human Decision Processes, 106,* 39–60.

Johnson, W., Bouchard, T. J. Jr., McGue, M., Segal, N. L., Tellegen, A., Keyes, M., & Gottesman, I. I. (2007). Genetic and environmental influences on the Verbal-Perceptual-Image Rotation (VPR) model of the structure of mental abilities in the Minnesota study of twins reared apart. *Intelligence, 35,* 542–562.

Johnson, W., Bouchard, T. J. Jr., Krueger, R. F., McGue, M., & Gottesman, I. I. (2004). Just one g: Consistent results from three test batteries. *Intelligence, 32*(1), 95–107.

Johnson, W., McGue, M., Krueger, R. F., & Bouchard, T. J. Jr. (2004). Marriage and personality: A genetic analysis. *Journal of Personality and Social Psychology. 86*(2), 285–294.

Jolliffe, C. D., & Nicholas, M. K. (2004). Verbally reinforcing pain reports: An experimental test of the operant conditioning of chronic pain. *Pain, 107,* 167–175.

Jonas, E., Traut-Mattausch, E., Frey, D., & Greenberg, J. (2008). The path or the goal? Decision vs. information focus in biased information seeking after preliminary decisions. *Journal of Experimental Social Psychology, 44,* 1180–1186.

Jones, B. C., DeBruine, L. M., & Little, A. C. (2007). The role of symmetry in attraction to average faces. *Perception & Psychophysics, 69,* 1273–1277.

Jones, D. G., Anderson, E. R., & Galvin, K. A. (2003). Spinal cord regeneration: Moving tentatively towards new perspectives. *Neuro-Rehabilitation, 18*(4), 339–351.

Jones, E. (2008). Predicting performance in first-semester college basic writers: Revisiting the role of self-beliefs. *Contemporary Educational Psychology, 33,* 209–238.

Jones, S. R., & Fernyhough, C. (2007). A new look at the neural diathesis-stress model of schizophrenia: The primacy of social-evaluative and uncontrollable situations. *Schizophrenia Bulletin, 33,* 1171–1177.

Jonides, J., Lewis, R. L., Nee, D. E., Lustig, C. A., Berman, M. G., & Moore, K. S. (2008). The mind and brain of short-term memory. *Annual Review of Psychology, 59,* 193–224.

Joy, L. A., Kimball, M. M., & Zabrack, M. L. (1986). Television and children's aggressive behavior. In T. M. Williams (Ed.), *The impact of television: A natural experiment in three communities* (pp. 303–360). Orlando, FL: Academic Press.

Jung, C. (1969). The concept of collective unconscious. In *Collected Works* (Vol. 9, Part 1). Princeton, NJ: Princeton University Press. (Original work published 1936.)

Jung, C. G. (1946). *Psychological types.* New York, NY: Harcourt Brace.

Jung, C. G. (1959). The archetypes and the collective unconscious. In H. Read, M. Fordham, & G. Adler (Eds.), *The collected works of C.G. Jung,* Vol. 9. New York, NY: Pantheon.

Jung, H. (2006). Assessing the influence of cultural values on consumer susceptibility to social pressure for conformity: Self-image enhancing motivations vs. information searching motivation. In L. R. Kahle & C-H. Kim (Eds.), Creating images and the psychology of marketing communication (pp. 309–329). *Advertising and Consumer Psychology.* Mahwah, NJ: Erlbaum.

Jung, R. E., & Haier, R. J. (2007). The Parieto-Frontal Integration Theory (P-FIT) of intelligence: Converging neuroimaging evidence. *Behavioral and Brain Sciences, 30,* 135–154.

Juntii, S. A., Coats, J. K., & Shah, N. M. (2008). A genetic approach to dissect sexually dimorphic behaviors. *Hormones and Behavior, 53,* 627–637.

Kagan, J., & Fox, N. A. (2006). Biology, culture, and temperamental biases. In W. Damon & R. M. Lerner (Series Eds.) & N. Eisenberg (Vol. Ed.), *Handbook of child psychology: Vol. 3. Social, emotional, and personality development* (6th ed., pp 167–225). Hoboken, NJ: Wiley.

Kahneman, D. (2003). Experiences of collaborative research. *American Psychologist, 58*(9), 723–730.

Kamdar, B. B., Kaplan, K. A., Kezirian, E. J., & Dement, W. C. (2004). The impact of extended sleep on daytime alertness, vigilance, and mood. *Sleep Medicine, 5*(5), 441–448.

Kanner, A. D., Coyne, J. C., Schaefer, C., Lazarus, R. S. (1981). Comparison of two modes of stress measurement: Daily hassles and uplifts versus major life events. *Journal of Behavioral Medicine, 4*, 1–39.

Kaplan, L. E. (2006). Moral reasoning of MSW social workers and the influence of education. *Journal of Social Work Education, 42*, 507–522.

Kapner, D. A. (2004). *Infofacts resources: Alcohol and other drugs on campus*. Retrieved from http://www.edc.org/hec//hec/pubs/factsheets/scope.html.

Kardong, K. (2008). *Introduction to biological evolution* (2nd ed.). New York, NY: McGraw-Hill.

Kareev, Y. (2000). Seven (indeed, plus or minus two) and the detection of correlations. *Psychological Review, 107*(2), 397–402.

Karmiloff, K, & Karmiloff-Smith, A. (2002). *Pathways to language: From fetus to adolescent*. Cambridge, MA: Harvard University Press.

Karon, B. P., & Widener, A. J. (1998). Repressed memories: The real story. *Professional Psychology: Research & Practice, 29*, 482–487.

Karremans, J. C., Stroebe, W., & Claus, J. (2006). Beyond Vicary's fantasies: The impact of subliminal priming and brand choice. *Journal of Experimental Social Psychology, 42*, 792–798.

Kassin, S., Fein, S., & Markus, H. R. (2008). *Social psychology* (7th ed.). Belmont, CA: Cengage.

Kastenbaum, R. J. (2007). *Death, society, and human experience* (9th ed.). Upper Saddle River, NJ: Prentice Hall.

Katzmarzyk, P. T., Gledhill, N., & Shephard, R. J. (2000). The economic burden of physical inactivity in Canada. *Canadian Medical Association Journal, 163*(11), 1435–1440.

Kaufman, J. C. (2002). Dissecting the golden goose: Components of studying creative writers. *Creativity Research Journal, 14*(1), 27–40.

Kaukiainen, A., Björkqvist, K., Lagerspetz, K., Österman, K., Salmivalli, C., Rothberg, S., et al. (1999). The relationships between social intelligence, empathy, and three types of aggression. *Aggressive Behavior, 25*(2), 81–89.

Kaye, W. (2008). Neurobiology of anorexia and bulimia nervosa. *Physiology & Behavior, 94*, 121–135.

Kaysen, D., Pantalone, D. W., Chawla, N., Lindgrren, K. P., Clum, G. A., Lee, C., & Resick, P. A. (2008). Posttraumatic stress disorder, alcohol use, and physical health concerns. *Journal of Behavioral Medicine, 31*, 115–125.

Kazdin, A. E. (1994). Methodology, design, and evaluation in psychotherapy research. In A. E. Bergin & S. L. Garfield (Eds.), *Handbook of psycho and behavior change* (4th ed.). New York, NY: Wiley.

Kazdin, A. E. (2008). *Behavior modification in applied settings*. Long Grove, IL: Waveland Press.

Keats, D. M. (1982). Cultural bases of concepts of intelligence: A Chinese versus Australian comparison. In P. Sukontasarp, N. Yongsiri, P. Intasuwan, N. Jotiban, & C. Suvannathat (Eds.), *Proceedings of the Second Asian Workshop on Child and Adolescent Development* (pp. 67–75). Bangkok: Burapasilpa Press.

Keller, J., & Bless, H. (2008). The interplay of stereotype threat and regulatory focus. In Y. Kashima, K. Fiedler, & P. Freytag (Eds.), *Stereotype dynamics: Language-based approaches to the formation, maintenance, and transformation of stereotypes* (pp. 367–389). Mahwah, NJ: Erlbaum.

Kellogg, S. H., & Young, J. E. (2008). Cognitive therapy. In J. L. Lebow (Ed.), *Twenty-first century psychotherapies: Contemporary approaches to theory and practice* (pp. 43–79). Hoboken, NJ: Wiley.

Kelly, G., Brown, S., Todd, J., & Kremer, P. (2008). Challenging behaviour profiles of people with acquired brain injury living in community settings. *Brain Injury, 22*, 457–470.

Keltner, D., Kring, A. M., & Bonanno, G. A. (1999). Fleeting signs of the course of life: Facial expression and personal adjustment. *Current Directions in Psychological Science, 8*(1), 18–22.

Kemeny, M. E. (2007). Psychoneuroimmunology. In H. S. Friedman & R. C. Silver (Eds.), *Foundations of health psychology*. New York, NY: Oxford University Press.

Kendler, K. S., & Prescott, C. A. (2006). *Genes, environment, and psychopathology: Understanding the causes of psychiatric and substance use disorders*. New York, NY: Guilford Press.

Kendler, K. S., Gallagher, T. J., Abelson, J. M., & Kessler, R. C. (1996). Lifetime prevalence, demographic risk factors, and diagnostic validity of nonaffective psychosis as assessed in a U. S. community sample. *Archives of General Psychiatry, 53*, 1022–1031.

Kenealy, P. M. (1997). Mood-state-dependent retrieval: The effects of induced mood on memory reconsidered. *Quarterly Journal of Experimental Psychology: Human Experimental Psychology, 50A*, 290–317.

Kerschreiter, R., Schulz-Hardt, S., Mojzisch, A., & Frey, D. (2008). Biased information search in homogeneous groups: Confidence as a moderator for the effect of anticipated task requirements. *Personality & Social Psychology Bulletin, 34*, 679–691.

Kershaw, S. (2008). Sharing their demons on the Web. *New York Times*. Retrieved from http://www.nytimes.com/2008/11/13/fashion/13psych.html

Kessler, R. C., McGonagle, K. A., Zhao, S., Nelson, C. B., Hughes, M., Eshleman, S., Wittchen, H., & Kendler, K. S. (1994). Lifetime and 12-month prevalence of *DSM-IIIR* psychiatric disorders in the United States. *Archives of General Psychiatry, 51*, 8–19.

Kezwer, G. (1998). Organic cigarettes new fad for "health conscious" smokers. *Canadian Medical Association Journal, 158*(1), 13.

Khalid, N., Atkins, M., Tredget, J., Giles, M., Champney-Smith, K., & Kirov, G. (2008). The effectiveness of electroconvulsive therapy in treatment-resistant depression. *Journal of ECT, 24*, 141–145.

Kieffer, K. M., Schinka, J. A., & Curtiss, G. (2004). Person-environment congruence and personality domains in the prediction of job performance and work quality. *Journal of Counseling Psychology, 51*(2), 168–177.

Kihlstrom, J. F. (2004). An unbalanced balancing act: Blocked, recovered, and false memories in the laboratory and clinic. *Clinical Psychology: Science & Practice, 11*(1), 34–41.

Kihlstrom, J. F. (2005). Dissociative disorders. *Annual Review of Clinical Psychology, 1*, 227–253.

Kim, J., & Hatfield, E. (2004). Love types and subjective well-being: A cross cultural study. *Social Behavior & Personality, 32*(2), 173–182.

Kim, S. U. (2004). Human neural stem cells genetically modified for brain repair in neurological disorders. *Neuropathology, 24*(3), 159–171.

Kim, Y. H. (2008). Rebounding from learned helplessness: A measure of academic resilience using anagrams. *Dissertation Abstracts International: Section B: The Sciences and Engineering. 68*(10-B), 6947.

Kimball, M. M. (1986). Television and sex-role attitudes. In T. M. Williams (Ed.), *The impact of television: A natural experiment in three communities* (pp. 265–302). Orlando, FL: Academic Press.

Kimmel, M. S. (2000). *The gendered society*. London: Oxford University Press.

Kimura, D. (1999). *Sex and cognition*. Cambridge, MA: MIT Press.

Kimura, D. (2004). Human sex differences in cognition: Fact, not predicament. *Sexualities, Evolution, and Gender, 6*, 45–53.

Kinder, L. S., Bradley, K. A., Katon, W. J., Ludman, E., McDonnell, M. B., & Bryson, C. L. (2008).

Depression, posttraumatic stress disorder, and mortality. *Psychosomatic Medicine, 70*, 20–26.

King, B. M. (2009). *Human sexuality today* (6th ed.). Boston, MA: Allyn & Bacon.

Kinsella, T., & Verhoef, M. (1999). Determinants of Canadian physicians' opinions about legalized physician-assisted suicide: A national survey. *Annals of the Royal College of Physicians and Surgeons of Canada, 32*, 211–215.

Kinsley, C. H., & Lambert, K. G. (2008). Reproduction-induced neuroplasticity: Natural behavioural and neuronal alterations associated with the production and care of offspring. *Journal of Neuroendocrinology, 20*(4), 515–525.

Kirk, K. M., Bailey, J. M., Dunne, M. P., & Martin, N. G. (2000). Measurement models for sexual orientation in a community twin sample. *Behavior Genetics, 30*(4), 345–356.

Kirkman, C. A. (2002). Non-incarcerated psychopaths: Why we need to know more about the psychopaths who live amongst us. *Journal of Psychiatric & Mental Health Nursing, 9*(2), 155–160.

Kirsch, I., & Braffman, W. (2001). Imaginative suggestibility and hypnotizability. *Current Directions in Psychological Science, 10*(2), 57–61.

Kirsch, I., Mazzoni, G., & Montgomery, G. H. (2006). Remembrance of hypnosis past. *American Journal of Clinical Hypnosis, 49*, 171–178.

Kirschenbaum, H. & Jourdan, A. (2005). The current status of Carl Rogers and the person-centered approach. *Psychotherapy: Theory, Research Practice, Training, 42*(1), 37–51.

Kisilevsky, B. S., Hains, S. M. J., Lee, K., Xie, X., Huang, H., Ye, H., Zhang, K., & Wang, Z. (2003). Effects of experience on fetal voice recognition. *Psychological Science, 14*(3), 220–224.

Klatzky, R. L. (1984). *Memory and awareness.* New York, NY: Freeman.

Kleider, H. M., Pezdek, K., Goldinger, S. D., & Kirk, A. (2008). Schema-driven source misattribution errors: Remembering the expected from a witnessed event. *Applied Cognitive Psychology, 22*, 1–20.

Klein, O., Pohl, S., & Ndagijimana, C. (2007). The influence of intergroup comparisons on Africans' intelligence test performance in a job selection context. *Journal of Psychology: Interdisciplinary and Applied, 141*, 453–467.

Klimes-Dougan, B., Lee, C-Y. S., Ronsaville, D., & Martinez, P. (2008). Suicidal risk in young adult offspring of mothers with bipolar or major depressive disorder: A longitudinal family risk study. *Journal of Clinical Psychology, 64*, 531–540.

Knekt, P., Lindfors, O., Laaksonen, M. A., Raitosalo, R., Haaramo, P., Järvikoski, A., & The Helsinki Psychotherapy Study Group, Helsinki, Finland. (2008). Effectiveness of short-term and long-term psychotherapy on work ability and functional capacity—A randomized clinical trial on depressive and anxiety disorders. *Journal of Affective Disorders, 107*, 95–105.

Knoblauch, K., Vital-Durand, F., & Barbur, J. L. (2000). Variation of chromatic sensitivity across the life span. *Vision Research, 41*(1), 23–36.

Kobasa, S. (1979). Stressful life events, personality, and health: An inquiry into hardiness. *Journal of Personality and Social Psychology, 37*, 1–11.

Köfalvi, A. (Ed.). (2008). *Cannabinoids and the brain.* New York, NY: Springer Science & Business Media.

Kofalvi, A. (Ed.). (2008). *Cannabinoids and the brain.* New York, NY: Springer Science + Business Media.

Kohlberg, L. (1964). Development of moral character and moral behavior. In L. W. Hoffman & M. L. Hoffman (Eds.), *Review of child development research* (Vol. 1). New York, NY: Sage.

Kohlberg, L. (1981). *The meaning and measurement of moral development.* Worcester, MA: Clark University Press.

Kohlberg, L. (1984). *The psychology of moral development: Essays on moral development* (Vol. 2). San Francisco, CA: Harper & Row.

Köhler, W. (1925). *The mentality of apes.* New York, NY: Harcourt, Brace.

Kohn, A. (2000). *Punished by rewards: The trouble with gold stars, incentive plans, A's, and other bribes.* New York, NY: Houghton Mifflin.

Komiya, N., Good, G. E., & Sherrod, N. B. (2000). Emotional openness as a predictor of college students' attitudes toward seeking psychological help. *Journal of Counseling Psychology, 47*(1), 138–143.

Konheim-Kalkstein, Y. L., & van den Broek, P. (2008). The effect of incentives on cognitive processing of text. *Discourse Processes, 45*, 180–194.

Koop, C. E., Richmond, J., & Steinfeld, J. (2004). America's choice: Reducing tobacco addiction and disease. *American Journal of Public Health, 94*(2), 174–176.

Kovacic, Z., Henigsberg, N., Pivac, N., Nedic, G., & Borovecki, A. (2008). Platelet serotonin concentration and suicidal behavior in combat related posttraumatic stress disorder. *Progress in Neuro-Psychopharmacology & Biological Psychiatry, 32*, 544–551.

Kraaij, V., Arensman, E., & Spinhoven, P. (2002). Negative life events and depression

in elderly persons: A meta-analysis. *Journals of Gerontology: Series B: Psychological Sciences & Social Sciences, 57B*(1), 87–94.

Kracher, B., & Marble, R. P. (2008). The significance of gender in predicting the cognitive moral development of business practitioners using the socioemotional reflection objective measure. *Journal of Business Ethics, 78*, 503–526.

Kramer, A. F., Hahn, S., Irwin, D. E., & Theeuwes, J. (2000). Age differences in the control of looking behavior. *Psychological Science, 11*(3), 210–217.

Krantz, D. S., & McCeney, M. K. (2002). Effects of psychological and social factors on organic disease: A critical assessment of research on coronary heart disease. *Annual Review of Psychology, (1)*, 341–369.

Kring, A. M., Davison, G. C., Neale, J. M., & Johnson, S. L. (2007). *Abnormal psychology* (10th ed.). Hoboken, NJ: Wiley.

Krishna, G. (1999). *The dawn of a new science.* Los Angeles, CA: Institute for Consciousness Research.

Kronenberger, W. G., Mathews, V. P., Dunn, D. W., Wang, Y., Wood, E. A., Larsen, J. J., Rembusch, M. E., Lowe, M. J., Giauque, A. L., & Lurito, J. T. (2005). Media violence exposure in aggressive and control adolescents: Differences in self- and parent-reported exposure to violence on television and in video games. *Aggressive Behavior, 31*(3), 201–216.

Krueger, J. I. (2007). From social projection to social behaviour. *European Review of Social Psychology, 18*, 1–35.

Krusemark, E. A., Campbell, W. K., & Clementz, B. A. (2008). Attributions, deception, and event related potentials: An investigation of the self-serving bias. *Psychophysiology, 45*, 511–515.

Ksir, C. J., Hart, C. I., & Ray, O. S. (2008). *Drugs, society, and human behavior.* New York, NY: McGraw-Hill.

Kubiak, T., Vögele, C., Siering, M., Schiel, R., & Weber, H. (2008). Daily hassles and emotional eating in obese adolescents under restricted dietary conditions—The role of ruminative thinking. *Appetite, 51*, 206–209.

Kübler-Ross, E. (1983). *On children and death.* New York, NY: Macmillan.

Kübler-Ross, E. (1997). *Death: The final stage of growth.* New York, NY: Simon & Schuster.

Kübler-Ross, E. (1999). *On death and dying.* New York, NY: Simon & Schuster.

Kudo, E., & Numazaki, M. (2003). Explicit and direct self-serving bias in Japan. Reexamination of self-serving bias for success and failure. *Journal of Cross-Cultural Psychology, 34*(5), 511–521.

Kuhn, C., Swartzwelder, S., & Wilson, W. (2003). *Buzzed: The straight facts about the most used and abused drugs from alcohol to ecstasy* (2nd ed.). New York, NY: Norton.

Kulik, L. (2005). Intrafamiliar congruence in gender role attitudes and ethnic stereotypes: The Israeli case. *Journal of Comparative Family Studies, 36*(2), 289–303.

Kumkale, G. T., & Albarracín, D. (2004). The sleeper effect in persuasion: A metaanalytic review. *Psychological Bulletin, 130*(1), 143–172.

Kuperstok, N. (2008). Effects of exposure to differentiated aggressive films, equated for levels of interest and excitation, and the vicarious hostility catharsis hypothesis. *Dissertation Abstracts International: Section B: The Sciences and Engineering 68*(7-B), 4806.

Kyle, A. (2009). Inkblot release sparks furor. *Regina Leader-Post*, August 1.

Lachman, M. E. (2004). Development in midlife. *Annual Review of Psychology, 55*, 305–331.

Lader, M. (2007). Limitations of current medical treatments for depression: Disturbed circadian rhythms as a possible therapeutic target. *European Neuropsychopharacology, 17*, 743–755.

Laidlaw, K., & Thompson, L. W. (2008). Cognitive behavior therapy with depressed older people. In K. Laidlaw & B. Knight (Eds.), *Handbook of emotional disorders in later life: Assessment and treatment*. New York, NY: Oxford University Press.

Lakein, A. (1998). *Give me a moment and I'll change your life: Tools for moment management*. New York, NY: Andrews McMeel Publishing.

Lamb, H. R. (2000). Deinstitutionalization and public policy. In R. W. Menninger & J. C. Nemiah (Eds.), *American psychiatry after World War II*. Washington, DC: American Psychiatric Press.

Landeira-Fernandez, J. (2004). Analysis of the cold-water restraint procedure in gastric ulceration and body temperature. *Physiology & Behavior, 82*(5), 827–833.

Lang, U. E., Bajbouj, M., Sander, T., & Gallinat, J. (2007). Gender-dependent association of the functional catechol-Omethyltransferase Val158Met genotype with sensation seeking personality trait. *Neuropsychopharmacology, 32*, 1950–1955.

Langenecker, S. A., Bieliauskas, L. A., Rapport, L. J., Zubieta, J-K., Wilde, E. A., & Berent, S. (2005). Face emotion perception and executive functioning deficits in depression. *Journal of Clinical & Experimental Neuropsychology, 27*(3), 320–333.

Latané, B., & Darley, J. M. (1970). *The unresponsive bystander: Why doesn't he help?* New York, NY: Appleton-Century-Crofts.

Laungani, P. D. (2007). *Understanding cross-cultural psychology*. Thousand Oaks, CA: Sage.

Lawrence, M. (2008). Review of the bifurcation of the self: The history and theory of dissociation and its disorders. *American Journal of Clinical Hypnosis, 50*, 281–282.

Lazar, S. W., Kerr, C. E., Wasserman, R. H., Gray, J. R., Greve, D. N., Treadway, M. T., McGarvey, M., Quinn, B. T., Dusek, J. A., Benson, H., Rauch, S. L., Moore, C. I., Fischl, B. (2005). Meditation experience is associated with increased cortical thickness. *Neuroreport, 16*(17), 1893–1897.

Leadbeater, B., & Hoglund, W. (2006). Changing the social contexts of peer victimization. *Journal of the Canadian Academy of Child and Adolescent Psychiatry, 15*, 21–26.

Leaper, C. (2000). Gender, affiliation, assertion, and the interactive context of parentchild play. *Developmental Psychology, 36*(3), 381–393.

Leaper, C., & Friedman, C. K. (2007). The socialization of gender. In J. Grusec & P. Hastings (Eds.), *Handbook of socialization: Theory and research* (pp. 561–587). New York, NY: Guilford Press.

Leary, C. E., Kelley, M. L., Morrow, J., & Mikulka, P. J. (2008). Parental use of physical punishment as related to family environment, psychological well-being, and personality in undergraduates. *Journal of Family Violence, 23*(1), 1–7.

Lecrubier, Y., Clerc, G., Didi, R., & Kieser, M. (2002). Efficacy of St. John's wort extract WS 5570 in major depression: A double-blind, placebo-controlled trial. *American Journal of Psychiatry, 159*(8), 1361–1366.

LeDoux, J. (1996a). *The emotional brain: The mysterious underpinnings of emotional life*. New York, NY: Simon & Schuster.

LeDoux, J. E. (1996b). Sensory systems and emotion: A model of affective processing. *Integrative Psychiatry, 4*, 237–243.

LeDoux, J. E. (1998). *The emotional brain*. New York, NY: Simon & Schuster.

LeDoux, J. E. (2002). *Synaptic self: How our brains become who we are*. New York, NY: Viking.

LeDoux, J. E. (2007). Emotional memory. *Scholarpedia, 2*, 180.

Lee, J-H., Kwon, Y-D., Hong, S-H., Jeong, H-J., Kim, H-M., & Um, J-Y. (2008). Interleukin-1 beta gene polymorphism and traditional constitution in obese women. *International Journal of Neuroscience, 118*, 793–805.

Lee, W-Y. (2002). One therapist, four cultures: Working with families in Greater China. *Journal of Family Therapy, 24*, 258–275.

Lefley, H. P. (2000). Cultural perspectives on families, mental illness, and the law. *International Journal of Law and Psychiatry, 23*, 229–243.

Leglise, A. (2008). *Progress in circadian rhythm research*. Hauppauge, NY: Nova Science.

Legrand, F. D., Gomà-i-freixanet, M., Kaltenbach, M. L., & Joly, P. M. (2007). Association between sensation seeking and alcohol consumption in French college students: Some ecological data collected in "open bar" parties. *Personality and Individual Differences, 43*, 1950–1959.

Lehnert, G., & Zimmer, H. D. (2008). Modality and domain specific components in auditory and visual working memory tasks. *Cognitive Processing, 9*, 53–61.

Lehto, S. M., Tolmunen, T., Joensuu, M., Saarinen, P. I., Valkonen-Korhonen, M., Vanninen, R., Ahola, P., Tiihonen, J., Kuikka, J., & Lehtonen, J. (2008). Changes in midbrain serotonin transporter availability in atypically depressed subjects after one year of psychotherapy. *Progress in Neuro-Psychopharmacology & Biological Psychiatry, 32*, 229–237.

Leichtman, M. D. (2006). Cultural and maturational influences on long-term event memory. In L. Balter & C. S. Tamis-LeMonda (Eds.), *Child psychology: A handbook of contemporary issues* (2nd ed., pp. 565–589). New York, NY: Psychology Press.

Lein, C., & Wills, C. E. (2007). Using patient-centered interviewing skills to manage complex patient encounters in primary care. *Journal of the American Academy of Nurse Practitioners, 19*, 215–220.

Lele, D. U. (2008). The influence of individual personality and attachment styles on romantic relationships (partner choice and couples' satisfaction). *Dissertation Abstracts International: Section B: The Sciences and Engineering, 68*, 6316.

Lemus, D. R. (2008). Communication during retirement planning: An information-seeking process. *Dissertation Abstracts International Section A: Humanities and Social Sciences, 68*(10-A), 4139.

Leonard, B. E. (2003). *Fundamentals of psychopharmacology* (3rd ed.). Hoboken, NJ: Wiley.

Lepper, M. R., Greene, D., & Nisbett, R. E. (1973). Undermining children's intrinsic interest with extrinsic rewards: A test of the overjustification hypothesis. *Journal of Personality and Social Psychology, 28*, 129–137.

Leri, A., Anversa, P., & Frishman, W. H. (Eds.) (2007). *Cardiovascular regeneration and stem cell therapy*. Hoboken, NJ: Wiley-Blackwell.

Lerner, H. D. (2008). Psychodynamic perspectives. In M. Hersen & A. M. Gross (Eds.), *Handbook of clinical psychology, vol 1: Adults* (pp. 127–160). Hoboken, NJ: Wiley.

Lerner, J. S., Gonzalez, R. M., Small, D. A., & Fischhoff, B. (2003). Effects of fear and anger on perceived risks of terrorism: A national field experiment. *Psychological Science, 14*, 144–150.

Leslie, M. (2000, July/August). The Vexing Legacy of Lewis Terman. *Stanford Magazine.* Retrieved from http://www.stanford alumni.org/news/magazine/2000/julaug/articles/terman.html

Lett, D. (2009, March 6). Following voices. *National Post*, p. A7.

LeVay, S. (2003). Queer science: The use and abuse of research into homosexuality. *Archives of Sexual Behavior, 32*(2), 187–189.

Levenson, R. W. (1992). Autonomic nervous system differences among emotions. *Psychological Science, 3*, 23–27.

Levenson, R. W. (2007). Emotion elicitation with neurological patients. In J. A. Coan & J. J. B. Allen (Eds.), *Handbook of emotion elicitation and assessment* (pp. 158–168). *Series in affective science.* New York, NY: Oxford University Press.

Leventhal, H., Weinman, J., Leventhal, E. A., & Phillips, L. A. (2008). Health psychology: The search for pathways between behavior and health. *Annual Review of Psychology, 59*, 477–505.

Levine, J. R. (2001). *Why do fools fall in love: Experiencing the magic, mystery, and meaning of successful relationships.* New York, NY: Jossey-Bass.

Levinson, D. J. (1977). The mid-life transition, *Psychiatry, 40*, 99–112.

Levinson, D. J. (1996). *The seasons of a woman's life.* New York, NY: Knopf.

Levinthal, C. (2008). *Drugs, behavior, and modern society* (5th ed.). Boston, MA: Allyn & Bacon.

Levitan, L. C. (2008). Giving prejudice an attitude adjustment: The implications of attitude strength and social network attitudinal composition for prejudice and prejudice reduction. *Dissertation Abstracts International: Section B: The Sciences and Engineering, 68* (8-B), 5634.

Lewis, C. (2009). Attempt to legalize euthanasia revived: Death by appointment. *National Post*, August 29, 2009.

Lewis, M. B., & Bowler, P. J. (2009). Botulinum toxin cosmetic therapy correlates with a more positive mood. *Journal of Cosmetic Dermatology, 8*(1), 24–26.

Lewis, S. (1963). *Dear Shari.* New York, NY: Stein & Day.

Libon, D. J., Xie, S. X., Moore, P., Farmer, J., Antani, S., McCawley, G., Cross, K., & Grossman, M. (2007). Patterns of neuropsychological impairment in frontotemporal dementia. *Neurology, 68*, 369–375.

Lieberman, P. (1998). *Eve spoke: Human language and human evolution.* New York, NY: Norton.

Lindberg, B., Axelsson, K., & Öhrling, K. (2008). Adjusting to being a father to an infant born prematurely: Experiences from Swedish fathers. *Scandinavian Journal of Caring Sciences, 22*, 79–85.

Linden, E. (1993). Can animals think? *Time, 141*(12), 54–61.

Links, P. S., Eynan, R., Heisel, M. J., & Nisenbaum, R. (2008). Elements of affective instability associated with suicidal behaviour in patients with borderline personality disorder. *The Canadian Journal of Psychiatry, 53*, 112–116.

Links, P. S., Heslegrave, R., & van Reekum, R. (1998). Prospective follow-up of borderline personality disorder: Prognosis, prediction outcome, and Axis II comorbidity. *Canadian Journal of Psychiatry, 43*, 265–270.

Linzer, M., Gerrity, M., Douglas, J. A., McMurray, J. E., Williams, E. S., Konrad, T. R., & Society of General Medicine Career Satisfaction Study Group. (2002). Physician stress: Results from the physician worklife study. *Stress & Health: Journal of the International Society for the Investigation of Stress, 18*(1), 37–42.

Lippa, R. A. (2007). The preferred traits of mates in a cross-national study of heterosexual and homosexual men and women: An examination of biological and cultural influences. *Archives of Sexual Behavior, 36*, 193–208.

Lipsanen, T., Korkeila, J., Peltola, P., Järvinen, J., Langen, K., & Lauerma, H. (2004). Dissociative disorders among psychiatric patients: Comparison with a nonclinical sample. *European Psychiatry, 19*(1), 53–55.

Lissek, S., & Powers, A. S. (2003). Sensation seeking and startle modulation by physically threatening images. *Biological Psychology, 63*(2), 179–197.

Liu, H., Mantyh, P., & Basbaum, A. I. (1997). NMDA-receptor regulation of substance P release from primary afferent nociceptors. *Nature, 386*, 721–724.

Liu, J. H., & Latané, B. (1998). Extremitization of attitudes: Does thought- and discussion-induced polarization cumulate? *Basic and Applied Social Psychology, 20*, 103–110.

Livesley, W. J., & Jackson, D. N. (2002). *Manual for the Dimensional Assessment of Personality Problems—Basic Questionnaire.* London, ON: Research Psychologists' Press.

Livingston, J. A. (1999). Something old and something new: Love, creativity, and the enduring relationship. *Bulletin of the Menninger Clinic, 63*, 40–52.

Livingston, R. W., & Drwecki, B. B. (2007). Why are some individuals not racially biased? Susceptibility to affective conditioning predicts nonprejudice toward Blacks. *Psychological Science, 18*, 816–823.

Lizarraga, M. L. S., & Ganuza, J. M. G. (2003). Improvement of mental rotation in girls and boys. *Sex Roles, 49*(5–6), 277–286.

Loftus, E. (1982). Memory and its distortions. In A. G. Kraut (Ed.), *The G. Stanley Hall Lecture Series Vol. 2* (pp. 123–154). Washington, DC: American Psychological Association.

Loftus, E. F. (2000). Remembering what never happened. In E. Tulving, et al. (Eds.), *Memory, consciousness, and the brain: The Tallinn Conference*, pp. 106–118. Philadelphia: Psychology Press/Taylor & Francis.

Loftus, E. F. (2001). Imagining the past. *Psychologist, 14*(11), 584–587.

Loftus, E. F. (2007). Memory distortions: Problems solved and unsolved. In M. Garry & H. Hayne (Eds.), *Do justice and let the skies fall.* Mahwah, NJ: Erlbaum.

Loftus, E. F., & Cahill, L. (2007). Memory distortion from misattribution to rich false memory. In J. S. Nairne (Ed.), *The foundations of remembering: Essays in honor of Henry L. Roediger, III* (pp. 413–425). New York, NY: Psychology Press.

Loftus, E., & Ketcham, K. (1994). *The myth of repressed memories: False memories and allegations of sexual abuse.* New York, NY: St. Martin's Press.

Lopez, S. R., & Guarnaccia, P. J. J. (2000). Cultural psychopathology: Uncovering the social world of mental illness. *Annual Review of Psychology, 51*, 571–598.

Lorenz, K. Z. (1937). The companion in the bird's world. *Auk, 54*, 245–273.

Lores-Arnaiz, S., Bustamante, J., Czernizyniec, A., Galeano, P., Gervasoni, M. G., Martinez, A. R., Paglia, N., Cores, V., & Lores-Arnaiz, M. R. (2007). Exposure to enriched environments increases brain nitric oxide synthase and improves cognitive performance in prepubertal but not in young rats. *Behavioural Brain Research, 184*, 117–123.

Loriaux, D. L. (2008). Historical note: Hans Hugo Bruno Seyle (1907–1982). *The Endocrinologist, 18*(2), 53–54.

Lott, D. A. (2000). *The new flirting game.* London, UK: Sage.

Loxton, N. J., Nguyen, D., Casey, L., & Dawe, S. (2008). Reward drive, rash impulsivity and punishment sensitivity in problem gamblers. *Personality & Individual Differences, 45*, 167–173.

Lu, Z. L., Williamson, S. J., & Kaufman, L. (1992). Behavioral lifetime of human auditory sensory memory predicted by physiological measures. *Science, 258*, 1668–1670.

Lubinski, D., & Benbow, C. P. (2000). States of excellence. *American Psychologist, 55*(1), 137–150.

Lucio, E., Ampudia, A., Durán, C., León, I., & Butcher, J. N. (2001). Comparison of the Mexican and American norms of the MMPI-2. *Journal of Clinical Psychology, 57,* 1459–1468.

Lucio-Gómez, E., Ampudia-Rueda, A., Durán Patiño, C., Gallegos-Mejía, L., & León Guzmán, I. (1999). La nueva versión del inventario multifásico de la personalidad de Minnesota para adolescentes mexicanos. [The new version of the Minnesota Multiphasic Personality Inventory for Mexican adolescents]. *Revista Mexicana de Psicología, 16*(2), 217–226.

Luecken, L. J., & Lemery, K. S. (2004). Early caregiving and physiological stress responses. *Clinical Psychology Review, 24*(2), 171–191.

Luria, A. R. (1968). *The mind of a mnemonist: A little book about a vast memory.* New York, NY: Basic Books.

Lutz, A., Greischar, L. L., Rawlings, N. B., Ricard, M., & Davidson, R. J. (2004). Long-term meditators self-induce high-amplitude gamma synchrony during mental practice. *Proceedings of the National Academy of Sciences, 101*(46), 16369–16373.

Lynn, R., & Harvey, J. (2008). The decline of the world's IQ. *Intelligence, 36,* 112–120.

Lynn, S. J. (2007). Hypnosis reconsidered. *American Journal of Clinical Hypnosis, 49,* 195–197.

Lyons-Ruth, K., Holmes, B. M., Sasvari-Szekely, M., Ronai, Z., Nemoda, Z., & Pauls, D. (2007). Serotonin transporter polymorphism and borderline or antisocial traits among low-income young adults. *Psychiatric Genetics, 17,* 339–343.

Lyoo, I. K., Kim, M. J., Stoll, A. L., Demopulos, C. M., Parow, A. M., Dager, S. R., Friedman, S. D., Dunner, D. L., & Renshaw, P. F. (2004). Frontal lobe gray matter density decreases in Bipolar I Disorder. *Biological Psychiatry, 55*(6), 648–651.

Lyubimov, N. N. (1992). *Electrophysiological characteristics of sensory processing and mobilization of hidden brain reserves. 2nd Russian-Swedish Symposium New Research in Neurobiology,* Moscow: Russian Academy of Science Institute of Human Brain.

Maas, J. B. (1999). *Power sleep.* New York, NY: HarperPerennial.

Macmillan, M. B. (2000). *An odd kind of fame: Stories of Phineas Gage.* Cambridge, MA: MIT Press.

Maddi, S. R., Harvey, R. H., Khoshaba, D. M., Lu, J. L., Persico, M., & Brow, M. (2006). The personality construct of hardiness, III: Relationships with repression, innovativeness, authoritarianism, and performance. *Journal of Personality, 74,* 575–597.

Maehr, M. L., & Urdan, T. C. (2000). *Advances in motivation and achievement: The role of context.* Greenwich, CT: JAI Press.

Maisto, S. A., Galizio, M., & Connors, G. J. (2008). *Drug use and abuse* (5th ed.). Belmont, CA: Cengage.

Major, B., Spencer, S., Schmader, T., Wolfe, C., & Crocker, J. (1998). Coping with negative stereotypes about intellectual performance: The role of psychological disengagement. *Personality & Social Psychology Bulletin, 24*(1), 34–50.

Maner, J. K., DeWall, C. N., & Gailliot, M. T. (2008). Selective attention to signs of success: Social dominance and early stage interpersonal perception. *Personality and Social Psychology Bulletin, 34,* 488–501.

Manly, J. J., Byrd, D., Touradji, P., Sanchez, D., & Stern, Y. (2004). Literacy and cognitive change among ethnically diverse elders. *International Journal of Psychology, 39*(1), 47–60.

Manning, J. (2007). The use of meridian-based therapy for anxiety and phobias. *Australian Journal of Clinical Hypnotherapy and Hypnosis, 28,* 45–50.

Marchand, A. (2007). Mental health in Canada: Are there any risky occupations and industries? *International Journal of Law and Psychiatry, 30*(4–5), 272–283.

Markle, A. (2007). Asymmetric disconfirmation in managerial beliefs about employee motivation. *Dissertation Abstracts International Section A: Humanities and Social Sciences, 68*(5-A), 2051.

Markovitz, P. J. (2004). Recent trends in the pharmacotherapy of personality disorders. *Journal of Personality Disorders, 18*(1), 99–101.

Marks, L. D., Hopkins, K. C., Monroe, P. A., Nesteruk, O., & Sasser, D. D. (2008). "Together, we are strong": A qualitative study of happy, enduring African American marriages. *Family Relations, 57,* 172–185.

Markstrom, C. A., & Marshall, S. K. (2007). The psychosocial inventory of ego strengths: Examination of theory and psychometric properties. *Journal of Adolescence, 30,* 63–79.

Markus, H. R., & Kitayama, S. (1998). The cultural psychology of personality. *Journal of Cross-Cultural Psychology, 29,* 63–87.

Markus, H. R., & Kitayama, S. (2003). Culture, self, and the reality of the social. *Psychological Inquiry, 14*(3–4), 277–283.

Marsee, M. A., Weems, C. F., Taylor, L. K. (2008). Exploring the association between aggression and anxiety in youth: A look at aggressive subtypes, gender, and social cognition. *Journal of Child and Family Studies, 17,* 154–168.

Marshall, L., & Born, J. (2007). The contribution of sleep to hippocampus-dependent memory consolidation. *Trends in Cognitive Sciences, 11,* 442–450.

Marshall, M., & Brown, J. D. (2008). On the psychological benefits of self-enhancement. In E. C. Chang (Ed.). *Self-criticism and self-enhancement: Theory, research, and clinical implications* (pp. 19–35). Washington, DC: American Psychological Association.

Martin, C. L., & Fabes, R. (2009). *Discovering child development* (2nd ed.). Belmont, CA: Cengage.

Martin, S. E., Snyder, L. B., Hamilton, M., Fleming-Milici, F., Slater, M. D., Stacy, A., Chen, M., & Grube, J. W. (2002). Alcohol advertising and youth. *Alcoholism: Clinical & Experimental Research, 26*(6), 900–906.

Martineau, J., Cochin, S., Magne, R., & Barthelemy, C. (2008). Impaired cortical activation in autistic children: Is the mirror neuron system involved? *International Journal of Psychophysiology, 68,* 35–40.

Martinelli, E. A. (2006). Paternal role development and acquisition in fathers of pre-term infants: A qualitative study. *Dissertation Abstracts International: Section B: The Sciences and Engineering 66*(9-B), 5125.

Maslow, A. H. (1954). *Motivation and personality.* New York, NY: Harper & Row.

Maslow, A. H. (1970). *Motivation and personality* (2nd ed.). New York, NY: Harper & Row.

Maslow, A. H. (1999). *Toward a psychology of being* (3rd ed.). New York, NY: Wiley.

Mason, P. T., & Kreger, R. (1998). *Stop walking on eggshells: Taking your life back when someone you care about has borderline personality disorder.* New York, NY: New Harbinger Publishers.

Massicotte-Marquez, J., Décary, A., Gagnon, J. F., Vendette, M., Mathieu, A., Postuma, R. B., Carrier, J., & Montplaisir, J. (2008). Executive dysfunction and memory impairment in idiopathic REM sleep behavior disorder. *Neurology, 70,* 1250–1257.

Masters, W. H., & Johnson, V. E. (1961). Orgasm, anatomy of the female. In A. Ellis & A. Abarbonel (Eds.), *Encyclopedia of Sexual Behavior,* Vol. 2. New York, NY: Hawthorn.

Masters, W. H., & Johnson, V. E. (1966). *Human sexual response.* Boston, MA: Little, Brown.

Masters, W. H., & Johnson, V. E. (1970). *Human sexual inadequacy.* Boston, MA: Little, Brown.

Mateer, C. A., & Kerns, K. A. (2000). Capitalizing on neuroplasticity. *Brain and Cognition, 42,* 106–109.

Mathews, A., & MacLeod, C. (2005). Cognitive vulnerability to emotional disorders. *Annual Review of Clinical Psychology, 1,* 167–195.

Matlin, M. W. (2008). *The psychology of women* (6th ed.). Belmont, CA: Cengage.

Mailin, M. W., & Foley, H. J. (1997). *Sensation and perception* (4th ed.). Boston, MA: Allyn and Bacon.

Matsumoto, D. (2000). *Culture and psychology: People around the world.* Belmont, CA: Wadsworth.

Matsumoto, D., & Juang, L. (2008). *Culture and psychology* (4th ed.). Belmont, CA: Cengage.

Matusov, E., & Hayes, R. (2000). Sociocultural critique of Piaget and Vygotsky. *New Ideas in Psychology, 18*(2–3), 215–239.

May, A., Hajak, G., Gänßlbauer, S., Steffens, T., Langguth, B., Kleinjung, T., & Eichhammer, P. (2007). Structural brain alterations following 5 days of intervention: Dynamic aspects of neuroplasticity. *Cerebral Cortex, 17,* 205–210.

Mayers, A. G., Baldwin, D. S., Dyson, R., Middleton, R. W., & Mustapha, A. (2003). Use of St John's wort (*Hypericum perforatum L*) in members of a depression self-help organization: A 12-week open prospective pilot study using the HADS scale. *Primary Care Psychiatry, 9*(1), 15–20.

Maynard, A. E., & Greenfield, P. M. (2003). Implicit cognitive development in cultural tools and children: Lessons from Maya Mexico. *Cognitive Development, 18*(4), 489–510.

Mays, V. M., Cochran, S. D., & Barnes, N. W. (2007). Race, race-based discrimination, and health outcomes among African Americans. *Annual Review of Psychology, 58,* 201–225.

Mazzoni, G., & Memon, A. (2003). Imagination can create false autobiographical memories. *Psychological Science, 14,* 186–188.

Mazzoni, G., & Vannucci, M. (2007). Hindsight bias, the misinformation effect, and false autobiographical memories. *Social Cognition, 25,* 203–220.

McAllister-Williams, R. H., & Rugg, M. D. (2002). Effects of repeated cortisol administration on brain potential correlates of episodic memory retrieval. *Psychopharmacology, 160*(1), 74–83.

McCabe, C., & Rolls, E. T. (2007). Umami: A delicious flavor formed by convergence of taste and olfactory pathways in the human brain. *European Journal of Neuroscience, 25,* 1855–1864.

McClelland, D. C. (1958). Risk-taking in children with high and low need for achievement. In J. W. Atkinson (Ed.), *Motives in fantasy, action, and society.* Princeton, NJ: Van Nostrand.

McClelland, D. C. (1987). Characteristics of successful entrepreneurs. *Journal of Creative Behavior, 3,* 219–233.

McClelland, D. C. (1993). Intelligence is not the best predictor of job performance. *Current Directions in Psychological Science, 2,* 5–6.

McCrae, R. R. (2004). Human nature and culture: A trait perspective. *Journal of Research in Personality, 38*(1), 3–14.

McCrae, R. R., & Costa, P. T. Jr. (1990). *Personality in adulthood.* New York, NY: Guilford Press.

McCrae, R. R., & Costa, P. T. Jr. (1999). A five-factor theory of personality. In L. A. Pervin & O. P. John (Eds.), *Handbook of personality: Theory and research.* New York, NY: Guilford Press.

McCrae, R. R., & Sutin, A. R. (2007). New frontiers for the five-factor model: A review of the literature. *Social and Personality Psychology Compass, 1,* 423–440.

McCrae, R. R., Costa, P. T. Jr., Hrebíčková, M., Urbánek, T., Martin, T. A., Oryol, V. E., Rukavishnikov, A. A., & Senin, I. G. (2004). Age differences in personality traits across cultures: Self-report and observer perspectives. *European Journal of Personality, 18*(2), 143–157.

McCrae, R. R., Costa, P. T. Jr., Martin, T. A., Oryol, V. E., Rukavishnikov, A. A., Senin, I. G., Hrebíčková, M., & Urbánek, T. (2004). Consensual validation of personality traits across cultures. *Journal of Research in Personality, 38*(2), 179–201.

McCrae, R. R., Costa, P. T. Jr., Ostendorf, F., Angleitner, A., Hrebickova, M., Avia, M. D., Sanz, J., Sanchez-Bernardos, M. L., Kusdil, M. E., Woodfield, R., Saunders, P. R., & Smith, P. B. (2000). Nature over nurture: Temperament, personality, and life span development. *Journal of Personality and Social Psychology, 78*(1), 173–186.

McDonald, J. W., Liu, X. Z., Qu, Y., Liu, S., Mickey, S. K., Turetsky, D., Gottlieb, D. I., & Choi, D. W. (1999). Transplanted embryonic stem cells survive, differentiate, and promote recovery in injured rat spinal cord. *Nature & Medicine, 5,* 1410–1412.

McDougall, W. (1908). *Social psychology.* New York, NY: Putnam's Sons.

McEvoy, P. M. (2007). Effectiveness of cognitive behavioural group therapy for social phobia in a community clinic: A benchmarking study. *Behaviour Research and Therapy, 45,* 3030–3040.

McFarlane, W. R. (2006). Family expressed emotion prior to onset of psychosis. In S. R. H. Beach, M. Z. Wamboldt, N. J. Kaslow, R. E. Heyman, M. B. First, L. G. Underwood, & D. Reiss (Eds.), *Relational processes and DSM-V: Neuroscience, assessment, prevention, and treatment* (pp. 77–87). Washington, DC: American Psychiatric Association.

McGrath, P. (2002). Qualitative findings on the experience of end-of-life care for hematological malignancies. *American Journal of Hospice & Palliative Care, 19*(2), 103–111.

McGue, M., Bouchard, T. J., Iacono, W. G., & Lykken, D. T. (1993). Behavioral genetics of cognitive ability: A life-span perspective. In R. Plomin & G. McClearn (Eds.), *Nature, nurture, and psychology.* Washington, DC: American Psychological Association.

McIntyre, M. (2009a, March 5). Fateful meeting on Greyhound. *Winnipeg Free Press.* Retrieved from http://www.winnipegfreepress.com/local/fateful_meeting_on_greyhound-40702917.html

McIntyre, M. (2009b, March 6). Li found not criminally responsible. *National Post,* p. A7.

McKellar, P. (1972). Imagery from the standpoint of introspection. In P. W. Sheehan (Ed.), *The function and nature of imagery* (pp. 35–61). New York, NY: Academic Press.

McKim, W. A. (2002). *Drugs and behavior: An introduction to behavioral pharmacology* (5th ed). Englewood Cliffs, NJ: Prentice Hall.

McKinney, C., Donnelly, R., & Renk, K. (2008). Perceived parenting, positive and negative perceptions of parents, and late adolescent emotional adjustment. *Child and Adolescent Mental Health, 13,* 66–73.

McNamara, J. M., Barta, Z., Fromhage, L., & Houston, A. I. (2008). The coevolution of choosiness and cooperation. *Nature, 451,* 189–201.

McNicholas, W. T., & Javaheri, S. (2007). Pathophysiologic mechanisms of cardiovascular disease in obstructive sleep apnea. *Sleep Medicine Clinics, 2,* 539–547.

Medina, J. J. (1996). *The clock of ages: Why we age.* Cambridge, MA: Cambridge University Press.

Meeus, W., & Raaijmakers, Q. (1989). Autoritätsgehorsam in Experimenten des Milgram-Typs: Eine Forschungsübersicht [Obedience to authority in Milgram-type studies: A research review]. *Zeitschrift für Sozialpsychologie, 20*(2), 70–85.

Mehrabian, A. (1968). A relationship of attitude to seated posture orientation and distance. *Journal of Personality and Social Psychology, 10,* 26–30.

Mehrabian, A. (1971). *Silent messages.* Belmont, CA: Wadsworth.

Mehrabian, A. (2007). *Nonverbal communication.* New Brunswick, NJ: Aldine Transaction.

Meltzer, G. (2000). Genetics and etiology of schizophrenia and bipolar disorder. *Biological Psychiatry, 47*(3), 171–178.

Meltzer, L. (2004). Resilience and learning disabilities: Research on internal and external protective dynamics. *Learning Disabilities Research & Practice, 19*(1), 1–2.

Meltzoff, A. N., & Moore, M. K. (1977). Imitation of facial and manual gestures by human neonates. *Science, 198,* 75–78.

Meltzoff, A. N., & Moore, M. K. (1985). Cognitive foundations and social functions of imitation and intermodal representation in infancy. In J. Mehler & R. Fox (Eds.), *Neonate cognition: Beyond the blooming buzzing confusion* (pp. 139–156). Hillsdale, NJ: Erlbaum.

Meltzoff, A. N., & Moore, M. K. (1994). Imitation, memory, and the representation of persons. *Infant Behavior and Development, 17,* 83–99.

Melzack, R. (1999). Pain and stress: A new perspective. In R. J. Gatchel & D. C. Turk (Eds.), *Psychosocial factors in pain: Critical perspectives.* New York, NY: Guilford Press.

Melzack, R., & Wall, P. D. (1965). Pain mechanisms: A new theory. *Science, 150,* 971–979.

Menec, V. H. (2003). The relation between everyday activities and successful aging: A 6-year longitudinal study. *Journals of Gerontology B: Psychological Sciences and Social Sciences, 58,* 574–582.

Messinger, L. M. (2001). *Georgia O'Keeffe.* London: Thames & Hudson.

Metcalf, P., & Huntington, R. (1991). *Celebrations of death: The anthropology of mortuary ritual* (2nd ed.). Cambridge, England: Cambridge University Press.

Meyer, U., Nyffeler, M., Schwendener, S., Knuesel, I., Yee, B. K., & Feldon, J. (2008). Relative prenatal and postnatal maternal contributions to schizophrenia-related neurochemical dysfunction after in utero immune challenge. *Neuropsychopharmacology, 33,* 441–456.

Migueles, M, & Garcia-Bajos, E. (1999). Recall, recognition, and confidence patterns in eyewitness testimony. *Applied Cognitive Psychology, 13,* 257–268.

Mikulincer, M., & Goodman, G. S. (Eds.). (2006). *Dynamics of romantic love: Attachment, caregiving, and sex.* New York, NY: Guilford Press.

Milgram, S. (1963). Behavioral study of obedience. *Journal of Abnormal and Social Psychology, 67,* 371–378.

Milgram, S. (1974). *Obedience to authority: An experimental view.* New York, NY: Harper & Row.

Miller, G. A. (1956). The magical number seven, plus or minus two: Some limits on our capacity for processing information. *Psychological Review, 63,* 81–97.

Miller, J. G., & Bersoff, D. M. (1998). The role of liking in perceptions of the moral responsibility to help: A cultural perspective. *Journal of Experimental Social Psychology, 34,* 443–469.

Miller, L. K. (2005). What the savant syndrome can tell us about the nature and nurture of talent. *Journal for the Education of the Gifted, 28,* 361–373.

Millon, T. (2004). *Masters of the mind: Exploring the story of mental illness from ancient times to the new millennium.* Hoboken, NJ: Wiley.

Miltenberger, R. G. (2008). *Behavior modification: Principles and procedures* (4th ed.). Belmont, CA: Cengage.

Milton, J., & Wiseman, R. (1999). Does psi exist? Lack of replication of an anomalous process of information transfer. *Psychological Bulletin, 125,* 387–391.

Milton, J., & Wiseman, R. (2001). Does psi exist? Reply to Storm and Ertel 2000. *Psychological Bulletin, 127* (3), 434–438.

Mineka, S., & Oehlberg, K. (2008). The relevance of recent developments in classical conditioning to understanding the etiology and maintenance of anxiety disorders. *Acta Psychologica, 127,* 567–580.

Mineka, S., & Oehman, A. (2002). Phobias and preparedness: The selective, automatic, and encapsulated nature of fear. *Biological Psychiatry, 51*(9), 927–937.

Mingo, C., Herman, C. J., & Jasperse, M. (2000). Women's stories: Ethnic variations in women's attitudes and experiences of menopause, hysterectomy, and hormone replacement therapy. *Journal of Women's Health and Gender Based Medicine, 9,* S27–S38.

Mingroni, M. A. (2004). The secular rise in IQ. *Intelligence, 32,* 65–83.

Minuchin, S., Lee, W-Y., & Simon, G. M. (2007). *Mastering family therapy: Journeys of growth and transformation* (2nd ed.). Hoboken, NJ: Wiley.

Minzenberg, M. J., Poole, J. H., & Vinogradov, S. (2008). A neurocognitive model of borderline personality disorder: Effects of childhood sexual abuse and relationship to adult social attachment disturbance. *Development and Psychopathology, 20,* 341–368.

Mirescu, C., Peters, J. D., Noiman, L., & Gould, E. (2006). Sleep deprivation inhibits adult neurogenesis in the hippocampus by elevating glucocorticoids. *PNAS Proceedings of the National Academy of Sciences of the United States of America, 103*(50), 19170–19175.

Mischel, W., Shoda, Y., & Ayduk, O. (2008). *Introduction to personality: Toward an integrative science of the person* (8th ed.). Hoboken, NJ: Wiley.

Mita, T. H., Dermer, M., & Knight, J. (1977). Reversed facial images and the mere-exposure hypothesis. *Journal of Personality and Social Psychology, 35*(8), 597–601.

Mitchell, J. P., Dodson, C. S., & Schacter, D. L. (2005). fMRI evidence for the role of recollection in suppressing misattribution errors: The illusory truth effect. *Journal of Cognitive Neuroscience, 17,* 800–810.

Mitchell, R. (2003). Ideological reflections on the DSM-IV-R (or pay no attention to that

man behind the curtain, Dorothy!). *Child & Youth Care Forum, 32*(5), 281–298.

Mittag, O., & Maurischat, C. (2004). Die Cook-Medley Hostility Scale (Ho-Skala) im Vergleich zu den Inhaltsskalen "Zynismus," "Ärger," sowie "Typ A" aus dem MMPI-2: Zur zukünftigen Operationalisierung von Feindseligkeit [A comparison of the Cook-Medley Hostility Scale (Ho-scale) and the content scales "cynicism," "anger," and "type A" out of the MMPI-2: On the future assessment of hostility]. *Zeitschrift für Medizinische Psychologie, 13*(1), 7–12.

Moffitt, T. E. (2005). The new look of behavioral genetics in developmental psychopathology: Gene-environment interplay in antisocial behaviors. *Psychological Bulletin, 131,* 533–554.

Mograss, M. A., Guillem, F., & Godbout, R. (2008). Event-related potentials differentiates the processes involved in the effects of sleep on recognition memory. *Psychophysiology, 45,* 420–434.

Möhler, H., Rudolph, U., Boison, D., Singer, P., Feldon, J., & Yee, B. K. (2008). Regulation of cognition and symptoms of psychosis: Focus on GABA-sub(A) receptors and glycine transporter 1. *Pharmacology, Biochemistry & Behavior, 90,* 58–64.

Moneta, G. B., & Siu, C. M. Y. (2002). Trait intrinsic and extrinsic motivations, academic performance, and creativity in Hong Kong college students. *Journal of College Student Development, 43*(5), 664–683.

Monin, B. (2003). The warm glow heuristic: When liking leads to familiarity. *Journal of Personality and Social Psychology, 85*(6), 1035–1048.

Monks, C. P., Ortega-Ruiz, R., & Rodríguez-Hidalgo, A. J. (2008). Peer victimization in multicultural schools in Spain and England. *European Journal of Developmental Psychology, 5,* 507–535.

Montgomery, S. A. (2008). The under-recognized role of dopamine in the treatment of major depressive disorder. *International Clinical Psychopharmacology, 23,* 63–69.

Moore, M. M. (1998). The science of sexual signaling. In G. C. Brannigan, E. R. Allgeier, & A. R. Allgeier (Eds.), *The sex scientists* (pp. 61–75). New York, NY: Longman.

Moore, S., Grunberg, L., & Greenberg, E. (2004). Repeated downsizing contact: The effects of similar and dissimilar layoff experiences on work and well-being outcomes. *Journal of Occupational Health Psychology, 9*(3), 247–257.

Morgenthaler, T. I., Lee-Chiong, T., Alessi, C., Friedman, L., Aurora, R. N., Boehlecke, B., Brown, T., Chesson, A. L. Jr., Kapur, V., Maganti, R., Owens, J., Pancer, J., Swick, T. J., Zak, R., &

Standards of Practice Committee of the AASM. (2007). Practice parameters for the clinical evaluation and treatment of circadian rhythm sleep disorders: An American academy of sleep medicine report. *Sleep: Journal of Sleep and Sleep Disorders Research, 30,* 1445–1459.

Morris, S. G. (2007). Influences on childrens' narrative coherence: Age, memory breadth, and verbal comprehension. *Dissertation Abstracts International: Section B: The Sciences and Engineering, 68*(6-B), 4157.

Morrison, C., & Westman, A. S. (2001). Women report being more likely than men to model their relationships after what they have seen on TV. *Psychological Reports, 89*(2), 252–254.

Moss, D. (2004). Biofeedback. *Applied Psychophysiology & Biofeedback, 29*(1), 75–78.

Mueser, K. T., & Jeste, D. V. (Eds.). (2008). *Clinical handbook of schizophrenia.* New York, NY: Guildford Press.

Munro, I., & Edward, K-L. (2008). Mental illness and substance use: An Australian perspective. *International Journal of Mental Health Nursing, 17,* 255–260.

Murakami, K., & Hayashi, T. (2002). Interaction between mind-heart and gene. *Journal of International Society of Life Information Science, 20*(1), 122–126.

Murdoch, S. (2007). *IQ: A smart history of a failed idea.* Hoboken, NJ: Wiley.

Murphy, L. L. (2006). Endocannabinoids and endocrine function. In E. S. Onaivi, T. Sugiura, & V. Di Marzo (Eds.), *Endocannabinoids: The brain and body's marijuana and beyond* (pp. 467–474). Boca Raton, FL: CRC Press.

Murray, H. A. (1938). *Explorations in personality.* New York, NY: Oxford University Press.

Myers, L. B., & Vetere, A. (2002). Adult romantic attachment styles and health-related measures. *Psychology, Health & Medicine, 7*(2), 175–180.

Myerson, J., Rank, M. R., Raines, F. Q., & Schnitzler, M. A. (1998). Race and general cognitive ability: The myth of diminishing returns to education. *Psychological Science, 9,* 139–142.

Nabi, R. L., Moyer-Gusé, E., & Byrne, S. (2007). All joking aside: A serious investigation into the persuasive effect of funny social issue messages. *Communication Monographs, 74,* 29–54.

Naglieri, J. A., & Ronning, M. E. (2000) Comparison of White, African American, Hispanic, and Asian children on the Naglieri Nonverbal Ability Test. *Psychological Assessment, 12*(3), 328–334.

Nahas, G. G., Frick, H. C., Lattimer, J. K., Latour, C., & Harvey, D. (2002). Pharmacokinetics of THC in brain and testis, male gametotoxicity and premature apoptosis of spermatozoa.

Human Psychopharmacology: Clinical & Experimental, 17(2), 103–113.

Naisch, P. L. N. (2007). Time to explain the nature of hypnosis? *Contemporary Hypnosis, 23,* 33–46.

Nakamura, K. (2006). The history of psychotherapy in Japan. *International Medical Journal, 13,* 13–18.

Nash, M., & Barnier, A. (Eds.). (2008). *The Oxford handbook of hypnosis.* New York, NY: Oxford University Press.

Näslund, E., & Hellström, P. M. (2007). Appetite signaling: From gut peptides and enteric nerves to brain. *Physiology & Behavior, 92,* 256–262.

Nathan, R., Rollinson, L., Harvey, K., & Hill, J. (2003). The Liverpool violence assessment: An investigator-based measure of serious violence. *Criminal Behaviour & Mental Health, 13*(2), 106–120.

National Institute of Mental Health. (2008). *Anxiety disorders.* Retrieved from http://www.nimh.nih.gov/health/publications/anxiety-disorders/summary.shtml

National Institute on Drug Abuse. (2005). *NIDA infofacts: Club drugs.* Retrieved from http://www.nida.nih.gov/infofacts/club drugs.html

National Organization on Fetal Alcohol Syndrome. (2008). *Facts about FAS and FASD.* Retrieved from http://www.nofas.org/family/facts.aspx

National Sleep Foundation. (2007). *Myths and facts about sleep.* Retrieved from http://www.sleepfoundation.org/article/hot-topics/myths-and-facts-about-sleep

Neale, J. M., Oltmanns, T. F., & Winters, K. C. (1983). Recent developments in the assessment and conceptualization of schizophrenia. *Behavioral Assessment, 5,* 33–54

Neenan, M. (2008). Tackling procrastination: An REBT perspective for coaches. *Journal of Rational-Emotive & Cognitive Behavior Therapy, 26,* 53–62.

Neher, A. (1991). Maslow's theory of motivation: A critique. *Journal of Humanistic Psychology, 31,* 89–112.

Neisser, U. (1967). *Cognitive psychology.* New York, NY: Appleton-Century-Crofts.

Nelson III, C. A., Zeanah, C. H., & Fox, N. A. (2007). The effects of early deprivation on brain-behavioral development: The Bucharest Early Intervention Project. In D. Romer & E. F. Walker (Eds.), *Adolescent psychopathology and the developing brain: Integrating brain and prevention science* (pp. 197–215). New York, NY: Oxford University Press.

Nelson, R. J., & Chiavegatto, S. (2001). Molecular basis of aggression. *Trends in Neurosciences, 24*(12), 713–719.

Neria, Y., Bromet, E. J., Sievers, S., Lavelle, J., & Fochtmann, L. J. (2002). Trauma exposure and posttraumatic stress disorder in psychosis: Findings from a first-admission cohort. *Journal of Consulting & Clinical Psychology, 70*(1), 246–251.

Nesse, R. M. (2000). Is depression an adaptation? *Archives of General Psychiatry, 57,* 14–20.

Nesse, R. M., & Jackson, E. D. (2006). Evolution: Psychiatric nosology's missing biological foundation. *Clinical Neuropsychiatry: Journal of Treatment Evaluation, 3,* 121–131.

Neto, F., & Furnham, A. (2005). Gender-role portrayals in children's television advertisements. *International Journal of Adolescence & Youth, 12*(1–2), 69–90.

Neubauer, A. C., Grabner, R. H., Freudenthaler, H. H., Beckmann, J. F., & Guthke, J. (2004). Intelligence and individual differences in becoming neurally efficient. *Acta Psychologica, 116*(1), 55–74.

Neugarten, B. L., Havighurst, R. J., & Tobin, S. S. (1968). The measurement of life satisfaction. *Journal of Gerontology, 16,* 134–143.

Neuringer, A., Deiss, C., & Olson, G. (2000). Reinforced variability and operant learning. *Journal of Experimental Psychology: Animal Behavior Processes, 26*(1), 98–111.

Ng, S. M., Li, A. M., Lou, V. W. Q., Tso, I. F., Wan, P. Y. P., & Chan, D. F. Y. (2008). Incorporating family therapy into asthma group intervention: A randomized waitlist-controlled trial. *Family Process, 47,* 115–130.

Niaura, R., Todaro, J. F., Stroud, L., Spiro, A., Ward, K. D., & Weiss, S. (2002). Hostility, the metabolic syndrome, and incident cornary heart disease. *Health Psychology, 21*(6), 598–593.

Nicholson, A., Pikhart, H., Pajak, A., Malyutina, S., Kubinova, R., Peasey, A., Topor-Madry, R., Nikitin, Y., Capkova, N., Marmot, M., & Bobak, M. (2008). Socioeconomic status over the life-course and depressive symptoms in men and women in Eastern Europe. *Journal of Affective Disorders, 105,* 125–136.

Nickerson, R. (1998). Confirmation bias: A ubiquitous phenomenon in many guises. *Review of General Psychology, 2,* 175–220.

Nicotra, A., Critchley, H. D., Mathias, C. J., & Dolan, R. J. (2006). Emotional and autonomic consequences of spinal cord injury explored using functional brain imaging. *Brain: A Journal of Neurology, 129,* 718–728.

Nishimoto, R. (1988). A cross-cultural analysis of psychiatric symptom expression using Langer's twenty-two item index. *Journal of Sociology and Social Welfare, 15,* 45–62.

Nishino, S., Ripley, B., Overeem, S., Lammers, G. L., & Mignot E. (2000). Hypocretin (orexin)

transmission in human narcolepsy. *Lancet, 355,* 39–40.

Nogueiras, R., & Tschöp, M. (2005). Separation of conjoined hormones yields appetite rivals. *Science, 310,* 985–986.

Nolen-Hoeksema, S., Larson, J., & Grayson, C. (2000). Explaining the gender difference in depressive symptoms. *Journal of Personality and Social Psychology, 77,* 1061–1072.

Norenzayan, A. (2006). Cultural variation in reasoning. In R. Viale, D. Andler, & L. Hirschfeld (Eds.), *Biological and cultural bases of human inference.* Mahwah, NJ: Erlbaum.

Norton, K. L., Olds, T. S., Olive, S., & Dank, S. (1996). Ken and Barbie at life size. *Sex Roles, 34,* 287–294.

Nouchi, R., & Hyodo, M. (2007). The congruence between the emotional valences of recalled episodes and mood states influences the mood congruence effect. *Japanese Journal of Psychology, 78,* 25–32.

O'Farrell, T. J., Murphy, M., Alter, J., & Fals-Stewart, W. (2008). Brief family treatment intervention to promote continuing care among alcohol-dependent patients in inpatient detoxification: A randomized pilot study. *Journal of Substance Abuse Treatment, 34,* 363–369.

O'Tuathaigh, C. M., Babovic, D., O'Meara, G., Clifford, J. J., Croke, D. T., & Waddington, J. L. (2006). Susceptibility genes for schizophrenia: Characterisation of mutant mouse models at the level of phenotypic behaviour. *Neuroscience and Biobehavioral Reviews, 31*(1), 60–78.

Oei, T. P. S., & Dingle, G. (2008). The effectiveness of group cognitive behaviour therapy for unipolar depressive disorders. *Journal of Affective Disorders, 107,* 5–21.

Oishi, K., Ohkura, N., Sei, H., Matsuda, J., & Ishida, N. (2007). CLOCK regulates the circadian rhythm of kaolin-induced writhing behavior in mice. *Neuroreport: For Rapid Communication of Neuroscience Research, 18,* 1925–1928.

Olds, J., & Milner, P. M. (1954). Positive reinforcement produced by electrical stimulation of septal area and other regions of rat brains. *Journal of Comparative and Physiological Psychology, 47,* 419–427.

Olfson, M., Marcus, S., Pincus, H. A., Zito, J. M., Thompson, J. W., & Zarin, D. A. (1998). Antidepressant prescribing practices of outpatient psychiatrists. *Archives of General Psychiatry, 55,* 310, 316.

Oliver, R. J. (2002). Tobacco abuse in pregnancy. *Journal of Prenatal Psychology & Health, 17*(2), 153–166.

Olweus, D. (1997). Bully/victim problems in school: Facts and intervention. *European Journal of Psychology of Education, 12,* 495–510.

Olweus, D. (2001). Peer harassment: A critical analysis and some important issues. In J. Juvonen & S. Graham (Eds.), *Peer harassment in school: The plight of the vulnerable and victimized.* New York: Guilford.

Olweus, D. (2004). The Olweus Bullying Prevention Programme: Design and implementation issues and a new national initiative in Norway. In P. K. Smith, D. Pepler, & K. Rigby (Eds.), *Bullying in schools: How successful can interventions be?* (pp. 13–36). New York: Cambridge University Press.

Ontario Lottery and Gaming Corporation. (2007). *Payout levels of slot machines at OLG gaming facilities: Fact sheet.* Retrieved from http://www.olg.ca/assets/documents/media/slots_payout_fact_sheet_2007.pdf

Oppenheimer, D. M. (2004). Spontaneous discounting of availability in frequency judgment tasks. *Psychological Science, 15*(2), 100–105.

Orne, M. T. (2006). The nature of hypnosis, artifact and essence: An experimental study. *Dissertation Abstracts International: Section B: The Sciences and Engineering, 67*(2-B), 1207.

Orth-Gomer, K. (2007). Job strain and risk of recurrent coronary events. *Journal of the American Medical Association, 298,* 1693–1694.

Oshima, K. (2000). Ethnic jokes and social function in Hawaii. *Humor: International Journal of Humor Research, 13*(1), 41–57.

Ostrov, J. M., & Keating, C. F. (2004). Gender differences in preschool aggression during free play and structured interactions: An observational study. *Social Development, 13*(2), 255–277.

Overmier, J. B., & Murison, R. (2000). Anxiety and helplessness in the face of stress predisposes, precipitates, and sustains gastric ulceration. *Behavioural Brain Research, 110*(1–2), 161–174.

Ozawa-de Silva, C. (2007). Demystifying Japanese therapy: An analysis of Naikan and the Ajase complex through Buddhist thought. *Ethos, 35,* 411–446.

Paice, E., Rutter, H., Wetherell, M., Winder, B., & McManus, I. C. (2002). Stressful incidents, stress and coping strategies in the pre-registration house officer year. *Medical Education, 36*(1), 56–65.

Palfai, T. P., Monti, P. M., Ostafin, B., & Hutchinson, K. (2000). Effects of nicotine deprivation on alcohol-related information processing and drinking behavior. *Journal of Abnormal Psychology, 109,* 96–105.

Palmer, S., & Gyllensten, K. (2008). How cognitive-behavioural, rational-emotive-behavioural or multimodal coaching could prevent mental health problems, enhance performance, and reduce work related stress. *Journal of Rational-Emotive & Cognitive Behavior Therapy, 26,* 38–52.

Panksepp, J. (2005). Affective consciousness: Core emotional feelings in animals and humans. *Consciousness & Cognition: An International Journal, 14*(1), 30–80.

Papadelis, C., Chen, Z., Kourtidou-Papadeli, C., Bamidis, P. D., Chouvarda, I., Bekiaris, E., & Maglaveras, N. (2007). Monitoring sleepiness with on-board electrophysiological recordings for preventing sleep-deprived traffic accidents. *Clinical Neurophysiology, 118,* 1906–1922.

Paquet, F., Soucy, J. P., Stip, E., Lévesque, M., Elie, A., & Bédard, M. A. (2004). Comparison between olanzapine and haloperidol on procedural learning and the relationship with striatal D-sub-2 receptor occupancy in schizophrenia. *Journal of Neuropsychiatry & Clinical Neurosciences, 16*(1), 47–56.

Park, C. (2007). In other (people's) words: Plagiarism by university students—literature and lessons. *Assessment and Evaluation in Higher Education, 28*(5), 231–241.

Parker, G. (1982). Re-searching the schizophrenogenic mother. *The Journal of Nervous and Mental Disease, 170*(8), 452–462.

Parker-Oliver, D. (2002). Redefining hope for the terminally ill. *American Journal of Hospice & Palliative Care, 19*(2), 115–120.

Parrott, A., Morinan, A., Moss, M., & Scholey, A. (2004). *Understanding drugs and behavior.* Hoboken, NJ: Wiley.

Patterson, C. J. (2009). *APA online public interest. Lesbian and gay parenting: Children of lesbian and gay parenting.* Retrieved from http://www.apa.org/pi/lgbc/publications/lgpchildren.html

Patterson, F., & Linden, E. (1981). *The education of Koko.* New York, NY: Holt, Rinehart and Winston.

Patterson, J. M., Holm, K. E., & Gurney, J. G. (2004). The impact of childhood cancer on the family: A qualitative analysis of strains, resources, and coping behaviors. *Psycho-Oncology, 13*(6), 390–407.

Patterson, P. (2002). *Penny's journal: Koko wants to have a baby.* Retrieved from http://www.koko.org/world/journal.phtml?

Paul, D. B., & Blumenthal, A. L. (1989). On the trail of little Albert. *The Psychological Record, 39,* 547–553.

Pearce, M. E., Christian, W. M., Patterson, K., Norris, K., Moniruzzaman, A., Craib, K. J. P., Schechter, M. T., & Spittal, P. M. (2008). The Cedar Project: Historical trauma, sexual abuse and HIV risk among young Aboriginal people who use injection and non-injection drugs in two Canadian cities. *Social Science and Medicine, 66*(11), 2185–2194.

Pearlman, C. (2002). Electroconvulsive therapy in clinical psychopharmacology. *Journal of Clinical Psychopharmacology, 22*(4), 345–346.

Pearson, N. J., Johnson. I. M., & Nahin, R. L. (2006). Insomnia, trouble sleeping, and complementary and alternative medicine: Analysis of the 2002 National Health Interview Survey data. *Archives of Internal Medicine, 166,* 1775–1782.

Pedrazzoli, M., Pontes, J. C., Peirano, P., & Tufik, S. (2007). HLA-DQB1 genotyping in a family with narcolepsy-cataplexy. *Brain Research, 1165,* 1–4.

Peleg, G., Katzir, G., Peleg, O., Kamara, M., Brodsky, L., Hel-Or, H., et al. (2006). Hereditary family signature of facial expression. *Proceedings of the National Academy of Sciences, 103,* 15921–15926.

Pellegrino, J. E., & Pellegrino, L. (2008). Fetal alcohol syndrome and related disorders. In P. J. Accardo (Ed.), *Caputo and Accardo's neurodevelopmental disabilities in infancy and childhood: Vol 1: Neurodevelopmental diagnosis and treatment* (3rd ed.) (pp. 269–284). Baltimore, MD: Paul H Brookes.

Pelletier, J. G., & Paré, D. (2004). Role of amygdale oscillations in the consolidation of emotional memories. *Biological Psychiatry, 55*(6), 559–562.

Penfield, W. (1947). Some observations in the cerebral cortex of man. *Proceedings of the Royal Society, 134,* 349.

Pepler, D., & Craig, W. (2000). *Making a difference in bullying.* LaMarsh Research Programme, Report Series, Report # 60. Toronto, ON: LaMarsh Centre for Research on Violence and Conflict Resolution. Retrieved from http://www.arts.yorku.ca/lamarsh/pdf/Making_a_Difference_in_Bullying.pdf

Pérez-Mata, N., & Diges, M. (2007). False recollections and the congruence of suggested information. *Memory, 15,* 701–717.

Persson, J., Lind, J., Larsson, A., Ingvar, M., Sleegers, K., Van Broeckhoven, C., Adolfsson, R., Nilsson, L-G., & Nyberg, L. (2008). Altered deactivation in individuals with genetic risk for Alzheimer's disease. *Neuropsychologia, 46,* 1679–1687.

Pettigrew, T. F. (1998). Reactions towards the new minorities of Western Europe. *Annual Review of Sociology, 24,* 77–103.

Pham, T. M., Winblad, B., Granholm, A-C., & Mohammed, A. H. (2002). Environmental influences on brain neurotrophins in rats. *Pharmacology, Biochemistry & Behavior, 73*(1), 167–175.

Phares, V. (2008). *Understanding abnormal child psychology* (2nd ed.). Hoboken, NJ: Wiley.

Phillips, S. T., & Ziller, R. C. (1997). Toward a theory and measure of the nature of nonprejudice. *Journal of Personality and Social Psychology, 72,* 420–434.

Piaget, J. (1962). *Play, dreams and imitation in Childhood.* New York, NY: Norton.

Pickel, D., Manucy, G. P., Walker, D. B., Hall, S. B., & Walker, J. C. (2004). Evidence of canine olfactory detection of melanoma. *Applied Animal Behaviour Science, 89,* 107–113.

Pierce, J. P. (2007). Tobacco industry marketing, population-based tobacco control, and smoking behavior. *American Journal of Preventive Medicine, 33,* 327–334.

Pinker, S. (2007). *The language instinct: How the mind creates language* (PS ed.). New York, NY: Harper-Collins.

Pinker, S., & Jackendoff, R. (2005) What's special about the human language faculty? *Cognition, 95*(2), 201–236.

Pittenger, D. J. (2005). Cautionary comments regarding the Myers-Briggs Type Indicator. *Consulting Psychology Journal: Practice and Research, 57,* 210–221.

Plomin, R. (1990). The role of inheritance in behavior. *Science, 248,* 183–188.

Plomin, R. (1999). Genetics and general cognitive ability. *Nature, 402,* C25–C29.

Plomin, R., & Crabbe, J. (2000). DNA. *Psychological Bulletin, 126,* 806–828.

Plomin, R., DeFries, J. C., & Fulker, D. W. (2007). *Nature and nurture during infancy and early childhood.* New York, NY: Cambridge University Press.

Plummer, D. C. (2001). The quest for modern manhood: Masculine stereotypes, peer culture and the social significance of homophobia. *Journal of Adolescence, 24*(1), 15–23.

Plutchik, R. (1984). Emotions: A general psychoevolutionary theory. In K. R. Scherer & P. Ekman (Eds.), *Approaches to emotion.* Hillsdale, NJ: Erlbaum.

Plutchik, R. (1994). *The psychology and biology of emotion.* New York, NY: HarperCollins.

Plutchik, R. (2000). *Emotions in the practice of psychotherapy: Clinical implications of affect theories.* Washington, DC: American Psychological Association.

Pomponio, A. T. (2002). *Psychological consequences of terror.* New York, NY: Wiley.

Ponzi, A. (2008). Dynamical model of salience gated working memory, action selection and reinforcement based on basal ganglia and dopamine feedback. *Neural Networks, 21,* 322–330.

Pope, H. G. Jr., Barry, S., Bodkin, J. A., & Hudson, J. (2007). "Scientific study of the dissociative disorders": Reply. *Psychotherapy and Psychosomatics, 76,* 401–403.

Popma, A., Vermeiren, R., Geluk, C. A. M. L., Rinne, T., van den Brink, W., Knol, D. L., Jansen, L. M. C., van Engeland, H., & Doreleijers, T. A. H. (2007). Cortisol moderates the relationship between testosterone and aggression in delinquent male adolescents. *Biological Psychiatry, 61,* 405–411.

Porzelius, L. K., Dinsmore, B. D., & Staffelbach, D. (2001). Eating disorders. In M. Hersen & V. B. Van Hasselt (Eds.), *Advanced abnormal psychology* (2nd ed.). Netherlands: Klewer Academic Publishers.

Posthuma, D., de Geus, E. J. C., & Boomsma, D. I. (2001). Perceptual speed and IQ are associated through common genetic factors. *Behavior Genetics, 31*(6), 593–602.

Posthuma, D., Neale, M. C., Boomsma, D. I., & de Geus, E. J. C. (2001). Are smarter brains running faster? Heritability of alpha peak frequency, IQ, and their interrelation. *Behavior Genetics, 31*(6), 567–579.

Powell, D. H. (1998), *The nine myths of aging: Maximizing the quality of later life.* San Francisco, CA: Freeman.

Prabhu, V., Sutton, C., & Sauser, W. (2008). Creativity and certain personality traits: Understanding the mediating effect of intrinsic motivation. *Creativity Research Journal, 20,* 53–66.

Pratt, M. W., Skoe, E. E., & Arnold, M. (2004). Care reasoning development and family socialisation patterns in later adolescence: A longitudinal analysis. *International Journal of Behavioral Development, 28*(2), 139–147.

Preuss, U. W., Zetzsche, T., Jäger, M., Groll, C., Frodl, T., Bottlender, R., Leinsinger, G., Hegerl, U., Hahn, K., Möller, H. J., & Meisenzahl, E. M. (2005). Thalamic volume in first-episode and chronic schizophrenic subjects: A volumetric MRI study. *Schizophrenia Research, 73*(1), 91–101.

Prigatano, G. P., & Gray, J. A. (2008). Predictors of performance on three developmentally sensitive neuropsychological tests in children with and without traumatic brain injury. *Brain Injury, 22,* 491–500.

Primavera, L. H., & Herron, W. G. (1996). The effect of viewing television violence on aggression. *International Journal of Instructional Media, 23,* 91–104.

Pring, L., Woolf, K., & Tadic, V. (2008). Melody and pitch processing in five musical savants with congenital blindness. *Perception, 37,* 290–307.

Prkachin, K. M. (2005). Effects of deliberate control on verbal and facial expressions of pain. *Pain, 114,* 328–338.

Prkachin, K. M., & Silverman, B. E. (2002). Hostility and facial expression in young men and women: Is social regulation more important than negative affect? *Health Psychology, 21*(1), 33–39.

Public Health Agency of Canada. (2006). *Awareness of the effects of alcohol use during pregnancy and awareness of fetal alcohol spectrum disorder: Results of a national survey* (PN4568). Retrieved from http://www.phac-aspc.gc.ca/publicat/fas-saf-natsurv-2006/pdf/ap-ag-finalreport06_e.pdf

Public Health Agency of Canada. (2007). *Fetal alcohol spectrum disorder (FASD)*. Retrieved from http://www.phac-aspc.gc.ca/fasd-etcaf/faq_e.html#7

Public Health Agency of Canada. (2008). *Common questions about smoking and pregnancy.* Retrieved from http://www.phac-aspc.gc.ca/hp-gs/faq/smoke-fumer-eng.php

Public Health Agency of Canada. (2003). Healthy living unit: Canada's physical activity guide to healthy active living. Retrieved from http://www.phac-aspc.gc.ca/pau-uap/paguide/index.html

Pullum, G. K. (1991). *The great Eskimo vocabulary hoax and other irreverent essays on the study of language.* Chicago: University of Chicago Press.

Qualls, S. H. (2008). Caregiver family therapy. In K. Laidlaw & B. Knight (Eds.), *Handbook of emotional disorders in later life: Assessment and treatment.* New York, NY: Oxford University Press.

Quinn, J., Barrowclough, C., & Tarrier, N. (2003). The Family Questionnaire (FQ): A scale for measuring symptom appraisal in relatives of schizophrenic patients. *Acta Psychiatrica Scandinavica, 108*(4), 290–296.

Quintanilla, Y. T. (2007). Achievement motivation strategies: An integrative achievement motivation program with first year seminar students. *Dissertation Abstracts International Section A: Humanities and Social Sciences, 68* (6-A), 2339.

Raevuori, A., Keski-Rahkonen, A., Hoek, H. W., Sihvola, E., Rissanen, A., & Kaprio, J. (2008). Lifetime anorexia nervosa in young men in the community: Five cases and their co-twins. *International Journal of Eating Disorders, 41,* 458–463.

Raine, A., & Yang, Y. (2006). The neuroanatomical bases of psychopathy: A review of brain imaging findings. In C. J. Patrick (Ed.), *Handbook of the psychopathy* (pp. 278–295). New York, NY: Guilford Press.

Ramirez, G., Zemba, D., & Geiselman, R. E. (1996). Judges' cautionary instructions on eyewitness testimony. *American Journal of Forensic Psychology, 14,* 31–66.

Ran, M. (2007). Experimental research on the reliability of the testimony from eyewitnesses. *Psychological Science (China), 30,* 727–730.

Rattaz, C., Goubet, N., & Bullinger, A. (2005). The calming effect of a familiar odor on full-term newborns. *Journal of Developmental & Behavioral Pediatrics, 26,* 86–92.

Rauer, A. J. (2007). Identifying happy, healthy marriages for men, women, and children. *Dissertation Abstracts International: Section B: The Sciences and Engineering, 67*(10-B), 6098.

Rechtschaffen, A., & Bergmann, B. M. (2002). Sleep deprivation in the rat: An update of the 1989 paper. *Sleep, 25*(1), 18–24.

Rechtschaffen, A., & Siegel, J. M. (2000). Sleep and dreaming. In E. R. Kandel, J. H. Schwartz, & T. M. Jessel (Eds.), *Principles of Neuroscience* (4th ed., pp. 936–947). New York, NY: McGraw-Hill.

Reeve, J. (2005). *Understanding motivation and emotion* (4th ed.). Hoboken, NJ: Wiley.

Regan, P. (1998). What if you can't get what you want? Willingness to compromise ideal mate selection standards as a function of sex, mate value, and relationship context. *Personality and Social Psychology Bulletin, 24,* 1294–1303.

Regier, D. A., Narrow, W. E., Rae, D. S., Manderscheid, R. W., Locke, B. Z., & Goodwin, F. K. (1993). The de facto US mental and addictive disorders service system. *Archives of General Psychiatry, 50,* 85–93.

Reich, D. A. (2004). What you expect is not always what you get: The roles of extremity, optimism, and pessimism in the behavioral confirmation process. *Journal of Experimental Social Psychology, 40*(2), 199–215.

Reifman, A. (2000). Revisiting the Bell Curve. *Psychology, 11,* 21–29.

Reissig, C. J., Strain, E. C., & Griffiths, R. R. (2009). Caffeinated energy drinks: A growing problem. *Drug and Alcohol Dependence, 99*(1–3), 1–10.

Renzetti, C., Curran, D., & Kennedy-Bergen, R. (2006). *Understanding diversity.* Boston, MA: Allyn & Bacon/Longman.

Resing, W. C., & Nijland, M. I. (2002). Worden kinderen intelligenter? Een kwart eeuw onderzoek met de Leidse Diagnostische Test [Are children becoming more intelligent? Twenty-five years' research using the Leiden Diagnostic Test]. *Kind en Adolescent, 23*(1), 42–49.

Ressler, K., & Davis, M. (2003). Genetics of childhood disorders: Learning and memory, part 3: Fear conditioning. *Journal of the American Academy of Child & Adolescent Psychiatry, 42*(5), 612–615.

Rest, J., Narvaez, D., Bebeau, M., & Thoma, S. (1999). A neo-Kohlbergian approach: The DIT and schema theory. *Educational Psychology Review, 11*(4), 291–324.

Reulbach, U., Bleich, S., Biermann, T., Pfahlberg, A., & Sperling, W. (2007). Late-onset schizophrenia in child survivors of the Holocaust. *Journal of Nervous and Mental Disease, 195,* 315–319.

Revonsuo, A. (2006). *Inner presence: Consciousness as a biological phenomenon.* Cambridge, MA: MIT Press.

Reynolds, M. R., Keith, T. Z., Ridley, K. P., & Patel, P. G. (2008). Sex differences in latent general and broad cognitive abilities for children and youth: Evidence from higher-order MG-MACS and MIMIC models. *Intelligence, 36,* 236–260.

Rhodes, G., Halberstadt, J., & Brajkovich, G. (2001). Generalization of mere exposure effects to averaged composite faces. *Social Cognition, 19*(1), 57–70.

Ridley, R. M., Baker, H. F., Cummings, R. M., Green, M. E., & Leow-Dyke, A. (2005). Mild topographical memory impairment following crossed unilateral lesions of the mediodorsal thalamic nucleus and the inferotemporal cortex. *Behavioral Neuroscience, 119*(2), 518–525.

Riebe, D., Garber, C. E., Rossi, J. S., Greaney, M. L., Nigg, C. R., Lees, F. D., Burbank, P. M., & Clark, P. G. (2005). Physical activity, physical function, and stages of change in older adults. *American Journal of Health Behavior, 29,* 70–80.

Riemann, D., & Voderholzer, U. (2003). Primary insomnia: a risk factor to develop depression? *Journal of Affective Disorders, 76*(1–3), 255–259.

Rigby, K. (2008). *Children and bullying: How parents and educators can reduce bullying at school.* Malden, MA: Blackwell.

Rizzolatti, G., Fadiga, L., Fogassi, L. & Gallese, V. (2002). From mirror neurons to imitation: Facts and speculations. In A. N. Meltzoff & W. Prinz (Eds.), *The imitative mind: Development, evolution, and brain bases.* Cambridge, MA: Cambridge University Press.

Rizzolatti, G., Fogassi, L. & Gallese, V. (2006, November). In the mind. *Scientific American,* 54–61.

Roberge, P., Marchand, A., Reinharz, D., & Savard, P. (2008). Cognitive-behavioral treatment for panic disorder with agoraphobia: A randomized, controlled trial and cost-effectiveness analysis. *Behavior Modification, 32,* 333–351.

Roberts, M. (2006, March). Idol dreams. *Schizophrenia Digest,* 30–33.

Roberts, W. W., & Nagel, J. (1996). First-order projections activated by stimulation of hypothalamic sites eliciting attack and flight in rats. *Behavioral Neuroscience, 110,* 509–527.

Robinson, F. P. (1970). *Effective study* (4th ed.). New York, NY: Harper & Row.

Robinson, R. J. (2008). Comorbidity of alcohol abuse and depression: Exploring the self-medication hypothesis. *Dissertation Abstracts International: Section B: The Sciences and Engineering, 68*(9-B), 6332.

Rodrigues, A., Assmar, E. M., & Jablonski, B. (2005). Social-psychology and the invasion of Iraq. *Revista de Psicología Social, 20,* 387–398.

Rogers, C. R. (1961). *On becoming a person.* Boston, MA: Houghton Mifflin.

Rogers, C. R. (1980). *A way of being.* Boston, MA: Houghton Mifflin.

Rogosch, F. A., & Cicchetti, D. (2004). Child maltreatment and emergent personality organization: Perspectives from the five-factor model. *Journal of Abnormal Child Psychology, 32*(2), 123–145.

Roid, G. H. (2003). *Stanford-Binet Intelligence Scales* (5th ed.). Itasca, IL: Riverside Publishing.

Romero, S. G., McFarland, D. J., Faust, R., Farrell, L., & Cacace, A. T. (2008). Electrophysiological markers of skill-related neuroplasticity. *Biological Psychology, 78,* 221–230.

Roques, P., Lambin, M., Jeunier, B., & Strayer, F. (1997). Multivariate analysis of personal space in a primary school classroom. *Enfance, 4,* 451–468.

Rosch, E. (1978). Principles of organization. In E. Rosch & H. L. Lloyd (Eds.), *Cognition and categorization* (pp. 27–48). Hillsdale, NJ: Erlbaum.

Rosch, E. H. (1973). Natural categories. *Cognitive Psychology, 4,* 328–350.

Rosenthal, C. J., & Gladstone, J. (2007). *Grandparenthood in Canada.* Ottawa, ON: The Vanier Institute of the Family. Retrieved from http://www.vifamily.ca/library/cft/grandparenthood.html

Rosenthal, H. G. (2007). The Tiger Woods analogy: The seven-minute active listening solution. In L. L. Hecker & C. F. Sori (Eds.), *The therapist's notebook: More homework, handouts, and activities for use in psychotherapy* (Vol. 2) (pp. 277–280). Haworth practical practice in mental health. New York, NY: Haworth Press.

Rosenzweig, M. R., & Bennett, E. L. (1996). Psychobiology of plasticity: Effects of training and experience on brain and behavior. *Behavioral Brain Research, 78*(1), 57–65.

Rosenzweig, M. R., Bennett, E. L., & Diamond, M. C. (1972). Brain changes in response to experience. *Scientific American, 226,* 22–29.

Rossato, M., Pagano, C., & Vettor, R. (2008). The cannabinoid system and male reproductive functions. *Journal of Neuroendocrinology, 20,* 90–93.

Rossignol, S., Barrière, G., Frigon, A., Barthélemy, D., Bouyer, L., Provencher, J., Leblond, H., & Bernard, G. (2008). Plasticity of locomotor sensorimotor interactions after peripheral and/or spinal lesions. *Brain Research Reviews, 57,* 228–240.

Roth, M. D., Whittaker, K., Salehi, K., Tashkin, D. P., & Baldwin, G. C. (2004). Mechanisms for impaired effector function in alveolar macrophages from marijuana and cocaine smokers. *Journal of Neuroimmunology, 147*(1–2), 82–86.

Roth, M. L., Tripp, D. A., Harrison, M. H., Sullivan, M., & Carson, P. (2007). Demographic and psychosocial predictors of acute perioperative pain for total knee arthroplasty. *Pain Research & Management, 12,* 185–194.

Rothstein, J. B., Jensen, G., & Neuringer, A. (2008). Human choice among five alternatives when reinforcers decay. *Behavioural Processes, 78,* 231–239.

Rotter, J. B. (1954). *Social learning and clinical psychology.* Englewood Cliffs, NJ: Prentice Hall.

Rotter, J. B. (1990). Internal versus external control of reinforcement: A case history of a variable. *American Psychologist, 45,* 489–493.

Rowe, R., Maughan, B., Worthman, C. M., Costello, E. J., & Angold, A. (2004). Testosterone, antisocial behavior, and social dominance in boys: Pubertal development and biosocial interaction. *Biological Psychiatry, 55*(5), 546–552.

Rozencwajg, P., Cherfi, M., Ferrandez, A. M., Lautrey, J., Lemoine, C., & Loarer, E. (2005). Age related differences in the strategies used by middle aged adults to solve a block design task. *International Journal of Aging & Human Development, 60*(2), 159–182.

Rubin, Z. (1970). Measurement of romantic love. *Journal of Personality and Social Psychology, 16,* 265–273.

Rubinstein, E. (2008). Judicial perceptions of eyewitness testimony. *Dissertation Abstracts International: Section B: The Sciences and Engineering, 68*(8-B), 5592.

Ruble, D. N., Martin, C. L., & Berenbaum, S. A. (2006). Gender development. In N. E. Eisenberg, W. E. Damon, & R. M. Lerner (Eds.), *Handbook of child psychology. Vol. 3: Social, emotional, and personality development* (6th ed., pp. 858–932). Hoboken, NJ: Wiley.

Ruffolo, J. S., Phillips, K. A., Menard, W., Fay, C., & Weisberg, R. B. (2006). Comorbidity of body dysmorphic disorder and eating disorders: Severity of psychopathology and body image disturbance. *International Journal of Eating Disorders, 39,* 11–19.

Rumbaugh, D. M., von Glasersfeld, E. C., Warner, H., Pisani, P., & Gill, T. V. (1974). Lana (chimpanzee) learning language: A progress report. *Brain & Language, 1*(2), 205–212.

Russo, N. F., & Tartaro, J. (2008). Women and mental health. In F. L. Denmark & M. A. Paludi (Eds.), *Psychology of women: A handbook of issues and theories* (2nd ed., pp. 440–483). *Women's psychology.* Westport, CT: Praeger/Greenwood.

Ruthig, J. C., Chipperfield, J. G., Perry, R. P., Newall, N. E., & Swift, A. (2007). Comparative risk and perceived control: Implications for psychological and physical well-being among older adults. *Journal of Social Psychology, 147,* 345–369.

Rutter, M. (2007). Gene-environment interdependence. *Developmental Science, 10,* 12–18.

Ryback, D., Ikemi, A., & Miki, Y. (2001). Japanese psychology in crisis: Thinking inside the (empty) box. *Journal of Humanistic Psychology, 41*(4), 124–136.

Rymer, R. (1993). *Genie: An abused child's first flight from silence.* New York, NY: HarperCollins.

Sabini, J., & Silver, M. (1993). Critical thinking and obedience to authority. In J. Chaffee (Ed.). *Critical thinking* (2nd ed., pp. 367–376). Palo Alto, CA: Houghton Mifflin.

Sacchetti, B., Sacco, T., & Strata, P. (2007). Reversible inactivation of amygdala and cerebellum but not perirhinal cortex impairs reactivated fear memories. *European Journal of Neuroscience, 25*(9), 2875–2884.

Sachdev, P., Mondraty, N., Wen, W., & Gulliford, K. (2008). Brains of anorexia nervosa patients process self-images differently from non-self-images: An fMRI study. *Neuropsychologia, 46,* 2161–2168.

Sack, R. L., Auckley, D., Auger, R. R., Carskadon, M. A., Wright, Jr., K. P., Vitiello, M. V., & Zhdanova, I. V. (2007). Circadian rhythm sleep disorders: Part I, basic principles, shift work and jet lag disorders: An American Academy of Sleep Medicine review. *Sleep: Journal of Sleep and Sleep Disorders Research, 30,* 1460–1483.

Sacks, O. (1995). *An anthropologist on Mars.* New York, NY: Vintage Books.

Salovey, P., & Mayer, J. D. (1990). Emotional intelligence. *Imagination, Cognition, and Personality, 9,* 185–211.

Salovey, P., Bedell, B. T., Detweiler, J. B., & Mayer, J. D. (2000). Current directions in emotional intelligence research. In M. Lewis & J. M. Haviland (Eds.), *Handbook of emotions* (2nd ed., pp. 504–520). New York, NY: Guilford Press.

Salvatore, P., Ghidini, S., Zita, G., De Panfilis, C., Lambertino, S., Maggini, C., & Baldessarini, R. J.

(2008). Circadian activity rhythm abnormalities in ill and recovered bipolar I disorder patients. *Bipolar Disorders, 10,* 256–265.

Sampselle, C. M., Harris, V. Harlow, S. D., & Sowers, M. F. (2002). Midlife development and menopause in African American and Caucasian women. *Health Care for Women International, 23*(4), 351–363.

Sanchez Jr., J. (2006). Life satisfaction factors impacting the older Cuban-American population. *Dissertation Abstracts International Section A: Humanities and Social Sciences, 67*(5-A), 1864.

Sangha, S., McComb, C., Scheibenstock, A., Johannes, C., & Lukowiak, K. (2002). The effects of continuous versus partial reinforcement schedules on associative learning, memory, and extinction in Lymnaea stagnalis. *Journal of Experimental Biology, 205,* 1171–1178.

Sangwan, S. (2001). Ecological factors as related to I.Q. of children. *Psycho-Lingua, 31*(2), 89–92.

Sarafino, E. P. (2005). *Health psychology: Biopsychosocial interactions* (5th ed.). Hoboken, NJ: Wiley.

Sarafino, E. P. (2008). *Health psychology: Biopsychosocial interactions* (6th ed.). Hoboken, NJ: Wiley.

Sassenberg, K., Moskowitz, G. B., Jacoby, J., & Hansen, N. (2007). The carry-over effect of competition: The impact of competition on prejudice towards uninvolved outgroups. *Journal of Experimental Social Psychology, 43,* 529–538.

Satcher, N. D. (2007). Social and moral reasoning of high school athletes and non-athletes. *Dissertation Abstracts International Section 7A: Humanities and Social Sciences, 68*(3-A), 928.

Sathyaprabha, T. N., Satishchandra, P., Pradhan, C., Sinha, S., Kaveri, B., Thennarasu, K., Murthy, B. T. C., & Raju, T. R. (2008). Modulation of cardiac autonomic balance with adjuvant yoga therapy in patients with refractory epilepsy. *Epilepsy & Behavior, 12,* 245–252.

Sato, S. M., Schulz, K. M., Sisk, C. L., & Wood, R. I. (2008). Adolescents and androgens, receptors and rewards. *Hormones and Behavior, 53,* 647–658.

Sattler, J. M. (1988). *Assessment of children* (3rd ed.). San Diego, CA: Jerome M. Sattler Publisher.

Sattler, J. M., & Hoge, R. D. (2006). *Assessment of children: Behavioral, social, and clinical foundations* (5th ed.). San Diego, CA: Jerome M. Sattler Publisher, Inc.

Saudino, K. J. (1997). Moving beyond the heritability question: New directions in behavioral genetic studies of personality. *Current Directions in Psychological Science, 6,* 86–90.

Savage-Rumbaugh, E. S. (1990). Language acquisition in a nonhuman species: Implications for the innateness debate. *Developmental Psychobiology, 23,* 599–620.

Savic, I., Berglund, H., & Lindström, P. (2007). Brain response to putative pheromones in homosexual men. In G. Einstein (Ed.), *Sex and the brain* (pp. 731–738). Cambridge, MA: MIT Press.

Savory, E. (2004, March 10). *Baby signing.* CBC News Online. Retrieved from http://www.cbc.ca/news/background/baby sign/

Schachter, S., & Singer, J. E. (1962). Cognitive, social, and physiological determinants of emotional state. *Psychological Review, 69,* 379–399.

Schaefer, R. T. (2008). Power and power elite. In V. Parillo (Ed.), *Encyclopedia of social problems.* Thousand Oaks, CA: Sage.

Schaie, K. W. (1994). The life course of adult intellectual development. *American Psychologist, 49,* 304–313.

Schaie, K. W. (2008). A lifespan developmental perspective of psychological ageing. In K. Laidlaw & B. Knight (Eds.), *Handbook of emotional disorders in later life: Assessment and treatment.* New York, NY: Oxford University Press.

Schmahl, C. G., Vermetten, E., Elzinga, B. M., & Bremner, J. D. (2004). A positron emission tomography study of memories of childhood abuse in borderline personality disorder. *Biological Psychiatry, 55*(7), 759–765.

Schmidt, U. (2004). Undue influence of weight on self-evaluation: A population-based twin study of gender differences. *International Journal of Eating Disorders, 35*(2), 133–135.

Schopp, L. H., Good, G. E., Mazurek, M. O., Barker, K. B., & Stucky, R. C. (2007). Masculine role variables and outcomes among men with spinal cord injury. *Disability and Rehabilitation: An International, Multidisciplinary Journal, 29,* 625–633.

Schülein, J. A. (2007). Science and psychoanalysis. *Scandinavian Psychoanalytic Review, 30,* 13–21.

Schunk, D. H. (2008). Attributions as motivators of self-regulated learning. In D. H. Schunk & B. J. Zimmerman (Eds.), *Motivation and self-regulated learning: Theory, research, and applications* (pp. 245–266). Mahwah, NJ: Erlbaum.

Scribner, S. (1977). Modes of thinking and ways of speaking: Culture and logic reconsidered. In P. N. Johnson-Laird & P. C. Wason (Eds.), *Thinking: Readings in cognitive science* (pp. 324–339). New York, NY: Cambridge University Press.

Scully, J. A., Tosi, H., & Banning, K. (2000). Life event checklists: Revisiting the Social Readjustment Rating Scale after 30 years. *Educational & Psychological Measurement, 60*(6), 864–876.

Sebre, S., Sprugevica, I., Novotni, A., Bonevski, D., Pakalniskiene, V., Popescu, D., Turchina, T., Friedrich, W., & Lewis, O. (2004). Crosscultural comparisons of child-reported emotional and physical abuse: Rates, risk factors and psychosocial symptoms. *Child Abuse & Neglect, 28*(1), 113–127.

Segerdahl, P., Fields, W., & Savage-Rumbaugh, E. S. (2006). *Kanzai's primal language: The cultural initiation of primates into language.* New York, NY: Palgrave Macmillan.

Segerstrale, U. (2000). *Defenders of the truth: The battle for science in the sociobiology debate and beyond.* London, UK: Oxford University Press.

Segerstrom, S. C., & Miller, G. E. (2004). Psychological stress and the human immune system: A meta-analytic study of 30 years of inquiry. *Psychological Bulletin, 130*(4), 601–630.

Seligman, M. E. P. (1971). Phobias and preparedness. *Behavior Therapy, 2,* 307–321.

Seligman, M. E. P. (1975) *Helplessness: On depression, development, and death.* San Francisco, CA: Freeman.

Seligman, M. E. P. (1994). *What you can change and what you can't.* New York, NY: Alfred A. Knopf.

Seligman, M. E. P. (2007). Coaching and positive psychology. *Australian Psychologist, 42,* 266–267.

Selye, H. (1936). A syndrome produced by diverse nocuous agents. *Nature, 138,* 32.

Selye, H. (1974). *Stress without distress.* New York, NY: Harper & Row.

Senko, C., Durik, A. M., & Harackiewicz, J. M. (2008). Historical perspectives and new directions in achievement goal theory: Understanding the effects of mastery and performance-approach goals. In J. Y. Shah & W. L. Gardner (Eds.), *Handbook of motivation science* (pp. 100–113). New York, NY: Guilford Press.

Sequeira, A., Mamdani, F., Lalovic, A., Anguelova, M., Lesage, A., Seguin, M., Chawky, N., Desautels, A., & Turecki, G. (2004). Alpha 2A adrenergic receptor gene and suicide. *Psychiatry Research, 125*(2), 87–93.

Shahim, S. (2008). Sex differences in relational aggression in preschool children in Iran. *Psychological Reports, 102,* 235–238.

Shakhar, K., Valdimarsdottir, H. B., Guevarra, J. S., & Bovbjerg, D. H. (2007). Sleep, fatigue, and NK cell activity in healthy volunteers: Significant relationships revealed by within subject analyses. *Brain, Behavior, and Immunity, 21*, 180–184.

Sharps, M. J., Hess, A. B., Casner, H., Ranes, B., & Jones, J. (2007). Eyewitness memory in context: Toward a systematic understanding of eyewitness evidence. *The Forensic Examiner, 16*, 20–27.

Shaver, P. R., & Mikulincer, M. (2005). Attachment theory and research: Resurrection of the psychodynamic approach to personality. *Journal of Research in Personality, 39*(1), 22–45.

Shea, D. J. (2008). Effects of sexual abuse by Catholic priests on adults victimized as children. *Sexual Addiction & Compulsivity, 15*, 250–268.

Shea, S. C. (1988). *Psychiatric interviewing: The art of understanding.* Philadelphia, PA: Saunders.

Shear, K., Halmi, K. A., Widiger, T. A., & Boyce, C. (2007). Sociocultural factors and gender. In W. E. Narrow, M. B. First, P. J. Sirovatka, & D. A. Regier (Eds.), *Age and gender considerations in psychiatric diagnosis: A research agenda for DSM-V* (pp. 65–79). Arlington, VA: American Psychiatric Publishing.

Sheehy, G. (1976). *Passages: Predictable crises of adult life.* New York, NY: Dutton.

Shepperd, J., Malone, W., & Sweeny, K. (2008). Exploring causes of the self-serving bias. *Social and Personality Psychology Compass, 2*, 895–908.

Sher, K. J., Grekin, E. R., & Williams, N. A. (2005). The development of alcohol use disorders. *Annual Review of Clinical Psychology, 1*, 493–523.

Sherif, M. (1966). *In common predicament: Social psychology of intergroup conflict and cooperation.* Boston, MA: Houghton Mifflin.

Sherif, M. (1998). Experiments in group conflict. In J. M. Jenkins, K. Oatley, & N. L. Stein (Eds.), *Human emotions: A reader* (pp. 245–252). Malden, MA: Blackwell.

Shields, C. D. (2008). The relationship between goal orientation, parenting style, and self-handicapping in adolescents. *Dissertation Abstracts International Section A: Humanities and Social Sciences, 68*(10-A), 4200.

Sias, P. M., Heath, R. G., Perry, T., Silva, D., & Fix, B. (2004). Narratives of workplace friendship deterioration. *Journal of Social & Personal Relationships, 21*(3), 321–340.

Siccoli, M. M., Rölli-Baumeler, N., Achermann, P., & Bassetti, C. L. (2008). Correlation between sleep and cognitive functions after hemispheric ischaemic stroke. *European Journal of Neurology, 15*, 565–572.

Siegala, M., & Varley, R. (2008). If we could talk to the animals. *Behavioral & Brain Sciences, 31*, 146–147.

Siegel, J. M. (2000, January). Narcolepsy. *Scientific American*, pp. 76–81.

Siegel, J. M. (2008). Do all animals sleep? *Trends in Neurosciences, 31*, 208–213.

Siever, L. J. (2008). Neurobiology of aggression and violence. *American Journal of Psychiatry, 165*, 429–442.

Sigall, H., & Johnson, M. (2006). The relationship between facial contact with a pillow and mood. *Journal of Applied Social Psychology, 36*, 505–526.

Silventoinen, K., Magnusson, P. K., Tynelius, P., Kaprio, J., & Rasmussen, F. (2008). Heritability of body size and muscle strength in young adulthood: A study of one million Swedish men. *Genetic Epidemiology, 32*(4), 341–349.

Silverman, W. K., Pina, A. A., & Viswesvaran, C. (2008). Evidence-based psychosocial treatments for phobic and anxiety disorders in children and adolescents. *Journal of Clinical Child and Adolescent Psychology, 37*, 105–130.

Silvestri, A. J., & Root, D. H. (2008). Effects of REM deprivation and an NMDA agonist on the extinction of conditioned fear. *Physiology & Behavior, 93*, 274–281.

Sim, T., & Wong, D. (2008). Working with Chinese families in adolescent drug treatment. *Journal of Social Work Practice, 22*, 103–118.

Singelis, T. M., Triandis, H. C., Bhawuk, D. S., & Gelfand, M. (1995). Horizontal and vertical dimensions of individualism and collectivism: A theoretical and measurement refinement. *Cross-Cultural Research, 29*, 240–275.

Skelhorn, J., Griksaitis, D., & Rowe, C. (2008). Colour biases are more than a question of taste. *Animal Behaviour, 75*, 827–835.

Skinner, B. F. (1948). Superstition in the pigeon. *Journal of Experimental Psychology, 38*, 168–172.

Skinner, B. F. (1953). *Science and human behavior.* New York, NY: Macmillan.

Skinner, B. F. (1961). Diagramming schedules of reinforcement. *Journal of the Experimental Analysis of Behavior, 1*, 67–68.

Skinner, B. F. (1992). "Superstition" in the pigeon. *Journal of Experimental Psychology: General, 121*(3), 273–274.

Slagter, H. A., Lutz, A., Greischar, L. L., Francis, A. D., Nieuwenhuis, S., Davis, J. M., & Davidson, R. J. (2007). Mental training affects distribution of limited brain resources. *PLoS Biology, 5*(6), e138. doi:10.1371/journal. pbio.0050138

Slováčková, B., & Slováček, L. (2007). Moral judgement competence and moral attitudes of medical students. *Nursing Ethics, 14*, 320–328.

Smart, D. W., & Smart, J. F. (1997). *DSM-IV* and culturally sensitive diagnosis: Some observations for counselors. *Journal of Counseling and Development, 75*, 392–398.

Smith, E. E. (1995). Concepts and categorization. In E. E. Smith & D. N. Osherson (Eds.), *Thinking: An invitation to cognitive science* (2nd ed., Vol. 3, pp. 3–33). Cambridge: MIT Press.

Smith, K. D. (2007). Spinning straw into gold: Dynamics of Rumpelstiltskin style of leadership. *Dissertation Abstracts International Section A: Humanities and Social Sciences, 68*(5-A), 1760.

Smith, M. T., Huang, M. I., & Manber, R. (2005). Cognitive behavior therapy for chronic insomnia occurring within the context of medical and psychiatric disorders. *Clinical Psychology Review, 25*, 559–592.

Smith, P., Frank, J., Bondy, S., & Mustard, C. (2008). Do changes in job control predict differences in health status? Results from a longitudinal national survey of Canadians. *Psychosomatic Medicine, 70*, 85–91.

Smith, R. A. (2002). *Challenging your preconceptions: Thinking critically about psychology* (2nd ed.). Toronto, ON: Nelson.

Smithson, M., & Baker, C. (2008). Risk orientation, loving, and liking in long-term romantic relationships. *Journal of Social and Personal Relationships, 25*, 87–103.

Snarey, J. R. (1985). Cross-cultural universality of social-moral development: A critical review of Kohlbergian research. *Psychological Bulletin, 97*, 202–233.

Snarey, J. R. (1995). In communitarian voice: The sociological expansion of Kohlbergian theory, research, and practice. In W. M. Kurtines & J. L. Gewirtz (Eds.), *Moral development: An introduction* (pp. 109–134). Boston, MA: Allyn & Bacon.

Snyder, C. R. (2003). "Me conform? No way": Classroom demonstrations for sensitizing students to their conformity. *Teaching of Psychology, 30*(1), 59–61.

Snyder, J. S., & Alain, C. (2007). Sequential auditory sense analysis is preserved in normal aging adults. *Cerebral Cortex, 17*, 501–512.

Solan, H. A., & Mozlin, R. (2001). Children in poverty: Impact on health, visual development, and school failure. *Issues in Interdisciplinary Care, 3*(4), 271–288.

Sollod, R. N., Monte, C. F., & Wilson, J. P. (2009). *Beneath the mask: An introduction to theories of personality* (8th ed.). Hoboken, NJ: Wiley.

Sotres-Bayón, F., & Pellicer, F. (2000). The role of the dopaminergic mesolimbic system in the affective component of chronic pain. *Salud Mental, 23*(1), 23–29.

Sowell, E. R., Mattson, S. N., Kan, E., Thompson, P. M., Riley, E. P., Edward, P., & Toga, A. W. (2008). Abnormal cortical thickness and brain-behavior correlation patterns in individuals with heavy prenatal alcohol exposure. *Cerebral Cortex, 18,* 136–144.

Spearman, C. (1923). *The nature of "intelligence" and the principles of cognition.* London: Macmillan.

Sperling, G. (1960). The information available in brief visual presentations. *Psychological Monographs, 74* (Whole No. 498).

Spiegel, D., & Maldonado, J. R. (1999). Dissociative disorders. In R. E. Hales, S. C. Yudofsky, & J. C. Talbott (Eds.), *American psychiatric press textbook of psychiatry.* Washington, DC: American Psychiatric Press.

Spitz, R. A., & Wolf, K. M. (1946). The smiling response: A contribution to the ontogenesis of social relations. *Genetic Psychology Monographs, 34,* 57–123.

Spokane, A. R., Meir, E. I., & Catalano, M. (2000). Person-environment congruence and Holland's theory: A review and reconsideration. *Journal of Vocational Behavior, 57*(2), 137–187.

Sprecher, S., & Regan, P. C. (2002). Liking some things (in some people) more than others: Partner preferences in romantic relationships and friendships. *Journal of Social & Personal Relationships, 19*(4), 463–481.

Squier, L. H., & Domhoff, G. W. (1998). The presentation of dreaming and dreams in introductory psychology textbooks: A critical examination. *Dreaming, 10,* 21–26.

Sroufe, L. A., Egeland, B., Carlson, E. A., & Collins, W. A. (2005). *The development of the person: The Minnesota study of risk and adaptation from birth to adulthood.* New York, NY: Guilford.

Stafford, J., & Lynn, S. J. (2002). Cultural scripts, memories of childhood abuse, and multiple identities: A study of role-played enactments. *International Journal of Clinical & Experimental Hypnosis, 50*(1), 67–85.

Statistics Canada. (2004). *Ranking and number of deaths for the ten leading causes, Canada.* Retrieved from Statistics Canada: http://www.statcan.gc.ca/daily-quotidien/081204/t081204c1-eng.htm

Statistics Canada. (2005). "Divorces." *The Daily,* March 9. Retrieved from http://www.statcan.ca/Daily/English/050309/d050309b.htm

Statistics Canada. (2007a). "2006 Census: Immigration, citizenship, language mobility, and migration." *The Daily,* December 4. Retrieved from http://www.statcan.ca/Daily/English/071204/td071204.htm

Statistics Canada. (2007b). *2006 Census: Families, marital status, households and dwelling characteristics.* Retrieved from: http://www.statcan.gc.ca/daily-quotidien/070912/dq070912a-eng.htm

Statistics Canada. (2008). "Study: Sedentary behaviour and obesity." *The Daily,* June 18. Retrieved from http://www.statcan.gc.ca/daily-quotidien/080618/dq080618b-eng.htm

Steele, C. M. (2003). Through the back door to theory. *Psychological Inquiry, 14*(3–4), 314–317.

Steele, C. M., & Aronson, J. (1995). Stereotype threat and the intellectual test performance of African Americans. *Journal of Personality and Social Psychology, 69,* 797–811.

Steele, J., James, J. B., & Barnett, R. C. (2002). Learning in a man's world: Examining the perceptions of undergraduate women in male-dominated academic areas. *Psychology of Women Quarterly, 26*(1), 46–50.

Steffens, D. C., McQuoid, D. R., Welsh-Bohmer, K. A., & Krishnan, K. R. R. (2003). Left orbital frontal cortex volume and performance on the Benton visual retention test in older depressives and controls. *Neuropsychopharmacology, 28*(12), 2179–2183.

Stein, D. J., & Matsunaga, H. (2006). Specific phobia: A disorder of fear conditioning and extinction. *CNS Spectrums, 11*(4), 248–251.

Steinberg, L. (2008). A social neuroscience perspective on adolescent risk-taking. *Developmental Review, 28,* 78–106.

Steinhart, P. (1986, March). Personal boundaries. *Audubon,* pp. 8–11.

Sternberg, R. J. (1985). *Beyond IQ: A triarchic theory of human intelligence.* New York, NY: Cambridge University Press.

Sternberg, R. J. (1998). Principles of teaching for successful intelligence. *Educational Psychologist, 33,* 65–72.

Sternberg, R. J. (1999). The theory of successful intelligence. *Review of General Psychology, 3,* 292–316.

Sternberg, R. J. (2005). The importance of converging operations in the study of human intelligence. *Cortex. 41*(2), 243–244.

Sternberg, R. J. (2007). Developing successful intelligence in all children: A potential solution to underachievement in ethnic minority children. In M. C. Wang & R. D. Taylor (Eds.), *Closing the achievement gap.* Philadelphia: Laboratory for Student Success at Temple University.

Sternberg, R. J. (2008). The triarchic theory of human intelligence. In N. Salkind (Ed.), *Encyclopedia of educational psychology* (Vol. 2, pp. 988–994). Thousand Oaks, CA: Sage.

Sternberg, R. J. (2009). *Cognitive psychology* (5th ed.). Belmont, CA: Wadsworth.

Sternberg, R. J., & Grigorenko, E. L. (2008). Ability testing across cultures. In L. Suzuki (Ed.), *Handbook of multicultural assessment* (3rd ed.). New York, NY: Jossey-Bass.

Sternberg, R. J., & Hedlund, J. (2002). Practical intelligence, g, and work psychology. *Human Performance, 15*(1–2), 143–160.

Sternberg, R. J., & Lubart, T. I. (1992). Buy low and sell high: An investment approach to creativity. *Current Directions in Psychological Science, 1*(1), 1–5.

Sternberg, R. J., & Lubart, T. I. (1996). Investing in creativity. *American Psychologist, 51*(7), 677–688.

Stetter, F., & Kupper, S. (2002). Autogenic training: A meta-analysis of clinical outcome studies. *Applied Psychophysiology & Biofeedback, 27*(1), 45–98.

Stiles, W. B., Barkham, M., Mellor-Clark, J., & Connell, J. (2008). Effectiveness of cognitive-behavioural, person-centered, and psychodynamic therapies in UK primary-care routine practice: Replication in a larger sample. *Psychological Medicine, 39,* 677–688.

Stompe, T. G., Ortwein-Swoboda, K., Ritter, K., & Schanda, H. (2003). Old wine in new bottles? Stability and plasticity of the contents of schizophrenic delusions. *Psychopathology, 36*(1), 6–12.

Stone, K. L., & Redline, S. (2006). Sleep-related breathing disorders in the elderly. *Sleep Medicine Clinics, 1*(2), 247–262.

Stoner, J. A. (1961). *A comparison of individual and group decisions involving risk.* Unpublished master's thesis, School of Industrial Management, MIT, Cambridge, MA.

Strack, F., Martin, L. L., & Stepper, S. (1988). Inhibiting and facilitating conditions of the human smile: A nonobstrusive test of the facial feedback hypothesis. *Journal of Personality and Social Psychology, 54,* 768–777.

Stratton, G. M. (1896). Some preliminary experiments on vision without inversion of the retinal image. *Psychological Review, 3,* 611–617.

Straub, R. O. (2007). *Health psychology: A biopsychosocial approach* (2nd ed.). New York, NY: Worth.

Streissguth, A. P., & Connor, P. D. (2001). Fetal alcohol syndrome and other effects of prenatal alcohol: Developmental cognitive neuroscience implications. In C. A. Nelson & M. Luciana (Eds.), *Handbook of developmental cognitive neuroscience* (pp. 505–518). Cambridge, MA: MIT Press.

Strickland, B. R. (1995). Research on sexual orientation and human development: A commentary. *Developmental Psychology, 31*(1), 137–140.

Subramanian, S., & Vollmer, R. R. (2002). Sympathetic activation fenfluramine depletes brown adipose tissue norepinephrine content in rats. *Pharmacology, Biochemistry & Behavior, 73*(3), 639–646.

Sue, D. W., & Sue, D. (2008). *Counseling the culturally diverse: Theory and practice* (5th ed.). Hoboken, NJ: Wiley.

Sullivan, M. J. L. (2008). Toward a biopsychomotor conceptualization of pain: Implications for research and intervention. *Clinical Journal of Pain, 24,* 281–290.

Sullivan, M. J. L., Tripp, D. A., & Santor, D. (1998). *Gender differences in pain and pain behavior: The role of catastrophizing.* Paper presented at the annual meeting of the American Psychological Association, San Francisco, CA.

Sullivan, T. P., & Holt, L. J. (2008). PTSD symptom clusters are differentially related to substance use among community women exposed to intimate partner violence. *Journal of Traumatic Stress, 21,* 173–180.

Suomi, S. J. (1991). Adolescent depression and depressive symptoms: Insights from longitudinal studies with rhesus monkeys. *Journal of Youth and Adolescence, 20,* 273–287.

Suzuki, W. A., & Amaral, D. G. (2004). Functional neuroanatomy of the medial temporal lobe memory system. *Cortex, 40*(1), 220–222.

Swami, V.. & Furnham, A. (2008). *The psychology of physical attraction.* New York, NY: Routledge/Taylor & Francis Group.

Swartz, K. L. & Margolis, S. (2004). *Depression and anxiety.* Johns Hopkins White Papers. Baltimore: Johns Hopkins Medical Institutions.

Swartz, K. L. (2008). *Depression and anxiety.* Johns Hopkins White Papers. Baltimore: Johns Hopkins Medical Institutions.

Szasz, T. (1960). The myth of mental illness. *American Psychologist, 15,* 113–118.

Szasz, T. (2000). Second commentary on "Aristotle's function argument." *Philosophy, Psychiatry, & Psychology, 7,* 3–16.

Szasz, T. (2004). The psychiatric protection order for the "battered mental patient." *British. Medical Journal, 327*(7429), 1449–1451.

Takano, Y., & Sogon, S. (2008). Are Japanese more collectivistic than Americans? Examining conformity in in-groups and the reference-group effect. *Journal of Cross-Cultural Psychology, 39,* 237–250.

Talarico, J. M., & Rubin, D. C. (2007). Flashbulb memories are special after all; in phenomenology, not accuracy. *Applied Cognitive Psychology, 21,* 557–578.

Tal-Or, N., & Papirman, Y. (2007). The fundamental attribution error in attributing fictional figures' characteristics to the actors. *Media Psychology, 9,* 331–345.

Tanaka, T., Yoshida, M., Yokoo, H., Tomita, M., & Tanaka, M. (1998). Expression of aggression attenuates both stress-induced gastric ulcer formation and increases in noradrenaline release in the rat amygdala assessed intracerebral microdialysis. *Pharmacology, Biochemistry & Behavior, 59*(1), 27–31.

Tandon, R., Keshavan, M. S., & Nasrallah, H. A. (2008). Schizophrenia, "just the facts" what we know in 2008. 2. Epidemiology and etiology. *Schizophrenia Research, 102,* 1–18.

Tang, Y.-P., Wang, H., Feng, R., Kyin, M., & Tsien, J. Z. (2001). Differential effects of enrichment on learning and memory function in NR2B transgenic mice. *Neuropharmacology, 41*(6), 779–790.

Tarbox, R. S. F., Ghezzi, P. M., & Wilson, G. (2006). The effects of token reinforcement on attending in a young child with autism. *Behavioral Interventions, 21,* 155–164.

Tatrow, K., Blanchard, E. B., & Silverman, D. J. (2003). Posttraumatic headache An exploratory treatment study. *Applied Psychophysiology & Biofeedback, 28*(4), 267–279.

Taub, E. (2004). Harnessing brain plasticity through behavioral techniques to produce new treatments in neurorehabilitation. *American Psychologist, 59*(8), 692–704.

Taylor, D. J., Lichstein, K. L., & Durrence, H. H. (2003). Insomnia as a risk factor. *Behavioral Sleep Medicine, 1,* 227–247.

Taylor, J. Y., Caldwell, C. H., Baser, R. E., Frison, N., & Jackson, J. S. (2007). Prevalence of eating disorders among Blacks in the national survey of American life. *International Journal of Eating Disorders, 40*(Supl), S10–S14.

Taylor, R. C., Harris, N. A., Singleton, E. G., Moolchan, E. T., & Heishman, S. J. (2000). Tobacco craving: Intensity-related effects of imagery scripts in drug abusers. *Experimental and Clinical Psychopharmacology, 8*(1), 75–87.

Teasdale, T. W., & Owen, D. R. (2008). Secular declines in cognitive test scores: A reversal of the Flynn effect. *Intelligence, 36,* 121–126.

Tebartz van Elst, L., Hesslinger, B., Thiel, T., Geiger, E., Haegele, K., Lemieux, L., Lieb, K., Bohus, M., Hennig, J., & Ebert, D. (2003). Frontolimbic brain abnormalities in patients with borderline personality disorder: A volumetric magnetic resonance imaging study. *Biological Psychiatry, 54*(2), 163–171.

Tecchio, F., Zappasodi, F., Pasqualetti, P., De Gennaro, L., Pellicciari, M. C., Ercolani, M., Squitti, R., & Rossini, P. M. (2008). Age dependence of primary motor cortex plasticity induced by paired associative stimulation. *Clinical Neurophysiology, 119,* 675–682.

Tellegen, A. (1985). Structures of mood and personality and their relevance to assessing anxiety with an emphasis on self-report. In A. H. Tuma & J. D. Maser (Eds.), *Anxiety and the anxiety disorders* (pp. 681–706). Hillsdale, NJ: Erlbaum.

Temcheff, C. E., Serbin, L. A., Martin-Storey, A., Stack, D. M., Hodgins, S., Ledingham, J., & Schwartzman, A. E. (2008). Continuity and pathways from aggression in childhood to family violence in adulthood: A 30-year longitudinal study. *Journal of Family Violence, 23,* 231–242.

Terman, L. M. (1916). *The measurement of intelligence.* Boston, MA: Houghton Mifflin.

Terman, L. M. (1954). Scientists and nonscientists in a group of 800 gifted men. *Psychological Monographs, 68*(7), 1–44.

Terrace, H. S. (1979, November). How Nim Chimpsky changed my mind. *Psychology Today, 13*(6), 65–76.

Terry, S. W. (2009). *Learning and memory* (4th ed.). Boston, MA: Allyn and Bacon.

Tett, R. P., & Murphy, P. J. (2002). Personality and situations in co-worker preference: Similarity and complementarity in worker compatibility. *Journal of Business & Psychology, 17*(2), 223–243.

Thomas, S. E., Randall, P. K., Book, S. W., & Randall, C. L. (2008). The complex relationship between co-occurring social anxiety and alcohol use disorders: What effect does treating social anxiety have on drinking? *Alcoholism: Clinical and Experimental Research, 32,* 77–84.

Thompson, R. F. (2005). In search of memory traces. *Annual Review of Clinical Psychology, 56,* 1–23.

Thomson, E. (2007). *Mind in life: Biology, phenomenology, and the sciences of mind.* Cambridge, MA: Belknap Press.

Thorndike, E. L. (1898). Animal intelligence. *Psychological Review Monograph, 2*(8).

Thorndike, E. L. (1911). *Animal intelligence.* New York, NY: Macmillan.

Thornhill, R., Gangestad, S. W., Miller, R., Scheyd, G., McCollough, J. K., & Franklin, M. (2003). Major histocompatibility complex genes, symmetry, and body scent attractiveness in men and women. *Behavioral Ecology, 14*(5), 668–678.

Thurstone, L. L. (1938). *Primary mental abilities.* Chicago: University of Chicago Press.

Tirodkar, M. A., & Jain, A. (2003). Food messages on African American television shows. *American Journal of Public Health, 93*(3), 439–441.

Tolin, D. F., Robison, J. T., Gaztambide, S., Horowitz, S., & Blank, K. (2007). Ataques de nervios and psychiatric disorders in older Puerto Rican primary care patients. *Journal of Cross-Cultural Psychology, 38*, 659–669.

Tolman, E. C., & Honzik, C. H. (1930). Introduction and removal of reward and maze performance in rats. *University of California Publications in Psychology, 4*, 257–275.

Tom, S. E. (2008). Menopause and women's health transitions through mid-life. *Dissertation Abstracts International Section A: Humanities and Social Sciences, 68*(8-A), 3605.

Torges, C. M., Stewart, A. J., & Duncan, L. E. (2008). Achieving ego-integrity: Personality development in late midlife. *Journal of Research in Personality, 42*, 1004–1019.

Torrey, E. F., & Yolken, R. H. (1998). Is household crowding a risk factor for schizophrenia and bipolar disorder? *Schizophrenia Bulletin, 24*, 321–324.

Torta, D. M., & Castelli, L. (2008). Reward pathways in Parkinson's disease: Clinical and theoretical implications. *Psychiatry and Clinical Neurosciences, 62*(2), 303–313.

Trainor, B. C., Bird, I. M., & Marler, C. A. (2004). Opposing hormonal mechanisms of aggression revealed through short-lived testosterone manipulations and multiple winning experiences. *Hormones & Behavior, 45*(2), 115–121.

Tremblay, P. F., Graham, K., & Wells, S. (2008). Severity of physical aggression reported by university students: A test of the interaction between trait aggression and alcohol consumption. *Personality and Individual Differences, 45*, 3–9.

Triandis, H. C. (2007). Culture and psychology: A history of the study of their relationship. In S. Kitayama & D. Cohen (Eds.), *Handbook of cultural psychology*. New York, NY: Guilford.

Troll, S. J., Miller, J., & Atchley, R. C. (1979). *Families in later life*. Belmont, CA: Wadsworth.

Trull, T., Sher, K. J., Minks-Brown, C., Durbin, J., & Burr, R. (2000). Borderline personality disorder and substance use disorders: A review and integration. *Clinical Psychology Review, 20*, 235–253.

Tryon, W. W. (2008). Whatever happened to symptom substitution? *Clinical Psychology Review, 28*, 963–968.

Tseng, W. (2004). Culture and psychotherapy: Asian perspectives. *Journal of Mental Health, 13*(2), 151–161.

Tsien, J. Z. (2000, April). Building a brainier mouse. *Scientific American*, pp. 62–68.

Tsuang, M. T., Stone, W. S., & Faraone, S. V. (2001). Genes, environment and schizophrenia. *British Journal of Psychiatry, Suppl 40*, s18–24.

Tulving, E. & Schacter, D. (1990). Priming and human memory systems. *Science, 247*(4940), 301–306.

Tulving, E. (2000). Concepts of memory. In E. Tulving & F. I. M. Craik (Eds.), *The Oxford handbook of memory* (pp. 33–44). New York, NY: Oxford University Press.

Tulving, E., & Thompson, D. M. (1973). Encoding specificity and retrieval processes in episodic memory. *Psychological Review, 80*, 352–373.

Tversky, A., & Kahneman, D. (1974). Judgment under uncertainty: Heuristics and biases. *Science, 185*, 1124–1131.

Tversky, A., & Kahneman, D. (1993). Probabilistic reasoning. In A. I. Goldman (Ed.), *Readings in philosophy and cognitive science* (pp. 43–68). Cambridge, MA: The MIT Press.

Twenge, J. M., Baumeister, R. F., Tice, D. M., & Stucke, T. S. (2001). If you can't join them, beat them: Effects of social exclusion on aggressive behavior. *Journal of Personality and Social Psychology, 81*(6), 1058–1069.

Uhlmann, E., & Swanson, J. (2004). Exposure to violent video games increases automatic aggressiveness. *Journal of Adolescence, 27*(1), 41–52.

Ulrich, R. E., Stachnik, T. J., & Stainton, N. R. (1963). Student acceptance of generalized personality interpretations. *Psychological Reports, 13*, 831–834.

Vaillend, C., Poirier, R., & Laroche, S. (2008). Genes, plasticity and mental retardation. *Behavioural Brain Research, 192*(1), 88–105.

Valeo, T., & Beyerstein, L. (2008). Curses! In T. Gordon (Eds.), *Your brain on cubs: Inside the players and fans* (pp. 59–74; 139–140). Washington, DC: Dana Press.

Van de Carr, F. R., & Lehrer, M. (1997). *While you are expecting: Your own prenatal classroom*. New York, NY: Humanics Publishing.

van der Sluis, S., Derom, C., Thiery, E., Bartels, M., Polderman, T. J. C., Verhulst, F. C., Jacobs, N., van Gestel, S., de Geus, E. J. C., & Dolan, C. V. (2008). Sex differences on the WISC-R in Belgium and the Netherlands. *Intelligence, 36*, 48–67.

van Lier, P., Boivin, M., Dionne, G., Vitaro, F., Brendgen, M., Koot, H., Tremblay, R. E., & Pérusse, D. (2007). Kindergarten children's genetic variabilities interact with friends' aggression to promote children's own aggression. *Journal of the American Academy of Child & Adolescent Psychiatry, 46*, 1080–1087.

van Stegeren, A. H. (2008). The role of the noradrenergic system in emotional memory. *Acta Psychologica, 127*, 532–541.

Vasta, R., Younger, A., Adler, S., Miller, S., & Ellis, S. (2009). *Child psychology* (2nd Cdn ed.). Toronto, ON: Wiley.

Vaughn, D. (1996). *The* Challenger *launch decision: Risky technology, culture, and deviance at NASA*. Chicago: University of Chicago Press.

Venkatesh, V., Morris, M. G., Sykes, T. A., & Ackerman, P. L. (2004). Individual reactions to new technologies in the workplace: The role of gender as a psychological construct. *Journal of Applied Social Psychology, 34*(3), 445–467.

Vertosick, F. T. (2000). *Why we hurt: The natural history of pain*. New York, NY: Harcourt.

Vickers, J. C., Dickson, T. C., Adlard, P. A., Saunders, H. L., King, C. E., & McCormack, G. (2000). The cause of neuronal degeneration in Alzheimer's disease. *Progress in Neurobiology, 60*(2), 139–165.

Vidmar, N. (1997). Generic prejudice and the presumption of guilt in sex abuse trials. *Law and Human Behavior, 21*(1), 5–25.

Vijgen, S. M. C., van Baal, P. H. M., Hoogenveen, R. T., de Wit, G. A., & Feenstra, T. L. (2008). Cost-effectiveness analyses of health promotion programs: A case study of smoking prevention and cessation among Dutch students. *Health Education Research, 23*, 310–318.

Vogt, D. S., Rizvi, S. L., Shipherd, J. C., & Resick, P. A. (2008). Longitudinal investigation of reciprocal relationship between stress reactions and hardiness. *Personality and Social Psychology Bulletin, 34*, 61–73.

Völker, S. (2007). Infants' vocal engagement oriented towards mother versus stranger at 3 months and avoidant attachment behavior at 12 months. *International Journal of Behavioral Development, 31*, 88–95.

von Hippel, W., Brener, L., & von Hippel, C. (2008). Implicit prejudice toward injecting drug users predicts intentions to change jobs among drug and alcohol nurses. *Psychological Science, 19*, 7–11.

Vorria, P., Vairami, M., Gialaouzidis, M., Kotroni, E., Koutra, G., Markou, N., Marti, E., & Pantoleon, I. (2007). Romantic relationships, attachment syles, and experiences of childhood. *Hellenic Journal of Psychology, 4*, 281–309.

Wachtel, P. L. (2008). *Relational theory and the practice of psychotherapy*. New York, NY: Guilford.

Wagg, J. (2008, October 30). *Challenge application: $1M challenge*. James Randi Educational Foundation. Retrieved from http://www.randi.org/site/index.php/1m-challenge/challenge-application.html

Wagner, U., Christ, O., & Pettigrew, T. F. (2008). Prejudice and group-related behaviors in Germany. *Journal of Social Issues, 64*, 403–416.

Wagstaff, G. G., Cole, J., Wheatcroft, J., Marshall, M., & Barsby, I. (2007). A componential approach to hypnotic memory facilitation: Focused meditation, context reinstatement and eye movements. *Contemporary Hypnosis, 24,* 97–108.

Wakefield, M., Flay, B., Nichter, M., & Giovino, G. (2003). Role of the media in influencing trajectories of youth smoking. *Addiction, 98*(Suppl 1), 79–103.

Waldau, B., & Shetty, A. K. (2008). Behavior of neural stem cells in the Alzheimer brain. *Cellular and Molecular Life Sciences, 65*(15), 2372–2384.

Walker, E., Kestler, L., Bollini, A., & Hochman, K. M. Schizophrenia: Etiology and course. (2004). *Annual Review of Psychology, 55,* 401–430.

Walker, F. R., Hinwood, M., Masters, L., Deilenberg, R. A., & Trevor, A. (2008). Individual differences predict susceptibility to conditioned fear arising from psychosocial trauma. *Journal of Psychiatric Research, 42,* 371–383.

Wallace, D. C. (1997, August). Mitochondrial DNA in aging and disease. *Scientific American,* 40–47.

Waller, M. R., & McLanahan, S. S. (2005). "His" and "her" marriage expectations: Determinants and consequences. *Journal of Marriage & Family, 67*(1), 53–67.

Waller, N. G., & Ross, C. A. (1997). The prevalence and biometric structure of pathological dissociation in the general population: Taxometric and behavior genetics findings. *Journal of Abnormal Psychology, 106,* 499–510.

Wallerstein, G. (2008). *The pleasure instinct: Why we crave adventure, chocolate, pheromones, and music.* New York, NY: Wiley.

Wang, Q. (2008). Emotion, knowledge and autobiographical memory across the preschool years: A cross-cultural longitudinal investigation. *Cognition, 108,* 117–135.

Wardlaw, G. M., & Hampl, J. (2007). *Perspectives in nutrition* (7th ed.). New York, NY: McGraw-Hill.

Warr, P., Butcher, V., & Robertson, I. (2004). Activity and psychological well-being in older people. *Aging & Mental Health, 8*(2), 172–183.

Wason, P. C. (1968). Reasoning about a rule. *Quarterly Journal of Experimental Psychology, 20*(3), 273–281.

Wass, T. S. (2008). Neuroanatomical and neurobehavioral effects of heavy prenatal alcohol exposure. In J. Brick (Ed.), *Handbook of the medical consequences of alcohol and drug abuse* (2nd ed.), (pp. 177–217). *The Haworth Press series in neuropharmacology.* New York, NY: Haworth Press/Taylor and Francis Group.

Waters, A. J., & Gobet, F. (2008). Mental imagery and chunks: Empirical and conventional findings. *Memory & Cognition, 36,* 505–517.

Watson, J. (1913). Psychology as the behaviorist views it. *Psychological Review, 20,* 158–177.

Watson, J. B., & Rayner, R. (1920). Conditioned emotional reactions. *Journal of Experimental Psychology, 3,* 1–14.

Waye, K. P. (2004). Effects of low-frequency noise on sleep. *Noise Health, 6,* 87–91.

Waye, K. P., Bengtsson, J., Rylander, R., Hucklebridge, F., Evans, P., & Clow, A. (2002). Low-frequency noise enhances cortisol among noise-sensitive subjects during work performance. *Life Sciences, 70*(7), 745–758.

Weaver, M. F., & Schnoll, S. H. (2008). Hallucinogens and club drugs. In M. Galanter & H. D. Kleber (Eds.), *The American Psychiatric Publishing textbook of substance abuse treatment* (4th ed., pp. 191–200). Arlington, VA: American Psychiatric Publishing.

Wechsler, D. (1944). *The measurement of adult intelligence* (3rd ed.). Baltimore: Williams & Wilkins.

Wechsler, D. (1977). *Manual for the Wechsler Intelligence Scale for Children* (Rev.). New York, NY: Psychological Corporation.

Wegener, D. T., Clark, J. K., & Petty, R. E. (2006). Not all stereotyping is created equal: Differential consequences of thoughtful versus nonthoughtful stereotyping. *Journal of Personality and Social Psychology, 90,* 42–59.

Wei, R. (2007). Effects of playing violent video games on Chinese adolescents' providence attitudes, attitudes toward others, and aggressive behavior. *CyberPsychology & Behavior, 10,* 371–380.

Weiner, B. (1972). *Theories of motivation.* Chicago: Rand-McNally.

Weiner, B. (1982). The emotional consequences of causal attributions. In M. S. Clark & S. T. Fiske (Eds.), *Affect and cognition.* Hillsdale, NJ: Erlbaum.

Weiner, G. (2008). *Handbook of personality assessment.* Hoboken, NJ: Wiley.

Weiner, M. F. (2008). Perspective on race and ethnicity in Alzheimer's disease research. *Alzheimer's & Dementia, 4,* 233–238

Weiss, A., Bates, T. C., & Luciano, M. (2008). Happiness is a personal(ity) thing: The genetics of personality and well-being in a representative sample. *Psychological Science, 19,* 205–210.

Weitlauf, J. C., Cervone, D., Smith, R. E., & Wright, P. M. (2001). Assessing generalization in perceived self-efficacy: Multidomain and global assessments of the effects of self-defense training for women. *Personality & So-*

cial Psychology Bulletin, 27(12), 1683–1691.

Wenger, A., & Fowers, B. J. (2008). Positive illusions in parenting: Every child is above average. *Journal of Applied Social Psychology, 38,* 611–634.

Wentz, E., Mellström, D., Gillberg, I. C., Gillberg, C., & Råstam, M. (2007). Brief report: Decreased bone mineral density as a long-term complication of teenage-onset anorexia nervosa. *European Eating Disorders Review, 15,* 290–295.

Werner, J. S., & Wooten, B. R. (1979). Human infant color vision and color perception. *Infant Behavior and Development, 2*(3), 241–273.

Werner, K. H., Roberts, N. A., Rosen, H. J., Dean, D. L., Kramer, J. H., Weiner, M. W., Miller, B. L., & Levenson, R. W. (2007). Emotional reactivity and emotion recognition in frontotemporal lobar degeneration. *Neurology, 69,* 148–155.

Werth, J. L. Jr., Wright, K. S., Archambault, R. J., & Bardash, R. (2003). When does the "duty to protect" apply with a client who has anorexia nervosa? *Counseling Psychologist, 31*(4), 427–450.

Westen, D. (1998). Unconscious thought, feeling, and motivation: The end of a century-long debate. In R. F. Bornstein & J. M. Masling (Eds.), *Empirical perspectives on the psychoanalytic unconscious.* Washington, DC: American Psychological Association.

Whishaw, I. Q., Alaverdashvili, M., & Kolb, B. (2008). The problem of relating and skilled reaching after motor cortex stroke in the rat. *Behavioural Brain Research, 192*(1), 124–136.

Whitbourne, S. K. (2009). *Adult development and aging: Biopsychosocial perspectives* (3rd ed.). Hoboken, NJ: Wiley.

White, L. K., & Rogers, S. J. (1997). Strong support but uneasy relationships: Coresidence and adult children's relationships with their parents. *Journal of Marriage and the Family, 59,* 62–76.

White, T., Andreasen, N. C., & Nopoulos, P. (2002). Brain volumes and surface morphology in monozygotic twins. *Cerebral Cortex, 12*(5), 486–493.

Whorf, B. L. (1956). Science and linguistics. In J. B. Carroll (Ed.), *Language, thought and reality* (pp. 207–219). Cambridge, MA: MIT Press.

Whyte, M. K. (1992, March–April). Choosing mates—the American way. *Society,* 71–77.

Wickramasekera II, I. (2008). Review of how can we help witnesses to remember more? It's an eyes open and shut case. *American Journal of Clinical Hypnosis, 50,* 290–291.

Wiederman, M. W. (1999). Volunteer bias in sexuality research using college student participants. *Journal of Sex Research, 36*(1), 59–66.

Wieseler-Frank, J., Maier, S. F., & Watkins, L. R. (2005). Immune-to-brain communication dynamically modulates pain: Physiological and pathological consequences. *Brain, Behavior, & Immunity, 19*(2), 104–111.

Williams, A. L., Haber, D., Weaver, G. D., & Freeman, J. L. (1998). Altruistic activity: Does it make a difference in the senior center? *Activities, Adaptation and Aging, 22*(4), 31–39.

Williams, G., Cai, X. J., Elliott, J. C., & Harrold, J. A. (2004). Anabolic neuropeptides. *Physiology & Behavior, 81*(2), 211–222.

Williams, J. E., & Best, D. L. (1990). *Sex and psyche: Gender and self viewed cross-culturally.* Newbury Park, CA: Sage.

Williams, S. S. (2001). Sexual lying among college students in close and casual relationships. *Journal of Applied Social Psychology, 31*(11), 2322–2338.

Williamson, A. M., & Feyer, A. M. (2000). Moderate sleep deprivation produces impairments in cognitive and motor performance equivalent to legally prescribed levels of alcohol intoxication. *Occupational and Environmental Medicine, 57*(10), 649–655.

Williamson, M. (1997). Circumcision an esthesia: A study of nursing implication for dorsal penile nerve block. *Pediatric Nursing, 23,* 59–63.

Willingham, D. B. (2001). *Cognition: The thinking animal.* Upper Saddle River, NJ: Prentice Hall.

Willis, M. S., Esqueda, C. W., & Schacht, R. N. (2008). Social perceptions of individuals missing upper front teeth. *Perceptual and Motor Skills, 106,* 423–435.

Wilson, E. O. (1975). *Sociobiology: The new synthesis.* Cambridge, MA: Harvard University Press.

Wilson, E. O. (1978). *On human nature.* Cambridge, MA: Harvard University Press.

Wilson, K. G., Chochinov, H. W., McPherson, C. J., Graham, M., Allard, P., Chary, S., Gagnon, P. R., Macmillan, K., DeLuca, M., O'Shea, F., Kuhl, D., Fainsinger, R. L., Karam, A. M., & Clinch, J. J. (2007). Desire for euthanasia or physician-assisted suicide in palliative cancer care. *Health Psychology, 26,* 314–323.

Wilson, R. S., Gilley, D. W., Bennett, D. A., Beckett, L. A., & Evans, D. A. (2000). Person-specific paths of cognitive decline in Alzheimer's disease and their relation to age. *Psychology & Aging, 15*(1), 18–28.

Wilson, S., & Nutt, D. (2008). *Sleep disorders.* Oxford, UK: Oxford University Press.

Winkelman, M. J., & Roberts, T. B. (2007). *Psychedelic medicine: New evidence for hallucinogenic substances as treatments* (Vol. 1). Westport, CT:

Praeger Publishers/Greenwood Publishing Group.

Winterich, J. A. (2003). Sex, menopause, and culture: Sexual orientation and the meaning of menopause for women's sex lives. *Gender & Society, 17*(4), 627–642.

Wise, D., & Rosqvist, J. (2006). Explanatory style and well-being. In J. C. Thomas, D. L. Segal, & M. Hersen (Eds.), *Comprehensive handbook of personality and psychopathology, Vol. 1: Personality and everyday functioning* (pp. 285–305). Hoboken, NJ: Wiley.

Wiste, A. K., Arango, V., Ellis, S. P., Mann, J. J., & Underwood, M. D. (2008). Norepinephrine and serotonin imbalance in the locus coeruleus in bipolar disorder. *Bipolar Disorders, 10,* 349–359.

Witelson, S. F., Kigar, D. L., & Harvey, T. (1999). The exceptional brain of Albert Einstein. *The Lancet, 353,* 2149–2153.

Wolf, G. (2008). Want to remember everything you'll ever learn? Surrender to this algorithm. *Wired Magazine.* Retrieved from http://www.wired.com/print/medtech/health/magazine/16-05/FF_Wozniak

Wolf, S. L., Winstein, C. J., Miller, J. P., Thompson, P. A., Taub, E., Uswatte, G., et al. (2008). Retention of upper limb function in stroke survivors who have received constraint-induced movement therapy: The EXCITE randomized trial. *Lancet Neurology, 7*(1), 33–40.

Wolpe, J., & Plaud, J. J. (1997). Pavlov's contributions to behavior therapy. *American Psychologist, 52*(9), 966–972.

Wood, J. M., Lilienfeld, S. O., Nezworski, M. T., & Garb, H. N. (2001). Coming to grips with negative evidence for the comprehensive system for the Rorschach: A comment on Gacono, Loving, and Bodholdt, Ganellen, and Bornstein. *Journal of Personality Assessment, 77*(1), 48–70.

Wood, V. F., & Bell, P. A. (2008). Predicting interpersonal conflict resolution styles from personality characteristics. *Personality and Individual Differences, 45,* 126–131.

Wood, W., Christensen, P. N., Hebl, M. R., & Rothgerber, H. (1997). Conformity to sex-typed norms, affect, and the self-concept. *Journal of Personality and Social Psychology, 73*(3), 523–535.

Woods, T., Coyle, K., Hoglund, W., & Leadbeater, B. (2007). Changing the contexts of peer victimization: The effects of a primary prevention program on school and classroom levels of victimization. In J. E. Zins, M. J. Elias, & C. A. Maher (Eds.), *Bullying, victimization, and peer harassment: A handbook of prevention and intervention* (pp. 369–388). New York: Haworth Press.

Woollams, A. M., Taylor, J. R., Karayanidis, F., & Henson, R. N. (2008). Event-related potentials associated with masked priming of test cues reveal multiple potential contributions to recognition memory. *Journal of Cognitive Neuroscience, 20,* 1114–1129.

Workman, L., & Reader, W. (2008). *Evolutionary psychology: An introduction.* New York, NY: Cambridge University Press.

World Health Organization. (2007). *Cultural diversity presents special challenges for mental health.* Retrieved from http://www.paho.org/English/DD/PIN/pr071010.htm

World Health Organization. (2008). *Mental health and substance abuse.* Retrieved from http://www.searo.who.int/en/section 1174/section1199/section1567_6741.htm

Wright, J. H., & Beck, A. T. (1999). Cognitive therapies. In R. E. Hales, S. C. Yudofsky, & J. A. Talbott (Eds.), *American Psychiatric Press textbook of psychiatry.* Washington, DC: American Psychiatric Press.

Wright, M. J., & Myers, C. R. (1982). *History of academic psychology in Canada.* Toronto, ON: Hogrefe.

Wu, J. C., Huang, W. C., Tsai, Y. A., Chen, Y. C., & Cheng, H. (2008). Nerve repair using acidic fibroblast growth factor in human cervial spinal cord: A preliminary Phase I clinical study. *Journal Neurosurgery of the Spine, 8,* 208–214.

Wyman, A. J., & Vyse, S. (2008). Science versus the stars: A double-blind test of the validity of the NEO Five Factor Inventory and computer-generated astrological natal charts. *Journal of General Psychology, 135,* 287–300.

Wynne, C. D. L. (2007). What the ape said. *Ethology, 113,* 411–413.

Yacoubian, G. S. Jr., Green, M. K., & Peters, R. J. (2003). Identifying the prevalence and correlates of Ecstasy and other club drug (EOCD) use among high school seniors. *Journal of Ethnicity in Substance Abuse, 2*(2), 53–66.

Yamada, H. (1997). *Different games, different rules: Why Americans and Japanese misunderstand each other.* London, England: Oxford University Press.

Yang, Y. K., Yao, W. J., Yeh, T. L., Lee, I. H., Chen, P. S., Lu, R. B, & Chiu, N. T. (2008). Decreased dopamine transporter availability in male smokers—A dual isotope SPECT study. *Progress in Neuro-Psychopharmacology & Biological Psychiatry, 32,* 274–279.

Yarmey, A. D. (2004). Eyewitness recall and photo identification: A field experiment. *Psychology, Crime & Law, 10*(1), 53–68.

Yegneswaran, B., & Shapiro, C. (2007). Do sleep deprivation and alcohol have the same effects on psychomotor performance? *Journal of Psychosomatic Research, 63,* 569–572.

Yeh, S. J., & Lo, S. K. (2004). Living alone, social support, and feeling lonely among the elderly. *Social Behavior & Personality, 32*(2), 129–138.

Yoo, S-S., Hu, P. T., Gujar, N., Jolesz, F. A., & Walker, M. P. (2007). A deficit in the ability to form new human memories without sleep. *Nature Neuroscience, 10,* 385–392.

Young, J. D., & Taylor, E. (1998). Meditation as a voluntary hypometabolic state of biological estivation. *News in Physiological Science, 13,* 149–153.

Young, T. (1802). Color vision. *Philosophical Transactions of the Royal Society,* p. 12.

Zalaquett, C. P., Fuerth, K. M., Stein, C., Ivey, A. E., & Ivey, M. B. (2008). Reframing the *DSM-IV-TR* from a multicultural/social justice perspective. *Journal of Counseling & Development, 86,* 364–371.

Zarrindast, M-R., Fazli-Tabaei, S., Khalilzadeh, A., Farahmanfar, M., & Yahyavi, S-Y. (2005). Cross state-dependent retrieval between histamine and lithium. *Physiology & Behavior, 86,* 154–163.

Zarrindast, M-R., Shendy, M. M., & Ahmadi, S. (2007). Nitric oxide modulates states dependency induced by lithium in an inhibitory avoidance task in mice. *Behavioural Pharmacology, 18,* 289–295.

Zeanah, C. H. (2000). Disturbances of attachment in young children adopted from institutions. *Journal of Developmental & Behavioral Pediatrics, 21*(3), 230–236.

Zillmer, E. A., Spiers, M. V., & Culbertson, W. (2008). *Principles of neuropsychology* (2nd ed.). Belmont, CA: Cengage.

Zimbardo, P. (2007). *The Lucifer effect: Understanding how good people turn evil.* New York, NY: Random House.

Zimbardo, P. G. (1993). Stanford prison experiment: A 20-year retrospective. Invited presentation at the meeting of the Western Psychological Association, Phoenix, AZ.

Zimbardo, P. G. (2004). A situationist perspective on the psychology of evil: Understanding how good people are transformed into perpetrators. In A. G. Miller (Ed.), *The social psychology of good and evil* (pp. 21–50). New York, NY: Guilford Press.

Zimbardo, P. G., Ebbeson, E. B., & Maslach, C. (1977). *Influencing attitudes and changing behavior.* Reading, MA: Addison-Wesley.

Zucker, K. J. (2008). Special issue: Biological research on sex-dimorphic behavior and sexual orientation. *Archives of Sexual Behavior, 37,* 1.

Zuckerman, L., &, Weiner, I. (2005). Maternal immune activation leads to behavioral and pharmacological changes in the adult offspring. *Journal of Psychiatric Research, 39*(3), 311–323.

Zuckerman, M. (1979). *Sensation seeking: Beyond the optimal level of arousal.* Hillsdale, NJ: Erlbaum.

Zuckerman, M. (1994). *Behavioral expressions and biosocial bases of sensation seeking.* New York, NY: Cambridge University Press.

Zuckerman, M. (2004). The shaping of personality: Genes, environments, and chance encounters. *Journal of Personality Assessment, 82*(1), 11–22.

Zuckerman, M. (2008). Rose is a rose is a rose: Content and construct validity. *Personality and Individual Differences, 45,* 110–112.

Genetic mutations, 41
Genetics and intelligence, 229
Genetics and schizophrenia, 372, 373
Genie, 241
Genital arousal, 65
Genital stage, 337
Genocide, 423
Genuineness, 397
Germinal period, 244
Gestalt, 108
Gestalt principles of organization, 108
gf, 222
Giftedness, 228
Glial cells, 42
Goals of psychology, 7
Good child orientation, 275
Grameen Bank, 298
Grammar, 216
Grande, 164
Group decision-making, 433–434
Group membership, 432
Group polarization, 433
Group therapy, 397–398
Groupthink, 433–434, 440
Growth spurt, 251
Gustation, 103

H

Habituation, 106, 107
Hallucinogens, 138, 140–141
Hardiness, 77
Hassles, 71
Hatha yoga, 143
Health psychologist, 80
Health psychology, 8, 80
Healthy living, 84, 85–87
Hearing, 98–102
Hearing loss, 95, 102
Heart attack, 76
Heart disease, 76
Height, 40
Heinz's dilemma, 274
Helping, 437
Herbal remedies, 406
Heritability, 40
Heroin, 139
Heuristic, 212, 214
Hierarchy of needs, 304
High-achievement-oriented people, 312
Higher-level needs, 304
Higher-order conditioning, 156
Hindbrain, 54–55
Hippocampus, 55, 57
Historical overview, 9–10
Holiday of Darkness: A Psychologist's Journey Out of His Depression (Endler), 369
Holland personality type, 288
Homeostasis, 301
Hospice, 293
Hostility, 77
HPA axis, 73, 74
Human sexual response cycle, 310

Humanistic perspective, 10
Humanistic theories, 341–343
Humanistic therapy, 394–397
Hunger, 305
Hyperopia, 98
Hypnosis, 144–145
Hypothalamus, 47, 55, 56, 305–306

I

Iconic memory, 184
Id, 335
Identical twins, 39
Identity crisis, 279
Illusion, 107
Imaginary audience, 261
Immigration, 423
Implicit/nondeclarative memory, 187, 188
Impossible figures, 109
Imprinting, 270
Impulse control disorders, 363
Inactivity, 84
Incentive theory, 302
Incus, 100
Independent variable (IV), 18
Individual psychology, 338
Individualistic cultures, 284, 285
Industrial/organizational psychology, 8
Industry *versus* inferiority, 278
Inferiority complex, 338
Information-processing approach, 10
Information-processing model, 182, 183
Information social influence, 428
Informed consent, 15
Ingroup, 422
Ingroup favouritism, 423
Inner ear, 100
Inner-ear deafness, 102
Insight, 165
Insight learning, 165
Insight therapies, 390–398
Insomnia, 132
Instinct, 300
Instinctive drift, 170
Institutionalization, 410–411
Instrumental conditioning, 157
Instrumental-exchange orientation, 274
Intellectualization, 336
Intelligence, 222. *See also* Thinking, and intelligence, language
Intelligence controversy, 227–231
Intelligence quotient (IQ), 224
Intelligence tests, 224–227
Interactionist perspective, 241
Interference theory, 195
Intermediate cultures, 285
Intermittent schedule of reinforcement, 159
Internal locus of control, 87
Interneuron, 52
Interpersonal attraction, 424–425
Interpersonal intelligence, 223
Interposition, 112
Interpersonal therapy (IPT), 392

Interpretation, 113–115, 391
Interval schedules of reinforcement, 159
Interview, 348, 350–351
Intimacy *versus* isolation, 279
Intrapersonal intelligence, 223
Intrinsic motivation, 313, 314
Investment theory, 215
IPT, 392
IQ, 224
Irrational misconceptions, 393
IV, 18

J

Jackson Personality Inventory-Revised, 349
James-Lange theory, 317–319
James Randi Educational Foundation, 5, 115
Japanese Naikan therapy, 409
Jerusalem syndrome, 371
Jet lag, 126
Just noticeable difference (JND), 95
Just-world phenomenon, 418, 436

K

Kinesthesia, 105
Kohlberg's stages of moral development, 274–277
Koko, 220, 221

L

Labelled lines, 94
Laboratory observation, 21
LAD, 219
Lana, 221
Language, 216–221
Language acquisition device (LAD), 219
Language development, 217–219
Language Instinct, The (Pinker), 219
Latency stage, 337
Latent content, 390
Latent learning, 165
Lateral hypothalamus (LH), 305, 306
Lateralization, 60
Law-and-order orientation, 275
Law of effect, 157
Learned helplessness, 163, 369
Learning, 150–179
    biology of, 168–170
    classical conditioning, 152–156, 171, 172
    cognitive-social theory, 164–167, 174
    defined, 152
    evolution, 169–170
    insight, 165
    latent, 165
    mirror neurons, 169
    neuroscience, 168–169
    observational, 166, 167
    operant conditioning, 157–163, 172–173
    punishment, 161–163
    real-life examples, 171–174
    reinforcement, 158–161
Left hemisphere, 62
Lesioning, 23, 25